Frommer's

Argentina

1st Edition

by Michael Luongo, Charlie O'Malley & Christie Pashby

Here's what the critics say about Frommer's:

"Amazingly easy to use. Very portable, very complete."

—*Booklist*

"Detailed, accurate, and easy-to-read information for all price ranges."
—*Glamour Magazine*

"Hotel information is close to encyclopedic."

—*Des Moines Sunday Register*

"Frommer's Guides have a way of giving you a real feel for a place."
—*Knight Ridder Newspapers*

BICENTENNIAL
1807
WILEY
2007
BICENTENNIAL

Wiley Publishing, Inc.

Published by:

Wiley Publishing, Inc.

111 River St.
Hoboken, NJ 07030-5774

ISBN: 978-0-470-12479-6

Editor: Maureen Clarke
Production Editor: Suzanna R. Thompson
Cartographer: Roberta Stockwell
Photo Editor: Richard Fox
Anniversary Logo Design: Richard Pacifico
Production by Wiley Indianapolis Composition Services

Front cover photo: Cerro Torre in Los Glaciares National Park (Patagonia)
Back cover photo: A tango demonstration in San Telmo, Buenos Aires

For information on our other products and services or to obtain technical support, please contact our Customer Care Department within the U.S. at 800/762-2974, outside the U.S. at 317/572-3993 or fax 317/572-4002.

Wiley also publishes its books in a variety of electronic formats. Some content that appears in print may not be available in electronic formats.

Manufactured in the United States of America

5   4   3   2   1

Contents

List of Maps   vii

1 The Best of Argentina   1

1 The Most Unforgettable Travel
Experiences in Argentina 1

2 The Best Charming Small Towns 3

3 The Best Outdoor Adventures 4

4 The Best Hotels 5

5 The Best Dining Experiences 7

2 Planning Your Trip to Argentina   9

1 The Regions in Brief 9

2 Visitor Information 12

3 Entry Requirements & Customs 13

4 Money 15

5 When to Go 17

6 Health & Insurance 18

7 Specialized Travel Resources 21

8 Planning Your Trip Online 25

*Frommers.com: The Complete
Travel Resource* 26

9 The 21st-Century Traveler 27

Online Traveler's Toolbox 29

10 Getting There 30

11 Independent Travel Packages &
Escorted General-Interest Tours 33

Fast Facts: Argentina 35

12 The Active Vacation Planner 37

3 Suggested Argentina Itineraries   42

1 Five Days in Buenos Aires 42

2 Northern Patagonia:
Lakes & Villages 43

3 Hiking Southern Argentine
Patagonia in 1 Week 47

4 Mendoza: Malbec & Mountains 49

5 Patagonia Wildlife: Península
Valdés & Los Glaciares
National Park 52

4 Buenos Aires   55

by Michael Luongo

1 Essentials 56

Fast Facts: Buenos Aires 60

2 Where to Stay 63

3 Where to Dine 89

4 What to See & Do 123

5 Shopping 134

6 Buenos Aires After Dark 144

Tango Lowdown 149

5 The Pampas, the Coast & Other Side Trips from Buenos Airies   152

by Michael Luongo

1 Mar del Plata 152
2 Miramar .159
3 La Plata .162
4 Tigre & the Delta 164
5 Puente del Este, Uruguay 167
6 Colonia del Sacramento, Uruguay . . .173
7 Montevideo, Uruguay 175
   Fast Facts: Montevideo 178
8 San Antonio de Areco &
   Pampas Estancias 183

6 Iguazú Falls & the Northeast   190

by Charlie O'Malley

1 Iguazú Falls & Puerto Iguazú 190
   Behind the Falls &
   into the Jungle 195
2 The Brazilian Side:
   Foz do Iguaçu 199
   Border Crossing 200
3 Resistencia & El Chaco 203

7 Salta & the Northwest   205

by Charlie O'Malley

1 Salta 205
   Train to the Clouds: Delayed
   until Further Notice 208
2 A Driving Tour of the Calchaquíes
   Valley via Cachi & Cafayate 215
3 San Salvador de Jujuy 221
4 Driving the Quebrada de
   Humahuaca (Humahuaca
   Gorge) 224
5 Tucumán 225
6 La Rioja .228

8 Córdoba & the Central Sierras   232

by Charlie O'Malley

1 Córdoba .232
   Fast Facts: Córdoba 234
   Touring the Jesuit Estancias 240
2 Villa Carlos Paz 242
   Parque Nacional Quebrada
   del Condorito 245
3 La Falda .246
4 La Cumbre 247
   Parque Nacional Sierra
   de las Quijadas 250
5 Alta Gracia 250

9 Mendoza, the Wine Country & the Central Andes   252

by Christie Pashby

1 Mendoza 254
  Fast Facts: Mendoza 256
  The Real Scoop 262
2 Touring the Wineries 266
  Taking Wine Home 268
  When to Visit 279
  The Story of Mendoza's Wine 281

3 San Rafael 282
4 The Alta Montaña
  Driving Circuit 284
  Roadside Shrines: Folk
  Saints of Argentina 285
  Hitting the Slopes in Las Leñas 288
  A Shared Backbone: Crossing
  into Chile 290

10 The Argentine Lake District   292

by Christie Pashby

1 San Carlos de Bariloche 294
  Fast Facts: Bariloche 297
  What's with All the Chocolate? . . .298
  Nah-Well What? 299
2 South of Bariloche 313
  Ruta 40: The Road South 314
3 Villa La Angostura 315

  Driving to Chile 319
4 Driving Bariloche to San Martín . . .320
5 San Martín de los Andes 322
  Fast Facts: San Martín
  de los Andes 324
6 Junín de los Andes 333

11 Península Valdés & Southern Patagonia   335

by Christie Pashby

1 Puerto Madryn 338
  Fast Facts: Puerto Madryn 340
2 Península Valdés 347
  Kayak Expedition: Up Close &
  Personal with Wildlife 349
3 Puerto Pirámides 350
4 Trelew 352
5 Gaiman .353
  High Tea in Gaiman 354

6 El Calafate 355
  Fast Facts: El Calafate 355
7 Parque Nacional los Glaciares &
  Perito Moreno Glacier 366
  How to See the Glacier 369
8 El Chaltén & the FitzRoy Area 370
  Patagonia's Famous Peaks 374
9 Torres del Paine National
  Park, Chile 377

12 Tierra del Fuego & Antarctica   386

by Charlie O'Malley

1 Ushuaia 386
   *Cruising from Punta Arenas
   to Ushuaia* 389
   Fast Facts: Ushuaia 390

*Monster Trout on the
Río Grande* 400
2 Puerto Williams, Chile 401
3 Antarctica 403

Appendix A: Argentina in Depth   410

by Michael Luongo

1 Settlement & Colonization 410
2 Independence & Warfare 411
3 Buenos Aires, the Capital 413

4 The Cultural Growth of the
   1920s & 1930s 414
5 The Perón Years 415
6 The Dirty War & Its Aftermath 417

Appendix B: Survival Spanish   421

Index   425

List of Maps

Argentina   11

Buenos Aires in 5 Days   44

Northern Patagonia Lakes &
 Villages   47

Hiking Southern Patagonia
 in 1 Week   49

Mendoza: Malbec & Mountains   51

Península Valdés & Los Glaciares   53

Where to Stay in Buenos Aires   64

Where to Stay & Dine in Palermo   86

Where to Dine in Buenos Aires   90

Buenos Aires Sightseeing   124

Buenos Aires Shopping &
 Nightlife   136

Palermo Shopping & Nightlife   140

Mar del Plata   154

Montevideo   177

The Iguazú Falls Region   191

Northwestern Argentina   207

Salta   209

Córdoba   233

Córdoba Province   243

Mendoza   253

Mendoza Province   267

Argentina's Lake District   293

Seven Lakes Route   321

Patagonia   337

Península Valdés/Puerto Madryn   339

Southern Patagonia   357

Los Glaciares National Park   367

Ushuaia   387

Antarctica   405

About the Authors

Michael Luongo has written on Argentina for the *New York Times*, the *Chicago Tribune*, *Frommer's Budget Travel*, *National Geographic Traveler*, *Bloomberg News*, *Out Traveler*, and many other publications. He is senior editor for Haworth Press's Out in the World Series, on gay and lesbian travel literature, and he also authors *Frommer's Buenos Aires*. His debut novel, *The Voyeur*, was published by Alyson Books in 2007. He has visited more than 80 countries and all seven continents, but few places have stolen his heart like Argentina. Highlights of his travels there include riding Juan Perón's coffin through the streets of Buenos Aires during his 2006 reburial, and wearing Evita's perfume to a dinner party. Visit him at www.michaelluongo.com.

Charlie O'Malley worked in theater for many years in England and Ireland. In 2002 he discovered South America—the most theatrical continent there is—and has traveled extensively throughout the region. He currently lives in Mendoza, Argentina, and is editor of the wine magazine *Wine Republic*.

Christie Pashby is the author of *Frommer's Banff & Jasper National Parks*. A freelance editor, journalist, and translator, she is the former editor of the *Canmore Leader* newspaper and the *WildLife* arts magazine, and she worked previously as a reporter in Costa Rica. Her freelance writing has appeared in many of Canada's major daily newspapers. She divides her time between the Canadian Rockies and Patagonia, Argentina, where she runs a small guiding business with her husband. Her websites include www.patagoniatravelco.com and www.patagonialiving.com.

Acknowledgments

A big thanks to my editor, Maureen Clarke, and to my Buenos Aires book editor, Jamie Ehrlich; to Kathleen Warnock for introducing me to them; and to Melinda Quintero and so many others at Frommer's. Thanks to Inés Segarra and Debora Pucheta for their endless help; to Alejandro, Verónica, Vicky, and everyone else in the Argentine Tourism and Consular Office in New York; and to Eduardo Piva in Miami. To Luciana Beiler and Carlos Enrique Mayer and everyone at the National Tourism Office; to Ruben, Jorge Giberti, Milciades Pena, and everyone at the Buenos Aires City Tourism office; and to Claudia Kuzmicz of BA Province. Thanks to Gabriel Miremont at Museo Evita, and to Luis and Lawrence for being big brothers to me over the years.

—Michael Luongo

Thanks to Alec Quinn and María Paz Muriel in Ushuaia; to the Beggs in Córdoba; Martha Chocobar in Cafayate; to winemakers Jason Mabbett and David Kingsbury for their driving skills on the Route 40; and to everybody at Frommer's—especially his editor Maureen Clarke—for their encouragement. A very special thanks to Ana Laura Aguilera—my traveling companion, assistant, researcher, driver, and girlfriend.

—Charlie O'Malley

I would like to thank Gabriela in Chacras; Charlie and Carolyn in Mendoza; La Rubia for emergency floor space; Max, for bringing me home to Bariloche; and my family in Toronto for supporting my ever-evolving wanderlust, and for picking me up at the airport at 6am.

—Christie Pashby

An Invitation to the Reader

In researching this book, we discovered many wonderful places—hotels, restaurants, shops, and more. We're sure you'll find others. Please tell us about them, so we can share the information with your fellow travelers in upcoming editions. If you were disappointed with a recommendation, we'd love to know that, too. Please write to:

Frommer's Argentina, 1st Edition
Wiley Publishing, Inc. • 111 River St. • Hoboken, NJ 07030-5774

An Additional Note

Please be advised that travel information is subject to change at any time—and this is especially true of prices. We therefore suggest that you write or call ahead for confirmation when making your travel plans. The authors, editors, and publisher cannot be held responsible for the experiences of readers while traveling. Your safety is important to us, however, so we encourage you to stay alert and be aware of your surroundings. Keep a close eye on cameras, purses, and wallets, all favorite targets of thieves and pickpockets.

Other Great Guides for Your Trip:

Frommer's Spanish PhraseFinder & Dictionary

Frommer's Buenos Aires

Frommer's Chile & Easter Island

Frommer's Ecuador & the Galápagos Islands

Frommer's Peru

Frommer's South America

Frommer's Star Ratings, Icons & Abbreviations

Every hotel, restaurant, and attraction listing in this guide has been ranked for quality, value, service, amenities, and special features using a **star-rating system.** In country, state, and regional guides, we also rate towns and regions to help you narrow down your choices and budget your time accordingly. Hotels and restaurants are rated on a scale of zero (recommended) to three stars (exceptional). Attractions, shopping, nightlife, towns, and regions are rated according to the following scale: zero stars (recommended), one star (highly recommended), two stars (very highly recommended), and three stars (must-see).

In addition to the star-rating system, we also use **seven feature icons** that point you to the great deals, in-the-know advice, and unique experiences that separate travelers from tourists. Throughout the book, look for:

Finds	Special finds—those places only insiders know about
Fun Fact	Fun facts—details that make travelers more informed and their trips more fun
Kids	Best bets for kids and advice for the whole family
Moments	Special moments—those experiences that memories are made of
Overrated	Places or experiences not worth your time or money
Tips	Insider tips—great ways to save time and money
Value	Great values—where to get the best deals

The following **abbreviations** are used for credit cards:

AE	American Express	DISC Discover	V Visa
DC	Diners Club	MC MasterCard	

Frommers.com

Now that you have this guidebook to help you plan a great trip, visit our website at **www. frommers.com** for additional travel information on more than 3,500 destinations. We update features regularly to give you instant access to the most current trip-planning information available. At Frommers.com, you'll find scoops on the best airfares, lodging rates, and car rental bargains. You can even book your travel online through our reliable travel booking partners. Other popular features include:

- Online updates of our most popular guidebooks
- Vacation sweepstakes and contest giveaways
- Newsletters highlighting the hottest travel trends
- Online travel message boards with featured travel discussions

The Best of Argentina

The distance from Argentina's northern tip to Tierra del Fuego spans 3,650km (2,263 miles). And the scope of experiences you can find here is no less grand, ranging from the cosmopolitan bustle of Buenos Aires to the tropical jungles and pounding falls of Iguazú or the thunderous splash of icebergs in Los Glaciares National Park. Whether you've come to meander the quiet towns of the Lake District or dance the night away in a smoky, low-lit Argentine tango bar, your trip to the Southern Hemisphere won't disappoint. In this chapter, we've selected the best that Argentina has to offer—museums, outdoor adventures, hotels, and even side trips to Chile.

1 The Most Unforgettable Travel Experiences in Argentina

- **Experiencing Tango in Buenos Aires:** *Milongas,* or tango salons, take place every night of the week throughout the Argentine capital; the most famous are in the San Telmo neighborhood. Most visitors will be content just to watch as dancers of all generations (most of them amateurs) go through the beautiful paces of traditional Argentine tango. Both the dance and the complex social ritual that frames it are mesmerizing. Brave onlookers can choose to dance as well; most *milongas* offer lessons before the floor opens up to dancers. **El Niño Bien,** Humberto I no. 1462 (© **11/4483-2588**), is like taking a step back in time, as you watch patrons dance in an enormous Belle Epoque–era hall under ceiling fans. The best dancers come here to show off, though you'll also find instructors looking to mingle with shy potential students who watch from the sidelines. See p. 148. For an authentic historical look, see the tango show **El Querandí,** Perú 302 (© **11/4345-0331**), which traces the dance's roots

  from brothel slums, when only men danced it, to its current leggy sexiness. See p. 146.

- **Paying Respects at a First-Class Necropolis:** In the beautiful Recoleta Cemetery in a chi-chi neighborhood in Buenos Aires, enormous, expensive mausoleums compete for grandeur. It's a place where the rich *can* "take it with them," in a sense, and continue displaying their wealth long after death. Among the scant few nonaristocrats buried here is Eva Perón, or "Evita." See p. 128.

- **The Capital's Best Nightlife Street:** Whether you want to dine at a *parrilla* (grill), try some nouvelle cuisine, barhop, or go dancing, **Calle Báez** in Las Cañitas is the place to go. This busy street in Palermo has great restaurants—such as **Novecento,** Báez 199 (© **11/4778-1900**), and **El Estanciero,** Báez 202 (© **11/4899-0951**)—and some of the most intensely packed nightlife on any 3 blocks of Buenos Aires. See chapter 4.

- **Visiting Iguazú Falls:** One of the world's most spectacular sights,

Iguazú boasts over 275 waterfalls fed by the Iguazú River. In addition to the falls, Iguazú encompasses a marvelous subtropical jungle with extensive flora and fauna. See chapter 6.

- **Driving the Quebrada de Humahuaca:** This rainbow-colored mountain range reveals dusty adobe villages and striking rock formations. With so many Quechuan women herding goats amid Inca ruins, you may think you have accidentally crossed into nearby Bolivia. See chapter 7.

- **Riding the Train to the Clouds:** The Tren a las Nubes is one of the world's great railroad experiences. The journey through Argentina's Northwest takes you 434km (269 miles) through tunnels, turns, and bridges, culminating in the breathtaking La Polvorilla viaduct. You will cross magnificent landscapes, making your way from the multicolored Lerma valley through the deep canyons and rugged peaks of the Quebrada del Toro, and on to the desolate desert plateau of La Puña. *Note:* Train service was suspended at press time, but it's due to start up again later in 2007. See chapter 7.

- **Touring the Jesuit ruins of Córdoba:** Magnificent colonial architecture set in the rolling green hills of the Córdoba sierras reveals a lost Utopia of arts and learning. It's one of the few examples of harmonious cooperation between indigenous people and European colonizers. See chapter 8.

- **Traveling the Wine Roads of Mendoza:** Less commercialized than their European and American counterparts, Mendoza's wineries are free to visit and easily accessible along roads known locally as Caminos del Vino. About 80 wineries formally offer tours and tastings. See chapter 9.

- **Wine Tasting in Valle de Uco:** While Maipú and Luján make wonderful day trips from Mendoza, driving another hour south to the incredibly picturesque Valle de Uco region makes for a sublime day. Hot spots, such as the villages of La Consulta and Villa Flores, are known as "Napa South," thanks to vineyards run by some of the world's great enologists. With the towering wall of the Cordillera de los Andes as a backdrop, and gentle rows of poplar trees marking the country roads, this route is a biking and driving destination without compare. See chapter 9.

- **Sailing to Chile on the Cruce de Lagos:** Why fly or drive when you can sail through the Andes? With three boats and three bus trips, you can go from Bariloche, Argentina, to Puerto Montt, Chile, in a day on the **Cruce de Lagos** tour. Turning it into an overnight trip, with a stay on the Chilean side, gives you time to take in the beauty of the temperate rainforest and the magic of these mountains. See chapter 10.

- **Whale-Watching at Península Valdés:** From April to December, the giant Southern Right Whale heads to the protected bays off the Península Valdés to relax, reproduce, and recharge. The boats that head out hourly from Puerto Pirámides get remarkably close to these friendly giants. You can spot sea elephants, penguins, ostrichlike *choiques,* and sometimes even orca whales on the peninsula as well. See chapter 11.

- **Seeing a Million Penguins Guarding Their Nests:** Every autumn, over a million penguins return to mate on a hillside overlooking the Atlantic, in a remote area of Patagonia. At Punta Tombo National Reserve, you can walk among these friendly creatures and, if you're lucky, get to see them guarding the babies in their nests. See chapter 11.

2 The Best Charming Small Towns

- **Colonia del Sacramento, Uruguay:** Just a short ferry trip from Buenos Aires, Colonia is Uruguay's best example of colonial life. The Old Neighborhood contains brilliant examples of colonial wealth and many of Uruguay's oldest structures. Dating from the 17th century, this beautifully preserved Portuguese settlement makes a perfect day trip. See chapter 5.

- **Salta:** Salta, which sits in the Lerma valley of Argentina's Northwest, has an eternal-spring-like climate and the nation's best-preserved colonial architecture. It's surrounded by the fertile valley of the provincial capital, the polychrome canyons of Cafayate, and the desolate plateau of La Puña. See chapter 7.

- **Cafayate:** Set amid a pink, sandy landscape of cactus-dotted vineyards, the sleepy town of Cafayate has donkeys grazing on the central plaza and heaps of unlocked bicycles outside schools and churches. The sun-drenched area offers palatial-style wineries and luxurious wine lodges. See chapter 7.

- **Villa Carlos Paz:** A quick getaway from Córdoba, Villa Carlos Paz surrounds the picturesque Ebalse San Roque. Although it's actually a reservoir, vacationers treat San Roque like a lake, and they swim, sail, and windsurf in its gentle waters. Year-round, visitors come to Carlos Paz to play outdoors by day and party by night. See chapter 8.

- **La Falda:** An excellent base from which to explore the Punilla, La Falda lies between the Valle Hermoso (Beautiful Valley) and the Sierras Chicas. Argentines come here for rest and relaxation, not wild entertainment. Crisp, clean air, wonderful hikes, and quiet hotels are the draw. See chapter 8.

- **Chacras de Coria:** Once considered a summer getaway for wealthy Mendoza families, Chacras de Coria is just 20 minutes from downtown Mendoza, but it's offset by its shady, gentle, rural lifestyle. The town has great bistros, excellent small inns, a lovely town square with an antiques market on Sundays, and a great ice-cream shop. See chapter 9.

- **Villa la Angostura:** It's becoming somewhat of a jet-set stop in Patagonia; its cottages are owned by a "who's who" of Porteños. Villa la Angostura has plenty of coast line along the north shores of Nahuel Huapi Lake for sailing, fishing, swimming, and sunning. The sweet main street is tidy and quaint, with good shops and some excellent restaurants. The eastern suburb of Bahia Manzano has a collection of cozy wooden lodges that hug the shore. In the winter, the local ski hill Cerro Bayo may be Patagonia's best-kept winter secret. See chapter 10.

- **San Martín de los Andes:** City planners in San Martín had the sense to do what Bariloche never thought of: to limit building height to two stories and to mandate continuity in the town's alpine architecture. The result? Bariloche is crass, whereas San Martín is class, and the town is a year-round playground, to boot. Relax, swim, bike, ski, raft, hunt, or fish—this small town has it all. See chapter 10.

- **El Chaltén:** If you've ever wanted to relive the Wild West, you just might get your chance here in El Chaltén. On the verge of modernity, the area is influenced above all by the ever-present wind and by the beautiful granite spires of Cerro Torre and

Mt. FitzRoy, which tower above town. It's a ramshackle place, with few paved roads, lots of half-built homes, and a remarkable selection of good restaurants. The vibe is for adventurers and nature lovers who are willing to sacrifice some comforts for awe-inspiring nature and friendly locals. See chapter 11.

3 The Best Outdoor Adventures

- **Best Park Walks:** The Palermo Park system, in Buenos Aires, is one of the world's most beautiful, running along Avenida Libertador. You could spend more than a day here, wandering this tree- and monument-lined part of the city, and still not see it all. Within the system are numerous small parks such as the Rose Garden and the Japanese Gardens, as well as museums such as the **Museo de Arte Latinoamericano de Buenos Aires** and the **Museo Nacional de Bellas Artes.** In the Argentine spring, from late September to early October, the weather is at its best; the jacaranda trees here are in their purple-bloomed glory, making this the best time for a stroll. In summer months, locals who can't escape the city come to jog, suntan, and while away the day in this area. See chapter 4.

- **Discovering Iguazú Falls by Raft:** A number of tour companies operate rafts that speed toward the falls, soaking their awestruck passengers along the way. This is the best way to experience the sound and fury of Iguazú's magnificent *cataratas*. See chapter 6.

- **Traveling beyond the Falls into the Iguazú Jungle:** This is a place where birds such as the great dusky swift and brilliant morpho butterflies spread color through the thick forest canopy. You can easily arrange an outing into the forest once you arrive in Iguazú. See chapter 6.

- **Paragliding in La Cumbre.** Jumping off a 300m (984-ft.) cliff and flying with condors is what attracts world-champion paragliders to this laidback

valley in the Córdoba sierra. See chapter 8.

- **Raging down the Mendoza River:** Mendoza offers the best white-water rafting in Argentina. During the summer months, when the snow melts in the Andes and fills the Mendoza River, rafters take on Class IV and V rapids here. Rafting is possible year-round, but the river is colder and calmer in winter months. See chapter 9.

- **Skiing Las Leñas:** One of South America's top ski destinations, Las Leñas boasts more slopes than any single resort in the Americas, with 40 miles of runs, excellent snow, and typically small crowds. Las Leñas also hosts an active nightlife in winter. See chapter 9.

- **Climbing Aconcagua:** At 6,960m (22,829 ft.), Cerro Aconcagua is the highest peak in the Western Hemisphere. Those hoping to reach the top must buy a 20-day permit, which costs $200 (£110), including emergency medical insurance. The climb is not technically difficult, but it demands strength and endurance. See chapter 9.

- **Skiing Cerro Catedral:** With a huge investment in new lifts, new development at the base, and consecutive years of heavy snowfall, Bariloche's Catedral can't be beat. The après-ski scene includes chocolate shops, live music, and happening slope-side lounges. And the views take in the Andes and the beautiful Nahuel Huapi Lake. Catedral is the best ski resort in Argentina. See chapter 10.

- **Rafting the Río Manso:** There are two sections to this gorgeous emerald river south of Bariloche. The Inferior makes for a great family outing, with bird-watching and fun paddling. The Frontera section takes you through an adrenaline-heavy set of 10 rapids towards the border with Chile, followed with a barbecue lunch. Either way, it's a trip through a beautiful undiscovered mountain valley. See chapter 10.

- **Hiking to Laguna Torre:** One of the world's finest day hikes takes you from the door of your inn in El Chaltén to the base of the needle-shaped granite spire of Cerro Torre, a legendary challenge for mountaineers and rock climbers. The hike's pinnacle is on the shores of the blustery Laguna Torre, where the wind feels like it just may blow you over. Back in the shelter of the FitzRoy River valley, you'll head back to town refreshed and exhilarated. See chapter 11.

- **Big Ice: Hiking in Perito Moreno Glacier:** Tour operators have been offering guided walks on the Perito Moreno Glacier for years, and guests from around the world strap on some crampons and head out for an hour or so. Those with a good level of fitness can now head much deeper into the glacier with a full-day hike. Peer into deep ice canyons, navigate your way along a frozen ridge, and try to grasp the sheer grandeur of this UNESCO World Heritage Site. See chapter 11.

4 The Best Hotels

- **The Faena Hotel & Universe:** Fashionistas flock to this Philippe Starck designed hotel, in the Puerto Madero district, to see and be seen. The lobby has lots of bars, and the pool is in the front of the hotel, so players making the rounds here can quickly size up who else is around. See p. 76.

- **Alvear Palace Hotel:** The most exclusive hotel in Buenos Aires and one of the top hotels in the world, the Alvear reflects the Belle Epoque era in which it was designed. Luxurious bedrooms and suites have private butler service, and the hotel's guest list reflects the top names in Argentina and visitors from abroad. See p. 77.

- **Four Seasons Hotel:** In 2002, the Four Seasons took over what was already one of Buenos Aires's most luxurious properties. This landmark hotel has two parts—the 12-story Park Tower, housing the majority of the guest rooms, and the turn-of-the-20th-century French-rococo La Mansión, with seven elegant suites and a handful of private event rooms. See p. 79.

- **Marriott Plaza Hotel:** This historic hotel was the grande dame of Buenos Aires for much of the 20th century— a gathering place for Argentine politicians, foreign dignitaries, and international celebrities. It remains one of the city's most impressive hotels. See p. 66.

- **Sheraton Internacional Iguazú:** The Sheraton International Iguazú is the only hotel on the Argentine side of the falls situated within the national park. From here, half the rooms overlook the falls, and guests are within easy walking distance of the waterfall circuits. See p. 196.

- **Patios de Cafayate:** Flower-adorned courtyards, connected by vaulted corridors that lead to luxury suites, make Patios de Cafayate the most palatial wine lodge in Argentina. A futuristic spa offers wine treatments and splendid views. See p. 220.

- **Park Hyatt Mendoza:** The best-located hotel in Mendoza looks out on the bustling Plaza Independencia. Sipping a glass of Malbec on the front courtyard patio, you're likely to feel like royalty. Rooms are modern, luxurious, and large. There are regular events held here that celebrate the amazing food and wine of the area. See p. 257.
- **Cavas Wine Lodge:** Many new wine lodges are opening up in the Mendoza area, but for now this remarkably luxurious and private inn is the crème de la crème. With its spectacular spa, ultra-isolated bungalows looking across the vineyards to the Andes, and one of the area's most extensive wine cellars, there's no reason to go anywhere else. It affords true romance for food and wine lovers. See p. 273.
- **Llao Llao Hotel & Resort:** With its stunning alpine style, top-notch service, a golf course, a lovely pool, and a plethora of activities, the Llao Llao has it all. It's regularly considered one of the top resorts in the world, with a price to match. Inside, the style is that of an upscale yet cozy hunting lodge. The unbeatable location, perched on a hill surrounded by mountain lakes, offers sublime views from every window. Come here for an unforgettable splurge. See p. 305.
- **Ten Rivers & Ten Lakes Lodge:** This small lodge, perched high on a hill above San Martín de los Andes, is like having your own cottage in an alpine paradise. The eight rooms are cozy and rustic, with warm blankets and private balconies overlooking Lago Lacar. Guests gather in the bright communal loft to watch DVDs. A sumptuous breakfast features homemade baked goods, served in the historic Arrayán teahouse next door. See p. 327.
- **Hotel Territorio:** With just under 40 rooms, this newest spot at Puerto Madryn on the Atlantic Coast means you can come see the whales and penguins and still live in style. The look is very natural: stone, washed cement, dark-wood furniture, and many, many windows overlooking the bay. Territorio is peaceful and modern, with a spa and gourmet restaurant. See p. 341.
- **EOLO Patagonia's Spirit:** A friendly and relaxed home amid the powerful emptiness of the Patagonian Steppe, EOLO is influenced by traditional *estancias* (Argentine ranch farms, dating mostly to the mid– to late 19th c.), but it has modern amenities such as a spa, a wine bar, a library, and an interesting menu. It's a place to come live, breathe, and be wowed by the vastness of Patagonia. See p. 360.
- **Cumbres del Martial:** These immaculate wood cabins are a very romantic place to stay, set in a forest of beech trees overlooking the Beagle Channel. Nearby is a famous tea shop and exhilarating ski lift to an Andean glacier. Unforgettable. See p. 390.
- **Los Notros,** Perito Moreno Glacier, near Calafate: Location is everything at the Los Notros hotel, which boasts a breathtaking view spanning one of Argentina's great wonders, Perito Moreno Glacier. The hotel blends contemporary folk art with a range of colorful hues. Impeccable rooms come with a dramatic view of the electric-blue tongue of the glacier, making this lodge one of the most upscale, unique lodging options in Argentina. The hotel arranges excursions around the area and occasional informative talks. Plenty of easy chairs and lounges are strewn around the property, so guests can sit and contemplate the glorious natural environment. See p. 370.

5 The Best Dining Experiences

- **Cabaña las Lilas,** Buenos Aires (© 11/4313-1336): Widely considered the best *parrilla* in Buenos Aires, Cabaña las Lilas is always packed. The beef comes exclusively from the restaurant's private *estancia,* and the steaks are outstanding. The cuts of beef are so soft, they almost melt in your mouth. Despite the high price of a meal here, it's casual; some guests even come in sneakers and shorts. See p. 94.

- **Katrine,** Buenos Aires (© 11/4315-6222): One of the capital's top dining choices, Katrine (named after its Norwegian chef-owner, who can be found almost every day in the kitchen) serves exquisite international cuisine in a loud and festive dining room. See p. 95.

- **Café Tortoni,** Buenos Aires (© 11/4342-4328): This legendary cafe might not have the best service in town, but its historic importance and old-world beauty more than make up for that. Café Tortoni was and remains Argentina's meeting place of choice among intellectuals; even the throngs of tourists don't overwhelm the space. See p. 116.

- **La Bourgogne,** Buenos Aires (© 11/4805-3857): Jean-Paul Bondoux is the top French chef in South America, brandishing his talents in the kitchen of the restaurant tucked inside the Alvear Palace Hotel. A member of Relais & Châteaux, La Bourgogne serves exquisite cuisine inspired by Bondoux's Burgundy heritage. See p. 96 and p. 273.

- **José Balcance,** Salta (© 387/421-1628): The best restaurant in Salta serves incredibly imaginative Andean cuisine in an elegant setting. Guests can sample llama carpaccio or roasted llama medallions with prickly pear sauce, accompanied by Andean potatoes grown in the verdant hills on the outskirts of the city. They're all delicious. See p. 214.

- **DOC Vinos y Cocina,** Córdoba (© 351/460-8012): This small, elegant restaurant is all about fine wines and finer foods. Modern art hangs from pink-washed walls, amid immaculate white tablecloths bearing wine glasses like waiting sentries. See p. 236.

- **1884,** Mendoza (© 261/424-2698): Celebrity chef Francis Mallmann's restaurant in Mendoza has been number one in town for a few years now, and it remains the ultimate Argentine dining experience in the country's food and wine capital. Located inside a century-old *bodega,* or wine cellar, the restaurant serves rugged and tasty local specialties such as *chivito* (kid) and *lechón* (piglet). See p. 260.

- **Lunch at a *Bodega:*** Mendoza is home to dozens of places where visitors can learn more about wine—from how the grapes are grown to how the barrels are chosen. And the lessons usually come with a relaxed outdoor lunch served on a *bodega* patio, with the towering Andes in the distance. The experience is indulgent, informative, and so very relaxing. Try the lunch at **Bodega Ruca Malen** or at **La Bourgogne** inside Carlos Pulenta's stunning Vistalba vineyard. See chapter 9.

- **Patagonian *Asado:*** The gaucho gets things going early. The coals take time to warm up, and then they place the lamb on a cross in front of the heat, and leave it there to roast for hours. Served with a simple salad and a few bottles of Malbec, it's home cooking like you've never eaten. *Estancias* from the Lakes District to

Los Glaciares National Park humbly offer this tradition daily to visitors. Don't miss it at **Estancia Cristina.** See chapter 11.

- **Luis Martial,** Ushuaia (© 2901/ 430710): Part of the splendid Las Hayas hotel, this elegant restaurant is an excellent choice, with great views and gourmet dining, as well as fixed meals and weekly changing menus. Service is always prompt and professional. See p. 390.

- **Kaupé Restaurant,** Ushuaia (© 02901/422704): King crab predominates on the menu at the Kaupé, in puff pastries, in soufflés, and fresh on the plate. Nearly every dish here is refined and delectable. The gracious, family-run service is as pleasant as the view of the Beagle Channel, and the restaurant's new wine bar really sets it apart from other dining establishments in town. See p. 395.

2

Planning Your Trip to Argentina

A little advance planning can make the difference between a good trip and a great trip. What do you need to know before you depart? When should you go? What's the best way to get there? How much should you plan to spend? What safety or health precautions are advised? This chapter outlines all the basics—the when, why, and how of traveling to and around Argentina.

1 The Regions in Brief

Argentina is the world's eighth-largest country. To the north, it is bordered by Bolivia, Paraguay, Brazil, and Uruguay (the latter situated directly northeast of Buenos Aires). The Andes run along Argentina's western border with Chile, where the continent's highest peaks stand. The multicolored hills and desert plateau of the nation's Northwest are as far removed from the bustling activity of Buenos Aires as are the flat grasslands of Las Pampas from the dazzling waterfalls and subtropical jungle of Iguazú. The land's geographic diversity is reflected in the people, too: Witness the contrast between the capital's largely immigrant population and the indigenous people of the Northwest.

Many people who spend at least a week in Argentina visit Buenos Aires and either Iguazú Falls, the Northwest, or one city in Patagonia. To see the spectacular falls of Iguazú from both the Argentine and Brazilian sides, you need at least 2 full days. A visit to the geographically stunning Northwest—centered around Salta and Jujuy, where Argentina's history began and traces of Inca influence still

appear—requires 3 or more days. If you choose to head south to see just one city in Patagonia (usually Bariloche, famous for ski resorts), you can do it in a few days, but you'd spend a good chunk of that time just getting down there. Ideally, if you want to combine the Lake District and Patagonia with a trip to Buenos Aires, it's better to allot 2 weeks minimum and allow time to savor the distinctive landscape.

BUENOS AIRES & THE PAMPAS Buenos Aires, a rich combination of South American energy and European sophistication, requires at least several days to explore (a week is best). In addition to seeing the city's impressive museums and architectural sites, take time to wander its grand plazas and boulevards, to stroll along its fashionable waterfront, and to engage in its dynamic culture and nightlife. A thick Argentine steak in a local *parrilla* (grill), a visit to a San Telmo antiques shop, a show on Corrientes, and a dance in a traditional tango salon— these are the small experiences that will connect you to the city's soul.

The heartland of the country is the Pampas, an enormous, fertile plain where the legendary gaucho (Pampas cowboy) roams. It includes the provinces of Buenos Aires, southern Santa Fe, southeastern Córdoba, and eastern La Pampa. The Pampas today contain many of the major cities, including the capital. One-third of Argentines live in greater Buenos Aires and exert a strong cultural and political influence over the entire country. For more, see chapter 4.

THE LAKE DISTRICT Argentina's Lake District extends from Junín de los Andes south to Esquel—an Alpine-like region of snowy mountains, waterfalls, lush forest, and, of course, glacier-fed lakes. San Martín de los Andes, Bariloche, and Villa La Angostura are the chief destinations here, but this isn't an area where you stay in one place for long. Driving tours, boating, skiing—you'll be on the move from the moment you set foot in the region. To avoid the crowds, I highly recommend that you plan a trip during the spring or fall (see "When to Go," later in this chapter). For more, see chapter 10.

MENDOZA WINE REGION Within the shadows of the Andes, some of the world's best grapes are grown. Once producing rough table wines best suited to home production, Argentina now produces wines rivaling those produced in California, France, or Italy. The rich and sensual Malbec is the country's signature wine. Trips to the region often use Mendoza as a base for exploring the wineries. Spas have also opened in the region, often using wine ingredients in the treatments. For more, see chapter 9.

NORTHEAST The small province of Misiones, in Argentina's northeastern Mesopotamian region, enjoys a subtropical climate responsible for the region's flowing rivers and lush vegetation. The spectacular Iguazú Falls are created by the merger of the Iguazú and Paraná rivers at the border of Argentina, Brazil, and Paraguay. The region takes its name from the Jesuit missions scattered in this frontier region shared by three countries. Trips here often take in both Argentina and Brazil to see the falls, though the two countries have different visa requirements, depending on the country you are from. If you're planning to see this region, be sure to double-check the requirements. For more, see chapter 6.

NORTHWEST The Andes dominate the Northwest, with ranges between 4,877m and 7,010m (15,997–22,993 ft.). It is here that South America's tallest mountain, Aconcagua, stands at 6,959m (22,826 ft.) above sea level. The two parallel mountain ranges are the Salto-Jujeña, cut by magnificent multicolored canyons called *quebradas*. This region is often compared with the "basin and range" region of the southwestern United States, and can be visited from the historic towns of Salta and Jujuy. For more, see chapter 7.

PATAGONIA Also known as Magallanes or the Deep South, this dry, arid region at the southern end of the continent has soared in popularity over the past 5 years. Patagonia is characterized by vast, open Pampa; the colossal Northern and Southern Ice Fields and hundreds of glaciers; the jagged peaks of the Andes as they reach their terminus; beautiful emerald fjords; and fierce winds. Getting here is an adventure—it usually takes 24 hours if you're coming directly from the United States or Europe. But the long journey pays off in the beauty and singularity of the region. El Calafate is a tourist-oriented village adjacent to Perito Moreno Glacier, which beckons visitors from around the world to stand face to face with its tremendous wall of ice, both a visual and aural spectacle as it slowly but brutally crunches down its path. El Chaltén is a tiny village of 200 whose numbers swell each summer with those who come to

Argentina

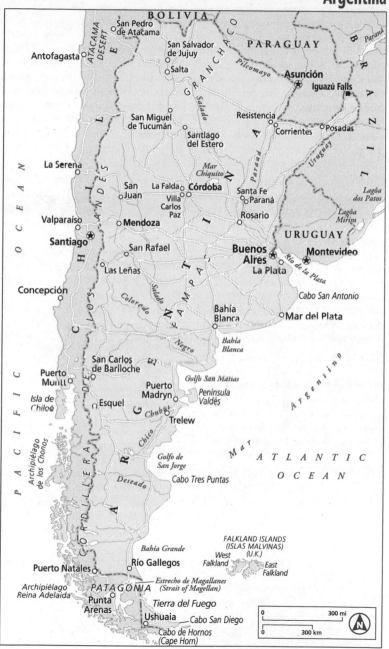

marvel at the stunning towers of mounts Fitz Roy, Cerro Torre, and Puntiagudo. This is the second-most-visited region of Argentina's Los Glaciares National Park and quite possibly its most exquisite, for the singular nature of the granite spires here that shoot up, torpedo-like, above massive tongues of ice that descend from the Southern Ice Field. Don't forget that Patagonia has two sides and water all along its eastern edge. Península Valdez, jutting out into the Atlantic, provides pristine whale-watching. For more, see chapter 11.

TIERRA DEL FUEGO & ANTARCTICA   Even more south than the Deep South, this archipelago at the southern extremity of South America is, like Patagonia, shared by both Chile and Argentina. The main island, separated from the mainland by the Strait of Magellan, is a triangle with its base on the Beagle Channel. Tierra del Fuego's main town is Ushuaia, the southernmost city in the world. Many use the city as a jumping-off point for trips to Antarctica or sailing trips around the Cape Horn. For more information, see chapter 12.

2 Visitor Information

IN THE U.S.   The Argentina Government Tourist Office has offices at 12 W. 56th St., New York, NY 10019 (© **212/ 603-0443;** fax 212/315-5545), and 2655 Le Jeune Rd., Penthouse Suite F, Coral Gables, FL 33134 (© **305/442-1366;** fax 305/441-7029). For more details, consult Argentina's Ministry of Tourism website (see "Websites of Note," below).

IN CANADA   Basic tourist information can be obtained by the Consulate General of Argentina, 2000 Peel St., Suite 600, Montreal, Quebec H3A 2W5 (© **514/842-6582;** fax 514/842-5797; www.consargenmtl.com); for more details, consult Argentina's Ministry of Tourism website (see "Websites of Note," below).

IN THE U.K.   For visitor information, contact the Embassy of Argentina in London (see "Entry Requirements & Customs," below) or consult Argentina's Ministry of Tourism website (see "Websites of Note," below).

IN BUENOS AIRES   The central office of the **City Tourism Secretariat,** Calle Balcarce 360, in Monserrat (© **11/ 4313-0187**), is responsible for all visitor information on Buenos Aires but is not open to the general public. Instead, the city uses several kiosks spread throughout various neighborhoods, which have

maps and hotel, restaurant, and attraction information.

The **Buenos Aires City Tourism Office** runs a hot line for information (© **11/4313-0187**) from 7:30am to 6pm Monday to Saturday, and Sunday 11am to 6pm.

WEBSITES OF NOTE

- **www.embassyofargentina.us**   Up-to-date travel information from the Argentine embassy in Washington, D.C.
- **www.turismo.gov.ar**   This Ministry of Tourism site has travel information for all of Argentina, including a virtual tour of the country's tourist regions, shopping tips, links to city tourist sites, and general travel facts.
- **www.mercotour.com**   A travel site focused on adventure and ecological excursions, with information on outdoor activities in both Argentina and Chile.
- **www.allaboutar.com**   This well-written site is packed with practical information about the country including skiing, golfing, and *estancia* (ranch) stays.
- **www.welcomepatagonia.com**   This fantastic website has extensive information about this region of

Argentina, including hotels, itineraries, and other details.

- **www.welcomeargentina.com** Great information about Argentina, and extensive details on things to do in Buenos Aires. Includes self-guided tour ideas, lists of hotels, and up-to-date information on restaurants and other trends.
- **www.bue.gov.ar** A comprehensive tourism website set up by the city of Buenos Aires with details on neighborhoods and a calendar of events in English and other languages. The website has lots of extremely detailed and useful information, but it can be cumbersome to work through its windows and pop-ups. Be patient with it.
- **www.palermoviejo.com** Find out what is going on in Buenos Aires's

trendiest neighborhood, full of the newest restaurants, shops, and boutique hotels.

- **www.google.com.ar** If you're good at Spanish, use this Argentina-based division of the popular Google search engine. Clicking on "Páginas de Argentina" will give you the most up-to-date, locally produced information.
- **www.subte.com.ar** This website explains in detail the workings of the Buenos Aires subway system and allows you to locate hotels and other sites of interest in relation to subway stops. It also includes downloadable maps and an interactive feature that helps you to calculate travel times between destinations.

3 Entry Requirements & Customs

ENTRY REQUIREMENTS

Citizens of the United States, Canada, the United Kingdom, Australia, New Zealand, and South Africa require a passport to enter the country. No visa is required for citizens of these countries for tourist stays of up to 90 days. For more information concerning longer stays, employment, or other types of visas, contact the embassies or consulates in your home country. Usually, a hop by boat into neighboring Uruguay or crossing into Brazil during an Iguazú Falls excursion will initiate a new 90-day tourist period. With the increasing amount of Americans and other foreigners living in Argentina, this has become one of the preferred quick-fix methods of bypassing visa extension bureaucracy. If you are planning to buy property, retire, or establish a business in Argentina, it is highly advisable to take care of the proper paperwork legally for your stay.

IN THE U.S. Contact the Consular Section of the Argentine Embassy, 1811

Q St. NW, Washington, DC 20009 (© **202/238-6400**). Consulates are also located in Los Angeles ((© **323/954-9155** or -9156), Miami (© **305/580-0530**), Atlanta (© **404/880-0805**), Chicago (© **312/819-2610**), New York City (© **212/603-0400**), and Houston (© **713/871-8935**). For more information, try www.embassyofargentina.us, with links to various consulates in the U.S.

IN CANADA Contact the Embassy of the Argentine Republic, Suite 910, Royal Bank Center, 90 Sparks St., Ottawa, Ontario K1P 5B4 (© **613/236-2351**; fax 613/235-2659).

IN THE U.K. Contact the Embassy of the Argentine Republic, 65 Brooke St., London W1Y 4AH (© **020/7318-1300**; fax 020/7318-1301; seruni@mrecic.gov.ar).

IN NEW ZEALAND Contact the Embassy of the Argentine Republic, Prime Finance Tower, Level 14, 142 Lambton Quay, P.O. Box 5430, Wellington (© **04/472-8330**; fax 04/472-8331; enzel@arg.org.nz).

IN AUSTRALIA Contact the Embassy of the Argentine Republic, John McEwen House, Level 2, 7 National Circuit, Barton, ACT 2600 (© **02/6273 9111;** fax 02/6273 0500; info@argentina.org.au).

CUSTOMS
WHAT YOU CAN TAKE INTO ARGENTINA
Travelers entering Argentina can bring personal effects—including clothes, jewelry, and professional equipment such as cameras and computers—without paying duty. In addition, they can bring in 21 liters of alcohol, 400 cigarettes, and 50 cigars duty-free.

WHAT YOU CAN TAKE HOME FROM ARGENTINA
Returning **U.S. citizens** who have been away for at least 48 hours are allowed to bring back, once every 30 days, $800 worth of merchandise duty-free. You'll be charged a flat rate of duty on the next $1,000 worth of purchases. Any dollar amount beyond that is dutiable at whatever rates apply. On mailed gifts, the duty-free limit is $200. Have your receipts handy to expedite the declaration process. *Note:* If you owe duty, you are required to pay on your arrival in the United States, either by cash, personal check, government or traveler's check, or money order, and in some locations, a Visa or MasterCard.

In Argentina this is rarely an issue unless you have a lot of electronics. To avoid having to pay duty on foreign-made personal items you owned before you left on your trip, bring along a bill of sale, insurance policy, jeweler's appraisal, or receipts of purchase. Or you can register items that can be readily identified by a permanently affixed serial number or marking—think laptop computers, cameras, and CD players—with Customs before you leave. Take the items to the nearest Customs office or register them with Customs at the airport from which

you're departing. You'll receive, at no cost, a Certificate of Registration, which allows duty-free entry for the life of the item.

You cannot bring fresh fruits and vegetables into the United States, with some exceptions. For specifics on what you can bring back, download the invaluable free pamphlet, *Know Before You Go,* online at **www.cbp.gov.** (Click on "Travel," and then on "Know Before You Go! Online Brochure.") Or contact the **U.S. Customs & Border Protection (CBP),** 1300 Pennsylvania Ave. NW, Washington, DC 20229 (© **877/287-8667**) and request the pamphlet.

For **Canadian** rules, write for the booklet *I Declare,* issued by the **Canada Border Services Agency** (© **800/461-9999** in Canada or 204/983-3500; www.cbsa-asfc.gc.ca). Canada allows its citizens a C$750 exemption, and you're allowed to bring back duty-free one carton of cigarettes, one can of tobacco, 40 imperial ounces of liquor, and 50 cigars. In addition, you're allowed to mail gifts to Canada valued at less than C$60 a day, provided they're unsolicited and don't contain alcohol or tobacco (write on the package "Unsolicited gift, under $60 value"). Declare all valuables on the Y-38 form before departure from Canada, including serial numbers of valuables you already own, such as expensive foreign cameras. *Note:* The C$750 exemption can only be used once a year and only after an absence of 7 days.

Citizens of the U.K. who are **returning from a non-E.U. country** have a Customs allowance of: 200 cigarettes; 50 cigars; 250 grams of smoking tobacco; 2 liters of still table wine; 1 liter of spirits or strong liqueurs (over 22% volume); 2 liters of fortified wine, sparkling wine, or other liqueurs; 60 cubic centimeters (ml) of perfume; 250 cubic centimeters (ml) of toilet water; and £145 worth of all other goods, including gifts and souvenirs. People under 17 cannot have the tobacco or alcohol allowance. For more information, contact HM Customs & Excise at ⓒ **0845/010-9000** (from outside the U.K., 020/8929-0152), or consult their website at www.hmce.gov.uk.

The duty-free allowance in **Australia** is A$400 or, for those under 18, A$200. Citizens can bring in 250 cigarettes or 250 grams of loose tobacco, and 1,125 milliliters of alcohol. If you're returning with valuables you already own, such as foreign-made cameras, you should file form B263. A helpful brochure available from Australian consulates or Customs offices is *Know Before You Go.* For more information, call the **Australian Customs Service** (ⓒ **1300/363-263;** www.customs.gov.au).

The duty-free allowance for **New Zealand** is NZ$700. Citizens over 17 can bring in 200 cigarettes, 50 cigars, or 250 grams of tobacco (or a mixture of all three if their combined weight doesn't exceed 250 grams); plus 4.5 liters of wine and beer, or 1.125 liters of liquor. New Zealand currency does not carry import or export restrictions. Fill out a certificate of export, listing the valuables you are taking out of the country; that way, you can bring them back without paying duty. Most questions are answered in a free pamphlet available at New Zealand consulates and Customs offices: *New Zealand Customs Guide for Travellers, Notice no. 4.* For more information, contact **New Zealand Customs,** The Customhouse, 17–21 Whitmore St., Box 2218, Wellington (ⓒ **04/473-6099** or 0800/428-786; www.customs.govt.nz).

4 Money

CASH & CURRENCY

The official Argentine currency is the **peso,** made up of 100 **centavos.** Money is denominated in notes of 2, 5, 10, 20, 50, and 100 pesos; and coins of 1, 2, and 5 pesos, and 1, 5, 10, 25, and 50 centavos. At the time this book went to press, the exchange rate was about 3 pesos to the dollar.

Prices have fallen across the board with the peso's devaluation in 2001, and Argentina is still a terrific bargain for foreign visitors. Often prices are only half what they were before the economic crisis, especially for dining in restaurants. Hotels, however, are guilty of wildly fluctuating rates. In fact, in many cases as of the time of this writing, hotels are no longer the bargain they once were. Many four- and five-star hotels have returned to their pre-devaluation prices, since the number of quality hotels has not kept up with demand as Argentina becomes one of the world's hottest travel destinations. As more and more Europeans (mostly from western Europe) flock to Argentina, hotels are jacking up their prices since they know the euro is so strong.

EXCHANGING MONEY

It's a good idea to exchange at least some money—just enough to cover airport incidentals and transportation to your hotel—before you leave home (though don't expect the exchange rate to be ideal), so you can avoid lines at airport ATMs (automated teller machines). You can exchange money at your local American Express or Thomas Cook office or your bank. If you're far away from a bank with currency-exchange services, American Express offers travelers checks and foreign currency, though with a $15 order fee and additional shipping costs, at www.americanexpress.com or ⓒ **800/807-6233.**

U.S. dollars are no longer as widely accepted in Buenos Aires as they were before and immediately after the December 2001 peso crisis. You can, however, still use them to pay in some business-class hotels, tourist-popular restaurants, and businesses catering to large numbers of tourists. Such places will often post their own daily exchange rate at the counter. (In fact, some ATMs in Buenos Aires dispense U.S. dollars as well as pesos.) For the vast majority of your purchases however, you will need pesos. You can convert your currency in hotels, *casas de cambio* (money-exchange houses), some banks, and at the Buenos Aires airport. Exchange American Express traveler's checks for pesos in Buenos Aires at **American Express,** Arenales 707 (© **11/4130-3135**). It is sometimes difficult to exchange traveler's checks outside the center of Buenos Aires, so plan ahead to have a sufficient amount of cash in pesos on day trips.

ATMs

ATMs are easy to access in Buenos Aires and other urban and touristic areas, but don't depend on finding them off the beaten path. Also, even if your bank allows a certain maximum daily amount to be withdrawn, usually in the range of $500, local ATM limits may be significantly lower (as little as $100), so plan ahead if you know you need large amounts of cash, or test various cash machines before an emergency. It is a good idea to let your bank know ahead of time that you will be using your ATM card overseas so that they do not block transactions in an effort to prevent fraudulent transactions.

The **Cirrus** (© **800/424-7787;** www. mastercard.com) and **PLUS** (© **800/843-7587;** www.visa.com) networks span the globe; look at the back of your bank card to see which network you're on, then call or check online for ATM locations at your destination. Be sure you know your personal identification number (PIN) before you leave home and be sure to find out your daily withdrawal limit before you depart. Also keep in mind that many banks impose a fee every time a card is used at a different bank's ATM, and that fee can be higher for international transactions (up to $5 or more) than for

domestic ones. On top of this, the bank from which you withdraw cash may charge its own fee. To compare banks' ATM fees within the U.S., use **www.bank rate.com**. For international withdrawal fees, ask your bank.

TRAVELER'S CHECKS

Traveler's checks are something of an anachronism from the days before the ATM made cash accessible at any time. Within the Pampas and rural areas of Buenos Aires Province, however, they're still welcomed by many establishments.

You can get traveler's checks at almost any bank. **American Express** offers denominations of $20, $50, $100, $500, and (for cardholders only) $1,000. You'll pay a service charge ranging from 1% to 4%. You can also get American Express traveler's checks over the phone by calling © **800/221-7282;** Amex gold and platinum cardholders who use this number are exempt from the 1% fee.

Visa offers traveler's checks at Citibank locations nationwide, as well as at several other banks. The service charge ranges between 1.5% and 2%; checks come in denominations of $20, $50, $100, $500, and $1,000. Call © **800/732-1322** for information. AAA members can obtain Visa checks for a $9.95 fee (for checks up to $1,500) at most AAA offices or by calling © **866/339-3378. MasterCard** also offers traveler's checks. Call © **800/223-9920** for a location near you.

Foreign-currency traveler's checks are useful if you're traveling to one country; they're accepted at locations such as bed-and-breakfasts where dollar checks may not be, and they minimize the amount of math you have to do at your destination. **American Express, Thomas Cook, Visa,** and **MasterCard** offer foreign currency traveler's checks. You'll pay the rate of exchange at the time of your purchase (so it's a good idea to monitor the rate before you take the plunge), and most companies charge a transaction fee per order (and a shipping fee if you order online).

If you choose to carry traveler's checks, be sure to keep a record of their serial numbers separate from your checks in the event that they are stolen or lost. You'll get a refund faster if you know the numbers.

CREDIT CARDS

Visa, American Express, MasterCard, and Diners Club are commonly accepted. However, bargain hunters take note: Some establishments—especially smaller businesses—will give you a better price if you pay cash. Credit cards are accepted at most hotels and the more expensive restaurants. But note that you cannot use credit cards in many taxis or at most attractions (museums, trams, and so on). Like ATM cards, many credit card companies are also now applying fees to international transactions, often as high as 3%. If you have more than one credit card and expect to charge a lot, call the credit card companies before you leave on your trip to find out which charges the lowest, if any, fee. Using the wrong card can make a bargain not such a bargain anymore.

You can get **cash advances** off your credit card at any bank, and you don't even need to go to a teller; you can get a cash advance at the ATM if you know your PIN. If you've forgotten your PIN or didn't even know you had one, call the phone number on the back of your credit card before your trip and ask the bank to send it to you. It usually takes 5 to 7 business days, although some banks will do it over the phone.

Another hidden expense to contend with: Interest rates for cash advances are often significantly higher than rates for credit card purchases. More importantly, you start paying interest on the advance *the moment you receive the cash.*

5 When to Go

The seasons in Argentina are the reverse of those in the Northern Hemisphere. Buenos Aires is ideal in fall (Mar–May) and spring (Sept–Nov), when temperatures are mild. The beaches and resort towns are packed with vacationing Argentines in summer (Dec–Mar), while Buenos Aires becomes somewhat deserted of locals. Plan a trip to Patagonia and the southern Andes in summer, when days are longer and warmer. Winter (June–Aug) is the best time to visit Iguazú and the Northwest, when the rains and heat have subsided; but spring (Aug–Oct) is also pleasant, as temperatures are mild and the crowds have cleared out.

CLIMATE Except for a small tropical area in northern Argentina, the country lies in the temperate zone, characterized by cool, dry weather in the south and warmer, humid air in the center. Accordingly, January and February are quite hot—often in the high 90s to more than 100°F (35°C–40°C)—while winter (approximately July–Oct) can be chilly.

HOLIDAYS Public holidays are January 1 (New Year's Day), Good Friday, May 1 (Labor Day), May 25 (First Argentine Government), June 10 (National Sovereignty Day), June 20 (Flag Day), July 9 (Independence Day), August 17 (Anniversary of the Death of General San Martín), October 12 (Día de la Raza), December 8 (Immaculate Conception Day), and December 25 (Christmas). Christmas is however usually celebrated on December 24, and called Noche Buena. Many stores and other services close this day.

FESTIVALS & SPECIAL EVENTS Several holidays and festivals are worth planning a trip around; the best place to get information for these events is through your local Argentine tourism office (see "Visitor Information," earlier in this chapter). **Carnaval (Mardi Gras),** the week before the start of Lent, is celebrated in many towns in Argentina, although to a much lesser extent than in neighboring Brazil. The main area for this is in Gulaeyguaychu, about 3 hours north of Buenos Aires in Entre Rios Province. In Salta, citizens throw a large parade, including caricatures of public officials and "water bomb" fights. The **Gaucho Parade** takes place in Salta on June 16, with music by folk artists and gauchos dressed in traditional red ponchos with black stripes, leather chaps, black boots, belts, and knives. For more gaucho madness, visit the city of San Antonio de Areco, about an hour and a half from Buenos Aires. **Día de la Tradición** is generally celebrated around November 10 when gauchos and the tourists who love them flock to the picturesque town.

Inti Raymi (Festival of the Sun) takes places in towns throughout the Northwest the night before the summer solstice (June 20) to give thanks for the year's harvest. **Día de Independencia (Independence Day)** is celebrated in Tucumán on July 9. **Exodo Jujeño (Jujuy Exodus)** takes place August 23 and 24, when locals re-enact the exodus of 1812. The **Batalla de Tucumán (Battle of Tucumán)** celebrates Belgrano's victory over the Spanish on September 24. And the **Fiesta Provincial del Turismo (Provincial Tourist Festival)** takes place in December in Puerto Iguazú.

The Buenos Aires version of Carnaval or Mardi Gras is called **Fiesta de las Murgas,** and though it's not as colorful as Rio de Janeiro's or even the one in Gualeyguaychu, it is celebrated every weekend in February. Various neighborhoods have costumed street band competitions full of loud music, drums, and dancing. Contact the Buenos Aires tourism office (www.bue.gov.ar) for more information.

The **World Tango Festival** is celebrated in early to mid-October, with various events, many concentrated in the tango neighborhood of San Telmo. See www.worldtangofestival.com.ar for more information and exact dates.

The world's biggest polo event, the **Argentine Open Polo Championships,** is held in the polo grounds in Palermo, near the Las Cañitas neighborhood, generally in late November, attracting moneyed crowds from around the world who get to mingle with visiting British royalty. Visit their website, www.aapolo.com.

The **National Gay Pride** parade is held in November, and can switch at the last minute from the first Saturday to the third Saturday of the month, so check Comunidad Homosexual de Argentina's website at www.cha.org.ar for updated information.

Though Argentina has little in the way of Christmas ritual, **Midnight Mass on Christmas Eve (Noche Buena)** at the Metropolitan Cathedral is a beautiful spectacle. It is usually held at 10pm on December 24.

6 Health & Insurance

Check your existing insurance policies and credit card coverage before you buy travel insurance. You may already be covered for lost luggage, canceled tickets, or medical expenses.

The cost of travel insurance varies widely, depending on the cost and length of your trip, your age and health, and the type of trip you're taking, but expect to pay between 5% and 8% of the vacation itself.

TRIP-CANCELLATION INSURANCE
Trip-cancellation insurance helps you get your money back if you have to back out

of a trip, if you have to go home early, or if your travel supplier goes bankrupt. Allowed reasons for cancellation can range from sickness to natural disasters to the State Department declaring your destination unsafe for travel. (Insurers usually won't cover vague fears, though, as many travelers discovered who tried to cancel their trips in Oct 2001 because they were wary of flying.) In this unstable world, trip-cancellation insurance is a good buy if you're getting tickets well in advance— who knows what the state of the world, or of your airline, will be in 9 months? Insurance policy details vary, so read the fine print—and make sure that your airline or cruise line is on the list of carriers covered in case of bankruptcy. A good resource is "Travel Guard Alerts," a list of companies considered high-risk by Travel Guard International (see website below). Protect yourself further by paying for the insurance with a credit card—by law, consumers can get their money back on goods and services not received if they report the loss within 60 days after the charge is listed on their credit card statement.

For more information, contact one of the following recommended insurers: Access America (© 866/807-3982; www.accessamerica.com); Travel Guard International (© 800/826-4919; www.travelguard.com); Travel Insured International (© 800/243-3174; www.travelinsured.com); and Travelex Insurance Services (© 888/457-4602; www.travelexinsurance.com).

MEDICAL INSURANCE

For travel overseas, most health plans (including Medicare and Medicaid) do not provide coverage, and the ones that do often require you to pay for services upfront and reimburse you only after you return home. Even if your plan does cover overseas treatment, most out-of-country hospitals make you pay your bills upfront, and send you a refund only after you've returned home and filed the necessary

paperwork with your insurance company. As a safety net, you may want to buy travel medical insurance. If you require additional medical insurance, try MEDEX Assistance (© 410/453-6300; www.medexassist.com) or Travel Assistance International (© 800/821-2828; www.travelassistance.com; for general information on services, call the company's Worldwide Assistance Services, Inc., at © 800/777-8710).

LOST-LUGGAGE INSURANCE   On domestic flights, checked baggage is covered up to $2,500 per ticketed passenger. On international flights (including U.S. portions of international trips), baggage coverage is limited to approximately $9.07 per pound, up to approximately $635 per checked bag. If you plan to check items more valuable than the standard liability, see if your valuables are covered by your homeowner's policy, get baggage insurance as part of your comprehensive travel-insurance package, or buy Travel Guard's "BagTrak" product. Don't buy insurance at the airport, as it's usually overpriced. Be sure to take any valuables or irreplaceable items with you in your carry-on luggage, as many valuables (including books, money, and electronics) aren't covered by airline policies.

If your luggage is lost, immediately file a lost-luggage claim at the airport, detailing the luggage contents. For most airlines, you must report delayed, damaged, or lost baggage within 4 hours of arrival. The airlines are required to deliver luggage, once found, directly to your house or destination free of charge.

STAYING HEALTHY

Argentina requires no vaccinations to enter the country, except for passengers coming from countries where cholera and yellow fever are endemic.

Some people who have allergies can be affected by the pollution in Buenos Aires's crowded Microcentro, where cars and buses remain mired in traffic jams, belching out pollution. The beautiful spring blossoms also bring with them **pollen,** and even people not usually affected by plants might be thrown off seasonally and by species of plants different from those in North America and Europe. It's a good idea to pack a decongestant with you, or asthma medicine if you require it. With the new anti-smoking laws, you will find indoor smoke not the hazard it once was.

Because motor vehicle crashes are a leading cause of injury among travelers, walk and drive defensively. Do not expect buses and taxis to stop for you when crossing the street. Always use a seat belt, which has now become the law in Buenos Aires, even in taxis.

Most visitors find that Argentine food and water are generally easy on the stomach. Water and ice are considered safe to drink in Buenos Aires. However, you should be careful with Argentine steak. Since it is generally served very rare, if not almost raw inside, people with delicate digestive systems or immune deficiency should request it well done *(bien cocido)*. You should also avoid street food and drinks served out of canisters by roving salespeople at the ubiquitous festivals all over the city. Vegetarians should take note that food that seems vegetarian often is not. With all those cows slaughtered for meat, there's plenty of cow fat finding its way as cooking oil for bread and biscuits. Read ingredients carefully and ask if in doubt.

Buenos Aires's streets and sidewalks can be disgustingly unsanitary. While there is a pooper-scooper law on the books, dog owners seem to take delight in letting their pets relieve themselves in the middle of the sidewalk. The rule of thumb also seems to be the better the neighborhood, the more poop there is, making Recoleta an obstacle course. Watch your step!

DRUGS & PRESCRIPTIONS   Many drugs requiring a prescription in the United States do not necessarily need one in Argentina. Hence, if you lose or run out of a medicine, it might not be necessary to schedule a doctor's appointment to get your prescription. The same goes if you become ill and are sure you know what you need. Many of the pharmacies in the Microcentro have staff members who speak English. Not all medicines, however, are a bargain in Argentina.

AUSTRAL SUN   The summer sun is hot and strong in Buenos Aires. It's best to bring sun block, though it is available in stores and pharmacies throughout the city. There are no beaches within the city proper, but many people go tanning in the Palermo and Recoleta parks or in the Ecological Preserve.

MALARIA & OTHER TROPICAL AILMENTS   Malaria is not an issue in most of Argentina. However, the humid summer months of January and February mean you will sometimes find swarms of mosquitoes, wherever you go. Bring repellant to avoid bites. To get shots or advice for various illnesses if you are traveling from Buenos Aires to the jungle for long periods of time, contact **Vacunar,** a chain of clinics specializing in vaccinations and preventative illness, with locations all over Buenos Aires (www.vacunar.com.ar). Keep in mind that many shots require a period of time before they become effective. They will also explain country by country what is required if you are traveling to other parts of South America.

WHAT TO DO IF YOU GET SICK AWAY FROM HOME

Any foreign consulate can provide a list of area doctors who speak English. If you get sick, consider asking your hotel concierge to recommend a local doctor— even his or her own. You can also try the emergency room at a local hospital. Many hospitals also have walk-in clinics for emergency cases that are not life-threatening; you may not get immediate attention, but you won't pay the high price of an emergency room visit.

If you suffer from a chronic illness, consult your doctor before your departure. For conditions like epilepsy, diabetes, or heart problems, wear a **MedicAlert identification tag** (© 888/ 633-4298; www.medicalert.org), which will immediately alert doctors to your condition and give them access to your records through MedicAlert's 24-hour hot line.

Pack **prescription medications** in your carry-on luggage, and carry prescription medications in their original containers, with pharmacy labels—otherwise they won't make it through airport security. Also bring along copies of your prescriptions in case you lose your pills or run out. Don't forget an extra pair of contact lenses or prescription glasses. Ask your doctor for the generic or chemical name of your prescription medicines, in case a local pharmacist is unfamiliar with the brand name.

The medical facilities and personnel in Buenos Aires and the other urban areas in Argentina are very professional. Argentina has a system of socialized medicine, where basic services are free. Private clinics are inexpensive by Western standards. For an English-speaking hospital, call **Clínica Suisso Argentino** (© 11/4304-1081). The **Hospital Británico** (© 11/ 4309-6600), established over 150 years ago during the British Empire's heyday, also has English-speaking doctors. If you worry about getting sick away from home, you may want to consider **medical travel insurance** (see the section on travel insurance above). In most cases, however, your existing health plan will provide all the coverage you need, but call to make sure. Be sure to carry your identification card in your wallet. You should also ask for receipts or notes from the doctors, which you might need for your claim.

7 Specialized Travel Resources

TRAVELERS WITH DISABILITIES

Buenos Aires is not a very accessible destination for travelers with disabilities. Four- and five-star hotels in Buenos Aires often have a few rooms designed for travelers with disabilities—check with the hotel in advance, and ask specific questions. Some hotels claim to be equipped for those with disabilities but still have one or two stairs leading to their elevator bays, making wheelchair access impossible. American-owned chains tend to be better at accessibility. Hotels with recent renovations sometimes will also have a room with limited capabilities and pull bars in the bathrooms. The tiny crowded streets of the Microcentro can often barely accommodate two people walking together, let alone a wheelchair, and sidewalk cutouts do not exist in all areas.

Fortunately, there are several organizations that can help.

Many travel agencies offer customized tours and itineraries for travelers with disabilities. **Flying Wheels Travel** (© 507/ 451-5005; www.flyingwheelstravel.com) offers escorted tours and cruises that emphasize sports and private tours in minivans with lifts. **Access-Able Travel Source** (© 303/232-2979; www.accessable.com) offers extensive access information and advice for traveling around the world with disabilities. **Accessible Journeys** (© 800/846-4537 or 610/521-0339; www.disabilitytravel.com) caters specifically to slow walkers and wheelchair travelers and their families and friends.

Organizations that offer assistance to travelers with disabilities include **Moss-Rehab** (www.mossresourcenet.org), which provides a library of accessible-travel resources online; **SATH** (Society for Accessible Travel & Hospitality; © **212/ 447-7284;** www.sath.org; annual membership fees: $45 adults, $30 seniors and students), which offers a wealth of travel resources for all types of disabilities and informed recommendations on destinations, access guides, travel agents, tour operators, vehicle rentals, and companion services; and the **American Foundation for the Blind (AFB;** © **800/232-5463;** www.afb.org), a referral resource for the blind or visually impaired that includes information on traveling with Seeing Eye dogs.

For more information specifically targeted to travelers with disabilities, the community website **iCan** (www.ican online.net/channels/travel/index.cfm) has destination guides and several regular columns on accessible travel. Also check out the quarterly magazine *Emerging Horizons* ($14.95 per year, $19.95/£11 outside the U.S.; www.emerginghorizons. com), and *Open World* magazine, published by SATH (see above; subscription: $13 per year, $21 outside the U.S.).

SENIOR TRAVEL

Argentines treat seniors with great respect, making travel for them easy. The Argentine term for a senior or retired person is *jubilado* or *jubilada*. Discounts are usually available; ask when booking a hotel room or before ordering a meal in a restaurant. There are often discounts at theaters and museums, too, or even free admission. **Aerolíneas Argentinas** (© **800/333-0276** in the U.S.; www. aerolineas.com.ar) offers a 10% discount on fares to Buenos Aires from Miami and New York for passengers 62 and older; companion fares are also discounted.

Members of **AARP** (formerly known as the American Association of Retired Persons), 601 E St. NW, Washington, DC 20049 (© **888/687-2277;** www.aarp.org),

get discounts on hotels, airfares, and car rentals. AARP offers members a wide range of benefits, including *AARP: The Magazine* and a monthly newsletter. Anyone over 50 can join.

The Alliance for Retired Americans, 8403 Colesville Rd., Suite 1200, Silver Spring, MD 20910 (© **301/578-8422;** www.retiredamericans.org), offers a newsletter six times a year and discounts on hotel and auto rentals; annual dues are $13 per person or couple. *Note:* Members of the former National Council of Senior Citizens receive automatic membership in the Alliance.

Many reliable agencies and organizations target the 50-plus market. **Elderhostel** (© **877/426-8056;** www.elder hostel.org) arranges study programs for those age 55 and over (and a spouse or companion of any age) in the U.S. and in more than 80 countries around the world. Most courses last 5 to 7 days in the U.S. (2–4 weeks abroad), and many include airfare, accommodations in university dormitories or modest inns, meals, and tuition. **ElderTreks** (© **800/741-7956;** www.eldertreks.com) offers small-group tours to off-the-beaten-path or adventure-travel locations, restricted to travelers 50 and older. **INTRAV** (© **800/ 456-8100;** www.intrav.com) is a high-end tour operator that caters to the mature, discerning traveler, not specifically seniors, with trips around the world that include guided safaris, polar expeditions, private-jet adventures, and small-boat cruises down jungle rivers.

Recommended publications offering travel resources and discounts for seniors include: the quarterly magazine *Travel 50 & Beyond* (www.travel50andbeyond. com); *Travel Unlimited: Uncommon Adventures for the Mature Traveler* (Avalon); *101 Tips for Mature Travelers,* available from Grand Circle Travel (© **800/221-2610** or 617/350-7500; www.gct.com); and *Unbelievably Good*

Deals and Great Adventures That You Absolutely Can't Get Unless You're Over 50 (McGraw-Hill), by Joann Rattner Heilman.

GAY & LESBIAN TRAVELERS

Though much has recently changed, Argentina remains a very traditional, Catholic society that is fairly closed-minded about homosexuality. Buenos Aires, however, is a more liberal exception to this rule, where gays and lesbians are part of the fabric of city life. Gay and lesbian travelers will find numerous clubs, restaurants, and even tango salons catering to them. Buenos Aires has become a major gay-tourism mecca since the peso crisis, outshining Rio de Janeiro in popularity for this market. Gay maps are now produced by the Buenos Aires Tourism Office for distribution with standard travel information. Most hotel concierges also easily provide this information, recognizing the importance of the emerging market. The locally produced website www.gayin buenosaires.com.ar also provides more details on many sites of interest.

In 2003 Buenos Aires enacted a Civil Unions law for gay and lesbian couples—the first major Latin American city to do so—and this law may eventually be made national. Still, throughout Argentina, while there are visible venues and efforts, for the most part many gays and lesbians remain fairly closeted. Violence is sometimes aimed at the transgendered, even by police.

Be aware of a few rules of thumb in a country where close contact is perfectly normal. Women walk hand in hand on the street, and it does not necessarily mean they are lesbians. It's simply common among women. Men kiss each other hello in public, and again this does not mean they are gay.

The **International Gay and Lesbian Travel Association** (IGLTA; © 800/448-8550 or 954/776-2626; www.iglta.org) is the trade association for the gay and lesbian travel industry, and offers an online directory of gay- and lesbian-friendly travel businesses.

The **Comunidad Homosexual de Argentina** (CHA; © 11/4361-6382; www.cha.org.ar) is the main gay- and lesbian-rights group in Argentina. They were the main proponents of the Civil Unions law, which they are attempting to expand to the entire country. They also run the annual Gay Pride March, known as Marcha del Orgullo Gay, in November.

Many agencies offer tours and travel itineraries specifically for gay and lesbian travelers. **Above and Beyond Tours** (© 800/397-2681; www.abovebeyond tours.com) is the exclusive gay and lesbian tour operator for United Airlines. **Olivia Cruises & Resorts** (© 800/631-6277; www.olivia.com) charters entire resorts and ships for exclusive lesbian vacations and offers smaller group experiences for both gay and lesbian travelers.

Pride Travel (© 11/5218-6556; www.pride-travel.com) is an Argentina-based company specializing in inbound Buenos Aires travel and other trips throughout South America. They also run the local gay guide publication *La Ronda* and started Argentina's first gay travel magazine, *Pride Travel,* in 2005. **BueGay Travel** (© 11/4184-8290; www.buegay.com.ar) handles upscale gay tourism within Buenos Aires and other parts of Argentina. **Viajeras Travel** (© 11/4328-1857; www.viajeras.net) is a woman-run travel company, specializing in travel for lesbian visitors to Buenos Aires. The women's scene is harder to tap than the men's scene, so this is a very useful resource.

Since 1992, **Gay.com Travel** and its predecessor **Out and About** (© 800/929-2268; www.outandabout.com) have provided gay and lesbian travelers with objective, timely, and trustworthy coverage of gay-owned and gay-friendly lodging, dining, sightseeing, nightlife, and shopping establishments in every important destination worldwide. *Out Traveler* (© 800/792-2760; www.outtraveler.com) is a gay travel magazine published by LPI Media, the owners of the U.S. gay news magazine the *Advocate. Spartacus International Gay Guide* (Bruno Gmünder Verlag; www.spartacusworld.com/gayguide) and *Odysseus* (Odysseus Enterprises Ltd.) are good, annual English-language guidebooks focused on gay men, with some information for lesbians. You can get them from most gay and lesbian bookstores, or order them from **Giovanni's Room** bookstore, 1145 Pine St., Philadelphia, PA 19107 (© **215/923-2960;** www.giovannisroom.com). Within Buenos Aires, the gay monthly magazine *Imperio* is available at central newspaper kiosks.

WOMEN TRAVELERS
In spite of recent female candidates for president like Elisa Carrió and the very visible women-owned and -run businesses in the restaurant and tourism industries, Argentina remains at heart a sexist country. There is a glass ceiling for women in many corporations, and female beauty is highly idealized above all other traits. Men are extremely flirtatious, and leering looks are common, owing perhaps to the strong Italian influence in the country. While disconcerting, any looks and calls you might get are rarely more than that. Drunk men in clubs can sometimes be physically harassing, however. If you seek to avoid unwanted attention, don't dress skimpily (as many Porteñas, or Buenos Aires natives, do). Women should be cautious when walking alone at night and should take radio-taxis, known as *remises* (p. 32), after dark.

In the rare and unlikely event of an assault or sexual attack, contact the police immediately. More help can also be received from the **Centro de Estudios Cultura y Mujer (CECYM),** Guatemala 4294 (© **11/4865-9102;** www.cecym.org.ar). It specializes in sexual violence against women, but not all of the staff members speak English.

Check out the award-winning website **Journeywoman** (www.journeywoman.com), a "real-life" women's travel information network where you can sign up for a free e-mail newsletter and get advice on everything from etiquette and dress to safety; or the travel guide *Safety and Security for Women Who Travel,* by Sheila Swan and Peter Laufer (Travelers' Tales, Inc.), offering common-sense tips on safe travel.

KIDS & TEENS
Argentines love and pamper their children in every way possible. Argentine kids are also trained from an early age to stay up late like their parents. Don't be surprised to find yourself passing a playground full of kids and their parents on the swing sets at 2am when you're trying to find your way back to your hotel.

Many hotels have programs for children, especially around the holidays. Most will also provide babysitting, as long as it is requested in advance.

STUDENT TRAVELERS
Student discounts are very common in Argentina, but usually only if one has appropriate ID. **STA Travel** (© **800/781-4040** in the U.S., 020/7361-6144 in the U.K., or 1300/360-960 in Australia; www.statravel.com) specializes in affordable airfares, bus and rail passes, accommodations, insurance, tours, and packages for students and young travelers, and issues the **International Student Identity Card (ISIC).** This is the most widely recognized proof that you really are a student. As well as getting you discounts on a huge range of travel, tours, and attractions, it comes with a 24-hour

emergency help line and a global voice/fax/e-mail messaging system with discounted international telephone calls. Available to any full-time student over 12, it costs $21.

Argentina is great for college students on vacation and on a budget. The legal drinking age in Argentina is 18. There are places to drink and socialize all over Argentina. Within Buenos Aires, the bars around Plaza Serrano (see chapter 4) in Palermo Soho offer inexpensive beers on tap and pitchers of sangria. This is often served up with inexpensive snacks and live music, meaning having fun won't break a student budget. In other cities, if it's not listed here in the book, ask around at the central square. You might make new friends in the process.

8 Planning Your Trip Online

SURFING FOR AIRFARES

The "big three" online travel agencies, **Expedia.com, Travelocity,** and **Orbitz,** sell most of the air tickets bought on the Internet. (Canadian travelers should try Expedia.ca and Travelocity.ca; U.K. residents can go to Expedia.co.uk and Opodo.co.uk.). Each has different business deals with the airlines and may offer different fares on the same flights, so it's wise to shop around. Expedia.com and Travelocity will also send you **e-mail notification** when a cheap fare becomes available to your favorite destination. Of the smaller travel agency websites, **SideStep** (www.sidestep.com) has gotten the best reviews from Frommer's authors. It's a browser add-on that purports to "search 140 sites at once," but in reality only beats competitors' fares as often as other sites do.

Also remember to check **airline websites.** Even with major airlines, you can often shave a few bucks from a fare by booking directly through the airline and avoiding a travel agency's transaction fee. But you'll get these discounts only by **booking online:** Most airlines now offer online-only fares that even their phone agents know nothing about. For the websites of airlines that fly to and from your destination, see "Getting There," later in this chapter.

Great **last-minute deals** are available through free weekly e-mail services provided directly by the airlines. Most of these are announced on Tuesday or Wednesday and must be purchased online. Most are only valid for travel that weekend, but some (such as Southwest's) can be booked weeks or months in advance. Sign up for weekly e-mail alerts at airline websites or check megasites that compile comprehensive lists of last-minute specials, such as **SmarterTravel.com.** For last-minute trips, **site59.com** and **lastminutetravel.com** in the U.S. and **lastminute.com** in Europe often have better air-and-hotel package deals than the major-label sites. A website listing numerous bargain sites and airlines around the world is **www.itravelnet.com**.

If you're willing to give up some control over your flight details, use what is called an **"opaque" fare service** like **Priceline** (www.priceline.com; www.priceline.co.uk for Europeans) or its smaller competitor **Hotwire** (www.hotwire.com). Both offer rock-bottom prices in exchange for travel on a "mystery airline" at a mysterious time of day, often with a mysterious change of planes en route. The mystery airlines are all major, well-known carriers—and the possibility of being sent from Philadelphia to Chicago via Tampa is remote; the airlines' routing computers have gotten a lot better than they used to be. But your chances of getting a 6am or 11pm flight are pretty high. Hotwire tells you flight prices before you buy; Priceline usually has better deals than Hotwire, but you

Frommers.com: The Complete Travel Resource

For an excellent travel-planning resource, we highly recommend **Frommers. com** (www.frommers.com), voted Best Travel Site by *PC Magazine*. We're a little biased, of course, but we guarantee that you'll find the travel tips, reviews, monthly vacation giveaways, bookstore, and online-booking capabilities thoroughly indispensable. Among the special features are our popular **Destinations** section, where you'll get expert travel tips, hotel and dining recommendations, and advice on the sights to see for more than 3,500 destinations around the globe; the **Frommers.com Newsletter**, with the latest deals, travel trends, and money-saving secrets; our **Community** area featuring **Message Boards**, where Frommer's readers post queries and share advice (sometimes even our authors show up to answer questions); and our **Photo Center**, where you can post and share vacation tips. When your research is done, the **Online Reservations System** (www.frommers.com/book_a_trip) takes you to Frommer's preferred online partners for booking your vacation at affordable prices.

have to play their "name our price" game. If you're new at this, the helpful folks at **BiddingForTravel** (www.biddingfor travel.com) do a good job of demystifying Priceline's prices and strategies. Priceline and Hotwire are great for flights within North America and between the U.S. and Europe. But for flights to other parts of the world, consolidators will almost always beat their fares. *Note:* In 2004 Priceline added nonopaque service to its roster. You now have the option to pick exact flights, times, and airlines from a list of offers—or opt to bid on opaque fares as before.

For much more about airfares and savvy air-travel tips and advice, pick up a copy of *Frommer's Fly Safe, Fly Smart* (Wiley Publishing, Inc.).

SURFING FOR HOTELS

Shopping online for hotels is generally done one of two ways: by booking through the hotel's own website or through an independent booking agency (or a fare-service agency like Priceline; see below). These Internet hotel agencies have multiplied in mind-boggling numbers of late, competing for the business of millions of consumers surfing for accommodations around the world. This competitiveness can be a boon to consumers who have the patience and time to shop and compare the online sites for good deals—but shop they must, for prices can vary considerably from site to site. And keep in mind that hotels at the top of a site's listing may be there for no other reason than that they paid money to get the placement.

Of the "big three" sites, **Expedia.com** offers a long list of special deals and "virtual tours" or photos of available rooms so you can see what you're paying for (a feature that helps counter the claims that the best rooms are often held back from bargain-booking websites). **Travelocity** posts unvarnished customer reviews and ranks its properties according to the AAA rating system. Also reliable are **Hotels.com** and **Quikbook.com**. An excellent free program, **TravelAxe** (www.travelaxe.net), can help you search multiple hotel sites at once, even ones you may never have heard of—and conveniently lists the total price of the room, including the taxes and service charges. Another booking site, **Travelweb** (www.travelweb.com), is partly owned by the hotels it represents (including the Hilton, Hyatt, and Starwood chains) and is therefore plugged directly into the hotels' reservations systems—unlike independent online agencies, which have to fax or e-mail reservation requests to the hotel, a good portion of which get misplaced in the shuffle. More than once, travelers have arrived at the hotel only to be told that they have no reservation. To be fair, many of the major sites are undergoing improvements in service and ease of use, and Expedia.com will soon be able to plug directly into the reservations systems of many hotel chains—none of which can be bad news for consumers. In the meantime, it's a good idea to **get a confirmation number** and **make a printout** of any online-booking transaction.

In the opaque-website category, **Priceline** and **Hotwire** are even better for hotels than for airfares; with both, you're allowed to pick the neighborhood and quality level of your hotel before offering up your money. Priceline's hotel product even covers Europe and Asia, though it's much better at getting five-star lodging for three-star prices than at finding anything at the bottom of the scale. On the downside, many hotels stick Priceline guests in their least desirable rooms. Be sure to go to the BiddingForTravel website (see above) before bidding on a hotel room on Priceline; it features a fairly up-to-date list of hotels that Priceline uses in major cities. For both Priceline and Hotwire, you pay upfront and the fee is nonrefundable. *Note:* Some hotels do not provide loyalty program credits or points or other frequent-stay amenities when you book a room through opaque online services.

SURFING FOR RENTAL CARS

For booking rental cars online, the best deals are usually found at rental-car company websites, although all the major online travel agencies also offer rental-car reservations services. Priceline and Hotwire work well for rental cars too; the only "mystery" is which major rental company you get, and for most travelers the difference between Hertz, Avis, and Budget is negligible.

9 The 21st-Century Traveler

INTERNET ACCESS ABROAD

Travelers have any number of ways to check their e-mail and access the Internet on the road. Of course, using your own laptop—or even a PDA (personal digital assistant) or electronic organizer with a modem—gives you the most flexibility. But even if you don't have a computer, you can still access your e-mail and even your office computer from cybercafes.

WITHOUT YOUR OWN COMPUTER

It's hard nowadays to find a city that *doesn't* have a few cybercafes. Although there's no definitive directory for cyber-cafes—these are independent businesses, after all—two places to start looking are at **www.cybercaptive.com** and **www.cyber cafe.com**.

Aside from formal cybercafes, most **youth hostels** nowadays have at least one computer you can get to the Internet on. And most **public libraries** across the world offer Internet access free or for a small charge. Avoid **hotel business centers** unless you're willing to pay exorbitant rates.

Most major airports now have **Internet kiosks** scattered throughout their gates. These kiosks, which you'll also see in shopping malls, hotel lobbies, and tourist information offices around the world, give you basic Web access for a per-minute fee that's usually higher than cybercafe prices. The kiosks' clunkiness and high prices mean they should be avoided whenever possible.

To retrieve your e-mail, ask your **Internet Service Provider (ISP)** if it has a Web-based interface tied to your existing e-mail account. If your ISP doesn't have such an interface, you can use the free **mail2web** service (www.mail2web.com) to view and reply to your home e-mail. For more flexibility, you may want to open a free, Web-based e-mail account with **Yahoo! Mail** (http://mail.yahoo.com). (Microsoft's Hotmail is another popular option, but Hotmail has severe spam problems.) Your home ISP may be able to forward your e-mail to the Web-based account automatically.

If you need to access files on your office computer, look into a service called **GoToMyPC** (www.gotomypc.com). The service provides a Web-based interface for you to access and manipulate a distant PC from anywhere—even a cybercafe— provided your "target" PC is on and has an always-on connection to the Internet (such as with Road Runner cable). The service offers top-quality security, but if you're worried about hackers, use your own laptop rather than a cybercafe computer to access the GoToMyPC system.

WITH YOUR OWN COMPUTER

Wi-Fi (wireless fidelity) is the buzzword in computer access, and more and more hotels, cafes, and retailers are signing on as wireless "hotspots" from where you can get high-speed connection without cable wires, networking hardware, or a phone line (see below). You can get Wi-Fi connection one of several ways. Many laptops sold in the last year have built-in Wi-Fi capability (an 802.11b wireless Ethernet connection). Mac owners have their own networking technology, Apple AirPort. Those with older computers can plug an 802.11b/**Wi-Fi card** (around $50) into their laptops. You sign up for wireless access service much as you do cellphone service, through a plan offered by one of several commercial companies that have made wireless service available in airports, hotel lobbies, and coffee shops, primarily in the U.S. (followed by the U.K. and Japan). **T-Mobile Hotspot** (www.t-mobile.com/hotspot) serves up wireless connections at more than 1,000 Starbucks coffee shops nationwide. **Boingo** (www.boingo.com) and **Wayport** (www.wayport.com) have set up networks in airports and high-class hotel lobbies. IPass providers (see below) also give you access to a few hundred wireless hotel-lobby setups. Best of all, you don't need to be staying at the Four Seasons to use the hotel's network; just set yourself up on a nice couch in the lobby. The companies' pricing policies can be Byzantine, with a variety of monthly, per-connection, and per-minute plans, but in general you pay around $30 a month for limited access— and as more and more companies jump on the wireless bandwagon, prices are likely to get even more competitive.

There are also places that provide **free wireless networks** in cities around the world. To locate these free hotspots, go to **www.personaltelco.net/index.cgi/ WirelessCommunities**.

If Wi-Fi is not available at your destination, most business-class hotels throughout the world offer dataports for laptop modems, and a few thousand hotels in the U.S. and Europe now offer free high-speed Internet access using an Ethernet network cable. You can bring your own cables, but most hotels rent them for around $10. **Call your hotel in advance** to see what your options are.

In addition, major ISPs have **local access numbers** around the world, allowing you to go online by simply placing a local call. Check your ISP's website or call its toll-free number and ask how you

Online Traveler's Toolbox

Veteran travelers usually carry some essential items to make their trips easier. Following is a selection of handy online tools to bookmark and use.

- **Airplane Seating & Food.** Find out which seats to reserve and which to avoid (and more) on all major domestic airlines at www.seatguru.com. And check out the type of meal (with photos) you'll likely be served on airlines around the world at **www.airlinemeals.net**.
- **Foreign Languages for Travelers (www.travlang.com).** Learn basic terms in more than 70 languages and click on any underlined phrase to hear what it sounds like.
- **Intellicast** (www.Intellicast.com) and **Weather.com** (www.weather.com). Provide weather forecasts for all 50 states and for cities around the world.
- **Subway Navigator** (www.subwaynavigator.com). Download subway maps and get savvy advice on using subway systems in dozens of major cities around the world.
- **Time & Date** (www.timeanddate.com). See what time (and day) it is anywhere in the world.
- **Travel Warnings** (http://travel.state.gov, www.fco.gov.uk/travel, www.voyage.gc.ca, www.dfat.gov.au/consular/advice). These sites report on places where health concerns or unrest might threaten American, British, Canadian, and Australian travelers. Generally, U.S. warnings are the most paranoid; Australian warnings are the most relaxed.
- **Universal Currency Converter** (www.xe.com/ucc). See what your dollar or pound is worth in more than 100 other countries.
- **Visa ATM Locator** (www.visa.com) for locations of PLUS ATMs worldwide, or **MasterCard ATM Locator** (www.mastercard.com) for locations of Cirrus ATMs worldwide.

can use your current account away from home, and how much it will cost.

If you're traveling outside the reach of your ISP, the **iPass** network has dial-up numbers in most of the world's countries. You'll have to sign up with an iPass provider, who will then tell you how to set up your computer for your destination(s). For a list of iPass providers, go to www.ipass.com and click on "Individuals Buy Now." One solid provider is **i2roam** (© **866/811-6209** or 920/235-0475; www.i2roam.com).

Wherever you go, bring a **connection kit** of the right power and phone adapters, a spare phone cord, and a spare Ethernet network cable—or find out whether your hotel supplies them to guests.

USING A CELLPHONE ABROAD

The three letters that define much of the world's **wireless capabilities** are GSM (Global System for Mobiles)—a big, seamless network that makes for easy cross-border cellphone use throughout Europe and dozens of other countries worldwide. In the U.S., T-Mobile, AT&T Wireless, and Cingular use this quasi-universal system; in Canada, Microcell and some Rogers customers are GSM, and all Europeans and most Australians use GSM.

If your cellphone is on a GSM system and you have a world-capable multiband phone such as many Sony Ericsson, Motorola, or Samsung models, you can make and receive calls across civilized areas on much of the globe, from Andorra to Uganda. Just call your wireless operator and ask for "international roaming" to be activated on your account. Unfortunately, per-minute charges can be high—usually $1 to $1.50 in western Europe and up to $5 in places such as Russia and Indonesia.

That's why it's important to buy an "unlocked" world phone from the get-go. Many cellphone operators sell "locked" phones that restrict you from using any other removable computer memory phone chip (called a **SIM card**) card other than the ones they supply. Having an unlocked phone allows you to install a cheap, prepaid SIM card (found at a local retailer) in your destination country. (Show your phone to the salesperson; not all phones work on all networks.) You'll get a local phone number—and much, much lower calling rates. Getting an already locked phone unlocked can be a complicated process, but it can be done; just call your cellular operator and say you'll be going abroad for several months and want to use the phone with a local provider.

For many, **renting** a phone is a good idea. (Even world-phone owners will have to rent new phones if they're traveling to non-GSM regions, such as Japan or Korea.) While you can rent a phone from any number of overseas sites, including kiosks at airports and at car-rental agencies, I suggest renting the phone before you leave home. That way you can give loved ones and business associates your new number, make sure the phone works, and take the phone wherever you go—especially helpful for overseas trips through several countries, where local phone-rental agencies often bill in local currency and may not let you take the phone to another country.

Phone rental isn't cheap. You'll usually pay $40 to $50 per week, plus airtime fees of at least a dollar a minute. If you're traveling to Europe, though, local rental companies often offer free incoming calls within their home country, which can save you big bucks. The bottom line: Shop around.

Two good wireless rental companies are **InTouch USA** (© **800/872-7626; www.intouchglobal.com**) and **RoadPost** (© **888/290-1606** or 905/272-5665; www.roadpost.com). Give them your itinerary and they'll tell you what wireless products you need. InTouch will also, for free, advise you on whether your existing phone will work overseas; simply call © 703/222-7161 between 9am and 4pm EST, or go to http://intouchglobal.com/travel.htm. For trips of more than a few weeks spent in one country, **buying a phone** becomes economically attractive, as many nations have cheap, no-questions-asked prepaid phone systems. Once you arrive at your destination, stop by a local cellphone shop and get the cheapest package; you'll probably pay less than $100 for a phone and a starter calling card. Local calls may be as low as 10¢ per minute, and in many countries incoming calls are free.

10 Getting There

BY PLANE
Argentina's main international airport is **Ezeiza Ministro Pistarini** (EZE; © **11/4480-9538**), located 42km (26 miles) to the west of Buenos Aires. Allot at least 45 minutes to an hour for travel between the airport and the city, more in rush hour. You will be assessed a departure tax of approximately $24 upon leaving the country, payable in pesos, dollars, or by

Visa credit card. For flights from Buenos Aires to Montevideo (in Uruguay), the departure tax is $5. Passengers in transit and children under 2 are exempt from this tax. However, visitors are advised to verify the departure tax with their airline or travel agent, as the exact amount changes frequently.

Below are the major airlines that fly into Argentina from North America, Europe, and Australia. Argentina's national airline is **Aerolíneas Argentinas** (© **800/333-0276** in the U.S., 0810/ 222-86527 in Buenos Aires, or 1800/ 22-22-15 in Australia; www.aerolineas. com.ar). The airline flies a few times a week from New York and daily from Miami. Aerolíneas Argentinas is an interesting introduction to the excitement of Argentina and its culture. The female flight attendants tend to be particularly glamorous, and the staff, mostly natives of Argentina, can offer excellent advice for you to use once you are on the ground. Argentine wine is free and liberally served in coach and all classes.

Other operators include **American Airlines** (© 800/433 7300 in the U.S. or 11/4318-1111 in Buenos Aires; www.americanair.com); **United Airlines** (© 800/241-6522 in the U.S. or 0810/ 777-8648 in Buenos Aires; www.ual.com); **Air Canada** (© 888/247-2262 in Canada or 11/4327-3640 in Buenos Aires; www. aircanada.ca); **British Airways** (© 0845/ 773-3377 in the U.K. or 11/4320-6600 in Buenos Aires; www.britishairways.com); and **Iberia** (© 0845/601-2854 in the U.K. or 11/4131-1000 in Buenos Aires; www.iberia.com). **LanChile** (© 866/ 435-9526 in the U.S. and Canada or 11/ 4378-2222 in Buenos Aires; www.lanchile. com) also provides connections from Miami and New York both direct and through Santiago to Buenos Aires. **Qantas Airlines** of Australia (© 13-13-13 in Australia or 11/4514-4730 in Buenos Aires) now has service from Sydney to Santiago with shared service continuing to Buenos Aires on LanChile.

Domestic airlines and flights to Uruguay use **Jorge Newbery Airport** (© **11/4514-1515**), located only 15 minutes to the north along the river from downtown.

The easiest way to travel Argentina's vast distances is by air. **Aerolíneas Argentinas** (see above) connects most cities and tourist destinations in Argentina, including Córdoba, Jujuy, Iguazú, Salta, and the beach resorts.

If you plan to travel extensively in Argentina from Buenos Aires, consider buying the **Visit Argentina Pass,** issued by Aerolíneas Argentinas. You must purchase the pass in your home country—it cannot be purchased once you are in Argentina. This pass offers discounts for domestic travel in conjunction with your international Aerolíneas Argentinas ticket. Passes are purchasable as one-way coupons for flights within Argentina. Each segment ranges in price from $27 to $294, depending on the destination, not including additional possible fees and taxes. Slightly higher, but still reduced rates, ranging from $38 to $382, are available if you fly into Argentina via other airlines as well. Tickets are exchangeable by date but not by destination and are nonrefundable. For more information, contact the Aerolíneas office in your home country or visit **www.aerolineas.com.**

BY BUS

The **Estación Terminal de Omnibus,** Av. Ramos Mejía 1680 (© **11/4310-0700**), located near Retiro Station, serves all long-distance buses. You would use this station when connecting to other parts of Argentina, or by long-distance coach from other countries. Due to the high cost of air transport for most South Americans, the continent is served by numerous companies offering comfortable, and at times luxurious, bus services to other capitals, often overnight. This is ideal for student and budget travelers.

Among the major bus companies that operate out of Buenos Aires are **La Veloz del Norte** (© 11/4315-2482), serving destinations in the Northwest, including Salta and Jujuy; **Singer** (© 11/4315-2653), serving Puerto Iguazú as well as Brazilian destinations; and **T.A. Chevallier** (© 11/4313-3297), serving points throughout the country.

The **Estación Terminal de Omnibus,** sometimes referred to as the Retiro Bus Station, is sprawling, enormous, and confusing. Just walking from one end to another takes about 15 minutes given the ramps, crowds and stairs you have to maneuver through. Routes and platform locations rarely make it to the overhead boards also so don't rely on them. Still, in spite of the chaos, there is an overarching order. A color-coded system used at the ticket counters explains in general which destinations of the country are served by which bus lines. Red, for instance, indicates the center of the country, including the province of Buenos Aires; dark blue, the south; orange, the north; green, the northeast; light blue, the central Atlantic coast; and gray, the international destinations. However, at their sales counters, many bus companies indicate names of cities on their destination lists that they no longer serve, so you may have to stand in a line to ask. Many companies also have more than one name, adding to the visual clutter at the ticket counters. To help you make sense of it all, use **www.tebasa.com.ar**, the terminal's website, while planning your trip. Click on the province where you are traveling and a list of bus companies and phone numbers will come up. Bus tickets can also be purchased at most travel agents. This can cost slightly more, but can save a lot of confusion if you're short on time.

BY CAR

In Buenos Aires, travel by *subte* (subway) or *remises* (radio-dispatched taxis, as opposed to street taxis) is easier and safer than driving yourself. Rush-hour traffic is chaotic, and parking is difficult. If you have rented a car for whatever reason, park it at your hotel or a nearby garage and leave it there. Most daily parking charges do not exceed $4 or $5. Many recently built hotels have parking on the premises; others use nearby garages.

If you're traveling outside of Buenos Aires, it's another story when it comes to having a car. Argentine roads and highways are generally in good condition, with the exception of some rural areas. Most highways have been privatized and charge nominal tolls. In Buenos Aires, drivers are aggressive and don't always obey traffic lanes or lights. Wear your seat belt, as required by Argentine law. U.S. driver's licenses are valid in greater Buenos Aires, but you need an Argentine or international license to drive in most other parts of the country. Fuel is expensive, at about $1 per liter (or $4 per gal.).

The **Automóvil Club Argentino (ACA),** Av. del Libertador 1850 (© 11/4802-6061), has working arrangements with international automobile clubs. The ACA offers numerous services, including roadside assistance, road maps, hotel and camping information, and discounts for various tourist activities.

CAR RENTALS Many international car-rental companies operate in Argentina with offices at airports and in city centers. Here are the main offices in Buenos Aires for the following agencies: **Hertz,** Paraguay 1122 (© **800/654-3131** in the U.S., or 11/4816-8001 in Buenos Aires); **Avis,** Cerrito 1527 (© **800/230-4898** in the U.S., or 11/4300-8201 in Buenos Aires); **Dollar,** Marcelo T. de Alvear 523 (© **800/800-6000** in the U.S., or 11/4315-8800 in Buenos Aires); and **Thrifty,** Av. Leandro N. Alem 699 (© **800/847-4389** in the U.S., or 11/4315-0777 in Buenos Aires). Car rental is expensive in Argentina, with standard rates beginning at about $50 to $60 per day for a subcompact with unlimited mileage (ask for any special promotions, especially on weekly rates). Check to see if your existing automobile insurance policy (or a credit card) covers insurance for car rentals.

11 Independent Travel Packages & Escorted General-Interest Tours

These days, so many people plan their trips via websites and e-mail that it's easy to forget that a computer can never replace the knowledge of a good travel agent.

RECOMMENDED U.S.-BASED OPERATORS The following U.S.-based tour companies offer solid, well-organized tours in various price categories, and they are backed by years of experience. All can arrange tours of Buenos Aires, the surroundings, and other parts of Argentina and South America.

- **Borello Travel & Tours,** 7 Park Ave., Suite 21, New York, NY 10016 ((℃ **800/405-3072** or 212/686-4911; www.borellotravel.com), is a New York–based travel firm specializing in upscale travel to South America. The owner, Sandra Borello, has run her company for nearly 20 years and is a native of Buenos Aires. Prices can vary, depending on the season, options, and hotel, but a 1-week package to Buenos Aires can cost about $1,500 per person. They maintain an additional office in Buenos Aires that can be reached at ℃ 11/5031-1988.
- **Travel Dynamics International,** 132 East 70th Street, New York NY 10021 (℃ **800/257-5767** or 212/517-0076; www.TravelDynamics International.com), is a luxury cruise operator that specializes in educational enrichment programs aboard small cruise ships. TDI voyages include expert guided land tours, and on-board lectures by distinguished scholars and guests. They cater to the traveler with an intellectual interest in history, culture, and nature. Operating for almost 40 years, this company offers voyages with destinations in South America and Antarctica. Their journeys to Antarctica usually open with an overnight stay in Buenos Aires and begin at $7,995 for a 14-day program (prices may vary).

RECOMMENDED BUENOS AIRES–BASED OPERATORS Even if you have arranged things at home, once you're in Buenos Aires, there are always last-minute changes or new things you would like to see. The following companies are all excellent and have English-speaking staff members. All can also provide trips to other cities in Argentina outside of Buenos Aires, as well as South America.

- **Say Hueque Tourism,** Viamonte 749, Office 601, 1053 Buenos Aires (℃ **11/5199-2517**; www.sayhueque. com), is a highly recommended small company with knowledgeable, friendly service and attention to personalized client care. The company began by catering to the young and adventurous on a budget, but has begun to deal with a more upscale yet independent-thinking clientele. Various tour themes include Literary Buenos Aires, Biking Buenos Aires, and Tango Buenos Aires, among many others. They also offer adventure tours within the vicinity of Buenos Aires such as to the Tigre Delta. Outside of Buenos Aires, they specialize in Patagonia and Iguazú, finding special out-of-the-way places for their clients. Based on their very personal service, this is among my favorite of the operators within Buenos Aires.

- **Euro Tur,** Viamonte 486, 1053 Buenos Aires (© **11/4312-6077;** www.eurotur.com), is one of the largest and oldest travel companies in Argentina, specializing in inbound travel, but they can also help walk-ins to accommodate travelers' needs directly while in Buenos Aires. They can arrange basic city tours to trips of all kinds throughout Argentina and South America.

- **Les Amis,** Maipú 1270, 1005 Buenos Aires (© **11/4314-0500;** www.lesamis.com.ar), is another large Argentine tour company, with offices throughout Buenos Aires and Argentina. They can arrange trips while you are in town for Buenos Aires, Argentina, and many other parts of South America. Within the U.S., they are represented by Gina Heilpern, who maintains an office in New York. She can be reached at © **718/857-5567.**

ORGANIZED ADVENTURE TRIPS
The advantages of traveling with an organized group are plentiful, especially for travelers who have limited time and resources. Tour operators take the headache out of planning a trip, and they iron out the wrinkles that invariably pop up along the way. Many tours are organized to include guides, transportation, accommodations, meals, and gear (some outfits will even carry gear for you, for example, on trekking adventures).

- **Abercrombie & Kent,** 1520 Kensington Rd., Oak Brook, IL 60521 (© **800/323-7308;** www.abercrombiekent.com), is a luxury tour operator that offers the "Patagonia: A Natural

Playground" trip that heads from Buenos Aires to Ushuaia for a 3-day cruise around Tierra del Fuego, followed by visits to Torres del Paine park, Puerto Varas, and Bariloche. Cost is $7,000 to $8,000 per person, double occupancy. This trip also features a 4-day extension to Iguazú Falls.

- **Butterfield and Robinson,** 70 Bond St., Toronto, Canada M5B 1X3 (© **800/678-1147;** www.butterfieldandrobinson.com), is another gourmet tour operator, with a walking-oriented, 10-day trip to Patagonia starting in El Calafate, Argentina, and finishing in Punta Arenas, Chile. In between, travelers visit national parks Los Glaciares and Torres del Paine, with visits to Perito Moreno Glacier and lodging in fine lodges and ranches. Cost is roughly $6,300 per person, double occupancy.

- **Mountain-Travel Sobek,** 6420 Fairmount Ave., El Cerrito, CA 94530 (© **888/MTSOBEK** or 510/527-8100; fax 510/525-7718; www.mtsobek.com), are the pioneers of organized adventure travel, and they offer trips that involve a lot of physical activity. One of their more gung-ho journeys traverses part of the Patagonian Ice Cap in Fitzroy National Park for 21 days; a more moderate "Patagonia Explorer" mixes hiking with cruising. Prices run from $1,500 to $3,000 and more. Sobek always comes recommended for their excellent guides.

- **Backroads Active Vacations,** 801 Cedar St., Berkeley, CA 94710-1800 (© **800/GO-ACTIVE** or 510/527-1555; www.backroads.com), offers a biking tour through the lake districts of Chile and Argentina, with stops in Villa La Angostura and San Martín de los Andes; an afternoon of rafting is included. There's also a hiking trip through the same region, and a 9-day hiking trip in Patagonia that begins in El Calafate and travels between the two countries. Guests lodge in luxury hotels and inns. Costs run from $3,800 to $5,300.

- **Wilderness Travel,** 1102 Ninth St., Berkeley, CA 94710 (© **800/ 368-2794** or 510/558-2488; www. wildernesstravel.com), offers a more mellow sightseeing/day-hiking tour around Patagonia, including Los Glaciares, Ushuaia, El Calafate, and Perito Moreno Glacier. The trip costs $4,600 to $5,200, depending on the number of guests (maximum 15).
- **Wildland Adventures,** 3516 NE 155th St., Seattle, WA 98155 (© **800/345-4453** or 206/365-0686; www.wildland.com), offers a few adventure tours of Argentina. The "Salta Trek Through Silent Valleys" tour takes in Salta, Jujuy, and the Andean plain. Two Patagonia tours are offered: "Best of Patagonia," which concentrates on Argentine Patagonia (including Península Valdés, Río Gallegos, Perito Moreno, and Ushuaia), and "Los Glaciares Adventure," which visits El Calafate, Fitzroy National Park, and Perito Moreno Glacier, among others. Accommodations range from hotels to camping to rustic park lodges. Eco-tourism is an integral part of Wildland tours. Prices start at $1,500 for the 8-day Salta tour and continue upward of $4,350 for the 2-week Patagonia trip.

PRIVATE TOUR GUIDES   It's easy to hire guides through your hotel or any travel agency in Buenos Aires. You may also want to contact **AGUITBA** (Asociación de Guías de Turismo de Buenos Aires), Carlos Pellegrini 833, sixth floor C, Buenos Aires (© **11/4322-2557;** aguitba@ sion.com), a professional society of tour guides that has tried to promote licensing and other credentials legislation to ensure the quality of guides. Its offices are open Monday to Friday from 1 to 6pm.

Private guides I recommend include Buenos Aires–based Marta Pasquali. (© **[011]11/15/4421-2486;** marpas@ uolsinectis.com.ar) and Monica Varela (© **[011]11/15/4407-0268;** monyliv@ hotmail.com). Both have conducted tours for several years in Buenos Aires. They offer high-quality specialized tours on various themes, and often work with corporations. I highly recommend them for their specialized knowledge of the city which goes far beyond what many other tour guides know.

FAST FACTS: Argentina

American Express Offices are located in Buenos Aires, Bariloche, Salta, San Martín, and Ushuaia. In Buenos Aires, the Amex office is at Arenales 707 (© **11/4130-3135**).

Business Hours Banks are open weekdays from 10am to 3pm. Shopping hours are weekdays from 9am to 8pm and Saturday from 9am to 1pm. Shopping centers are open daily from 10am to 8pm. Some stores close for lunch.

Climate See "When to Go," earlier in this chapter.

Currency See "Money," earlier in this chapter.

Documents See "Entry Requirements & Customs," earlier in this chapter.

Driving Rules In cities, Argentines drive exceedingly fast and do not always obey traffic lights or lanes. Seat belts are mandatory, although few Argentines actually wear them. When driving outside the city, remember that *autopista* means motorway or highway, and *paso* means mountain pass. Don't drive in rural areas at night, as cattle sometimes overtake the road to keep warm and are nearly impossible to see.

Drugstores Ask your hotel where the nearest pharmacy *(farmacia)* is; they are generally ubiquitous in city centers, and there is always at least one open 24 hours. In Buenos Aires, the chain **Farmacity** is open 24 hours, with locations at Lavalle 919 (© **11/4821-3000**) and Av. Santa Fe 2830 (© **11/4821-0235**). Farmacity will also deliver to your hotel.

Electricity If you plan to bring any small appliance with you, pack a transformer and a European-style adapter because electricity in Argentina runs on 220 volts. Note that most laptops operate on both 110 and 220 volts. Luxury hotels usually have transformers and adapters available.

Embassies All in Buenos Aires: **U.S. Embassy,** Av. Colombia 4300 (© 11/4774-5333); **Australian Embassy,** Villanueva 1400 (© 11/4777-6580); **Canadian Embassy,** Tagle 2828 (© 11/4805-3032); **New Zealand Embassy,** Carlos Pellegrini 1427, 5th Floor (© 11/4328-0747); **United Kingdom Embassy,** Luis Agote 2412 (© 11/4803-6021).

Emergencies The following emergency numbers are valid throughout Argentina. For an **ambulance,** call © **107;** in case of **fire,** call © **100;** for **police** assistance, call © **101.**

Information See "Visitor Information," earlier in this chapter.

Internet Access Cybercafes called "Locuturios" are found on every corner in Buenos Aires and in other cities and towns as well, so it won't be hard to stay connected while in Argentina. Access is reasonably priced (usually averaging just under $1 per hour) and connections are reliably good.

Mail Airmail postage for a standard letter from Argentina to North America and Europe is about $1.50. Mail takes, on average, between 7 and 10 days to get to the U.S. and Europe.

Maps Reliable maps can be purchased at the offices of the **Automóvil Club Argentino,** Av. del Libertador 1850, in Buenos Aires (© **11/4802-6061** or 11/4802-7071).

Safety Petty crime has increased significantly in Buenos Aires and other cities as a result of Argentina's economic crisis. Travelers should be especially alert to pickpockets and purse snatchers on the streets and on buses and trains. Tourists should take care not to be overly conspicuous, walking in pairs or groups when possible. In Buenos Aires, do not take taxis off the street. You should call for a radio-taxi instead. Take similar precautions when traveling in Argentina's other big cities.

Smoking People who hate smoke can rejoice. Anti-smoking laws have finally been passed in Buenos Aires, as well as a few other Argentine cities. It's among the few laws actually paid attention to in Argentina.

Taxes Argentina's value added tax (VAT) is 21%. You can recover this 21% at the airport if you have purchased certain local products totaling more than

70 pesos (per invoice) from stores participating in tax-free shopping. Forms are available at the airport and participating stores.

Telephone The country code for Argentina is **54**. When making domestic long-distance calls in Argentina, place a 0 before the area code. For international calls, add 00 before the country code. Direct dialing to North America and Europe is available from most phones. International, as well as domestic, calls are expensive in Argentina, especially from hotels (rates fall 10pm–8am). Holders of AT&T credit cards can reach the money-saving **USA Direct** from Argentina by calling toll-free ✆ **0800/555-4288** from the north of Argentina or 0800/222-1288 from the south. Similar services are offered by **MCI** (✆ **0800/555-1002**) and **Sprint** (✆ **0800/555-1003** from the north of Argentina, or 0800/222-1003 from the south).

Public phones take either phone cards (sold at kiosks on the street) or coins (less common). Local calls cost 20 centavos to start and charge more the longer you talk. Telecentro offices—found everywhere in city centers—offer private phone booths where calls are paid when completed. Most hotels offer fax services, as do all Telecentro offices. Dial ✆ **110** for directory assistance (most operators speak English) and ✆ **000** to reach an international operator.

Time Argentina does not adopt daylight saving time, so the country is 1 hour ahead of Eastern Standard Time in the United States in northern summer and 2 hours ahead in northern winter.

Tipping A 10% tip is expected at cafes and restaurants. Give at least $1 to bellboys and porters, 5% to hairdressers, and leftover change to taxi drivers.

Water In Buenos Aires, the water is perfectly safe to drink. But if you are traveling to more remote regions of Argentina, it's best to stick with bottled water for drinking.

12 The Active Vacation Planner

With so many climate zones and such a wide variety of terrain, Argentina is a haven for outdoor activities of all kinds. Locals have a healthy sense of adventure, and recreational outdoor sports are an important part of life here. Activities around Iguazú Falls range from easy hiking along the waterfall circuits and on San Martín Island to speed-rafting along the river and trekking into the jungle. The high plains of the northwest draw adventurers seeking a little-traveled wilderness that can be explored by bike, on horseback, or in a 4WD vehicle. Near Mendoza are the tallest mountains in the Western Hemisphere, with spectacular rivers and high plains. And of course, Argentine Patagonia has more kayaking, climbing, and trekking opportunities than you could possibly fit in one lifetime.

Here is a brief introduction to the main outdoor activities in Argentina. Many will require you to hire a local guide to help you navigate the local terrain—and the sometimes-confusing local permit process. For more information, visit the website of the Argentine National Parks Service at **www.parquesnacionales.gov.ar**.

TREKKING/HIKING
With the spine of the Andes as a western backdrop, Argentina offers many options for hikers. The north of the country offers good trails heading out of virtually

every town—from the high *altiplano* of the northwest, and the tallest mountains in the Western Hemisphere near Mendoza, to the rolling hills of Córdoba. Farther south, the Lakes District has dozens of good day hikes that wind through lush valleys and along high ridges. The El Chaltén area of Los Glaciares National Park is one of the world's top trekking destinations. Don't forget Tierra del Fuego, where the national park blends coastal marine life with high mountains.

BACKPACKING

Overnight hiking trips will take you even deeper into the mountains, and farther away from the hustle and bustle of life. Organized campsites dot most national parks and have rustic facilities. Camping is a popular activity for young Argentines, who flock to the peaks for their summer holidays in droves. There are excellent backpacking trips in the Lakes District, where you can connect rustic and friendly mountain huts in Nahuel Huapi National Park. In the El Chaltén area, overnight trekking can take you beneath the granite spires of Mt. FitzRoy and Cerro Torre. Be sure to head out well prepared, with appropriate clothing and safety gear, a good map, and a reliable weather report. Always tell someone where you are going.

BIKING

The wide-open spaces and notoriously long distances can make for some adventurous two-wheel trips. With so many seldom-traveled dirt roads, a good suspension bike will certainly come in handy here. The most popular area for recreational mountain biking is the Lakes District, where you can cross the Andes to Chile and back or pedal the stunning (albeit dusty) Seven Lakes Route, camping lakeside each night. Mountain biking is also popular in the Nahuel Huapi National Park area near Bariloche, as well as in the northern province of Salta, where tours take you from the clouds to the jungle. Biking in the wine country near Mendoza is also fun. And cities like Córdoba have established bike routes. Virtually every town has a local bike shop where you can rent a bike and ask locals for trail ideas.

FISHING

Argentine Patagonia is one of the world's premiere destinations for fishing, and particularly for fly-fishing. Trout and salmon populate the picturesque and isolated rivers and lakes from Junín de los Andes south to Esquel. Tierra del Fuego also draws fly-fishing fanatics. The fishing season runs from November through April, generally, and strict catch-and-release policies are in place in certain places. Fishing on the Atlantic Coast is popular anywhere there is a dock, and the giant dorado fish in Entre Rios province is a legendary lure for both foreign and national fishers.

SCUBA DIVING

The Atlantic Coast of Argentina offers some good scuba diving at Puerto Madryn, where experienced divers can have close-up contact with marine wildlife. There are also a number of places in the Lakes District for fresh-water diving.

MOUNTAINEERING & ROCK CLIMBING

Alpine climbers are drawn to a few hot spots in Argentina: to the mighty summit of Mt. Aconcagua in Mendoza, the tallest mountain in the world outside the Himalaya, to the glaciated volcanoes like Mt Tronador or Volcán Lanín in the Lakes District, and to the famous granite spires near El Chaltén.

SURFING

Riding the breaks off the Atlantic Ocean is a growing sport, and there is a healthy beach culture to accompany the local surfing scene. The most popular area is near Mar del Plata, but there are a dozen interesting surfing spots in the Buenos Aires province as well.

WINDSURFING/KITE-SURFING

Another growing sport, the wind- and kite-surfing scene just outside Buenos Aires at Peru Beach is popular. In the notoriously windy expanses of Patagonia, these sports are somewhat challenged by daunting gusts and cold water, although Bariloche hosts an annual Wind Riders Festival each January.

SKIING/SNOWBOARDING

Alpine skiing and snowboarding in Argentina offer plenty of choices for foreigners. The biggest resort, Las Leñas, is nestled in a high altitude valley. Farther south, the biggest ski resort is at Bariloche's Catedral, and gems such as Chapelco in San Martín or Cerro Bayo in Villa La Angostura are nearby, allowing travelers to visit a few different resorts over the period of one visit. Finally, Cerro Castor in Ushuaia is the southernmost ski resort in the world. The Austral ski season runs from late June to September. When snow conditions are good, you'll find a lively slope-side scene with good restaurants, cozy inns, and beautiful scenery. Nordic or cross-country skiing is not as popular, as it requires a deeper snow base. Backcountry skiing, or ski-touring, is also on the rise.

PADDLING

Thanks to the steep eastern slopes of the Andes, there are many fun rivers with bubbling rapids to entertain enthusiasts here. The Mendoza and Atuel rivers in Mendoza Province, and the Juramento River in Salta are important spots. In the Lakes District, the main river for rafting and kayaking is the Manso, south of Bariloche, although there are dozens of nearby rivers to keep a river rat happy.

HORSEBACK RIDING

Argentina has one of the world's great horse cultures, from the polo fields of Buenos Aires to the gauchos roaming the Pampas and Patagonia. And so the terrain is ideal for horseback riding, and horses are well cared for and very common. Hour-long trail rides are offered at *estancias* throughout the country. In the wilder areas of the Northwest, the Mendozan Andes and Patagonia, visitors can sign up for multiday pack trips.

ORGANIZED ADVENTURE TRIPS & OPERATORS

The advantages of traveling with an organized group are plentiful, especially for travelers who have limited time and resources. Tour operators take the headache out of planning a trip, and they iron out the wrinkles that invariably pop up along the way. Many tours are organized to include guides, transportation, accommodations, meals, and gear (some outfits will even carry gear for you, for example, on trekking adventures). Independent travelers tend to view organized tours as antithetical to the joy of discovery, but leaving the details to someone else does free up substantial time to concentrate on something else. Besides, your traveling companions are likely to be kindred souls interested in similar things.

Remember to be aware of what you're getting yourself into. A 5-day trek in the remote Patagonian wilderness may look great on paper, but are you physically up to it? Tour operators are responsible for their clients' well-being and safety, but that doesn't let you off the hook in terms of personal responsibility. Inquire about your guide's experience, safety record, and insurance policy. Remember, no adventure trip is 100% risk-free.

NORTH AMERICAN OPERATORS

The following North America–based outfitters offer solid, well-organized tours around the world, and they are backed by years of experience. Most of these operators are expensive, a few are exorbitant (remember that prices do not include airfare), but that usually is because they include luxury accommodations and gourmet dining. Many of them have dozens and dozens of itineraries around the world; they are not necessarily Argentina experts. Most offer trips to hot spots like Patagonia, and operators with trips to that region often combine Argentina and Chile in the same trip.

- **Abercrombie & Kent,** 1520 Kensington Rd., Oak Brook, IL 60521 (© **800/554-7016;** www.abercrombie kent.com), is a luxury tour operator that offers a "Patagonia: A Luxury Adventure" trip that heads from Buenos Aires to Ushuaia for a 3-day cruise around Tierra del Fuego, followed by visits to Chile's Torres del Paine park and Puerto Varas in the Lakes District, before heading back across the border to Bariloche. Cost is $10,580 per person, double occupancy. It's a 16-day trip. They also have half-a-dozen other itineraries around Argentina.

- **Butterfield and Robinson,** 70 Bond St., Toronto, Canada M5B 1X3 (© **866/551-9090;** www.butterfield. com), is another exclusive gourmet tour operator, with a walking-oriented, 10-day trip to Patagonia starting in El Calafate, Argentina, and finishing in Punta Arenas, Chile. In between, travelers visit national parks Los Glaciares and Torres del Paine, with visits to the Perito Moreno glacier and lodging in fine lodges and ranches. It runs $7,995 per person, double occupancy. They also have a week-long biking trip in the Northwest for $4,995 per person, double occupancy.

- **Mountain-Travel Sobek,** 1266 66th St., Emeryville, CA 94608 (© **888/ MTSOBEK** or 510/527-8100; fax 510/525-7718; www.mtsobek.com), are the pioneers of organized adventure travel, and they offer trips that involve a lot of physical activity. One of their more interesting trips includes 4 days cruising the Beagle Channel before disembarking in Ushuaia. The price starts at $5,550 per person, based on double occupancy. Sobek always comes recommended for their excellent guides.

- **Backroads Active Vacations,** 801 Cedar St., Berkeley, CA 94710-1800 (© **800/GO-ACTIVE** or 510/ 527-1555; www.backroads.com), offers a biking tour through the lake districts of Chile and Argentina, with stops in Villa La Angostura and San Martín de los Andes; an afternoon of rafting is included. There's also a hiking trip through the same region, and a 9-day hiking trip in Patagonia that begins in El Calafate and travels between Chile and Argentina. Guests lodge in luxury hotels and inns. Costs run from $4,498 to $6,698.

- **Wilderness Travel,** 1102 Ninth St., Berkeley, CA 94710 (© **800/ 368-2794** or 510/558-2488; www. wildernesstravel.com), offers a more mellow sightseeing/day hiking tour around Patagonia, including Los Glaciares, Ushuaia, El Calafate, and Perito Moreno Glacier. The trip starts at $4,995, depending on the number of guests (maximum 15).

- **Wildland Adventures,** 3516 NE 155th St., Seattle, WA 98155 (© **800/345-4453** or 206/365-0686; www.wildland.com), offers a few adventure tours of Argentina. The "Salta Trek through Silent Valleys" tour takes in Salta, Jujuy, and the Andean plain. Two Patagonia tours are offered: "Best of Patagonia," a lodge-based trip which concentrates on Argentine Patagonia (including Península Valdés, Río Gallegos, Perito Moreno, and Ushuaia); and "In the Wake of Magellan," which explores Patagonia by land and sea. Prices start at $1,380 for the 8-day

Salta tour and continue upwards of $6,000 for the 2-week Patagonia sailing and hiking trip.

- **Whitney and Smith Legendary Expeditions,** P.O. Box 8576, Canmore, Alberta T1W2V3 (© **800/713-6660** or 403/678-3052; www.legendaryex.com) has two unique trips in Patagonia for more serious adventurers. The first is a rare chance to sea kayak on the coast of the Península Valdés. This 15-day trip costs $4,250 per person. The other is a hiking trip in southern Patagonia that includes a challenging yet spectacular 5-day trek into the rarely traveled area between the Viedma and Upsala glaciers. The trip costs $4,250 per person. You can also stay on and hike on little-traveled trails (yes, they do still exist!) in Torres del Paine. They have long-standing relationships with the locals here, and travel lightly, with little impact and far from the beaten path.
- **PowderQuest Tours,** 7108 PineTree Rd., Richmond, VA 23229 (© **888/565-7158** or 206/203-6065; www.powderquest.com), runs top-notch guided skiing adventures in Argentina, including resort-focused tours that visit a number of different ski hills. A week-long trip that includes guides, hotels, ski passes, food, and transfers starts at $2,595.

ARGENTINE OPERATORS

In general, all of the above-listed North American operators have a partner on the ground in Argentina and they also always have a local guide who is certified in Argentine national parks. If you sign up with a tour run directly by a local agency, you'll find it is often cheaper and usually provides an equally good service with guides and planners who know the territory inside out; after all, it's their own backyard. Bilingual guides can provide plenty of useful insight into what you are seeing and discovering. Be sure to take advantage of customized itinerary planning.

- **Clark Expeditions,** Caseros 121, Salta (© **0387/4215390;** www.clarkexpediciones.com), is the leader in nature tours in the north of Argentina. Their natural-history-focused tours take in the high deserts on both sides of the Andes, and they have a week-long trekking trip that reaches 6,000m (1,800 ft.) above sea level.
- **Experience Patagonia,** Arenales 1457, third floor, Buenos Aires (© **011/4814-3934;** www.experiencepatagonia.com), offers high-end trips that link their three stellar and truly unique properties in southern Argentina: Los Notros, which is right in front of Perito Moreno Glacier, the outstanding Estancia Cristina, and the new Los Cerros del Chalten. They mix adventures like hiking with great food and accommodations.
- **Huala Adventure Tourism,** San Martín 86, Bariloche (© **02944/522-438;** www.huala.com.ar), has unique backcountry expeditions mainly in the Lakes District. They run white-water-rafting trips, horseback-riding expeditions, biking tours, and multisport adventures. Their trips are fun and take you to little-traveled areas.
- **Patagonia Travel Company,** Sarmiento 3974, Bariloche, Río Negro (© **02944/584-784;** www.patagoniatravelco.com), is run by a Canadian-Argentine couple based in Bariloche. They customize trips that range from challenging backpacking expeditions to "soft" multisport adventures combining hiking, rafting, fishing, and horseback riding.

3

Suggested Argentina Itineraries

by Michael Luongo

No length of time ever seems like enough in a city as wonderful as Buenos Aires. This itinerary takes you through 5 days in the capital—ideally a Wednesday to a Sunday. This route guides you through the best features of various neighborhoods—from the MicroCentro and Palermo Viejo to Recoleta and San Telmo. You'll eat several great meals, go shopping, and take in some breathtakingly beautiful sites. I've scheduled in plenty of downtime, too, in case you want to tango all night long and take it easy the following day (Buenos Aires, like New York, is a city that doesn't sleep).

Day ❶: Relaxing & Settling In

More than likely, you've arrived early in the morning after an all-night flight. Before you head out for the day, make reservations at **Cabaña las Lilas** 𝕲𝕲𝕲 (p. 94) for dinner tonight. Afterwards, head to Calle Florida, checking out the shops at **Galerías Pacífico** (p. 135), and have a snack at **Il Gran Caffe** 𝕲 (p. 116). Wander down to **Plaza de Mayo** (p. 128) and take a look at historic sites such as the **Cabildo** (p. 129), Buenos Aires's original city hall, the **Metropolitan Cathedral** 𝕲𝕲 (p. 129), and the **Casa Rosada** 𝕲𝕲𝕲 (p. 128), with Evita's famous balcony. Head back to the hotel for a much-needed nap before heading out to Cabaña las Lilas for dinner. Certainly you've admired the view of **Puerto Madero** (p. 130) from your table, so have a wander dockside.

Day ❷: Historical Buenos Aires

I highly recommend exploring the historic center of Buenos Aires with a professional guide, such as **Borello Travel & Tours** (© 800/405-3072 or 212/686-4911; www.borellotravel.com; see p. 33), **Say Hueque Tours** (© 11/5199-2517; www. sayhueque.com; p. 33), or private freelance tour guides **Marta Pasquali** (© 11/15/4421-2486) or **Monica Varela** (© 11/15/4407-0268). As they lead you through the historic center of Buenos Aires, passing the **Plaza de Mayo** (p. 128) and the turn-of-the-20th-century marvel **Avenida de Mayo** to **Congreso,** they'll explain how architecture, history, and the lost glory of a powerful Argentina is reflected in the streets of Buenos Aires. Ride the **A line subway**'s (p. 58) wooden trains down to station Avenida de Mayo. Have a coffee and *medialunas* at **Café Tortoni** 𝕲𝕲𝕲 (p. 116), one of the city's most historic and scenic cafes, and try to catch the conversation of Buenos Aires locals discussing the latest issues. At 3:30pm, head back to Plaza de Mayo for the **Madres of Plaza de Mayo,** a weekly protest held by the mothers of the 30,000 young people who disappeared during the military regime between 1976 to 1982. Head back and take a nap at the hotel. In the evening, have dinner in the glorious gilded dining hall of **Club-Español** ☆☆ (p. 111).

Day ❸: A Day in Recoleta

Sleep in and have a late breakfast at your hotel. Have your hotel make dinner reservations at **La Bourgogne** ☆☆☆ (p. 96), a fine French restaurant in the **Alvear Palace Hotel** ☆☆☆ (p. 77). Then head to **Recoleta Cemetery** ☆☆☆ (p. 128), in the Recoleta neighborhood. Pay homage to the most famous tomb of all, Evita's. Make sure to wander around and see many of the other tombs, all glorious works of art. Around the corner from the cemetery, head to the **Centro Cultural Recoleta** ☆ (p. 145) and check out the newest art exhibit. If you've brought the kids along or you're feeling young at heart, don't forget to visit the children's section inside, with its interactive science exhibits. Afterwards, head across **Plaza Francia** and take a coffee at **La Biela** ☆☆☆ (p. 98), one of the most famous cafes in the city. After this much-needed break, it's time to do some shopping along **Avenida Alvear,** stopping into stores like **Polo Ralph Lauren** (p. 139), built into a grand mansion. If you've been shopping for hours, you're just in time for your reservation at La Bourgogne.

Day ❹: Palermo

After breakfast, head to **Plaza Italia** and take a brief walk around, enjoying the contrast of the green trees against the white-marble buildings lining this part of Avenida Santa Fe. Head to the **Zoological Gardens** ☆ (p. 127) and check out all the animals, after buying special food for them at the entrance. Afterwards, stroll down Avenida Libertador and wander among the parks, heading to **Museo Nacional de Bellas Artes** ☆☆ (p. 132). It's a long walk, but beautiful all along the way. Head back to the hotel, freshen up, and head for dinner to **Casa Cruz** ☆☆ (p. 102), in Palermo Viejo, one of the city's best places to be seen on a night out.

Day ❺: San Telmo & Tango

Head to **Plaza Dorrego** (p. 126) for the Sunday **San Telmo antiques fair** ☆☆☆ (p. 126), one of the most enjoyable highlights of Buenos Aires. In this open-air bazaar, you can buy small antiques and souvenirs to bring home, and watch live tango performances. (Keep an eye on your pockets while you watch.) Then, grab a late lunch at the atmospheric **Bar El Federal** ☆☆ (p. 117). Head up **Calle Defensa** to take a look at more antiques in the numerous shops lining the street, such as **Galería El Solar de French** (p. 138). Head back to the hotel and freshen up. You're having dinner tonight at **El Viejo Almacén** (p. 147). Watching their show is a great way to end your 5-day stay in Buenos Aires.

2 Northern Patagonia: Lakes & Villages

by Christie Pashby

One of the world's great Alpine playgrounds, the Argentina Lakes District has plenty to discover. Visitors can combine adventure activities with scenic drives and other more chilled-out explorations. In the evenings, enjoy great food and wine, and stay in lovely local inns. You'll need a rental car to get from San Carlos de Bariloche to San Martín de los Andes and back. Pick one up at the Bariloche airport, but be ready for dirt roads and some of the most aggressive drivers in Bariloche.

Buenos Aires in 5 Days

Day 1
1. Galerías Pacífico
2. Plaza de Mayo
3. Cabildo
4. Metropolitan Catedral
5. Casa Rosada
6. Cabaña Las Lilas

Day 2
7. Congreso
8. Café Tortoni
9. Plaza de Mayo
10. Club Español

Day 3
11. Recoleta Cemetery
12. La Biela
13. Avenida Alvear
14. La Bourgogne

Day 4
15. Plaza Italia
16. Zoological Gardens
17. Museo Nacional de Bellas Artes
18. Casa Cruz

Day 5
19. Plaza Dorrego
20. San Telmo Antiques Market
21. Bar El Federal
22. Galería El Solar de French
23. El Viejo Almacén

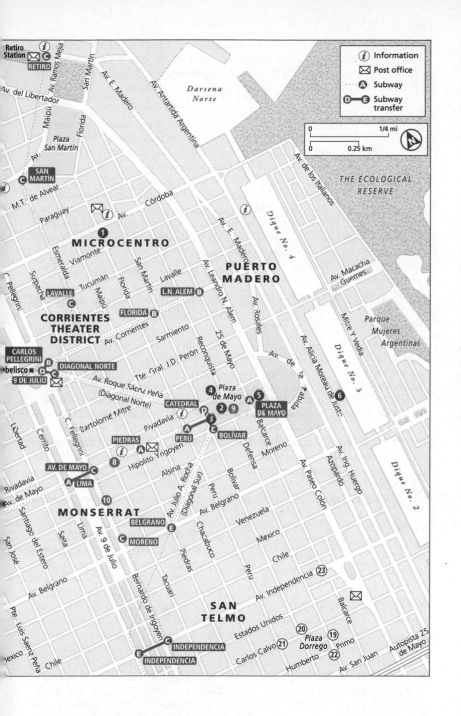

Legend

- (i) Information
- ✉ Post office
- ···Ⓐ··· Subway
- Ⓓ●—●Ⓔ Subway transfer

0 — 1/4 mi
0 — 0.25 km

Retiro Station ✉ Ⓒ RETIRO (i)

Av. del Libertador

San Martín
Av. Ramos Mejía
Av. E. Madero
Av. Antártida Argentina

Darsena Norte

Plaza San Martín

Maipú
Florida

SAN MARTÍN Ⓒ (i)

M.T. de Alvear

Paraguay ✉ (i) Av. Córdoba

THE ECOLOGICAL RESERVE

Av. de los Italianos

Dique No. 4

(i)

MICROCENTRO ①

Esmeralda
Viamonte
Tucumán
Florida
San Martín
Lavalle

LAVALLE Ⓒ

C. Pellegrini
Suipacha
Maipú

PUERTO MADERO

Av. Leandro N. Alem

L.N. ALEM Ⓑ

Av. Rosales

CORRIENTES THEATER DISTRICT

FLORIDA Ⓑ

Av. Corrientes

Sarmiento

25 de Mayo

Reconquista

Av. Macacha Güemes

Parque Mujeres Argentinas

Mitre Y Vedia

Dique No. 3

CARLOS PELLEGRINI Ⓑ
belisco ■ Ⓓ Ⓒ
9 DE JULIO ✉

DIAGONAL NORTE Ⓒ

Tte. Gral. J.D. Perón

Av. Roque Saenz Peña (Diagonal Norte)

Av. de la Rábida

Av. Alicia Moreau de Justo

⑥

Libertad
Cerrito
C. Pellegrini

Bartolomé Mitre

CATEDRAL (i)

④ Plaza de Mayo ⑤ Ⓐ

② ⑨ **PLAZA DE MAYO**

Rivadavia

PIEDRAS (i) Ⓐ

PERÚ ③ Ⓔ BOLÍVAR

Balcarce

Hipólito Yrigoyen

Defensa

Moreno

Av. Ing. Huergo

AV. DE MAYO Ⓒ
Ⓐ LIMA

Alsina

Bolívar
Perú

Av. Paseo Colón

Azopardo

Dique No. 2

Rivadavia
Santiago del Estero
Salta
Lima
San José

⑧

Av. de Mayo

⑩

MONSERRAT

BELGRANO Ⓔ

Av. 9 de Julio

Ⓒ MORENO

Av. Julio A. Rocha (Diagonal Sur)

Av. Belgrano

Venezuela

Chacabuco

Mexico

Chile

Av. Belgrano

Piedras

Tacuari

Bernardo de Irigoyen

Perú

Av. Independencia ㉓

✉

Pte. Luis Saenz Peña
Mexico
Chile

SAN TELMO

Estados Unidos

⑳ Plaza Dorrego ⑲

Carlos Calvo ㉑

Humberto ㉒

Balcarce

Primo

Av. San Juan

Autopista 25 de Mayo

INDEPENDENCIA Ⓒ
Ⓔ INDEPENDENCIA

The trip starts with some orientation in Bariloche, the area's main city. After exploring there for a few days, you'll continue on to two nearby towns: Villa la Angostura and San Martín de los Andes. The entire driving route is spectacular, with tall forests, expansive mountain lakes, and photo opportunities at every turn.

Day ❶: Bariloche

Fly into San Carlos de Bariloche from Buenos Aires. Pick up a rental car at the airport and drive into town along the shores of the spectacular Lago Nahuel Huapi. Check into an inn with a lake view such as **Villa Huinid** ⟨★★⟩ or **El Sol del Nahuel** ⟨★⟩ (p. 307). If you can afford it, head along Avenida Bustillo for 25km (16 miles) to the incredible **Llao Llao Hotel & Resort** ⟨★★★⟩ (p. 305). After relaxing by the pool, make reservations for dinner at **Il Gabbiano** ⟨★★⟩ (p. 311) near the Llao Llao, or at the hidden **Naan** ⟨★★⟩ (p. 308) in town.

Day ❷: Bariloche

After a lovely breakfast at your hotel, make a reservation for your next day's activities (see below). Then hop into your car and explore the **Circuito Chico** ⟨★★⟩ (p. 299), a leisurely loop that takes you past the many bays of Nahuel Huapi Lake. Take the beautiful sightseeing chair lift to the top of **Cerro Campanario** ⟨★⟩, to get a stunning view of the area before heading west past the Llao Llao Resort. Stop in **Colonia Suiza** for lunch—a traditional *curanto* if it's a Wednesday or Sunday. After a siesta at your hotel room, head out for dinner, Argentine-style, sometime after 9pm. Tonight, choose a traditional Argentine *asado* at either **Tarquino** (p. 310) or **El Patacón** (p. 311).

Day ❸: Bariloche Rafting

There are many active adventures to choose from in Bariloche: sea kayaking, hiking, or fishing, to name a few. My absolute favorite is white-water rafting on the emerald **Manso River,** south of Bariloche, with **Huala Adventure Tourism** (p. 298). They'll pick you up at your hotel at 9am and drive south through the lush valleys past lakes Gutiérrez, Mascardi, and Guillelmo, before turning west toward the height of the Andes. The rafting is intense and adrenaline-packed, for good swimmers only! After lunch, a big barbecue will recharge you before you head back to town. You may be up for a lighter dinner tonight after that big lunch. Try **Kandahar** ⟨★⟩ or **Vegetariano** ⟨★⟩ (p. 311).

Day ❹: Villa La Angostura

Eat breakfast, check out, and give yourself some time to explore the shops and markets of Bariloche. Take a step back in time by stopping for lunch at **El Boliche Viejo** ⟨★⟩ (p. 309), where Butch Cassidy and the Sundance Kid apparently stopped en route to Bolivia. The drive continues along Ruta Nacional 231 along the north shore of Nahuel Huapi Lake to the swish town of Villa la Angostura, which is definitely an upscale joint. Check into **Las Balsas** ⟨★⟩ (p. 317), or into the more economical **Hostería Puerto Sur** ⟨★⟩ (p. 318), in the lakeside suburb of Bahia Manzano. Enjoy an afternoon of fishing or hiking, then head to the excellent **Tinto Bistro** ⟨★⟩ (p. 320) for dinner.

Day ❺: Ruta de los Siete Lagos

Eat breakfast, check out, and stop at a supermarket for picnic supplies. Then head north on RN 234, the spectacular Ruta de los Siete Lagos. It's 110km (68 miles) to San Martín de los Andes, but give yourself most of the day to get there. Plan to stop frequently to explore the lakeshores at Lago Correntoso and Lago Falkner. The Vuliñaco waterfall is a great picnic spot. You'll arrive in San Martín de los Andes, Bariloche's tidier and smaller sister, in time for an afternoon tea at the historic **Arrayán Tea House** ⟨★⟩ (p. 325).

Northern Patagonia Lakes & Villages

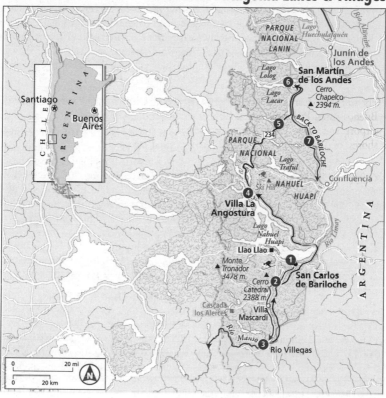

Make your plans for the following day's activities. Check into your inn at **La Casa de Eugenia** (p. 328). San Martín has many good restaurants; try **La Tasca** (p. 331) or **La Reserva** (p. 331).

Day ⑥: San Martín de los Andes

Eat breakfast and leave the car behind. Your hiking guide is here to drive you to the lovely trails of Lanín National Park. In the evening, head to **La Fondue de Betty** (p. 331) for the San Martín classic—a bubbling and scrumptious fondue dinner, with *vino tinto* of course!

Day ⑦: Bariloche & Home

Check out, fill up the tank, and take the "other" way back to Bariloche. You can either go via the lovely mountain village of **Villa Trafúl**, or via the marvelous raw canyons of the **Paso Córdoba.** You'll be back in Bariloche in time to catch a mid-afternoon flight to Buenos Aires.

3 Hiking Southern Argentine Patagonia in 1 Week

by Christie Pashby

Hikers from all over the world make the long journey to Patagonia, for some of the best trekking on the planet. The terrain is simply world class: stunning granite spires, expansive glaciers, thick forests, and wide-open plains. There is much to see here, enough to keep hard-core hikers and backpackers busy for a month.

This itinerary starts with a day spent visiting the stunning Perito Moreno Glacier and hiking on the ice itself. Then head north to El Chaltén, the "National Capital of Trekking." The hikes are demanding, but easily manageable for fit people with some trekking experience. Each day ends back in town for a good meal and a hot shower.

The best time of year for this trip is either November or March, when the winds are relatively calm, and the trails are less busy than in high season (Jan–Feb).

Day ❶: El Calafate

After your trip from Buenos Aires, settle into a nice local inn; try **Esplendor de Calafate** ✿ (p. 361) or the economical **Kau Kaleshen** (p. 363). Head out for a stroll around town and sign yourself up for the "Big Ice" experience the following day. Pop in for dinner at the excellent **Casimiro Biguá** ✿ (p. 363), where you can enjoy king crab from Tierra del Fuego or the local specialty, Patagonian lamb. Get a good night's sleep; tomorrow is a big day.

Day ❷: Perito Moreno Glacier ✿✿✿

You'll be picked up right after breakfast and driven out to Lago Argentino for the **"Big Ice"** ✿✿ adventure outfitter with **Hielo y Aventura.** Once you spot your first jaw-dropping views of Perito Moreno Glacier, there's no turning back. After traveling by boat across the lake, hike up the southern side of the glacier. Your guides will set you up with crampons and lead you deep onto the seemingly endless mass of ice. You'll skirt crevasses and explore its frozen horizons. Book tomorrow's trip to Estancia Cristina upon return. After a good siesta back in town, head out for a well-deserved dinner of Argentine classics such as chorizo and blood sausages, and a big piece of tenderloin with red wine at **La Tablita** ✿✿ (p. 365).

Day ❸: Estancia Cristina

Another early morning! After boarding the catamaran and heading out on the shores of Lago Argentino, you'll enjoy breakfast overlooking icebergs and glaciers. Back on ground at the awesome **Estancia Cristina** ✿✿ (p. 360), hop into

a 4WD truck and drive to a lookout over the massive **Upsala Glacier.** The hiking starts here and heads along the ancient ridges before dropping into a spectacular glacier-carved canyon. Keep your eye out for condors and fossils. Guides provide your lunch en route. The trek ends with enough time left for you to visit the *estancia* museum, before boarding the boat and heading back to El Calafate. For dinner tonight? How about pizza and a few *cervezas* at **El Puesto** (p. 365)?

Day ❹: El Chaltén & Hiking

The first bus of the day heads to El Chaltén at 8am, delivering you to El Chaltén early enough that you'll have time to drop off your luggage at your hotel—we highly recommend **El Puma** ✿ (p. 375)— pick up picnic supplies, and hit the trail. Today's trek will take you along the FitzRoy River up to the **Cerro Torre Lookout** (p. 373). It takes about 4 hours. Back in town, stop by **Patagonicus** for a coffee and a sweet treat. After your now-regular siesta, head to the cozy and historic **Ruca Mahuida** (p. 377) for dinner.

Day ❺: Hiking

Up early again, you've got a spectacular day ahead of you on the trail. Your inn will give you a good breakfast and pack you a picnic lunch if you ask the previous day. The trail today is **Laguna de los Tres** (p. 375), affording a close-up view of **Mt. FitzRoy.** You'll be on the trail for 10 hours, a good full day. But you'll be home in time for a hot shower, a rest (siesta?), and then dinner at **Fuegia** (p. 377), which serves abundant salads and creative curries.

Hiking Southern Patagonia in 1 Week

Day ⑥: Hiking

Your last day hiking in El Chaltén will be unforgettable. After filling up on breakfast and loading your pack with lunch and good rain gear (no matter what the morning weather is like, pack a good rain jacket), your transfer takes you 17km (11 miles) south of El Chaltén to the **Río Eléctrico** and the Hostería El Pilar. From here, you'll hike up a gradual climb and over the pass, stopping at the lovely **Laguna Capri** for rest. Back at the lodge, head for pizza at **Estepa** (p. 377) for dinner.

Day ⑦: El Calafate & Home

If your flight leaves El Calafate in the afternoon, you'll need to be on the first bus out of El Chaltén. Back in El Calafate, you may have time for lunch before transferring to the airport and flying to Buenos Aires, exhausted but invigorated from a week of trekking amid fine peaks and grand glaciers.

4 Mendoza: Malbec & Mountains

by Christie Pashby

You can practically do it all here in Mendoza—live large, indulge your palate, and experience thrilling adventures and marvelous scenery. This journey starts with a few nights based out of Mendoza, a marvelous city with excellent restaurants, charming cafes, and plenty of plazas and parks. Then head out of town to relax in the wine country and explore the three principal wine areas: Luján de Cuyo, Maipú, and the lovely Valle de Uco. You'll also want time to relax and get a good look at the spectacular Andes Mountains, which make a majestic backdrop for the rural countryside here. Good restaurants are another hallmark of the region. Tables are in high demand, so I recommend that you plan ahead by making dinner reservations each morning before you head out. Ask your hotel reception to do so for you, and plan to take a taxi to dinner so you can drink wine. Driving the high mountain roads requires some attention and care. Keep a good map on hand, and don't be afraid to ask for directions. Mendocinos are very friendly, proud, and happy to have you visiting them.

Day ❶: Mendoza

A midmorning flight will have you in Mendoza, from either Buenos Aires or Santiago, in time for a leisurely lunch in town. Check into a downtown hotel; the swish **Park Hyatt** ￼￼￼ (p. 257) and the midrange **Hotel Argentino** ￼￼ (p. 258) have the best locations, in front of the Plaza Independencia. Head to the outdoor tables in front of **Azafrán** ￼ (p. 261) to acquaint yourself with the local specialties. After an afternoon exploring the parks and plazas of Mendoza, relax by the pool. Then stop by one of the local wine stores for some sampling. The Wines of Mendoza runs tastings and offers glasses by the flight. It's a good place to mingle and grab some light dinner. If you've still got room, indulge in some of the continent's best ice cream.

Day ❷: Wines of Luján

After a nice breakfast in your hotel, head out for a day exploring the wines of **Luján de Cuyo** (p. 272). This is the "Tierra del Malbec," where Argentina's signature varietal has found its most harmonic home. Since it's your first day in the area, it's worth signing up for an organized tour to help you get the lay of the land. Ask for a tour that includes three vineyard stops and lunch (I highly recommend **Catena Zapata** and **Ruca Malen**). In the afternoon, relax in a plaza or by the pool. Then hit the funky **Las Negras** ￼ (p. 261) for dinner, and stroll the sidewalk cafes and bars of Calle Aristides before hitting the sack.

Day ❸: Wines of Maipú

Today is a good day to switch to a more rural inn. After breakfast, check out of your hotel and pick up a rental car. Then head south of town and drop your bags off at your inn in either Chacras de Coria, at **Finca Adalgisa** ￼￼ (p. 271), or in Maipú at **Club Tapiz** ￼￼ (p. 277). From either one, you can head out on bicycle or in your car to explore more vineyards. Visit the outstanding wine museum at **Bodega La Rural.** Don't forget an afternoon by the pool! Dine nearby at **Terruños** ￼￼ (p. 277) if you're at Club Tapiz, or stroll into the charming heart of the village of Chacras de Coria and follow your nose. Either way, nighttime amid the vines is romantic and relaxing.

Day ❹: Alta Montaña

Eat breakfast, pack a sweater, and pick up supplies for a picnic (local olives, local jam, local cheese, local bread—it's all right here!), and drive west into the Andes. The road first heads south out of town and then west on RN 7 to Porterillos and on to the Chilean border. After Uspallata, it's a wild and winding mountain road that takes you to the base of the highest mountain in the world outside the Himalayas, the mighty **Mt. Aconcagua.** Don't miss the photo opportunity at the mystical **Puente de Inca.** If you're a confident driver, return via the

Mendoza: Malbec & Mountains

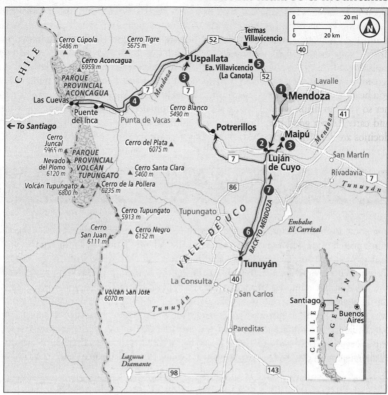

winding spiral cliff-hanging Ruta 52 past the thermal springs at Villavicencio. When you're back in the Mendoza area, it's worth the effort to dine at **La Bourgognel** ✿✿✿ (p. 273). Take a taxi so you can enjoy the excellent wines at the Vistalba vineyard.

Day ❺: Day Off

You'll be tired, perhaps, from driving and indulging. If you're still raring to go, head out for horseback riding or white-water rafting on the Mendoza River. Or rent a bike and explore the rural roads. Give yourself time for a leisurely outdoor lunch at **Almacén del Sur** (p. 276) or **Mi Tierra** (p. 262). Eat light, though, because you're saving room for a spectacular dinner at celebrity chef Francis

Mallman's outstanding **1884** ✿✿✿ (p. 260)—another excellent reason to call a taxi.

Day ❻: Wines of the Valle de Uco

It may be the most scenic area of Mendoza, and well worth the 2-hour drive south of town. After breakfast at your inn, follow the Panamerican Highway RN 40 towards the town of Tunuyán. It's a land of rolling hills, poplar-lined country roads, and in-your-face close-ups of the high Andes. Your first stop should the impressive **Bodega Salentein** ✿✿ (p. 280), which includes an interesting art gallery and one of the spookiest and most fascinating cellars in the country. Either their vineyard cafe or at the nearby Posada Salentein makes a good stop for lunch.

Drop in at another "it" vineyard such as **Lurton** or **Le Clos de los Siete** in the afternoon. A light dinner may be in order: How about a *tabla de picadas*—a sampling of local cheeses and meats, served with a glass of Malbec on a patio at your inn?

Day ❼: Shopping & Home
If this is your only stop in Argentina, it's worth checking out the shops in town for leather goods and other souvenirs. After eating breakfast and checking out of your hotel, stop by the **Palmares Open Mall** (p. 265) and then park in downtown Mendoza for one more stroll down the shop-lined pedestrian mall. Then head to the airport to drop off your car and catch your flight home.

5 Patagonia Wildlife: Península Valdés & Los Glaciares National Park

by Christie Pashby

Patagonia is for nature lovers, particularly in November—the single month of the year when you can see whales and penguins on the Atlantic Coast and still see the peaks and glaciers of southern Patagonia without freezing. Start your trip on the coast at Puerto Madryn, and spend a full day exploring the Península Valdés. This time should include a whale-watching trip and a visit to sea lion colonies. You will need a second day to see the penguin colony at the northern tip of the peninsula, making it worthwhile to stay on the Península Valdés itself. Then you'll need a full day to travel south to El Calafate. If you are a keen bird-watcher and can afford deluxe lodgings, stay at the spectacular new *estancia* Eolo. I saw eight condors at once there in November! From there, you can explore the remote areas of Los Glaciares National Park.

Day ❶: Puerto Madryn & Eco Centro
After flying in from Buenos Aires, you have no real choice but to spend the first night on the beachside town of Puerto Madryn. The nicest spot is the new **Hotel Territorio** ☆ (p. 341). A bit more economical, the **Hotel Bahía Nueva** ☆☆ (p. 342) is centrally located. After transferring from the airport at Trelew and checking in, you'll arrive with time to explore the coastal waters and make a visit to the outstanding **Ecocentro Museum** ☆☆ (p. 345), which will orient you to the wonders of the local oceans. Be sure to book tomorrow's full-day tour of Península Valdés, asking the agency to drop you off at your inn the following night. For dinner, indulge in something from the sea at **Mar y Meseta** ☆☆ (p. 343), and stroll back along the beach.

Day ❷: Península Valdés
Tours always get an early start; most would have you leaving your hotel in Madryn at around 8am. Your first stop will likely be the easy-going beach town of **Puerto Pirámides,** from where all the whale-watching tours head out to catch the annual congregation of Southern Right Whales. These are remarkably social mammals, and they'll no doubt get incredibly close to your boat. Later, your guide will head on to the far eastern coast of the peninsula to visit the sea lion and elephant seal colonies. They usually stop at a cafeteria-style restaurant. Keep your eye out for other wildlife, such as ostrich-resembling *choiques* and the strange *mara,* which looks like a mix of a rabbit with a dog. Afterward, they'll drop you off at the outstanding **Faro Punta Delgada** ☆☆

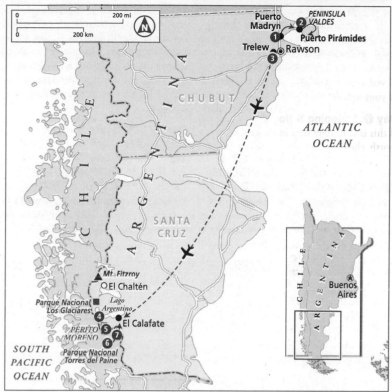

(p. 349) lighthouse inn, where you can hike along the beach. After a nice dinner in the hotel, climb to the top of the lighthouse for a starry view.

Day ❸: Penguins & El Calafate

Eat breakfast at the inn, then ask to be taken to the remote **Estancia San Lorenzo** (p. 348) for a private viewing of their 200,000-strong Magellan penguin colony. From there, head all the way back to Trelew for your flight to El Calafate, and grab lunch en route. You'll arrive in El Calafate in time to be transferred to your *estancia* for dinner. The excellent new rural hotel called **Eolo: Patagonia's Spirit** 𝕬𝕬 (p. 360) will take care of it all.

Day ❹: Condor-Viewing

Eat breakfast, and then head out with your bird-watching guide in search of the majestic condor, with its 3m (10-ft.) wing span. You'll look for shorebirds on the coast of Lago Argentino and the mighty predators amid the high peaks of Cerro Frías. In the afternoon, enjoy a leisurely tea in the ranch's living room, with binoculars nearby. Dinner will also be served in the *estancia*.

Day ❺: Perito Moreno Glacier

You can't come to El Calafate without seeing the world-famous Perito Moreno Glacier, a UNESCO World Heritage Site. After breakfast, you'll be driven west to the glacier's lookout point. Plan ahead and sign up for a **"mini trekking"** (p. 368), where you strap on crampons and go for a short hike on the glacier itself. It also includes a short boat trip beneath the southern wall of the glacier. Return to the *estancia* with time to relax, read, and get back to those binoculars. For dinner, don't miss the local specialty, barbecued Patagonian lamb.

Day ❻: Torres del Paine in 1 Day

It looks close, and as the crow flies, Chile's **Torres del Paine National Park** 𝕮𝕮 (p. 377) is right there on the horizon. Of course, this is Patagonia, and roads are long and dirty. It takes a few hours, in fact, to reach Torres del Paine, but it's

well worth the drive, especially if you're looking to see guanacos, the Patagonian cousin of the llama. You'll also see the black rock peaks—known as *torres* and *cuernos* (towers and horns)—of this very popular park, and get to do some short hikes. Return for a late dinner at the *estancia*.

Day ❼: El Calafate & Home

After breakfast, pack your bags and snap a few more photographs of the incredible emptiness on every horizon. Then stop in the town of El Calafate to stroll the shops along the main tourist drag, Avenida Del Libertador, before heading to the airport for your flight to Buenos Aires.

4

Buenos Aires

by Michael Luongo

A country's tragedy has become a traveler's opportunity, and in between the two is a vastly improved economy for Buenos Aires, the glamorous capital of Argentina. Up until the peso crisis of December 2001, Buenos Aires was regarded as Latin America's most expensive city, with some hotel and restaurant prices rivaling those in New York and Paris. Many on the South American tourist crawl avoided this sophisticated and beautiful metropolis, staying in the cheaper capitals of the countries that surrounded it. But now that the peso, once on par with the U.S. dollar, has fallen to a third of its former value and stabilized there, visitors from all over the world are flocking to the Argentine capital, which in many ways lives up to its reputation as the Paris of South America. In just the last 2 years, prices have gone up in Buenos Aires, most considerably in terms of hotels. Still, it's a relative bargain destination, as the enormous number of travelers here will tell you. Tourism has become the third most important component of Argentina's economy, and Buenos Aires receives the majority of its visitors.

Despite the 2001 peso crisis, the city's beauty remains a constant. With the pending 2010 bicentennial, the capital is busily renovating to renew its wealth of architecture, much of which dates from nearly a century ago. Stroll through the neighborhoods of Recoleta or Palermo, full of buildings with marble neoclassical facades on broad, tree-lined boulevards, or tour the historic Avenida de Mayo, which was designed to rival Paris's Champs-Elysées. European immigrants to Buenos Aires, mostly from Spain and Italy, brought with them the warm ways of Mediterranean culture, wherein friends, family, and conversation were the most important things in life. Whiling away the night over a long meal was the norm, and locals had always packed into cafes, restaurants, and bars until the early-morning hours. The peso crisis hit the locals that much harder because of this, making the lifestyle and good times that they cherished almost unattainable for a period of time.

But don't think that the new Buenos Aires is a depressing shell of its formerly glorious self: Old cafes and restaurants are still full of patrons and competing with the many new restaurants and cafes opening up at a breakneck pace all over town.

Since the peso crisis, Argentines as a whole are becoming more self-reflective, examining themselves and the reasons why their country fell into so much trouble, and seeking answers. This has led, ironically, to a flourishing of all things Porteño (the word Buenos Aires locals use to describe both themselves and the culture of their city). Unable to import expensive foods from overseas anymore, Buenos Aires's restaurants are concentrating instead on cooking with Argentine staples such as Pampas grass-fed beef, and using locally produced, organic ingredients as seasonings. What has developed is a spectacular array of Argentine-nouvelle cuisine of incredible quality and originality. Chefs can't seem to produce it fast enough in the ever-expanding array of restaurants, particularly in the trendy Palermo Viejo district on the city's north side.

This new Argentine self-reliance and pride has transformed the country's fashion, as well as its food. In the go-go 1990s, when the peso was pegged to the U.S. dollar, Argentines loaded up on European labels and made shopping trips to the malls of Miami for their clothing. Now, however, even members of the middle class cannot afford to do this anymore. Instead, young Argentine designers are opening up their own shops and boutiques in the Palermo Soho neighborhood, putting other Argentines to work sewing, selling, and modeling their designs. Women, especially, will find fantastic unique fashions, at unbelievably low prices. And when it comes to leather goods, the buck stops here: The greatest variety and quality in the world are available all over town.

Importantly, the most Porteño thing of all, the tango, has witnessed an explosive growth as well. Until recent years, Argentines had worried that the dance would die out as young people bopped instead to American hip-hop and European techno. But the peso crisis and the self-reflection it created helped bolster the art form's popularity: New varieties of shows for tourists mean you can now see a different form of tango every night of your stay. And, more importantly to residents, traditional, 1930s-style tango salons, called *milongas,* have opened in spaces all over town. They're drawing not only the older, traditional tango dancers but young Argentines, who have rediscovered their grandparents' favorite dance, as well as young ex-pats from all over the world who are making Buenos Aires the world's new hot city, the way Prague was at the end of the Cold War.

The capital is also home to an incomparable array of theaters and other traditional venues. Its vast arrays of museums, many in beautiful neoclassical structures along broad tree-lined Avenida Libertador, are as exquisite as the treasures they hold inside.

All of this means there is no time like now to visit Buenos Aires, a city rich in culture at a bargain price unheard of just a few short years ago. With prices on the upswing, the situation will change soon enough, so get there soon!

1 Essentials

GETTING THERE

BY PLANE   International flights arrive at **Ezeiza International Airport** (© 11/ 4480-0224), located 34km (20 miles) west of downtown Buenos Aires. You can reach the city by shuttle or *remise* (private, unmetered taxi); you will see official stands with set fares in the airport once you clear Customs. Taxis from the airport to the center of town cost about $15 to $20 (£8.25–£11). See Safe Rides, below.

Domestic airlines and flights to Uruguay use **Jorge Newbery Airport** (© 11/ 4514-1515), located only 15 minutes to the north along the river from downtown. Taxis and *remises* cost $8 to $12 (£4.40–£6.60) to the city center. **Manuel Tienda León** (© 11/4314-3636) is the most reliable transportation company, offering buses and *remises* to and from the airports, starting at about $6 (£3.30) for bus rides to the city center.

BY BUS   The **Estación Terminal de Omnibus,** Av. Ramos Mejía 1680 (© 11/ 4310-0700), located near Retiro Station, serves all long-distance buses connecting

---

Tips **Safe Rides**

Buenos Aires has its share of dishonest taxi drivers. At both airports, take only officially sanctioned transportation. Do not accept rides from private individuals.
Even if freelance taxi drivers approach you offering cheaper fares, play it safe and
use the official *remise* stands. For more details, see "Traveling by Taxi," below.

Buenos Aires with the suburbs, the coasts and interior of Argentina, and even international destinations. Rates are very affordable.

BY CAR   In Buenos Aires, it's easier and safer to travel by *subte* (subway), *remise,* or
radio-taxi (radio-dispatched taxis, as opposed to street taxis) than by driving yourself.
Rush-hour traffic is chaotic, and parking is difficult. If you do rent a car, park it at
your hotel or a nearby garage and leave it there.

CITY LAYOUT

Although Buenos Aires is a vastly expansive city, the main tourist neighborhoods are
concentrated in a small, comparatively wealthy part of town that hugs the Río de la
Plata. The city's "MicroCentro" extends from Plaza de Mayo to the south and Plaza
San Martín to the north, and from Plaza del Congreso to the west and Puerto Madero
to the east. The neighborhoods of San Telmo, La Boca, Puerto Madero, Recoleta, and
Palermo surround the MicroCentro. The city layout follows a wobbly grid pattern;
avenidas are the wide boulevards where most traffic flows and the subways lines generally run; *calles* are narrower one-way streets; and *diagonales* cut across streets and
avenues at 45-degree angles, providing beautiful vistas onto many tourist sites. Each
city block extends 100m (328 ft.), and building addresses indicate relative location on
the street.

The **MicroCentro** includes Plaza de Mayo (the political and historic center of
Buenos Aires), Plaza San Martín, and Avenida 9 de Julio, generally claimed to be the
widest street in the world. *Note:* Addresses on this thoroughfare generally take on
those of its parallel service streets, such as Carlos Pelligrini, Cerrito, and Bernardo de
Irogoyen. Most commercial activity is focused in this busy zone, as are the majority of
hotels and restaurants. Next to the MicroCentro, the newly renovated riverfront area
called **Puerto Madero** boasts excellent restaurants and nightlife, as well as new commercial and residential zones. Farther south, **La Boca, Monserrat,** and **San Telmo** are
the historic neighborhoods where the first immigrants arrived and *milonga* and tango
originated. These areas are somewhat run-down and considered by some locals to be
dangerous at night. They are nonetheless beautiful and loaded with areas of interest to
tourists, but take caution if exploring them after sunset.

The city's most European neighborhood, **Recoleta,** offers fashionable restaurants,
cafes, and evening entertainment on tree-lined streets. It's home to the city's cultural
center, built into a former church, as well as the Recoleta Cemetery, the necropolis
where key personalities, such as Evita and many former presidents, are buried. Bordering Recoleta, **Barrio Norte** is famous for its Avenida Santa Fe shopping and nightlife.
Fast becoming the city's trendiest area, **Palermo,** to the northwest, is a sprawling, mul-
ticentered neighborhood of parks, mansions, and cobblestone streets lined with tiny
stucco homes. It is vastly wealthy in some parts and gracefully bohemian in others.
Palermo is a catch-all term for many neighborhoods in Buenos Aires. Today when

Tips **Websites for Your Trip**

We have included as many useful websites as possible in this section. The Buenos Aires city government site (**www.bue.gov.ar**) provides additional tourist information, with links to businesses in town, and a calendar of events. For tourist maps, check out **www.dediosonline.com**. Subway *(subte)* information is available through the interactive website **www.subte.com.ar**, which offers maps, estimated times, and transfer information between stations. A new website with great self-guided tours of Buenos Aires and shopping tips is **www.welcomeargentina.com**. If your Spanish is excellent, use the Argentine version of Google, **www.google.com.ar**, and click on "páginas de Argentina" for the latest locally produced online information on Buenos Aires.

most people say Palermo, they are not referring to the wealthy European-style section of the city along Avenida Libertador, but instead to **Palermo Viejo** and its further subdivisions of **Palermo Hollywood** and **Palermo Soho**, newly hip parts of the city full of chic restaurants and tiny boutiques owned by young up-and-coming designers. When anyone says "meet me in Palermo," it's crucial to clarify exactly which part of the neighborhood they mean.

STREET MAPS   At the front desk of your hotel, ask for a copy of "The Golden Map" and *QuickGuide Buenos Aires.* To help you plan your trip before you leave home, the Buenos Aires–based company **De Dios** (www.dediosonline.com) sells laminated street guides, available from Amazon (www.amazon.com).

GETTING AROUND

The Buenos Aires **Metro**—called the *subte*—is the fastest, cheapest way to get around. Buses are also convenient, though less commonly used by tourists. Get maps of Metro and bus lines from tourist offices and most hotels. (Ask for the *QuickGuide Buenos Aires.*) All Metro stations are supposed to have maps, but they are rarely in good supply.

BY METRO   The *subte* is the fastest and cheapest way to travel in Buenos Aires. Five lines connect commercial, tourist, and residential areas in the city Monday through Saturday from 5am to 11pm, and on Sunday and holidays from 8am to 11pm. These are the official hours, but in fact many lines stop running after 10:30pm. Because they don't close the stations after hours, you could end up waiting for trains that never come if you're not mindful of the service schedule. See the inside back cover of this guide for a map of the system.

The flat fare is 70 *centavos* (25¢/15p). Every station has a staffed ticket window. Some stations have ticket vending machines, but they're unreliable. You can also buy a *subte* pass for 7 pesos ($2.30/£1.25), valid for 10 trips. The passes demagnetize easily, however, and don't work well in intense humidity, which is common through most of the summer. Lines also back up considerably during the summer. Considering the low cost of cards, it's worth buying extra cards as backup. Trains get crowded during rush hours. Cars are not air-conditioned and get unbearably hot in summer. Try to ride the A line at least once; it's a tourist attraction in itself. It's the oldest line, running along Avenida de Mayo on the original rickety wooden cars. Peru station, in particular, retains most of the original ornamentation and copies of advertisements from the turn of the 20th century.

Neither Recoleta nor Puerto Madero has *subte* access. Most of Puerto Madero, however, is accessible via the L. N. Alem *subte* stop on the B line. It's a 5- to 20-minute walk, depending on which dock you're going to. (Puerto Madero is a renovated port district that stretches far along the Río de la Plata waterfront downtown.) The D runs through Barrio Norte, which borders Recoleta. Visit www.subte.com.ar for maps before heading to Argentina. The interactive site also gives estimated times and transfer information between stations.

BY BUS   Buenos Aires has about 140 bus lines that run 24 hours a day. The fare is 80 centavos and up, depending on distance traveled. Pay your fare inside the bus at the electronic ticket machine, which accepts coins only. Some machines don't give change, so it's ideal to have lots of change on hand. Many bus drivers will tell you the fare for your destination and direct you where to get off, but most speak only Spanish. Locals are just as helpful and sometimes make an almost comical effort to ensure you don't get lost. The *Guia T* is a comprehensive guide to the city bus grid and bus lines. Buy it at bookstores, newspaper kiosks, or on the *subte* from peddlers.

BY TAXI   The streets of Buenos Aires are swarming with taxis. Fares are low, with an initial meter reading of 2.16 pesos increasing 24 centavos every 200m (656 ft.) or each minute. *Remises* and radio-taxis are much safer than street taxis (see "Traveling by Taxi," below). Most of what the average tourist needs to see in the city is accessible for $2 to $3 (£1.10–£1.65). Radio-taxis, when hailed on the street, are recognizable by the plastic light boxes on their rooftops, though not all will have them. If a cab is available, the word *libre* will flash in red on the windshield. Ordinary taxis, more likely to be run by members of Buenos Aires's infamous taxi mafia, do not have these special lights at all. I personally have had few problems, but it's always best to err on the side of caution. If you speak English loudly with fellow passengers, identifying yourself as a tourist, expect your ride to take longer than it should, with strange diversions ensuring a higher fare than normal. You can prevent this by being vigilant, having a general idea where you are going, and keeping in mind the one-way street system. Drivers often use traffic problems as their excuse for the run-around. A rarely enforced law means taxi drivers can stop only if their passenger side is facing the curb. If available cabs are ignoring you, cross to the other side of the street and hail again. To request a

---

Tips   Traveling by Taxi

At the risk of sounding repetitive, we strongly recommend that if you need a taxi, you call in advance for a *remise* or radio-taxi (see "By Taxi," above, for numbers). Even better: Ask an employee of your hotel, restaurant, or other venue to call on your behalf, as a representative of that establishment, which ensures greater accountability from drivers. If you must hail taxis off the street, use only those with plastic light boxes on their roofs, indicating that they are radio-taxis. Since the economic crisis began, robberies by street taxi drivers have increased sharply. *Remises* are only slightly pricier than street cabs, but far safer. Most hotels have contracts with *remise* companies, and they're accustomed to calling for patrons.

taxi by phone, consider **Taxi Premium** (② 11/4374-6666), the service used by the Four Seasons Hotel, or **Radio Taxi Blue** (② 11/4777-8888), contracted by the Alvear Palace Hotel.

BY CAR   Buenos Aires is not a place where you need a car. We don't advise driving yourself unless you're heading out of the city. If you must rent a car, contact one of the international rental companies at either airport, as well as those listed in the next paragraph. Most hotels can also arrange car rentals. *Note:* Most local motorists disregard traffic rules except for one: no turn on red.

Rental cars are available from **Hertz,** Paraguay 1122 (② **800/654-3131** in the U.S., or 11/4816-8001); **Avis,** Cerrito 1527 (② **800/230-4898** in the U.S., or 11/4300-8201); **Dollar,** Marcelo T. de Alvear 523 (② **800/800-6000** in the U.S., or 11/4315-8800); and **Thrifty,** Av. Leandro N. Alem 699 (② **800/847-4389** in the U.S., or 11/4315-0777).

ON FOOT   You'll probably find yourself walking more than you'd planned to in this pedestrian-friendly city. Most of the center is small enough to navigate on foot, and you can connect to adjacent neighborhoods by catching a taxi or using the *subte.* Based on the Spanish colonial plan, the city is a wobbly grid expanding from the Plaza de Mayo, so you are not likely to get too lost. Plazas and parks all over the city supply a wonderful place to rest, people-watch, and meet the locals.

VISITOR INFORMATION

The central office of the **City Tourism Secretariat,** responsible for all visitor information on Buenos Aires, is located at Calle Balcarce 360 in Monserrat but is not open to the general public (② 11/4313-0187). Instead, the city uses several kiosks spread in various neighborhoods, which have maps and hotel, restaurant, and attraction information. These are found at J.M. Ortiz and Quintana in Recoleta, Puerto Madero, the central bus terminal, Caminito in La Boca, and Calle Florida 100, where it hits Diagonal Norte. Most are open Monday through Friday from 10am to 5pm, although some open and close later. Others are also open on weekends as well, including the one in San Telmo at Defensa 1250. The center on Caminito in La Boca is open weekends only, usually Saturday and Sunday from 10am to 5pm.

The **Buenos Aires City Tourism Office** runs a hot line for information (② 11/4313-0187) from 7:30am to 6pm Monday to Saturday, and Sunday 11am to 6pm. The city also runs free tours (for details, call ② 11/4114-5791 Mon–Fri 10am–4pm). The majority of the tours are in Spanish, but a few are also in English.

When you arrive in Buenos Aires at Eizeza, there is also a central tourism station just outside of customs run by the **Tourism Secretariat of the Nation,** with information on Buenos Aires and the rest of Argentina

FAST FACTS: Buenos Aires

American Express   The huge American Express building is next to Plaza San Martín, at Arenales 707 (② 11/4312-1661). The travel agency is open Monday through Friday from 9am to 6pm; the bank is open Monday through Friday from 9am to 5pm. In addition to card-member services, the bank offers currency exchange (dollars only), money orders, check cashing, and refunds.

Area Code The city area code for Buenos Aires, known locally as a *característica*, is **011**. Drop the 0 when combining from overseas with Argentina's country code, **54**. The number **15** in front of a local number indicates a cellular phone. This will need the addition of the **011** if you're calling from outside Buenos Aires. Cellular phones become complicated when dialing from overseas. Dial whatever international code you need from your country (011 from the U.S. and Canada), then 54 for Argentina, then 9 to indicate a cell phone, then the area code of the cell phone, then the number. Thus, to call Buenos Aires cell phones from the U.S., you would dial 011-54-9-11 and then the eight-digit number.

Business Hours Banks are generally open weekdays 10am to 3pm, and ATMs work 24 hours. Shopping hours are Monday through Friday from 9am to 8pm or 10pm, and Saturday from 10am to midnight. Shopping centers are open daily from 10am to 10pm. Most independent stores are closed on Sunday, and some close for lunch. Some kiosks, selling water, candy, and packaged food are open 24 hours. Most neighborhoods have a 24-hour pharmacy or *locutorio*.

Currency Exchange Although American dollars are often accepted in major hotels and businesses catering to tourists, you will need Argentine pesos for ordinary transactions. Credit cards are widely used, although some businesses charge a small additional fee. It's easiest to exchange money at the airport, your hotel, or an independent exchange house rather than at an Argentine bank. Traveler's checks can be difficult to cash: **American Express** (see above) offers the best rates on its traveler's checks and charges no commission. It offers currency exchange for dollars only. ATMs are plentiful in Buenos Aires, but you should use those only in secure, well-lit locations. At some ATMs, you can withdraw pesos or dollars. Even if your bank allows you to make larger daily withdrawals, Argentine ATMs generally only give out pesos in the value range $100 to $200 maximum at a time or on a daily basis, so plan accordingly if you know you will need large amounts of cash while in Buenos Aires. You can have money wired to **Western Union**, Av. Córdoba 975 (℡ **0800/800-3030**).

Embassies & Consulates See "Fast Facts: Argentina" in chapter 2.

Emergencies For an **ambulance**, call ℡ **107**; in case of **fire**, call ℡ **100**; for **police** assistance, call ℡ **101**; for an English-speaking hospital, call **Clínica Suisso Argentino** (℡ **11/4304-1081**).

Language Shops, hotels, and restaurants are usually staffed by at least one or two fluent English speakers, and many people speak at least a few words of English. A rule of thumb though is that less expensive venues will have fewer, if any, English speakers. With the massive influx of tourism since the peso crisis, English has become ubiquitous on the streets of the city.

Post Office You never have to venture more than a few blocks to find a post office, open weekdays from 10am to 8pm and Saturday until 1pm. The main post office, or Correo Central, is at Av. Sarmiento 151 (℡ **11/4311-5040**). In addition, the post office works with some *locutorios*, which offer limited mailing services. The purple-signed and ubiquitous **OCA** is a private postal service.

Safety If the daughter of the president of the world's most powerful nation, surrounded by Secret Service and cops, can still get robbed, it says a lot about crime in Buenos Aires. Visitors need to be aware at all times. Crime in Buenos Aires—especially pickpocketing, robberies, and car thefts—has increased sharply in recent years as the economy has collapsed, although it's generally safe to walk around Recoleta, Palermo, and the MicroCentro by both day and night. Some tourist areas deemed safe by day, such as La Boca, should be avoided at night. Be careful at night when in San Telmo, especially in outdoor restaurants. Never leave a bag or purse unattended or on the ground. (Though official accounts differ and/or deny the Bush daughters were robbed at all, the method by which they were likely hoodwinked was the "soccer" method: A purse on the ground under a chair is kicked to another thief who then takes it away.) I also would warn tourists against walking around at night in Monserrat, though with increasing gentrification and tourist spillover from San Telmo, the area will continue to become safer. Visitors should walk in pairs or groups when possible and avoid the conspicuous appearance of being a tourist. Do not flaunt expensive possessions, particularly jewelry. Call for a radio-taxi or *remise* when leaving a place of business. The number-one rule is that thieves take advantage of naiveté and opportunity, but real violence is unlikely.

Taxes The 21% sales tax (or VAT) is already included in the sales price of your purchase. Foreign tourists are entitled to a VAT tax return for certain purchases over 70 pesos, but you must request a refund check at the time of purchase from participating shops (the shop should display a "Global Refund" logo). Before departing the country, present these refund checks (invoices) to Customs, and then your credit card will be credited for the refund, or you'll receive a check by mail. Be aware when checking into hotels that the posted or spoken price may or may not reflect this tax, so make sure to ask for clarification.

Taxis See "Getting Around," above.

Telephone Unless you are calling from your hotel (which will be expensive), the easiest way to place calls in Buenos Aires is by going to a *locutorio* or *telecentro,* found on nearly every city block. Private glass booths allow you to place as many calls as you like by dialing directly, after which you pay an attendant. A running meter tells you what you'll owe. Most *locutorios* also have fax machines and broadband Internet computers. Calls to the U.S. or Canada run about a peso or less per minute.

Although some coin-operated public phones still exist in Buenos Aires, most require a calling card, available at kiosks, which are specifically branded for the various communication companies. Local calls, like all others, are charged by the minute. Dial ⓒ **110** for information and ⓒ **000** to reach an international operator. To dial another number in Argentina from Buenos Aires, dial the area code first, then the local number; this applies to cellular numbers too. *Note:* If you call someone's cellular phone in Argentina, the call is also charged to you and can cost significantly more than a standard landline call.

Tipping A 10% to 15% tip is common at cafes and restaurants. Taxis do not require tips, but many people round up to the nearest peso or 50 centavo figure. If a taxi driver helps you with bags, a small tip might be a nice touch.

2 Where to Stay

International tourism to Buenos Aires has been increasing by as much as 20% a year since the devaluation of the peso. As a result, hotels in Buenos Aires often fill up in high season, so it's more crucial than ever to book ahead. Most of the best and most convenient hotels are in Recoleta and the MicroCentro. Recoleta is more scenic and not quite as noisy as the MicroCentro, but you might spend more money on cabs, as it is not near the *subte* lines. Prices listed below are rack rates in high season and include the 21% tax levied on hotel rooms. The prices listed here can differ considerably based on many factors—from type of room, events in the city, views, and the hotel management's discretion, based on overall availability in the city. Do not be surprised if rates vary considerably, up or down, from what I've listed here; many factors can affect the final price, including whether you book online using the Spanish versus the English version of a hotel's website. Discounts are almost always available in low season, and sometimes even in high season. Web packages and specials are also available on various hotel sites. Most hotels charge about $4 a night for valet parking or, at the very least, recommend nearby self-parking facilities. You should avoid parking long-term on the street.

Buenos Aires accommodations have improved tremendously in the past few years, following a series of renovations among many of the city's government-rated four- and five-star hotels. Most five- and four-star hotels in Buenos Aires offer in-room safes, cable TV, direct-dial phones with voice mail, and in-room Internet access at varying prices. Most hotels in this chapter boast four or five stars. Wi-Fi, often free, is becoming standard in the lobbies and public areas of most hotels, including two- and three-star venues.

You love Buenos Aires, and so does everyone else. That means that hotel bargains are much harder to find now. Exponentially increasing numbers of tourists have made available rooms a scarce commodity, and hotels are trending their rates up in accordance. In fact, many hotel prices are running at, or just under, their pre-peso crisis levels. Still, bargains can be had—especially from four-star establishments off the beaten path and locally owned (rather than international) hotel chains. And of course, every traveler knows never to accept the first price offered. Always ask for a better rate and whether your AAA card, student ID, or other discounts might also apply.

BARRIO NORTE
INEXPENSIVE

Bauen Hotel   The number-one reason for staying in this hotel is that it gives you the best glimpse into a post-peso-crisis phenomenon in Argentina: worker *cooperativas,* in which employees take over a failed business abandoned by the owners in order to keep their jobs. The Bauen, a disco-era hotel, never made a lot of money, and the peso crisis drove it under. The workers reacted by taking over and keeping it open. Virtually everything dates from its late-1970s opening: the lobby signs, the curves of the front desk, avocado Formica furniture, shiny globe-shape lamps, old televisions, and the pièce de résistance: the underground disco lounge where you'd expect to find John Travolta "staying alive." Upper floors have fantastic views of the surrounding city. The staff is also exceptionally friendly and helpful. Some rooms also connect, which is ideal for families and friends staying in large groups.

Av. Callao 360 (at Corrientes), 1022 Buenos Aires. © 11/4372-1932. Fax 11/4372-3883. www.bauenhotel.com.ar. 160 units, including 18 suites. From $55 (£30) single; $60 (£33) double; from $80 (£44) suite. Rates include continental breakfast. AE, MC, V. Metro: Callao. **Amenities:** Restaurant; bar; disco lounge; small health club; sauna; concierge; business center; room service; laundry service; theater; convention center. *In room:* A/C, TV w/cable; Internet; select suites have minibar and kitchens.

Where to Stay in Buenos Aires

Alvear Palace Hotel **3**
Amerian Buenos Aires Park Hotel **33**
Amerian Congreso **15**
Aspen Towers **25**
Auge Buenos Aires **12**
Bauen Hotel **13**
Bel Air Hotel **10**
Caesar Park **5**
Claridge Hotel **34**
Dazzler Hotel **11**
Dolmen Hotel **44**
El Lugar Gay **25**
Etoile Hotel **1**
The Faena Hotel and Universe **27**
Four Seasons Hotel **6**
The Golden Tulip Savoy **14**
Gran Hotel Vedra **18**
Grand Boulevard Hotel **22**
Hilton Buenos Aires **29**
Holiday Inn Express **38**
Hostel Carlos Gardel **24**
Hostel Nomade **26**
Hotel Castelar **20**
Hotel Colon **31**
Hotel de Los Dos Congresos **16**
Hotel Emperador **7**
Hotel Ibis **17**
Hotel Reconquista Plaza **36**
Hotel Ritz **39**
Howard Johnson Florida Street **40**
InterContinental Hotel Buenos Aires **21**
Lafayette Hotel **35**
Lina's Tango Guesthouse **23**
Loi Suites **2**
Loi Suites Esmeralda **41**
Marriott Plaza Hotel **46**
Meliá Confort Buenos Aires **47**
NH City Hotel **28**
NH Florida **39**
NH Hotel Crillon **45**
Obelisco Center Suites Hotel and Apartments **30**
Pan Americano **32**
Park Hyatt **4**
Park Tower Buenos Aires (The Luxury Connection) **20**
The Recoleta Hostel **9**
The Regente Palace Hotel **43**
Sheraton Buenos Aires Hotel and Convention Center **48**
Sofitel **8**
V&S Hostel **33**

MICROCENTRO
VERY EXPENSIVE

Marriott Plaza Hotel 🏨🏨   The historic Plaza was the grande dame of Buenos Aires for most of the 20th century, and the Marriott management has maintained much of its original splendor. (The hotel still belongs to descendants of the first owners, from 1909.) The intimate lobby, decorated in Italian marble, crystal, and Persian carpets, is a virtual revolving door of Argentine politicians, foreign diplomats, and business executives. The veteran staff offers outstanding service, and the concierge will address needs ranging from executive business services to sightseeing tours. All the rooms are spacious and well appointed. In August of 2006, the hotel spent about $100,000 (£55,000) adding more luxurious bedding, featuring plusher mattresses, softer white Egyptian cotton sheets with a 300-thread count, more pillows, and duvets. Twenty-six rooms overlook Plaza San Martín, providing dreamlike views of the green canopy of trees in the spring and summer. This view is at its most magical in October, when the jacaranda trees are in their majestic purple bloom. The **Plaza Grill** (p. 112) remains a favorite spot for a business lunch and offers a reasonably priced multicourse dinner menu as well. The **Plaza Bar** (p. 151) is among the most famous in the city; *Forbes* rated it among the world's best for 2005. The hotel's enormous health club is one of the city's best, with a large heated indoor pool, specialized dance and aerobics rooms, and a punching bag. Guests whose rooms are not ready can wait in the special health club lounge, where they can rest and shower. (The value of this unique service becomes most apparent if you've arrived very early after an overnight flight from North America.) The hotel lobby has free Wi-Fi access, but in-room Internet access costs about $16 (£8.80) a day, decreasing with the purchase of additional days. The exterior of the hotel, with its historic landmark facade, is currently undergoing a renovation. The complexity of the process means there is no current endpoint for this slow procedure, though management hopes to finish by the end of 2007. The hotel also offers free high-quality historical tours of Buenos Aires, though space is limited.

Calle Florida 1005 (at Santa Fe overlooking Plaza San Martín), 1005 Buenos Aires. ℂ **11/4318-3000.** Fax 11/4318-3008. www.marriott.com. 325 units. $300 (£165) double; from $400 (£220) suite. Rates include buffet breakfast. AE, DC, MC, V. Valet parking $16 (£8.80). Metro: San Martín. **Amenities:** 2 restaurants; cigar bar; excellent health club w/outdoor pool; exercise room; sauna; concierge; business center; salon; room service; massage service; laundry service; dry cleaning. *In room:* A/C, TV, Internet, minibar, coffeemaker, hair dryer, safe.

Park Tower Buenos Aires (The Luxury Connection) 🏨🏨🏨   One of the most beautiful hotels in Buenos Aires, the Park Tower is connected to the Sheraton next door. The hotel combines traditional elegance with technological sophistication and offers impeccable service. Common areas as well as private rooms feature imported marble, Italian linens, lavish furniture, and impressive works of art. The lobby—with its floor-to-ceiling windows, potted palms, and Japanese wall screens—contributes to a sense that this is the Pacific Rim rather than South America. Tastefully designed guest rooms are equipped with 29-inch color TVs, stereo systems with CD players, and cellphones. The rooms have stunning views of the city and the river. Guests also have access to 24-hour private butler service. The hotel boasts three restaurants, including Crystal Garden, serving refined international cuisine; El Aljibe, cooking Argentine beef from the grill; and Cardinale, offering Italian specialties. The lobby lounge features piano music, a cigar bar, tea, cocktails, and special liquors.

Av. Leandro N. Alem 1193 (at Della Paolera), 1104 Buenos Aires. ℂ **11/4318-9100.** Fax 11/4318-9150. www.luxury collection.com/parktower. 181 units. From $350 (£193) double. AE, DC, MC, V. Metro: Retiro. **Amenities:** 3 restaurants; snack bar; piano bar; 2 pools; putting green; 2 lighted tennis courts; fitness center w/gym; wet and dry saunas;

B & B in Buenos Aires = Beautiful & Bargain-Priced

Buenos Aires has a growing number of intimate, chic bed-and-breakfast-type guesthouses for $20 to $60 a night (U.S. dollars). Unlike American B&Bs—which are so often fusty and cluttered with bric-a-brac and cats—those in Buenos Aires tend to have hip, young owners with very clean, cosmopolitan taste. Many owners are designers who open their homes to the traveling public. Their places tend to be airy and bright, and many have Spanish-style interior gardens and patios. Unless you demand the ultimate in five-star luxury, many private guesthouses are nicer than most hotels charging three or four times the price. They also ensure authenticity, in that you can have a more personal exchange with the owners and other guests. Many offer weekly or monthly rates.

For a selective list of properties and their websites, explore **Stay in Buenos Aires** (www.stayinbuenosaires.com.ar/english.html). Many of the best digs are in San Telmo—which was the city's ritzy neighborhood in the 19th century, with the architectural interiors you see in tango photo spreads. Palermo Viejo, Palermo Soho, and Palermo Hollywood also have many great guesthouses. These neighborhoods are a hub for young creative types—especially designers. Their beautiful, with-it websites alone convey a sense of what these places have over the five-star marble palaces.

Casa Monserrat (www.casa-monserrat.com) is in one of the city's surprisingly few Spanish Colonial–style structures, with Spanish tile floors and an interior garden, flourishing with vines and flowers, running the length of the place. Rooms, radiating off the garden, are simple and lovingly appointed (request the suite with private balcony on the second floor). We also recommend: **Casa Vaiven** (http://casavaiven.com), a bright, open loft with rooms, in San Telmo, and **Che Lulu** (www.luluguesthouse.com), between Palermo Soho and Palermo Viejo. See individual websites for additional information and prices.

---

concierge; business center and secretarial services; room service; massage therapy; laundry service; dry cleaning. *In room:* A/C, TV/VCR, Internet, minibar, hair dryer, safe.

Sofitel ⭐⭐⭐ The first Sofitel in Argentina opened in late 2002. This classy French hotel near Plaza San Martín joins two seven-story buildings to a 20-story neoclassical tower dating from 1929, linked by a glass atrium lobby. The lobby resembles an enormous gazebo, with six ficus trees, a giant iron-and-bronze chandelier, an Art Nouveau clock, and Botticcino and black San Gabriel marble filling the space. Adjacent to the lobby, you will find an elegant French restaurant, **Le Sud** (p. 112), and the early-20th-century-style Buenos Aires Café. The cozy library, with its grand fireplace and dark woods, offers guests an enchanting place to read outside their rooms. These rooms vary in size, mixing modern French decor with traditional Art Deco styles; ask for one of the "deluxe" rooms or suites if you're looking for more space. Beautiful marble bathrooms have separate showers and bathtubs and feature Roger & Gallet amenities. Rooms above the eighth floor enjoy the best views, and the 17th-floor suite, *L'Appartement,* covers the whole floor. Many of the staff members speak Spanish, English, and French.

Arroyo 841/849 (at Juncal), 1007 Buenos Aires. ℂ **11/4909-1454.** Fax 11/4909-1452. www.sofitel.com. 144 units. From $300 (£165) double; from $450 (£248) suite. AE, DC, MC, V. **Amenities:** Restaurant; cafe; bar; indoor swimming pool; fitness center; concierge; business center; room service; laundry service. *In room:* A/C, TV, Internet, minibar, hair dryer, safe.

EXPENSIVE

Claridge Hotel 𝒢   The Claridge is living testimony to the once-close ties between England and Argentina. The grand entrance, with its imposing Ionic columns, mimics a London terrace apartment. The lobby was renovated in 2002 in a classical style with colored marbles. Guest rooms are spacious, tastefully decorated, and equipped with all the amenities expected of a five-star hotel. The restaurant's hunting-themed wood-paneled interior is a registered city landmark with a good-value menu of carefully prepared international food for as little as $8 (£4.40) and an inviting breakfast buffet, included in the room rates. Because it occasionally hosts conventions, the Claridge can become very busy. The rates at this hotel can go down significantly when booking promotions via the website, pushing it into the moderate category.

Tucumán 535 (at San Martín), 1049 Buenos Aires. ℰ 11/4314-7700. Fax 11/4314-8022. www.claridge.com.ar. 165 units. $170 (£94) double; from $355 (£195) suite. Rates include buffet breakfast. AE, DC, MC, V. Metro: Florida. **Amenities:** Restaurant; bar; health club w/heated outdoor pool; exercise room; sauna; concierge; business center; room service; massage service; laundry service; dry cleaning. *In room:* A/C, TV, minibar, safe.

Meliá Buenos Aires Boutique Hotel 𝒢𝒢   Within easy walking distance of Plaza San Martín and Calle Florida, the Meliá is among the best of the city's four-star hotels. Spacious guest rooms colored in soft earth tones feature overstuffed chairs, soundproof windows, and marble bathrooms. Large desks, two phone lines, and available cellphones make this a good choice for business travelers. Some of the rooms are also wheelchair accessible, but you should call to make sure of specifics. The staff offers friendly, relaxed service. The Meliá has a small Spanish restaurant and bar.

Reconquista 945 (at Paraguay), 1003 Buenos Aires. ℰ 11/4891-3800. Fax 11/4891-3834. www.solmelia.com. 125 units. $145 (£80) double; from $190 (£105) suite. Rates include buffet breakfast. AE, DC, MC, V. Parking $4 (£2.20). Metro: San Martín. **Amenities:** Restaurant; bar; exercise room; concierge; business services; room service; babysitting; laundry service; dry cleaning. *In room:* A/C, TV, Internet, minibar, coffeemaker, hair dryer, safe.

Pan Americano 𝒢𝒢𝒢   An enormous hotel, the Pan Americano faces both the Obelisco and the Teatro Colón, offering convenient access to tourist sites as well as virtually all the *subte* lines that converge on this part of town. Once part of the American Crowne Plaza chain, it's now independent, and prices have dropped considerably for some of the rooms, though the quality and service remains as high as before. The South Tower rooms are a good size, but the North Tower rooms are even larger and better appointed (for the small difference in price, it's worth asking for one). Decor also varies here; some are fully carpeted; others offer elegant hardwood floors. Bathrooms are also larger, with whirlpool tubs and separate shower units, and marble counters and floors. Valet presses are also standard in the North Tower rooms. All rooms in both towers come with desks, extra side chairs, and ample closet space. In a three-story glass box atop the North Tower, the hotel health club, spa, and sauna are perhaps the most amazing and magical in the city. They must be experienced, if only for the view. Swimming in the heated pool, which is both indoors and outdoors, or working out in the gym makes you feel as though you're floating above Avenida 9 de Julio. The health club restaurant, **Kasuga,** becomes a sushi bar at night. Two other restaurants are located in the gracious and inspiring lobby with Greek frescoes and dark-wood and marble accents. **Lucíernaga,** the main lobby bar where breakfast is served, is enormous, but the space has an intimate feeling due to its niche-filled layout and Jacobean tapestry-upholstered furniture. **Tomo I** has a modern decor. Both spaces serve international, Argentine, and Italian cuisine.

Carlos Pelligrini 551 (at Corrientes), 1009 Buenos Aires. © **11/4348-5115.** Fax 11/4348-5250. www.panamericano. us. 386 units. $163 (£90) double; from $300 (£165) suite. Rates include sumptuous buffet breakfast. AE, DC, MC, V. Free valet parking. Metro: Lavalle, Diagonal Norte. **Amenities:** 3 restaurants; enormous health club w/indoor-outdoor pool; exercise room; spa; sauna; concierge; business center; salon; room service; massage service; babysitting; laundry service; dry cleaning. *In room:* A/C, TV, Internet, minibar, coffeemaker, hair dryer, safe.

Sheraton Buenos Aires Hotel and Convention Center ✪

Situated in the heart of the business, shopping, and theater district, the Sheraton is an ideal location for business travelers and tourists. Guest rooms are typical of a large American chain— well equipped but charmless. What the hotel lacks in intimacy, however, it makes up for in the wide range of guest services. It shares three restaurants with the neighboring Park Tower Buenos Aires (The Luxury Collection), and its "Neptune" pool and fitness center are among the city's best.

Av. San Martín 1225 (at Leandro N. Alem), 1104 Buenos Aires. © **11/4318-9000.** Fax 11/4318-9353. www.sheraton. com. 741 units. $210 (£116) double; from $320 (£176) suite. AE, DC, MC, V. Metro: Retiro. **Amenities:** 3 restaurants; snack bar; piano bar; 2 heated pools (1 indoor, 1 outdoor); putting green; 2 lighted tennis courts; fitness center w/gym; wet and dry saunas; concierge; activities desk; car-rental desk; business center; shopping arcade; salon; room service; massage therapy; babysitting; laundry service; dry cleaning. *In room:* A/C, TV, Wi-Fi, minibar, hair dryer, safe.

MODERATE

Amerian Buenos Aires Park Hotel ✪✪ *Finds*

One of the best four-star hotels in the city, the modern Amerian is a good bet for tourists as well as business travelers. Prices here have climbed significantly recently, pushing up to pre-peso-crisis prices, so the hotel is no longer the bargain it once was. The warm atrium lobby looks more like California than Argentina, and the highly qualified staff offers personalized service. Soundproof rooms are elegantly appointed with wood, marble, and granite. All boast comfortable beds, chairs, and work areas. The Argentine-owned hotel is just blocks away from Calle Florida, Plaza San Martín, and the Teatro Colón.

Reconquista 699 (at Viamonte), 1003 Buenos Aires. © **11/4317-5100.** Fax 11/4317-5101. www.amerian.com. 152 units. $140 (£77) double; from $220 (£121) suite. Rates include buffet breakfast. AE, DC, MC, V. Parking $4 (£2.20). Metro: Florida. **Amenities:** Restaurant; pub; exercise room; sauna; concierge; business center; room service; laundry service; dry cleaning. *In room:* A/C, TV, Internet, minibar.

Aspen Towers ✪✪

Built in 1995, the Aspen Towers is one of the city's newer and more refined hotels. Its 13-floor tower is contemporary in design, with a light-filled atrium lobby, elegant restaurant, and inviting rooftop pool. Guest rooms are small but classically decorated, with faux-antique furniture and soft-colored linens. All rooms feature marble bathrooms with whirlpool baths—something you're unlikely to find anywhere in the city at this price. The hotel is popular with Brazilians, Chileans, and Americans, and lies within easy walking distance of downtown's attractions.

Paraguay 857 (at Suipacha), 1057 Buenos Aires. © **11/4313-1919.** Fax 11/4313-2662. www.aspentowers.com.ar. 105 units. $125–$175 (£69–£96) double. Rates include buffet breakfast. AE, DC, MC, V. Metro: San Martín. **Amenities:** Restaurant; cafe; rooftop pool; exercise room; sauna; concierge; business center; room service; laundry service; dry cleaning. *In room:* A/C, TV, Wi-Fi, Internet, minibar.

Dolmen Hotel ✪

This four-star hotel's central location in the MicroCentro, 1 block from Plaza San Martín, offers two things you usually do not find in this price category—quiet and a heated indoor swimming pool. The rooms are not the largest, nor are they the nicest, decorated in bright florals and blond woods. Nevertheless, you'll find desk/vanity combinations and a single control panel over the bed for all lights and the air-conditioning unit. Bathrooms are large, with spacious counters, and well stocked with supplies. Surrounded by buildings of the same size, you won't get great views from most of the rooms. A few of the rooms are also suitable for those with special needs. Suites offer considerably more space for only a little more money than the standard rooms. Head upstairs to the pool and gym area for the best views from this glass-enclosed space. The hotel offers free parking in a building next door and free Internet in the business center. Select rooms have free Internet access, as will all rooms eventually, according to plan. Public areas are set for Wi-Fi. The lobby bar, recessed in a space behind the concierge, offers another quiet retreat, with a splashy marble-and-brass decor.

Suipacha 1079 (at Santa Fe), 1003 Buenos Aires. ℂ **11/4315-7117.** Fax 11/4315-6666. www.hoteldolmen.com.ar. 146 units, including 22 suites. From $157 (£86) double; from $193 (£106) suite. Rates include buffet breakfast. AE, MC, V. Free parking. Metro: San Martín. **Amenities:** Restaurant; bar; small heated indoor swimming pool; small health club; sauna; concierge; business center; room service; laundry service; dry cleaning. *In room:* A/C, TV, Internet (select rooms), minibar, hair dryer, safe.

Holiday Inn Express Puerto Madero ⋇

This hotel enjoys a convenient location next to Puerto Madero, bustling with restaurants and nightlife. Although it lacks room service, concierge, or bellhop, the hotel is friendly, modern, and inexpensive. Guest rooms have large, firm beds; ample desk space; and 27-inch cable TVs. Half of them boast river views. Coffee and tea are served 24 hours, and the buffet breakfast is excellent. Pets are also allowed. The gym is on the roof of the building, with excellent views over the city. Passcards allow 24-hour access to the gym.

Av. Leandro N. Alem 770 (at Viamonte), 1057 Buenos Aires. ℂ **11/4311-5200.** Fax 11/4311-5757. www.holiday-inn.com. 116 units. From $160 (£88) double; $215 (£118) suite. Children under 18 stay free in parent's room. Rates include buffet breakfast. AE, DC, MC, V. Metro: L. N. Alem. Free parking. **Amenities:** Deli; 24-hr. rooftop gym; whirlpool; sauna; business center; room service. *In room:* A/C, TV, Internet.

Hotel Colón

This hotel is in the heart of the city, on Avenida 9 de Julio overlooking the Obelisco, which gives guests here convenient access to virtually all of the city's *subte* lines. Corner rooms are more spacious, and many of the very large suites come with terraces. The decor varies throughout, and renovations are ongoing in this property, opened in 1984 in an older building. As such, some rooms are hit-or-miss: Some come with very sleek modern interiors, others are traditional, but the color theme throughout is creamy white, giving a luminescence to some of the rooms. Double-glazed windows means quiet despite busy surroundings, but don't worry about oversleeping, because each room comes with an alarm clock. Bathrooms are very large, and some of the suite bathrooms have Jacuzzis. The restaurant offers international cuisine and a wraparound view overlooking the Obelisco. Lifeguards oversee the medium-size heated rooftop pool, but this amenity's location, in the back of the building, means there is no view from up here. A small business center offers Internet access at roughly $1.35 (75p) per half-hour.

Carlos Pellegrini 507 (at Corrientes), 1009 Buenos Aires. ℂ **11/4320-3500.** Fax 11/4320-3507. www.colon-hotel.com.ar. 173 units, including 35 suites. From $150 (£83) double; from $216 (£119) suite. Rates include buffet breakfast. AE, DC, MC, V. Parking $4 (£2.20). Metro: Carlos Pellegrini or 9 de Julio. **Amenities:** Restaurant; bar; pool; small health club; concierge; business center; room service; laundry service; dry cleaning. *In room:* A/C, TV, minibar, hair dryer, safe.

Hotel Reconquista Plaza ⋇

Near busy Calle Florida, this hotel provides a good location and clean, modern amenities. The decor is harvest gold with dark wooden trim. All rooms have enormous rounded windows looking out onto the street. Suites are merely oversize rooms partially separated by a large wardrobe unit. A sleeper couch in this area provides extra bed space. Some suites have enormous terraces, with views overlooking the MicroCentro. Though the balconies are wonderful amenities, the hotel unfortunately does not provide chairs and tables for enjoying them. All rooms have tub/shower combinations, but the tubs are small in standard rooms. Suite bathrooms are equipped with whirlpools. Double-glazing on the windows blocks out noise, an important consideration in this area. Staff is exceptionally friendly and helpful. High-speed Internet access is available from all rooms for about $3 (£1.65) per day, and desks provide a workspace. For the money, this hotel is a good option for business travelers who do not need full services and want a convenient central location. In-room safes are oversize, providing space for a laptop. A small gym and sauna are also part of the offerings, and access to a pool can be arranged for a fee of about $5 (£2.75), though the hotel doesn't have one of its own. Cat lovers who travel with their pets are in luck, but dog owners will have to leave the canine at home.

Reconquista 602 (at Tucumán), 1003 Buenos Aires. © **11/4311-4600.** Fax 11/4311-3302. 60 units, including 9 suites. From $150 (£83) double; from $185 (£102) suite. Rates include buffet breakfast. AE, MC, V. Parking $4 (£2.20). Metro: Florida. **Amenities:** Restaurant; bar; small health club; sauna; concierge; business center; room service; laundry service. *In room:* A/C, TV, Internet, minibar, coffeemaker, hair dryer, large safe.

Howard Johnson Florida Street ★★ (Value)   Having taken over this property from Courtyard by Marriott, this Howard Johnson is an excellent choice for travelers who don't require many special services. It has a great location off Calle Florida near Plaza San Martín, with access through a shopping-and-restaurant gallery on the ground level. Guest rooms come equipped with sleeper chairs (in addition to the bed), large desks and dressers, and well-appointed bathrooms. Room size is above average in this category. Each room has two phones, and local calls and Internet use are free—a rarity in Buenos Aires. There's a small, airy cafe and bar in the lobby, with additional food served in the gallery below. Four small budget-priced function rooms off the lobby are available for business and social events. The hotel also advertises extensively as gay-friendly. There is no pool or health club on premises, but access is offered free of charge to a nearby facility. Wi-Fi is free in the lobby.

Calle Florida 944 (at Alvear), 1005 Buenos Aires. © **11/4891-9200.** Fax 11/4891-9208. www.hojoar.com. 77 units. $160 (£88) double. Rates include buffet breakfast. AE, DC, MC, V. Metro: San Martín. Small pets accepted for fee (about $35/£19) on pre-arrangement with the hotel. **Amenities:** Restaurant; bar; business services; room service; laundry service; dry cleaning; conference center. *In room:* A/C, TV, high-speed Internet, minibar, coffeemaker, hair dryer, iron, large safe.

Lafayette Hotel ★ (Kids)   Popular with European and Brazilian travelers, the Lafayette Hotel is a good value for a midprice hotel. Rooms are spacious (some are even large enough to accommodate an entire family), exceedingly clean, and well maintained. Each has a desk, and all rooms have Wi-Fi. A small combination meeting room and business center has 24-hour Internet access on one computer. Bathrooms are hit-or-miss—some are large, others seem like jammed-together afterthoughts. Street-side rooms are great for people-watching in the MicroCentro, though you should expect some noise. Back rooms are quieter but offer no views. The location is ideal for Micro-Centro's Lavalle and Calle Florida shopping, and the subway is only a few blocks away. The buffet breakfast is generous and varied, offering made-to-order omelets on request. The hotel is built in two parts with two different elevator bays, so if you're staying with friends or family, request rooms in the same division of the hotel.

Reconquista 546 (at Viamonte), 1003 Buenos Aires. © **11/4393-9081.** Fax 11/4322-1611. www.lafayettehotel.com.ar. 82 units, including 6 suites. From $85 (£47) double; from $100 (£55) suite. Rates include generous buffet breakfast. AE, DC, MC, V. Metro: Florida. **Amenities:** Restaurant; bar; concierge; small business center; room service; laundry service; dry cleaning. *In room:* A/C, TV, Wi-Fi, minibar, hair dryer, safe.

NH Florida   This is a simple, well-located, four-star hotel less than a block away from the Galerías Pacífico. It opened in 2001 in an older apartment hotel, but the original old building was completely gutted. Views are not the focus at NH Florida, surrounded by buildings of the same size, but the rooms are larger than most in this price category. Almost all have wood floors with small carpets, adding a simple elegance to the modern decor. All rooms have free high-speed Internet access and a good workstation. Suites are much larger, with large doors to wall off the guest areas from the sitting room. At the time of this writing, this hotel had plans to expand by adding new rooms on the first floor. The hotel offers many good services, but its main disadvantage, compared to other accommodations in this category, is its lack of a gym or pool. However, for a fee of about $3 (£1.65) per day, clients can access nearby facilities. Eleven rooms are equipped for those with special needs, but I recommend calling and asking specific questions about your needs before booking here. With its MicroCentro location, this is among the most accessible hotels, for all travelers, in Buenos Aires.

San Martín 839 (at Córdoba), 1004 Buenos Aires. ℂ **11/4321-9850.** Fax 11/4321-9875. www.nh-hotels.com. 148 units, including 20 suites. $155 (£85) double; from $200 (£110) suite. Rates include buffet breakfast. AE, DC, MC, V. Valet parking $4 (£2.20). Metro: San Martín. **Amenities:** Restaurant; bar; concierge; business center; room service; babysitting; laundry service; dry cleaning. *In room:* A/C, TV, minibar, hair dryer, safe.

NH Hotel Crillón ⟨   This 50-year-old French-style hotel enjoys an outstanding location adjacent to Plaza San Martín, next to some of the city's best sights and shops, and recently joined the NH company, a Spanish hotel chain with several properties in town. Having completed a renovation in 2002, the Crillón has become more comfortable, since guest rooms were refitted with nicer furniture and better linens. A business center, racquetball and squash courts, gym, and sauna have been added. The hotel is popular with European and Brazilian business travelers, and offers high-tech conveniences such as wireless Internet access and cellphones. Deluxe rooms enjoy views of calles Santa Fe and Esmeralda; the suites (with Jacuzzis) overlook Plaza San Martín. Stay away from interior rooms, which have no views. The hotel staff is extremely helpful.

Av. Santa Fe 796 (at Plaza San Martín), 1059 Buenos Aires. ℂ **11/4310-2000.** Fax 11/4310-2020. www.nh-hotels.com. 96 units. $120 (£66) double; $150 (£83) suite. Rates include buffet breakfast. AE, DC, MC, V. Metro: San Martín. **Amenities:** Restaurant; bar; concierge; business services; room service; laundry service; dry cleaning. *In room:* A/C, TV, Wi-Fi, minibar, hair dryer, safe.

Obelisco Center Suites Hotel and Apartments   As its name implies, the location of this Argentine-owned hotel puts you right in the center of the city, close to the Obelisco. However, the property does not directly overlook this monument, and only a few rooms offer views of it. The hotel is in two parts, an older apartment complex and the newer hotel section. Both are accessible via the same lobby. Very big on security issues, the hotel has several fire protection procedures proudly in place. Rooms are large and have a bright, flowery decor. Bathroom countertops come with a lot of surface space, and tubs are unusually deep. Whirlpools are available in the large superior rooms, which also have terraces with views to the Obelisco. Though the hotel is near all the major subway lines and theaters, the area and the rooms facing the street can be noisy. Free high-speed Internet access is available in the small business center, which is open 24 hours a day. A gym, sauna, spa, and pool are available for free in a large shared facility a block away from the hotel. Apartments have small efficiency kitchens and come in various sizes and configurations. All are simply decorated, with a bright, open feel.

Av. Roque Sáenz Peña 991 (Diagonal Norte at Av. 9 de Julio), 1035 Buenos Aires. © **11/4326-0909.** Fax 11/4326-0269. www.obeliscohotel.com.ar. 101 units. From $121 (£67) double; $210 (£116) apt. Rates include buffet breakfast. AE, DC, MC, V. Parking $4 (£2.20). Metro: Carlos Pellegrini or Diagonal Norte. **Amenities:** Restaurant; bar; concierge; room service; laundry service; dry cleaning; conference center. *In room:* A/C, TV, kitchen (in apts), minibar, hair dryer, safe.

The Regente Palace Hotel   Walking into the four-star Regente is like stepping back into the disco era, with its 1970s-style brass-and-neutral-toned rounded brick decor. Plus, the porthole windows in the building's hallways might make you think you're on the *Love Boat*. This place is funky but fashionable in a retro kind of way. Even though many of the furnishings seem outdated, all room carpets were replaced in late 2004. Rooms can be on the small side, but all come with desks/vanities as work surfaces. Suites have been renovated in gray tones, and some have Jacuzzi bathtubs. What sets this hotel apart is the brilliant amount of light that comes through the floor-to-ceiling windows that form a virtual glass wall to the outside. Double-glazed windows silence street noise. Guests can use the hotel's free Internet access from the lobby business center. A small gym is down in the basement, and there is event space for about 400 people in three rooms. The restaurant area, where breakfast is served, is on a brass mezzanine with catwalks suspended over the lobby. A cascading waterfall in this area provides a pleasant atmosphere. You'll find a few shops and travel services here also. Free parking is provided. Because of oddly placed steps throughout the building, including the passages that lead to the elevators, this is not an ideal location for people with limited mobility.

Suipacha 964 (at Córdoba), 1008 Buenos Aires. © **11/4328-6800.** Fax 11/4328-7460. www.regente.com. 137 units, including 28 suites. From $140 (£77) double; from $180 (£99) suite. Rates include buffet breakfast. AE, MC, V. Free parking. Metro: Lavalle. **Amenities:** Restaurant; bar; small health club; concierge; business center; shopping gallery; room service; laundry service; dry cleaning. *In room:* A/C, TV, minibar, hair dryer, large safe.

INEXPENSIVE

V&S Hostel ★★ *(Finds*   Privately owned, but part of an Argentine network of hostels, V&S provides exceptionally friendly service in a convenient MicroCentro location. The hostel is inside of a gorgeous turn-of-the-20th-century apartment building, with lavish touches such as molded plaster, curved doorway entries, stained-glass ornamentation, and balconies. Five private bedrooms with attached shower-stall bathrooms are also available. A kitchen is available for making meals. Guests can mingle in the quiet library, TV sitting room, or patio. Several computers are also available for Internet access. This place is a great value, with air-conditioning throughout the rooms (rare for a hostel).

Viamonte 887 (at Maipú), 1053 Buenos Aires. © **11/4322-0994.** Fax 11/4327-5131. www.hostelclub.com. 60 bed spaces, including 10 in 5 bedrooms with attached bathroom. From $9 (£4.95) per bed; $45 (£25) per private room. Rates include continental breakfast. No credit cards. Metro: Lavalle. **Amenities:** Concierge; Internet; shared kitchen; lockers. *In room:* A/C, hair dryer.

MONSERRAT
EXPENSIVE

Inter-Continental ★★★   Opened in 1994, this luxurious tower hotel was built in one of the city's oldest districts, Monserrat, and decorated in the Argentine style of the 1930s. The marble lobby is beige and apricot, with heavy black and brass accents, and handsome carved-wood furniture and antiques inlaid with agates and other stones. The lobby's small Café de las Luces sometimes offers evening tango performances. The Inter-Continental is the only five star in walking distance to the San Telmo tango district. The **Restaurante y Bar Mediterráneo** (p. 111) serves healthful, gourmet Mediterranean cuisine on an outdoor patio under a glassed-in trellis. Stop by the Brasco & Duane wine bar for an exclusive selection of Argentine vintages. Guest rooms continue the 1930s theme, with elegant black woodwork, comfy king-size beds, marble-top nightstands, large desks, and black-and-white photographs of the city. Marble bathrooms have separate showers and bathtubs, and extensive amenities.

Moreno 809 (at Piedras), 1091 Buenos Aires. © **11/4340-7100.** Fax 11/4340-7119. www.buenos-aires. interconti.com. 312 units. $240 (£132) double; from $400 (£220) suite. AE, DC, MC, V. Parking $10 (£5.50). Metro: Moreno. **Amenities:** Restaurant; wine bar; lobby bar; health club w/indoor pool; exercise room; sauna; concierge; business center; room service; massage service; laundry service; dry cleaning; executive floors; sun deck. *In room:* A/C, TV, Internet, minibar, hair dryer, safe.

NH City Hotel ⊛⊛   Of all the hotels near the political center of the city, this is the best. The Spanish-owned NH hotel chain opened the property in June 2001 in the old City Hotel, an Art Deco masterpiece that was once one of Buenos Aires's grandest hotels. Its jagged ziggurat exterior calls to mind buildings more associated with Jazz Age New York than Argentina. Its lobby has been meticulously renovated, a combination of Art Deco and collegiate Gothic popular in that time period, with simple beige and brown furnishings offsetting the burnished woods, stained-glass ceiling, and honey-colored marble floors. Many of the large rooms are on the dark side, with a masculine combination of simple materials in red and black. Others are brighter, with white walls and burnt-sienna offsets. All the bathrooms are spacious and luminous, with large counters and an excellent range of toiletries. A new building was also added to the hotel in 2006, giving it more capacity. The safes are among the biggest in the city, with ample room for laptops. The rooftop, with its small outdoor heated pool, is a delight. Attendants make sure you feel comfortable as you take in the fantastic view of the river and Uruguay on a clear day, as well as the nearby Plaza de Mayo and the domes of the buildings lining Diagonal Norte. A small health club, complete with a spa, sauna, and Jacuzzi, is also on this level, as is the executive area. You can get a massage here or arrange to have one in your room. Views from many of the rooms, however, leave something to be desired, and rooms in the back of the hotel afford views of only construction on an adjacent building. You have a choice of high-speed Internet or Wi-Fi connections within the rooms, and the small business center also has free 24-hour access through its two computers. A small conference center has meeting rooms for functions of up to 400 people. There are two restaurants in the building. One is casual, while the other, named Clue, is a large, minimalist space, with 1930s style, where patrons are forbidden from dining in shorts.

Bolívar 160 (at Alsina), 1066 Buenos Aires. © **11/4121-6464.** Fax 11/4121-6450. www.nh-hotels.com. 370 units, including 38 suites. From $140 (£77) double; from $194 (£107) suite. Generous buffet breakfast included. AE, DC, MC, V. Parking $5 (£2.75). Metro: Bolívar or Plaza de Mayo. **Amenities:** 2 restaurants; bar; small gym facility w/open-air pool deck; spa; sauna; concierge; business center; room service; babysitting; laundry service; dry cleaning; executive floor; conference center. *In room:* TV, high-speed Internet or Wi-Fi, minibar, hair dryer, large safe.

MODERATE

Grand Boulevard Hotel ⊛ (Value)   The Grand Boulevard offers a location similar to the Inter-Continental (see above) at a much lower price, while still offering a convenient set of services for both business and leisure travelers. Double-glazed German-made windows lock out noise from Avenida 9 de Julio while offering incredible views of that street and the river from higher floors. The restaurant/bar is open 24 hours, and it offers both international cuisine and a special spa menu of light, nutritious foods, detailing caloric content for health-conscious travelers. All rooms offer desks and vanities of varying sizes, and a single bedside panel that controls all room lights. The Argentine queen beds, slightly larger than an American full, are comfortable but not the firmest. All rooms have large closets. High-speed Internet access is free in all rooms, as well as in the 24-hour business center. Some of the rooms have Wi-Fi, and some have cabled Internet. Subway access is easy. With the *autopista* (highway) nearby, this is also the city's closest four-star hotel to the airport. Parking is free in the hotel's garage. Some of the rooms here have limited wheelchair accessibility. A small, glassed-in meeting-room space sits on the roof of the building, with beautiful views of the city.

Bernardo de Irogoyen 432 (at Belgrano), 1072 Buenos Aires. (C) **11/5222-9000.** www.grandboulevardhotel.com. 85 units. $110 (£61) double; from $195 (£107) suite. AE, DC, MC, V. Free parking. Metro: Moreno. **Amenities:** Restaurant; bar; small health club w/personal trainer; sauna; concierge; business center; room service; massage service; babysitting; laundry service; dry cleaning. *In room:* A/C, TV, free Internet, free Wi-Fi in some rooms, minibar, hair dryer, safe.

Hotel Castelar   Despite its current condition, which tends toward shabby, the 1929 Hotel Castelar has historic significance: It was once a popular stopping point for Spanish-language literary stars during Argentina's golden years as an intellectual center in the 1930s. It is most famously associated with Spanish playwright Federico García Lorca, who took refuge here during the Spanish Civil War for several months in 1934. The room he lived in has also been preserved, though with a slight sense of kitsch. The lobby retains much of the brass, marble, and heavy plaster elements from its opening. These details extend into the dining area, which was once a *confitería* (cafe) as culturally important as the Café Tortoni (p. 116), farther down Avenida de Mayo. Mario Palanti, the eccentric architect of the nearby Palacio Barolo, designed the Castelar. While the golden years of Avenida de Mayo are long over, the hotel allows you to bask in its residual charms. The Castelar's spa in the hotel's basement is free for all guests of the hotel (men and women are separated in this area), with additional fees for various services. Enormous, full of white Carrera marble, and built in the Turkish style, it is worth paying the entrance fee of about $8 (£4.40) just to see the place, even if you are not a hotel guest. Renovations in all of the units were completed in early 2005; all now have new color patterns, new mattresses, and comfortable furniture. The old wooden touches, speckled glass, and tiled floors in the bathrooms were retained. The rooms are not very large, but the setup—a small antechamber with the bedroom to one side, the bathroom to the other—adds a sense of privacy to the spaces, even when shared by a couple. Suites are similar, but with an added living area. No rooms are truly equipped for those with special needs, but some units have slight accommodations such as wider spaces and a few grip bars in the bathroom. Internet access is free in the rooms, as is Wi-Fi in the lobby.

Av. de Mayo (at Lima and Av. 9 de Julio), 1152 Buenos Aires. (C) **11/4383-5000.** Fax 11/4383-8388. www.castelar hotel.com.ar. 151 units, including 70 suites. $89 (£49) double; $123 (£68) suite. Rates include buffet breakfast. AE, DC, MC, V. Parking $3 (£1.65). Metro: Lima. **Amenities:** Restaurant; bar; small health club; extensive spa; business services; room service; laundry service; dry cleaning. *In room:* A/C, TV, Internet, minibar.

INEXPENSIVE

Hotel Ritz ☆   This is one of my favorite bargain hotels in Buenos Aires, due to its price, the warmth of the staff, and its location at the juncture of 9 de Julio and Avenida de Mayo. The building originally opened at the turn of the last century as a doctor's office and became a hotel in the 1920s. This has lent character to the place, although it has also led to some unusual room shapes and arrangements—some bathrooms are off the rooms, for example, and units are often either enormous or small.

Of the 38 rooms, 30 are large enough for doubles or triples, and 24 rooms have balconies facing the street (anyone who saw the really awful movie *Testosterone,* starring Antonio Sabato, Jr., and Sonia Braga, will recognize the balconies). Ceilings are very high, and some rooms still maintain intricate plaster work, French doors, and brass fixtures. The bathrooms are hit or miss—some have only showers with low water pressure. Management is planning to install air-conditioning in early 2007, which may impact the rates. For now, ceiling fans do the trick well. Wi-Fi is free in the breakfast room, and the small-budget meeting center holds about 60 people. The maids here are very much like second mothers overseeing your stay in Buenos Aires. There is an elevator, but staircases lead to it, making it hard to access for those with limited mobility. Most of the clients are Europeans or Argentines on business but on a budget. The hotel is exceedingly clean. Rooms do not have safes, but front desk staff will guard valuables and arrange side trips and city tours as well.

Av. de Mayo 1111 (at 9 de Julio), 1085 Buenos Aires. ⓒ/fax **11/4383-9001.** 38 units. From $40 (£22) double. Rates include continental breakfast. AE, DC, MC, V. Off-site parking $3 (£1.65). Metro: Lima. **Amenities:** Concierge; room service; dry cleaning; laundry service; small meeting center; Wi-Fi. *In room:* Ceiling fans, TV w/cable.

PUERTO MADERO

There are no convenient Metro stops to this neighborhood.

VERY EXPENSIVE

The Faena Hotel and Universe ⓕⓕⓕ   The Faena opened to much fanfare among fashionistas in October 2004. International travel magazines gave it page upon page of coverage, with its Philippe Starck design and handsome, camera-ready owner, who gave the hotel his name. Only time will tell if the glamour and buzz last. The hotel is built into El Porteño, an old grain silo, one of the once-dilapidated historic buildings lining Puerto Madero. The Faena is different from Starck's typical barren, all-white environments. In the public spaces, decayed Edwardian elegance meets country chic—with tin metal sheeting, peeling paint, new ornamental plaster ceiling molding made to look old, and antique Queen Anne–style cabinets. Many original elements of the grain building were maintained. In the rooms, mid-century classical meets modern—with white Empire-style furnishings in modern surroundings, and cut-glass mirrors reminiscent of colonial Mexico. White and red are key color elements throughout the oversize rooms, with interesting touches such as heavy velvet curtains controlled electronically. Each room has a home entertainment center. Bathrooms are enormous, completely mirrored, outfitted with oversize tubs, and stocked with bath products chosen by guests, from among a variety of brands, upon making their reservations. Some of the rooms facing the city skyline and the port have incredible vistas; others overlook the nearby Ecological Reserve and the Río de la Plata. Rooms have desks as well as dial-up, high-speed, and Wi-Fi Internet access. The Faena was designed as a sort of resort within the confines of the city. The staff member who tends to guests' needs is called an "experience manager," rather than a concierge. The spa is spacious and unique, using the round shapes of the silos to great effect, with Turkish-style hammam baths and a special stone Incan-style sauna shaped like an igloo. The array of special services is vast, treatment rooms are numerous, and the on-site health club is huge, with the latest equipment. An outdoor pool graces the building's entrance. The hotel also has a residential section, with properties for sale. These vary in size and price, and 20 are available for rent on a nonscheduled basis. The lobby houses several dining, bar, and entertainment areas. The "Universe" in the hotel's name refers to these shared elements open to guests, residents, and the general public. Guests also receive free private transfers from the airport.

Martha Salotti 445 (at Av. Juana Manso), 1107 Buenos Aires. © **11/4010-9000**. Fax 11/4010-9001. www.faenahotelanduniverse.com. 103 units, including 14 suites and 20 apts of varying size, space, and price. From $480 (£264) double; from $700 (£385) suite. Rates include continental breakfast. AE, MC, V. Parking $12 (£6.60). No Metro access. **Amenities:** 3 restaurants; 3 bars; outdoor heated pool; large health club; spa w/extensive treatments; large sauna w/unique elements; business center w/secretarial services; room service; laundry service, dry cleaning. *In room:* A/C, home theater TV, high-speed Internet, Wi-Fi, minibar, hair dryer, large safe, individualized bath treatments.

EXPENSIVE

Hilton Buenos Aires 🎯🎯 The Hilton opened in mid-2000 as the first major hotel and convention center in Puerto Madero. Within easy walking distance of some of the best restaurants in Buenos Aires, it's an excellent choice for steak and seafood connoisseurs. The strikingly contemporary hotel—a sleek silver block hoisted on stilts—features a seven-story atrium with more than 400 well-equipped guest rooms and an additional number of private residences. Spacious guest rooms offer multiple phone lines, walk-in closets, and bathrooms with separate showers and tubs. Those staying on the executive floors receive complimentary breakfast and have access to a private concierge. Next to the lobby, the El Faro restaurant serves California cuisine with a focus on seafood. The hotel has the largest in-hotel convention center in the city.

Av. Macacha Güemes 351 (at Malecón Pierina Dealessi), 1106 Buenos Aires. © **800/445-8667** in the U.S. or 11/4891-0000. Fax 11/4891-0001. www.buenos.hilton.com. 418 units. From $360 (£198) double; from $530 (£292) suite. AE, DC, MC, V. Parking $8 (£4.40). No Metro access. **Amenities:** Restaurant; bar; modern gym facility w/openair pool deck and a service of light snacks and beverages; concierge; business center and secretarial services; room service; babysitting; laundry service; dry cleaning. *In room:* TV, minibar, hair dryer, safe.

RECOLETA

There are no convenient Metro stops to this neighborhood.

VERY EXPENSIVE

Alvear Palace Hotel 🎯🎯🎯 In the center of the upscale Recoleta district, the Alvear Palace is the most exclusive hotel in Buenos Aires and one of the top hotels in the world. A gilded classical confection full of marble and bronze, the Alvear combines Empire- and Louis XV-style furniture with exquisite French decorative arts. After a long process, the historically important facade was restored in 2004 to its original glory. The illustrious guest list has included Antonio Banderas, Donatella Versace, the emperor of Japan, and Robert Duvall, to name a few. Recently renovated guest rooms combine modern conveniences with luxurious comforts, such as chandeliers, Egyptian cotton linens, and silk drapes. All rooms come with personal butler service, cellphones that can be activated on demand, fresh flowers and fruit baskets, and daily newspaper delivery. Large marble bathrooms contain Hermès toiletries, and most have Jacuzzi baths. The formal hotel provides sharp, professional service, and the excellent concierges go to great lengths to accommodate guest requests. It's pricey, but the website sometimes offers discounts when occupancy is low. The Alvear Palace is home to one of the best restaurants in South America (**La Bourgogne;** p. 96) and offers an excellent, expensive Sunday brunch and afternoon tea in L'Orangerie. Kosher catering and dining is also available at the Alvear.

Av. Alvear 1891 (at Ayacucho), 1129 Buenos Aires. © **11/4808-2100**. Fax 11/4804-0034. www.alvearpalace.com. 210 units (85 palace rooms and 125 suites). From $450 (£248) double; from $520 (£286) suite. Rates include luxurious buffet breakfast. AE, DC, MC, V. No Metro access. **Amenities:** 2 restaurants; bar; small health club; spa; concierge;

elaborate business center; shopping arcade; room service; massage service; laundry service; dry cleaning; private butler service. *In room:* A/C, TV, Internet, minibar, hair dryer, safe.

Buenos Aires Park Hyatt 🌟🌟🌟   This is the second reincarnation of the Buenos Aires Park Hyatt, originally located in what is now the Four Seasons, just down the block. This hotel opened on July 12, 2006, after many construction delays, but it was worth the wait. An intense amount of thought went into the design of the rooms throughout the main tower facing Posadas Street and the Palacio Duhau, one of the most important mansions along Avenida Alvear. The two buildings are connected above ground by a terraced and layered garden, and below ground by an art-filled tunnel flooded with natural light. This Hyatt has two lobbies, one in the new tower and another frightfully dark one in the Palace, accessed by a gorgeous double staircase that fronts the building. The side rooms and waiting areas that spill from it are magnificent, however, utilizing the best of the original spaces in the Palacio Duhau, once owned by the powerful Duhau family, who oversaw the Agricultural Ministry. Because lobby furnishings are spartan and staff members tend to usher guests to the side rooms, the Hyatt lacks the lobby culture that thrives in some of the other five stars, such as the Alvear and Four Seasons. You'll see agricultural and cattle elements in the design of the palace. This is most evident in what had been the ballroom, with its carved limestone walls and colored marble floor.

Rooms in the mansion exhibit the mix of modern and classical elements found throughout the hotel. Brass handles on French doors, heavy wooden molding, and a mix of Louis XV–style and contemporary furnishings adorn the rooms. Within the tower, the color palette is a modern and slightly masculine use of leather browns, charcoals, and silver-grays, including the Shantung silk curtains imported from France, which open and close at the touch of a button. Rooms are spacious, and suites come with extra bathrooms for use during business meetings. Some tower rooms have breathtaking views of the Río de la Plata. Bathrooms in both buildings are enormous, with both a walk-in shower and a bathtub. In fact, the bathroom takes up 30% to 40% of each guest room.

One of the hotel restaurant/bars is in the Piano Nobile, a side room off the lobby, painted light gray with silver accents along its intricate classical molding in the style of Versailles. Piano Nobile is overseen by Maximo Lopez May, considered one of the city's best young chefs Another is the Oak Bar, masculine and Gothic with a fine selection of liquors. In spite of the new anti-smoking law, this is one of the few bars in Buenos Aires with a filtration system effective enough to allow smoking among guests. The walls are made from panels that originally adorned a medieval Normandy palace purchased by the Duhau family. Gioia offers modern Italian cuisine for breakfast, lunch, and dinner; and the Duhau Restaurant, international with French touches, is open for lunch and dinner. Murano glass chandeliers adorn the space. The executive chef overseeing all of the kitchens is Cyril Cheype. The back of the palace, with its original terrace overlooking the layered gardens with their gently cascading water-lily-filled pools, is another pleasant place for a drink or an informal meeting. The entire garden is shaded by a 120-year-old tree, which projects from the adjacent property. A gazebo contraption goes directly from the terrace into the underground garage. It can be used for bringing up models for fashion shows, automobiles for product launches, and other corporate promotions.

Within the spaces connecting the buildings underground, a wine-and-cheese bar stocks about 45 artisanal cheeses produced in Argentina, along with wine to enhance the selection. This area then leads to the actual passageway, lined with art in the style of a museum. The art changes every 40 days, and all of it is for sale. In the middle of the passageway is the flower preparation area. The spa, called Ahin, takes its name from a Mapuche Indian word meaning "welcome ceremony for honored guests." It and the adjacent health facilities are enormous, offering a range of treatments beginning at about $80 (£44) to nearly $270 (£149). Treatments rooms are spas in themselves, with no need to leave for showering, and there is even a room so that couples or friends can jointly receive treatments. The gym houses a large heated swimming pool. A full-service business center offers translation and secretarial functions. Computers and faxes can be rented here and brought to the rooms. Internet access is also available in all the rooms, beginning at $12 (£6.60) a day and decreasing with multi-day purchases. All public areas of the hotel have Wi-Fi. Breakfast, a huge multicourse spread, is not included in the rates and runs about $20 (£11) per day. Valet parking on-site runs $15 (£8.25) a day.

Av. Alvear 1661 (at Montevideo), 1014 Buenos Aires. (€ **11/5171-1234.** Fax 11/5171-1235. http://buenosaires. park.hyatt.com/hyatt/hotels/index.jsp. 165 units, including 23 mansion units, 23 suites in both towers. $500 (£275) double; from $700 (£385) suite; from $2,200 (£1,210) select suites. AE, DC, MC, V. No Metro access. **Amenities:** 3 restaurants; lobby bar; heated indoor pool; exercise room; health club; sauna; concierge; multilingual business center; salon; room service; massage service; babysitting; laundry service; dry cleaning. *In room:* A/C, TV/VCR, Internet, Wi-Fi, minibar, hair dryer, safe.

Four Seasons Hotel *★★★ (Kids* In 2002, the Four Seasons took over the original Park Hyatt, which was already one of the city's most luxurious properties. This landmark hotel consists of two parts—the 12-story "Park" tower housing the majority of the guest rooms, and the 1916 French style "La Mansión," with seven elegant suites and a handful of private event rooms. A French-style garden and a pool separate the two buildings, and a well-equipped health club offers spa treatments, including a wine massage and facial. The spa was renovated in mid-2004, and all the guest rooms were renovated to reflect the Four Seasons style. The spa is named Pachamama, in honor of the native earth goddess. Specialties include treatments using wine and other Argentine ingredients. The hotel's restaurant, **Le Mistral** (p. 97), serves excellent Mediterranean cuisine in a casual environment. Spacious guest rooms offer atypical amenities such as walk-in closets, wet and dry bars, stereo systems, and cellphones. Large marble bathrooms contain separate water-jet bathtubs and showers. People staying on the Library Floor, formerly known as the Executive area, enjoy exclusive check-in and checkout; additional in-room amenities including a printer, fax machine, Argentine wine, complimentary breakfast, and evening cocktails. On the seventh floor of the tower, the Library itself offers guests in Preferred Rooms and Suites a lounge area in which to relax and conduct business meetings. A selection of international newspapers and magazines is available in this area, as is complimentary Internet access and complimentary non-alcoholic beverages and coffee. The Library is open from 8am to 9pm. Attentive staff will assist you in arranging day tours of Buenos Aires, as well as access to golf courses, tennis, boating, and horseback riding. Kids receive bedtime milk and cookies. While new competition has opened up around the corner in the form of the new Buenos Aires Park Hyatt, the Four Seasons holds its own and continues to win top honors from *Condé Nast Traveler, Travel + Leisure,* and other magazines.

Posadas 1086/88 (at Av. 9 de Julio), 1011 Buenos Aires. (€ **11/4321-1200.** Fax 11/4321-1201. www.fourseasons.com. 165 units, including 49 suites (7 suites in La Mansión). $380 (£209) double; from $570 (£314) suite; $3,500 (£1,925) mansion suite. Prices include breakfast. AE, DC, MC, V. No Metro access. **Amenities:** Restaurant; lobby bar; heated outdoor pool; exercise room; health club; sauna; concierge; multilingual business center; room service; massage service; babysitting; laundry service; dry cleaning. *In room:* A/C, TV/VCR, Internet, minibar, hair dryer, safe.

EXPENSIVE

Caesar Park 🍴 This classic hotel sits opposite Patio Bullrich, the city's most exclusive shopping mall. Guest rooms vary in size and amenities, but all have been tastefully appointed with fine furniture and elegant linens, marble bathrooms with separate bathtubs and showers, and entertainment centers with TVs and stereos. Larger rooms come with a fresh fruit basket on the first night's stay. The art in the lobby and on the mezzanine is for sale, and a few boutique shops are located on the ground level. Internet access is available in the rooms for an additional $20 (£11) per day.

Posadas 1232/46 (at Montevideo), 1014 Buenos Aires. 📞 11/4819-1100. Fax 11/4819-1121. www.caesar-park.com. 170 units. $400 (£220) double; from $480 (£264) suite. Buffet breakfast included. AE, DC, MC, V. Free valet parking. No Metro access. **Amenities:** Restaurant; 2 bars; small fitness center w/indoor pool and sauna; concierge; business center; room service; laundry service; dry cleaning. *In room:* A/C, TV, Internet, minibar, hair dryer, safe.

Hotel Emperador 🍴🍴 Located on Avenida Libertador, this hotel is Spanish-owned, with a sister hotel in Madrid. It opened in 2001 a few blocks from the Patio Bullrich shopping center in an area some would call Retiro, because it is near the train station complex, and others would call Recoleta. The theme here is "Empire with a modern update." A bust of Julius Caesar overlooks the concierge desk. The lobby evokes a sense of the Old World. Behind the main restaurant, the lobby opens onto a large overgrown patio with a gazebo and outdoor seating. The English-hunting-lodge-style lobby bar is a place for ladies who lunch and businesspeople to gather for informal discussions. The imperial theme continues in the spacious rooms. Royal-blue carpets with wreath patterns, and elegant furnishings with rich veneers, brass fittings, and gold velvet upholstery await the visitor. The suites, with their walls, multiple doors and entrances, and extra sinks, are ideal for doing business without incurring on the sleeping quarters. All bathrooms are oversize, with cream-and-green marble, and well stocked with fine supplies. Suite bathrooms are even larger, with separate tub and shower stalls. Each room comes with a large desk and high-speed Internet and Wi-Fi access, which will cost you about $12 (£6.60) a day. The enormous and impressive top-floor nuptial suites have kitchens. Three wheelchair-accessible rooms are available. The gym is small, very clean, and well lit, with a wet and dry sauna and separate areas for men and women. A medium-size heated indoor swimming pool is also here; with the space's modern columns, it gives the impression of a Roman bath.

Av. del Libertador 420 (at Suipacha), 1001 Buenos Aires. 📞 11/4131-4000. Fax 11/4131-3900. www.hotel-emperador. com.ar. 265 units, including 36 suites. $194 (£107) double; from $300 (£165) suite; $1,000 (£550) nuptial suite. Buffet breakfast $24 (£13). AE, DC, MC, V. Valet parking $4 (£2.20). Metro: Retiro. **Amenities:** Restaurant; bar; small fitness center w/medium-size indoor heated pool and sauna; concierge; business center; room service; massage; babysitting; laundry service; dry cleaning; garden patio. *In room:* A/C, TV, high-speed Internet and Wi-Fi at $12 (£6.60) a day, minibar, coffeemaker, hair dryer, safe.

Loi Suites 🍴🍴 Part of a small local hotel chain, the Loi Suites Recoleta is a contemporary hotel with spacious rooms and personalized service. A palm-filled garden atrium and covered pool adjoin the lobby, which is bathed in various shades of white. Breakfast and afternoon tea are served in the "winter garden." Management uses the term "suites" rather loosely to describe rooms with microwaves, sinks, and small fridges. But the hotel does offer some traditional suites in addition to its more regular studio-style rooms. Loi Suites lies just around the corner from Recoleta's trendy restaurants and bars, and the staff will provide information on city tours upon request. In-room Internet is free, and there are also CD players.

Vicente López 1955 (at Ayacucho), 1128 Buenos Aires. ℂ 11/5777-8950. Fax 11/5777-8999. www.loisuites.com.ar. 112 units. From $300 (£165) double; from $450 (£248) suite. Rates include buffet breakfast. AE, DC, MC, V. Parking $4 (£2.20). No Metro access. **Amenities:** Restaurant; indoor pool; exercise room; sauna; small business center; room service; laundry service; dry cleaning. *In room:* A/C, TV, Internet, minibar, fridge, hair dryer, safe.

MODERATE

Bel Air Hotel   Opened in late 2000, the intimate Bel Air has the ambience of a boutique hotel, but it's no longer the bargain it once was. Although the lobby and building's exterior are more extravagant than the rooms, guests can still look forward to comfortable, quiet accommodations. Superior rooms are bigger than standards and only slightly more expensive, and suites have separate sitting areas. Certain rooms contain showers only (no tubs). Next to the lobby, Bis-a-Bis restaurant and bar features window-side tables, great for people-watching along the fashionable Calle Arenales. The majority of the hotel's guests hail from Peru, Chile, and Colombia.

Arenales 1462 (at Paraná), 1061 Buenos Aires. ℂ 11/4021-4000. Fax 11/4816-0016. www.hotelbelair.com.ar. 76 units. $150 (£83) double; from $180 (£99) suite. Rates include buffet breakfast. AE, DC, MC, V. No parking. Metro: Callao. **Amenities:** Restaurant; bar; gym; business services; room service; laundry service; dry cleaning. *In room:* A/C, TV, Internet, minibar, safe.

Etoile Hotel ★ *(Value)*   In the heart of Recoleta, steps from the neighborhood's fashionable restaurants and cafes, the 14-story Etoile is an older hotel with a Turkish flair. It's not as luxurious as the city's other five-star venues, but it's not as expensive, either—making it a good value for the neighborhood. Colored in gold and cream, guest rooms are fairly large—although they're not really "suites," as the hotel describes them. Executive rooms have separate sitting areas, large tile-floor bathrooms with whirlpool baths, and balconies. Rooms facing south have balconies overlooking Plaza Francia and the Recoleta Cemetery.

Roberto M. Ortiz 1835 (at Guido overlooking Recoleta Cemetery), 1113 Buenos Aires. ℂ 11/4805-2626. Fax 11/4805-3613. www.etoile.com.ar. 96 units. $110 (£61) double; from $160 (£88) suite. Rates include buffet breakfast. AE, DC, MC, V. Free parking. No Metro access. **Amenities:** Restaurant; rooftop health club w/indoor pool; exercise room; concierge; executive business services; room service; laundry service; dry cleaning. *In room:* A/C, TV, minibar, hair dryer.

INEXPENSIVE

The Recoleta Hostel ★ *(Finds)*   This is a great inexpensive choice for young people who want to be in a beautiful neighborhood close to everything but can't ordinarily afford such a location. Accommodations are simple, with 22 bunk bed–filled rooms for 8 to 12 people each. Two double rooms with private bathrooms can also be rented, but they have bunk beds, too, so lovers wishing to cozy up will have to get really cozy. Rooms are simple, with bare floors and walls, beds, and a small wooden desk in the private rooms. The decor is reminiscent of a convent. Public areas have high ceilings, and there is a public kitchen, a TV room, laundry service, lockers, and an outdoor patio. The hostel is also a Wi-Fi hot spot.

Libertad 1216 (at Juncal), 1012 Buenos Aires. ℂ 11/4812-4419. Fax 11/4815-6622. www.trhostel.com.ar. 75 bed spaces, including 4 in 2 bedrooms with attached bathroom. From $8 (£4.40) per bed; $18 (£9.90) per private room. Rates include continental breakfast. No credit cards. Metro: Lavalle. **Amenities:** Concierge; Internet; Wi-Fi; shared kitchen; outdoor patio; lockers. *In room:* Hair dryer.

SAN TELMO
INEXPENSIVE

El Lugar Gay 🏾   This is Buenos Aires's first exclusively gay hotel, but it is open only to men. It's inside a historical turn-of-the-last-century building less than a block from Plaza Dorrego, the heart of San Telmo. It has a homey feeling, with industrial chic well blended into a century-old interior. Nestor and Juan, the gay couple who own the building, run a friendly staff, but most don't speak much English. Ask for the rooms in the back with the beautiful views of the Church of San Telmo, which is beside the building. Rooms are small and sparse. Some share bathrooms with adjacent rooms, but one group has a Jacuzzi. They do not provide shampoo or hair dryers in the bathroom. Rooms do not have phones, but some have small desks or tables for use as work stations. Small in-room safes, TVs, and air-conditioners complete the rooms. There is 24-hour free use of an Internet station. Several flights of narrow stairs leading to the hotel's lobby and the rooms might be a problem for people with limited mobility. The hotel becomes a de facto gay community center at times, with its small cafe and Sunday evening tango lessons at 7pm conducted by the gay tango group La Marshall. These are open to the public, so even if you don't stay here, you can still visit this hotel when in town.

Defensa 1120 (at Humberto I), 1102 Buenos Aires. ℂ **11/4300-4747.** www.lugargay.com.ar. 7 rooms, some with shared bathrooms. From $35–$50 (£19–£28) double. Rates include continental breakfast. No credit cards. Metro: Independencia. **Amenities:** Restaurant; bar; business center. *In room:* A/C, TV w/cable, small safe.

Hostel Carlos Gardel 🏾   If you can't get enough of Gardel in the tango clubs, then stay here, where a red wall full of his pictures is the first thing to greet you. This hostel is built into a renovated old house, and though it has been severely gutted, a few charming elements, such as marble staircases, wall sconces, and stained-glass windows remain. The location is also very new, having opened in March 2004. Two rooms with private bath are available in this location, but at $43 (£24), they are expensive, considering the lack of amenities other than a bathroom. The staff is friendly, and a large TV room off the concierge area allows for chatting with them and other patrons. A shared kitchen and an *asado* on the rooftop terrace provide more spaces for interacting and sharing stories of your adventures in Buenos Aires. Towels and sheets are provided for guests, but of all the hostels, this seems to have the fewest bathrooms for the number of guests. Internet is available on-site.

Carlos Calvo 579 (at Perú), 1102 Buenos Aires. ℂ **11/4307-2606.** www.hostelcarlosgardel.com.ar. 45 bed spaces, including 10 in 2 private rooms with bathroom. From $8 (£4.40) per bed; $35 (£19) for room. Rates include continental breakfast. No credit cards. Metro: Independencia. **Amenities:** Concierge; self-service drink station; TV room; free Internet; shared kitchen. *In room:* Lockers.

Hostel Nómade 🏾   Painted green on the outside and all over the inside, the clean and basic Hostel Nómade is in a charming little house a few blocks from Plaza Dorrego. There are several rooms with bunk beds scattered about, and three of the rooms can be rented privately, but none come with bathrooms. A TV room, complete with a pool table and self-service drink station, creates an environment where guests feel comfortable sharing stories about their adventures in the city. The majority of patrons are young Europeans, mostly Germans. As is the case with most hostels, there aren't enough bathrooms for all the beds in this place. A narrow staircase from the center of the house leads to the enormous rooftop terrace, complete with an *asado* (grill). Towels and sheets are provided for guests.

Carlos Calvo 430 (at Defensa), 1102 Buenos Aires. ℂ **11/4300-7641.** www.hostelnomade.com. 31 bed spaces, including 12 in 3 private rooms. From $7 (£3.85) per bed; $17 (£9.35) private room. Rates include continental breakfast. No credit cards. No parking. Metro: Independencia. **Amenities:** Concierge; self-service drink station; free Internet; shared kitchen; TV room. *In room:* Lockers.

Lina's Tango Guesthouse ★★★ *Finds*   If you want to immerse yourself in the tango scene, this is the place to stay. Owner Lina Acuña, who hails from Colombia, opened this charming little spot in 1997. She herself is a tango dancer and wanted to create a space where the tango community from around the world could come together, enjoy each other's company, and share in Buenos Aires's unique tango history. As a woman-owned space, it's also great for women traveling alone, and Lina often goes with her guests on informal trips to the *milongas* of San Telmo and other neighborhoods, offering a unique inside view. Lina lives in the house, and its 1960s exterior hides the fact that the building dates from the turn of the last century. In the rooms off the back garden, the original doors and other elements remain. She has painted these in kitschy colors reminiscent of La Boca, and vines and trees add to the authentic Porteño atmosphere. Guests and Lina's friends gather here for conversation, impromptu help with each other's dance techniques, and *asados* on holidays and weekends. Three of the eight guest rooms share bathrooms. Rooms come in different sizes but all are big enough to share. Breakfast is included, and guests can use the small kitchen and a washing machine. Lina is most proud of the shelves she created in all the rooms for her guests' tango shoes. It is not a full-service location; it's lacking Internet service and in-room phones. The TV is in the shared living room, and it can be noisy with people talking and dancing in the courtyard. Guests may also encounter the periodic barking of Lina's very friendly dog. No other pets but hers are allowed, however. If you're all about tango, however, this is where you should stay.

Estados Unidos 780 (at Piedras), 1011 Buenos Aires. ℂ **11/4361-6817** and 11/4300-7367. www.tangoguesthouse. com.ar. 8 units, 5 with bathrooms. $30–$60 (£17–£33) double. Rates include continental breakfast. No credit cards. Metro: Independencia. **Amenities:** Continental breakfast; self-service laundry; self-service kitchen; tango tours.

CONGRESO
MODERATE
Amerian Congreso   Part of the Argentine-owned Amerian hotel chain, this establishment offers very large standard hotel rooms as well as apartments. A former office building, it opened as a hotel in 2003, after extensive renovations. The decor is simple. None of the rooms have great views, due to the hotel's location on a side street surrounded by buildings of the same height. But it's very quiet. An unheated covered rooftop swimming pool is a nice touch, and there's a small sauna on the premises, too. Most of the rooms also have kitchens or microwaves, making it ideal for long-term stays. Internet access is not available in the rooms, but they plan to add in-room access by the end of 2007. Internet access is free in the business center, which is small, meaning you might have to rely on *locutorios* (phone centers). The lobby has free Wi-Fi. Stairs to the elevator bay also make this a bad option for people with limited mobility. Because the hotel is new and in a renovated structure, however, the chain is making improvements as they go, so you may find added amenities in the near future. Overall, it's a good-value hotel in terms of size, price, and amenities, in spite of its few deficiencies. On-site parking is $4 (£2.20).

Bartolomé Mitre 1744 (at Callao), 1037 Buenos Aires. ℂ **11/5032-5200.** www.amerian.com. 89 units, including 8 apts. From $98 (£54) double; from $98 (£54) apt. Rates include buffet breakfast. AE, DC, MC, V. Parking $4 (£2.20). Metro: Congreso. **Amenities:** Restaurant; rooftop pool; sauna; concierge; business center w/free Internet; room service; massage service; laundry service; dry cleaning. *In room:* A/C, TV, full kitchens or microwaves in most rooms, minibar, hair dryer, large safe.

The Golden Tulip Savoy   Ever since Dutch Crown Prince William married the beautiful Argentine commoner Maxima in 2002, Netherlands natives have been flocking to Argentina in droves. The Dutch-owned Golden Tulip, opened in the faded but historic hotel Savoy, is an attempt by Dutch investors to catch that traffic, and the majority of the hotel's clients are from Europe. The original hotel opened in 1910, built in an eclectic style, with largely Art Nouveau elements. It was just one small part of the glamorous rebuilding of Avenida Callao in the aftermath of the opening of the nearby Congreso. The hotel became part of the Golden Tulip chain in 2000, and the company has upgraded and renovated the hotel completely, with an eye toward maintaining as much of the structure as possible. Gorgeous moldings, ornamental metal details, and stained glass are part of the original decoration, though the lobby was severely altered in the 1960s and retains none of this now. The rooms are very large, in keeping with the old grandeur, and each is entered through its own antechamber, adding to the sense of space, and sports a color pattern of light grays and blues. Rooms facing the street have tiny French balconies, but half of the hotel faces an interior courtyard and therefore offers no views. All rooms are soundproofed and have Wi-Fi. Suite bathrooms include a whirlpool bathtub. A small spa offers facials. The hotel's Madrigales restaurant offers Argentine cuisine with interesting Latin American fusion elements. There is no pool, sauna, or gym here, but the hotel has an agreement with a nearby establishment in case you're interested in these amenities.

Av. Callao 181 (at Juan Perón), 1022 Buenos Aires. © 11/4370-8000. Fax 11/4370-8020. www.gtsavoyhotel.com.ar. 174 units, including 15 suites. From $145 (£80) double; $242 (£133) suite. Rates include buffet breakfast. AE, DC, MC, V. Parking $4 (£2.20). Metro: Congreso. **Amenities:** Restaurant; bar; spa; concierge; small business center; room service; laundry service; conference center. *In room:* A/C, TV, Wi-Fi, minibar, hair dryer, safe.

INEXPENSIVE

Gran Hotel Vedra (Value)   Owing to its low cost, convenient location, and excellent service, this small two-star hotel is best in its category. The hotel offers both "Classic" rooms, in the older wing, and "Superior" rooms, in the newer part of the building. Classic rooms, which face the Avenida de Mayo, are undergoing renovations. They can be noisy, but they afford beautiful views of this historic area. They are small, however, and the furniture is arranged tightly in some of them. Superior rooms are larger, but some face an interior airshaft, with no other windows onto the outside world. Classic rooms have only showers, but Superior rooms have tub/shower combinations. Your best bet is to ask to see the room before checking in. The staff is very friendly and most of them speak English. A small meeting center holds 40 people. A new Internet station offers free Internet access, and the lobby has free Wi-Fi. The hotel offers an evening checkout for people with night flights for a 50% additional charge. The small restaurant offers basic Argentine food and snacks.

Av. de Mayo 1350 (at San José), 1085 Buenos Aires. © 11/4383-0883. www.hotelvedra.com.ar. 35 units. From $35–$40 (£19–£22) double. Rates include buffet breakfast. AE, MC, V. No parking. Metro: Sáenz Peña. **Amenities:** Restaurant; bar; concierge; room service; laundry service; dry cleaning; conference center. *In room:* A/C, TV, minibar, hair dryer, safe.

Hotel de Los Dos Congresos (Value)   This hotel opened in 1999 in a historically listed building just across from Congreso. This hotel is a relative bargain, but some units come in odd shapes and arrangements, so ask to see a room before taking it. A few rooms are split levels, with the bed in lofts; others have very large bathrooms, others small. Some bathrooms have only showers, while others have tub/shower combinations. Suites come with Jacuzzi tubs. Hair dryers are available at the front desk.

Rooms facing Congreso have fantastic views, but the windows are not double-glazed, meaning it can be noisy, especially given the constant protests in front of Congreso. There is no price differential for rooms with or without views. Staff members are exceptionally helpful. Most patrons hail from Europe and South America as part of tour groups, and the hotel also heavily advertises itself as gay-friendly. The hotel no longer accepts pets. Each room has a safe, but they are very small, holding not much more than a wallet. You can stash additional items at the front desk. Wi-Fi runs throughout the establishment.

Rivadavia 1777 (at Callao), 1033 Buenos Aires. © 11/4372-0466 or 11/4371-0072. Fax 11/4372-0317. www.hotel doscongresos.com. 50 units, including 2 suites. $55–$65 (£30–£36) double; from $85 (£47) suite. Rates include buffet breakfast. AE, DC, MC, V. Metro: Congreso. Pets permitted. **Amenities:** Restaurant; bar; concierge; room service; laundry service; dry cleaning. *In room:* A/C, TV, Wi-Fi, minibar, coffeemaker, small safe.

Hotel Ibis 𝒦𝒦 *Value* *Kids*   The French budget hotelier Ibis has done it again, bringing their inexpensive chain to the Argentine capital. The hotel opened ceremoniously on May 25, 2001, and though it looks like every other Ibis in the world, the friendliness and helpfulness of the staff is strictly Argentine. Well located on Plaza Congreso, adjacent to the Madres de Plaza de Mayo office, all rooms here have street views, and many face the plaza directly. High floors offer good views of the surrounding city and Congreso. Double-glazed windows lock out noise in this busy location. Rooms are a good size for this price range, and all are identical, with a peach-and-mint color pattern. They are all doubles, but an extra bed is available, for a few pesos more, for children. Some rooms also connect, which is an ideal option for a family or group of friends traveling together. Three rooms are also geared to accommodate travelers with disabilities. All rooms have cable TV, dial-up Internet service, and a small desk workspace. High-speed Internet is also available in the small business center, along with Wi-Fi access, for about $1.50 (85p) an hour. Bathrooms are bright and clean, all with shower stalls only (no tubs). The hotel supplies only small packets of shampoo or tiny soap bars, so you may want to bring your own trial-size packets. The beds are not the city's firmest, and rooms don't have minibars. No bellboys are on hand to help with luggage, which might be a drawback for the elderly or travelers with disabilities. Safes and hair dryers are available in the lobby concierge area. The basic Argentine restaurant is an incredible value at about $6 (£3.30) for a prix-fixe dinner, and $1 to $3 (55p–£1.65) for most lunch items a la carte. Breakfast is not included in the rates but costs only about $3.50 (£1.95) per person. The hotel is naturally popular with French tourists, and most of the staff speaks Spanish, English, and French. You'll find lots of college-aged backpackers here.

Hipólito Yrigoyen 1592 (at Ceballos), 1089 Buenos Aires. © 11/5300-5555. Fax 11/5300-5566. www.ibishotel.com. 147 units. From $50 (£28) double. AE, DC, MC, V. Parking $4 (£2.20) in a nearby garage. Metro: Congreso. **Amenities:** Restaurant; bar; concierge; business center; laundry service. *In room:* A/C, TV.

TRIBUNALES
EXPENSIVE

Dazzler Hotel 𝒦   This basic hotel, built in 1978, is virtually unknown to the North American market. The majority of clients come from South America, though all staff members speak English. Since our last edition, however, this hotel has doubled its prices, in keeping with a citywide trend. The hotel is conveniently situated overlooking Plaza Libertad, which is set against Avenida 9 de Julio, a few blocks from Teatro Colón (p. 146). Front rooms have excellent views, but they can be noisy, as there is no double glazing on the windows. All rooms are on the small side, but they're exceptionally

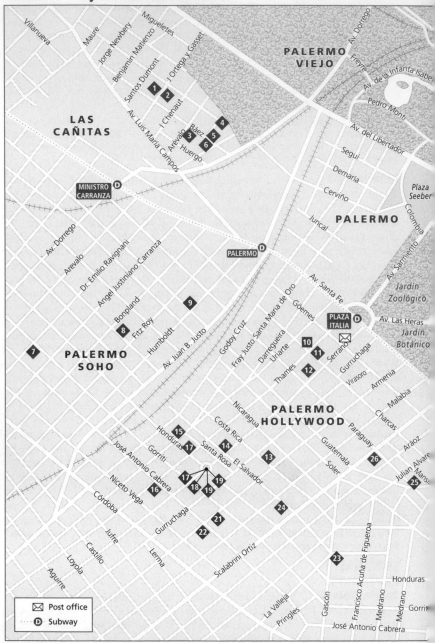

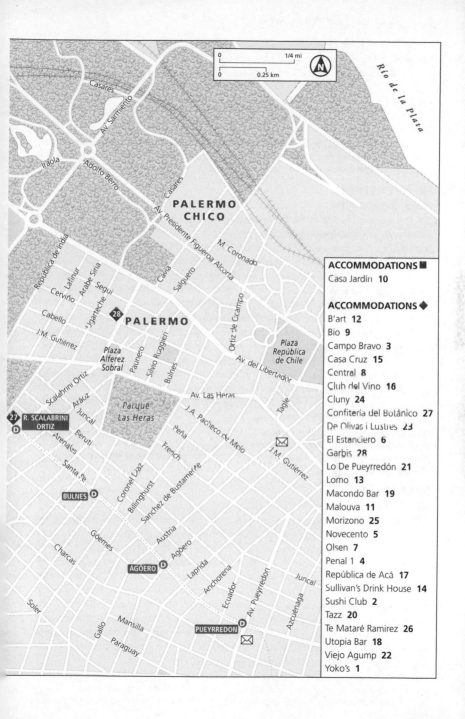

ACCOMMODATIONS ■
Casa Jardín **10**

ACCOMMODATIONS ◆
B'art **12**
Bio **9**
Campo Bravo **3**
Casa Cruz **15**
Central **8**
Club del Vino **16**
Cluny **24**
Confitería del Botánico **27**
De Olivas i Lustres **23**
El Estanciero **6**
Garbis **28**
Lo De Pueyrredón **21**
Lomo **13**
Macondo Bar **19**
Malouva **11**
Morizono **25**
Novecento **5**
Olsen **7**
Penal 1 **4**
República de Acá **17**
Sullivan's Drink House **14**
Sushi Club **2**
Tazz **20**
Te Mataré Ramirez **26**
Utopia Bar **18**
Viejo Agump **22**
Yoko's **1**

bright, with floor to ceiling windows, which also makes the rooms feel larger. Corner rooms offer the most space. Ask about connecting rooms if you're traveling in a group or with family. Large closets and a combination desk and vanity space round out the rooms. Lights and air-conditioning are controlled by a single panel over the bed. The small smoke-glass mirrored lobby has a staircase leading to the large and bright restaurant, where breakfast is served. They also offer an excellent value on their prix-fixe lunches and dinners, which run about $3 to $5 (£1.65–£2.75).

Libertad 902 (at Paraguay), 1012 Buenos Aires. © **11/4816-5005**. www.dazzlerhotel.com. 88 units. From $160 £88) double. Rates include buffet breakfast. AE, MC, V. Metro: Tribunales. **Amenities:** Restaurant; bar; small health club; sauna; concierge; small business center; room service; laundry service; dry cleaning. *In room:* A/C, TV, minibar, hair dryer.

INEXPENSIVE

Auge Buenos Aires 🄰   Alejandro Guiggi opened this private-room pension in 2004 in a renovated apartment building near the Supreme Court. His idea was to create *conventillo*-style lodgings (Italian immigrant rooming house), to foster better understanding of turn-of-the-20th-century Buenos Aires. He expanded the size of his small hotel in 2006. Faithfully restored details include wooden sashes on the windows, ceiling moldings, and stained-glass details throughout the rooms and public areas. The color pattern and antique furniture he has chosen call to mind a bordello, adding a bit of kitsch to the complex. Many of the rooms also have balconies and French doors. Rooms are available for the day, week, or month. Prices vary, dropping significantly the longer you rent. Bathrooms for 10 of the rooms are shared, with whimsical sinks made from buckets and stools. Six rooms have private bathrooms, and these are quieter than the main areas of the pension. Breakfast is included, and guests have 24-hour access and full use of the communal kitchen. Rooms don't have air-conditioning, though public areas do, and they are planning to install A/C throughout the hotel in the future. Wi-Fi access is free through most of the hotel, but the strength of the signal will vary depending on the room.

Paraná 473, Floor 3 (at Lavalle), Buenos Aires 1017. © **11/4373-6812**, 11/4361-4535, or 15/5055-8810. augebuenos aires@yahoo.com.ar. 16 units, 6 with private bathroom. From $30 (£17) with shared bathroom; from $50 (£28) with private bathroom. Rates include continental breakfast. No credit cards. Metro: Tribunales. **Amenities:** Laundry service; kitchen; Wi-Fi.

PALERMO VIEJO
INEXPENSIVE

Casa Jardín 🄰   Owner Nerina Sturgeon wanted to create an "artist hostel" in the heart of Palermo Viejo, and she has succeeded in doing so. Built into an old house, this intimate hostel boasts extremely high ceilings—all the better to display Nerina's paintings, as well as the artwork of others, throughout the space. The gallery atmosphere is furthered by exhibitions held here periodically, complete with rooftop parties on the garden-wrapped terrace overlooking the street. Guest rooms are accessed by old French doors, and each has just a few beds. There are 10 bed spaces, including 1 single. As a woman-owned-and-run business, it's an ideal location for young women travelers. The only drawback is the low bathroom-to-bed ratio. No breakfast is served either, but a 24-hour cafe sits across the street, and there is a shared kitchen. The living room has an Internet station with Wi-Fi capability.

Charcas 4416 (at Scalabrini Ortiz), 1425 Buenos Aires. © **11/4774-8783**. Fax 11/4891-9208. www.casajardinba. com.ar. 10 bed spaces, including 1 single unit. $10 (£5.50) per bed; $15 (£8.25) for single space. No credit cards. Metro: Plaza Italia. **Amenities:** Concierge; free Internet; self-service drink station; shared kitchen; TV room. *In room:* Wi-Fi; lockers.

ABASTO

EXPENSIVE

Abasto Plaza Hotel 🏨   This hotel, opened in 2002, is off the beaten path, but it shows how the Buenos Aires tourism boom has been spreading beyond the city's usual tourist haunts. This location is associated with Buenos Aires's tango history, even if on the surface there seems little that is of tourist value nearby. A block away from the hotel are both the Abasto Shopping Center and Esquina Carlos Gardel—both locations built over sites related to the tango crooner. The hotel takes this to heart, with a unique tango shop for shoes, dresses, and other *milonga* accessories. Free tango lessons and shows take place Thursday evenings at 9pm in the lobby. Every day at 8pm a free tango show goes down in the restaurant. The rooms are a good size, with rich dark woods and deep-red carpets, giving an overall masculine feel to the decor. Few rooms offer great views, but the firm beds will ensure you get a good night's sleep. Superior rooms come with whirlpool bathtubs. The restaurant, Volver, named for a Gardel song, is brilliantly sunny, decorated in a funky design, complete with silver hands holding up shelves of liquor behind the bar. The small heated outdoor pool sits on the rooftop with access through a small gym. Wi-Fi access is available throughout the building, and free 24-hour Internet access is available via three computers in the business center. One wheelchair-accessible room is available. While this hotel does not offer much of interest in itself for Jewish travelers, it is the closest full-service hotel to Once and Abasto's historic Jewish communities and sites.

Av. Corrientes 3190 (at Anchorena), 1193 Buenos Aires. (📞 **11/6311-4465.** Fax 11/6311-4465. www.abastoplaza.com. 126 units. From $140 (£77) double; from $160 (£88) suite. Rates include buffet breakfast. AE, DC, MC, V. Parking $4 (£2.20). Metro: Carlos Gardel. **Amenities:** Restaurant; bar; heated outdoor pool; small health club; concierge; business center; room service; laundry service; dry cleaning. *In room:* A/C, TV, Wi-Fi, Internet, minibar, coffeemaker, hair dryer, iron, safe.

3 Where to Dine

Buenos Aires offers world-class dining with a variety of Argentine and international restaurants and cuisines. With the collapse of the peso, fine dining in Buenos Aires has also become marvelously inexpensive.

Nothing matches the meat from the Pampas grass-fed Argentine cows, and that meat is the focus of the dining experience throughout the city, from the humblest *parrilla* (grill) to the finest business-class restaurant. Empanadas, dough pockets filled with ground beef and other ingredients, are another staple, sold almost everywhere.

Buenos Aires's most fashionable neighborhoods for dining are all in Palermo. Las Cañitas provides a row of Argentine and Nouvelle-fusion cuisine concentrated on Calle Báez. Palermo Hollywood is quickly matching this with even more trendy hot spots combining fine dining with a bohemian atmosphere in small, renovated, turn-of-the-20th-century houses. These restaurants are attracting some of the city's top chefs, many of whom trained in France and Spain. Some of the most exquisite and interesting cuisine is in Palermo Viejo. Both Palermo Viejo and Las Cañitas are near the D metro line, but the best restaurants are often a long walk from the stations, which close at 11pm. All things considered, cabs are the best way to reach these restaurants.

Puerto Madero's docks are lined with more top restaurants, along with a mix of chains and hit-or-miss spots. The MicroCentro and Recoleta offer many outstanding restaurants and cafes, some of which have been on the map for decades. Buenos Aires's cafe life, where friends meet over coffee, is as sacred a ritual to Porteños as it is to

Where to Dine in Buenos Aires

Asia de Cuba **44**
Bar El Federal **55**
Broccolino **29**
Cabaña las Lilas **47**
Café de la Ciudad **39**
Café de Madres de
    Plaza de Mayo **20**
Café Literario **35**
Café Retiro **21**
Café Tortoni **42**
Café Victoria **4**
Casa de Estéban
    de Luca **58**
Clark's **5**
Clásica y Moderna **15**
Confitería Exedra **27**
Desnivel **50**
Don Galindez **36**
Dora **33**
El Mirasol **8**
Empire **32**
Filo **26**
Gran Victoria **43**
Il Gran Caffé **30**
Inside Resto-Bar **16**
Juana M **11**
Katrine **34**
La Americana **17**
La Biela **1**
La Bisteca **51**
La Bourgogne **2**
La Brigada **52, 6**
La Chacra **28**
La Coruña **56**
La Farmacia **53**
La Moncloa **19**
La Sortija **37**
La Vieja Rotisería **54**
Las Nazarenas **25**
Le Mistral **10**
Le Sud **13**
Ligure **14**
Lola **3**
Los Chilenos **22**
Maru Botana **12**
Medio y Medio **49**
Morizono **31**
Palacio Española **45**
Pappa Deus **57**
Petit Paris Café **23**
Piegari **7**
Plaza Asturias **41**
Plaza del Carmen **18**
Plaza Grill **24**
Puerto Cristal **48**
Restaurante y Bar
    Mediterráneo **46**
Richmond Café **38**
Sorrento del Puerto **9, 40**

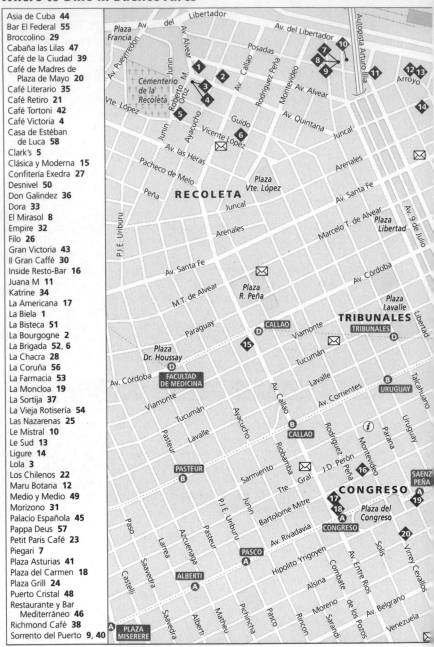

Parisians. Favorite local meeting spots include La Biela in Recoleta, across from the world-famous Recoleta Cemetery, and Café Tortoni, one of the city's most beautiful and traditional cafes, on Avenida de Mayo close to Plaza de Mayo. These places were once smoke-filled, but a new anti-smoking law was enacted in early 2006. If this is your first time in a Buenos Aires cafe, you may not notice. If you have been here before, you may agree with me that something unique has been lost to Porteño cafes—once smoky, but now sterile as hospitals.

Porteños eat breakfast until 10am, lunch between noon and 4pm, and dinner late—usually after 9pm, though some restaurants open as early as 7pm. If you are an early-bird diner in the North American and British style, wanting to eat from 5pm on, look for restaurants in our listings that remain open between lunch and dinner. If you can make a reservation, I highly recommend doing so. If you do not want to commit, get to places close to their usual 8pm opening time, when you will almost always arrive to a nearly empty restaurant. However, once the clock hits 9pm, virtually every table at the best restaurants will suddenly be full.

Many restaurants serve executive lunch menus (usually fixed-price, three-course meals) at noon, but most dinner menus are a la carte. There is sometimes a small "cover" charge for bread and other items placed at the table. In restaurants that serve pasta, the pasta and sauce are sometimes priced separately. Standard tipping is 10% in Buenos Aires, more for exceptional service. When paying by credit card, you will often be expected to leave the *propina* (tip) in cash, since many credit card receipts don't provide a place to include the tip. Be aware that some new restaurants are not yet accepting credit cards, due to fears still resonating from the peso collapse. Many restaurants close between lunch and dinner, and some close completely on Sunday or Monday, or only offer dinner. In January and February, many restaurants offer very limited hours or close for vacations, because most Porteños flee to the beach this time of year. It's best to call ahead during these months, to make sure a restaurant is open.

In early 2006, Buenos Aires passed an anti-smoking law. I never thought it could be enforced, considering the clouds of smoke that once hung over public spaces here. But both patron and restaurant get fined for violations, and so most restaurants strictly enforce the rules, and most patrons follow them. A very few restaurants have special smoking areas, which require a special ventilation system. More smokers are simply sitting outdoors, which was always common in Buenos Aires, but more so now.

Though Buenos Aires is a very cosmopolitan city, it is not very ethnically diverse, at least on the surface. However, a few areas reflect the influences of Middle Eastern and Jewish immigrants who came to this city in the wake of World War I and the Ottoman Empire's collapse. Middle Eastern restaurants are clustered in Palermo Viejo near the *subte* station Scalabrini Ortiz, and also on Calle Armenia. I list several of them below. Since Once and Abasto were the traditional neighborhoods for Jewish immigrants, you'll find many kosher restaurants (some traditional, others recently opened by young people trying to bring back the cuisine they remember their grandparents cooking) along Calle Tucumán in particular. Because many Buenos Aires Jews are Sephardic or of Middle Eastern descent, you'll also find Arabic influences here along with Ashkenazi, or eastern European Jewish, touches.

With a renewed definition of what it means to be Argentine, native Indian and Incan influences are also finding their way into some Argentine restaurants. The best of these are in Palermo Viejo. Try the *parrilla* Lo De Pueyrredón (p. 104), owned by a descendant of one of the country's most important families, and Bio (p. 108), a vegetarian restaurant using the Incan grain quinoa in many dishes.

With as many local Italian last names as Spanish ones, it's hard to distinguish those of Italian descent as a specific ethnic group within Argentina, as you can in the United States, Canada, or Australia. As such, Buenos Aires's Italian food is Argentine food in essence, and pastas and other Italian dishes are usually folded in with traditional Argentine offerings such as grilled beef. La Boca is Buenos Aires's historic Little Italy, the place where Italian immigrants first settled at the end of the 19th and early 20th centuries. The atmosphere in these restaurants plays on this past and caters to tourists, but this is not where the city's best Italian food is served. Instead, it is usually found in old, simple *parrillas* that have operated for decades and include pastas on their menus. Throughout this chapter, most of these are in the Inexpensive categories all over the city. Additionally, though it is on the pricey side, check out Piegari in Recoleta's La Recova restaurant area, which has some of the best northern Italian cuisine in the city.

Asians only make up a tiny portion of Buenos Aires's population, with little effect on local cuisine. Still, in keeping with international trends, sushi bars and other restaurants with Japanese and Chinese influences have cropped up. All over the city, you will find various sushi fast-food-chain restaurants as well. For authenticity, I also describe a few restaurants in Belgrano's very tiny and little-known Chinatown district.

If you are looking through these listings and still cannot decide what you want to eat, head to one of these three neighborhoods, and you are bound to find something that pleases you: **Puerto Madero**'s historical dock buildings are one such place, and many of the restaurants here are a bargain; **Calle Báez** in the Las Cañitas area of Palermo is another such area, and is also one of the most happening restaurant scenes in the whole city; finally, **Plaza Serrano,** in Palermo Hollywood, has many a good choice for the young, funky, and bargain minded. All of these areas also have plenty of places for after-dinner drinks and dancing.

For even further opinions, check out **www.restaurant.com.ar**. It provides information in English and Spanish on restaurants in Buenos Aires and other major cities, and allows you to search by neighborhood as well as cuisine type. Once in Buenos Aires, look for the **De Dios** map company's excellent restaurant map in bookstores everywhere, or order it ahead of time at **www.dediosonline.com**.

I list exact prices for main courses, and categorize restaurants by price. However, it's all relative: Restaurants in the Expensive and Very Expensive categories would not be considered pricey by North American or European standards. In some cases, Inexpensive and Moderate places overlap, or a single menu item, such as lobster, might push an ordinarily Inexpensive restaurant into a Very Expensive category. In short, take a look at our specific prices, which are expressed in a range.

With the current exchange rates, it is very difficult to overspend on food in Argentina. Inexpensive restaurants serve main courses from less than $1 (55p) to about $5 (£2.75). Moderate restaurants serve entrees from around $3 (£1.65) to about $9 (£4.95). Expensive restaurants' main courses cost about $7 to $13 (£3.85–£7.15). Very Expensive means dishes run from $13 (£7.15) up to almost $25 (£14). Remember that in all restaurants, lunch is usually cheaper. Also ask about Executive or Tourist menus, which provide a very reasonably priced three-course meal, sometimes including wine. Tips, drinks, desserts, other menu items, as well as table service and the unavoidable cover charge will add to your costs.

Note: While English is becoming obscenely prevalent in Buenos Aires, less expensive restaurants tend to have fewer English speakers on staff.

Tips Wine Tasting

Part of what makes a meal in Buenos Aires so good is the fine wine selection, specially chosen to complement beef, chicken, fish, and other items on the menu. Most Argentine wine comes from the Mendoza district, bordering the Andean mountains. Malbecs make up most of the best, with cabernets, champagnes, and even grappas on the menus in the humblest restaurants. If you know nothing about wine, you may want to take a wine-tasting class, to make sense of the selections and suggestions offered by the waiter or sommelier. I recommend these two above the many available. On the high end of the scale, go to the **Hotel Alvear's Cave de Vines,** which will run you about $65 (£36) per person. My other choice is out of the wine-based restaurant **Club del Vino,** which will only cost about $12 (£6.60) per person. You'll get about an hour with a sommelier who will explain the grape-growing process, the harvest, and how the wine is actually produced. Like fine diamonds, wine is judged by color and clarity, and you'll learn what to look for in every glass, as well as how to pair wines with food. Other points include discerning taste and scent points as well as how to hold a glass of wine without damaging its contents with your hand's body heat.

PLAZA DE MAYO AREA

Gran Victoria *A* CAFE/ARGENTINE   Watch the political world of Argentina pass by your window at this great cafe overlooking Plaza de Mayo. This cafe sits in the middle of one of the country's most important historic areas, with stunning views of the Cabildo, Plaza de Mayo, Casa Rosada, and the Metropolitan Cathedral, in addition to the excellent people-watching opportunities. Food is basic Argentine, with Italian touches, and a great dessert selection. I'd recommend coming here for a break after sightseeing in the area. What's more, the waitresses have a pleasant sense of humor.

Hipólito Yrigoyen 500 (at Diagonal Sur). ℂ **11/4345-7703.** Main courses $3–$10 (£1.65–£5.50). AE, MC, V. Mon–Sat 7am–9pm. Metro: Bolívar.

PUERTO MADERO

There are no convenient Metro stops to this neighborhood.

EXPENSIVE

Cabaña las Lilas *AAA* ARGENTINE   Widely considered the best *parrilla* in Buenos Aires, Cabaña las Lilas is always packed. The menu pays homage to Argentine beef, which comes from the restaurant's private *estancia* (ranch). The table "cover"— which includes dried tomatoes, mozzarella, olives, peppers, and delicious garlic bread—nicely whets the appetite. Clearly, you're here to order steak: The best cuts are the rib-eye, baby beef, and thin skirt steak. Order sautéed vegetables, grilled onions, or Provençal-style fries separately. Service is hurried but professional; ask your waiter to match a fine Argentine wine with your meal. The enormous eatery offers indoor and outdoor seating. In spite of its high prices, it's casual and informal; patrons come in suits or shorts. They also offer a large and very good salad bar, so even vegetarians can be happy here.

Alicia Moreau de Justo 516 (at Villaflor in Dique 3). ℂ **11/4313-1336.** Reservations recommended. Main courses $9–$14 (£4.95–£7.70). AE, DC, V. Daily noon–midnight. Metro: L. N. Alem.

Katrine ☆☆☆ INTERNATIONAL   One of the top dining choices in Buenos Aires, Katrine (named after the restaurant's Norwegian chef-owner) serves exquisite cuisine. Yet for such an exclusive restaurant, the dining room is surprisingly loud and festive. You won't go wrong with any of the menu choices, but a couple of suggestions include marinated salmon Scandinavian style, followed by shrimp with vegetables and saffron, or thinly sliced beef tenderloin with portobello mushrooms, onions, and a cabernet sauvignon reduction. All of the pasta dishes are excellent, too. Katrine's modern dining room and outdoor terrace overlook the water. Service is outstanding.

Av. Alicia Moreau de Justo 138 (at Thompson on Dique 4). 🕓 11/4315-6222. Reservations recommended. Main courses $8–$15 (£4.40–£8.25). AE, DC, MC, V. Mon–Fri noon–3:30pm and 8pm–midnight; Sat 8pm–12:30am. Metro: L. N. Alem.

MODERATE

Asia de Cuba ☆ ASIAN/JAPANESE   Though not associated with the other Asia de Cubas around the world, this place offers an exciting environment in which to dine. Opened in 2001, the interior is red and black with disco balls and Chinese lanterns hanging from the ceiling. In the back there's a sushi bar and a VIP lounge. Glamorous hostesses glide you to your dining table. Lunchtime is more casual, and less expensive, than at night. Daytime sushi prices start at about $3 (£1.65) per person, doubling to $6 (£3.30) in the evening. A table sushi menu, with 110 different items, is about $113 (£62). Dinner comes with all kinds of exotic entertainment, from Arabian belly dancers to stripteasing women suspended above the crowd. Asia de Cuba is also one of the most important clubs in the Puerto Madero area, ideal for an older crowd because a large portion of its clientele is over the age of 40. Dancing begins at about 1:30am Tuesday to Saturday. If you do not eat here, admission ranges from $7 to $9 (£3.85–£4.95), depending on the day. The dining area overlooks the dance area. In addition to the standard Argentine assortment of red wines, you can choose from among many white wines and mixed drinks as well. Drinks are more expensive by about 10% to 20% if you are not having a meal. The ideal is to come here late in the evening, dine, and stay around for a night of dancing.

P. Dealessi 750 (at Guemes on Dique 3). 🕓 11/4894 1320 or 11/4894-1329. www.asiadecuba.com.ar. Reservations recommended. Main courses $3–$10 (£1.65–£5.50). AE, MC, V. Daily 1pm–5am, often later on weekends. No Metro access.

La Bisteca ☆☆ (Value) PARRILLA   Puerto Madero's La Bisteca offers a wide range of meal choices at incredible value for the money. This is an all-you-can-eat establishment, locally called a *tenedor libre*. A three-course lunch is about $9 (£4.95), and dinner ranges from about $12 to $14 (£6.60–£7.70). If you came to Argentina for beef, definitely stop here. The high quality of the meat surprised me, considering the price and bottomless portions. There really was no limit to the number of times I could fill my plate at the various grills in the restaurant. For vegetarians, there is also a diverse salad bar. In spite of the restaurant's large size, the lighting and seating arrangements work to create small intimate spaces. At lunchtime, the place is full of businesspeople, while at night you'll find a mix of couples, friends, and families. This is a chain, with other locations throughout the city and country.

Av. Alicia Moreau de Justo 1890 (at Peñaloza on Dique 1). 🕓 11/4514-4999. Main courses $5–$7 (£2.75–£3.85). AE, DC, MC, V. Daily noon–4pm and 8pm–1am. No Metro access.

Sorrento del Puerto ☆☆ ITALIAN   The only two-story restaurant in Puerto Madero enjoys impressive views of the water from both floors. When the city decided to reinvigorate the port in 1995, this was one of the first five restaurants opened (today you'll find more than 50). The sleek modern dining room boasts large windows, modern blue lighting, and tables and booths decorated with white linens and individual roses. The outdoor patio accommodates only 15 tables, but the inside is enormous. People come here for two reasons: great pasta and even better seafood. Choose your pasta and accompanying sauce: seafood, shrimp scampi, pesto, or four cheeses. The best seafood dishes include trout stuffed with crabmeat, sole with a Belle Marnier sauce, Galician-style octopus, paella Valenciana, and assorted grilled seafood for two. A three-course menu with a drink costs $7 (£3.85). Sorrento has a second location in Recoleta at Posadas 1053 (© **11/4326-0532**).

Av. Alicia Moreau de Justo 430 (at Guevara on Dique 4). © **11/4319-8731**. Reservations recommended. Main courses $5–$9 (£2.75–£4.95). AE, DC, MC, V. Mon–Fri noon–4pm and 8pm–1am; Sat 8pm–2am. Metro: L. N. Alem.

INEXPENSIVE
Puerto Cristal ✿ INTERNATIONAL/SEAFOOD   The menu here has everything, but fish is why patrons choose this restaurant amid all the others in Puerto Madero. The place is enormous, with friendly hostesses and theatrical waiter service; a constant flurry of fresh silverware and dishes will cross your table between courses, befitting a much pricier establishment. Windows overlooking the port and glassed-in central garden amid the dining area lend tranquillity to the industrial-chic design. Great lunch specials are part of the draw here; their executive menu runs about $6 (£3.30) and usually includes a glass of champagne (though other drinks and the table cover will be additional). You'll pay a slight surcharge for credit card payments here.

Av. Alicia Moreau de Justo 1082 (at Villaflor in Dique 3). © **11/4331-3669**. www.puerto-cristal.com.ar. Main courses $3–$5 (£1.65–£2.75). AE, MC, V. Sun–Fri 6:30am–midnight; Sat 6:30am–2am. No Metro access.

RECOLETA
There are no convenient Metro stops in this neighborhood.

VERY EXPENSIVE
Piegari ✿✿ ITALIAN   You would not expect to find such a fine restaurant under a highway overpass in a part of Recoleta dubbed "La Recova," meaning poultry business. Piegari has two restaurants located across the street from each other; the more formal focuses on Italian dishes while the other (Piegari Vitello e Dolce) is mainly a *parrilla*. Both restaurants are excellent, but visit the formal Piegari for outstanding Italian cuisine, with an emphasis on seafood and pastas. Homemade spaghetti, six kinds of risotto, pan pizza, veal scallops, and black salmon ravioli are just a few of the mouthwatering choices. Huge portions are made for sharing, and an excellent eight-page wine list accompanies the menu. If you decide to try Piegari Vitello e Dolce instead, the best dishes are the short rib roast and the leg of Patagonian lamb.

Posadas 1042 (at Av. 9 de Julio in La Recova, near the Four Seasons Hotel). © **11/4328-4104**. Reservations recommended. Main courses $14–$35 (£7.70–£19). AE, DC, MC, V. Daily noon–3:30pm and 7:30pm–1am. No Metro access.

EXPENSIVE
La Bourgogne ✿✿✿ FRENCH   The only Relais Gourmand in Argentina, chef Jean Paul Bondoux serves the finest French and international food in the city here. *Travel + Leisure* magazine rated La Bourgogne the number-one restaurant in South America, and *Wine Spectator* called it one of the "Best Restaurants in the World for Wine Lovers." Decorated in elegant pastel hues, the formal dining room serves the city's top gourmands. To begin your meal, consider a warm foie gras scallop with

honey-wine sauce, or perhaps the succulent *ravioli d'escargots*. Examples of the carefully prepared main courses include *chateaubriand béarnaise*, roasted salmon, veal steak, and lamb with parsley-and-garlic sauce. The kitchen's fresh vegetables, fruits, herbs, and spices originate from Bondoux's private farm. Downstairs, **La Cave** offers a less formal experience, with a different menu, though the food comes from the same kitchen. Wine tastings are offered Thursday in the restaurant's wine-cellar area called **Cave de Vines;** contact La Bourgogne directly for details.

Av. Alvear 1891 (at Ayacucho in the Alvear Palace Hotel). © **11/4805-3857.** www.alvearpalace.com. Reservations required. Jacket and tie required for men. Main courses $9–$14 (£4.95–£7.70). AE, DC, MC, V. Free valet parking. Mon–Fri noon–3pm; Mon–Sat 8pm–midnight. Closed Jan. No Metro access.

Lola 🍴 INTERNATIONAL   Among the best-known international restaurants in Buenos Aires, Lola recently completed a makeover, turning its dining room into one of the city's brightest and most contemporary. Caricatures of major personalities adorn the walls, and fresh plants and flowers give Lola's dining room a springlike atmosphere. A French-trained chef offers creative dishes such as chicken fricassee with leek sauce, grilled trout with lemon-grass butter and zucchini, and beef tenderloin stuffed with Gruyère cheese and mushrooms. The chef will prepare dishes for those with special dietary requirements as well.

Roberto M. Ortiz 1805 (at Guido). © **11/4804-5959** or 11/4802-3023. Reservations recommended. Main courses $7–$12 (£3.85–£6.60). AE, DC, MC, V. Daily noon–4pm and 7pm–1am. No Metro access.

MODERATE
El Mirasol 🍴🍴 PARRILLA   One of the city's best *parrillas*, this restaurant serves thick cuts of fine Argentine beef. Like Piegari (see above), El Mirasol is also located in La Recova, but its glassed-in dining area full of plants and trellises gives the impression of dining outdoors. Your waiter will guide you through the selection of cuts, among which the rib-eye, tenderloin, sirloin, and ribs are most popular. A mammoth 2½-pound serving of tenderloin is a specialty, certainly meant for sharing. El Mirasol is part of a chain that first opened in 1967. The best dessert is an enticing combination of meringue, ice cream, whipped cream, *dulce de leche*, walnuts, and hot chocolate sauce. The wine list pays tribute to Argentine Malbec, Wyrah, merlot, and cabernet sauvignon. El Mirasol, frequented by business executives and government officials at lunch and a more relaxed crowd at night, remains open throughout the afternoon.

Posadas 1032 (at Av. 9 de Julio in La Recova, near the Four Seasons Hotel). © **11/4326-7322.** www.el-mirasol.com.ar. Reservations recommended. Main courses $6–$15 (£3.30–£8.25). AE, DC, MC, V. Daily noon–2am. No Metro access.

Le Mistral 🍴🍴 MEDITERANNEAN   Formerly known as Galani, this elegant but informal restaurant in the Four Seasons Hotel serves Mediterranean cuisine with Italian and Asian influences. It has been completely redesigned from its previous incarnation, paying homage to Argentine materials such as leather and native woods. The executive lunch menu includes an antipasto buffet with seafood, cold cuts, cheese, and salads followed by a main course and dessert. From the dinner menu, the aged angus New York strip makes an excellent choice. All grilled dishes come with béarnaise sauce or *chimichurri* (a thick herb sauce) and a choice of potatoes or seasonal vegetables. Organic chicken and fresh seafood join the menu, along with a terrific selection of desserts. Live harp music often accompanies meals, and tables are candlelit at night. Enjoy an after-dinner drink in Le Dôme, the split-level bar adjacent to the lobby featuring live piano music and occasional tango shows. The Sunday brunch, which runs about $35 (£19), is one of the best in Buenos Aires.

Posadas 1086 (at Av. 9 de Julio, in the Four Seasons Hotel). ℂ **11/4321-1234**. Reservations recommended. Main courses $6–$20 (£3.30–£11). Sun brunch $35 (£19). AE, DC, MC, V. Daily 7–11am, noon–3pm, and 8pm–1am. No Metro access.

INEXPENSIVE

Café Victoria ✦ CAFE   Perfect for a relaxing afternoon in Recoleta, the cafe's outdoor patio is surrounded by flowers and shaded by an enormous tree. Sit and drink a coffee or enjoy a complete meal. The three-course express lunch menu offers a salad, main dish, and dessert, with a drink included. Afternoon tea with pastries and scones is served daily from 4 to 7pm. The cafe remains equally popular in the evening, with excellent people-watching opportunities, when live music enlivens the patio. It's a great value for the area—the Recoleta Cemetery and cultural center are next door.

Roberto M. Ortiz 1865 (at Quintana). ℂ **11/4804-0016**. Main courses $3–$5 (£1.65–£2.75). AE, DC, MC, V. Daily 7:30am–11:30pm. No Metro access.

Clark's ✦ INTERNATIONAL   The dining room here is an eclectic mix of oak, yellow lamps, live plants, and deer antlers. A slanted ceiling descends over the English-style bar with a fine selection of spirits; in back, a 3m-high (9[bf]¾-ft.) glass case showcases a winter garden. Booths and tables are covered with green-and-white checkered tablecloths and are usually occupied by North Americans. Specialties include tenderloin steak with goat cheese, sautéed shrimp with wild mushrooms, and sole with a sparkling wine, cream, and shrimp sauce. A number of pasta and rice dishes are offered as well. A large terrace attracts a fashionable crowd in summer.

Roberto M. Ortiz 1777 (at Quintana). ℂ **11/4801-9502**. Reservations recommended. Main courses $4–$8 (£2.20–£4.40). AE, DC, MC, V. Daily noon–3:30pm and 7:30pm–midnight. No Metro access.

Juana M ✦✦ Value PARRILLA   This *parrilla* is hard to find but worth the effort. A family-owned affair, it takes its name from its chic matriarch owner and is known almost solely to Porteños who want to keep this place all to themselves. Located in the basement of a former orphanage, which was once part of the city's Catholic University, this neoclassical building is one of the few saved from the highway demolition that created the nearby La Recova area where Avenida 9 de Julio intersects with Libertador. This cavernous industrial-chic space is white and luminous by day, with seating for more than 210 patrons. At night, when the space is lit only by candlelight, trendy young patrons flood in, chattering the night away. The menu is simple, high-quality, and amazingly inexpensive, with a free unlimited salad bar with several healthy options.

Carlos Pellegrini 1535 (basement), at Libertador, across from the La Recova area. ℂ **11/4326-0462**. Main courses $3–$4 (£1.65–£2.20). AE, MC, V. Sun–Fri noon–4pm and 8pm–12:30am; Sat 8pm–12:30am. No Metro access.

La Biela ✦✦✦ CAFE   Originally a small sidewalk cafe opened in 1850, La Biela earned its distinction in the 1950s as the rendezvous choice of race-car champions. Black-and-white photos of these Argentine racers decorate the huge dining room. Today artists, politicians, and neighborhood executives (as well as a very large number of tourists) all frequent La Biela, which serves breakfast, informal lunch plates, ice cream, and crepes. The outdoor terrace sits beneath an enormous 19th-century gum tree opposite the church of Nuestra Señora del Pinar and the adjoining Recoleta Cemetery. This place ranks among the most important cafes in the city, with some of the best sidewalk viewing anywhere in Recoleta. You might just feel like you're in Paris when you come here. La Biela is a protected *bar notable*.

Av. Quintana 596 (at Alvear). © 11/4804-0449. www.labiela.com.ar. Main courses $3–$5 (£1.65–£2.75). V. Daily 7am–3am. No Metro access.

Maru Botana ☞ CAFE/INTERNATIONAL   A pleasant little cafe on a small out-of-the-way street in Recoleta, Maru Botana is owned by an Argentine television cooking-show personality. In spite of her fame, the cafe is unpretentious and quiet, with only a few nods to its celebrity chef owner. You'll find a small inside seating area where you can sip tea and have excellent baked goods or light items such as salads and sandwiches. It's also near the Israeli Embassy Monument commemorating the fatal 1992 bombing, and makes a great place to contemplate the memorial.

Suipacha 1371 (at Arroyo). © 11/4326-7134. www.marubotana.com.ar. Main courses $1–$5 (55p–£2.75). AE, MC, V. Mon–Fri 9am–8pm. Metro: San Martín.

BARRIO NORTE
MODERATE

Clásica y Moderna ☞☞ *Finds* ARGENTINE   This restaurant represents an interesting way to save an important bookstore from extinction—by opening a restaurant inside. The bookstore opened in this location in 1938, though the company dates from 1918. Emilio Robert Diaz was original owner, and now his grandchildren run the place. In 1988 books were relegated to the back to make way for diners, but this is one of the best bookstores for English-speaking tourists in the city. You'll find Buenos Aires photo and history books, as well as Argentine short-story collections, all translated into English. While this is a protected *café notable*, the interior has been completely stripped down to the exposed brick, giving the place a dark, industrial feel. Decorations overhead include old bicycles and signs, but it is a pleasant relaxed space where it's easy to chat with the staff as you dine or sit at the bar. There are many light and healthful choices such as salads and soy burgers on the menu, though since all come with fries, it evens out the caloric content. Mixed drinks start at about $4 (£2.20). Events of all kinds are held here too, from literary readings to plays, dance shows, and art exhibitions. Shows are held Wednesday to Saturday around 10pm, and there are sometimes two shows, the second one beginning after midnight. Show prices vary from $5 to $8 (£2.75–£4.40) and are not included in the price of dining here.

Callao 892 (at Córdoba). © 11/4812-8707 or 11/4811-3670. Reservations recommended for shows. Main courses $3–$10 (£1.65–£5.50). AE, MC, V. Daily 8am–1am. Bookstore hours: Mon–Sat 9am–1am; Sun 5pm–1am. Metro: Callao.

CONGRESO
MODERATE

Inside Resto-Bar ☞ INTERNATIONAL/ARGENTINE   This place is very popular with a largely gay clientele, though of course anyone is welcome. The waitstaff and the owners provide great, attitude-free service here; in fact, the two co-owners work along with their staff, with Diego serving and Matias cooking. There is a low-key red-and-black decor, with dim moody lighting, and a second level of tables they open up when it gets crowded. The food is a mix of French and Italian influences and is very flavorfully prepared. This is also a good place to go just for drinks at their small bar, where many locals gather for conversation. On weekends they have special tango shows and male strippers too, after 12:30am. Reservations are accepted and recommended for weekends. Ask about their return coupons, offering great discounts for people who come back during their slow early weeknights.

Bartolomé Mitre 1571 (at Montevideo). ✆ 11/4372-5439. Main courses $5–$8 £2.75–£4.40). No credit cards. Daily 7pm–2am, later on weekends depending on the crowds. Metro: Congreso.

La Moncloa ✦ *Value* CAFE The surrounding trees here give a calming sense to sidewalk eating in what is normally a busy area on a street just off Plaza Congreso. La Moncloa takes its name from a famous Spanish palace. Basic Argentine fare such as empanadas, steaks, and salads are on offer, along with croissant sandwiches and an extensive dessert menu. There is also a large selection of pork dishes, including the tempting pork in white-wine sauce. Still, for the diet conscious, there is also a low-calorie menu with vegetarian offerings. Whatever you order, I recommend taking the time for a break in this restaurant's parklike setting. Coffee runs about a dollar and mixed drinks start at $3 (£1.65). Flavored and alcoholic coffees, another of their specialties, are about $5 (£2.75). If you don't have time to eat, stop by and grab a menu, as they'll deliver to local hotels.

Av. de Mayo 1500 (at Sáenz Peña). ✆ 11/4381-3357 or 11/4382-7194. Main courses $3–$9 (£1.65–£4.95). AE, DC, MC, V. Daily 7:30am–2am. Metro: Sáenz Peña.

Plaza Asturias ✦✦ *Finds* SPANISH/ITALIAN/ARGENTINE This decades-old place on Avenida de Mayo is about as authentic as it gets, packed mostly with only Porteños who want to keep this place to themselves. It's all about the food here, with touches of Italian, Argentine, and most importantly, authentic Spanish cuisine. They are so busy and have to keep so much food on hand here that there are legs of cured ham literally hanging from the rafters over the diners' heads. Steaks are as thick as the crowds waiting to get into this place, and among their specialties are Spanish casseroles and lots of food with various sauces. Fish is also a big highlight. **Be warned:** The staff is so busy yelling out orders to the kitchen and bringing food to the tables that you can get hurt trying to find the bathroom.

Av. de Mayo 1199 (at San José). ✆ 11/4382-7334. Main courses $6–$10 (£3.30–£5.50). No credit cards. Daily noon–3am. Metro: Sáenz Peña.

Plaza del Carmen CAFE/ARGENTINE This is part of a chain, slightly sterile and clean. However, the best part of this cafe is not inside but the view from this corner overlooking Congreso outside. Generally open 24 hours, no matter what time of day it is you can find people having nothing more than croissants and coffee here. Weekdays, the outdoor seating area is a little overwhelming, since there is a huge amount of traffic flowing by this corner. But inside, protected from the noise and the bus and car fumes, everything is just fine. Wait until the weekends, when the sidewalk is less busy, and the outdoor area becomes more ideal. This restaurant offers standard Argentine cuisine in addition to a healthy choice of salads and diet and other light items on its menu. Pizzas, pastas, and other Italian items round out the menu.

Rivadavia 1795 (at Callao). ✆ 11/4374-8477. Main courses $5–$8 (£2.75–£4.40). AE, MC, V. Daily 24 hr. Metro: Congreso.

INEXPENSIVE

Café de Madres de Plaza de Mayo ✦✦ *Moments* CAFE The official name of this cafe is Café Literario Osvaldo Bayer, named for an Argentine political intellectual. This cafe is located inside the lobby of the headquarters and teaching center of the Madres de Plaza de Mayo, just off of Plaza Congreso. What makes the place so special is its location and its left-wing political atmosphere. In few other places in Buenos Aires will you so easily be able to speak with people who had family members disappear during Argentina's military dictatorship, or with young students who have come to study in this building and continue seeking justice in this cause. The Madres bookstore is just to the side of the cafe, and it's full of books and newspapers on liberal causes from throughout Latin America. It also has one of the largest collections of books on Che Guevara anywhere in the world. An Argentine native, he is a personal hero to many of the Madres, and his image adorns walls throughout the building. The restaurant here recently expanded. It used to be just snacks and sandwiches and some desserts, all self-service from the snack bar. Waitress service has been added along with an outdoor seating area, one of the side effects of the smoking ban. Prices have gone up slightly, and new offerings include simple pasta dishes and a new selection of Italian pastries.

Hipólito Yrigoyen 1584 (at Ceballos). © 11/4382-3261. Main courses $3–$5 (£1.65–£2.75). No credit cards. Mon–Fri 8:30am–10:30pm; Sat (and some Sun) 11am–5pm. Metro: Congreso.

La Americana *Finds* ARGENTINE/ITALIAN   This place calls itself "La Reina de las Empanadas" (the Queen of Empanadas), and that indeed it is. They offer an enormous range of empanadas, all made with a very light dough and slightly burnt edges; they're never heavy or greasy. The place is busy and loud, with the constant din of conversation bouncing off the tile and stone walls and the glass-plate windows looking out over Callao. There are tables here as well as a takeout section and an area for standing and eating—some people just can't be bothered sitting and simply scarf down these delicious creations once they get them. The place looks like many of the fast-food-chain emporiums, but don't confuse it with them; this is the only one of its kind. Waiters are frantic, scurrying from table to table as people change their minds after one bite and order extra rounds. You'll have to keep reminding them of what you ordered if you feel it's taking too much time, but don't blame them. It's just too busy for normal humans to keep up with the pace of the place. Italian specialties such as calzones and pizzas round out the menu choices. Deliveries can be made to nearby hotels.

Callao 83 (at Bartolomé Mitre). © 11/4371-0202. Main courses 40¢–$5 (20p–£2.75). No credit cards. Sun–Thurs 7am–2am; Fri–Sat 7am–3am. Metro: Congreso.

PALERMO
EXPENSIVE

B'art *Finds* ARGENTINE/SPANISH/INTERNATIONAL   B'art's owner Adrián Fuentes might have worked for the McDonald's corporation during his 20 years living in the United States, but nothing about this unique place would seem to show that. He returned to his native Argentina after the terrorist attacks of September 11, 2001, seeking to do something to connect himself back to his culture. So he opened this restaurant serving the best Argentine meats, many of which are used for dishes prepared with both Argentine methods and old-world Spanish traditions. Among the menu items are tapas, casseroles, and *pinchos,* a kind of kabob. In addition to the usual meats, chefs cook up rabbit in various forms. Pastas, salads, and other vegetable dishes complete the eclectic menu. The restaurant sits in an 1885 building near the area of Palermo that the famous Argentine writer Jorge Luis Borges said once marked the edge of Buenos Aires proper. Adrián has beautifully restored the building, and he uses antiques such as turn-of-the-20th-century brick pulleys for decorative but functional tasks, such as carrying wine. He also invites artists to perform on a periodic basis, but some patrons just simply sit at the piano in the waiting area and play the keys while waiting for a table at this delightful restaurant.

Borges 2180 (at Paraguay). € 11/4777-1112. Main courses $6–$10 (£3.30–£5.50). No credit cards. Mon–Thurs 10:30am–1am; Fri–Sat 10:30am–2:30am; Sun noon–1am. Metro: Scalabrini Ortiz.

Casa Cruz *★★ (Finds* ITALIAN/INTERNATIONAL   Opened in December 2004, Casa Cruz is one of the city's chicest restaurants. With its enormous polished-brass doors and lack of a sign on the door, you almost feel like you are entering a nightclub, and inside, the dark modern interior maintains the theme. The impressive round bar, always decorated with fresh flower arrangements, is the first thing you'll see before continuing on into the spacious dining area full of polished woods and red upholstery. The place takes its name from its owner, Juan Santa Cruz. This is his first venture into restaurants, and with the attention this restaurant has received in the national and international press, he has done exceedingly well. The menu here is eclectic and interesting, overseen by Germán Martitegui, the same chef who oversees the kitchen at Olsen. Rabbit, sea bass, Parma ham rolls, and other interesting and exotic ingredients go into the many flavorful dishes.

Uriarte 1658 (at Honduras). € 11/4833-1112. www.casa-cruz.com. Reservations highly recommended. Main courses $10–$14 (£5.50–£7.70). AE, MC, V. Mon–Sat 8:30pm–3am, later on weekends. No Metro access.

Central *★★★ (Finds* MEDITERRANEAN/LATINO   If you only have one night to go out for dinner in Palermo Viejo, this is the place you should choose. Federico Olabarrieta opened his restaurant in 2000 and oversees the service and the food here each night from the busy bar. The severe architecture, cold grays, steel elements, and clean white-marble slabs belie the warm, wonderful service and food you will receive here. A small patio out back also offers outdoor dining. Lit entirely by candles once darkness sets, the place is transformed and soon fills with a young sophisticated crowd. The building was once the atelier of the daughter of Fernando Botero, the Colombian artist famed for his rounded portraits of people, and Colombian influences in the food celebrate this connection. Federico's Basque heritage is also evident in some of the menu items. The location of the restaurant was previously a fruit market, hence the name "Central" for Central Market, and bins of fresh fruits and vegetables in the vestibule celebrate this previous usage of the space. Food portions are large, and the menu has only eight main selections, which rotate seasonally. All are very good, with complex and contrasting ingredients. Salads are superb, sometimes with bitter flowers thrown in with the greens for colorful, tasty touches. Dinner prices push this into the expensive category, but lunch is a bargain at $4 (£2.20) for a prix-fixe menu. If you've already eaten elsewhere, come for drinks and enjoy them in the lounge area with its low, white leather sofas. Happy hour is from 6:30 to 8:30pm Monday to Friday. The large wine selection offers 25 Malbecs, 12 cabernet sauvignons, 6 merlots, and local champagnes.

Costa Rica 5644 (at Fitzroy). € 11/4776-7374 or 11/4776-7370. Reservations recommended. Main courses $8–$10 (£4.40–£5.50). AE, MC, V. Daily 12:30pm–2 or 3am. Metro: Palermo.

Club del Vino *★ ARGENTINE/ITALIAN   In Palermo Viejo, Club del Vino brings a touch of Italian charm. This restaurant has several pretty dining rooms with a Tuscan rustic feel to them with simple sculptures and tables and chairs draped in red- and wheat-colored cloth. Birds chirp in the overgrown trees and vines in the interior gardens as you eat, giving an outdoor feel even inside. Federico Heinzmann is the executive chef, and before working here, he was at the Marriott Plaza Grill. He received his training throughout Spain, in the Basque region in particular. Because of this, his favorite thing to cook is fish, not a usual item on an Argentine menu, but his meat dishes are very well done, too. Naturally, wine tastings are a major part of the offerings, and they are held regularly in an upstairs gallery for $12 (£6.60) a person, lasting about an hour. Make sure to check out the basement, where there is a small museum with old winemaking instruments such as presses and corking machines. The area also holds their extensive wine cellar. Over 350 kinds of wines are stored here; a staff sommelier can help you make your choice. Bottle prices range from $6 to $100 (£3.30–£55), but the majority of them fall in the range of $6 to $12 (£3.30–£6.60). Twenty percent of the wines are also available in glasses. Club del Vino was established in 1985 and opened in this location in 1994. Music and dancing shows are held Wednesday through Sunday beginning at 7 or 9pm, so make sure to call ahead and make a reservation.

Cabrera 4737 (at Thames). ⓒ 11/4833-0048. Reservations recommended. Main courses $8–$13 (£4.40–£7.15). AE, MC, V. Daily 7pm–1am, sometimes later on weekends. No Metro access.

Cluny ✸✸✸ INTERNATIONAL/ARGENTINE   Cluny is casual but elegant, looking more like a modernist living room than a dining room, with neutral color patterns and bursts of burnt orange to brighten things up. A loft space sits above it all and is excellent for hiding away for private conversations or romance. Others choose to dine outside in the patio garden in the restaurant's front space. Sinatra and bossa nova music from the 1960s add to the soft, casual atmosphere. The food, overseen by chef Matias Zuccarino, is the highlight here, and much of it is exotic, with complex offerings such as stuffed quail or duck with grilled pumpkin. There are also many salmon dishes and lamb ravioli on offering. Beef, unlike in other Argentine restaurants, seems to be a second thought here, though it is well prepared, with the sirloin grills as a highlight. The extensive wine list runs over eight pages, offering the finest Argentine vintages from Catena Zapata to French imports hitting more than $250 (£137) a bottle. In the afternoon they have a fine British tea service, a distinctive feature more associated with the old dowager hotels in the center of the city rather than young and chic Palermo Viejo. While dinner is expensive, budget-priced executive menus (as low as $5–$6/£2.75–£3.30) are on offer in the afternoon, with smaller, less complex versions of the late-evening meals.

El Salvador 4618 (at Malabia). ⓒ 11/4831-7176. Reservations highly recommended. Main courses $8–$12 (£4.40–£6.60). AE, MC, V. Mon–Sat 12:30–3:30pm, 4–7:30pm for tea time, and 8:30pm–2am. Metro: Plaza Italia.

La Corte ✸✸ ARGENTINE/INTERNATIONAL   Located on a quiet side street in the Las Cañitas area of Palermo, away from the chaos of Calle Báez, La Corte has a well-prepared menu and is a romantic choice for a night out. Candlelight and other soft lighting and slow music offer an opportunity for a couple to talk and relax after a day of sightseeing. Still, anyone will enjoy the long white lounges and deep chairs as they sit at the tables. Huge bookshelves with antique clocks and other odds and ends are in the front part of the restaurant, giving a sense of being in a library and adding comfort to the seating arrangements. The tiny bar is beautifully backlit, and many people stop in for drinks from the extensive wine-and-mixed-drink list. The cuts of meat are enormous and tasty, but there is a strong emphasis on the vegetable components of the meal to add texture and flavor. There are starters such as sautéed mushrooms and vegetables. Before you begin your meal, the waiters offer a puréed vegetable shot to clean your palate. The very friendly and attentive staff is great at answering questions and attending to your needs. Desserts are very heavy and rich and though well worth it, they're on the expensive side, costing as much as many of the main dishes. The restaurant itself is large, divided up into various levels and spaces, with a few tables on the narrow sidewalk for outdoor dining.

Arévalo 2977 (at Báez). © 11/4775-0999. Reservations recommended. Main courses $7–$9 (£3.85–£4.95). AE, MC, V. Winter daily noon–1am, later on weekends; summer daily 6pm–1am. Metro: Carranza.

Lo De Pueyrredón ★★ *Finds* PARRILLA/ARGENTINE   You may recognize the name of this place from one of the main streets of Buenos Aires. It's owned by Horacio Pueyrredón, a descendant of one of Argentina's most important political families. The place appears humble in spite of Horacio's lineage, and he says very proudly that it is strictly Argentine, serving up the best and most typical food his country can produce. The *parrilla* serves up thick slabs of meat eaten on rustic tables. The building itself is incredible, a restored house that still maintains its ornate floor tiles and stained-glass windows within its doors and patio exit. Exposed brick walls hold changing works by local artists, all of which are for sale. Salads, empanadas, and pastas make up the bulk of the other offerings. They also serve a very traditional and heavy stew called *locro*. It takes over 5 hours to prepare and is a slow-simmered mix of corn, pumpkin, pork, beans, chorizo, blood sausage, and other ingredients. Though this is usually considered a winter dish, they offer it year-round. With the belief that the Indians who once lived in the Pampas are just as Argentine as Horacio is, he also offers items with native influences, such as tamales and *humitas* with *choclo,* a type of corn. He is also vehemently proud of his long wine list, all of it produced in Argentina. The wide range of unusual, hard-to-find, local cuisine pushes this place into the expensive category, but *parrilla* items begin at a mere $4 (£2.20) a serving. The $25 (£14) three-course menú turístico is among the most expensive in this part of the city but is worth it for the high-quality meat and interesting items on the menu. Thursday evenings around 11pm, there is an open mic and guitar playing. Friday and Saturday beginning at 11:30pm, there is a folkloric dance show that lasts about 2 hours.

Armenia 1378 (at Cabrera). © 11/4773-7790. Reservations highly recommended. Main courses $4–$25 (£2.20–£14). AE, MC, V. Wed–Sat noon–3pm and 8pm–5am, often later Fri–Sat. No Metro access.

Lomo ★ ARGENTINE   The full name of this restaurant is "Lomo, the Holy Argentine Word," in reference to the worship of meat throughout Argentina. Inside a former cheese factory bankrupted by the peso crisis, this is one of the most interesting reuses of any old building in Palermo Viejo. While the cheese-drying shelves are gone, the joints that held them in the cracking concrete walls remain. The place is lit by a soaring atrium, and stairs lead to the more intimate upper floor with a fireplace and an outdoor section, decorated with indigenous textiles calling to mind the Indians who once roamed the land where cows now graze. Ironically, the restaurant opened on October 17, 2002, the anniversary date of the rise of Peronism, but the high prices and slightly pretentious attitude of the staff are far from the Peronist ideal. A small record shop is on a mezzanine, and patrons can choose music to listen to and buy if they like it. Chef Guillermo González serves up *lomo,* a cut of beef, in interesting ways, including *lomo* ravioli and *lomo* in various crème sauces. Several fish dishes are also on the menu, but the main specialty is wild boar in fennel stock, which takes over 7 hours to prepare. There's also an afternoon *mate* service, which many locals, especially fashionable young mothers with baby strollers, come for. It's like a British tea service, but with *mate* (a South American tea made from a strong herbal grass) and salted toasts instead, bringing an elegant touch to a gaucho tradition. A cover charge of about $1 per person is added to your bill here.

Costa Rica 4661 (at Armenia). © **11/4833-3200.** Reservations highly recommended. Main courses $6–$14 (£3.30–£7.70). AE, MC, V. Mon 8:30pm–2am; Tues–Sun 1pm–2am. No Metro access.

Olsen 𝓴𝓴 SCANDINAVIAN/SEAFOOD   A bit of Scandinavia has landed in Argentina. Olsen is built into what was once a warehouse, and it soars to churchlike proportions and has a mezzanine with a few tables overlooking the main dining area. The interior, complete with a central round metal fireplace, has a 1960s mod feel to it with blond woods, straight lines, and funky dish settings with orange, brown, and black circles on them. The place is set apart from the street by a large wooden fence, which leads into a patio garden overgrown with vines, complete with a metal sculpture fountain on an adjacent wall. It's an extremely tranquil space, with only a few chairs and tables set out here. They sink into the grass, giving the feeling of a living room that has succumbed to nature. Olsen is very popular with tourists and locals alike, and all of the extremely attractive staff members speak English. Starters are fun and meant to be shared, such as an excellent selection of bagels, tiny pancakes, smoked salmon, smoked herring, caviar, and flavored cheeses and butters. Fish is the main point of this place, and a few of the meat dishes, though flavorful, tend to be on the dry side. Many people come just for the bar, and there is an enormous vodka selection. Absolut rules this part of the restaurant and is available by the shot or the bottle. On Sunday try their brunch, which begins at 10am.

Gorriti 5870 (at Carranza). © **11/4776-7677.** restaurantolsen@netizon.com.ar. Reservations recommended. Main courses $7–$12 (£3.85–£6.60). AE, DC, MC, V. Tues–Thurs noon–1am; Fri–Sat 12:30pm–2:30am, sometimes later if busy; Sun 10am–1am. No Metro access.

Sullivan's Drink House 𝓴𝓲𝓭𝓼 IRISH/INTERNATIONAL   Amid this decor, as green as the Emerald Isle, and the international staff full of young people from all over Europe, you'll feel as though you've left Argentina when you step into this place. Traditional Irish food and herb-marinated meat make up the bulk of the offerings here. Cordero Longueville is one of their specialties, based on an old Irish recipe using Patagonian lamb. Sandwiches and children's meals are also on the menu. Windows to the street give great views, and a VIP lounge, decorated in Old English style, is upstairs, serving as a cigar bar. On the rooftop there's a covered terrace offering even more dining space. No matter what part of the restaurant you choose, Sullivan's has one of the most extensive imported whiskey menus in town, beginning at about $5 (£2.75) per serving. The luck of the Irish is indeed evident in the history of this restaurant: They opened on December 20, 2001, just days before the peso crisis, yet they have survived. If you're in Buenos Aires on St. Patrick's Day, this is definitely the place to be.

El Salvador 4919 (at Borges). © **11/4832-6442.** Main courses $7–$12 (£3.85–£6.60). AE, DC, MC, V. Mon–Thurs 10:30am–1am; Fri–Sat 10:30am–2:30am; Sun noon–1am. Metro: Scalabrini Ortiz.

Te Mataré Ramírez 𝓴𝓴𝓴 𝓕𝓲𝓷𝓭𝓼 INTERNATIONAL/FRENCH   This is perhaps the most interesting and creative dining experience in Buenos Aires. Its symbol, an aroused fork with an extended and upright prong, gives you a clue as to the erotic nature of the restaurant. The name of the restaurant literally means "I am going to kill you, Ramírez." It comes from playful arguments the owner would have with a friend who was a sort of Casanova, and this was a threat the friend often heard from the husbands whose wives he was carrying on affairs with. It's an erotic restaurant, both in its food and decor. Carlos DiCesare, the owner, is himself a devilishly handsome man, looking much younger and fit than his late-40s age. The food he puts out is an interesting mix of flavors and textures. Sensual combinations include garlic and sun-dried tomatoes mixed with sweet elements and poured over sautéed or marinated meats with deeply embedded flavor. This emphasis on contrasts creates some of the most flavorful cooking in town. The ceilings are decorated with paintings of naked men and women with nothing more than high-heeled shoes, mixed in with naughty cherubs. Erotic art hangs on the walls, all of it for sale. The lighting is boudoir red, and wine is consumed out of antique cut-crystal glasses that cast red sparkles on the tablecloths. Black-clothed actors perform playfully racy shows on a small stage here, using hand-held puppets that do very naughty things. It's hard to describe this place as romantic, but certainly a dinner here could lead to post-meal hanky-panky when discussing the play's theme. Slow, soft music such as jazz and bossa nova plays as you eat, adding to the mood for love. There's another location in the suburbs in San Isidro, at Primera Junta 702 (© **11/4747-8618**).

Paraguay 4062 (at Scalabrini Ortiz). © **11/4831-9156**. www.tematareramirez.com. Reservations recommended. Main courses $6–$12 (£3.30–£6.60). AE, MC, V. Sun–Wed 9pm–midnight; Thurs–Fri 9pm–1am; Sat 9pm–2am. Metro: Scalabrini Ortiz.

MODERATE

De Olivas i Lustres ★★ MEDITERRANEAN   This magical restaurant opened in Palermo Viejo several years ago, setting the trend for the gastronomic paradise the neighborhood would soon become. The small, rustic dining room displays antiques, olive jars, and wine bottles, and each candlelit table is individually decorated—one resembles a writer's desk, another is sprinkled with seashells. The reasonably priced menu celebrates Mediterranean cuisine, with light soups, fresh fish, and sautéed vegetables as its focus. The breast of duck with lemon and honey is mouthwatering; there are also a number of *tapeos*—appetizer-size dishes. Best of all: For about $9 (£4.95) a person, you and your partner can share 15 sensational small plates—brought out individually, and building in adventurousness—over the course of a couple of hours. What I find most unique in the restaurant beyond the Mediterranean fare is the use of native and Incan ingredients in various dishes. If you have ever wanted to try alligator or llama, this is the place to do it.

Gascón 1460 (at El Salvador). © **11/4867-3388**. Reservations recommended. Main courses $3–$5 (£1.65–£2.75); fixed-price menu $8 (£4.40). AE, V. Mon–Sat 7:30pm–1:30am. Metro: Scalabrini Ortiz.

El Estanciero ★ *Finds* PARRILLA   In most of the restaurants in the Las Cañitas section of Palermo, it's all about the glamour. Here, however, in the *parrilla* El Estanciero, it's all about the beef, which I would argue is the best in the neighborhood. The portions are not the largest, but the cuts are amazingly flavorful, with just the right mix of fat to add tenderness. If you order the steak rare *(jugoso)*, they know not to serve it nearly raw. The restaurant is in two levels, with sidewalk seating at the entrance and a covered open-air terrace above. Both floors have a subtle gaucho-accented decor that does not overwhelm the senses with kitsch. Never as crowded as the other restaurants lining the street, it's a great option when the lines are too long at nearby hot spots.

Báez 202 (at Arguibel). © **11/4899-0951**. Main courses $5–$10 (£2.75–£5.50). AE, MC, V. Daily noon–4pm and 8pm–1am (to 2am weekends). Metro: Ministro Carranza.

Garbis ★★ *Kids* MIDDLE EASTERN   If you're looking for great Middle Eastern food at reasonable prices or a spot to entertain the kids, Garbis has the answer. Kabobs, falafel, lamb, and other Middle Eastern mainstays are all on the menu, along with great, friendly service. The desert kitsch—in the form of tiled walls and brilliant colors—makes you think you've wound up far away from Argentina. A children's entertainment center will keep the kids happy while you dine. Tarot card readings on select days add fun for the adults. Call to find out the soothsayer's schedule. This is a chain, with additional restaurants in Belgrano and Villa Crespo.

Scalabrini Ortiz (at Cerviño). © 11/4511-6600. www.garbis.com.ar. Main courses $3–$8 (£1.65–£4.40). AE, MC, V. Daily 11am–3pm and 7–11:30pm. Metro: Scalabrini Ortiz.

Novecento 🖈🖈🖈 INTERNATIONAL   With a sister restaurant in Soho, Novecento was a pioneer restaurant in Palermo's Las Cañitas neighborhood. Fashionable Porteños pack the New York–style bistro by 11pm, clinking wineglasses under a Canal Street sign or opting for the busy outdoor terrace. Waiters rush to keep their clients happy, with dishes such as salmon carpaccio and steak salad. The pastas and risotto are mouthwatering, but you may prefer a steak au poivre or a chicken brochette. Other wonderful choices include filet mignon, grilled Pacific salmon, and penne with wild mushrooms. Top it off with an Argentine wine. At night, by candlelight, it makes a romantic choice for couples. A large, separate but slightly sterile side room is available for spillover or to rent for private parties.

Báez 199 (at Arguibel). © 11/4778-1900. Reservations recommended. Main courses $4–$7 (£2.20–£3.85). AE, DC, MC, V. Daily noon–4pm and 8pm–2am; Sun brunch 8am–noon. Metro: Ministro Carranza.

Penal1 🖈🖈 PARRILLA/ARGENTINE   If you can't get enough of Argentine polo, come to this restaurant, just a block from the back entrance to one of the nation's world-famous polo grounds. Taking its name from a play in polo, Penal1 has various owners, including Horacio and Bautista Heguy, two brothers who play for the Indios Chapaleuful team. Every now and then, they come by to check things out. In season, during November and early December, you can often find them celebrating here with fellow players. Service is extremely friendly and casual. Besides the owners' ties to the game, you won't find much about polo itself here, except for a mantle with a few trophies and a polo painting that looks more like a Marlboro ad. The food is simple and inexpensive, consisting mostly of pastas, salads, and meat grilled on the *parrilla*. Lomito Penal1 is their signature sandwich, with *lomo*, lettuce, tomato, cheese, egg, and bacon. The large, expensive selection of wine and mixed drinks includes champagne. In fact, drinking seems to be the point here, more than eating. The place is at its height in season when the bar section, graced by an enormous television, hosts rowdy and happy patrons after games. A disco ball hangs from the ceiling, somewhat incongruous with the rest of the building, located in an old house that still retains some of its original elements. The large overgrown garden in front of the restaurant has several tables, making it an excellent spot for late-night summer dining.

Arguibel 2851 (at Báez). © 11/4776-6030. Main courses $3–$6 (£1.65–£3.30). No credit cards. Tues–Sun 9pm–2am, much later on weekends depending on crowds. Metro: Carranza.

República de Acá 🖈🖈 INTERNATIONAL/ARGENTINE/COMEDY CLUB   Charcoal drawings of Hollywood actors and other stars decorate the walls of this place, a fun comedy club and karaoke bar overlooking Plaza Serrano. Drinks are the main event here, but food offerings include pizzas, *picadas* (small cuts of cheese and meat that you "pick" at), salads, and other easy-to-make small items. Drinks come with free use of the Internet, and the menu will tell you how many minutes of Internet use are included with each drink. About half of this club is taken up by computers. Prices of drinks rise after 11pm by about 10%. At night the shows begin, with entertainment of all kinds.

On weekends, live music shows begin at 10pm, followed by comedy routines at 12:30am, karaoke at 3am, and then dancing until way past sunrise. There is a $5 (£2.75) entrance fee after 10pm on weekends, which includes one drink. After 2am this drops to a little over $3 (£1.65) to enter and still includes one drink. Many mixed drinks are made with ice cream, like very adult interpretations of soda floats. TVs wrap around the whole space, so there is always something to watch. Fine champagnes and a selection of cigars at the bar make this a place to head to when you've got something to celebrate.

Serrano 1549 (at Plaza Serrano). © 11/4581-0278. www.republicadeaca.com.ar. Main courses $2–$5 (£1.10–£2.75). No credit cards. Sun–Thurs 9am–2am; Fri–Sat 9am–7am. Metro: Plaza Italia.

Sushi Club JAPANESE   This restaurant is part of a very popular chain, with many locations throughout the city, but this is one of its nicest outlets. The Sushi Club serves sushi and other Japanese cuisine in a modern clublike interior, with orange, black, and metallic elements. Fish is a big highlight of the menu, as is beef with Japanese seasonings. The sushi roll selection is enormous and creative; many of the offerings pay tribute to other international cuisines, using ingredients to match.

Ortega Y Gasset 1812 (at Arce). © 0-810/222-SUSHI (toll-free). Main courses $4–$8 (£2.20–£4.40). AE, DC, MC, V. Daily noon–5pm and 8pm–3am. Metro: Carranza.

Utopia Bar ARGENTINE/INTERNATIONAL   More cozy and calm than some of the other bars that surround Plaza Serrano, this is an excellent place to grab a drink and a bite in this very trendy and busy neighborhood. Yellow walls and soothing rustic wooden tables add a sense of calm, though the live music, scheduled on an irregular basis, can be loud at times. There is an emphasis on the drinks here, and breakfast has a large selection of flavored coffees, some prepared with whiskey. At night, pizza and sandwiches make up the bulk of the offerings. The upstairs, open-air terrace on the roof of the bar is one of the best places to sit, but it's small and hard to claim a spot. If a table is open, nab it.

Serrano 1590 (at Plaza Serrano). © 11/4831-8572. Main courses $2–$8 (£1.10–£4.40). AE, MC, V. Daily 24 hr. Metro: Plaza Italia.

Yoko's ✦ JAPANESE/CHINESE   This elegant, upscale eatery combines elements of Japanese and Chinese cuisines with California accents. The setting is mod, romantic, and chic all at once, with black-lacquered tables, red walls, and black metal sculpture with red accents. The service is friendly, with a large number of servers to attend to patrons. Try their rolls, which are like California wraps, mixing seafood and cheeses. Healthy wok-cooked food and sushi round out the menu.

J. Ortega y Gasset 1813 (at Calle Báez). © 11/4776-0018 or 11/4778-0036. Main courses $4–$7 (£2.20–£3.85). AE, DC, MC, V. Mon–Sat 10am–1am; Sun 6pm–1am. Metro: M. Carranza.

INEXPENSIVE

Bio ✦✦ *Finds* VEGETARIAN/MEDITERRANEAN   In a nation where meat reigns supreme, finding an organic vegetarian restaurant is a near impossibility. Bio, opened in 2002, is the exception. Their "meat" is made on the premises from wheat, then marinated to add more flavor, making for an elevated, tasty variation on a hamburger. All the ingredients are organic, grown or produced strictly in Argentina. Piles of organic cheese line the counters near the chefs, Gaston and Maximo, who are happy to explain the processes by which they work. Quinoa, the ancient Incan grain, is also used in many of the dishes, some of which they describe as Mediterranean-Asian fusion, though with the combinations of so many unusual ingredients, anything goes.

You have to try the quinoa risotto, one of the restaurant's main specialties, though everything here is simply delicious and fresh. Chairs and tables are painted a spring green, and, on warm days, a few tables are scattered on the sidewalk outside. This is also a great place for veg-heads to go shopping for snacks to bring back to their hotel. They have a small shop inside with organic chips, teas, cheeses, and even organic wine. They also do takeout—a delight if you want to bring something home with you.

Humboldt 2199 (at Guatemala). (© 11/4774-3880. Main courses $4–$6 (£2.20–£3.30). No credit cards. Tues–Sun noon–3:30pm; daily 8pm–1am, often later on weekends. No Metro access.

Campo Bravo 🏵🏵 _Value_ PARRILLA/ARGENTINE   Everyone I know who knows Buenos Aires tests me on this place. Do I know of it, and what do I think? Well, I know it, and I love it! This place serves as the virtual center of the Las Cañitas dining scene. It's relaxed during the day but insane at night. Dining on the sidewalk here, you'll get a great view of the glamorous crowds emerging from taxis to kick off their night in this exciting neighborhood. The _parrilla_ serves up basic Argentine cuisine, and its enormous slabs of meat are served on wooden boards. A large, efficient wait-staff will take care of you, but they can't do anything about the long wait for an outside table on weekends—sometimes as long as 40 minutes to an hour. There's no way around that, since they don't accept reservations. So do as the locals do on Saturday night: Get a glass of champagne and sip it on the street amid what looks like a well-dressed and overage frat party. A limited wine selection and imported whiskeys are also part of the drink selection. Can't handle the late nights in Argentina? Well, then you're in luck—they don't close between lunch and dinner, so people used to North American dining schedules can still enjoy a great meal here without a wait.

Báez 292 (at Arévalo). (© 11/4514-5820. Main courses $3.50–$5 (£1.95–£2.75). MC. Mon 6pm–4am; Tues–Sun 11:30am–4am, often later on weekends depending on crowds. Metro: Carranza.

Coanico Bar ARGENTINE/INTERNATIONAL   The movie posters on the outside of this bar are probably the first thing you'll notice. Inside, you'll find a busy place where people eat and drink off tables painted with nude women in the style of Picasso. The bar has overlooked Plaza Serrano for over 20 years, and offers typical bar food such as sandwiches and hamburgers but has a larger menu than most of the surrounding bars. Live rock music sometimes entertains the crowd.

Borges 1646 (at Plaza Serrano). (© 11/4833-0708. Main courses $1–$3 (55p–£1.65). No credit cards. Daily 10am–4am, sometimes later on weekends. Metro: Plaza Italia.

Confitería del Botánico CAFE/ARGENTINE   Stop here after visiting the nearby zoo or Botanical Gardens. It's on a pleasant corner on busy Santa Fe, but the green spaces of the gardens and Plaza Siria give it a more tranquil feel. Enormous windows seem to bring the park inside. Continental breakfast here is inexpensive, and you can also order from the entire menu any time of day (omelets from the dinner menu make a hearty breakfast). Lunch specials run $3 to $4 (£1.65–£2.20). They also do takeout, which makes a great picnic for the park or zoo.

Av. Santa Fe (at República Siria). (© 11/4833-5515. Main courses $2–$4 (£1.10–£2.20). AE, MC, V. Sun–Fri 6:30am–midnight; Sat 6:30am–2am. Metro: Plaza Italia.

Macondo Bar 🏵🏵 INTERNATIONAL/ARGENTINE   Macondo Bar is one of the stars of Plaza Serrano, with sidewalk seating and lots of levels overlooking the action. Inside, the restaurant twists around several staircases and low ceilings. It's a loud and busy place, for sure, but the setup creates a sense of intimacy if you come here with friends, to share conversation over drinks and a meal. Sandwiches, pizzas, salads, and *picadas* make up the menu. DJs blast music of all kinds through the bar, from folkloric to techno to electrónica. Technically, there's no live music, but sometimes people come around and play on the street in front of the bar.

Borges 1810 (at Plaza Serrano). ℂ 11/4831-4174. Main courses $1–$5 (55p–£2.75). No credit cards. Mon–Thurs 6pm–4am; Fri–Sat 5pm–7am; Sun 5pm–3am. Metro: Plaza Italia.

Malouva CAFE   This is a great location at any time, but it's best late at night when you have the munchies after barhopping in Palermo Viejo. Malouva is open 24 hours and was here long before the neighborhood around it got trendy. As such, you're not here for sophistication but, rather, for the simple menu items and the drink selection. Cheap offerings include salads, pastries, sandwiches, and pizzas. On the downside, service can be slow, and they don't seem to have enough staff for both the indoor and outdoor seating sections. Nevertheless, lots of young local people come here, making weekends especially crowded, with kids conversing over large bottles of Quilmes beer. If you're not staying nearby, don't worry about getting a cab from here: It's across the street from a gas station where taxi drivers clean and fuel up, so it's easy to get a car from here to anywhere. In fact, the table next to yours may be full of taxi drivers taking a break from their long days.

Charcas 4401 (at Thames). ℂ 11/4774-0427. Main courses $1–$3 (55p–£1.65). No credit cards. Daily 24 hr. Metro: Plaza Italia.

Tazz ℝ MEXICAN   In an old house, like so many other restaurants in Palermo Viejo, Tazz is one of the best spots for outdoor seating on all of Plaza Serrano. Step inside, however, and you'll think you've entered the dining hall of a spaceship, with blue glowing lights and walls, mod aluminum panels, and billiard table after billiard table. The booths look like little emergency space capsules that can be released if the mother ship gets attacked. The bulk of the menu is Mexican (there are hardly any other Mexican restaurants in Buenos Aires). Pitchers of sangria and margaritas add to the fun More of a bar than a restaurant, this place is very popular, with a very young clientele.

Serrano 1556 (at Plaza Serrano). ℂ 11/4833-5164. www.tazzbars.com. Main courses $2–$4 (£1.10–£2.20). No credit cards. Sun–Thurs noon–3am; Fri–Sat noon–6am. Metro: Plaza Italia.

Viejo Agump ℝ Finds MIDDLE EASTERN   In the heart of the old Armenian section of Buenos Aires, owner Elizabeth Hounanjian offers authentic Middle Eastern cuisine and a new hub for her compatriots ("agump" means "club" or "meeting place" in Armenian), in the shadows of the Armenian church and the community center. The exposed brick interior of the old house adds a touch of comfort to the dining area, where mainstays include kabobs and baklava. Sidewalk seating on this tree-lined street is a delight in warm weather. On weekends, Arabic belly dancing and coffee-bean readings heighten the exotic atmosphere. To arrange a reading, contact the mystic Roxana Banklian and schedule an appointment (ℂ **11/15/4185-2225** cell; roxanabanklin@arnet.com.ar).

Armenia 1382 (at José Antonio Cabrera). ℂ **11/4773-5081.** Main courses $2–$5 (£1.10–£2.75). No credit cards. Mon–Sat 8am–midnight. Metro: Scalabrini Ortiz.

BELGRANO
EXPENSIVE
Buddha BA ℝ CHINESE   In the heart of Belgrano's Chinatown, this very elegant, two-level Chinese teahouse and restaurant is built into a house, with an adjacent garden and art gallery selling fine Asian art and antiques. The interesting and creatively named menu includes items such as Dragon Fire, a mix of spicy chicken and curried

lomo; or Buddha Tears, squid in a soy and chicken broth sauce with seasoned vegetables. The atmosphere is very welcoming, and makes a great rest stop if you're exploring this neighborhood in depth.

Arribeños 2288 (at Mendoza). © **11/4706-2382.** www.buddhaba.com.ar. Main courses $6–$10 (£3.30–£5.50). MC, V. Wed–Sun 8:30–11:30pm; Sat–Sun 12:30–3:30pm; tea service Wed–Sun 4–7:30pm. Metro: Juramento.

MODERATE

Club Español *✿✿* SPANISH   This restaurant has one of the most magnificent dining rooms in Buenos Aires. It's located in the Club Español, one of the grandest buildings along 9 de Julio. An orgy of brass, marble, agate lighting fixtures, carved oak bas-reliefs and molded plaster ornaments will surround you. Interspersed are Spanish paintings of major battles, and graceful Art Nouveau maidens who stare down from the tops of pilasters. Despite the restaurant's architectural grandeur, the atmosphere is surprisingly relaxed and often celebratory; don't be surprised to find a table of champagne-clinking Argentines next to you. Tables have beautiful silver place settings, and tuxedo-clad waiters offer friendly but formal service. Although the menu is a tempting sample of Spanish cuisine—including paella and Spanish omelets—the fish dishes are best. Special salads are meals in themselves; a few include calamari. The wine list is pages long, with a large selection of whites to complement the fish offerings. Bills include a table service of about $1.50 (85p).

Bernardo de Yrigoyen 180 (at Alsina). © **11/4334-4876.** Reservations recommended. Main courses $5–$12 (£2.75–£6.60). AE, DC, MC, V. Daily noon–4pm and 8pm–midnight, sometimes until 1am Fri–Sat. Metro: Lima.

Todos Contentos CHINESE   If you're looking for that busy, authentic Chinatown feel, come to this place, with crowded tables full of patrons eating noodle dishes and other Chinese cuisine. Waitresses in embroidered Chinese silk shirts make sure everyone is well tended. The very large selection of standards includes pork dishes and chow mein, in addition to interesting items such as salted tripe. The very reasonable weekend special, for about $3 (£1.65) per person, includes a starter such as egg rolls, a noodle meat dish, and a drink. I list this restaurant as moderate, but they also sell lobster, which is considerably more expensive (about $15/£8.25 per person, which would push it into the very expensive category). But the vast majority of dishes are reasonable.

Arribeños 2177 (at Mendoza). © **11/4780-3437.** Main courses $3–$15 (£1.65–£8.25). No credit cards. Mon–Fri 11:30am–3:30pm and 7:30–9:30pm; Sat–Sun 9:30am–midnight. Metro: Juramento.

MONSERRAT
MODERATE

Restaurante y Bar Mediterráneo *✿✿* MEDITERRANEAN   The Inter-Continental Hotel's exclusive Mediterranean restaurant and bar were built in colonial style, resembling the city's famous Café Tortoni. The downstairs bar, with its hardwood floor, marble-top tables, and polished Victrola playing tango, takes you back to Buenos Aires of the 1930s. A spiral staircase leads to the elegant restaurant, where subdued lighting and well-spaced tables create an intimate atmosphere. Mediterranean herbs, olive oil, and sun-dried tomatoes are among the chef's usual ingredients. Dishes might include carefully prepared shellfish bouillabaisse; black hake served with ratatouille; chicken casserole with morels, fava beans, and potatoes; or duck breast with cabbage confit, wild mushrooms, and sautéed apples. Express menus (items ready within minutes) are available at lunch.

Moreno 809 (at Piedras in the Inter-Continental Hotel). © **11/4340-7200.** Reservations recommended. Main courses $6–$9 (£3.30–£4.95). AE, DC, MC, V. Daily 7–11am, 11:30am–3:30pm, and 7pm–midnight. Metro: Moreno.

MICROCENTER
EXPENSIVE

Dora 🌟🌟 ARGENTINE/SEAFOOD   This restaurant looks like nothing inside or outside, but nobody comes here for the decor: Dora is all about the food. On the ground floor of an office building, with plain brown wooden interiors lined with bottles of wine, Dora has been open since the 1940s, run by the same family (the third generation is now in charge). It's loud, noisy, crazy, and chaotic—an odd mix of businesspeople from nearby offices and casually dressed older locals who have been regulars for decades. The specialty is fish, with a few beef, chicken, and pasta dishes thrown in almost as an afterthought. The Cazuela Dora is the specialty—a casserole of fish, shellfish, and shrimp thrown into one pot. It's expensive for Buenos Aires; appetizers alone run from $4 to $14 (£2.20–£7.70), though some of the starters are made with caviar. The dessert menu includes a surprisingly varied choice of light fruits in season. Because they serve so much fish, Dora has one of the city's largest white-wine selections.

Leandro N. Alem 1016 (at Paraguay). 🕐 11/4311-2891. Main courses $8–$20 (£4.40–£11). V. U.S. dollars accepted. Mon–Thurs 12:30pm–1am; Fri–Sat noon–2am. Metro: San Martín.

Le Sud 🌟🌟 FRENCH/MEDITERRANEAN   Executive Chef Thierry Pszonka earned a gold medal from the National Committee of French Gastronomy and gained experience at La Bourgogne before opening this gourmet restaurant in the new Sofitel Hotel. His simple, elegant cooking style embraces spices and olive oils from Provence, to create delicious entrees such as stewed rabbit with green pepper and tomatoes, polenta with Parmesan and rosemary, and spinach with lemon ravioli. Le Sud's dining room is as sophisticated as the cuisine: The design is contemporary, with chandeliers and black-marble floors, tables of Brazilian rosewood, and large windows overlooking Calle Arroyo. After dinner, consider a drink in the adjacent wine bar.

Arroyo 841/849 (at Suipacha in the Sofitel Hotel). 🕐 11/4131-0000. Reservations recommended. Main courses $10–$20 (£5.50–£11). AE, DC, MC, V. Daily 6:30–11am, 12:30–3pm, and 7:30pm–midnight. Metro: San Martín.

Plaza Grill 🌟🌟 INTERNATIONAL   For nearly a century, the Plaza Grill dominated the city's power-lunch scene, and it remains the first choice for government officials and business executives. The dining room is decorated with dark-oak furniture, the owners' 90-year-old Dutch porcelain collection, Indian fans from the British Empire, and Villeroy & Boch china place settings. Tables are well spaced, allowing for intimate conversations. Order a la carte from the international menu or off the *parrilla*—the steaks are perfect Argentine cuts. Marinated filet mignon, thinly sliced and served with gratinéed potatoes, is superb. Another interesting choice is venison with crispy apple sauce, served during the November and December holiday season, though seemingly incongruous in the heat of Buenos Aires's summer. The "po parisky eggs" form another classic dish—two poached eggs in a bread shell topped with a rich mushroom-and-bacon sauce. The restaurant's wine list spans seven countries, with the world's best Malbec coming from Mendoza. The restaurant previously sold wine only by the bottle, but now will sell it by the glass. While a la carte choices can add up, ranging from $7 to $10 (£3.85–£5.50), with select items spiking to $20 (£11), a prix-fixe lunch menu of $25 (£14) with appetizer, main course, and desert, not including wine, is a bargain

Marriott Plaza Hotel, Calle Florida 1005 (at Santa Fe overlooking Plaza San Martín). 🕐 11/4318-3070. Reservations recommended. Main courses $7–$10 (£3.85–£5.50). AE, DC, MC, V. Daily noon–4pm and 7pm–midnight. Metro: San Martín.

MODERATE

Broccolino 🏵 ITALIAN   The name of this restaurant doesn't mean little broccoli; it's a corruption of Italian immigrant slang for New York's biggest and once most heavily Italian borough (notice the Brooklyn memorabilia filling the walls and the mural of Manhattan's skyline). This casual trattoria near Calle Florida is popular with North Americans, including Robert Duvall. Many of the waiters speak English, and the restaurant has a distinctly New York feel. Three small dining rooms are decorated in quintessential red-and-white-checkered tablecloths, and the smell of tomatoes, onions, and garlic fills the air. The restaurant is known for its spicy pizzas, fresh pastas, and, above all, its sauces (*salsas* in Spanish). The restaurant also serves 2,000 pounds per month of baby calamari sautéed in wine, onions, parsley, and garlic.

Esmeralda 776 (at Córdoba). © **11/4322-7652.** Reservations recommended. Main courses $3–$7 (£1.65–£3.85). No credit cards. Daily noon–4pm and 7pm–1am. Metro: Lavalle.

Café de la Ciudad CAFE/ARGENTINE   The city's only restaurant with outdoor dining directly overlooking the Obelisco, Café de la Ciudad opened 40 years ago on one of the six corners around the landmark, on Avenida 9 de Julio. It's like Buenos Aires's Times Square, where you can watch the myriad flashing electronic ads for Japanese and American companies. Sure, it's noisy, and, sure, you're a target for beggars, but you'll be dining under the symbol of the city. The food comes in large portions; sandwiches, pizzas, and specially priced executive menus are made fast, so it's a great stop if you're short on time. The subway station Carlos Pellegrini is right here too. On nights after the Boca Juniors have won a game, it's a great free show when locals gather to cheer under the Obelisco, as cars and taxis hurtle by, beeping at the crowd. The cafe is also a 24-hour place, so you can stop by after clubbing or a show at one of the nearby theaters, and watch the parade of Porteños passing by.

Corrientes 999 (at Carlos Pellegrini, Av. 9 de Julio). © **11/4322-8905** or 11/4322-6174. Main courses $1.50–$7 (85p–£3.85). AE, DC, MC, V. Daily 24 hr. Metro: Carlos Pellegrini.

Confitería Exedra 🏵🏵 CAFE/ARGENTINE   The tag name for this place is "La Esquina de Buenos Aires" (the corner of Buenos Aires). Every walk of life seems to pass through this exciting cafe, like a busy city street corner. It's graced by a stained-glass-and-blond-wood wall mural, reminiscent of something out of a 1970s church, and topped off with a glitzy Vegas ceiling. The old waiter, Victor, with more than 20 years experience here, says, "We serve all." And they do. The crowd here is boisterous, in a mix of formal and informal dress, all enjoying each other's company and checking out the crowds walking by on Avenida 9 de Julio through the huge glass windows. Because this place is popular late at night, surrounded by some of the special men's clubs, you might find some call girls and a few other dubious creatures hanging out. Still, it's definitely a spot to hit on weekends if you're looking for a bite to eat after club hopping. The drink selection is huge, and the prices go up slightly late at night. The menu is a combination of snacks, fast food, and more interesting and substantial things too, such as chicken with pumpkin sauce. The executive lunch menu is $5 to $7 (£2.75–£3.85), and dinner is a similar bargain.

Av. Córdoba 999 (at Carlos Pellegrini/Av. 9 de Julio). © **11/4322-7807.** Main courses $3–$5 (£1.65–£2.75). AE, MC, V. Sun–Thurs 7am–5am; Fri–Sat 24 hr. Metro: Lavalle.

Empire 🏵 ASIAN/THAI   This restaurant is interesting, but it's in a surprisingly desolate part of the MicroCentro—steps away from the action, on a very small street that gets little foot traffic and therefore seems remote. Enter this dark space, with paintings of elephants and mosaic decorations made from broken mirrors on the columns, and you'll feel as though you've stepped into some kind of funky club. For vegetarians seeking a break from the meat offerings everywhere else, it's is an ideal stop, with its many all-vegetable or noodle offerings. Many come for drinks alone and sit at the large bar with shelves of backlit bottles casting a warm glow. Empire's advertising symbol is the Empire State Building, but there's nothing New York–like about it. It's also one of the city's most popular restaurants among gay locals.

Tres Sargentos 427 (at San Martín). ⓒ 11/5411-4312 or 11/5411-5706. empire_bar@hotmail.com. Main courses $6–$10 (£3.30–£5.50). AE, MC, V. Mon–Fri 9am–1am; Sat 10:30am–3am. Metro: San Martín.

La Chacra 🅰 ARGENTINE   Your first impression will be either the stuffed cow begging you to go on in and eat some meat, or the open-fire spit grill glowing through the window. Professional waiters clad in black pants and white dinner jackets welcome you into what is otherwise a casual environment, with deer horns and wrought-iron lamps adorning the walls. Dishes from the grill include sirloin steak, T-bone with red peppers, and tenderloin. Barbecued ribs and suckling pig call out from the open-pit fire, as do a number of hearty brochettes. Steaks are thick and juicy. Get a good beer or an Argentine wine to wash it all down.

Av. Córdoba 941 (at Carlos Pelligrini/9 de Julio). ⓒ 11/4322-1409. Main courses $4–$7 (£2.20–£3.85). AE, DC, MC, V. Daily noon–1:30am. Metro: San Martín.

Las Nazarenas 🅰 ARGENTINE   This is not a restaurant, an old waiter will warn you; it's an *asador.* More specifically, it's a steakhouse with meat on the menu, not a pseudo-*parrilla* with vegetable plates or some froufrou international dishes for the faint of heart. You have two choices: cuts grilled on the *parrilla* or meat cooked on a spit over the fire. Argentine presidents and foreign ministers have all made their way here. The two-level dining room is handsomely decorated with cases of Argentine wines and abundant plants. Service is unhurried, offering you plenty of time for a relaxing meal.

Reconquista 1132 (at Leandro N. Alem). ⓒ 11/4312-5559. Reservations recommended. Main courses $4–$6 (£2.20–£3.30). AE, DC, MC, V. Daily noon–1am. Metro: San Martín.

Ligure 🅰🅰 (Finds) FRENCH   Painted mirrors look over the long rectangular dining room, which since 1933 has drawn ambassadors, artists, and business leaders by day and a more romantic crowd at night. A nautical theme prevails, with fishnets, dock ropes, and masts decorating the room; captain's wheels substitute for chandeliers. Portions are huge and meticulously prepared—an unusual combination for French-inspired cuisine. Seafood options include the Patagonian tooth fish sautéed with butter, prawns, and mushrooms, or the trout glazed with an almond sauce. The chateaubriand is outstanding, and the *bife de lomo* (filet mignon) can be prepared seven different ways (pepper sauce with brandy is delightful, made at your table).

Juncal 855 (at Esmerelda). ⓒ 11/4393-0644 or 11/4394-8226. Reservations recommended. Main courses $4–$6 (£2.20–£3.30). AE, DC, MC, V. Daily noon–3pm and 8–11:30pm. Metro: San Martín.

Los Chilenos 🅰 SEAFOOD/CHILEAN   A taste of the long country next door is what you'll find here, and because of that, this restaurant is popular with Chileans who live here or are visiting. It's a simple place, with a home-style feeling. The dining room has long tables where everyone sits together, and it's decorated with posters of

Chilean tourist sites and draped with Chilean flags. Fish is one of the restaurant's fortes, and one of the most popular dishes is abalone in mayonnaise.

Suipacha 1024 (at Santa Fe). ℂ 11/4328-3123. Main courses $1–$7 (55p–£3.85). AE, DC, MC, V. Mon–Sat noon–4pm and 8pm–1am. Metro: San Martín.

Richmond Cafe ✿✿ CAFE/ARGENTINE   Enter this place and find the pace and atmosphere of an older Buenos Aires. The Richmond Cafe, a *café notable,* is all that is left of the Richmond Hotel, an Argentine-British hybrid that opened in 1917 and once catered to the elite. The cafe sits in the lobby of the former hotel, whose upstairs area has been converted into offices. The menu here is traditionally Argentine, and there is a *confitería,* or cafe, section in the front, serving as a cafe and fast-food eatery. You'll find locals of all kinds here, from workers grabbing a quick bite to well-dressed seniors who must recall Calle Florida's more elegant heyday. The decor is that of a gentlemen's club, full of wood, brass, and red-leather upholstery. Patrons can still let loose downstairs, in a bar area full of billiard tables. The menu of high-quality pastries is extensive. The restaurant offers hearty basics such as chicken, fish, and beef. A la carte, the food tends to be expensive, but three-course executive menus with a drink included are a good bargain, running between $6 and $10 (£3.30–£5.50), depending on what you choose.

Calle Florida 468 (at Corrientes). ℂ **11/4322-1341** or 11/4322-1653. www.restaurant.com.ar/richmond. Main courses $5–$8 (£2.75–£4.40). AE, MC, V. Mon–Sat 7am–10pm. Metro: Florida.

INEXPENSIVE

Café Literario CAFE/ARGENTINE   This quiet little cafe takes advantage of its location next door to the place where Argentine literary great Jorge Luis Borges was born. It sort of has a loose affiliation with the Fundación Internacional Jorge Luis Borges, which works to preserve the writer's memory and work. Literature-themed, the cafe hosts readings and art events on an irregular basis. A range of publications lie on shelves and racks for patrons to peruse while they eat. The idea according to the owners was to have a place where people could come to read and eat and be more relaxed than in a library. Fare includes light items such as sandwiches, snacks, desserts, and Argentine steak. The building is modern but opens into the patio of the adjacent YWCA (Tucumán 844; ℂ **11/4322-1550**), inside a gorgeous early-20th-century building built over the now demolished house where Borges was born. Café Literario serves as the cafeteria for the YWCA. Stop in for information on plays, art shows, other events aimed at the general public, and exercise programs strictly for women.

Tucumán 840 (at Suipacha). ℂ **11/4328-0391.** Main courses $2–$5 (£1.10–£2.75). No credit cards. Mon–Fri 8am–6pm. Metro: Lavalle.

Café Retiro ✿✿ (Finds) CAFE/ARGENTINE   This cafe is part of a chain, the Café Café consortium. As such, there is nothing spectacular about the food, but it is high quality, consistent, and inexpensive. The main point of dining here is to enjoy the restored elegance of the original cafe, which was part of Retiro Station when it was built in 1915. The place had been closed for many years but was restored in 2001 with the help of a government program. It is now one of the *cafés notables,* the interiors of which are considered historically important to the nation. The marble has been cleaned, the bronze chandeliers polished, and the stained-glass windows have been restored, allowing a luminescent light to flow in. This cafe is ideal if you are taking a train from here to other parts of Argentina and the province, such as Tigre, or if you came to admire the architecture of Retiro and the other classical stations in this enormous transportation complex. It's also worth checking out if you came to see the nearby English Clock Tower, which sits in the plaza just outside. The staff is friendly and full of advice on things to do in town. An attached art gallery in the hallway outside also has changing exhibitions. A tango show takes place on Fridays at 7pm.

Ramos Meija 1358 (at Libertador, in the Retiro Station Lobby). *C* 11/4516-0902. Main courses $1.35–$3 (75p–£1.65). No credit cards. Daily 6:30am–10pm. Metro: Retiro.

Café Tortoni ✦✦✦ *(Moments* CAFE   You cannot come to Buenos Aires without visiting this Porteño institution. The artistic and intellectual capital of Buenos Aires since 1858, this historic cafe has served guests such as Jorge Luis Borges, Julio de Caro, Cátulo Castillo, and José Gobello. Its current location opened in the 1890s, when Avenida de Mayo was created as the main thoroughfare of a rich and powerful emerging Buenos Aires. Wonderfully appointed in woods, stained glass, yellowing marble, and bronzes, the place itself exudes more history than any of the photos and artifacts hanging on its walls. It's the perfect place for a coffee or a small snack after wandering along Avenida de Mayo. Twice-nightly tango shows in a cramped side gallery, where the performers often walk through the crowd, are worth attending, though tight seating means you'll get to know the patron next to you almost too well. What makes the Tortoni all the more special is that locals and tourists exist side by side, and one never seems to overwhelm the other. Do not, however, expect great service: Sometimes, the only way to get attention is to jump up and down, even if your server is a few feet from you. And management seems to be limiting who can gain entry now: If a show is taking place in the gallery, they may turn away touristy-looking people who want a snack in the cafe. Or if you mention you just want to look inside at the architecture, they might refuse you. All told, it's a beautiful place but service and treating people well has never been the Tortoni's forté.

Av. de Mayo 825 (at Esmeralda). *C* 11/4342-4328. Main courses $2–$7 (£1.10–£3.85). AE, DC, MC, V. Mon–Thurs 8am–2am; Fri–Sat 8am–3am; Sun 8am–1am. Metro: Av. de Mayo.

Filo ✦ *(Finds* PIZZA   Popular with young professionals, artists, and anyone looking for cause to celebrate, Filo presents its happy clients with mouthwatering pizzas, delicious pastas, and potent cocktails. The crowded bar hosts occasional live music, and tango lessons take place downstairs a few evenings per week.

San Martín 975 (at Alvear). *C* 11/4311-0312. Main courses $2–$5 (£1.10–£2.75). AE, MC, V. Daily noon–4pm and 8pm–2am. Metro: San Martín.

Il Gran Caffe ✦ CAFE/ITALIAN   As its name implies, this largely Italian restaurant sells an extensive selection of pastries, pastas, and paninis, as well as more traditional Argentine fare. On a busy corner across the street from Galerías Pacífico, it is also one of the best perches from which to watch the crowds passing by on Calle Florida. A covered canopy on the Córdoba side also provides further outdoor seating, rain or shine. The people-watching is so good, in fact, that the restaurant charges 15% more for outdoor dining. If that bothers the budget-conscious spy in you, the best compromise is to sit inside, on their upper-floor level, with its bird's-eye view of the street and the Naval Academy, one of the city's most beautiful landmarks. Mixed drinks start at about $3 (£1.65) each. They have an excellent Italian pastry menu; the Neapolitan *sfogliatella* is especially good.

Calle Florida 700 (at Córdoba). *C* 11/4326-5008. Main courses $3–$8 (£1.65–£4.40). AE, MC, V. Daily 7am–2am. Metro: Florida.

(Tips Bares y Cafés Notables

If you want to dine in an atmosphere recalling the glory days of Buenos Aires's past, investigate the list of nearly 40 *bares y cafés notables*—historic restaurants, cafes, and bars specially protected by a law stating that their interiors cannot be altered. Known as Law No. 35, this special protection, granted by the city of Buenos Aires, passed in 1998 and was updated in 2002. Many of these special establishments appear in this chapter, including **Café Tortoni, La Biela, La Perla,** and **Bar El Federal.** They tend to be clustered in the city's oldest neighborhoods, such as Monserrat, Congreso, La Boca, and San Telmo. Ask the tourism office for the map *Bares y Cafés Notables de Buenos Aires,* which lists them all, with photographs of the interiors. All the venues also sell a coffee-table book with additional photographs.

La Sortija (Value) PARRILLA/ARGENTINE   This very basic, small *parrilla* opened in 2000. Decorations are minimal, with an emphasis on the food and courteous service instead. Shelves full of wine and soda bottles are the only clutter in the mostly wood interior. Most of the patrons are working-class locals who have jobs in the area. It's very busy after 5pm, when they stop in for a bite before making their way home. La Sortija prides itself on what it calls *cocina casera,* or home cooking, and serves well-prepared cuts of meat, such as *bife de chorizo.* They also have sandwiches for takeout. This place offers tremendous value, considering the small amount of money it costs to eat here. Pizza, pasta, and chicken round out the menu.

Lavalle 663 (at Maipú). (C) 11/4328-0824, Main courses $3–$5 (£1.65–£2.75). No credit cards. Daily 8am–midnight. Metro: Lavalle.

Morizono (Value) JAPANESE   A casual Japanese restaurant and sushi bar, Morizono offers treats such as dumplings stuffed with pork, shrimp and vegetable tempuras, salmon with ginger sauce, and a variety of sushi and sashimi combination platters. Morizono also has locations in Palermo at Paraguay 3521 ((C) **11/4823-4250**) and Lacroze 2173, in Belgrano ((C) **11/4773-0940**).

Reconquista 899 (at Paraguay). (C) 11/4314-0924. Reservations recommended. Main courses $3–$6 (£1.65–£3.30). AE, DC, MC, V. Mon–Fri 12:30–3:30pm and 8pm–midnight; Sat 8pm–1am. Metro: San Martín.

Petit Paris Café SNACKS/AFTERNOON TEA   Marble-top tables with velvet-upholstered chairs, crystal chandeliers, and bow tie–clad waiters give this cafe a European flavor. Large windows look directly onto Plaza San Martín, placing the cafe within short walking distance of some of the city's best sights. The menu offers a selection of hot and cold sandwiches, pastries, and special coffees and teas. Linger over your coffee as long as you like—nobody will pressure you to move.

Av. Santa Fe 774 (at Esmeralda). (C) 11/4312-5885. Main courses $2–$4 (£1.10–£2.20). AE, DC, MC, V. Daily 7am–2am. Metro: San Martín.

SAN TELMO
MODERATE
Bar El Federal (Moments) CAFE/ARGENTINE   This bar and restaurant, on a quiet corner in San Telmo, represents a beautiful step back in time. Fortunately, as another *café notable,* it will stay that way forever. The first thing that will strike you

here is the massive carved wood and stained glass ornamental stand over the bar area, which originally came from an old pastry shop. Local patrons while away their time at the old tables, looking out onto the streets, chatting, or reading while nursing tea or espresso. The original tile floor remains. Old signs, portraits, and small antique machines decorate the space, which has been in business since 1864. Bar El Federal is among the most Porteño of places in San Telmo, a neighborhood that has more of these establishments than any other. Some of the staff has been here for decades, and proudly so. Food is a collection of small, simple things, mostly sandwiches, steaks, *lomos* (sirloin cuts), and a very large salad selection. High-quality pastries complement the savory menu.

Corner of Perú and Carlos Calvo. © 11/4300-4313. Main courses $2–$6 (£1.10–£3.30). AE, MC, V. Sun–Thurs 7am–2am; Fri–Sat 7am–4am. Metro: Independencia.

Desnivel ⍟ PARRILLA   This place brings new meaning to the term "greasy spoon." Everything in here has an oily sheen—from the slippery floor to the railings, glasses, and dishes. Even the walls and the artwork seem to bleed grease. Thankfully, the food more than makes up for the atmosphere: Serving mostly thick, well-cooked, and fatty steaks, this is one of San Telmo's best *parrillas*. A flood of locals and tourists, often lined up at the door, keeps the place hopping. On Sunday or when a game is on television, especially large crowds come to watch and eat under the blaring TV screen suspended over the dining area. The decor in this two-level restaurant is unassuming, home-style, and full of mismatched wooden chairs, tablecloths, and silverware. Though prices here are slightly higher than in other *parrillas*, your meal will be worth the price.

Defensa 858 (at Independencia). © 11/4300-9081. Main courses $5–$8 (£2.75–£4.40). No credit cards. Daily noon–4pm and 8pm–1am. Metro: Independencia.

La Brigada ⍟⍟⍟ ARGENTINE   The best *parrilla* in San Telmo is reminiscent of the Pampas, with gaucho memorabilia filling the restaurant. White-linen tablecloths and tango music complement the atmosphere. An upstairs dining room faces an excellent walled wine rack. The professional staff makes sure diners are never disappointed. Chef-owner Hugo Echevarrieta, known as *el maestro parrillero*, carefully selects meats. The best choices include the *asado* (short rib roast), *lomo* (sirloin steak, prepared with a mushroom or pepper sauce), baby beef (an enormous 850g/30 oz., served for two), and the *mollejas de chivito al verdero* (young goat sweetbreads in a scallion sauce). The Felipe Rutini merlot goes perfectly with baby beef and chorizo. The waiters are exceedingly nice, but management tends to be caustic.

Estados Unidos 465 (at Bolívar). © 11/4361-5557. Reservations recommended. Main courses $4–$8 (£2.20–£4.40). AE, DC, MC, V. Daily noon–3pm and 8pm–midnight. Metro: Constitución.

La Coruña ⍟⍟ *Moments* CAFE/ARGENTINE   This extremely authentic old cafe and restaurant bar, another of the *cafés notables* protected by law, is the kind of place where you'd expect your grandfather to have eaten when he was a teenager. This neighborhood hub draws young and old alike, who catch soccer games on television or quietly chat away as they order beer, small snacks, and sandwiches. The TV seems to be the only modern thing in here. Music plays from a wooden table-top radio that must be from the 1950s, and two wooden refrigerators, dating from who knows when, are still used to store food. José Moreira and Manuela Lopéz, the old couple who own the place, obviously believe that if it ain't broke, there's no reason for a new one.

Bolívar 994 (at Carlos Calvo). © 11/4362-7637. Main courses $2–$4 (£1.10–£2.20). No credit cards. Daily 9am–10pm. Metro: Independencia.

La Farmacia *CAFE/ITALIAN/ARGENTINE* Artwork by local San Telmo artists hangs all around the dining area. The restaurant has several levels, including an upstairs lounge with a 1930s Art Deco feel, painted red with mismatched furniture, and an air-conditioned lounge for respite in the hot summer. Windows overlook the street corner, allowing for great people-watching, as slow traffic rumbles by soothingly. Some people prefer to take their drinks onto the rooftop terrace, where there's no view to the street, but where you will get a wonderful outdoor dining experience. Many patrons come here for small, easy-to-prepare items such as sandwiches, pastries, and *fiambres* (cut-up bits of cheese and meat meant to be shared over drinks). Italian-inspired items, however, make up the bulk of the main courses, such as spinach crepes, *lomo* medallions, and gnocchi. This gathering spot is considered one of the most gay-friendly restaurants in the neighborhood. A small clothing boutique full of vintage and clubby items shares the main floor, opening onto the cafe/lounge.

Bolívar 898 (at Estados Unidos). ✆ **11/4300-6151**. www.lafarmaciarestobar.com.ar. Main courses $2–$6 (£1.10–£3.30). AE, MC, V. Tues–Sun 9am–3am; much later on weekends, depending on crowds. Metro: Independencia.

La Vieja Rotisería *Value PARRILLA/ITALIAN/ARGENTINE* The slabs of meat sizzling at this *parrilla* are so huge you hope the cook doesn't drop one on his foot, which would put him out of commission and deprive you from eating at one of the best *parrillas* in San Telmo. Following the rule "simple is best," this place concentrates on the food, not the decor, and prices are reasonable. Mismatched vinyl table-cloths and old tacky prints and mirrors in baroque frames are part of the visual disorder here. But your eyes should be on the food. Steaks are thick and well prepared, but they also offer interesting twists on the meat here, such as *lomo* in a tasty Roquefort sauce. Pastas, salads, fish, and chicken are offered here, too—and the latter is served boneless so you don't have to waste any time chowing down on it. The place gets very crowded at night, so make reservations if you're coming after 9pm, to make sure you're not waiting outside the window looking in.

Defensa 963, at Estados Unidos. ✆ **11/4362-5660**. Reservations recommended. Main courses $2–$5 (£1.10–£2.75). No credit cards. Mon–Thurs noon–4:30pm and 7:30pm–12:30am; Fri–Sat noon–4pm and 7:30pm–1:30am; Sun 11:30am–5:30pm and 7:30pm–12:30am. Metro: Independencia.

Pappa Deus *INTERNATIONAL/ARGENTINE* An interesting menu every day of the week, live music shows, folkloric dancing, and jazz on Friday and Saturday nights make this place one of the best alternatives to tango venues along Dorrego Plaza. The upstairs loft offers a more romantic setting, especially for couples who want a break from strolling along the streets of San Telmo. Built in 1798, the house in which the restaurant is located is among the oldest still standing in all of Buenos Aires.

Bethlem 423 (at Defensa, on Plaza Dorrego). ✆ **11/4361-2110**. www.pappadeus.com.ar. Main courses $5–$8 (£2.75–£4.40). No credit cards. Sun–Thurs 9am–2am; Fri–Sat 9am–4am, often later. Metro: Independencia.

INEXPENSIVE

Casa de Esteban de Luca *ARGENTINE* This historic house, once inhabited by Argentina's beloved poet and soldier Esteban de Luca (who wrote the country's first national anthem, the "Marcha Patriótica"), was built in 1786 and declared a National Historic Monument in 1941. Today it's a popular restaurant serving pasta and meat dishes. Come on Thursday, Friday, or Saturday night after 9pm for the fun-spirited piano show.

Calle Defensa 1000 (at Bethlem). ✆ **11/4361-4338**. Main courses $4–$6 (£2.20–£3.30). AE, DC, MC, V. Tues–Sun noon–4pm and 8pm–1am. Metro: Independencia.

Medio y Medio ✦ URUGUAYAN   This place serves Uruguayan *chivitos*, which are *lomo* sandwiches. *Lomo* takes on a different meaning in Uruguay than in Argentina. In Argentina, it is only a cut of beef; in Uruguay, it can be steer, pork, or chicken, cut flat as a filet, served as a hot sandwich with a slice of ham, cheese, and an egg, with a garnish of tomatoes and lettuce. This is a crowded, busy place, especially at night when patrons sit outside, under a canopy, at tables painted with *fileteado*, an Italian art of painted filigree borders that has become quintessentially Argentine. At night, starting at 10pm, as you stuff yourself you'll be entertained by Spanish and folkloric singers and guitar players. They charge a 1.50 peso service for this pleasure, but don't worry: Beer gets cheaper here if you buy it with a meal at that time, which more than makes up for the charge.

Chile 316 (at Defensa). ✆ 11/4300-7007. Main courses $1.50–$4 (85p–£2.20). No credit cards. Mon–Tues noon–2am; Wed noon–3am; Thurs noon–4am; Fri noon–8am; Sat 24 hr. Metro: Independencia.

LA BOCA

There is no convenient subway service to this neighborhood. Wandering at night is not recommended.

MODERATE

Barbería *Overrated* ARGENTINE/ITALIAN   This is a La Boca institution, with a very colorful interior, old-style banisters, and a waitstaff that prides itself on its Italian La Boca heritage. It's very touristy, though, just steps away from El Caminito's flood of out-of-town visitors and tacky souvenir stands. The owner, Nancy, is quite a local character, in constantly changing acting and tango costumes. The walls are full of photos of her with visiting stars. Tango, folkloric, and even drag shows run from noon until 5pm on the sidewalk dining area in front of the cafe, which overlooks the harbor. The food is overpriced for what it is, but the show is included in the price. Pastries, such as the Neapolitan *sfogliatella*, a local tradition, tend to be on the soggy side, but every dish comes with a generous helping of history, and the staff is friendly enough.

Pedro de Mendoza 1959 (at Caminito). ✆ 11/4303-8256. www.barberia.com.ar. Main courses $2–$7 (£1.10–£3.85). AE, DC, MC, V. Daily 11am–6pm, later in summer if busy. No Metro access.

La Perla *Overrated* CAFE/ARGENTINE   This ancient cafe and bar is one of Buenos Aires's *cafés notables*. It dates from 1899 and has a beautiful interior, loaded with photos of the owners mingling with important visitors from around the world who have come to visit La Boca and this important stop on the tourist circuit. Like most things in La Boca, the food is overpriced for what you get. Pizzas, *picadas*, and a range of coffees and drinks are on offer. Hillary Clinton is among the luminaries, and her image is among those most highlighted. If you're in La Boca, it's not a bad place to have a drink and soak up some atmosphere, but I would skip this place if you want a major meal.

Pedro de Mendoza 1899 (at Caminito). ✆ 11/4301-2985. Main courses $6–$10 (£3.30–£5.50). No credit cards. Daily 7am–9pm. No Metro access.

INEXPENSIVE

Corsario ✦ ARGENTINE/ITALIAN/SEAFOOD   This restaurant takes La Boca's old port heritage to an extreme, adding family-owned charm and warmth to the kitsch. The place was originally a museum, full of old nautical items saved by the family as Boca's connection to the waterfront began to deteriorate. In 1993, they also opened a restaurant serving a mix of Italian, Argentine, and seafood cuisine. Now the purpose of eating outweighs the purpose of seeing the nautical items, many of which are for sale, so wander around and check them out while waiting for your meal. If Popeye were alive and local, this is the type of place he'd patronize.

Av. Pedro de Mendoza 1981 (at Caminito). ℭ 11/4301-6579. Main courses $3–$5 (£1.65–£2.75). No credit cards. Daily noon–7pm. No Metro access.

El Obrero (★★★ (Kids) PARRILLA/ITALIAN/ARGENTINE   Grandfathers are not on the menu in this place, but they come free with every meal. Two old brothers from Barcelona, Spain, who own the place—Marcelino and Francisco Castro—putter around making sure everyone is okay. Did you have enough to eat, do you need more bread, are you being taken care of? These are just some of the questions they ask as you dine on thick, juicy, perfectly cooked steaks. Italian food, fish, and chicken are also in the offerings. You can order one-half and one-quarter portions of many items, which is great both because they give you so much and because it means you can bring the kids along without wasting food. Lots of Boca Juniors and other sports memorabilia hanging on the walls remind you that you're in one of the most important soccer/football neighborhoods in the world. This is one of the only places I recommend for serious eating in La Boca, but tables fill up rapidly at 9pm, so reserve or come earlier than that. Note that you should arrive here by cab and have the restaurant call a cab for you when you leave. El Obrero is one of the best restaurants in Buenos Aires and should not be missed. However, though I have never personally had a problem in La Boca, it is considered a dangerous neighborhood to wander at night.

Agustin R. Caffarena 64 (at Caboto). ℭ 11/4362-9912. Main courses $3–$4 (£1.65–£2.20). No credit cards. Mon–Sat noon–5pm and 8pm–2 or 3am, depending on crowds. No Metro access.

ABASTO & ONCE
MODERATE

El Galope (★ ARGENTINE/PARRILLA/MIDDLE EASTERN/KOSHER   This place is best described as an Argentine *parrilla*, with Middle Eastern accents and the added twist of being kosher. It's located in what was once the main area of Buenos Aires's Jewish community. The *parrilla* serves wonderfully juicy and kosher slabs of beef (my experience in the United States has always been that beef plus kosher equals dry, so I am not sure how they do it). This is one of Buenos Aires's most popular kosher restaurants. The interior is simple, wood paneled, and home-style. The family that owns the restaurant oversees its operations; sometimes they argue right in front of you. The menu also features a selection of kosher Argentine wines, and you can take a bottle home with you if you'd like. Middle Eastern fare—such as pitas and hummus as starters or sides, and baklava desserts—is also on hand, as well as fast food such as pastrami sandwiches and salads. Service is low-key; unusually quiet waiters almost seem afraid to approach the tables, but the food more than makes up for it.

Tucumán 2633 (at Pueyrredón). ℭ 11/4963-6888. Main courses $2–$8 (£1.10–£4.40). No credit cards. Sun–Fri noon–3pm; Sun–Thurs 8pm–1am; Sat 9pm–midnight, but times will vary seasonally depending on sunset. Metro: Pueyrredón.

Mamá Jacinta (★★ (Finds) INTERNATIONAL/ITALIAN/KOSHER/MIDDLE EASTERN/PARRILLA   Owner José Mizrahi opened this restaurant in 1999 and named it in honor of his Syrian Sephardic grandmother. His idea was to bring to the public the kind of food he remembers eating while growing up, updating it with the international influences that are all the rage in Argentina. He does much of the cooking himself, and chicken dishes are his favorite thing to make. After that, he recommends his fish and rice salad dishes, served in large enough portions for a table full of patrons to share and enjoy together. French, Japanese, and Italian sausages are grilled on the *parrilla* and can be sampled as starters. Pasta lovers can choose from a wide selection, all custom-made in the restaurant. Try also the *kibbe*, a kind of meat-filled dumpling.

Tucumán 2580 (at Pueyrredón). ℂ **11/4962-9149** or 11/4962-7535. mamajacintakosher@hotmail.com. Main courses $2–$8 (£1.10–£4.40). No credit cards. Mon–Thurs noon–3:30pm and 8–11:30pm; Fri noon–3:30pm; Sat 1 hr. after sunset until midnight; Sun noon–3:30pm. Metro: Pueyrredón.

INEXPENSIVE

Gardel de Buenos Aires 🏵 ARGENTINE/ITALIAN   You won't see tango here, but this cafe celebrates Carlos Gardel, the famous tango singer, in other ways. A clock with his face at the 12 o'clock position overlooks the dining area, with its brilliant red tablecloths and rich wood trim. Gardel photos adorn red walls like icons in a Russian church. A papier-mâché mannequin of his likeness juts out from one of the walls. On top of that, his songs play nonstop from loudspeakers. It's a cute diversion, and in spite of the overwhelming kitsch, the food is good. The menu offers Argentine standards such as beef and empanadas, salads, pastas, desserts, sandwiches, pizzas, and other Italian specialties. The house specialty is *fugazzata*—a kind of stuffed pizza. Service is fast and friendly, so this is a great place for grabbing a quick coffee or a sandwich. It's open 24 hours Friday and Saturday, so come by and toast Gardel, after a night on the town, with a drink from their extensive liquor selection. They also have a takeout menu.

Entre Ríos 796 (at Independencia). ℂ **11/4381-4170** or 11/4381-9116. Main courses $2–$6 (£1.10–£3.30). AE, MC, V. Sun–Thurs 6am–2am; Fri–Sat 24 hr. Metro: Entre Ríos.

Kosher McDonald's 🏵🏵 *Finds* AMERICAN/KOSHER   Certainly you didn't come all this way to eat at McDonald's. I wouldn't ordinarily tell a traveler to eat here on vacation, but this franchise is clearly unique: This is the only kosher McDonald's outside of Israel in the world, underscoring Buenos Aires's reputation as one of the world's greatest Jewish centers. Rabbi supervision makes sure that kosher rules are strictly followed here. It's typical McDonald's fare—burgers, fries, salads, fish sandwiches—except that no dairy at all is served here. They also sell souvenir mugs and other items to bring home. Locals of all kinds, Jewish or not, patronize the place. If you only came to gawk and think you couldn't stand a Big Mac without cheese, fret not: It's in the Abasto Shopping Center's Food Court, so all you have to do is turn around and walk to the regular McDonald's on the other side.

Abasto Shopping Center Food Court, Av. Corrientes 3247 (at Agüero). ℂ **11/4959-3709** or 0800/777-6236 for McDonald's Argentina information hot line. Main courses $1–$3 (55p–£1.65). No credit cards. Sun–Thurs 10am–midnight; Fri 10am–2pm; Sat 9pm–midnight, but times will vary seasonally depending on sunset. Metro: Carlos Gardel.

Shefa Abasto 🏵 *Finds* INTERNATIONAL/ITALIAN/KOSHER/VEGETARIAN Next door to Kosher McDonald's, this is another great kosher option in Buenos Aires. The menu is varied, with a large range of pizzas, pastas, and numerous fish dishes. Salads and other light vegetarian menu items make this a healthy choice for anyone. Typical eastern European Jewish items, such as knishes, are unusually light, rather than the heavy fare you might find in New York delis. This place also delivers, so pick up a menu if you are staying in the area.

Abasto Shopping Center Food Court, Av. Corrientes 3247 (at Agüero). ℂ **11/4959-3708**. Main courses 75¢–$3 (40p–£1.65). No credit cards. Sun–Thurs 10am–midnight; Fri 10am–3:30pm; Sat 9pm–midnight, but times will vary seasonally depending on sunset. Metro: Carlos Gardel.

4 What to See & Do

Buenos Aires is wonderful to explore and fairly easy to navigate. The most impressive historical sites surround Plaza de Mayo, although you will certainly experience Argentine history in neighborhoods such as La Boca and San Telmo, too. Don't miss a walk along the riverfront in Puerto Madero or an afternoon among the plazas and cafes of Recoleta or Palermo. Numerous sidewalk cafes offer respite for weary feet, and good public transportation is available to carry you from neighborhood to neighborhood.

Your first stop should be one of the city tourism centers (see "Visitor Information," earlier in this chapter) to pick up a guidebook, city map, and advice. You can also ask at your hotel for a copy of "The Golden Map" and *QuickGuide Buenos Aires,* to help you navigate the city and locate its major attractions.

NEIGHBORHOODS TO EXPLORE
LA BOCA

La Boca, on the banks of the Río Riachuelo, developed originally as a trading center and shipyard. This was the city's first Little Italy, giving the neighborhood its distinct flavor. La Boca is most famous for giving birth to the tango in the numerous bordellos, known as *quilombos,* which once served the largely male population.

The focus of La Boca is the **Caminito,** a pedestrian walkway, named ironically after a tango song about a rural village. The walkway is lined with humorously sculpted statues and murals explaining its history. Surrounding the cobblestone street are corrugated metal houses painted in a hodge-podge of colors, recalling a time when the poor locals decorated with whatever paint was left over from ship maintenance in the harbor. Today many artists live or set up their studios in these houses. Art and souvenir vendors work side by side with tango performers along the Caminito; this Caminito "Fine Arts Fair" is open daily from 10am to 6pm.

A victim of its own success, La Boca has become an obscene tourist trap. While the area is historically important, most of what you will encounter are overpriced souvenir and T-shirt shops and constant harassment from people trying to hand you flyers for mediocre restaurants. In the summer, the smell from the heavily polluted river becomes almost overbearing. This area is a requisite stop, for at least a quick look, but if you are short on time, don't let the visit take up too much of your day.

The city of Buenos Aires has wonderful plans to rebuild the La Boca waterfront, replant dead and decaying trees on many thoroughfares, and open new museums throughout the neighborhood. Much of this work will begin in 2007 and 2008, slated for completion by the 2010 national centennial celebrations. How it will impact the neighborhood—including gentrification to push out the poor local residents—remains to be seen. It will certainly reduce crime, however, by bringing more foot traffic through the area at night. Enhanced police presence is another suggestion, in addition to the infrastructure changes.

For now, what remains authentic in La Boca is off the beaten path, such as the art galleries and theaters that cater both to locals and tourists, or the world-famous **Estadio Boca Juniors,** 4 blocks away in a garbage-strewn lot at the corner of Calles Del Valle Iberlucea and Brandsen. This is the home of the *fútbol* or soccer club Boca Juniors, the team of Diego Maradona who, like his country, went from glory to fiery collapse rather quickly. Go on game day, when street parties and general debauchery take over the area. For information on football (soccer) games, see the *Buenos Aires Herald.* Wealthy businessman Mauricio Macri, president of the Boca Juniors Fútbol

Buenos Aires Sightseeing

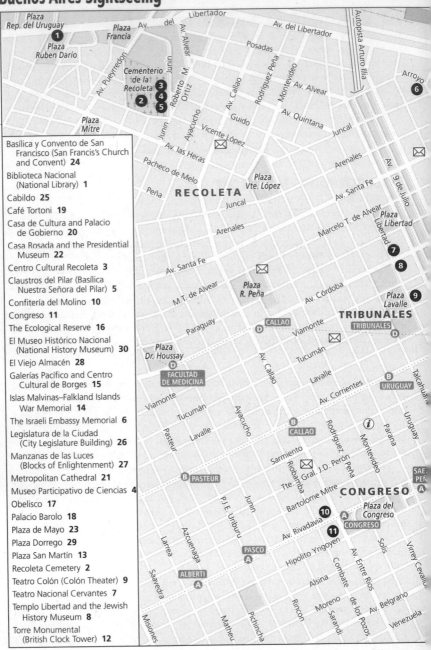

Basílica y Convento de San Francisco (San Francis's Church and Convent) **24**

Biblioteca Nacional (National Library) **1**

Cabildo **25**

Café Tortoni **19**

Casa de Cultura and Palacio de Gobierno **20**

Casa Rosada and the Presidential Museum **22**

Centro Cultural Recoleta **3**

Claustros del Pilar (Basílica Nuestra Señora del Pilar) **5**

Confitería del Molino **10**

Congreso **11**

The Ecological Reserve **16**

El Museo Histórico Nacional (National History Museum) **30**

El Viejo Almacén **28**

Galerías Pacífico and Centro Cultural de Borges **15**

Islas Malvinas–Falkland Islands War Memorial **14**

The Israeli Embassy Memorial **6**

Legislatura de la Ciudad (City Legislature Building) **26**

Manzanas de las Luces (Blocks of Enlightenment) **27**

Metropolitan Cathedral **21**

Museo Participativo de Ciencias **4**

Obelisco **17**

Palacio Barolo **18**

Plaza de Mayo **23**

Plaza Dorrego **29**

Plaza San Martín **13**

Recoleta Cemetery **2**

Teatro Colón (Colón Theater) **9**

Teatro Nacional Cervantes **7**

Templo Libertad and the Jewish History Museum **8**

Torre Monumental (British Clock Tower) **12**

Retiro
Station

RETIRO

12
13
14

Av. Ramos Mejía
San Martín
Av. E. Madero
Florida
Av. del Libertador
Av. Maipú

Plaza
San Martín

SAN MARTÍN

M.T. de Alvear
Esmeralda
Paraguay
Av. Córdoba

*Darsena
Norte*

15

MICROCENTRO

Viamonte
Tucumán
San Martín
Florida
Maipú
Suipacha
C. Pellegrini
Lavalle

LAVALLE

Av. Corrientes

FLORIDA

L.N. ALEM

Sarmiento

25 de Mayo
Reconquista

**CORRIENTES
THEATER DISTRICT**

17

CARLOS PELLEGRINI
DIAGONAL NORTE

9 DE JULIO

Tte. Gral. J.D. Perón

Av. Roque Sáenz Peña
(Diagonal Norte)

20

CATEDRAL

21 Plaza
de Mayo

22

PLAZA DE MAYO

Libertad
Cerrito
C. Pellegrini
Bartolome Mitre
Rivadavia

19

PIEDRAS
PERÚ

AV. DE MAYO

LIMA

25
26

23
BOLÍVAR

24

Balcarce
Moreno

MONSERRAT

Hipólito Yrigoyen
Alsina

Av. Julio A. Roca
(Diagonal Sur)

BELGRANO

MORENO

27

Av. Belgrano
Perú
Venezuela
Bolívar
Defensa
Av. Paseo Colón

Rivadavia
Av. de Mayo
Santiago del Estero
Salta
Lima
Av. 9 de Julio

**PUERTO
MADERO**

Av. E. Madero
Av. Leandro N. Alem
Av. Rosales

Av. de la Rábida
Av. Alicia M.creau

36

Av. de los Italianos

*ECOLOGICAL
RESERVE*

16

Dique No. 4

T. Guevara
Av. Macacha
Guemes

*Parque
Mujeres
Argentinas*

Mitre y Vedia

de Justo

Dique No 3

Bvd. A
Villaflor

Dique No. 2

Av. Ing. Huergo
Azopardo

Pte. Luis Saenz Peña
Chile
exico Saenz Peña
San José
Av. Belgrano

MONSERRAT

Chacabuco
México
Perú
Piedras
Tacuarí
Chile

**SAN
TELMO**

Estados Unidos
Carlos Calvo
Humberto

28

Plaza
Dorrego **29**

Primo
Balcarce

30

Av. San Juan
Autopista 25
de Mayo

↓(6 blocks)

INDEPENDENCIA
INDEPENDENCIA

Bernardo de Irigoyen

Legend:

ⓘ Information
✉ Post office
Ⓐ Subway
Ⓓ—Ⓔ Subway transfer

0 — 1/4 mi
0 — 0.25 km

Club, opened a museum in the stadium. He claims to love soccer, but as a political aspirant who ran for mayor of Buenos Aires and lost, who still hopes to one day be president of Argentina, the Juniors are a public relations tool.

Use caution, however, if you stray off the Caminito. Surrounding areas can be unsafe, without police presence. Once the shopkeepers go home, so do the police officers. At dusk, away from the Caminito, neighborhood residents quietly reclaim the streets and stroll along the waterfront. Most come not from Italy now, but from the poor interior provinces of the country. You may have your most interesting interactions with locals at this time, but it's risky.

Caution: After nightfall, avoid La Boca altogether.

SAN TELMO

Buenos Aires's oldest neighborhood, San Telmo originally housed the city's elite. When yellow fever struck in the 1870s—aggravated by substandard hygienic conditions in the area—the aristocrats moved north. Poor immigrants soon filled the neighborhood, and the houses were converted to tenements, called *conventillos.* In 1970, the city passed regulations to restore some of San Telmo's architectural landmarks. Still, gentrification has been a slow process, and the neighborhood maintains a gently decayed, very authentic atmosphere, reminiscent of Cuba's old Havana. It's a bohemian enclave, attracting tourists, locals, and performers daily. The collapse of the peso has also meant that a glut of antiques, sold for ready cash, is available for purchase and export. The best shops and markets line **Calle Defensa.**

After Plaza de Mayo, **Plaza Dorrego** is the oldest square in the city. Originally the site of a Bethlehemite monastery, the plaza is also where Argentines met to reconfirm their Declaration of Independence from Spain. On Sunday from 10am to 5pm, the city's best **antiques market** takes over the square. You can buy leather, silver, handicrafts, and other products here along with antiques, and tango and *milonga* dancers perform on the square. The tall, darkly handsome dancer nicknamed El Indio is the star of the plaza.

San Telmo is full of tango clubs; one of the most notable is **El Viejo Almacén** (at Independencia and Balcarce). The colonial structure was built in 1798 as a general store and hospital, before its reincarnation as the quintessential Argentine tango club. Make sure to go for a show at night (see "Buenos Aires After Dark," later in this chapter). If you get the urge for a tango course while you're in San Telmo, look for signs advertising lessons in the windows of clubs. If you look foreign enough, teachers might find their way to you anyway.

PALERMO

"Palermo" is a catchall term for a nebulously defined large chunk of northern Buenos Aires. It encompasses **Palermo** proper, with its park system; **Palermo Chico; Palermo Viejo,** which is further divided into **Palermo Soho** and **Palermo Hollywood;** and **Las Cañitas,** next to the city's world-famous polo field.

Palermo Chico is an exclusive neighborhood of elegant mansions off Avenida Libertador, where prices were seemingly unaffected by the peso crisis. This small set of streets, tucked behind the Malba museum area, has little of interest to tourists besides the beauty of the homes and a few embassy buildings.

Palermo is a neighborhood of parks filled with magnolias, pines, palms, and willows, where families picnic on weekends and couples stroll at sunset. Designed by French architect Charles Thays, the parks take their inspiration from London's Hyde

Park and Paris's Bois de Boulogne. Take the Metro to Plaza Italia, which lets you out next to the **Botanical Gardens** (© 11/4831-2951) and **Zoological Gardens** (© 11/4806-7412), open dawn to dusk. Stone paths wind their way through the botanical gardens, where a student might escape hurried city life to study on a park bench. Flora from throughout South America fills the garden, with over 8,000 plant species from around the world represented. Next door, the city zoo features an impressive diversity of animals, including indigenous birds and monkeys, giant turtles, llamas, elephants, and a polar bear and brown bear habitat. The eclectic kitschy architecture housing the animals, some designed as exotic temples, is as much of a delight as the inhabitants. Peacocks and some of the small animals are allowed to roam free, and feeding is allowed (special food for sale at kiosks).

Parque Tres de Febrero , a 400-hectare (1,000-acre) paradise of trees, lakes, and walking trails, begins just past the Rose Garden off Avenida Sarmiento. In summer, paddleboats are rented by the hour. The Jardin Botánico, off Plaza Italia, is another paradise, with many specially labeled South American plants. It is famous for its population of abandoned cats, tended by little old ladies from the neighborhood—a delight for kids to watch. Nearby, small streams and lakes meander through the **Japanese Garden** (© 11/4804-4922; daily 10am–6pm; admission $1/55p), where children can feed the fish (*alimento para peces* means "fish food") and watch the ducks. Small wood bridges connect classical Japanese gardens surrounding the artificial lake. A simple restaurant offers tea, pastries, sandwiches, and a few Japanese dishes such as sushi and teriyaki chicken. You'll also find notes posted for various Asian events throughout the city.

Palermo Viejo   once a run-down neighborhood of warehouses, factories, and tiny decaying stucco homes where few cared to live as recently as 15 years ago—has transformed into the city's most chic destination. Railroad tracks and Avenida Juan B. Justo Palermo Viejo further divide the neighborhood into **Palermo Soho** to the south and **Palermo Hollywood** to the north. The center of Palermo Hollywood is Plazaleto Jorge Cortazar, better known by its informal name, Plaza Serrano, a small oval park at the intersection of calles Serrano and Honduras. Young people gather here late at night for impromptu singing and guitar sessions, often fueled by drinks at the many funky bars and restaurants around the plaza. A crafts festival runs on weekends, but you'll always find someone selling bohemian jewelry and leather goods, no matter the day. The neighborhood gained its name because many Argentine film studios were initially attracted to its once cheap rents and easy parking. Palermo Soho is better known for boutiques owned by local designers, with some restaurants mixed in.

Las Cañitas was once the favored location of the military powers during the dictatorship, and the area remains the safest and most secure of all of the central Buenos Aires neighborhoods. While the military powers no longer control the country, their training base, hospital, high school, and various family housing units still remain and encircle the neighborhood. Today the area is far better known among the hip, trendy, and nouveau riche as the place to dine out, have a drink and party, and be seen along the fashionable venues built into converted low-rise former houses on Calle Báez. Located near the polo grounds, it's a great place for enthusiasts to catch polo stars dining on the sidewalks in season.

RECOLETA

The city's most exclusive neighborhood, La Recoleta wears a distinctly European face. Tree-lined avenues lead past fashionable restaurants, cafes, boutiques, and galleries, many housed in French-style buildings. Much of the activity takes place along the pedestrian walkway Roberto M. Ortiz and in front of the Cultural Center and Recoleta Cemetery. This is a neighborhood of plazas and parks, where tourists and wealthy Argentines spend their leisure time outdoors. Weekends bring street performances, art exhibits, fairs, and sports, especially near the entrance to the cemetery.

The **Recoleta Cemetery** 🎭🎭🎭 (℃ **11/4804-7040** or 11/7803-1594), open daily from 8am to 6pm, pays tribute to some of Argentina's most important historical figures and gives its richest citizens one last chance to show off their wealth. The cemetery was once the garden of the adjoining church. Created in 1822, it's the city's oldest grave site—more of a necropolis, with tall mausoleums abutting, lining the paths that run through the walled-in area. You can spend hours wandering the grounds, which cover 4 city blocks, adorned with works by local and international sculptors. More than 6,400 mausoleums form an architectural free-for-all, including Greek temples and pyramids. The most popular site is the tomb of Eva "Evita" Perón, which is always heaped with flowers and letters from adoring fans. To prevent her body from being stolen, as it had been many times, she is buried in a concrete vault 8.1m (27 ft.) underground. In spite of this, people peek through the glass doors and swear they see her. Many other rich or famous Argentines are buried here as well, including a number of Argentine presidents (many names on tombs correspond to names on city street signs). The dead are not the only residents of the cemetery—about 75 cats roam among the tombs. The cats here are plumper than most strays, thanks to a few women from the area who come to feed them at 10am and 4pm. The cats gather in anticipation at the entrance, and this is a good time to bring children who might otherwise be bored in the cemetery. Weather permitting, free English guided tours take place every Tuesday and Thursday at 11am from the cemetery's Doric-columned entrance at Calle Junin 1790.

Adjacent to the cemetery, the **Centro Cultural Recoleta** 🎭 (p. 145) holds permanent and touring art exhibits along with theatrical and musical performances. Designed in the mid-18th century as a Franciscan convent, it was reincarnated as a poorhouse in 1858, serving that function until it became a cultural center in 1979. The first floor houses an interactive children's science museum, where it is "forbidden not to touch." Next door, Buenos Aires Design Center features shops specializing in home decor. Among the best is Puro Diseno Argentina, featuring high-quality items, designed and manufactured strictly in Argentina.

PLAZA DE MAYO

Juan de Garay founded the historic core of Buenos Aires, the Plaza de Mayo, in 1580. The plaza's prominent buildings create an architectural timeline: the Cabildo, Pirámide de Mayo (Pyramid of May), and Metropolitan Cathedral are vestiges of the colonial period (18th and early 19th c.), while the seats of national and local government reflect the styles of the late 19th and early 20th centuries. In the center of the plaza, you'll find palm trees, fountains, and benches. Plaza de Mayo remains the political heart of the city, serving as a forum for protests. The mothers of the *desaparecidos,* victims of the military dictatorship's war against leftists, have demonstrated here since 1976. You can see them march, speak, and set up information booths Thursday afternoons at 3:30pm.

The Argentine president, whose residence is now in Los Olivos, in the suburbs, goes to work at the **Casa Rosada (Pink House)** 🎭🎭🎭. It is from a balcony of this mansion that Eva Perón addressed adoring crowds of Argentine workers, and former President Carlos Menem allowed Madonna to use it for the 1996 movie. Now, however, most

Argentines associate the balcony with military dictator Leopoldo Galtieri's ill-fated declaration of war against the United Kingdom over the Falkland Islands, known here as the Islas Malvinas. You can watch the changing of the guard in front of the palace every hour on the hour. Around back is the **Presidential Museum** (© 11/4344-3802), with information on the history of the building and items owned by various presidents over the centuries. It's open Monday through Friday from 10am to 6pm; admission is free.

The original structure of the **Metropolitan Cathedral** ✴✴ (© 11/4331-2845) was built in 1745; it was given a new facade with carvings that tell the story of Jacob and his son Joseph, and was designated a cathedral in 1836. Inside lies a mausoleum containing the remains of Gen. José de San Martín, South American liberator regarded as the "Father of the Nation." (San Martín fought successfully for freedom in Argentina, Peru, and Chile.) His body was moved here in 1880 to become a symbol of Argentina's unification and rise to greatness when Buenos Aires became the capital of Argentina at the end of a civil war. The tomb of the unknown soldier of Argentine independence is also here.

The **Cabildo** ✴, Bolívar 65 (© 11/4334-1782), was the original seat of city government established by the Spaniards. Completed in 1751, the colonial building proved significant in the events leading up to Argentina's declaration of independence from Spain in May 1810. Parts of the Cabildo were demolished to create space for Avenida de Mayo and Diagonal Sur. The remainder of the building was restored in 1939 and is worth a visit. The small informal museum offers paintings and furniture from the colonial period, and its ledges and windows offer some of the best views of the Plaza de Mayo (the museum is open to the public Tues–Fri 12:30–7pm and Sun 2–6pm; admission is $1/55p). The Cabildo is the only remaining public building dating back to colonial times. On Thursday and Friday, the Cabildo's back patio is home to a crafts fair (11am–6pm).

A striking neoclassical facade covers the **Legislatura de la Ciudad (City Legislature Building)**, at Calle Perú and Hipólito Yrigoyen, which houses exhibitions in several of its halls. Ask about tours, offered on an informal basis in English or Spanish. Legend has it that the watchtower was made so high so that the city could keep on eye on the nearby president in the Casa Rosada. In front of the Legislatura, you'll see a bronze statue of Julio A. Roca. He is considered one of Argentina's greatest presidents and generals, but one of his legacies is slaughtering tens of thousands of Indians in the name of racial purity within the province. He is why Argentina, unlike most of Latin America, is a largely white society rather than mestizo.

Farther down Calle Perú are the **Manzanas de las Luces (Blocks of Lights)** ✴✴, Calle Perú 272, which served as the intellectual center of the city in the 17th and 18th centuries. This land was granted in 1616 to the Jesuits, who built **San Ignacio**—the city's oldest church—still standing at the corner of calles Bolívar and Aslina. San Ignacio has a beautiful altar carved in wood with baroque details. It is currently under renovation after years of neglect and was nearly destroyed in the revolution that took Perón out of power in 1955, which also sought to reduce the power of the Catholic Church. The **Colegio Nacional de Buenos Aires (National High School of Buenos Aires)** is also located here. Argentina's best-known intellectuals have gathered and studied here. The name "block of lights" recognizes the contributions of the National School's graduates, especially in achieving Argentina's independence in the 19th century. Tours, usually led on Saturday and Sunday at 3 and 4:30pm, include a visit to the Jesuits' system of underground tunnels, which connected their churches to strategic spots in the city (admission $2/£1.10). Speculation remains as to whether the tunnels also served a military purpose or funneled pirated goods into the city, and their full extent is still unknown. *Ratearse,* the Argentine slang for playing hooky, which literally means becoming a rat, comes from the tunnels, as this is where students hid to skip class. In addition to weekend tours, the Comisión Nacional de la Manzana de las Luces organizes a variety of cultural activities during the week, including folkloric dance lessons, open-air theater performances, art expositions, and music concerts. Call ✆ **11/4331-9534** for information.

PUERTO MADERO

Puerto Madero became Buenos Aires's second major gateway to trade with Europe when it was built in 1880, replacing in importance the port at La Boca. By 1910, the city had already outgrown it. The Puerto Nuevo (New Port) was established to the north to accommodate growing commercial activity, and Madero was abandoned for almost a century. Urban renewal saved the original port in the 1990s with the construction of a riverfront promenade, apartments, and offices. Bustling and businesslike during the day, the area attracts a fashionable, wealthy crowd at night. It's lined with elegant restaurants serving Argentine steaks and fresh seafood specialties, and there is a popular cinema showing Argentine and Hollywood films, as well as several dance clubs such as **Opera Bay** and **Asia de Cuba.** The entire area is rapidly expanding, with high-rise luxury residences making this a newly fashionable, if somewhat isolated and artificial, neighborhood to live in. Note that all the streets in Puerto Madero are named for important women in Argentine history. Look for the Buenos Aires City Tourism brochure "Women of Buenos Aires" to learn more about some of them. At sunset, take a walk along the eastern, modern part of the renovated area, and watch the water shimmer in brilliant reds as the city forms a backdrop.

As you walk out from the port, you'll also come across the **Ecological Preserve** ★★. This area is an anomaly for a modern city and exists as proof that nature can regenerate from an ecological disaster. In the 1960s and 1970s, demolished buildings and debris were dumped into the Río de la Plata after the construction of the *autopista,* or highway system. Over time, sand and sediment began to build up, plants and grasses grew, and birds now use it as a breeding ground. Ask travel agents about bird-watching tours. In the summer, adventurous Porteños use it as a beach, but the water is too polluted to swim in and you must be careful of jagged debris and the homeless who set up camp here. In spite of limited protection, Puerto Madero development is slowly creeping onto the preserve.

PLAZA SAN MARTIN ★★★ & THE MICROCENTRO

Plaza San Martín, a beautiful park at the base of Calle Florida in the Retiro neighborhood, acts as the nucleus of what's called the city's MicroCentro. In summer months, Argentine businesspeople flock to the park on their lunch hour, loosening their ties, taking off some layers, and sunning for a while amid the plaza's flowering jacaranda trees. A monument to Gen. José de San Martín towers over the scene. The park is busy at all hours; even after midnight, the playground will be teeming with kids and their parents out for a late-night stroll. Plaza San Martín was once the location of choice for the most elite families at the beginning of the 20th century. The San Martín Palace, now used by the Argentine Ministry of Foreign Affairs; the Circulo Militar, once the home of the Paz family who own the *La Prensa* newspaper; and the elegant Plaza Hotel testify to this former grandeur. The construction of the modern American Express building unfortunately destroyed this once completely classical area.

Plaza San Martín cascades down a hill, at the base of which sits the **Islas Malvinas War Memorial,** a stark circular wall engraved with the names of the nearly 750 dead and an eternal flame, overseen by guards from the various branches of the military. The memorial directly faces the Elizabethan-style **British Clock Tower,** since renamed the **Torre Monumental,** though most locals still use the old name. It was a gift from the British, who built and ran the nearby Retiro train station complex. Oddly, it remained unscathed during the war but was attacked by a mob years later, which also toppled an accompanying statue of George Canning, the British foreign secretary who recognized Argentina's independence from Spain. The tower is open to the public and provides a view of the city and river.

Calle Florida 𝒦𝒦𝒦 is the city's main pedestrian thoroughfare and a shopper's paradise. The busiest section, extending south from Plaza San Martín to Avenida Corrientes, is lined with boutiques, restaurants, and record stores. It extends all the way through Avenida de Mayo to the south, forming into **Calle Perú,** where many international banks have retail branches. Day and night, street performers walk on glass, tango, and offer comedy acts. You'll find the upscale Galerías Pacífico fashion center here, where it intersects Calle Viamonte (see "Shopping," below). Most of the shopping on the street itself, however, is middle of the road. Leather stores abound, so compare prices and bargain by stopping into a few before finalizing your purchase. Florida intersects with **Calle Lavalle,** a smaller version of itself. You'll find even more stores, most of lesser quality, and some inexpensive *parrillas* worth visiting. The street is also home to numerous video and electronic game arcades, so it's a good place for teenagers to hang out while you shop around.

Avenida Corrientes 𝒦 is a living diary of Buenos Aires's cultural development. Until the 1930s, Avenida Corrientes was the favored hangout of tango legends. When the avenue was widened in the mid-1930s, it made its debut as the Argentine Broadway, and Evita's first apartment was here. Today Corrientes, lined with Art Deco cinemas and theaters, pulses with cultural and commercial activity day and night. It is also home to many bookstores, from the chains that sell bestsellers and offer English-language guidebooks, to independent bargain outlets and rare booksellers. The **Obelisco,** Buenos Aires's defining monument, marks the intersection of Corrientes with **9 de Julio.** Whenever locals have something to celebrate, they gather here.

MUSEUMS

Note that several of these museums are in Recoleta, which has no Metro stations.

El Museo Histórico Nacional (National History Museum) 𝒦𝒦   Argentine history from the 16th through the 19th centuries comes to life in the former Lezama family home. The expansive Italian-style mansion houses 30 rooms with items saved from Jesuit missions, paintings illustrating clashes between the Spaniards and Indians, and relics from the War of Independence against Spain. The focal point of the museum's collection is artist Cándido López's series of captivating scenes of the war against Paraguay in the 1870s.

Calle Defensa 1600 (at Caseros). ⓒ 11/4307-1182. Free admission. Tues–Sun noon–6pm. Closed Jan. Metro: Constitución.

Malba-Colección Constantini 𝒦𝒦𝒦   The airy and luminescent Museo de Arte Latinoamericano de Buenos Aires (Malba) houses the private art collection of Eduardo Constantini. One of the most impressive collections of Latin American art anywhere, its temporary and permanent exhibitions showcase names such as Antonio Berni,

Pedro Figari, Frida Kahlo, Cândido Portinari, Diego Rivera, and Antonio Siguí. Many of the works confront social issues and explore questions of national identity. Even the benches are modern pieces of art, and the enormous atrium offers access to the various floors under a metal sculpture of a man doing pushups over the escalator bay. In addition to the art exhibitions, Latin films are held Tuesday through Sunday at 2pm and 10pm. This wonderful museum, which opened in late 2001, is located in Palermo Chico.

Av. Figueroa Alcorta 3415 (at San Martín de Tours). © 11/4808-6500. www.malba.org.ar. Admission $1.75 (95p). Free admission Wed. Wed–Mon noon–8pm. No Metro access.

Museo Evita ✸✸✸   It is almost impossible for non-Argentines to fathom that it took 50 years from the time of her death for Evita, the world's most famous Argentine, to finally get a museum. The Museo Evita opened July 26, 2002, in a mansion where her charity, the Eva Perón Foundation, once housed single mothers with children. While the museum treats her history fairly, looking at both the good and the bad, it is obvious that love is behind the presentation. Indeed, Evita's grandniece Cristina Alvarez Rodríguez is often in the building meeting with the staff. The museum divides Evita's life into several parts, looking at her childhood; her arrival in Buenos Aires to become an actress; her assumption as Evita, first lady and unofficial saint to millions; and finally her death and legacy. You will be able to view her clothes, remarkably preserved by the military government, which took power after Perón. Other artifacts of her life include her voting card—significant because only through Evita did Argentine women gain the right to vote. There are also toys and schoolbooks adorned with her image, given to children to indoctrinate them with the Peronist ideology. The most touching artifact of all is a smashed statue of Evita hidden for decades by a farmer in his barn, despite the possibility of his being jailed for housing it. Whether you hate, love, or remain indifferent to Evita, you shouldn't miss this museum; digesting the exhibitions will help you understand why she remains such a controversial figure within the Argentine psyche.

Calle Lafinur 2988 (at Gutiérrez). © 11/4807-9433. www.evitaperon.org. Admission $2 (£1.10). Tues–Sun 2–7:30pm. Metro: Plaza Italia.

Museo Nacional de Arte Decorativo (National Museum of Decorative Art) ✸   French architect Rene Sergent, who designed some of the grandest mansions in Buenos Aires, envisioned and developed this museum. The building's 18th-century French design provides a classical setting for the diverse decorative styles represented within. Breathtaking sculptures, paintings, and furnishings round off the collection, and themed shows rotate seasonally. The **Museo de Arte Oriental (Museum of Eastern Art)** displays art, pottery, and engravings on the first floor of the building. The building is itself a work of art and gives an idea of the incredible mansions that once lined the avenue, overlooking the extensive Palermo park system.

Av. del Libertador 1902 (at Bustamante). © 11/4801-8248. Admission $1 (55p). Mon–Fri 2–8pm; Sat–Sun 11am–7pm. No Metro access.

Museo Nacional de Bellas Artes (National Museum of Fine Arts) ✸✸   This building, which formerly pumped the city's water supply, metamorphosed into Buenos Aires's most important art museum in 1930. The museum contains the world's largest collection of Argentine sculptures and paintings from the 19th and 20th centuries. It also houses European art dating from the pre-Renaissance period to the present day. The collections include notable pieces by Renoir, Monet, Rodin,

Toulouse-Lautrec, and van Gogh, as well as a surprisingly extensive collection of Picasso drawings.

Av. del Libertador 1473 (at Puerreydón). © 11/4803-0802. Free admission. Tues–Sun 12:30–7:30pm. No Metro access.

OTHER ATTRACTIONS

Basílica y Convento de San Francisco (San Francisco's Church and Convent) ⚜

The San Roque parish is one of the oldest in the city. A Jesuit architect designed the church in 1730, but a final reconstruction in the early 20th century added a German baroque facade, along with statues of Saint Francis of Assisi, Dante, and Christopher Columbus. Inside you'll find a tapestry by Argentine artist Horacio Butler, along with an extensive library.

Calle Defensa and Alsina. © 11/4331-0625. Free admission. Hours vary. Metro: Plaza de Mayo.

Biblioteca Nacional (National Library) ⚜

Opened in 1992, this modern architectural oddity stands on the land of the former Presidential Residence in which Eva Perón died. With its underground levels, the library's 13 floors can store up to five million volumes. Among its collection, the library stores 21 books printed by one of the earliest printing presses, dating from 1440 to 1500. Visit the reading room—occupying two stories at the top of the building—to enjoy an awe-inspiring view of the city. The library also hosts special events in its exhibition hall and auditorium.

Calle Aguero 2502 (at Libertador). © 11/4807-0885. Free admission. Mon–Fri 9am–9pm; Sat–Sun noon–8pm. No Metro access.

Congreso (Congress) ⚜

The National Congress towers over Avenida de Mayo, forming the end of the Avenida de Mayo processional route, which begins at the president's Casa Rosada down the street. The capitol building, built in 1906, combines elements of classical Greek and Roman architecture, topped with an immense central dome modeled after its counterpart in Washington, D.C. Today the building cannot accommodate the entire congressional staff, some of whom had to spill over into neighboring structures.

Plaza Congreso was designed in 1910 to frame the congress building and memorialize the centennial of a revolutionary junta that helped overthrow Spanish rule in Argentina. Stroll around the square and its surroundings to see a number of architectural landmarks, theaters, sidewalk cafes, and bars.

Plaza Congreso. Free hourly tours daily 11am–4pm. Metro: Congreso.

Teatro Colón (Colón Theater) ⚜⚜⚜ *Moments*

Buenos Aires's golden age of prosperity gave birth to this luxurious opera house. It's one of the crowning visual delights of 9 de Julio, though its true entrance faces a park on the opposite side of the building. Over the years, the theater has been graced by the likes of Enrico Caruso, Luciano Pavarotti, Julio Bocca, Maria Callas, Plácido Domingo, Arturo Toscanini, and Igor Stravinsky. Work began in 1880 and took close to 18 years to complete, largely because the first two architects died during the building process. The majestic building opened in 1908 and combines a variety of European styles, from the Ionic and Corinthian capitals and stained-glass pieces in the main entrance to the Italian marble staircase and French furniture, chandeliers, and vases in the Golden Hall. In the main theater—which seats 3,000 in orchestra seats, stalls, boxes, and four rises—an enormous chandelier hangs from the domed ceiling painted by Raúl Soldi in 1966 during a previous renovation. The theater's acoustics are world-renowned. In addition to hosting visiting performers, the Colón has its own philharmonic orchestra, choir, and ballet company. Opera and symphony seasons last from February to late December. The building is undergoing an ongoing renovation in preparation for its 100th anniversary in 2008, and will not host any shows in 2007 and parts of 2008. Through hourly **guided tours,** you can view the main theater, backstage, and costume and underground stage-design workshops. Tours run between 11am and 3pm weekdays, and from 9am to noon Saturday. Call ✆ **11/4378-7130** for more information and to see if any tours are taking place, which depends on the progress of the renovation.

Calle Libertad 621 (or Calle Toscanini 1180). ✆ 11/4378-7100. www.teatrocolon.org.ar. Tour admission $2.50 (£1.40). Seating for events $2–$45 (£1.10–£25). Metro: Tribunales.

SPECTATOR SPORTS & OUTDOOR ACTIVITIES

GOLF   Argentina has more than 200 golf courses. Closest to downtown are **Cancha de Golf de la Ciudad de Buenos Aires,** Av. Torquist 1426 and Olleros (✆ **11/ 4772-7261**), 10 minutes from downtown with great scenery and a 71-par course; and **Jockey Club Argentino,** Av. Márquez 1700 (✆ **11/4743-1001**), in San Isidro, which offers two courses (71 and 72 par) designed by Allister McKenzie.

HORSE RACING   Throughout much of the 20th century, Argentina was famous for its thoroughbreds. It continues to send prize horses to competitions around the world, although you can watch some of the best right here in Buenos Aires. Races take place at two tracks: **Hipódromo de San Isidro,** Av. Márquez 504 (✆ **11/4743-4010**), and **Hipódromo Argentino de Palermo,** Av. del Libertador 4205 (✆ **11/4778-2839**), in Palermo. Check the *Buenos Aires Herald* for race information.

POLO   Argentina has won more international polo tournaments than any other country, and the **Argentine Open Championship,** held late November through early December, is the world's most important polo event. Argentina has two seasons for polo: March through May and September through December, held at the **Campo Argentino de Polo,** Avenida del Libertador and Avenida Dorrego (✆ **11/4576-5600**). Tickets can be purchased at the gate. Contact the **Asociación Argentina de Polo,** Hipólito Yrigoyen 636 (✆ **11/4331-4646** or 11/4342-8321), for information on polo schools and events. **La Martina Polo Ranch** (✆ **11/4576-7997**), located 60km (37 miles) from Buenos Aires near the town of Vicente Casares, houses more than 80 polo horses, as well as a guesthouse with a swimming pool and tennis courts.

SOCCER   One cannot discuss soccer in Argentina without paying homage to Diego Armando Maradona, Argentina's most revered player and one of the sport's great (if fallen) players. Any sense of national unity dissolves when Argentines watch their favorite clubs—River Plate, Boca Juniors, Racing Club, Independiente, and San Lorenzo—battle on Sunday. Passion for soccer could not run hotter, and you can catch a game at the **Estadio Boca Juniors,** Brandsen 805 (✆ **11/4362-2260**), in San Telmo, followed by raucous street parties. Ticket prices start at $3 (£1.65) and can be purchased in advance or at the gate.

5 Shopping

Porteños consider their city one of the fashion capitals of the world. Although the wealthiest Argentines still fly to Miami for their wardrobes, Buenos Aires boasts many of the same upscale stores you would find in New York or Paris. Do not expect to find a city full of indigenous textiles and crafts, as you would elsewhere in Latin America;

Hermès, Louis Vuitton, Versace, and Ralph Lauren are more on the mark in wealthy districts such as Recoleta or Palermo. The European boutiques also sell much better-quality clothes than their Argentine counterparts, with the exception of furs, wool, and some leather goods, which are excellent across the country.

STORE HOURS & SHIPPING

Most stores are open weekdays from 9am to 8pm and Saturday from 9am until midnight, with some still closing for a few hours in the afternoon. You might find some shops open Sunday along Avenida Santa Fe, but few will be open on Calle Florida. Shopping centers are open daily from 10am to 10pm.

Certain art and antiques dealers will crate and ship bulky objects for an additional fee; others will tell you it's no problem to take that new sculpture directly on the plane. If you don't want to take any chances, contact **UPS** (© **800/222-2877**) or **FedEx** (© **810/333-3339**). Various stores participate in a tax-refund program for purchases over 70 pesos. In such a case, ask for a special receipt, which can entitle you to a refund of the hefty 21% tax (IVA) when you leave the country.

GREAT SHOPPING AREAS

MICROCENTRO Calle Florida, the pedestrian walking street in the MicroCenter, is home to wall-to-wall shops from Plaza San Martín past Avenida Corrientes. The **Galerías Pacífico** mall is on Calle Florida 750 and Avenida Córdoba (© **11/ 4319-5100**), with a magnificent dome and stunning frescoes painted by local artists. Over 180 shops are open Monday through Saturday from 10am to 9pm and Sunday from noon to 9pm, with tango and folk-dancing shows held on Thursday at 8pm. As you approach Plaza San Martín from Calle Florida, you find a number of well-regarded shoe stores, jewelers, and shops selling leather goods.

RECOLETA Avenida Alvear is Argentina's response to the Champs-Elysées, and—without taking the comparison too far—it is indeed an elegant, Parisian-like strip of European boutiques and cafes. Start your walk from Plaza Francia and continue from Junín to Cerrito. Along Calle Quintana, French-style mansions share company with upscale shops. Nearby **Patio Bullrich,** Av. del Libertador 750 (© **11/4814-7400**), is one of the city's best malls. Its 69 elegant shops are open daily 10am to 9pm.

AVENIDA SANTA FE Popular with local shoppers, Avenida Santa Fe offers a wide selection of clothing stores at down-to-earth prices. You will also find bookstores, cafes, ice-cream shops, and cinemas. The **Alto Palermo Shopping Center,** Av. Santa Fe 3253 (© **11/5777-8000**), is another excellent shopping center, with 155 stores open daily from 10am to 10pm.

SAN TELMO & LA BOCA These neighborhoods offer excellent antiques, artists' studios, and arts and crafts celebrating tango. Street performers and artists are omnipresent. Avoid La Boca at night.

OUTDOOR MARKETS

The **antiques market in San Telmo** ★★, which takes place every Sunday from 10am to 5pm at Plaza Dorrego, is a vibrant, colorful experience that will delight even the most jaded traveler. As street vendors sell their heirlooms, singers and dancers move amid the crowd to tango music. Among the 270-plus vendor stands, you will find antique silver objects, porcelain, crystal, and other antiques.

Plaza Serrano Fair is at the small plaza at the intersection of Calle Serrano and Honduras, which forms the heart of Palermo Hollywood. Bohemian arts and crafts

Buenos Aires Shopping & Nightlife

SHOPPING
Asociación Argentina de Cultura Inglesa (British Arts Centre) **13**
Café Tortoni **44**
Candido Silva **57**
Casa Lopez **30**
Clásica y Moderna **18**
Cousiño Jewels **29**
Emporio Armani **7**
Erminio Zegna **5**
Escada **12**
Galería El Solar de French **56**
Galería Promenade de Alvear **3**
Galería Ruth Benzacar **32**
Galerías Pacífico **35**
Gianni Versace **9**
Gran Bar Danzón **15**
Grand Cru **8**
H. Stern **28, 31**
Henry J. Beans **2**
Louis Vuitton **4**
Luna Park **42**
Pallarols **58**
Polo Ralph Lauren **6**
Rossi & Caruso **16, 36**
Tonel Privado **10, 37**
Winery **27, 43**

NIGHTLIFE
Asia de Cuba **47**
Bar El Federal **51**
Café Tortoni **44**
Centro Cultural de Borges **33**
Centro Cultural Recoleta (Recoleta Cultural Center) **1**
Chandon Bar **38**
Chicharron Disco Bar **24**
El Arranque **25**
El Beso Nightclub **21**
El Niño Bien **53**
El Nochero **11**
El Querandí **46**
El Viejo Almacén **49**
Grupo de Teatro Catalinas Sur **59**
Inside Resto-Bar **26**
Julio Bocca and Ballet Argentino **34**
La Coruña **52**
La Farmacia **50**
Medio y Medio **48**
Opera Bay **39**
Palacio **45**
Pappa Deus **54**
Plaza Dorrego Bar **55**
Señor Tango **60**
Teatro Coliseo **17**
Teatro Colón. **20**
Teatro Gran Rex **40**
Teatro Municipal General San Martín **23**
Teatro Nacional Cervantes **19**
Teatro Opera **41**
Teatro Presidente Alvear **22**
The Shamrock **14**

are sold here while dread-headed locals sing and play guitars. Officially, it's held Saturday and Sunday from 10am to 6pm, but impromptu vendors set up at night, too, when the restaurants are crowded.

Recoleta Fair ★★, which takes place Saturday and Sunday in front of Recoleta Cemetery from 10am until sunset, offers every imaginable souvenir and craft, as well as food. This has become the city's largest fair, completely taking over all the walkways in the area—even the Iglesia Pilar gets involved. Live bands sometimes play on whatever part of the hill is not taken over by vendors.

La Boca Fair is open daily from 10am to 6pm or sundown. It's the most touristy of all the fairs, and most of the items are terribly overpriced. Still, if you need tacky souvenirs in a hurry, you can do all your shopping here quickly. Besides, tango singers and other street performers will keep your mind off the inflated prices. When the vendors start leaving at the end of the day, you should, too, for safety reasons.

SHOPPING A TO Z

Almost all shops in Buenos Aires accept credit cards. However, you will often get a better price if you offer to pay with cash (including U.S. dollars, in certain cases). You won't be able to use credit cards at outdoor markets.

ANTIQUES

Throughout the streets of San Telmo, you will find the city's best antiques shops; don't miss the antiques market that takes place all day Sunday at Plaza Dorrego (see "Outdoor Markets," above). A number of fine antiques stores are scattered along Avenida Alvear in Recoleta, including a collection of boutique shops at **Galería Alvear,** Av. Alvear 1777.

Galería El Solar de French   Built in the early 20th century in a Spanish colonial style, this is where Argentine patriot Domingo French lived. Today it's a gallery, with antiques shops and photography stores depicting the San Telmo of yesteryear. Calle Defensa 1066. No phone. Metro: Constitución.

Pallarols   Located in San Telmo, Pallarols sells an exquisite collection of Argentine silver and other antiques. Calle Defensa 1015 at Carlos Calvo. ✆ 11/4362-5438. Metro: Constitución.

ART GALLERIES

Cándido Silva ★★★   Filled with antiques and religious objects, this store is the standout in the Galería El Solar de French. Objects come in a range of materials—from wood, to marble, to silver. Many items are centuries-old antiques. Others are tasteful and exquisite reproductions, including a wide selection of canvases painted by indigenous people from throughout South America: Renaissance portraiture comes together with Frida Kahlo's magical realism, in representations of saints, angels, Christ, and numerous renditions on the Virgin Mary. Rural silver and gaucho items are also part of the items on display. Don't worry about fitting it all on the plane—they ship around the world. Calle Defensa 1066 (at Humberto I in Galería El Solar de French). ✆ 11/4361-5053; cell 11/15-5733-0696. www.candidosilva.com.ar. Metro: Independencia.

Tips **Shopping Tip**

Most antiques stores will come down 10% to 20% from the listed price if you try to bargain.

Galería Ruth Benzacar   This avant-garde gallery, in a hidden underground space at the start of Calle Florida next to Plaza San Martín, hosts exhibitions of local and national interest. Among the best-known Argentines who have appeared here are Alfredo Prior, Miguel Angel Ríos, Daniel García, Graciela Hasper, and Pablo Siguier. Calle Florida 1000 (at Alvear). © 11/4313-8480. Metro: San Martín.

FASHION & APPAREL

Palermo Soho is fast becoming the place for boutiques showcasing young designers who seem to have done well in spite of, or perhaps because of, the peso crisis. Women's fashion as a whole is flirty, fun, and, above all, feminine, made for a thin figure. You will find the city's top international fashion stores along Avenida Alvear and Calle Quintana in Recoleta, including **Gianni Versace** (Av. Alvear 1901), **Polo Ralph Lauren** (Av. Alvear 1780), and **Emporio Armani** (Av. Alvear 1750).

Ermenegildo Zegna   This famous Italian chain sells outstanding suits and jackets made of light, cool fabrics. If you've landed in Buenos Aires without your suit, this is among your best options. Av. Alvear 1920 (at Ayacucho). © 11/4804-1908. No Metro access.

Escada   This boutique shop sells casual and elegant selections of women's clothing, combining quality and comfort. Av. Alvear 1516 (at Parera). © 11/4815-0353. No Metro access.

JEWELRY

The city's finest jewelry stores are in Recoleta and inside many five-star hotels. You can find bargains on gold along Calle Libertad, near Avenida Corrientes.

Cousiño Jewels   Located along the Sheraton hotel's shopping arcade, this Argentine jeweler features a brilliant collection of art made of the national stone, the rhodochrosite, or Inca Rose. In the Sheraton Buenos Aires Hotel, Av. San Martín. © 11/4318-9000. Metro: Retiro.

H.Stern   This upscale Brazilian jeweler, with branches in major cities around the world, sells an entire selection of South American stones, including emeralds and the unique imperial topaz. It's the top jeweler in Latin America. Branches in the Marriott Plaza (© 11/4318 3083) and the Sheraton (© 11/4312-6762). No Metro access.

LEATHER

With all that beef in its restaurants, Argentina could not be anything but one of the world's best leather centers. If you're looking for high-quality, interestingly designed leather goods, especially women's shoes, accessories, and handbags, few places beat Buenos Aires's selection. Many leather stores will also custom-make jackets and other items for interested customers, so do ask if you see something you like in the wrong size or want to combine ideas from pieces. Most can do this in a day or two, but if you are intent on bringing something home from Argentina, you should start checking out stores and prices early on in your trip. Some stores take a week for custom orders, and if something is complicated to make, it might take even longer.

Ashanti Leather Factory ℛ   This small store on Calle Florida offers a wide selection of leather goods, from men's and women's jackets to funky and interesting women's pocketbooks. Their prices on jackets are not the best, but women's accessories are very competitively priced, and you can always bargain. Best of all, their factory is in the basement of the shop, so they can easily custom-make almost anything for you. Ask them for a tour, through which you can meet the craftspeople Roberto, Victor, and Oscar, who sit surrounded by sewing machines and colorful bolts of leather. Open daily from 10am to 10pm. Calle Florida 585 (at Lavalle). © 11/4394-1310. Metro: San Martín.

Palermo Shopping & Nightlife

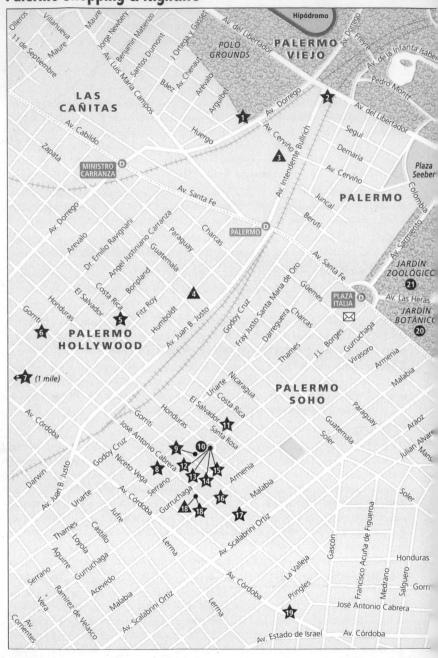

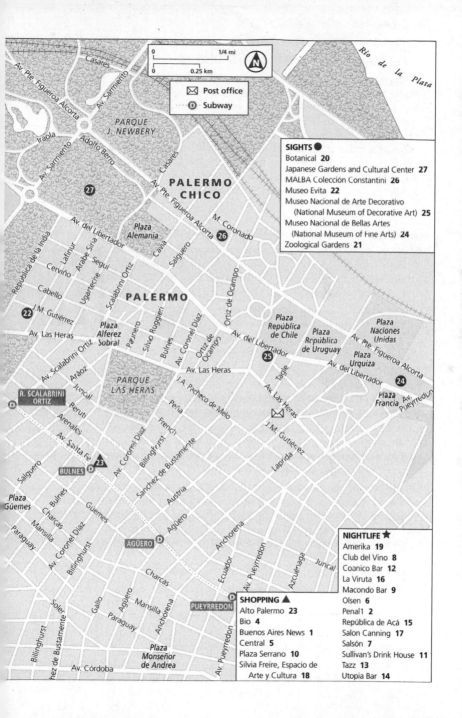

Post office

Subway

PARQUE
J. NEWBERY

PALERMO
CHICO

PALERMO

SIGHTS ●
Botanical **20**
Japanese Gardens and Cultural Center **27**
MALBA Colección Constantini **26**
Museo Evita **22**
Museo Nacional de Arte Decorativo
  (National Museum of Decorative Art) **25**
Museo Nacional de Bellas Artes
  (National Museum of Fine Arts) **24**
Zoological Gardens **21**

NIGHTLIFE ★
Amerika **19**
Club del Vino **8**
Coanico Bar **12**
La Viruta **16**
Macondo Bar **9**
Olsen **6**
Penal1 **2**
República de Acá **15**
Salon Canning **17**
Salsón **7**
Sullivan's Drink House **11**
Tazz **13**
Utopia Bar **14**

SHOPPING ▲
Alto Palermo **23**
Bio **4**
Buenos Aires News **1**
Central **5**
Plaza Serrano **10**
Silvia Freire, Espacio de
  Arte y Cultura **18**

Tips The Murillo Street Leather District

Looking to compare prices and selection in a hurry? Then head to the **Murillo Street Leather Warehouse** district in the Villa Crespo neighborhood. We've listed several individual stores in the area below, in the leather section, including the large Murillo 666, one of the street's main outlets. Items are often made above the store front, or in a factory nearby. Don't be afraid to bargain, or ask for custom orders if you don't find exactly what you like on the shop floor. The densest concentration of stores is on Murillo between Malabia and Acevedo, but a total of about 50 stores fan out from there, selling everything from leather jackets, to purses, to luggage, furniture, and more.

Beith Cuer   You'll find an excellent selection of women's coats and accessories in this store, from hats to purses to even items such as fur gloves and hats. For men, you'll find coats, hats, wallets, and belts, too. The staff is very attentive. Open Monday to Saturday 9am to 7pm; closed Sunday. Murillo 525 (between Malabia and Acevedo in Villa Crespo). ℃ 11/4854-8580. Metro: Malabia.

Casa López *★★*   Widely considered among the best *marroquinería* (leather-goods shop) in Buenos Aires, Casa López sells an extensive range of Argentine leather products. There is also a shop in the Patio Bullrich Mall. Open Monday to Saturday 10am to 2pm and Monday to Friday 3 to 7pm. Marcelo T. de Alvear 640, at Maipú (near Plaza San Martín). ℃ 11/4312-8911. Metro: San Martín.

Chabeli   This store offers a wide selection of women's shoes and pocketbooks, and nothing costs more than $75 (£40). They also offer an interesting selection of handmade Argentine jewelry from crystals and semiprecious stones. Designs of both leather accessories and jewelry fall into two main categories: native Argentine to very pretty and feminine, with pink and pastel materials. They also have another branch in the Patagonian resort town of Bariloche. Open Monday through Saturday from 10am to 8pm, and Sunday from noon to 7pm. Calle Florida 702. ℃ 11/4328-0805. Metro: San Martín.

El Nochero   All the products sold at El Nochero are made with first-rate Argentine leather and manufactured by local workers. Shoes and boots, leather goods and clothes, and decorative silverware (including *mates,* for holding the special herbal tea Argentines love) fill the store. Open Monday through Saturday from 10am to 9pm, Sunday and holidays noon to 9pm. Posadas 1169 (in the Patio Bullrich Mall). ℃ 11/4815-3629. No Metro access.

Gloria Lopes Sauqué *★*   Beautiful exclusive designs await you in this unique leather-design gallery. Gloria Lópes Sauqué is one of Argentina's most creative designers and exhibits her work in various countries. She is also the only Argentine designer whose work is sold in Galleries Lafayette in Paris. Open Monday through Friday from 10am to 8pm, Saturday 10am to 6pm. Posadas 1169 (between Libertad and Cerritos). ℃ 11/4815-3007. www.glorialopezsauque.com. No Metro access.

Hard Leather *★*   The name might make you wonder if you walked into a Buenos Aires S&M shop, but there's nothing hardcore or even hard about the leather; all of it is soft and supple. While there are coats for men, women will find a much larger selection of outerwear. Open Monday to Saturday 9am to 8pm; Sunday 10am to 7pm. Murillo 627 (between Malabia and Acevedo in Villa Crespo). ℃ 11/4856-8920. Metro: Malabia.

Louis Vuitton   The famous Parisian boutique sells an elite line of luggage, purses, and travel bags here. It's located alongside Recoleta's most exclusive shops. Open Monday through Friday from 10am to 8pm, Saturday from 11am to 6pm. Av. Alvear 1901 (at Ayacucho). ✆ 11/4802-0809. No Metro access.

Murillo 666 ⭐⭐   This store is the main outlet in the Murillo Street Leather District in Villa Crespo neighborhood. They have a large selection of women's coats and accessories, and one of the largest assortments of men's jackets, which they will custom-make. They also have the largest furniture showroom as well. Unlike many stores in the district, they offer the same prices for cash or for credit, but sometimes you can still bargain a price down slightly. Open daily 9:30am to 8pm. Murillo 666 (between Malabia and Acevedo in Villa Crespo). ✆ 11/4856-4501. www.murillo666.com.ar. Metro: Malabia.

Outlet ⭐   The name says it all for this store just off Murillo: This is definitely a place to bargain, and shopping with friends might save you even more money, because they offer group discounts. In addition to large selections of jackets, handbags, gloves, and other items, this store also carries a small selection of shoes. Those couches you're sitting on as your friends try everything on? You can buy those in various colors as well. There is also a small selection of women's fur coats here. Open Monday to Friday 10am to 7:30pm, and Saturday 10am to 6:30pm. Scalabrini Ortiz 5 (at Murillo in Villa Crespo). ✆ 11/4857-1009. Metro: Malabia.

Outlet de Cuero   Smaller than some of the other stores, this shop still provides great service, though the selection is better for women than men. Items range from jackets to handbags. If you can't find what you want, this is a perfect place to ask about what can be made from their various leather swatches on hand. Open Monday to Saturday 9am to 8pm. Murillo 643 (between Malabia and Acevedo in Villa Crespo). ✆ 11/4854-8436. Metro: Malabia.

Paseo Del Cuero ⭐   Along with coats and the usual items for men and women, this factory outlet in the Murillo district also has a great selection of men's and women's small luggage carry-ons and gym bags. Feel free to bargain, as the staff often gives you a slightly lower price if you hesitate or offer to pay in cash. Looking for cowhide throw rugs? They've got those too. Open Monday to Saturday 9:30am to 7:30pm. Murillo 624 (between Malabia and Acevedo in Villa Crespo). ✆ 11/4855-9094. www.paseodelcuero.com.ar. Metro: Malabia.

Pasión Argentina–Diseños Etnicos ⭐⭐   With chain stores overrunning Palermo Viejo, it's good to see this small independent shop thriving in the heart of it all. Owner Amadeo Bozzi concentrates on leather goods primarily for women, accessories for men and women, and the home. All produced in Argentina, they are well designed and well made. Some combine leather with other native materials, made by members of the Wichi tribe, a native group in the Chaco region. I highly recommend a visit to this store if you're in Palermo Viejo. Open Monday through Friday from 10am to 6pm, and Saturday 10am to 2pm. Ravignani 1780 (between Honduras and El Salvador in Palermo Viejo). ✆ 11/4773-1157 or 11/4777-7550. www.pasion-argentina.com.ar. Metro: Carranza.

Rossi & Caruso   Offering some of the best leather products in the city, this store is the first choice for visiting celebrities—the king and queen of Spain and Prince Philip of England among them. Products include luggage, saddles, and accessories as well as leather and chamois clothes, purses, wallets, and belts. There is another branch in the Galerías Pacífico mall (p. 135). Open daily 9:30am to 8:30pm. Av. Santa Fe 1377 (at Uruguay). ✆ 11/4811-1965. www.rossicaruso.com. Metro: Bulnes.

626 Cueros   The blasting disco music here tells you you're in a place with a little edge compared to some of the other leather stores in the Murillo district. Here you'll find interestingly designed men's and women's coats, many slightly less expensive than in the other stores. You'll also pay less if you pay cash. Open Monday to Saturday 10am to 6pm. Murillo 626 (between Malabia and Acevedo in Villa Crespo). © **11/4857-6972.** Metro: Malabia.

WINE SHOPS

Argentine wineries, particularly those in Mendoza and Salta, produce some excellent wines. Stores selling Argentina wines abound, and three of the best are **Grand Cru,** Av. Alvear 1718; **Tonel Privado,** in the Patio Bullrich Shopping Mall; and **Winery,** which has branches at L. N. Alem 880 and Av. Del Libertador 500, both downtown.

6 Buenos Aires After Dark

From the Teatro Colón (Colón Theater) to dimly lit tango salons, Buenos Aires offers an exceptional variety of nightlife. Porteños eat late and play later: Theater performances start around 9pm, bars and nightclubs open around midnight, and no one shows up until after 1am. Thursday, Friday, and Saturday are the big going-out nights, with the bulk of activity in Recoleta, Palermo, and Costanera. Summer is quieter, because most of the town flees to the coast.

Performing arts in Buenos Aires are centered on the highly regarded Teatro Colón, home to the National Opera, National Symphony, and National Ballet. In addition, the city boasts nearly 40 professional theaters (many located along Av. Corrientes between 9 de Julio and Callao and in the San Telmo and Abasto neighborhoods) showing Broadway- and off-Broadway-style hits, Argentine plays, and music reviews, although most are in Spanish. Buy tickets for most productions at the box office or through **Ticketmaster** (© **11/4321-9700**). The **British Arts Centre,** Suipacha 1333 (© **11/4393-0275**), runs productions in English.

For current information on after-dark entertainment, consult the *Buenos Aires Herald* (in English) or any of the major local publications. The *QuickGuide Buenos Aires* also has information on shows, theaters, and nightclubs.

THE PERFORMING ARTS
THEATERS, EXHIBITIONS & OTHER VENUES

There is no shortage of exciting theater and art exhibitions in Buenos Aires. It's high quality, varied, and extremely inexpensive considering what you get. Check out the options below, or head to Corrientes, Buenos Aires' answer to Broadway, and look at whatever is currently running in town. Besides the offerings at the British Arts Centre, virtually everything will be in Spanish.

Asociación Argentina de Cultura Inglesa (British Arts Centre) 🕿🕿🕿   This multifunctional facility was established over 77 years ago by a British ambassador who wanted to do more to promote British culture within Argentina. He was highly successful in his efforts, and today the AACI teaches English to over 25,000 students a year; runs several film, theater, culture, and art programs; and generally provides a very welcoming environment for any English speaker who is homesick. Events can range from upper crust (Shakespeare) to raunchy (*Absolutely Fabulous* TV program showings). You can pick up brochures and event listings at the center, or look up listings in the English-language *Buenos Aires Herald.* Suipacha 1333 (at Arroyo). © **11/4393-2004.** www.aaci.org.ar and www.britishartscentre.org.ar. Tickets $2–$10 (–(£1.10–£5.50). Metro: San Martín.

Centro Cultural de Borges 🎭🎭 Not only can you shop all you want in Galerías Pacífico, but, if it's culture you're after, you can find that there too. The shopping mall houses this arts center named for Jorge Luis Borges, Argentina's most important literary figure. You'll find art galleries; lecture halls with various events; an art cinema; art bookstore; the **Escuela Argentina de Tango,** which offers a schedule of lessons tourists can take with ease (© 11/4312-4990; www.eatango.org); and the ballet star **Julio Bocca's Ballet Argentino** performance space and training school, full of young ballet stars (© 11/5555-5359; www.juliobocca.com). Enter through Galerías Pacífico or at the corner of Viamonte and San Martín. © 11/5555-5359. www.ccborges.com.ar. Various hours and fees. Metro: San Martín.

Centro Cultural Recoleta (Recoleta Cultural Center) 🎭 The distinctive building—originally designed as a Franciscan convent—hosts Argentine and international art exhibits, experimental theater works, occasional music concerts, and an interactive science museum for children called Museo de Tocar, where children are encouraged to touch and play with the displays. The Hard Rock Cafe is behind the Cultural Center in the Recoleta Design Shopping Center. Junín 1930. © 11/4803-1041. Tickets $2–$3. No Metro access.

Grupo de Teatro Catalinas Sur This theater company presents outdoor weekend performances in La Boca. It's in Spanish, but it's mostly comedy, and both adults and children are likely to enjoy the productions. Av. Benito Pérez Galdós 93 (at Caboto). © 11/4300-5707. www.catalinasur.com.ar. Tickets $1–$5 (55p–£2.75). No Metro access.

Julio Bocca and Ballet Argentino 🎭🎭🎭 Julio Bocca is Argentina's greatest ballet and dance star. Many of his performances combine tango movements with classical dance, creating a style uniquely his own, and uniquely Argentine. He runs a studio in the Centro Cultural de Borges for classical dance and ballet performances, as well as another performance space in Teatro Maipo on Calle Esmeralda, offering a range of events from dance to comedy plays. It is hard to catch Mr. Bocca himself in Buenos Aires, because he is so often traveling to perform in cities around the world. If he is in town, make sure to book a spot to see one of his shows. (He plans to retire at the end of 2007, so catch him while you can.) Even without him, however, his Ballet Argentino troupe is a must-see for lovers of ballet and dance, especially the performances featuring Claudia Figaredo and Hernan Piquin. Ballet Argentino at the Centro Cultural Borges, within Galerías Pacífico (at the corner of Viamonte and San Martín). © 11/5555-5359. www.juliobocca.com. Tickets $5–$19 (£2.75–£10). Metro: San Martín. Teatro Maipo spaces, Esmeralda 449, at Corrientes. © 11/4394-5521. Metro: Lavalle.

Luna Park Once the home of international boxing matches, the Luna is the largest indoor stadium in Argentina, hosting some of the biggest shows and concerts in Buenos Aires. Many of these are classical music concerts, and the National Symphonic Orchestra often plays here. Legend has it that a 1944 fundraiser here, for the victims of the San Juan earthquake, was where Juan Perón first met a very young Eva Duarte, changing Argentine history forever. Av. Corrientes and Bouchard. © 11/4311-1990. Tickets $3–$12. Metro: L. N. Alem.

Silvia Freire, Espacio de Arte y Cultura A little religious, a little New Age-y, this Palermo institution sells avant-garde art and hosts theater presentations. Silvia Freire is considered a bit of an eccentric mystic, and she is interesting to meet if she happens to be in the building when you arrive. Store hours: Wednesday and Thursday 10am to 3pm. Performance hours vary based on programs; call for information. Cabrera 4849 (at Acevedo). © 11/4831-1441. Tickets $2–$4 (£1.10–£2.20). Metro: Plaza Italia.

Teatro Coliseo   This Recoleta theater puts on classical music productions. Marcelo T. de Alvear 1125 (at Cerrito). ✆ **11/4816-5943**. Tickets $2–$8 (£1.10–£4.40). Metro: San Martín.

Teatro Colón (Colón Theater) ✯✯✯ *Moments*   A more detailed description of this venue appears in "Other Attractions," earlier in this chapter. The building itself is a major tourist stop, in addition to being a performance space. The building is under ongoing renovations, in preparation for its 100th anniversary in 2008, with a moratorium on performances in 2007 and parts of 2008. If you're lucky enough to be traveling when the work is complete, don't miss this venue: The memory of an opera or musical in the Teatro Colón will last a lifetime. Calle Libertad 621 (at Tucumán). ✆ **11/4378-7100**. www.teatrocolon.org.ar. Tickets $2–$15 (£1.10–£8.25). Metro: Tribunales.

Teatro Gran Rex   Within this large theater, you'll be able to see many national and foreign music concerts. Av. Corrientes 857 (at Suipacha). ✆ **11/4322-8000**. Tickets $3–$9 (£1.65–£4.95). Metro: Carlos Pellegrini.

Teatro Municipal General San Martín   This entertainment complex has three theaters staging drama, comedy, ballet, music, and children's plays. The lobby in itself, which often hosts exhibitions of photography and art, is worth a special visit during the daytime. Lobby exhibitions are usually free. Corrientes 1530 (at Paraná). ✆ **0800/333-5254**. Tickets $3–$9 (£1.65–£4.95). Metro: Uruguay.

Teatro Nacional Cervantes   Some of the city's best theater takes place here, in this production house originally built by a group of Spanish actors as a thank-you to Buenos Aires. The building is sumptuous, in an ornate Spanish Imperial style, using materials brought from Spain. Calle Libertad 815 (at Córdoba). ✆ **11/4816-4224**. Tickets $3–$15 (£1.65–£8.25). Metro: Tribunales.

Teatro Opera   This theater has been adapted for Broadway-style shows. Av. Corrientes 860 (at Suipacha). ✆ **11/4326-1335**. Tickets $2–$14 (£1.10–£7.70). Metro: Carlos Pellegrini.

Teatro Presidente Alvear   Tango and other music shows take place at this theater. Av. Corrientes 1659 (at Montevideo). ✆ **11/4374-6076**. Tickets $3–$16 (£1.65–£8.80). Metro: Callao.

THE CLUB & MUSIC SCENE
TANGO SHOWS

In Buenos Aires, you can *watch* the tango or *dance* the tango. You'll have many opportunities to see the dance during your visit: Tango and *milonga* dancers frequent the streets of La Boca and San Telmo, some hotels offer tango shows in their lobbies and bars, and tango salons blanket the city. San Telmo's are the most famous (besides Café Tortoni), and they usually combine dinner and a show. Call a radio-taxi or *remise* to get to San Telmo, La Boca, or Barracas at night. For safety's sake, don't take the Metro there or walk. Most of the tango shows also offer direct transportation. Ask your hotel concierge for ticket prices, which include transportation (usually a shuttle bus).

Café Tortoni   High-quality yet inexpensive tango shows take place in the back room of the Café Tortoni. They do not include dinner. Shows are every day at 9pm except Tuesday. Av. de Mayo 829. ✆ **11/4342-4328**. No cover. Metro: Plaza de Mayo.

El Querandí   El Querandí offers the best historically based tango show in the city, tracing the tradition from its early roots in bordellos, when only men danced it, to its current leggy, sexy style. A great slab of beef and glass of wine come with the show. Open Monday through Saturday; dinner begins at 8:30pm, followed by the show at 10:15pm. Perú 302 at Moreno. ✆ **11/4345-0331**. Tickets $60–$80 (£33–£44). Metro: Moreno or Bolívar.

El Viejo Almacén   The most famous of the city's tango salons, the Almacén offers what some consider the city's most authentic performance. Shows involve traditional Argentine-style tango (many other shows feature international-style tango). Sunday through Thursday shows are at 10pm; Friday and Saturday shows are at 9:30 and 11:45pm. Dinner is served each night before the show starts, in the three-story restaurant across the street. Guests may opt for dinner-show or show only. Some hotels offer transportation. Independencia and Balcarce. (C) 11/4307-6689. Tickets $60–$80 (£33–£44). Metro: Independencia.

Esquina Carlos Gardel (<i>Finds</i>   In my opinion, this is one of the most elegant tango shows. It's on the former site of the Chanta Cuatro—a restaurant where Carlos Gardel used to dine with his friends—though the building is new. The luxurious old-time-style dining room features high-tech acoustics and superb dancers, creating a wonderful environment for this excellent performance. Doors open at 8pm. Carlos Gardel 3200 at Anchorena, across from the Abasto Shopping Center. (C) 11/4876-6363. Tickets $60–$80 (£33–£44). Metro: Carlos Gardel.

Señor Tango   This enormous theater is more akin to a Broadway production hall than a traditional tango salon, but the dancers are fantastic. The owner, who clearly loves to perform, is also a good singer. Walls are covered with photos of what appears to be every celebrity who's ever visited Buenos Aires—and all seem to have made it to Señor Tango! Diners choose among steak, chicken, or fish for dinner. Despite the huge crowd, the food quality is commendable. Have dinner or come only for the show (dinner is at 8:30pm; shows start at 10pm). Vieytes 1653 at Domingo. (C) 11/4303-0212. Tickets $90 (£50). No Metro access.

TANGO DANCE CLUBS (MILONGAS)

Tango palaces and dance performances are wonderful, but nothing compares to the lure of a *milonga* (tango salon), and Buenos Aires seems to have more now than ever. Rather than destroy tango, the peso crisis has heightened its popularity, here and abroad. Just as the early Porteños turned to tango a century ago to alleviate their pain and isolation, so too modern residents are dancing their melancholy away. With the increase in tourism and the enormous number of European and North Americans lured here by the dance, the number of *milongas* is unprecedented.

The numbers listed here are not necessarily those of the venues, but rather the dance organizations that organize the events, often with rotating venues. For further details, check the listings in *La Milonguera* or *El Tangauta,* the city's tango magazines. There's usually a $2 to $4 (£1.10–£2.20) fee to get into a *milonga*. Tango, like most nightlife in Buenos Aires, is a very late affair; most *milongas* don't get busy until 2am—even on weeknights.

Most importantly: Note that this scene is not without its rules and obstacles. Tango is an art form and a unique part of Buenos Aires culture. You should never enter a *milonga* with the obvious air of a clueless tourist, which might alter the atmosphere of a venue. In fact, you might even be refused entry or asked to leave if your behavior or appearance upsets the balance of a place. In fact, some of the city's best *milongas* aren't listed anywhere and require a contact to get in, akin to a 1920s speakeasy. If possible, attend a *milonga* with a local who knows the scene.

El Arranque (<i>Finds</i>   This dance venue looks like a Knights of Columbus hall, but it's one of the most authentic venues for *milongas;* it's also one of the few places that hosts afternoon dancing. Tango's late-night schedule could drive even a vampire crazy, but here you can dance and still get a real night's sleep afterward. No matter how old and pot-bellied a man is, he can be with any woman in the crowd as long as he dances well. Even older women, however, tend to keep up appearances here, dressing beautifully and stylishly. This place will be very comfortable for older crowds. They strictly enforce traditional tango rules about separating the sexes, however; couples might not even be allowed to sit together. Dancing begins most afternoons at 3pm. Closed Monday. Bartolomé Mitre 1759 (at Callao). (*) **11/4371-6767.** Admission $5 (£2.75). Metro: Congreso.

El Beso Nightclub *(Finds* The way to this club may be a little confusing, but follow my directions and you'll be fine. It's unmarked, so the street address is your only indication that you're in the right spot. Walk upstairs, pay your fee, and squeeze past the crowded bar blocking your view. The small space beyond maintains the air of a 1940s nightclub, updated for the modern era with brilliant reds and modern abstractions painted on some of its walls. Ceiling lamps made from car air filters cast a golden glow on the dancers. Some of the best performers drag their egos with them to the floor, so if you're not so good on your feet, just watch; the last thing you want is to bump into someone. The divisions between the *milongueras* and *milongueros* are not so strong, and the sexes tend to mix informally. Reserve a table ahead of time if you can. Different *milongas* take place on different nights. Check their calendar in advance for details. Snacks, wines, and beers are on sale. Riobamba 416 (at Corrientes). (*) **11/4953-2794** or 11/15-4938-8108 (cell). Admission $5 (£2.75). Metro: Callao.

El Niño Bien *(★★ (Finds* If you want to travel back in time, to an era when tango ruled Buenos Aires, few places will do you better than El Niño Bien. The beautiful main dance hall is straight from the Belle Epoque; you'll half-expect Carlos Gardel himself to show up behind the mike. Dressed in black, men and women tango as patrons at side tables respectfully study their techniques. Don't look too closely at anyone, however, unless you know what you're doing: *Milonga* eyes—staring across a room to attract a partner onto the dance floor—are taken seriously. Food is served, but don't bother unless you're famished; it's only so-so. Unfortunately, Niño Bien is becoming a victim of its own success, and many tour groups are starting to unload here. If you're looking to find a tango teacher, one will probably find you first at this venue; many instructors come here seeking students for private lessons. Centro Región Leonesa, Humberto I no. 1462 (at San José). (*) **11/4483-2588.** Admission $5–$6 (£2.75–£3.30). No Metro access.

La Viruta *(Finds* This is one of the most interesting *milongas*. It is authentic, but it attracts a very young crowd of Porteños and ex-pats who have come from all over the world to dance their lives away in Buenos Aires, where the living is good and cheap. Many nights it is just a *milonga*. Other nights host shows and competitions, many involving tango, folkloric, and modern dance. La Viruta is in the cellar of the Armenian Community Center. When decorated with balloons for some events, it looks a little like a high school prom from the 1970s. Armenia 1366 (at Cabrera). (*) **11/4774-6357.** Admission $3–$5 (£33–£44). No Metro access.

Salón Canning *(Finds* This is among the most authentic of all of the *milongas*. At the end of a long hallway, spectators crowd around the main dance floor to watch couples make their way around it. Salón Canning is known for its extremely smooth, high-quality wooden parquet floor, considered one of the best for dancing in all of Buenos Aires. This tango hall is among the few things left in Buenos Aires that still bear the

(Moments) Tango Lowdown

It seems impossible to imagine Argentina without thinking of tango, its greatest export to the world. First danced by working-class men in La Boca, San Telmo, and the port area, tango originated with a guitar and violin toward the end of the 19th century. Combining African rhythms with the *habanera* and *candombe,* it was not the sophisticated dance you know today. It originated in brothels, known locally as *quilombos,* and was considered too obscene for women—even "working" women. Men would actually dance it with each other as they waited their turn in the lounges of brothels.

Increasing waves of immigrants added Italian elements to tango, which helped the dance make its way to Europe. It was eventually internationalized in Paris. With a sense of approval from Europe, Argentine middle and upper classes began to accept the newly refined dance as part of their cultural identity. The form blossomed under the extraordinary voice of Carlos Gardel, who brought tango to Broadway and Hollywood. Astor Piazzola further heightened the international recognition of tango music, increasing its complexity by incorporating classical elements.

Tango music usually involves a piano and *bandoneón*—an instrument akin to an accordion. If a singer is participating, the lyrics might come from one of Argentina's great poets, such as Jorge Luis Borges, Homero Manzi, or Horacio Ferrer. Themes focus on a downtrodden life or a woman's betrayal, making it akin to American jazz and blues, which developed at the same time. The dance itself is improvised, consisting of a series of long walks and intertwined movements, usually in eight-step. The man and woman glide across the floor, with the man leading the way through early flirtatious movements that give way to dramatic leads and heartfelt turns. These movements—including kicks that simulate knife movements, or the sliding, shuffled feet that mimic a gangster silently stealing up to murder someone—reflect the dance's rough origins, even though tango today is refined and beautiful. The dancing style in salons is much more subtle and subdued than "show tango."

Tango lessons are an excellent way for a visitor to get a sense of what makes the music—and the dance—so alluring. Most respectable dancers would not show up before midnight, giving you the perfect opportunity to sneak in for a group lesson, offered at most of the salons starting around 8 or 9pm. They usually cost between $1 and $3 (55p–£1.65) for an hour; you can request private instruction for between $10 and $20 (£5.50–£11) per hour, depending on the instructor. In summer, the city of Buenos Aires promotes tango by offering free classes in many locations. Visit the nearest tourist information center for updated information.

name of George Canning—a British diplomat who opened relations between Argentina and Great Britain after independence from Spain. Scalabrini Ortiz 1331 (at Gorriti). (℡ 11/4832-6753. Admission $5 (£2.75). No Metro access.

OTHER DANCE CLUBS

Dancing in Buenos Aires is not just about tango; the majority of the younger population prefers salsa and European beats. Of course, nothing in life changes quite so fast as the "in" discos, so ask around for the latest hot spots. The biggest nights out are Thursday, Friday, and Saturday. Here are some of the hottest clubs as this book went to press: **Opera Bay,** Cecilia Grierson 225 in Puerto Madero (no phone), is among the city's top clubs, attracting an affluent and fashionable crowd. Built along the waterfront and resembling the Sydney opera house, Opera Bay features an international restaurant, tango show, and disco. The city's best salsa dancers head to **Salsón,** Av. Alvarez Thomas 1166 (© **11/4637-6970**), which offers lessons on Wednesday and Friday at 9pm. In Palermo, **Buenos Aires News,** Av. del Libertador 3883 (© **11/4778-1500**), is a rocking late-night club with Latin and European mixes. **Chicharron Disco Bar,** Bartolomo Mitre 1849 (© **11/4373-4884**), is a wild Dominican salsa club that mostly packs in locals who have relocated to Buenos Aires from the Caribbean. **Tequila,** Costanera Norte and La Pampa (© **11/4788-0438**), is packed every night. A number of popular discos are also nearby. Ladies who just want to dance and avoid lechery should head to **Mambo,** Báez 243 (© **11/4778-0115**), in Las Cañitas, where most patrons are groups of friends. The most popular gay and lesbian club is **Amerika,** Gascón 1040 (© **11/4865-4416;** www.mambobar.com.ar), which has three floors of dance music and all-you-can-drink specials on Friday and Saturday. Straight Porteños come often too, claiming it has the best music. **Palacio,** Alsina 934 (© **11/4331-3231;** www.palaciobuenosaires.com), is giving Amerika a run for the money, but it's open only on Friday.

THE BAR SCENE

Buenos Aires has no shortage of popular bars, and Porteños need little excuse to party. The following are only a few of the bars and pubs worthy of recommendation. Strolling along, you'll find plenty on your own. Most smoking now takes place outside, though you'll still find plenty of people breaking the ban indoors.

Chandon Bar   This intimate champagne lounge serves bottles and flutes of Chandon, produced in France and Argentina. In Puerto Madero, adjacent to some of the city's best restaurants, Chandon is perfect for drinks before or after dinner. Light fare is offered as well. Av. Alicia Moreau de Justo 152 at Alvear. © **11/4315-3533.** Metro: L. N. Alem.

Gran Bar Danzon   A small, intimate bar, Danzon attracts a fashionable crowd with its small selection of international food and smart, relaxing lounge music. An excellent barman serves exquisite cocktails. Libertad 1161 at Santa Fe. © **11/4811-1108.**

Henry J. Beans   A favorite of the expat-American community and visiting foreigners, this casual Recoleta bar serves burgers, sandwiches, and nachos, along with cocktails and beer. Old Coca-Cola ads, Miller and Budweiser neon signs, and model airplanes hang from the ceilings. The waiters do occasional impromptu dances, and the place is packed after midnight. A number of other popular restaurants, bars, and discos are strung along Junín. Junín 1749 at Las Heras. © **11/4801-8477.**

The Kilkenny   This trendy cafe-bar is more like a rock house than an Irish pub, although you will still be able to order Guinness, Kilkenny, and Harp draft beers. It's packed with locals and foreigners, and you are as likely to find people in suits and ties as in jeans and T-shirts. The Kilkenny offers happy hour from 6 to 8pm and live bands every night after midnight; it stays open until 5am. Marcelo T. de Alvear 399 at Reconquista. © **11/4312-9179** or 11/4312-7291. Metro: San Martín.

Plaza Bar   Nearly every Argentine president and his cabinet have come here, in addition to visiting celebs such as the queen of Spain, the emperor of Japan, Luciano Pavarotti, and David Copperfield. A vague mix of Art Deco and English country, the bar features mahogany furniture and velvet upholstery, where guests sip martinis and other high-end drinks. Tuxedo-clad waiters recommend a fine selection of whiskeys and brandies. In 2005, *Forbes* magazine declared it among the world's top nine hotel bars, based on several factors—the clientele, the beverage selection, and the way the staff makes everyone feel welcome, even if they come only once in a lifetime. This was at one time the city's most famous cigar bar, but the 2006 anti-smoking law put an end to that decades-long tradition. Nevertheless, add it to your list of things to do. Inside the Marriott Plaza Hotel, Calle Florida 1005 at Santa Fe, overlooking Plaza San Martín. © 11/4318-3000. Metro: San Martín.

Plaza Dorrego Bar ⊛   Representative of a typical Porteño bar from the 19th century, Plaza Dorrego displays portraits of Carlos Gardel, antique liquor bottles in cases along the walls, and anonymous writings engraved in the wood. Stop by on Sunday, when the crowd spills onto the street and you can catch the San Telmo antiques market on the plaza in front. Calle Defensa 1098 at Humberto Primo overlooking Plaza Dorrego. © 11/4361-0141. Metro: Constitución.

The Shamrock   The city's best-known Irish pub is lacking in authenticity; you're more likely to hear hot Latin rhythms than soft Gaelic music here. That said, it remains hugely popular with both Argentines and foreign visitors, and it's a great spot to begin the night. There is an enormous game room with pool tables and other attractions in the basement. Rodríguez Peña 1220 at Juncal. © 11/4812-3584. Metro: Callao.

5

The Pampas, the Coast & Other Side Trips from Buenos Aires

by Michael Luongo

If you're spending more than 4 or 5 days in Buenos Aires, you might want to consider a side trip—especially if you're visiting in summer, when many Porteños hit the beach resorts. **Mar del Plata** is the country's most popular stretch of shore, and musicians and other entertainers follow the beachgoers there. To describe Mar del Plata as crowded in summer is an understatement, as more than eight million people visit in December, January, and February alone. Nearby, the town of **Miramar** offers a quieter beach vacation at a slower pace. Or you can follow the glitterati to **Punta del Este,** just over the border in Uruguay (whose capital, **Montevideo,** also makes for a compelling and manageable side trip from Buenos Aires).

La Plata is the capital of Buenos Aires Province, planned in 1880 along neoclassical lines. Full of diagonals and parks, it is an interesting and open city with various museums and other sites of historical interest, which you can visit year-round.

Just outside Buenos Aires's suburbs is the **Tigre Delta,** a beautiful complex of islands and marshland full of small bed-and-breakfasts, resorts, and adventure trails. You can make a day trip here on mass transit from Buenos Aires, or you can choose to stay overnight. It is busiest in the summer season, but most sites and hotels are open year-round.

The Pampas surround Buenos Aires, and here you'll find gauchos and the stuff of Argentine cowboy lore. The region's main town is **San Antonio de Areco,** about 90 minutes north of the capital. Few people stay in town, preferring to lodge at the surrounding *estancias* (19th-c. ranch farms), several of which are detailed here.

1 Mar del Plata

400km (248 miles) S of Buenos Aires

Argentina's most popular beach resort is a sleepy coastal city of about 700,000 long-term residents—until mid-December, when Porteños flock here through March for their summer vacation. Nearly eight million vacationers will pass through in the summer season, the vast majority of them Argentines. Although it's not as luxurious as Uruguay's Punta del Este—the beach favorite of many jet-setting Argentines—Mar del Plata is closer to Buenos Aires and far cheaper. Its long, windy coastline is known for its crowded, tan-bodied beaches and quieter seaside coves, and beautiful landscapes farther inland, leading to the edge of the grassy Pampas. The resort was at one time very exclusive, but during the Perón era many hotels and high-rises were built for labor unions and the middle class, changing both the social and physical makeup of the city forever. Some of the magnificent French-style residences, which housed Argentina's summer elites in the early 20th century, have been meticulously preserved as museums.

Mar del Plata offers excellent nightlife in summer, when independent theater companies from Buenos Aires come to town, and nightclubs open their doors to passionate Latin partygoers. The months of December, January, and February are the most crowded, wild, and expensive for visiting. In March, families with children and retired couples on vacation make up the bulk of visitors, who take advantage of a more relaxed atmosphere and the slight reduction in prices. Many hotels and restaurants remain open year-round; though the weather is chillier, people do vacation here on weekends in winter too. The city was hit hard by the peso crisis, when unemployment hit about 20%. The economy is on an upswing, however, with summer unemployment at only 6%. The city hit the international radar recently during the 2005 Summit of the Americas, when special protests took place against George Bush's presence. Much of the city was blocked off during that time period, disrupting locals from their daily lives, and many people still have much to say about the visit.

ESSENTIALS

GETTING THERE   You can reach Mar del Plata by plane, car, bus, train, or boat. The airport lies 10 minutes from downtown and is served by **Aerolíneas Argentinas** (© **800/333-0276** in the U.S. or 0810/222-86527 in Argentina; www.aerolineas. com). Flights last just under an hour, and there are about three flights a day. Cabs will cost about $5 to $7 (£2.75–£3.85) into the center of town. The RN2 is the main highway from Buenos Aires to Mar del Plata; it takes about 4 to 5 hours to drive between these cities. More than 50 bus companies link Mar del Plata with the rest of the country. Buses to Buenos Aires, which leave from the central bus terminal at Alberti 1602 (© **223/451-5406**), are comfortable and cost under $15 (£8.25) each way. They arrive in Buenos Aires at the Retiro Bus Station. A train run by the company Ferrobaires also connects Mar del Plata with Buenos Aires, and it's only slightly more expensive than the buses. It leaves Buenos Aires from **Constitución**, in the southern part of the capital, and runs three times a day. In Mar del Plata, purchase tickets at the train station, located at avenidas Luro and Italia (© **223/475-6076** in Mar del Plata, or 11/4304-0028 in Buenos Aires). Bus and train trips take about 4 to 5 hours.

VISITOR INFORMATION   The **Centro de Información Turística,** Bulevar Marítimo PP Ramos 2270, at the Casino building (© **223/495-1777;** www.mardelplata.gov.ar), has a knowledgeable, helpful staff offering maps and suggested itineraries. It is open daily from 10am to 5pm (until 8pm in summer). There is also a branch at the airport.

GETTING AROUND   La Rambla marks the heart of the city, the seaside walk in front of the casino and main city beach. This area is walkable on its own, with restaurants and other businesses clustered here and between the nearby bus station and Plaza San Martín. Farther south, the Los Troncos neighborhood houses the city's most prominent residences as well as Playa Grande (the main beach), the Sheraton hotel, and the Mar del Plata Golf Club. Mar del Plata has 47km (29 miles) of Atlantic coastline, so if you plan to go to that part of the city, you'll need to take a taxi or rent a car. **Avis** (© **223/470-2100**) rents cars at the airport.

Mar del Plata

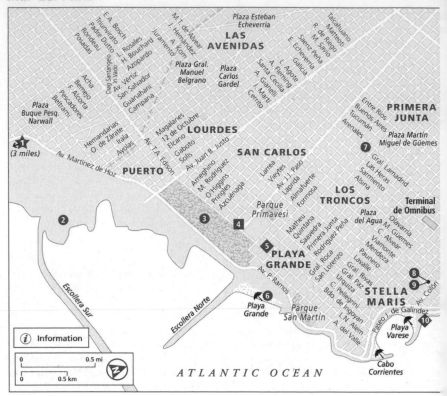

WHAT TO SEE & DO

The main reason to visit Mar del Plata is the beaches, all of which spread out from the city's heart at **Plaza Colón.** Here, you'll find the **Mar del Plata Casino** (© 223/495-7011; www.loteria.gba.gov.ar). The red brick–and-granite structure guarded by sea lion sculptures is the social center of the city. Walkways and steps lead from here to the beach. In the early evening, as the crowds head home from the beach, you'll often see street performers and musicians here. (Watch your pockets if you stand and admire.) With long, slow breaks, **Waikiki** is the best spot for surfing. The coastline is nice, but you should not come expecting to find the Caribbean—the Atlantic remains fairly cold, even during summer. Once you've brushed off the sand, visit the **fishing harbor,** where hundreds of red and yellow boats unload their daily catches. The harbor houses a colony of 800 male sea lions that come to bathe on the rocky shores. (Be warned that between the sea lions and the fishing boats, it's an olfactory disaster.) Next to the colony, there's an ugly but intriguing boat graveyard where rusty boats have been left to rest.

In the Los Tronces neighborhood, **Villa Victoria,** at Matheu 1851, at Arenales (© 223/492-0569), showcases the early-20th-century summerhouse of wealthy Argentine writer Victoria Ocampo. Some of Argentina's greatest authors have stayed

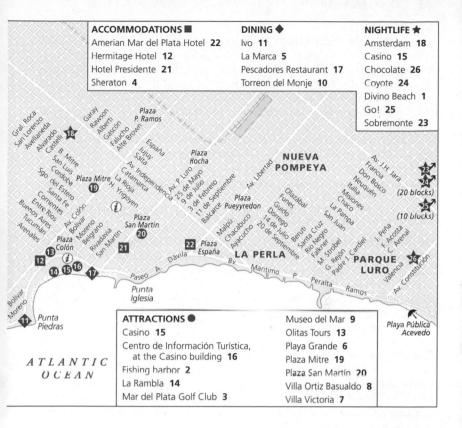

here, including Jorge Luis Borges. It is open year-round Thursday to Tuesday from 1 to 8pm, with an admission charge of 65¢ (36p). In summer, musical and theatrical performances are held in the gardens. **Villa Ortiz Basualdo,** Av. Colón 1189 (© 223/486-1636), is an English-style Victorian mansion decorated with exquisite Art Nouveau furniture from Belgium. In the same neighborhood, the **Museo del Mar,** Av. Colón 1114, at Viamonte (© 223/451-9779), houses a collection of 30,000 seashells. In summer it is open Sunday to Friday 9am to 7pm and Saturday 9am to 10pm. During the winter it's open daily from 9am to 1pm. Admission is $1 (55p). Stop in for a bite at their cafe surrounded by tanks of sharks staring at you and your meal.

Twenty minutes from the city center, **De Los Padres Lake and Hills** is a picturesque forest with wide parks surrounding the lake, perfect for an afternoon picnic. Nearby, the **Zoo El Paraíso,** Ruta 266, Km 16.5 (© 223/463-0347), features a wonderful collection of flora and fauna, including plants and trees from all over Argentina as well as lions, pumas, monkeys, llamas, and other animals. For information on surfing, deep-sea fishing, mountain biking, horseback riding, trekking, and other adventure sports, contact the tourism office.

The tour company **Olitas Tours** also does half-day city tours, as well as a special tour for children on a bus filled with clowns. Visit their kiosk at Plaza Colón or call © 223/472-6810.

WHERE TO STAY

Amerian Mar del Plata Hotel   The Amerian is an Argentine chain hotel, and this branch in Mar del Plata overlooks Plaza España and La Perla Beach. The hotel is surrounded by several nightclubs, so it can be noisy at night. Prices can differ depending on sea or city view. Rooms are spacious, however, especially for the price category. Junior suites, positioned at angles, all have some form of sea view, even if it's not direct. Suites come with Jacuzzi tubs, and all the bathrooms are on the large size no matter the category. Parking is free on-site. There is no Internet access in the rooms, but a small computer station in the lobby provides free Wi-Fi access. There is no gym or pool either, though staff will help guests arrange to visit one nearby. There is also a small event room for conventions and other functions.

Av. Libertad 2936 (at La Rioja and Yrigoyen), 7600 Mar del Plata. ℰ **223/491-2000.** Fax 223/491-2300. www.amerian.com. 58 units (52 doubles, 6 suites). From $105 (£58) double; from $182 (£100) suite. Rates include buffet breakfast. AE, DC, MC, V. Free parking. **Amenities:** Restaurant; bar; concierge; business center; limited room service; laundry service; dry cleaning. *In room:* A/C, TV, minibar, hair dryer, safe.

The Hermitage Hotel   Every city has a grande dame hotel, and for Mar del Plata, this complex overlooking the casino is it. The hotel isn't as glamorous as in years past, when it was built in 1943. But it's still the place where local celebrities often choose to make an appearance, timed for when they know the maximum amount of cameras and people are coming back from a day at the beach. Some choose to make a very dramatic entrance into town via the rooftop helipad. The lobby is rendered in a classical style, with gilded friezes of fishermen and Louis XV elements throughout, along with a very ornate lobby bar. Art and photos of old Mar del Plata adorn the walls, and the flow of spaces might remind visitors of Rio's Copacabana Palace Hotel. The extremely ornate Salon Versailles was also used during the 2005 Summit of the Americas. The hotel added the Torre Colón to its property in 2002, and renovated all the rooms in the old building at the same time. The rooms in the new building are nicer and pricier, affording both sea and city views. The formal restaurant Luis Alberto, where breakfast is served as well as lunch and dinner, is in an atrium connecting the two buildings. Rooms are spacious, with Wi-Fi capability, jumbo TVs, and oversize bathrooms. All have tub-and-shower combinations. The hotel has its own private casino and beach area, connected to the hotel via an underground passageway. The beach area has a bar and towel service open from 8am to 10pm. The casino is open 3pm to midnight Sunday to Thursday, and until 4am Friday and Saturday. Torre Colón has three rooms for the disabled. While the hotel faces the ocean via its original lobby, the door is often locked, and the new Torre Colón lobby serves as the main entrance. There is a small gym and spa on the premises, and the rooftop heated pool has a spectacular view to the sea.

Bulevar PP Ramos 2657 and Av. Colón 1643 overlooking the Casino, 7600 Mar del Plata. ℰ **223/451-9081.** Fax 223/451-7235. www.hermitagehotel.com.ar. 300 units (240 doubles, 60 suites). From $130 (£72) doubles in old building, from $154 (£85) new building; from $194 (£107) suites. Rates include buffet breakfast. AE, DC, MC, V. Parking $7 (£3.85). **Amenities:** Restaurant; bar; health club; concierge; business center; 24-hr. room service; massage service; babysitting; laundry service; dry cleaning. *In room:* A/C, TV, Internet, Wi-Fi, minibar, hair dryer, large safe.

Hotel Presidente   This small four-star hotel, owned by the Spanish chain Hoteles Alvarez, is about a block from the beach. An older property, it's full of dark woods, and some of the rooms are on the small side. The pleasant staff more than makes up for any faults in the decor. Some amenities—such as the restaurant Tartufu, where breakfast is served, and the small gym—are shared with the neighboring Hotel Iruña, owned by the same company. Some rooms also have Wi-Fi capability as the two hotels share antennas as well. Breakfast is included in the rates, and even some of the side rooms have sea views. Rooms facing the sea cost a little more, but overall this hotel is a good choice for those who want good service on a reasonable budget. Each room comes with a small desk and vanity, and while there is no air-conditioning, the ceiling fan keeps the room comfortable. Parking is available for an additional 20 Argentine pesos a day (about 7¢/4p). A small convention center on the eighth floor hosts meetings, and the lobby bar can be very busy. Here, you'll also find two computer terminals with free Internet access.

Corrientes 1516 at Diagonal J. B. Alberdi, 7600 Mar del Plata. ℂ **223/491-1060.** Fax 223/491-1183. www.hotel presidente.com. 53 units (45 doubles, 8 suites). From $71 (£39) double with city view, $80 (£44) with sea view; from $105 (£58) suites. Rates include buffet breakfast. AE, DC, MC, V. Parking for $7 (£3.85). **Amenities:** Restaurant; lobby bar; small health club; spa; concierge; car-rental desk; business center; 24-hr. room service; massage; babysitting; laundry service; dry cleaning. *In room:* TV, Wi-Fi in select rooms, hair dryer, safe.

Sheraton 𝒦𝒦 The 10-year-old Sheraton sits overlooking the golf course and the military port, near Playa Grande. It's a long but pleasant walk from the beach, a few blocks away. Its position near the golf course means this is the hotel of choice for golfers. Rooms have recently undergone a renovation, including the trademark Sheraton Suite Sleeper beds. The lobby has Wi-Fi access, at a charge, and includes a small shopping arcade and business center. The soaring atrium setting makes for a beautiful place to meet. The hotel has a children's area and a video arcade, making it a great choice if you have the family in tow. There are two pools, an indoor and outdoor pool. A $5 (£2.75) charge applies to use of the indoor pool, connected to the spa and sauna complex. Two restaurants are in the hotel: the informal **La Pampa,** open for breakfast, lunch, and dinner, with an international menu, as well as the formal **Las Barcas,** only open for dinner Wednesday to Sunday. The gym received all-new equipment in 2007. With its view to the sea, it's simply stunning for a workout. A garden surrounds the outdoor pool, free of charge to use, but it's only open in the summer. The hotel often hosts barbecues and other events at the pool for guests to participate in. Rooms have Internet access by cable or Wi-Fi, at a fee of $18 (£9.90). Rooms are light and airy. Even standards seem oversize, and suites have Jacuzzi tubs. Additional business functions of the hotel include an executive floor. The hotel also has the largest convention center in Argentina outside of Buenos Aires, with room for 4,500 people. Many famous international guests have stayed here including President George Bush during the October 2005 Summit of the Americas. The Sheraton will accept small pets and also has two rooms for the disabled.

Alem 4221 overlooking the golf course, 7600 Mar del Plata. ℂ **0800/777-7002** or 223/414-0000. Fax 223/499-0009. www.sheratonmardelplata.com.ar. 191 units (160 doubles, 31 suites). From $160 (£88) doubles; from $290 (£160) suites. Rates do not always include buffet breakfast. AE, DC, MC, V. Parking $7 (£3.85). **Amenities:** 2 restaurants; bar; large health club w/heated outdoor pool; golf; game room; concierge; business center; shopping arcade; 24-hr. room service; massage service; babysitting; laundry service; dry cleaning. *In room:* A/C, TV, dataport, Wi-Fi, minibar, hair dryer; safe.

WHERE TO DINE

Ivo Cafe 𝒦𝒦 GREEK/ARGENTINE I can't say enough about this fantastic Greek restaurant, only a few years old, at the bottom of a high-rise condo overlooking the ocean. It's a two-level restaurant, with sidewalk seating. The Greek owners serve Greek food along with an Argentine *parrilla* (grill). They have oversize Greek salads, excellent souvlaki, and many other Greek choices. The chic black table is also set with olives and eggplant pastes for dipping in bread. Also, while they have an English-language menu, ask for the Spanish one if you can read it; it has more and better choices. From the plate-glass windows, diners have a view of the sweeping arc of lights on the Mar del Plata shoreline. They also have dinner shows each Thursday, beginning at 9pm, with Greek dancing for a charge of about $12 (£6.60), which includes a meal but not the cost of drinks. Still, come in the wee hours on any day, and you'll find the staff breaks into piano playing, singing, and traditional dancing.

Bulevar Marítimo 3027 at Güemes. © **223/486-3160.** www.ivocafe.com. Main courses $6–$10 (£3.30–£5.50). AE, MC, V. Daily 24 hr. in summer; winter Sun–Thurs 8am–3am, 24 hr. Fri–Sat.

La Marca ★★ ARGENTINE   This restaurant became famous for serving a whole cow upon special request, for large groups of 50 or more people. While they rarely do this anymore, La Marca is still the town's best *parrilla,* serving thick rump steaks, tenderloins, barbecued ribs of beef, flanks, and other cuts of beef. The tender filet mignon with mushroom sauce is delicious. The menu includes pork chops, sausages, sweetbreads, black pudding, and other delights as well. The salad bar is extensive. Service is polite and unhurried. Make sure to try the *dulce de leche* before you leave.

Almafuerte 253. © **223/451-8072.** Main courses $3–$6 (£1.65–£3.30). AE, DC, MC, V. Daily noon–3pm and 8:30pm–1am.

Pescadores Restaurant ★★ SEAFOOD   You see this restaurant the moment you pull into Mar del Plata, only because it's under the enormous Quilmes neon billboard sign on the pier. This three-level seafood restaurant juts into the ocean and is one of the best seafood restaurants in town. Built into the Fisherman's Club, it's the next best thing to catching the fish yourself. Fish of all kinds—sole, salmon, calamari, lobster, oysters, and everything else local or shipped in—is here. Landlubbers will find pasta, salads, and *parrilla* offerings too, and some of the same sauces for fish double as pasta sauces. Naturally, there are a lot of white wines on the menu.

Bulevar Marítimo and Av. Luro in the Club de Pesca on the city pier. © **223/493-1713.** Main courses $3–$22 (£1.65–£12). AE, DC, MC, V. Daily noon–3pm and 8pm–midnight

Torreon del Monje ★★ ARGENTINE   It's hard not to notice this restaurant in Mar del Plata, inside a castlelike structure dating from 1904 overlooking the Atlantic Ocean. Day or night, the plate-glass windows over the sea and opening onto the street offer a fantastic view. Food runs from simple sandwiches to a *parrilla* with steak, chicken, and, of course, locally caught seafood. Almost each night, dinner shows take place while you dine, beginning at 10pm. Some are tango, others flamenco and folkloric. There is no additional charge for the shows; they're part of the experience of dining here. If you've dined elsewhere, stop in for drinks at the beautiful oak bar. During the day, many people come for the flavored and alcoholic coffee specials in the Esmeralda lounge.

Paseo Jesús de Galíndez at the Puente del Monje on the seafront. © **223/451-9467.** www.torreondelmonje.com. Main courses $4–$10 (£2.20–£5.50). AE, DC, MC, V. Daily 8am–2am; until 4am Fri–Sat.

MAR DEL PLATA AFTER DARK

Nightlife follows closely behind beaches as Mar del Plata's biggest draw. In summer, theater companies leave Buenos Aires to perform in this coastal resort; ask the tourism office for a schedule of performance times and places. The city's most popular bars are south of Plaza Mitre, off Calle San Luis. The best dance clubs are along Avenida Constitución, 3km (2 miles) from downtown, including **Chocolate,** Av. Constitución

4451 (© **223/479-4848**); **Divino Beach,** Paseo Costanero Sur Presidente Illia (© **223/467-1506**); **Go!,** Av. Constitución 5780 (© **223/479-6666**); and **Sobremonte,** Av. Constitución 6690 (© **223/479-7930**). **Amsterdam,** Castilli 3045 (© **15/527-8606**), is the best gay disco. **Coyote,** Av. Constitución 6670 (© **223/ 479-7930**), is a favorite local bar, which breaks into salsa and merengue dancing as the night goes on.

2 Miramar

450km (279 miles) SE of Buenos Aires

As Mar del Plata becomes more crowded and decidedly downscale, upper-middle-class Porteños have been looking for new vacation spots. Among them is Miramar, approximately 45km (28 miles) away from Mar del Plata down the Atlantic coast on Ruta 11. The city is green and quiet, with a relatively limited number of high-rise condominiums along its short waterfront. Most of the town's center is walkable, a few blocks from the beach. It's an ideal location for families or couples seeking a quiet vacation. The town is also blessed with a large forest reserve called the **Bosque Vivero Dunícola Florentino Ameghino** to the south, which helps to limit development. Jetties protect its shoreline, keeping the waters tranquil along the *balnearios,* or private beach kiosks peppering the shore. With the tranquillity come decidedly higher prices than you'll find in Mar del Plata.

ESSENTIALS

GETTING THERE   **Plusmar** (www.plusmar.com.ar) bus company runs several buses a day from Buenos Aires Retiro bus terminal. The trip takes about 5 hours, similar to heading to Mar del Plata. Contact them at [tel] 2291/433-709 in Miramar or at © 11/4315 3494 in Buenos Aires. Other bus companies connecting Buenos Aires to Miramar include **Micromar,** at © 2291/432-211 in Miramar or at © 11/ 4313-3130 in Buenos Aires; and **Turismo Parque,** at © 2291/431-333 in Miramar or at © 11/4315-4133 in Buenos Aires. There is no central bus station in Miramar, but most buses stop on the **Plaza Central** or on the wide diagonal streets leading from it. You can also take a train from Buenos Aires's **Constitución** station to Miramar, using Ferrobaires rail services. Contact them at © 11/4304-0028 in Buenos or at © 2291/420-657, or visit www.ferrobaires.gba.gov.ar. Trains leave Miramar Station, on Avenida 40 between streets 13 and 17. **Aeroparque Juan Domingo Perón** is a small private airport serving Miramar a few kilometers north. Call them at © **2291/ 432-599** for information about airplane services.

VISITOR INFORMATION   The **Dirección Municipal de Turismo** has its office on Plaza Central at the intersections of calles 28 and 21. They are open daily from 7am to 9pm 365 days a year. Call them at © **2291/420-190** (www.mga.gov.ar is the city's official site, and www.miramarense.com.ar and www.ciudad-de-miramar.com.ar also offer more tourism information).

GETTING AROUND   Most of what you need in this very compact city is accessible on foot. For longer distances, contact **Alvarado Remis** at © 2291/430-327, **Miramar Remis** at © 2291/430-400, or **Pronto Remis** at © 2291/432-452. You can't rent cars in Miramar directly, but you can arrange for rentals through travel agencies. The cars come from Mar del Plata, so arrange for one ahead of time. Call **Cosmopolitan Travel Agency** at © 2291/420-571, **Mabitur** at © 2291/422-709, or **La Plaza** at

© 2291/431-080. **Panda Viajes,** an adventure travel company, will rent cars along with other services. They also offer an interesting 4WD beach excursion through the wooded dunes surrounding Miramar. Contact them at © 2291/431-080 or visit www.pandaviajes.com. Bikes are a big deal here, and many hotels and travel companies provide them.

WHAT TO SEE & DO

Beyond the beach, there is not much to do in Miramar. You can see most of the city's non-aquatic sites within an hour. Before you begin your walk, keep in mind that even streets and avenues run parallel to the ocean, and odd ones run perpendicular. The city's **Plaza Central** is really four squares in one, surrounded by the calles 28, 24, 23, and 21. In the middle is a statue of **General Rudecindo Alvarado,** a hero in the Argentine independence movement. Other statues and busts of important national and local figures are scattered throughout the pine- and palm-tree-planted plaza. Kids will find plenty to do at the various local playgrounds or on the small merry-go-round nearby.

Most of the buildings surrounding the square are modern. Among them is the **Casino Miramar** at Calle 21, no. 1335, next door to the **Tourism Office** at Calle 28 (© **2291/420-477;** in summer daily 5pm–3am). The pedestrianized street called **9 de Julio,** which is really the continuation of Calle 21, connects the Plaza Central with the beach. It's lined with shops and ice-cream places. A few blocks away is **Iglesia San Antonio,** at the intersection of calles 22 and 29. Dating from 1891, it's a small cream-colored Spanish colonial building that wouldn't look out of place in the Southern California suburbs. It has a simple interior with modern stained-glass windows and a wooden roof. Giant holy water–filled clam shells at the door casually remind you that you're in a beach town. Miramar also has a large summertime Jewish population with the **Miramar Synagogue** serving as a community center. Its interior is small and starkly modern. It's on Calle 27 between calles 14 and 15 (© **2291/431-820**).

Two kilometers (1¼ miles) to the southwest of the town center, accessible by foot from many streets and by 4WD from Avenida 26, is the 80-hectare (200-acre) forest reserve **Vivero Dunícola Florentino Ameghino.** You can walk along the trails or take a 4WD dune excursion with Panda Viajes, mentioned in the "Getting Around" section. About 12km (7 miles) in the same direction is the historical town of **Mar del Sud,** full of interesting turn-of-the-20th-century buildings. Golfers will want to head 2km (1¼ miles) northeast along the Atlantic coast from the center of town to **Links Miramar** (© **2291/422-244**). The city also has a summer season inaugural parade a few days before Christmas every year, to celebrate the season in a spectacular way. Contact the tourism office for details.

WHERE TO STAY

Refugio de Mar ⒼR   This apartment/hotel complex is a great choice for families or large groups. Each apartment is designed as its own *cabaña,* with two bathrooms, sleeping up to six people. The apartments opened in June 2006, and all are wooden interiors, with green bedspreads and tile floors. Apartments are fully stocked with dishes, an iron, a TV, and a DVD player. All rooms also have Wi-Fi. The two-level apartments have balconies and face a central courtyard with a heated outdoor pool, and there is even a small gym and game room. Maid service and breakfast are included, but the apartments rent out by the week, which is negotiable in low season. All apartments are also alarmed.

Av. 9 (between calles 14 and 16), 7607 Miramar. ℂ 2291/434-115. www.refugiodemarmiramar.com.ar. 10 units. From $1,150 (£633) for 1 week for 6 people. Rates include continental breakfast and maid service. No credit cards. Free parking. **Amenities:** Outdoor pool; gym; bicycles; children's programs; game room; concierge; babysitting; laundry. *In room:* A/C, TV, Wi-Fi, kitchen, hair dryer, safe, alarm system, video games.

Villasol Hostería ⟨ℛ⟩   This is one of the nicest properties in Miramar, and it only opened in 2006. It's not directly on the beach, but it's very close, and its corner location means many rooms have sea views. The pseudo-Victorian structure of the property gives it the feel of an oversized bed and breakfast. Rooms are large and have a neutral color pattern with native accents, giving them a Southwestern feel. All floors are terra cotta tiled. Bathrooms are large, and some have hydro-massage tubs. A few rooms have balconies, with wicker furniture so you can lounge in the sun or take in a view of the ocean. There are two restaurants, one downstairs for lunch and dinner, offering simple international cuisine. The breakfast room, in the attic with terraces overlooking the ocean, is a delightful place to start the morning. There is a small lounge and gym here too, along with a snack bar. Rooms are not air-conditioned, but all come with fans. Some of the rooms are also apartments, with two bedrooms but without kitchens; they're good for families or groups of friends.

Calle 6, no. 1701 (at the corner of 33); 7607 Miramar. ℂ 2291/433-017. www.hosteriavillasol.com.ar. 8 units (4 doubles, 4 apts). From $95 (£52) double; $155 (£85) apt. Breakfast included. AE, MC, V. Free parking. **Amenities:** Bicycles; concierge; babysitting; laundry; dry cleaning. *In room:* A/C, TV, Wi-Fi, kitchen, minibar, hair dryer, safe, alarm system.

WHERE TO DINE

Círculo de Amigos ⟨ℛ⟩ ARGENTINE/SEAFOOD   This is one of the best seafood restaurants in Miramar, just a block from the Plaza Central. Some of the fish are international and come frozen; others are caught in Mar del Plata and driven in. The menu lists more than 30 fish recipes. Sole and bass are the highlights; other specialties include oysters cooked with mushrooms and lobster casserole. Some beef and vegetable dishes round out the offerings. The restaurant is enormous, and the white, blue, and gold tablecloths and furniture give it a Provençal air. Naturally, there is a large selection of white wine, much of which is stored on shelves in the back, so you can take a look and decide what you want.

Calle 21, no. 1246 (at 28th St.). ℂ 2291/422-226. Main courses $2.50–$8 (£1.40–£4.40). No credit cards. Daily noon–3pm and 8pm–midnight (sometimes later on weekends).

Van Dyke Resto Bar ARGENTINE/INTERNATIONAL   On a corner plot of a diagonal street, with enormous plate-glass windows, this fun restaurant and bar feels like the center of it all, with great food and live music every Thursday night. In summer, it's open 24 hours a day, and from 6:30am to 2am in winter. It's the only bar in Miramar with *torre jirafas* (giraffe towers), elongated funnel-shaped beer kegs with spigots that sit at tables and stand a meter tall. They also have an extensive mixed drink menu. Pizza, empanadas and a *parrilla* round out the food offerings. There's also sidewalk seating with a view of the Plaza Central. Even when the music isn't live, there's always music blasting. The owners say that on some nights, patrons just start dancing between the tables when they feel like it.

Calle 21, no. 1401 (at Diagonal Fortunato near the corner of Calle 30). ℂ 2291/423-255. Main courses $1.50–$4.50 (85p–£2.50). No credit cards. Daily 24 hr. in summer; daily 6:30am–2am in winter.

3 La Plata

55km (34 miles) S of Buenos Aires

La Plata began its history with the unification of Argentina in 1880. The new nation's leaders decided that if Buenos Aires was to be the capital of the new country, then Buenos Aires province needed a new capital of its own. Thus was born La Plata, south of Buenos Aires along the Río de la Plata. Construction began in 1882. Many residents in La Plata claim it is the first planned city in Argentina, but in fact it was the first planned city in Argentina created after independence from Spain. Part of what will strike you about this metropolis is the large number of parks and plazas, as well as its diagonal streets which cut across the city, creating vista points and complex intersections. This urban pattern earned La Plata the nickname "The Checkerboard City." The town is centered around the enormous Plaza Moreno, defined by the cathedral and municipal palace that face each other across this vast grassy expanse.

ESSENTIALS

GETTING THERE   You can reach La Plata by car, bus, or train. The highway, simply known as the **Autopista,** that begins at the southern end of Avenida 9 de Julio in Buenos Aires connects the capital to La Plata. By car the trip takes 45 minutes to an hour. Buses between Buenos Aires and La Plata leave the capital from **Retiro** and arrive at the **La Plata Terminal de Omnibus** at the intersections of Diagonal 74 and avenidas 4 and 42 (© **221/421-0992**). The main company serving La Plata is **Costera Metropolitana,** which also owns **Chevallier** (© **0800/222-6565;** www.costerametropolitana.com). The ride can last from 1 to 2 hours, depending on traffic or whether the bus is a local or an Autopista express. Buses generally run about every 10 minutes, and tickets are roughly $5 (£2.75) round-trip. A train also connects La Plata with Buenos Aires from **Constitución,** in the southern part of the capital, with **Estación La Plata** at the intersection of avenidas 1 and 44. Ticket prices are similar to bus fares. Trains run about every 15 to 30 minutes, depending on the day, and take about an hour and 20 minutes. However, the trains connecting La Plata and Buenos Aires have a high pickpocketing rate, and I don't recommend them for visitors. In Buenos Aires call © **11/1959-0800** for train tickets and in La Plata call © **221/423-2575.**

VISITOR INFORMATION   There are two **Centros de Información Turística** in La Plata. One is in the Terminal de Omnibus, at the intersections of Diagonal 74 and avenidas 4 and 42, open daily 9am to 5pm (© **221/427-3198**). The main center, open only on weekdays from 9am to 5pm, is in a building called the **Palacio Campodónico,** at the intersection of Diagonal 79 and avenidas 5 and 56 (© **221/422-9764**). You can also visit **www.laplata.gov.ar** for more information about the city.

GETTING AROUND   La Plata is a relatively compact city, and most of what you'll want to see will be about a 15-minute walk from either the train or bus station. You may, however, want to take a taxi to a few points in the suburbs, including the **República de los Niños** amusement park. Cabs are easy to find at the bus and train stations and all over town, but if you need to call one, try the 24-hour company **Remises Horizonte** (© **221/453-2800**). La Plata's streets are named with numbers according to a grid pattern with overlaying diagonals. Depending on the map or the person with whom you are speaking, the streets are either *calles* or *avenidas,* and the terms are used interchangeably, which can become confusing. The saving grace is that no street number is used twice for streets and avenues (like 8th St. and 8th Ave. in New Manhattan). Portions of **Calle 8** are now a pedestrianized shopping street—a good place to stop for ice cream or a drink at any of the numerous cafés in the vicinity.

WHAT TO SEE & DO

The city's most imposing building, the **Catedral de la Inmaculada Concepción,** at avenidas 14 and 51 and 52 (℗ **221/427-3504**), hovers over the **Plaza Moreno** in the center of the city. It was built in a medieval Gothic style more along the lines of a northern European church than a Spanish colonial one. It is free for visits, but the lookout tower in one of the spires, known as the **Torre de Jesús (Jesus Tower),** costs about $2 (£1.10) to climb. Across the plaza, the architecture of the **Palacio Municipal** warrants a look, at Avenida 12 between avenidas 51 and 53. The **City Park (Paseo del Bosque),** on the edge of the center of town, is home to the **Museo de Ciencias Naturales.** This museum (℗ **221/425-7744;** Tues–Sun 10am–6pm; admission $1/55p) has the feel of an old Victorian institution, with its mix of stuffed animals, archaeological relics, and other items displayed in the building's dusty, soaring, wrought-iron interior. Nearby in the park, the **City Zoo** (℗ **221/4257-3925;** Tues–Sun 9am–6pm; admission $1 (55p), free for children), shelters more than 180 kinds of animals. The **Teatro Nuevo Argentino,** Avenida 51 at avenidas 9 and 10 (℗ **221/429-1700**), stages various productions and exhibits paintings and other art in its lobby. Built into an old train station, the enormous **Dardo Rocha Cultural Center,** on Avenida 50 at avenidas 6 and 7 (℗ **221/427-1210** for all institutions), houses the **Contemporary Art Museum** and the **Municipal Art Museum.** Hours and admission fees vary depending on the venue, but the place is always busy with something to do. A few miles from downtown is the amusement park that inspired Walt Disney, when he created Disneyland in California. Juan and Evita Perón built the **República de los Niños,** at Belgrano and Calle 501 (℗ **221/484-1409;** www.republica.laplata.gov.ar), as a learning and entertainment center for children. The small-size buildings imitate government buildings in Buenos Aires, with themes related to various nations. Naturally, the rides and attractions make the place a great stop for kids.

CITY TOURS

The travel company **For Export,** Calle 5 no. 1241, between avenidas 57 and 58 (℗ **221/425-9393;** www.forexport.net.ar), offers city tours in La Plata. Various themes include the Panoramic City Tour, which lasts half a day; the Full Day City Tour; and the Religious City Tour. They also arrange excursions outside of the city, hotel accommodations, and car rentals.

WHERE TO STAY

Hotel del Rey　An Argentine-owned three-star property, the Hotel del Rey is a bargain considering its location and services. Rooms are of an average size; those on the upper floors come with nice views of the surrounding parts of the city. A travel agency is located in the lobby, which makes it easy to arrange excursions.

Plaza Paso 180 (at avs. 13 and 44), 1900 La Plata. ℗ **221/427-0177.** www.hoteldelrey.com.ar. 40 units. From $25 (£14) double. Rates include buffet breakfast. AE, DC, MC, V. Free parking. **Amenities:** Restaurant; bar; concierge; business center; 24-hr. room service; laundry service; dry cleaning. *In room:* A/C, TV, minibar.

Howard Johnson (Inn Corregidor)　A few blocks off Plaza Moreno, this Howard Johnson is very well situated near many of La Plata's government buildings and tourist sites. Rooms are well equipped, and many have a light, airy feeling to them. This place is sometimes known by its old name, Inn Corregidor.

Calle 6 no. 1026 (at avs. 53 and 54), 1900 La Plata. ℂ 221/425-6800. Fax 221/425-6805. www. hotelcorregidor.com.ar and www.hojoar.com. 110 units (109 doubles, 1 apt). From $50 (£28) double. Rates include buffet breakfast. AE, DC, MC, V. Free parking. **Amenities:** Restaurant; bar; health club; concierge; business center; 24-hr. room service; laundry service; dry cleaning. *In room:* A/C, TV, high-speed Internet, minibar, hair dryer, safe.

WHERE TO DINE

Hook ARGENTINE/IRISH/SEAFOOD   With a vague pirate-and-shipwreck theme, Hook is a restaurant/pub with very friendly staffers who like to chat with patrons at the bar. Seafood as well as Irish and Argentine items are the main draws here. During the lunch hours, they also have an inexpensive Executive menu, which is a bargain at about $4 to $5 (£2.20–£2.75).

Av. 53 no. 538, between avs. 5 and 6. ℂ 221/482-2160. Main courses $2–$5 (£1.10–£2.75). No credit cards. Mon–Sat 8am–2am; Sun 8pm–2am.

Restaurant Modelo ARGENTINE/ITALIAN   You won't find any models lurking around here, as the name of the place might imply. You will find professional service and high-quality food in an interior that looks more English than Argentine. At night, the bar becomes the focus, filling up with a young crowd drinking beer, shelling peanuts, and throwing the remains all over the floor.

Calle 5, at Av. 54. ℂ 221/421-1321. Main courses $2–$5 (£1.10–£2.75). No credit cards. Daily 8am–3am.

4 Tigre & the Delta

36km (22 miles) NE of Buenos Aires

The Tigre River Delta is in essence a wild natural suburb of Buenos Aires, but it seems a world apart from the city. The delta is formed by the confluence of five rivers, where they flow from the Pampas into the Río de la Plata. This marshy complex is full of silt and hundreds of tiny islands. Over time, it's continuing to grow down the Río de la Plata. The delta area has grown considerably since the Spanish Conquest. In theory, within several hundred years, the Río Tigre Delta will actually reach the capital. The islands here are a mix of grassland, swamp, and true forest, with a variety of animal and plant life.

The development of the Tigre Delta into a resort area owes to two concurrent historical circumstances in Buenos Aires in the 1870s. One was the construction of railroads from Buenos Aires into the rest of the country. The other was the 1877 outbreak of yellow fever, which caused wealthy Porteños to seek out new parts of the city for new year-round homes as well as summer vacation spots. The English were in charge of much of the construction here, so many of the older neo-Gothic and mock-Tudor mansions and bed-and-breakfasts that line the banks of the river passages look like Victorian London buildings transplanted into the wild marshes of the Pampas.

Today, many Porteños come here on weekends to relax, ride horseback, hike, fish, swim, or do nothing at all. It's also an attractive destination, since it's easy to come here just for the day, tour the islands by boat, and return to Buenos Aires in time for dinner. There is a year-round population of residents on these car-free inner islands, and they go to school, work, and shop for groceries using a system of boats and docks.

ESSENTIALS

GETTING THERE The Tigre Delta is best reached by train from Buenos Aires and then a boat or launch from the train station. Trains from Buenos Aires leave from **Estación Retiro** for Estación Tigre, at Avenida Naciones Unidas, every 10 to 20 minutes along the Mitre Line. Tickets run about $1 (55p) round-trip. Call © **11/ 4317-4445** for schedules and information, or visit www.tbanet.com.ar. Within Tigre, the **Estación Fluvial Tigre,** where the boats depart to head through the various rivers and islands, is on the next block over from **Estación Tigre,** at Mitre 305. Many companies run launches and services on both banks of the river here; you have to know where you want to go, or simply choose one and go wherever it takes you. Among the many companies are **Catamaranes Interisleña** (© **11/4731-0261); Líneas Delta** (© **11/4749-0537);** and **Catamaranes Río Tur** (© **11/4731-0280).** To reach **Martín García Island,** one of the most remote parts of the delta, you have to travel with **Cacciola** (© **11/4749-0329).** Most of these companies service the various islands but allow you to ride on the boat until the end of the trip and then simply return. Ticket prices vary but range from less than $1 (55p) and up. I highly recommend that you find out when the last few boats leave from your destination; toward the end of the day, boats can fill up quickly, leaving some passengers to wait for the next boat. Extra boats are dispatched at peak times, but you still may have to wait a few extra hours at the end of the day, especially on Sunday. Build this time into your plans. Many tour companies in Buenos Aires also provide excursions to the Tigre Delta, and I have included that information below.

VISITOR INFORMATION In theory, there are two **Centros de Información Turística** in Tigre. There is one in Estación Tigre, but it never seems to be open. Within Estación Fluvial Tigre, at Mitre 305 (© **0800/888-TIGRE** or 11/4512-4497; www.tigre.gov.ar), another office is open daily from 9am to 5pm. It is a very busy office, providing information on the islands, hotels and rentable bungalows, and other activities. You may have to wait a little while for help, but most of the staff speaks English. Another useful tourism website is **www.puntodelta.com.ar.**

GETTING AROUND Within the town of Tigre itself, where both the train station and the docks are, one can easily walk along both banks. There are restaurants, playgrounds for children, and a few tourist-oriented shops along the waterfront and on the streets heading to the Puerto de Frutos (see below). To get around and see the delta, however, you will need a boat. I have listed the companies that provide these services above. Of course, if you have the skills and stamina, swimming is another option.

WHAT TO SEE & DO

The main thing to see in Tigre is the delta itself and the various islands and resorts that dot the area. Within the town of Tigre, where the train station and boat docks are, there are a few services and various other places of interest. Many people simply stay in this area and dine in the restaurants, sunbathe along the shoreline, or wander the town. Ponies march up and down the eastern shoreline in the city center, near the intersection of calles Lavalle and Fernández (no address or phone); children love riding them. From this area, head along what is called **Paseo Victórica,** a collection of Victorian mansions along the waterfront of Río Lujan, until it intersects with Río Conquista. This is one of the prettiest parts of Tigre, and you will find many people sunbathing along the shore here also. In the midst of all this Victorian splendor is the

Naval Museum, Paseo Victorica 602, at Martínez (© **11/4749-0608**). On the other bank, across from here, is the **Parque de la Costa,** Vivanco, at Montes de Oca (© **11/4732-6000**), full of rides for kids and grownups. Just outside of the center of Tigre is the famous **Puerto de Frutos,** at 150 Calle Sarmiento, along Río Lujan. Fruit farming was integral to the early development of the Tigre Delta, and this market is a leftover from those days. Most people rave about seeing this site, but in general, I have always found it disappointing, with almost no fruit. Besides the traditional basket weavers who create their wares using the reeds growing in the delta, the market is now mostly full of odds and ends and less interesting crafts.

A 3-hour boat ride each way from the center of Tigre will take you to **Martín García Island.** It is famous for its upscale political prison where various Argentine presidents, including Juan Perón, have been incarcerated, but exploring here will take a full day once you account for the round-trip boat ride.

If you are doing any trekking on the islands, you will need hiking boots, long pants, and long-sleeved shirts. Saw grass and other very sharp forms of plants inhabit the area and will rip into unprotected skin. You should also bring mosquito repellent. It's also a good idea to pack binoculars, to view birds and other wildlife.

EXCURSION COMPANIES SERVING TIGRE DELTA

Various travel companies in Buenos Aires provide day-trip excursions to the Río Tigre delta or will arrange longer stays in the numerous bed-and-breakfasts, bungalows, and adventure lodges in the area. **Say Hueque Tourism,** Viamonte 749, Office 601, 1053 Buenos Aires (© **11/5199-2517** to -2520; www.sayhueque.com), is one that I highly recommend, especially for longer trips and adventure excursions to see the natural beauty of the area. **Travel Line** (© **11/4393-9000;** www.travelline.com.ar) offers Tigre Delta day tours, among many other excursions. The full-day Tigre tours are Sundays only (ask for an English-speaking guide), and include lunch, a ride to and from Tigre by train, and a boat ride among the rivers of the Tigre delta for about $40 (£22) per person.

WHERE TO STAY

Bonanza Deltaventura ✦✦ If you want to get away from it all, head to this hotel on one of the islands in the Río Tigre delta. It has miles of walkways through the grasslands for bird-watching and horses for riding along the shoreline. Or you can just swim off the dock out front. Guests can rent four small but comfortable rooms as either singles or doubles, for a total of eight people in the lodge. The living style is communal, with shared bathrooms and kitchen. The price includes breakfast and some excursions, but other meals and drinks cost extra. The staff also speaks English. You will need to call ahead of time to stay here, to ensure that space is available and that you take the right boat company. The hotel is on the Carapachay River islands section of the delta, about a 1-hour boat ride from the center of the town of Tigre.

Carapachay River Islands, 1648 Tigre. © **11/4798-2254** or 11/15-5603-7176 (cell). www.deltaventura.com. 4 units for up to 8 people. From $55 (£30) a person including breakfast and trekking. No credit cards. **Amenities:** Horses; trekking; use of kitchen.

Casona La Ruchi ✦✦ This charming bed-and-breakfast overlooks the waterfront across the bank from the Estación Fluvial. Owners Dora and Jorge Escuariza and their children run the place, treating guests who stay in the six-room, 1893 mansion like family. In the back, guests can gather and barbecue at the pool and grill. Rooms are furnished with quaint Victorian antiques, and some have windows looking out onto the waterfront. The place is open year-round, but it's busiest during summer weekends. Guests have 24-hour access to the hotel, though the family does not have an actual overnight staff person. Call if you're arriving late in the day to verify that someone can let you in. You will enjoy the warmth and hospitality at this place. Some rooms share a bathroom.

Lavalle 557 (at Av. Libertador), 1648 Tigre. ℂ **11/4749-2499**. www.casonalaruchi.com.ar. 6 units, some with shared bathroom. **$35 (£19) double.** Rates include continental breakfast. No credit cards. **Amenities:** Outdoor pool; use of kitchen and backyard grill.

WHERE TO DINE
Don Emilio Parrilla ARGENTINE/PARRILLA   A rustic interior and a casual atmosphere with tables in bright Provençal yellow await you in this *parrilla* overlooking the waterfront. The food here is great, and a complete meal will run you just a little over $5 (£2.75) a person. Unfortunately, it's only open on weekends.

Lavalle 573, at Av. Libertador. ℂ **11/4631-8804**. Main courses $1–$3 (55p–£1.65). No credit cards. Fri 8pm–1am; Sat–Sun 11:30am–5pm and 8pm–2am.

El Moño Rojo ⋆ ARGENTINE/INTERNATIONAL   An enormous restaurant complex overlooking the waterfront near the Estación Fluvial, this is one of the best places to come for a meal with entertainment. The atmosphere is brilliantly red, festive, and very kitschy, full of posters of tango stars, pictures of Argentine actors and actresses, and old Peronist memorabilia. On Friday they stage a tango show. The food is a mixture of pizzas, snacks, sandwiches, and traditional *parrilla* grilled meat, so there should be something to please everyone here.

Av. Mitre 345, at Estación Fluvial Tigre. ℂ **11/15-5135-7781** (cell). Main courses $2–$3 (£1.10–£1.65). No credit cards. Daily 8am–2am.

5 Punta del Este, Uruguay
320km (198 miles) NE of Buenos Aires

Few resorts in South America rival Punta del Este for glamour. It might be geographically located in Uruguay, but it's where the gliterrati and elite of Buenos Aires make their homes for the summer. As Mar del Plata's reputation downscales, this Uruguayan resort area has become the new place to see and be seen.

Punta is actually a reference to several towns located near each other. The main town of Punta del Este is on a small peninsula where the Río de la Plata meets the Atlantic Ocean. The town is connected to Maldonado, the capital of the Department of Maldonado. Punta del Este and its surrounding towns have over 50km (31 miles) of waterfront, stretching along both coasts. The majority of the city's major hotels are on the calmer river side. The sprawling Conrad Hotel and Casino complex dominates the riverbanks, and serves as a defacto social center even for those who aren't staying at the hotel. Sandy dunes stretch out along the Atlantic side, with rougher waves. The beaches on this side are less crowded. At night, as the tide gets stronger, you'll see many youths carrying surfboards and heading to catch the waves along the coastal highway Ruta 10. As a general rule, the farther you get from the center, the less crowded the beaches. Little of historical value is left anymore in this former fishing village, filled with high-rise hotels and condominiums, reminiscent of development in south Florida. The very heart of the peninsula still has a few historical buildings, such as the Faro or Lighthouse, churches, schoolhouses, and turn-of-the-20th-century buildings—a reminder of earlier, quieter times, before mass development in the 1950s and 1960s forever changed the way of life here. The port is often jammed with yachts in the summer.

Like any place that gets a reputation and becomes a part of package tours, Punta has lost some of its higher-end clients, who have gone elsewhere to look for greater exclusivity. About 10km (6 miles) up from Punta del Este is the small town of La Barra. It looks more like a little town grown up on Ruta 10, which serves as its main street, lined with bars, small hotels, clubs, and art galleries. It's more expensive to stay here. Visitors who have been to California's Laguna Beach will see more than a passing resemblance. Many young beachgoers flock here; at night, in high season, teenagers throw tailgate parties, parking their cars along the road to drink, hang out, dance along the road's shoulders, and blare car stereos. It's never quiet in La Barra in high season.

Farther along Ruta 10 is the very exclusive Jose Ignacio, a small quiet community that's even more expensive than La Barra. Many celebrities keep second homes here, including international stars such as the supermodel Naomi Campbell. And when the mood strikes and they want to be seen, they head to La Barra.

Most hotels and restaurants in Punta del Este itself are open year-round, regardless of the weather, and Punta maintains a permanent year-round community. In La Barra and Jose Ignacio however, many places close up for the winter. Summer season lasts from October to March, but "the Season," as it is known in the area, is a very specific time. From a few days after Christmas through the first 2 weeks of January, the Punta, La Barra, and Jose Ignacio swell with movie stars and models from all over South America, though mostly from Argentina. Film crews, photographers, and magazine staff follow them and watch their every movement, and parties abound. You may not know who most of them are if you are not from around here, but there are few places in the world with more glamour and beautiful women than Punta in season. Prices at this time are at their highest, needless to say, so if you plan to see this phenomenon, book in advance and prepare to blow your travel budget.

For dialing numbers in Uruguay from overseas, use the country code ✆ **598.** You also need to drop the "0" in the city codes listed here, **02** for Montevideo and **042** for Punta del Este, when you're dialing from outside the country.

ESSENTIALS

GETTING THERE   The easiest way to reach Punta del Este from Buenos Aires is by catching a **Buquebús** ferry to either Montevideo or Colonia, and then continuing by bus. **Buquebús**'s number is ✆ **02/916-1910** in Montevideo; its fast-service number is ✆ **02/130.** Within Argentina, dial ✆ 54/11/4316-**6500.**

COT (✆ **02/409-4949** in Montevideo; ✆ **042/486810** in Punta del Este; www.cot.com.uy) also offers bus service from Montevideo. **Copsa** (✆ **02/1975** in Montevideo; ✆ **042/1975** in Punta del Este; www.copsa.com.uy) is another bus company that offers service between Montevideo and Punta del Este. (These unusual numbers can not be dialed from overseas, but only within Uruguay.)

You can also fly between Buenos Aires' Jorge Newberry Airport and Punta's **Laguna del Sauce Airport,** about 16km (10 miles) from the city center. Airport information is ✆ **042/559777. Aerolineas Argentinas** services the airports (✆ **000-4054-86527** in Punta, or 0810/222-86527 in Buenos Aires; www.aerolineas.com.ar). **Pluna**

> ### *Tips* Locating Addresses in Punta del Este
>
> Many locations in Punta del Este are not listed with addresses but with *parada* numbers (a reference to the closest traffic light along the coast to their location). Many shops, hotels, and businesses don't seem to know their addresses, only their *paradas*. In other cases, many stores and businesses don't list the number of their building in a street address, referring only to the street they are on and the nearby cross streets (you'll actually perplex them if you press them for a numbered street address). Streets in Punta del Este are also labeled two different ways—as numbers and as names. For instance, Calle 31 is also called Inzaurraga; the main street, Avenida Gorlero, is called Avenida 22. Maps may or may not reflect both names. When in doubt about any address, ask for more information, such as a nearby store or landmark.

Airlines is another carrier (© **042/492050** in Punta, or 11/4342-4420 in Buenos Aires; www.pluna.aero). Be aware that as of this writing Argentina and Uruguay are in a diplomatic dispute over the construction of a paper mill that might pollute the Río Uruguay, near the Argentine town of Gualeguaychú. Access to Uruguay is at times restricted because of ongoing protests, and extra security is sometimes in place at crossings, airline gates, and the Buquebús terminal.

VISITOR INFORMATION   Punta del Este has several tourist information centers. Within the bus station **Terminal Punta Del Este** (© **042/494042**), there is a very small one with a very helpful staff. Overlooking the ocean at Parada 1 near Calle 21, the **Liga de Fomento** has a **Tourist Information Center** (© **042/446519**). Another city office is at Plaza Artigas, on Gorlero between calles 25 and 23 (© **042/446519**). The city's offices are open from 10am to 10pm 7 days a week. The government of Uruguay also maintains a tourist information office for the whole country at Gorlero 942 between calles 30 and 29 (© **042/441218**). The national office is open 10am to 7pm every day in the summer, and in winter daily from 10am to 5pm. The city government website (**www.maldonado.gub.uy**) has a section on tourist information; also visit **www.uruguaynatural.com**. Pick up *Liga News* or *Qué Hacemos Hoy,* two free tourist publications available all over the city with information on events around town.

Note: Citizens of the United States, the United Kingdom, Canada, and New Zealand need only a passport to enter Uruguay (for tourist stays of up to 90 days). Australian citizens must get a tourist visa before arrival.

GETTING AROUND   If you're staying in Punta del Este itself, most things you need are within walking distance. The hotels generally have great restaurants in them, and the beaches are just a quick walk over either the **Rambla Claudio Williman** on the Río de la Plata side, or the **Rambla Lorenzo Batlle Pacheco** on the Atlantic side. Although these two *ramblas* have different names, they are part of the same coastal highway, Ruta 10. The city's main shopping street is **Avenida Gorlero,** lined with stores and cafes. Another shopping street is **El Remanso,** 1 block parallel. Slightly more upscale and with a lot less foot traffic, it's nicknamed "the Little Paris," but you'll be hard-pressed to see any similarities between this thoroughfare and the French capital.

Many people hitchhike; you'll see a lot of young folk out there with their thumbs up. It's not considered dangerous at all here. It's best to rent a car, though, if you want to do some exploring or head to La Barra or Jose Ignacio without the threat of being stranded or sleeping on the beach. Car rental can be expensive, however, starting at $90 (£50) a day in high season. **Europcar** has an office at Gorlero and Calle 20 (© **042/495017** and 042/445018; www.europcar.com.uy). **Dollar Rent a Car** is at Gorlero 961 (© **042/443444;** www.dollar.com.uy).

Taxis are hard to come by, especially in high season. Keep the following numbers handy: **Shopping** (© 042/484704); **Parada 5** (© 042/490302), and **Aeropuerto** (© 042/559100). The bus company **COT** (© 042/486810) runs a service up and down the coastal routes, connecting the various towns in the area. You may have to wait a long time for one to pass by though. The company **Taller Rego,** Lenzina and Artigas, Parada 2 (© 042/486732) rents motorcycles and bicycles.

MONEY   The official currency is the **Uruguayan peso** (designated NP$, $U, or simply $); each peso is comprised of 100 **centavos.** Uruguayan pesos are available in $10, $20, $50, $100, $200, $500, $1,000, and $5,000 notes; coins come in 10, 20, and 50 centavos, and 1 and 2 pesos. The Uruguayan currency devalued by half in July 2002, due to its close kinship with the Argentine peso. The exchange rate as this book went to press was approximately 24 pesos to the dollar. Because the value of the peso fluctuates greatly with inflation, all prices in this chapter are quoted in U.S. dollars (with British pound conversions in parentheses).

WHAT TO SEE & DO

The main point behind a trip to Punta del Este is the beach, but if you must do other things besides lie in the sun, work on your tan, and check out hot bodies, then you'll find a few sights of interest. The symbol of Punta del Este is **La Mano,** a giant concrete hand sculpture rising out of the sands of the Atlantic across from the bus station. Creepy or playful, depending on your mood, it's a favorite photo-op for tourists and professional fashion shoots alike. The sculpture, by the Chilean artist Mario Irrarazabal, was inaugurated in 1981. On the tip of the peninsula, **Puerto Punta del Este** is pleasant for strolling and watching the boats come in, or trying to figure out who's who on the various yachts in season. A tranquil change of pace from the beach is the church **Nuestra Señora de la Candelaria,** at the corner of Calle 12 or Virazon and Calle 5 El Faro, a beautiful sky-blue-and-white Victorian structure. Inside, you'll find high white arches and yellow walls punctuated by simple golden stained-glass crosses in the windows. Across the street is the **Meteorological Station,** Calle 5 (or El Faro) and Calle 10 (or Calle Dos de Febrero), a modern lookout tower built over a 100-year-old schoolhouse. Entry is free to the museum at its base, with old pictures of Punta and weather instruments. The tower is not always open, but it has a great view of the surroundings. Directly across the street is **Faro de Punta del Este,** the city's symbolic lighthouse, dating from 1860, at Calle 5 (or El Faro) and Calle 10 (or Calle Dos de Febrero). There is a lookout tower with free admission open to the public, but opening hours are sporadic. **Plaza Artigas,** at Gorlero and Arrecifes, has a daily artist market with souvenirs and crafts. Along Ruta 10, just outside of downtown La Barra is the **Museo del Mar** *Kids* (© **042/771-817**), an interesting museum with sea shells and other marine items that kids seem to like. It's open daily in summer from 10am to 10:30pm, and in winter from 11am to 6pm daily.

TRAVEL COMPANIES IN PUNTA

Various travel companies in Punta del Este provide excursions and city tours. **Novo-turismo** (© 042/493154) is in the Terminal de Omnibus and offers city tours. **Alvaro Gimeno Turismo** (© 042/490570; www.alvarogimenoturismo.com) is also located in the Terminal de Omnibus. They offer city tours as well as day trips to nearby cities such as Piriapolis. Call both ahead of time about English-language tours, which are not offered on a daily basis. Both pick up clients at their hotels for city tours, which generally last about 4 hours and cost $15 (£8.25).

WHERE TO STAY

The Awa Hotel 🏵🏵 This small, well-designed boutique hotel is the newest property in Punta del Este. It opened just before Christmas in 2006, and it instantly booked up fully through its first season. The building has clean lines—a sort of 1950s interpretation of Alpine architecture, set on a landscaped hill with soaring pine trees. Its lobby is modern yet inviting, with polished concrete floors and teak walkways, and a large window overlooks the front garden. Rooms are a good size, set in pure radiant white, with African-made cotton wall-to-wall carpeting in neutral tones. Furnishings are stark ebonies, made in Italy with simple lines, giving the rooms what co-owner Analia Suarez calls a "zen" mood. Little touches include table lamps with swiveling shades that make them double as work spaces. Bathrooms are large and come with Gilchrist & Soames amenities, and the suites have hydro-massage tubs. Within the lobby and restaurant, this same multifunction idea comes out in the tables, which pivot up to become laptop work spaces, once you've finished having a drink with friends or eating breakfast. One of the most amazing things about the hotel is its theatre. If you want to watch a movie, you can certainly do so in your room, but why not come down to the small built-in theater and watch it on a big screen, in surround-sound, in a leather lounge chair? The owners say it's the only thing of its kind in a South American boutique hotel. The lobby restaurant is open for breakfast, lunch, and dinner, with a light international menu, and an emphasis on designer sandwiches. Rooms and public areas have Wi-Fi, and the business center has a terminal open 24 hours. The back garden is home to an outdoor heated pool, with a teakwood deck for suntanning. The hotel is a bit of a walk from the beach, but it's surrounded by several restaurants, and it's close to the Punta Shopping Mall. A small 80-person convention center rounds out the offerings.

Pedragosa Sierra and San Ciro; CP 20100, Punta del Este. © 042/499999. www.awahotel.com. 48 units, including 4 suites and 8 executive corner oversize rooms. In low season from $110 (£61) double; from $210 (£116) suite; high season from $265 (£146) double, from $530 (£292) suite. Rates include buffet breakfast. AE, DC, MC, V. Free on-site parking. **Amenities:** Restaurant; heated outdoor pool; small health club; spa; concierge; business center; room service; massage service; laundry service; dry cleaning; mini-theater; Wi-Fi in lobby. *In room:* A/C, TV, Wi-Fi, minibar, hair dryer, safe.

The Conrad Hotel and Casino 🏵🏵🏵 I can't say enough about this enormous, 14-story complex—a blue streamlined structure dominating the scene within Punta del Este. Upon its opening in the mid-'90s, it became the defacto town center. Rooms come in a variety of layouts and designs. Some have a California vibe, with casual decor in terra cottas and neutral tones; others are modern and more severe; and others have a tropical playfulness to them. All rooms facing the Río de la Plata have balconies, and the suites have balconies enormous enough for entertaining several guests, which is common in the summertime. Select suites also have kitchens, making them either ideal for corporate entertaining or long-term stays if you have the budget. Rooms in the back of the complex have views of the city and the Atlantic beyond but do not have balconies. All rooms have high-speed Internet access and robes. There are several restaurants in the lobby and other areas of the hotel. **St. Tropez** is open for lunch and dinner with fine dining. **Las Brisas** is more casual and international, with meat as the emphasis; it has a view to the Río de la Plata and the Rambla. Many people meet for sandwiches, snacks, or just drinks at **Los Veleros,** the lounge just off the lobby. **Gaucho's** is the name of the pool restaurant and bar, outside on the second floor terrace, where people gather for drinks, grilled meat, and light snacks. The pool and spa complex is a combination of indoor and outdoor spaces, with a view to the Río de la Plata. Built over the casino, it maintains a garden feel, with landscaping, grass, and paved walkways. In summer season, you might catch a few stars sunbathing here, hoping to be recognized. A heated indoor pool is also part of the complex, with a spacious gym and sauna offering several treatments and exercise programs. Here on this level is also the Children's Complex, where you can leave your kids and gain some free time. The 24-hour casino has 450 slot machines and 63 gaming tables; it's definitely worth visiting even if you're not staying here. (During your time in Punta, you'll likely hear "meet me at the Conrad" more than once.) If you *are* staying here, with so many things to do, you might even forget about the city around you. A convention center and theater complex round out some of the other offerings on the premises, with lots of shows and modeling events in the summer season; they're among the best in South America. Two rooms are equipped for special-needs travelers.

Parada 4 on Rambla Claudio Williman (between Chivert and Biarritz on Playa Mansa), CP 20100, Punta del Este. (C) 042/491111. Fax 042/490803. www.conrad.com.uy. 302 units, including 24 suites. In low season from $180 (£99) double; from $400 (£220) suite; high season from $340 (£187) double, from $500 (£275) suite with $7,500 (£4,125) for Conrad suite. Rates can fluctuate drastically within various date ranges. Rates include luxurious buffet breakfast. AE, DC, MC, V. **Amenities:** 5 restaurants; several bars; indoor and outdoor heated pools; large health club; spa; children's center; concierge; business center; shopping arcade; 24-hr. room service; massage service; babysitting; laundry service; dry cleaning; 24-hr. casino; theater and show complex; Wi-Fi in lobby. *In room:* A/C, TV, high-speed Internet access, kitchens in select suites, minibar, hair dryer, safe.

WHERE TO DINE

El Viejo Marino ✦ SEAFOOD/PARRILLA   This charming seafood restaurant and *parrilla* has a strong sailor theme. The smiling friendly waitresses all wear dresses inspired by sailor unforms. The dark interior mimics a ship, with navy-blue walls, dark woods, rope-back chairs, and old marine equipment scattered about. The menu has interesting combinations, such as sole cooked with Roquefort or mozzarella, several varieties of salmon, and catches of the day, much of it from the Río de la Plata. A standout specialty is Paella Viejo Marino—made with a variety of fish and other ingredients. Those who don't want fish can choose from plenty of grill options. A covered outdoor seating area is in front.

Calle 11 at Calle 14. (C) 042/443565. Main courses $11–$26 (£6.05–£14). AE, MC, V. Daily noon–3pm and 8pm–2am (in summer, if busy, they will remain open between lunch and dinner).

Lo de Tere ✦ INTERNATIONAL   Overlooking the yacht-filled port, this elegant but casual restaurant is a good choice. The menu includes fish, *parrilla,* pasta, and sandwiches named for celebrities (including the hunky beef sandwich called the Brad Pitt). A very large wine selection complements the food offerings. It's very often busy, with long lines stretching out the door.

Rambla de Puerto at Calle 21. ℂ 042/440492. www.lodetere.com. Main courses $8–$30 (£4.40–£17). AE, DC, MC, V. Daily noon–4pm and 8pm–1 or 2am.

Mika Restaurant—Espacio Torreón ✿ INTERNATIONAL   *Mika* means happy in the Spanish Basque dialect, and you'll certainly feel that way when you see the view from this revolving restaurant on the 22nd floor of the Espacio Torreón. There are few items on the menu, but they can be elaborate, with flavors ranging from sweet to salty to tangy. Leonardo, one of the chefs, recommended the Uruguayan lamb cooked with smoked sweet potatoes, followed by a dessert which combines pears and Roquefort cheese, which he calls a "harmonic combination." The restaurant is only open for dinner. Tea and drinks are served before dinner starts, beginning at 6:30pm. Around midnight, part of the restaurant transforms into a nightclub. Admission is free if you came for dinner; if not, it's $10 (£5.50). Expect the a la carte meals to run about $50 (£28) a person, when all is said and done. On a clear day, the view extends to almost 40km (25 miles) from Punta del Este. It's simply stunning—but then that's the point.

Edificio Torreón on Rambla Claudio Williman at Parada 1. ℂ 042/494949. www.espaciotorreon.com. Main courses $23–$33 (£13–£18). AE, DC, MC, V. Daily 9:30pm–1:30am; daily from 6:30pm for drinks; from midnight as a disco until 5am. Reservations required.

SHOPPING IN PUNTA

Shopping can be a major after-beach sport in Punta. The majority of shops run along Avenida Gorlero and Calle 20, also known as El Remanso or the Little Paris. Shop hours vary considerably from winter to summer, and many stores do not open until the evening, after most of their potential customers leave the beach. For leather goods, try **Leather Corner,** Calle 31 at Inzaurraga and Gorlero (ℂ 042/441901). **Duo,** Calle 20 at Calle 30 (ℂ 042/447709), is an upscale sportswear store for men and women, with a large selection of Diesel clothes. **100% Uruguayo,** Gorlero 883 at Calle 28 (ℂ 042/446530), has a large collection of handmade and distinctive locally produced goods; leather is the highlight. **Punta Shopping** is the main mall, with dozens of shops, along the wide pine-tree-lined boulevard Avenida Roosevelt, a few kilometers from the main part of town in the Playa Mansa area (Av. Roosevelt at Parada 7; ℂ 042/489666; www.puntashopping.com.uy). **Plaza Artigas,** at Gorlero and Arrecifes, has a daily artist market with souvenirs and crafts. The town of La Barra is better known for its art galleries, including the popular **Trench Gallery,** Ruta 10, Km 161, Parada 45 (ℂ 042/771597; www.trenchgallery.com). Gallery Night is every Friday in the summer in La Barra, when all the galleries have wine tastings.

6 Colonia del Sacramento, Uruguay

140km (87 miles) W of Buenos Aires

The tiny gem of Colonia del Sacramento, declared a World Heritage Site by UNESCO, appears untouched by time. Dating from the 17th century, the old city boasts beautifully preserved colonial artistry down its dusty streets. A leisurely stroll into the **Barrio Histórico (Historic Neighborhood)** leads you under flower-laden windowsills to churches dating from the 1680s, past simple single-story homes from Colonia's time as a Portuguese settlement, and on to local museums detailing the riches of the town's past. The Barrio Histórico contains brilliant examples of colonial wealth and many of Uruguay's oldest structures. A mix of lovely shops and delicious cafes makes the town more than a history lesson.

ESSENTIALS
GETTING THERE

The easiest way to reach Colonia from Buenos Aires is by **ferry. FerryLíneas** (© 02/ **900-6617**) runs a fast boat that arrives in 45 minutes. **Buquebús** (© **02/916-1910**) also offers two classes of service. Prices range from $18 to $40 (£9.90–£22) each way. A new ferryboat and bus combination service opened in 2006 to compete with what had been a monopoly for Buquebús. **Colonia Express** (in Buenos Aires © **54/11/ 4313-5100;** in Montevideo © 02/901-9597; www.coloniaexpress.com) offers similar prices but a less frequent schedule.

Colonia is a good stopping-off point if you're traveling between Buenos Aires and Montevideo. **COT** (© **02/409-4949** in Montevideo) offers **bus service** from Montevideo and from Punta del Este.

VISITOR INFORMATION

The **Oficina de Turismo,** General Flores and Rivera (© **052/27000** or 052/27300), is open daily from 8am to 8pm. Speak with someone at the tourism office to arrange a guided tour of the town.

WHAT TO SEE & DO
A WALK THROUGH COLONIA'S BARRIO HISTORICO

Your visit to Colonia will be concentrated in the **Barrio Histórico (Old Neighborhood),** located on the coast at the far southwestern corner of town. The sites, which are all within a few blocks of each other, can easily be visited on foot within a few hours. Museums and tourist sites are open Thursday through Monday from 11:30am to 5:45pm. For less than $1 (55p), you can buy a pass at the Portuguese or municipal museums, which will get you into all the sites.

Start your tour at **Plaza Mayor,** the principal square that served as the center of the colonial establishment. To explore Colonia's Portuguese history, cross the Calle Manuel Lobo on the southeastern side of the plaza and enter the **Museo Portugués (Portuguese Museum),** which exhibits European customs and traditions that influenced the town's beginnings. Upon exiting the museum, turn left and walk to the **Iglesia Matriz,** among the oldest churches in the country and an excellent example of 17th-century architecture and design.

Next, exit the church and turn left to the **Ruinas Convento San Francisco (San Francisco convent ruins).** Dating from 1696, the San Francisco convent was once inhabited by Jesuit and Franciscan monks, two brotherhoods dedicated to preaching the gospel to indigenous people. Continue up Calle San Francisco to the **Casa de Brown (Brown House),** which houses the **Museo Municipal (Municipal Museum).** Here, you will find an impressive collection of colonial documents and artifacts, a must-see for history buffs.

For those with a more artistic bent, turn left on Calle Misiones de los Tapes and walk 2 blocks to the **Museo del Azulejo (Tile Museum),** a unique museum of 19th-century European and Uruguayan tiles housed in a gorgeous 300-year-old country house. Then stroll back into the center of town along Calle de la Playa, enjoying the shops and cafes along the way, until you come to the **Ruinas Casa del Gobernador (House of the Viceroy ruins).** The House of the Viceroy captures something of the city's 17th- and 18th-century magistrates, when the port was used for imports, exports, and smuggling. Complete your walk with a visit to the **UNESCO–Colonia** headquarters, where exhibits on the city's newly acquired Historic Heritage of Humanity status will place your tour in the larger context of South American history.

WHERE TO STAY & DINE

Few people stay in Colonia, preferring to make a day trip from Buenos Aires or stop along the way to Montevideo. If you'd rather get a hotel, however, your best bets are the colonial-style **Hotel Plaza Mayor,** Calle del Comercio 111 (© 052/23193), and **Hotel La Misión,** Calle Misiones de los Tapes 171 (© 052/26767), whose original building dates from 1762. Both hotels charge from $80 (£44) for a double. A small **Sheraton** recently opened in the heart of Colonia (Continuación de la Rambla de Las Américas s/n; © 052/29000). The **Four Seasons** operates a luxury resort in nearby Carmelo, about 45 minutes away (Ruta 21, Km 262, Carmelo, Uruguay; © 0542/9000). For dining, **Mesón de la Plaza,** Vasconcellos 153 (© 052/24807), serves quality international and Uruguayan food in a colonial setting. **Pulpería de los Faroles,** Calle Misiones de los Tapes 101 (© 052/25399), in front of Plaza Mayor, specializes in beef and bean dishes and homemade pasta.

7 Montevideo, Uruguay

215km (133 miles) E of Buenos Aires

Montevideo, the southernmost capital on the continent, along with its suburbs, is home to half of Uruguay's population of 3 million people. On the banks of the Río de la Plata, Montevideo first existed as a fortress of the Spanish empire and developed into a major port city in the mid-18th century. European immigrants—including Spanish, Portuguese, French, and British—influenced the city's architecture. A walk around the capital reveals architectural styles ranging from colonial to Art Deco. Indeed, the richness of Montevideo's architecture is unrivaled in South America.

Although Montevideo has few must-see attractions, its charm lies in wait for the observant traveler. A walk along La Rambla, stretching from the Old City to the neighborhood of Carrasco, takes you along the riverfront past fishermen and their catch to parks and gardens where children play and elders sip *mate* (a tealike beverage). Restaurants, cafes, bars, and street performers populate the port area, where you will also discover the flavors of Uruguay at the afternoon and weekend Mercado del Puerto (Port Market). Many of the city's historic sites surround Plaza Independencia and can be visited in a few hours.

ESSENTIALS
GETTING THERE

International flights and those from Buenos Aires land at **Carrasco International Airport** (© 02/604-0386), located 19km (12 miles) from downtown Montevideo. Uruguay's national carrier is **Pluna,** Colonia and Julio Herrera (© 0800/118-811 or 02/604-4080), which operates several flights daily from Aeroparque. **Aerolíneas Argentinas** (© 02/901-9466) connects both Aeroparque and Ezeiza with Montevideo; the flight takes 50 minutes. The fare ranges between $150 and $250 (£83–£140) round-trip, depending on how far in advance you make reservations.

A taxi or *remise* (private, unmetered taxi) from the airport to downtown costs about $15 (£8.25).

BY BOAT OR HYDROFOIL The most popular way to get to Montevideo is by ferry. **Buquebús,** Calle Río Negro 1400 (© 02/916-8801), operates three to four hydrofoils per day from Buenos Aires; the trip takes about 2½ hours and costs about $110 (£61) round-trip. Montevideo's port is about 1.5km (1 mile) from downtown.

BY BUS   **Terminal Omnibus Tres Cruces,** General Artigas 1825 (© **02/409-7399 or 02/401-8998**), is Montevideo's long-distance bus terminal, connecting the capital with cities in Uruguay and throughout South America. Buses to Buenos Aires take about 8 hours. **COT** (© **02/409-4949**) offers the best service to Punta del Este, Maldonado, and Colonia.

ORIENTATION

Montevideo is surrounded by water on three sides, a testament to its earlier incarnation as an easily defended fortress for the Spanish empire. The Old City begins near the western edge of Montevideo, found on the skinny portion of a peninsula between the Rambla Gran Bretaña and the city's main artery, Avenida 18 de Julio. Look for Plaza Independencia and Plaza Constitución to find the center of the district. Many of the city's museums, theaters, and hotels reside in this historic area, although a trip east on Avenida 18 de Julio reveals the more modern Montevideo with its own share of hotels, markets, and monuments. Along the city's long southern coastline runs the Rambla Gran Bretaña, traveling 21km (13 miles) from the piers of the Old City past Parque Rodó and on to points south and east, passing fish stalls and street performers along the way.

GETTING AROUND

It's easy to navigate around the center of Montevideo on foot or by bus. Safe, convenient buses crisscross Montevideo, making it easy to venture outside the city center, for 15 Uruguayan pesos (about 60¢/35p). Taxis are safe and relatively inexpensive, but it can be difficult to hail one during rush hour. I recommend calling **Remises Carrasco** (© **09/440-5473**). To rent a car, try **Thrifty** (© **02/204-3373**). For roadside emergencies or general information on driving in Uruguay, contact the **Automóvil Club de Uruguay,** Av. Libertador 1532 (© **02/902-4792**), or the **Centro Automovilista del Uruguay,** E. V. Haedo 2378 (© **02/408-2091**).

VISITOR INFORMATION

Uruguay's **Ministerio de Turismo** is at Av. Libertador 1409, corner of Colonia (© **02/908-9105**). It assists travelers with countrywide information, and it's open daily from 8am to 8pm in winter, from 8am to 2pm in summer. There's also a branch at Carrasco International Airport and Tres Cruces bus station. The **municipal tourist office,** Explanada Municipal (© **1950**), offers city maps and brochures of tourist activities. It's open weekdays from 11am to 6pm, and weekends from 10am to 6pm. It also organizes cultural city tours on weekends. In the event of an emergency, the **Tourist Police** can be reached at (© **0800-8226**), and their office is at Colonia 1021.

TOUR COMPANIES

In business for more than 50 years, **Buemes Travel Services,** Colonia 979 (© **02/ 902-1050**), is among the largest full-service tour companies in Uruguay. Much of their business involves planning trips and tours for passengers coming into Montevideo by cruise ship. Contact them for day trips or history tours on various themes or for booking hotels and airline flights. They also arrange trips to other parts of Uruguay, including Colonia, Punta del Este, and the range of *estancias* near Montevideo that only a few foreigners have discovered. Private docent **Tamara Levinson**

Montevideo

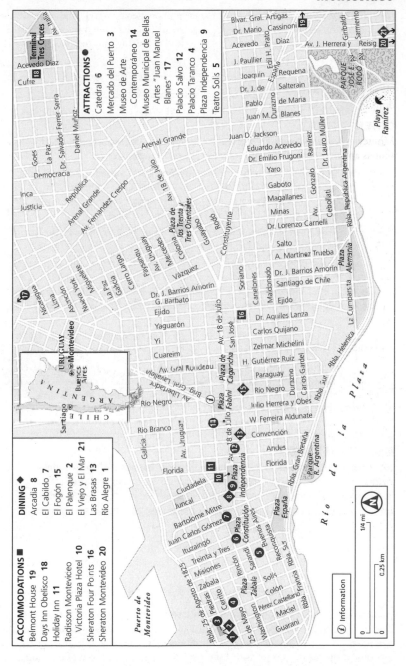

ATTRACTIONS ●

Catedral **6**
Mercado del Puerto **3**
Museo de Arte
Contemporáneo **14**
Museo Municipal de Bellas
Artes "Juan Manuel
Blanes" **17**
Palacio Salvo **12**
Palacio Taranco **4**
Plaza Independencia **9**
Teatro Solís **5**

ACCOMMODATIONS ■

Belmont House **19**
Days Inn Obelisco **18**
Holiday Inn **11**
Radisson Montevideo
Victoria Plaza Hotel **10**
Sheraton Four Points **16**
Sheraton Montevideo **20**

DINING ◆

Arcadia **8**
El Cabildo **7**
El Fogón **15**
El Palenque **2**
El Viejo y El Mar **21**
Las Brasas **13**
Río Alegre **1**

ⓘ **Information**

(© 02/710-3312 or 099/696-6518; tamaral@montevideo.com.uy) conducts individual custom tours of Montevideo and other parts of Uruguay. She works for Buemes, but visitors can hire her, in her spare time, to lead individualized travel experiences.

FAST FACTS: Montevideo

Area Code The country code for Uruguay is **598**; the city code for Montevideo is **2**.

ATMs ATMs are plentiful; look for **Bancomat** and **Redbrou** banks. Most have access to the Cirrus network. The Plus system is harder to find.

Currency Exchange To exchange money, try **Turisport Limitada** (the local Amex representative), San José 930 (© **02/902-0829**); **Gales Casa Cambiaria**, Av. 18 de Julio 1046 (© **02/902-0229**); or one of the airport exchanges. About 24 Uruguayan pesos equaled US$1 at the time of this writing.

Hospital The **British Hospital** is located at Av. Italia 2420 (© **02/487-1020**) and has emergency room services.

Internet Access Internet cafes appear and disappear faster than discos, but you won't walk long before coming across one in the city center. Reliable cybercafes include **El Cybercafé**, Calle 25 de Mayo 568; **Arroba del Sur**, Guayabo 1858; and **El Cybercafé Softec**, Santiago de Chile 1286. The average cost is $2 (£1.10) per hour of usage.

Post Office The main post office is at Calle Buenos Aires 451 (© **0810/444-CORREO**), open weekdays from 9am to 6pm.

Safety Although Montevideo remains very safe by big city standards, street crime has risen in recent years. Travelers should avoid walking alone, particularly at night, in Ciudad Vieja, Avenida 18 de Julio, Plaza Independencia, and the port vicinity. Take a taxi instead.

WHAT TO SEE & DO

Catedral ☆ Also known as Iglesia Matriz, the cathedral was the city's first public building, erected in 1804. It houses the remains of some of Uruguay's most important political, religious, and economic figures, and it's distinguished by its domed bell towers.

Calle Sarandí at Ituzaingó, overlooking Plaza Constitucion. Free admission. Mon–Fri 8am–8pm.

El Cabildo (Town Hall) ☆ Uruguay's constitution was signed in the old town hall, which also served as the city's jailhouse in the 19th century. Now a museum, the Cabildo houses the city's historic archives, as well as maps and photos, antiques, costumes, and artwork.

Juan Carlos Gómez 1362, overlooking Plaza Constitucion. © **02/915-9685**. Free admission. Tues–Sun 2:30–7pm.

Museo de Arte Contemporáneo (Museum of Contemporary Art) ☆ Opened in 1997, this museum is dedicated to contemporary Uruguayan art, and it exhibits the country's biggest names. To promote cultural exchange across the region, a section of the museum is set aside for artists who hail from various South American countries.

Av. 18 de Julio 965, 2nd floor. © **02/900-6662**. Free admission. Daily noon–8pm.

Museo Municipal de Bellas Artes "Juan Manuel Blanes" (Municipal Museum of Fine Arts) 𝒜 The national art history museum displays Uruguayan artistic styles from the nation's inception to the present day. Works include oils, engravings, drawings, sculptures, and documents. Among the great Uruguayan artists exhibited are Juan Manuel Blanes, Pedro Figari, Rafael Barradas, José Cúneo, and Carlos Gonzales.

Av. Millán 4015. ℂ 02/336-2248. Free admission. Tues–Sun 2–7pm.

Palacio Salvo 𝒜 Often referred to as the symbol of Montevideo, the Salvo Palace was once the tallest building in South America. Although its 26 stories might not impress you, it was once the city's tallest structure. It was the work of eccentric Italian architect Mario Palanti, who also designed the very similar structure Palacio Barolo on Buenos Aires's Avenida de Mayo.

Plaza Independencia.

Palacio Taranco 𝒜 Now the decorative arts museum, the Taranco Palace was built in the early 20th century and represents the trend toward French architecture during that period. The museum displays Uruguayan furniture, draperies, clocks, paintings, and other cultural works.

Calle 25 de Mayo 379. ℂ 02/915-1101. Free admission. Tues–Sat 10am–6pm.

Plaza Independencia 𝒜𝒜 Originally the site of a Spanish citadel, Independence Square marks the beginning of the Old City, and it's a good point from which to begin your tour of Montevideo. Only one gate to the old fortress remains on the Plaza. An enormous statue of Gen. José Gervasio Artigas, father of Uruguay and hero of its independence movement, stands in the center. His ashes are displayed in a mausoleum underground beneath the monument. It's a severe, modern structure with eerie lighting reminiscent of a horror movie. A changing-of-the-guards ceremony takes place every few hours. You'd be lucky to catch it.

Bordered by Av. 18 de Julio, Florida, and Juncal.

Teatro Solís 𝒜𝒜 Montevideo's main theater and opera house, opened in 1852, underwent an extensive renovation a few years back. It hosts Uruguay's most important cultural events, and it's the site of the **Museo Nacional de Historia Natural (National Museum of Natural History).** While the structure on its outside remains historical, the interior is a thoroughly modern contrast.

Calle Buenos Aires 652. ℂ 02/916-0908. Free admission. Museum Mon–Fri 2–6pm.

SHOPPING

The **Villa Biarritz fair,** at Parque Zorilla de San Martín-Ellauri, takes place Saturday from 9:30am to 3pm, featuring handicrafts, antiques, books, fruit and vegetable vendors, flowers, and other goodies. The **Mercado del Puerto (Port Market)** 𝒜 opens afternoons and weekends at Piedras and Yacaré, letting you sample the flavors of Uruguay, from small empanadas to enormous barbecued meats. Saturday is the best day to visit. **Tristán Narvaja,** Avenida 18 de Julio in the Cordón neighborhood, is the city's Sunday flea market (6am–3pm), initiated more than 55 years ago by Italian immigrants. **De la Abundancia/Artesanos** is a food-and-handicrafts market. It takes place Monday through Saturday from 10am to 8pm at San José 1312. Leather goods at great prices are at **Casa Mario Leather Factory**, Piedras 641 at Bartolomo Mitre

(© 02/916-2356; www.casamarioleather.com). **Tres Cruces Shopping Mall** is part of the bus terminal complex, with dozens of shops. It's at Avenida Serra with Acevedo Diaz (© **02/408 8710;** www.trescruces.com.uy).

WHERE TO STAY

Parking is included in the rates of most Uruguay hotels. In 2005, Montevideo repealed its hotel tax for foreigners. (Locals still pay this.)

EXPENSIVE

Belmont House ★★ *(Finds*   A boutique hotel in Montevideo's peaceful Carrasco neighborhood, Belmont House offers its privileged guests intimacy and luxury. Small elegant spaces with carefully chosen antiques and wood furnishings give this hotel the feeling of a wealthy private home. Beautiful guest rooms feature two- or four-poster beds; rich, colorful linens; and marble bathrooms with small details such as towel warmers and deluxe toiletries. Many of the rooms feature balconies overlooking the pretty courtyard and pool, and two of the rooms have Jacuzzis. Belmont House is a skip and a jump away from the beach, golf, and tennis. Gourmands will find an excellent international restaurant, afternoon tea, and a *parrilla* open weekends next to the pool. The gracious staff assists guests with outdoor activities and local itineraries.

Av. Rivera 6512, 11500 Montevideo. © **02/600-0430.** Fax 02/600-8609. www.belmonthouse.com.uy. 28 units. $160 (£88) double; from $186 (£102) suite. Rates include gourmet breakfast. AE, DC, MC, V. **Amenities:** Restaurant; tearoom; bar; beautiful outdoor pool; discounts for tennis and golf; small fitness center; sauna; business center; babysitting; laundry service; dry cleaning. *In room:* A/C, TV, minibar, hair dryer.

Radisson Montevideo Victoria Plaza Hotel ★★   The Victoria Plaza has long been one of Montevideo's top hotels. Standing in the heart of the financial district, this European-style hotel makes a good base from which to do business or explore the capital. Its convention center and casino also make it the center of the city's business and social activity. Ask for a room in the new tower, built in 1995, which houses spacious guest rooms and executive suites with classic French-style furnishings and panoramic city or river views. The busy hotel has a large multilingual staff that attends closely to guests' needs. Inquire about weekend spa packages. Plaza Victoria is famous for its casino, with French roulette tables, blackjack, baccarat, slot machines, horse races, and bingo. There are two lobby bars, in addition to the casino bars. **Arcadia** (p. 182), on the 25th floor, is the city's most elegant dining room.

Plaza Independencia 759, 11100 Montevideo. © **02/902-0111.** Fax 02/902-1628. www.radisson.com/montevideouy. 254 units. $175 (£96) double; from $210 (£116) suite. Rates include breakfast at rooftop restaurant. AE, DC, MC, V. **Amenities:** Restaurant; cafe; 2 bars; excellent health club w/skylit indoor pool; fitness center; aerobics classes; Jacuzzi; sauna; concierge; travel agency; business center w/high-speed Internet access; room service; massage service; laundry service; dry cleaning; executive floors. *In room:* A/C, TV, dataport, minibar, hair dryer, safe.

Sheraton Montevideo ★★   Opened in 1999, the Sheraton Montevideo has replaced Plaza Victoria as Montevideo's most luxurious hotel. A walkway connects the hotel to the Punta Carretas Shopping Center, one of the city's best malls. Spacious guest rooms have imported furniture, king-size beds, sleeper chairs, marble bathrooms, 25-inch televisions, and works by Uruguayan artists. Choose among views of the Río de la Plata, Uruguay Golf Club, or downtown Montevideo; views from the 20th through 24th floors are the most impressive. Rooms on the top two executive floors feature Jacuzzis and individual sound systems. Hotel service is excellent, particularly for guests with business needs. The main restaurant, Las Carretas, serves Continental cuisine with a Mediterranean flair. Don't miss the dining room's spectacular murals by contemporary Uruguayan artist Carlos Vilaro. Next door, the lobby bar is a popular spot for casual business meetings and afternoon cocktails.

Calle Víctor Soliño 349, 11300 Montevideo. © **02/710-2121.** Fax 02/712-1262. www.sheraton.com. 207 units. From $200 (£110) double; from $230 (£127) suite. Rates include buffet breakfast. AE, DC, MC, V. **Amenities:** Restaurant; bar; indoor pool; deluxe health club w/fitness center; sauna; concierge; car-rental desk; business center and secretarial services; room service; massage service; babysitting; laundry service; dry cleaning; executive floors; emergency medical service. *In room:* A/C, TV, dataport, minibar, hair dryer, safe.

MODERATE

Holiday Inn ⭐ This colorful Holiday Inn is actually one of the city's best hotels, popular both with tourists and business travelers. It's in the heart of downtown, next to Montevideo's main square. Bilingual staff members greet you in the marble lobby, which is attached to a good restaurant and bar. Guest rooms have simple, contemporary furnishings typical of an American chain. Because the hotel doubles as a convention center, it can become very busy. On the flip side, rooms are heavily discounted when the hotel is empty; be sure to ask for promotional rates, which can be as low as $50 (£28) per night.

Colonia 823, 11100 Montevideo. © **02/902-0001.** Fax 02/902-1242. www.holidayinn.com.uy. 137 units. From $90 (£50) double. Rates include buffet breakfast. AE, DC, MC, V. **Amenities:** Restaurant; bar; heated indoor pool; fitness center; sauna; business center; room service; laundry service; dry cleaning; Wi-Fi in public areas. *In room:* A/C, TV, Internet, minibar, safe.

Sheraton Four Points Montevideo ⭐⭐ Opened in 2005, the Sheraton Four Points is the newest of Montevideo's international hotels. It's considered a four-star property, but it falls somewhere between four and five, save for its smaller size. Whether you are on business dealing with the government, or visiting downtown as a tourist, the location across the street from city hall is convenient. The lobby is stark and modern, with polished black-granite panels over white walls in the soaring atrium. Walkways open on to the atrium on each floor, all connected by a glass elevator. Rooms are on the dark side, with charcoal carpeting, dark woods, and rust-colored bedspreads, giving a masculine feel overall. The bathrooms are spacious, however, and suite bathrooms have hydro-massage bathtubs. Select suites also have sofabeds in their second rooms. All rooms have high-speed Internet access, at a charge of $16 (£8.80) a day. The desks make a great work space. Very large TVs and stereos are part of the room's amenities. While small, the enclosed rooftop gym and spa has an unparalleled view of the city, and you'll also find the indoor heated pool more than adequate. There is a $5 (£2.75) charge for using these areas of the hotel. Breakfast is an additional $8 (£4.40) in the lobby's restaurant, which is also open for lunch and dinner, offering international cuisine. A small business center sits in the lobby with several computer terminals. Wi-Fi access is also available, all at the same price as an in-room connection. Parking is free. One room is available for the travelers with disabilities, and security is rigorous, with a camera system wrapped around the building.

Ejido 1275 at Soriano, across from the Intendencia or City Hall, 11000 Montevideo. © **02/901-7000.** Fax 02/903-2247. www.fourpoints.com/montevideo. 135 units, including 18 suites. From $120 (£66) double; from $200 (£110) suite. AE, DC, MC, V. Free parking. **Amenities:** Restaurant; bar; indoor pool; health club w/fitness center; sauna; concierge; business center; 24-hr. room service; babysitting; laundry service; dry cleaning. *In room:* A/C, TV, dataport, minibar, hair dryer, safe.

INEXPENSIVE

Days Inn Obelisco *(Value)*   This modern Days Inn caters to business travelers looking for good-value accommodations. The hotel is located next to the Tres Cruces bus station, not far from downtown or the airport. Rooms are comfortable and modern, if not overly spacious. Free local calls are permitted.

Acevedo Díaz 1821, 11800 Montevideo. © 02/400-4840. Fax 02/402-0229. www.daysinn.com. 60 units. From $45 (£25) double. Rates include buffet breakfast. AE, DC, MC, V. **Amenities:** Coffee shop; small health club; business center; room service. *In room:* A/C, TV, minibar, hair dryer.

WHERE TO DINE

Restaurants in Montevideo serve steak that's just as high in quality as Argentine beef, and they usually include a number of stews and seafood selections as well. You will find the native barbecue, in which beef and lamb are grilled on the fire, in any of the city's *parrilladas* (the name for *parrillas* in Uruguay). Sales tax on dining in Montevideo is a whopping 23%. There's also usually a table cover charge *(cubierto)* of about $1 (55p) per person.

MODERATE

Arcadia *(★★ (Moments)* INTERNATIONAL   Virgil and Homer wrote that Arcadia was a quiet paradise in ancient Greece; this elegant restaurant atop the Plaza Victoria is a quiet paradise and the best restaurant in Montevideo. Tables are nestled in semi-private nooks with floor-to-ceiling bay windows. The classic dining room is decorated with Italian curtains and crystal chandeliers; each table has a fresh rose and sterling silver place settings. Creative plates such as terrine of pheasant marinated in cognac are followed by grilled rack of lamb glazed with mint and garlic, or duck confit served on a thin strudel pastry with red cabbage.

Plaza Independencia 759. © 02/902-0111. Main courses $6–$11(£3.30–£6.05). AE, DC, MC, V. Daily 7pm–midnight.

El Fogón *(★* URUGUAYAN   This brightly lit *parrillada* and seafood restaurant is popular with Montevideo's late-night crowd. The extensive menu includes calamari, salmon, shrimp, and other fish, as well as generous steak and pasta dishes. Food here is priced well and prepared with care. The express lunch menu comes with steak or chicken, dessert, and a glass of wine.

San José 1080. © 02/900-0900. Main courses $6–$9 (£3.30–£4.95). AE, DC, MC, V. Daily noon–4pm and 7pm–1am.

El Palenque *(★* SEAFOOD/PARRILLADA   Located in the Mercado del Puerto, this is one of the area's most popular restaurants, crowded with locals and tourists alike. It gets especially crowded when the cruise ships come in. It has been around since 1958. Fish is the highlight, but they also have tapas, pastas, paellas, and lots of grilled meats. A specialty is the Paella Exotica made with rabbit.

Perez Castellano 1579 (at Rambla 25 de Agosto 400 in the Mercado del Puerto). © **02/917-0190** and 02/915-4704. www.elpalenque.com.uy. Main courses $6–$13 (£3.30–£7.15). AE, DC, MC, V. Daily noon–4pm and 8pm–1am.

El Viejo y el Mar *(★* SEAFOOD   Resembling an old fishing club, El Viejo y el Mar is on the riverfront near the Sheraton. The bar is made from an abandoned boat, while the dining room is decorated with dock lines, sea lamps, and pictures of 19th-century regattas. You'll find every kind of fish and pasta on the menu, and the restaurant is equally popular for evening cocktails. An outdoor patio is open most of the year.

Rambla Gandhi 400. © 02/710-5704. Main courses $5–$8 (£2.75–£4.40). MC, V. Daily noon–4pm and 8pm–1am.

Los Leños *Value* URUGUAYAN   Hillary Clinton once visited this restaurant; a picture of her with the staff hangs proudly on the wall. This casual *parrillada* resembles one you'd find in Buenos Aires—except that this one also serves an outstanding range of *mariscos* (seafood), such as the Spanish paella or *lenguado Las Brasas* (a flathead fish) served with prawns, mushrooms, and mashed potatoes. From the *parrilla*, the *filet de lomo* is the best cut—order it with Roquefort, mustard, or black-pepper sauce. The restaurant's fresh produce is displayed in a case near the kitchen.

San José 909. © **02/900-2285.** Main courses $5–$8 (£2.75–£4.40). AE, DC, MC, V. Daily 11:45am–3:30pm and 7:30pm–midnight.

INEXPENSIVE

Río Alegre *Value* SNACKS   This casual, inventive lunch stop specializes in quick steaks off the grill. Ribs, sausages, and most cuts of beef are cooked on the *parrilla*, made to order. Río Alegre is a local favorite because of its large portions, good quality, and cheap prices.

Calle Pérez Castellano and Piedras, at the Mercado del Puerto, Local 33. © **02/915-6504.** Main courses $2–$4 (£1.10–£2.20). No credit cards. Daily 11am–3pm.

MONTEVIDEO AFTER DARK

As in Buenos Aires, nightlife in Montevideo means drinks after 10pm and dancing after midnight. For earlier entertainment, ask at your hotel or call the **Teatro Solís,** Calle Buenos Aires 652 (© 02/916-0908), the city's center for opera, theater, ballets, and symphonies, for performance information. **SODRE,** Av. 18 de Julio 930 (© 02/901-2850), is the city's "Official Radio Service," which hosts classical music concerts from May to November. Gamblers should head to the **Plaza Victoria Casino,** Plaza Independencia (© 02/902-0111), a fashionable venue with French roulette tables, blackjack, baccarat, slot machines, horse races, and bingo. It opens at 2pm and keeps going through most of the night. **Mariachi,** Gabriel Pereira 2964 (© 02/709-1600), is one of the city's top bars and discos, with live bands or DJ music Wednesday to Sunday after 10pm. **Café Misterio,** Costa Rica 1700 (© 02/600-5999), is another popular bar. **New York,** Calle Mar Artico 1227 (© 02/600-0444), combines a restaurant, bar, and dance club under one roof and attracts a slightly older crowd. Montevideo's best tango clubs are **La Casa de Becho,** Nueva York 1415 (© 02/400-2717; Fri–Sat after 10:30pm), where composer Gerardo Mattos Rodríguez wrote the famous "La Cumparsita," and **Cuareim,** Zelmar Michelini 1079 (no phone; Wed and Fri–Sat after 9pm), which offers both tango and *candombe,* a lively dance indigenous to the area with its roots in early slave culture. The tourist office can give you schedule information for Montevideo's other tango salons.

8 San Antonio de Areco & Pampas Estancias

111km (69 miles) NW of Buenos Aires

San Antonio de Areco is a quiet little town about 90 minutes north of Buenos Aires, deep in the heart of Argentina's famous Pampas. The city is best known as the center for gaucho culture, Argentina's version of American cowboy tradition. Few people stay in San Antonio, choosing to visit it as a day trip from Buenos Aires, or as a base for exploring the nearby *estancias* that surround the town.

The city is compact, built in 1730 around an old colonial church dedicated to San Antonio of Padua, from which the town takes its name. Colonial and turn-of-the-20th-century buildings abound, all reached on walkable cobblestone streets that radiate from the church and Plaza Ruiz de Arellano, the town's main square. The Río Areco divides the town in two parts. Here along the river is a monument-lined green space called Parque San Martín, crossed by an old pedestrian bridge to Parque Criollo, where the city's most famous site, the Museo Gauchesco Ricardo Güiraldes, sits.

The city's main shopping streets are Alsina and Arellano, heading south from Plaza Arellano. It's a year-round tourism destination, but it lives for the annual **Día de la Tradición,** generally held around November 10. Gauchos real and wanna-be fill the town, playing gaucho games of skill such as the *sortija,* in which they catch rings from poles while riding horses, giving them as gifts to beautiful women in the audience. San Antonio doesn't have many hotels, and those it has fill up fast at this time of year. (Of course, there is always the gaucho's pad, if he hands you his *sortija* ring.) See also the section on *estancias,* below; all are within a short drive of the center of San Antonio.

ESSENTIALS

GETTING THERE   San Antonio de Areco can be reached by car from Buenos Aires by driving north along Ruta 8. The drive takes about an hour and a half. Most people come by bus, however. **Chevallier** offers hourly bus service from Buenos Aires's Retiro Bus depot (© **2326/453-904** in San Antonio, 11/4000-5255 in Buenos Aires, or 0800/222-6565 toll-free). The bus company **Pullman General Belgrano** (© **2326/454-059** in San Antonio, or 11/4315-6522 in Buenos Aires) provides less frequent service, also from Retiro Station in Buenos Aires.

VISITOR INFORMATION   The **Dirección de Turismo de San Antonio de Areco** tourism information center (© **2326/453-165;** www.pagosdeareco.com.ar) is in Parque San Martín along the Río Areco water front, near the intersection of Avenida Zerboni with Calle Zapiola and Calle Arellano. It is open 7 days a week from 8am to 8pm.

GETTING AROUND   Within San Antonio itself, your feet can take you most of the places you need to go. Even the most distant actual attraction, the Museo Gauchesco, is only a 15-minute walk from the center of town. Because many people use the town as a base for exploring other parts of the Pampas, such as the numerous *estancias, remises* are a must. Contact the 24-hour **Remis Zerboni,** Zerboni 313 near Alsina (© **2326/453-288**). The town is also great for bike riding; most hotels provide free bicycle loans.

WHAT TO SEE & DO

The center of San Antonio de Areco is the leafy **Plaza Arellano,** surrounded by cobblestone streets and overseen by a statue of Juan Hipólito Vieytes, a local involved in the Argentine war for independence from Spain. His memorial sits in an acoustic circle, so you'll have fun talking here, especially if you bring kids. The statue faces south to Mitre Street, staring at the church from which the town draws its name, **San Antonio de Padua,** rebuilt in the late 1800s over the original 1730 colonial version. Colonial on the outside, the interior mixes gothic and neoclassical styles with frescoes of angels and saints in niches on the walls, all overseen by a coffered ceiling. On the plaza's north side is the Belle Epoque **Municipal Hall,** a long pink building at Lavalle 363 with an attractive central courtyard. Nearby is the **Draghi Museum and Shop,** Lavalle 387 between Alsina and Arellano (© **2326/454-219;** daily approximately 10am–5pm, though technically by appointment only). It's owned by Juan Jose Draghi, a master silversmith who began his career more than 45 years ago, making ornamental items for gauchos. The material in the museum is in itself a work of art, with its exquisite stained-glass ceiling. The museum also has its own hotel (see below). A few blocks away, you can watch other silversmiths at work in the small **Artesano Platero,** Alsina at Zerboni, facing the Parque San Martín (© **2326/454-843,** or 2325/15-656-995 [cell]; www.arecoplateria.com.ar; daily 9:30am–12:30pm and 3–9pm).

From here, head to **Parque San Martín,** on the south side of the Río Areco. It's tree and monument lined, full of vine-covered walkways called *glorietas.* Families picnic, and kids play soccer or climb over the small dam constructed in the river. Two bridges cross the park here, but the most picturesque is the **Puente Viejo,** originally constructed in the 1850s as a toll crossing. The other end of the river has Parque Criollo, and here sits the city's most famous site, the **Museum of the Gaucho** (aka **Museo Ricardo Güiraldes,** in honor of the author of *Don Segundo Sombra*), Camino Ricardo Güiraldes at Sosa (© **2326/455-839;** Wed–Mon 11am–5pm). Written in 1926, the novel immortalized the noble gaucho, making him an honored part of Argentine history. The museum combines an authentic 1830 *pulpería,* or country general store, where gauchos gathered, with a museum designed in a colonial style by Argentine architect José María Bustillo in 1936. Here you will find the author's personal effects, photos, books, and other gaucho memorabilia. It's a bit kitschy (think rooms filled with gaucho mannequins), but if you speak Spanish, a conversation with the museum's guide and historian, Omar Tapia, will help you put the gauchos in their proper historical context.

EXCURSIONS TO SAN ANTONIO & *ESTANCIAS*

Various travel companies in Buenos Aires arrange day trips to San Antonio de Areco, with or without overnight stays on nearby *estancias.* **Borello Travel & Tours,** 7 Park Ave., Suite 21, New York, NY 10016 (© **800/405-3072** or 212/686-4911; www.borellotravel.com), is a New York–based travel firm specializing in upscale travel. They can include a visit to San Antonio with stays in the local *estancias.* They maintain an additional office in Buenos Aires (© 11/5031-1988). Buenos Aires–based **Say Hueque Tourism,** Viamonte 749, Office 601, 1053 Buenos Aires (© **11/5199-2517;** www.sayhueque.com), also provides trips to this area.

WHERE TO STAY

Draghi Paradores (★)   The Draghi Paradores is a small apartment hotel opened in 2006 behind the Draghi museum and store. It is the newest and one of the nicest of San Antonio's hotels, though it costs a few dollars more than its competitors. Built in a Spanish colonial style, the entrance is graced by a small pool and fountain in an enclosed courtyard. It looks a little like a miniature version of the *Melrose Place* apartment building, minus backstabbing blondes in high heels and miniskirts. The five rooms are clean with a country feel to them, with a rich use of woods, frilly white bedding, and terra-cotta tiles on the floor. All bathrooms are tub-and-shower combinations, and have ample space. Two of the rooms also come with small kitchens, making them ideal for families or for longer-term stays in San Antonio. All rooms are air-conditioned and have cable TV. Breakfast is included in the rate.

Lavalle 387 (between Alsina and Arellano), 2760 San Antonio de Areco. © 2326/455-583 or 02326/454-515. www.sanantoniodeareco.com/paradores. 5 units, including 2 with kitchens. From $53 (£29) per double, including breakfast. AE, DC, MC, V. Free parking. **Amenities:** Heated outdoor pool; free bicycle loans; concierge; limited room service; laundry service; dry cleaning. *In room:* A/C, TV, minibar, hair dryer, safe.

Hostal de Areco   This small family-style hotel is in an historical turn-of-the-20th-century red house, set back from the street and surrounded by a small garden. There are seven small, spartan, tile-floor rooms, each equipped with a full-size bed and a bathroom. Dark-green curtains and bedspreads give the rooms an even smaller appearance. The accommodations are very basic, with no air-conditioning and only a ceiling fan, but each comes with cable TV.

Zapioli 25 near the intersection of Zerboni, 2760 San Antonio de Areco. © **2326/456-118.** 7 units. From $30 (£17) per double, including breakfast. No credit cards. Free parking. **Amenities:** Free bicycle loans; concierge; laundry service. *In room:* TV.

Hotel San Carlos *&*   This motel-like hotel, overlooking the Parque San Martín, is the most businesslike hotel in town. It's also the only one with an Internet station and Wi-Fi in the lobby as well as some of the rooms (those nearest to the lobby, of course). You'll find a sun deck equipped with an *asado* grill, Jacuzzi, and two outdoor heated swimming pools in the courtyard, with a fountain decorated with a mosaic of San Antonio de Padua. (It's one of the few places in all of Argentina where you're likely to see bikini-clad women frolicking in front of religious icons, unless you belong to a particularly liberal church.) Some rooms are on the small side, but they're larger in the hotel's new wing. Many come with hydro-massage tubs or Jacuzzis in the bathrooms, and a few double bedroom apartments have kitchens. Breakfast, included in the rates, is served in the lobby. All the rooms have TV and air-conditioning, but only some have minibars.

Avenida Zerboni (on the west corner at the intersection of Zapiola), 2760 San Antonio de Areco. © **2326/456-119.** www.hotel-sancarlos.com.ar. 30 units (25 doubles, 5 apts). From $30 (£17) double; from $40 (£22) per apartment; includes breakfast. AE, MC, V. Free covered parking. **Amenities:** 2 heated outdoor pools; Jacuzzi; free bicycle rental; concierge; 24-hr. room service; laundry service; *asado* grill Internet station; Wi-Fi in lobby. *In room:* A/C, TV, Wi-Fi (select rooms), minibar (select rooms), hair dryer.

WHERE TO DINE

Almacén de Ramos Gerelos ARGENTINE/SPANISH   This is one of the best-known restaurants in San Antonio de Areco, with a *parrilla* and international items on the menu. It also offers a broad selection of paellas. The restaurant is in a turn-of-the-20th-century building. Its interior, with rich wooden details, will take you back in time.

Zapiola 143 at Segundo Sombra. No phone. Main courses $4–$8 (£2.20–£4.40). AE. Daily noon–3pm and 8–11pm.

Corner Pizza ARGENTINE/INTERNATIONAL   This simple place overlooks the Parque San Martín and the Río Areco. You'll find a selection of fast-food items on the menu, from hot dogs and hamburgers to pizza. Many people just come here to down a beer and look at the park. It's ideal if you're on a low budget.

Av. Zerboni at Alsina, overlooking Parque San Martín. No phone. Main courses $1–$2 (55p–£1.10). No credit cards. Daily 10am–11pm.

La Esquina de Merti *&* ARGENTINE   This restaurant has an old turn-of-the-20th-century feel to it, with exposed brick walls, an ancient copper coffeemaker on the bar, wooden tables overlaid with black-and-white-checkered tablecloths, and shelves full of apothecary jars. But it's all a trick: La Esquina de Merti just opened in December 2005, in the location of an old *almacén,* or Argentine general store. In any case, the food (primarily Argentine) is great. You'll find a beef and chicken *parrilla,* and a selection of pastas and empanadas. The house specialty is *mollejas* with cream, lemon, and champagne (*mollejas* are the pancreas or thymus of a cow, which might be worth trying for an only-in-Argentina experience). A large wine selection complements everything on the menu.

Arellano 147 at Segundo Sombra (overlooking Plaza Arellano). ⓒ 2326/456-705. Main courses $4–$8 (£2.20–£4.40). AE, V. Daily 9am–2am; until 3am Fri–Sat.

PAMPAS & *ESTANCIAS*

San Antonio is a popular base for exploring Argentina's famous *estancias*, which doubled historically as both farms and fortresses, built throughout the country along trails from Buenos Aires as a means of conquering and stabilizing territory originally controlled by the Indians. The majority of Argentina's *estancias* date from the middle to late 1800s. After General Roca's Campaign of the Desert in the 1870s, in which he murdered most of the Indian population within 150 miles of Buenos Aires, *estancia* culture, and the cattle and grain tended on them, flourished. Despite the bloody history that gave birth to them, today they're seen as a retreat from the chaos and stress of Buenos Aires. They are popular among Porteños on weekends or for day trips. With the increasing boom of tourism to Argentina, many foreigners are beginning to delight in them as well.

Most of the *estancias* listed here are a half-hour from San Antonio, and no more than 2 hours from Buenos Aires. You can drive to all of them on your own, or use a bus service from Buenos Aires to San Antonio and then catch a taxi from there. For a fee in the range of $50 (£28), almost all the estancias will also provide transportation from your hotel or the airport in Buenos Aires. Because many *estancias* are accessed by dirt roads, it is advisable to rent a 4WD vehicle, especially if rain is predicted during the time of your visit. The websites of the *estancias* listed here post detailed driving maps.

Services and features vary, but the atmosphere at most *estancias* is a cross between a rustic resort and a bed-and-breakfast. Nothing relieves stress like a day or a few in the country, and horseback riding, trekking, lounging by the pool, and eating and drinking aplenty are all part of a day's work in the Pampas. In general, the rates for *estancias* include a full board of four meals—breakfast, lunch, afternoon tea, and dinner—and sometimes all drinks including alcohol. Lunch, the highlight of a dining experience on an *estancia,* is usually an *asado* or barbecue where everyone, including the workers, gathers to socialize. Day rates generally include only lunch and limited activities. Most *estancias* are real working farms, with hundreds of acres and cows, horses, and other animals attended by real gauchos (not all of whom dress in the traditional way). If you're in the mood to milk a cow or watch the birth of colt, you just might have the chance.

El Cencerro ⓖⓖⓖ   Smaller, cozier, and more rustic than some of the other places listed here, this working *estancia* will make you feel like you're part of the farm's daily goings-on. It's owned by Buenos Aires–based psychologist Liliana Herbstein, who spends her weekends here. The ranch takes its name from the *cencerro,* a bell used by gauchos to tame horses. Rooms and public areas are filled with antiques and odd objects Liliana and her husband Eduardo have collected over the years, including antique luggage from Liliana's family's old store in Buenos Aires. Eduardo is an architect and artist whose work also hangs throughout the main house. Activities include horseback riding, helping with the animals if you want, carriage rides, bicycle rides, and trekking. Only 3km (2 miles) away is the historical Capilla del Señor, a charming town established in the early 1700s. You can walk or bike there on your own, or ask for optional guided tours. Similar to San Antonio de Areco in feel, it's virtually unknown to non-Argentines, and thus more authentic. Real gauchos wander the downtown, going about their business after a day tending cattle. Every second Tuesday of the month, the town has an animal auction, which Liliana attends with some of her guests. The area is also the center of Argentine ballooning, offered as an option for another $80 (£44). Four bedrooms, some with shared bath, are in the main house, where Liliana also spends her time, making you feel like a guest in her private home. By the end of 2007, they will have added four more rooms designed by Eduardo. One of the charms of this property is the wooded creek flowing through it; it makes a relaxing place for a nap, a picnic, or an afternoon spent reading or listening to the water and the cows in the distance. The property is 21 hectares (52 acres). You can access the *estancia* by bus from Buenos Aires to Capilla del Señor and then a $4 (£2.10) taxi ride. By *remise* from Buenos Aires, 80km (50 miles) away, it's about $45 (£24).

Buenos Aires Provincial Ruta 39; 2812 Capilla del Señor. ℂ **11/4743-2319** or 11/15-6093-2319 (in Buenos Aires). www.estanciaelcencerro.com.ar. 4 units. From $95 (£50) including all meals and some drinks; $45 (£24) day rate includes lunch. No credit cards. Free parking. **Amenities:** Outdoor pool; bicycles; game rooms; limited room service; laundry service; dry cleaning; bird-watching; carriage riding; horseback riding. *In room:* Ceiling fan.

El Ombú de Areco ✦✦✦   El Ombú takes its name from the tree that dominates the Pampas. It's among the most historic *estancias* near Buenos Aires. General Pablo Riccheri, an Italian military man who came to Argentina during the unification wars, built the original vine-covered house in 1880. The general atmosphere and the overgrown row of trees out front will remind you of a plantation in the Southern U.S. The rooms in the old house are best, with their high ceilings. But you really can't go wrong here; all the rooms have romantic appeal, decorated with brass beds, floral linens, and a strong country atmosphere. Now the house is owned by Eva Boelcke, whose family bought the property in 1934, and overseen by manager Patricia Bond. There are two pools, one in a small courtyard, another on the edge of the main garden with a fantastic view of the sun setting over horses in the fields. Several game rooms are on the grounds, with TVs, movies, and other activities, and it's easy to mingle with the very friendly staff. This is a working ranch, with 300 hectares (741 acres) of land and more than 400 cows and other animals. Patricia says, "What you see is what goes on," from horses giving birth to animal vaccinations. Horseback riding, carriage riding, bicycling, and many other activities are available, and all four meals and drinks are included in the rate. They also accept pets. Some rooms have hydro-massage tubs, or combination tub and showers. Rooms are not air-conditioned but they have ceiling fans. The estancia is about 10km (6 miles) from San Antonio and 120km (74 miles) from Buenos Aires. Their *remise* service costs $60 (£33) from Buenos Aires. A taxi from San Antonio de Areco is about $8 (£4.40).

Buenos Aires Provincial Ruta 31, Cuartel 6, 2760 San Antonio de Areco. ℂ **2326/492-080** or Buenos Aires ℂ 11/4737-0436. www.estanciaelombu.com. 9 units. From $140 (£77) single, $220 (£121) double, including all meals and drinks; $50 (£28) day rate includes lunch. AE, V. Free parking. **Amenities:** 2 outdoor pools; bicycles; game rooms; concierge; 24-hr. room service; babysitting; laundry service; carriage riding; horseback riding. *In room:* Ceiling fan, hair dryer.

El Rosario de Areco ✦✦✦   You'll quickly recognize the last name of English speaking Francisco and Florencia de Guevara, the owners of El Rosario de Areco. Francisco will just as quickly laugh and acknowledge his very distant relative Che, adding that he has "another ideological position." Unlike most *estancia* owners who live in Buenos Aires, Francisco and Florencia live year-round on their *estancia*, along with some of their nine children. This *estancia* is among the most pleasant to visit, with its barn red buildings and bougenvilleas scattered among the grounds. The *estancia* dates from 1892, but the rooms, many of which are in former horse stalls, have surprisingly modern interiors. The waitstaff is a little different here too. Instead of running around in gaucho outfits, they wear chic black uniforms, as if they popped in part-time from another job in Palermo Soho. The owners regularly greet guests, and Francisco tends the grill during the lunch *asado*. The public rooms and even some of the gardens have Wi-Fi, which is rare for an *estancia*. For now, they have 18 double rooms, all with large private bathrooms. Rooms are not air-conditioned, but they come with ceiling fans, and some rooms also have fireplaces. The owners are building a small hotel with 40 rooms on the 80-hectare (198-acre) grounds; it's set to open in early 2008. Presently, the property offers a small polo field, horseback riding, carriage riding, two pools, several public rooms with TVs, and other recreational activities such as pool and video games. The hotel is 7km (4⅓ miles) from San Antonio de Areco and 100km (62 miles) from Buenos Aires. From San Antonio, a taxi will run about $7 (£3.85), and the *estancia's remise* service is $50 (£28) from Buenos Aires. They accept only cash now, but they plan to take plastic by 2008.

Buenos Aires Provincial Ruta 41 (mailing address is Castilla de Correo 85), 2760 San Antonio de Areco. © 2326/451-000. www.rosariodeareco.com.ar. 18 units. From $150 (£83) per double, including all meals and drinks; $70 (£39) day rate includes lunch. No credit cards. Free parking. Amenities: 2 outdoor pools; bicycles; game room; concierge; limited room service; babysitting; laundry service; dry cleaning; carriage riding; horseback riding. *In room:* Ceiling fan, Wi-Fi (select rooms), hair dryer, safe, fireplace (select rooms).

La Bamba 🏵🏵🏵 This is one of the most gorgeous and romantic *estancias* near Buenos Aires, dating to 1830, when its original building opened as a stagecoach stop. The buildings are all painted a Pompeiian red with white trim, contrasting with the rich green landscape. The Argentine movie *Camila,* about a forbidden romance in the 1840s, was filmed here and nominated for Best Foreign Film in the 1984 Academy Awards. Rooms have brass beds with delft blue and/or white bedding. If you are in Argentina on a honeymoon, this place is an ideal choice—especially the isolated Torre Room in the main house, on the third floor, in what had been a lookout tower with windows on all sides opening onto the expansive Pampas. Or choose the master room, with its crowned and canopied bed, and furnishings that supposedly once belonged to Bernardino Rivadavia, Argentina's first president. Crosses and saints adorn all of the rooms. The very large and attentive staff constantly sees to your needs. The *estancia* was where the Bush twins stayed during their infamous romp through Argentina. Owner Isabel Aldao de Carcavallo lives in Buenos Aires, but she often comes by to share meals and chat with visitors. Swimming, horseback riding, carriage riding, trekking, and other activities are all available. For an additional fee, you can hire private guides. They also offer a massage service. All meals and alcohol are included with the fee, and lunch comes with the day rate. Patricia Foster, who looks a little like an Argentine Sigourney Weaver, oversees the 150-hectare (371-acre) property with cows, soy, and wheat fields for you to play around on. Some rooms are air-conditioned, and there is also an Internet station in one of the game rooms. The estancia is 13km (8 miles) from San Antonio, and 123km (76 miles) from Buenos Aires. A taxi from San Antonio is about $8 (£4.40), and a *remise* service from Buenos Aires is $55 (£30).

Buenos Aires Provincial Ruta 31, 2760 San Antonio de Areco. © 2326/456-293. www.la-bamba.com.ar. 12 units. $212–$350 (£117–£193) double, including all meals and drinks; $73 (£40) day rate includes lunch. AE, DC, MC. Free parking. Amenities: Outdoor pool; spa; bicycles; game rooms; concierge; limited room service; babysitting; laundry service; carriage riding; horseback riding; Internet. *In room:* A/C (select rooms), ceiling fan, hair dryer, safe.

6

Iguazú Falls & the Northeast

by Charlie O'Malley

"**A**wesome" is a word English speakers tend to overuse, but Iguazú Falls embodies the term in its fullest sense: In a spectacular subtropical setting, 23km (14 miles) of deafening waterfalls plummet up to 70m (229 ft.) into a giant gorge. The sheer power is overwhelming. You come face to face with raging sheets of water, with sprays so intense it seems as though geysers have erupted from below. Forget Niagara Falls (a mere toilet flush), forget Angel Falls (a faucet); think Grand Canyon with way too much water. Iguazú is a must-see on any trip to Argentina, and the well-run national park with howler monkeys and elusive pumas is another top national tourist draw.

It's shocking that this ecological blockbuster is 90 minutes from the civilized, cosmopolitan buzz of Buenos Aires. Many people drop into this humid corner of Misiones province on a day trip or for 2 days max. Yet this fascinating jungle zone of red soil, giant butterflies, and comical toucans has more to offer than jaw-dropping waterfalls. Misiones Province is a heady mix of strong indigenous tribal culture, blond eastern European settlers, and tropical frontierland. Its abundant wildlife and the mystery of its long-fallen Jesuit ruins are worth exploring. With its multitude of isolated national parks and huge swaths of untouched rainforest, it is an eco-tourist's paradise, with several genuine jungle lodges. Civilization has encroached in the form of tea plantations and pine forests, yet it is not too difficult to get off the beaten track and visit isolated wonders such as the stunning Mocona falls (a mere 3km/1¾ miles wide). Farther west of Misiones are the sprawling lowlands of El Chaco, a vast savannah of endless wetlands, cotton plantations, and sunflower prairies that could draw you as far as Bolivia.

1 Iguazú Falls & Puerto Iguazú

1,330km (825 miles) NE of Buenos Aires

A dazzling panorama of cascades whose power overwhelms the sounds of the surrounding jungle, Las Cataratas del Iguazú (Iguazú Falls) refers to the spectacular canyon of waterfalls fed by the Río Iguazú. Declared a World Heritage Area by UNESCO in 1984, these 275 waterfalls were shaped by 120 million years of geological history, forming one of Earth's most unforgettable sights. Iguazú Falls are shared by Argentina and Brazil, and are easily accessible from nearby Paraguay as well. Excellent walking circuits on both the Argentine and Brazilian sides allow visitors to peek over the tops and almost touch the torrent. A five-star hotel overlooks the falls in both the Argentine and Brazilian national parks, but many visitors looking for less expensive accommodations stay in the towns of Puerto Iguazú in Argentina or Foz do Iguaçu in Brazil.

The Iguazú Falls Region

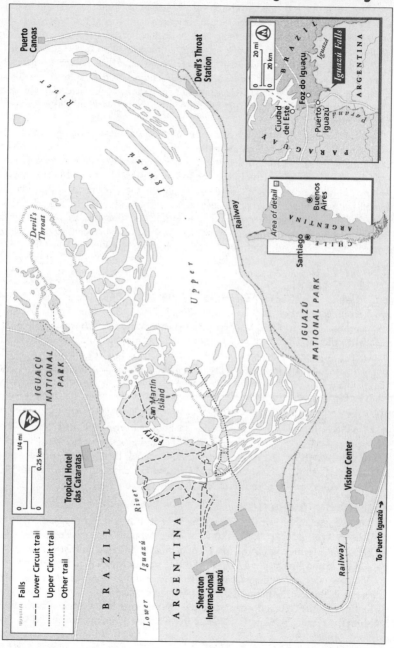

Legend:
- Falls
- Lower Circuit trail
- Upper Circuit trail
- Other trail

Puerto Canoas

Devil's Throat Station

Devil's Throat

Iguazú River

Railway

Upper

IGUAZÚ NATIONAL PARK

IGUAÇU NATIONAL PARK

Tropical Hotel das Cataratas

San Martín Island

Ferry

BRAZIL

ARGENTINA

Iguazú River

Lower

Sheraton Internacional Iguazú

Visitor Center

Railway

To Puerto Iguazú →

1/4 mi
0.25 km

Inset maps:

BRAZIL

Iguazú Falls

Iguaçu

ARGENTINA

Foz do Iguaçu

Ciudad del Este

Puerto Iguazú

PARAGUAY

Paraná

20 mi
20 km

Area of detail

ARGENTINA

Buenos Aires

CHILE

Santiago

Worth exploring is the park's subtropical jungle (see "Behind the Falls and into the Jungle," below). Here, *cupay* trees (South American hardwoods) tower over the various layers of life that compete for light; and the national park is known to contain 200 species of trees, 448 species of birds, 71 species of mammals, 36 species of reptiles, 20 species of amphibians, and more than 250 species of butterflies. Iguazú's climate also provides for the flowering of plants year-round, lending brilliant color to the forest. Because spray from the waterfall keeps humidity levels over 75%, there's a tremendous growth of epiphytes, or plants that grow on other plants without taking nutrients from their hosts.

You can visit the waterfalls on your own, but you will most certainly need a tour operator to explore the jungle. Allow at least 1 full day to explore the waterfalls on the Argentine side, another to visit the Brazilian side, and perhaps half a day for a jungle tour. Many visitors base themselves in the sedate, ramshackle town of Puerto Iguazú, 18km (11 miles) from the park. Though hardly the most memorable place, Puerto Iguazú has a subdued charm, pretty vegetation, and friendly people, and it's not yet ruined by the tourist trade. Accommodation options are improving all the time. If you want something more vibrant, expensive, and dangerous, go to the Brazilian town of Foz do Iguaçu on the other side (see "Border Crossing," later in this chapter).

ESSENTIALS
GETTING THERE
BY PLANE Aerolíneas Argentinas (✆ 0810/222-86527 or 3757/420-194; www.aerolineas.com.ar), and **LanChile** (✆ 3757/424-296) offer up to five daily flights from Buenos Aires to **Aeropuerto Internacional Cataratas** (✆ 3757/ 422-013); the trip takes 1½ hours. Round-trip fares cost approximately $245 (£135), depending on whether any specials are on offer. Aerolíneas Argentinas occasionally offers flights to Iguazú from Ezeiza international airport, usually on Saturday or Sunday. Catch a taxi (for about $12/£6.60) or one of the shuttle buses from the airport to town ($3/£1.65), a 20-minute drive.

BY BUS The fastest bus service from Buenos Aires is with **Vía Bariloche** (✆ 11/ 4315-4456 in Buenos Aires), which takes 18 hours and costs $50 to $70 (£28–£39) one-way, depending on the seat you choose. (The more expensive fare gets you a fully reclining *cama* [bed] seat.) Less pricey but longer (21 hr.) are **Expreso Singer** (✆ 011/4313-3927 in Buenos Aires) and **Expreso Tigre Iguazú** (✆ 011/4313-3915 in Buenos Aires), which both run for about $44 (£24) one-way.

VISITOR INFORMATION
In Puerto Iguazú, obtain maps and park information from the **Parque Nacional** office at Victoria Aguirre 66 (✆ 3757/420-722), open Monday through Friday from 8am to 9pm. For information on the town, contact the **municipal tourist office**, at Victoria Aguirre and Brañas (✆ 3757/420-800). It's open Monday to Friday from 8am to 9pm, Saturday and Sunday from 8am to noon and 3 to 9pm. Visitor information is also available near the national park entrance (see below).

In Buenos Aires, get information about Iguazú from **Casa de la Provincia de Misiones,** Av. Santa Fe 989 (✆ 11/4322-0686), open Monday through Friday from 10am to 5pm.

GETTING AROUND
El Práctico local buses run every 45 minutes from 7am to 8pm between Puerto Iguazú and the national park; the cost is $2 (£1.10). **Parada 10** (✆ 3757/421-527)

provides a 24-hour taxi service. You can rent a car at the airport, although this is much more a luxury than a necessity. Within both Puerto Iguazú and the national park, you can easily walk.

VISITING THE NATIONAL PARK ✿✿✿

Your first stop will likely be the recently opened (and environmentally friendly) **visitor center,** where you'll find maps and information about the area's flora and fauna. The visitor center is .8km (½ mile) from the park entrance, close to the parking lot and footbridges for the waterfall circuits. Adjacent to the visitor center, you will find a restaurant, snack shops, and souvenir stores. A natural-gas train takes visitors to the path entrance for the Upper and Lower circuits and to the footbridge leading to Devil's Throat. (If you'd rather walk, footpaths are available, but note that the walk to Devil's Throat is about 3km/1.75 miles). The visitor center is staffed with a number of English-speaking guides, available for individual and private tours. You may opt to see the falls on your own or with an experienced local guide. A guide is not really necessary, however, unless your time is limited or you want to ask detailed questions about the region's geography and fauna. The entrance fee is $10 (£5.50), which covers the train ride for non-Argentines to enter the national park. The national park is open from 8am to 7pm in summer, and from 8am until 6pm in winter.

The two main paths from which to view the waterfalls are the **Circuito Superior (Upper Circuit)** ✿ and the **Circuito Inferior (Lower Circuit)** ✿, both of which begin within walking distance (less than .8km/½ mile) from the visitor center. You may want to save your energy, however, and catch the train to the path entrance. There's a small snack shop near the beginning of the trails. The Upper Circuit winds its way along the top of the canyon, allowing you to look down the falls and see the area's rich flora, including cacti, ferns, and orchids. The Lower Circuit offers the best views, as magnificent waterfalls come hurtling down before you in walls of silvery spray. The waterfalls are clearly marked by signs along the way.

The best time to walk the **Upper Circuit** is early in the morning or late in the afternoon, and rainbows often appear near sunset. This .9km (.5-mile) path takes 1 to 2 hours, starting at the viewing tower and leading past **Dos Hermanos (Two Brothers), Bossetti, Chico (Small), Ramírez,** and **San Martín** (the park's widest) falls. You can come right to the edges of these falls and look over them as they fall as far as 60m (197 ft.) below. Along your walk, you can also look across to San Martín Island and the Brazilian side, and you'll pass a number of small streams and creeks.

The 1.8km (1¼-mile) **Lower Circuit** takes 2 hours to walk, leading you first past **Lanusse** and **Alvar Núñez** falls, then along the Lower Iguazú River past the raging **Dos Mosqueteros (Two Musketeers)** and **Tres Mosqueteros (Three Musketeers)** falls. The trail winds its way toward **Ramírez, Chico,** and **Dos Hermanos** falls. Here, you'll find an inspiring view of the **Garganta del Diablo (Devil's Throat)** and **Bossetti** falls. From the Salto Bossetti waterfall, a small pathway leads down to a small pier where you can catch a free boat to **San Martín Island.**

Once on the island, climb the stairs and walk along clearly marked trails for remarkable views of the surrounding *cataratas* (falls). To the left, you see the enormous **Garganta del Diablo, Saltos Brasileros (Brazilian Falls),** and **Ventana;** to the right, you overlook the mighty **Salto San Martín,** which sprays 30m (98 ft.) high after hitting the river below. This panoramic view looks out at dozens of falls forming an arch before you. San Martín Island also has a small, idyllic beach perfect for sunbathing and swimming.

Garganta del Diablo is the mother of all waterfalls in Iguazú, visible from observation points in both the Brazilian and Argentine parks. You'll notice that the water is calm as it makes its way down the Iguazú River, then begins to speed up as it approaches the gorge ahead. In front of you, Mother Nature has created a furious avalanche of water and spray that is the highest waterfall in Iguazú and one of the world's greatest natural spectacles. You might want to bring a raincoat, because you *will* get wet.

OUTDOOR ACTIVITIES

The area's main tour operator is **Iguazú Jungle Explorer** (© 3757/421-696; www. iguazujunglexplorer.com), located both inside the national park and in the Sheraton Internacional Iguazú. This company offers the Nautical Adventure tour ($15/£8.25) that visits the falls by inflatable raft, the Ecological Tour ($20/£11) that takes you to Devil's Throat and lets you paddle rubber boats along the Upper Iguazú Delta, and the Gran Aventura (Great Adventure) tour ($23/£13). This last tour begins with an 8km (5-mile) safari ride along the Yacoratia Path, the original dirt road that led through the forest and on to Buenos Aires. During the ride, you'll view the jungle's extensive flora and might catch a glimpse of some of the region's indigenous wildlife (see "Behind the Falls & into the Jungle," below). You will then disembark at Puerto Macuco, where you'll hop into an inflatable boat with your tour group and navigate 6.5km (4 miles) along the lower Iguazú River, braving 1.6km (1 mile) of rapids as you approach the falls in Devil's Throat Canyon. After a thrilling and wet ride, the raft lets you off across from San Martín Island. From there, catch a free boat to this island with excellent hiking trails and a small beach for swimming and sunbathing. You can combine the Ecological Tour and Great Adventure by buying a full-day Pasaporte Verde for $27 (£15). An increasingly popular tour is a guided walk around the falls under a full moon, where nighttime rainbows appear.

If you want to arrange a private adventure tour for your specific interests, the best outfit is **Explorador Expediciones,** with offices in the Sheraton Internacional Iguazú and in Puerto Iguazú at Perito Moreno 217 (© 3757/421-632). The guides are experts on life in the Iguazú jungle. A jungle safari costs $30 (£17) and an excursion to the waterfall $20 (£11). English guides are available, and tours last 2 hours. For other tours of the area, including the Jesuit ruins of San Ignacio, try **Cataratas Turismo,** Tres Fronteras 301 (© 3757/420-970). With this company, you must prebook English speaking guides if you need a translator.

WHERE TO STAY

Peak season for hotels in Iguazú extends through January and February (summer holiday) and also includes July (winter break), Semana Santa (Holy Week, the week before Easter), and long weekends. On the Argentine side, the Sheraton Internacional Iguazú is the only hotel inside the national park; the rest lie in Puerto Iguazú, 18km (11 miles) away. Discounts are common in the off season.

EXPENSIVE

Hotel Cataratas (R) (Kids)   Although it's not next to the falls, Hotel Cataratas, on the outskirts of town, deserves consideration for its excellent service, from its helpful receptionists to its meticulous housekeepers. None of the stuffiness you sometimes feel at luxury hotels is evident here. Despite the hotel's unimpressive exterior, rooms are among the most modern and spacious in the area—especially the 30 "master rooms" that feature two double beds, handsome wood furniture, colorful artwork, large bathrooms with separate toilet rooms, in-room safes, and views of the pool or gardens. These rooms are only slightly more than the standard rooms—called "superior"—and

Behind the Falls & into the Jungle

Dawn in Iguazú brings the first rays of light through the forest canopy, as orchids, butterflies, frogs, lizards, parrots, and monkeys awake and spread color and life through the forest. Binoculars in hand, step softly into this wonderland, where most sounds are masked by the roar from the falls.

You'll see parakeets long before entering the jungle. Their green bodies and loud song make them easy to spot; macaws, parrots, and toucans also live here. Look and listen carefully for the great dusky swift, which nests near the waterfalls, and the great yellow-breasted kiskadee, whose family name—*Tyrannidae*—tells much about its hunting prowess. Look below the canopy to observe an enormous population of butterflies, the other flying wonders of the park. Brilliant blue flyers known as morpho butterflies flit between deciduous trees and above lines of leaf-cutter ants, along with beautiful red, black, and yellow butterfly species.

It's close to impossible to walk through the park without running across some local indigenous reptiles. Ubiquitous tropidurus lizards, which feed on bird eggs, scamper everywhere. Colorful tree frogs hop and croak the nights away. Only patient and persistent visitors, however, will discover larger and rarer creatures, such as the 1.5m-long (5 ft.) tegu lizard and the caiman, a crocodile-like reptile.

Warm-blooded creatures share this forest as well. Coatis—aardvarklike mammals that travel in groups searching for insects and fruit—are frequent and fearless visitors to the trails. Swinging above the footpaths are brown capuchin monkeys, whose chatter and gestures make them seem more human than most primates. The predators of this warm-blooded group range from vampire bats to endangered jaguars and pumas. For your safety, stay on the walking paths and, when you're in the jungle, with your tour operator.

An array of subtropical flora surrounds Iguazú's resident animals and insects. Bamboo, ficus, fig, and ancient rosewood trees—up to 1,000 years old—are but a few of the trees that grow near the river and compete for light, along with a proliferation of epiphytes (plants growing on other plants), such as bromeliads, güembés, and orchids. Eighty-five species of orchid thrive in the park, mostly close to the damp and well-lit waterfalls.

the staff is often willing to offer promotional rates. The hotel's many facilities, including outdoor pool, spa, tennis and volleyball courts, putting green, playroom, and gymnasium, make this a great choice for families. The Cataratas restaurant offers a fine selection of regional and international dishes, and you can dine inside or out. The hotel lies 4km (2½ miles) from the center of Puerto Iguazú and 17km (11 miles) from the national park entrance. Bus service is available.

Ruta 12, Km 4, 3370 Misiones. ☎ 3757/421-100. Fax 3757/421-090. www.hotelcataratas.com.ar. 130 units. $130 (£72) double superior; from $200 (£110) suite. Rates include buffet breakfast. AE, DC, MC, V. **Amenities:** Restaurant; outdoor pool; putting green; tennis court; spa; Jacuzzi; sauna; game room; concierge; secretarial services; room service; massage; laundry service; conference room. *In room:* A/C, TV, minibar, hair dryer, safe.

Iguazú Grand Hotel Resort and Casino ☆ *(Kids)*   This large, red-brick, mansion-style hotel is on a low slope with lawns running down to an attractive pool area. The lobby is stunning and elegant, with white pillars and sparkling marble floors. The gracious and efficient receptionist speaks good English. So far so good, and it only gets better: What makes this five-star hotel stand out from the rest is its rooms, or should we say suites; they do not do rooms. Even the junior suites have 40 sq. m (431 sq. ft.) worth of impeccable decor, stylish period furniture, and ample light. The immaculate bathrooms have two washbasins and a separate section for toilet and bidet. A delicious fruit drink awaits you upon arrival, as do a fresh bathrobe and pair of slippers. All the bathtubs have a hydro-massage. The hotel grounds are delightful, and the three pools are immaculate and well maintained. The breakfast buffet is superb, with a large variety of international dishes, including bacon. The food in general is very good, though the menu does not change. All in all, the Iguazú Grand Hotel is an excellent, world-standard hotel, its main attraction being its large sumptuous rooms. It is on the road to the falls.

Ruta 12, 1640, 3370 Puerto Iguazú. ✆ **3757/498-050.** www.casinoiguazu.com. 120 units. $350 (£193) junior suite; $420 (£231) garden suite. Rates include buffet breakfast. AE, DC, MC, V. **Amenities:** Restaurant; 3 outdoor pools; putting green; tennis court; spa; Jacuzzi; sauna; game room; concierge; secretarial services; room service; massage; laundry service; casino; conference room; business center, health club, playland, baby sitter, shopping. *In room:* A/C, TV, minibar, hair dryer, safe.

Sheraton Internacional Iguazú ☆☆   Once the famous Internacional Cataratas de Iguazú, the Sheraton enjoys a magnificent and exclusive location inside the national park (read: It's the *only* hotel inside the park). Guests have little need to leave the resort, a self-contained paradise overlooking the falls; and you have the added advantage of being able to explore the park when the daily crowds have left. The hotel is only steps from the Upper and Lower circuit trails, and half of the guest rooms have direct views of the water (the others have splendid views of the jungle). The only drawback to the rooms is that the decor is fairly standard Sheraton-issue. Three restaurants include the stunning Garganta del Diablo, which peers over Devil's Throat and serves outstanding, if pricey, international dishes. The hotel also offers daytime activities, including swimming, golf, tennis, shopping, and access to national park tour operators. The service here can be patchy, and a better five-star accommodation is outside the park, yet this location is unbeatable. Book early, because this hotel is busy year-round.

Parque Nacional Iguazú, 3370 Misiones. ✆ **0800/888-9180** local toll-free, or 3757/491-800. Fax 3757/491-848. www.sheraton.com. 180 units. $250 (£138) double with jungle view; $320 (£176) double with view of waterfalls; from $510 (£281) suite. Rates include buffet breakfast. AE, DC, MC, V. **Amenities:** 3 restaurants; outdoor and indoor pools; 2 tennis courts; basketball court; fitness center; spa; concierge; car-rental desk; shopping arcade; room service; babysitting; laundry service; conference rooms. *In room:* A/C, TV, minibar, hair dryer, safe.

MODERATE

Hotel Esturion   Hotel Esturion is spacious, well equipped, and just a 10-minute walk from the town center. The main building has the look of a modern, tropical schoolhouse, but in general the facilities have a pleasing aesthetic. The huge pool and surrounding grounds have a Caribbean feel, though the safari-style staff uniforms are a little over the top. Rooms are decent, if a little functional and dated. Some have pleasant balconies. The lobby bar is very stylish and appealing. Service can be patchy, however; some staff members are helpful and efficient, and others are plain rude. Do not expect much English. The grounds are as expansive as the breakfast buffet, which is an excellent spread, and the food in general is good—particularly the *asado* (Argentine barbecue).

Av. Tres Fronteras 650, 3370 Puerto Iguazú. ℂ 3757/420-100. Fax 3757/421-468. www.hotelesturion.com. 128 units. $117 (£64) double; $164 (£90) suite. All rates include buffet breakfast. AE, DC, MC, V. **Amenities:** Restaurant; outdoor pool. *In room:* A/C, TV, minibar.

Hotel Saint George ℜ *Finds*   A modest hotel in the heart of Puerto Iguazú, the Saint George features colorful, slightly dated rooms with single beds. The walls are not super thick, but everything is sparkling clean with well-lit bathrooms with toiletries. An inviting pool is surrounded by lush vegetation and a commendable international restaurant that serves tasty fish from the local river. The breakfast buffet is not the most memorable, however, and needs improving. The friendly and enthusiastic staff will answer questions about the national park and help arrange tours, if requested.

Av. Córdoba 148, 3370 Puerto Iguazú. ℂ 3757/420-633. Fax 3757/420-651. www.hotelsaintgeorge.com. 80 units. $80 (44£) double ($100/£55 including dinner); $135 (£74) suite. All rates include buffet breakfast. AE, DC, MC, V. **Amenities:** Restaurant; outdoor pool; Jacuzzi; sauna; playroom; Wi-Fi. *In room:* A/C, TV, minibar.

Orquídeas Palace   This resort-style hotel with manicured lawns and low modern buildings has a pared-down, functional feel. At the same time, it's well equipped, pleasant, and relaxing. The decor is simple and elegant, if a little worn around the edges. It has a glass-fronted reception area with comfy couches and well lit, spacious rooms with tiled floors and small window tables. The fixtures and features, however, could use updating. The bathrooms are all ceramic and clean with shower and bath. The 5-hectare (12-acre) garden offers lots of greenery with fruit-laden trees, lush shrubbery, and tropical flowers. A cool, lagoon-shaped pool has deckchairs. Set amid the well-trimmed grounds are some very agreeable cottages with white walls and tiled roofs. Some are older than others and priced accordingly. Beds vary from queen-size to double bunk, and the interiors are well presented with attractive drapes and bed covers. Each cottage has a small open porch with plastic garden seating. Staff members are friendly and helpful but speak little English. Breakfast is a decent buffet with yogurt and fruit, but evening meals are very pedestrian fare. The hotel is a $2.50 (£1.40) taxi ride from town, on the way to the falls. Buses pass frequently in either direction.

Ruta 12, Km 5, 3370 Puerto Iguazú. ℂ 3757/420-472. Fax 3757/420-651. www.orquideashotel.com. 80 units. $50–$120 (£28–£66) double. All rates include buffet breakfast. AE, DC, MC, V. **Amenities:** Restaurant; outdoor pool. *In room:* A/C, TV, minibar.

INEXPENSIVE
Hotel Lilian *Value*   Sometimes being on a budget does have its advantages—one of them being that you escape the tourist bubble and meet some real locals who are not in uniform. Hotel Lilian's big plus is a very helpful owner who will do her best to make sure your stay is as comfortable and rewarding as possible. Six blocks from the town center, this hotel has immaculate rooms surrounding a central courtyard. Some are brighter than others, so ask for one with plenty of light. Wardrobes are a little bit too big for most travelers' needs. Do not get frustrated by the lack of clothes hangers— you must ask for them at reception. Bathrooms are a decent size and more than adequate, but occasionally water pressure is low. Besides the owner, no one on staff speaks English. The neighbourhood could use some sprucing up, but it is by no means unpleasant.

Fray Luis Beltran 183, 3370 Puerto Iguazú. ℂ/fax 3757/420-968. hotelliliana@yahoo.com.ar. 24 units. $30 (£17) double. Rates include breakfast. No credit cards. *In room:* A/C, TV.

Los Helechos *(Value* Family-run Los Helechos is a great bargain for those seeking comfortable, inexpensive accommodations in Puerto Iguazú. Located in the city center, this intimate hotel offers simple rooms, many of which surround a plant-filled courtyard and offer a sense of sleeping near the jungle. If you dislike humid nights, be sure to splurge for a room with air-conditioning (request it at the time of booking, but be ready to cough up an additional $6/£3.30).

Paulino Amarante 76, 3370 Puerto Iguazú. ©/fax 3757/420-338. www.hosterialoshelechos.com.ar. 60 units. $25 (£14) double without A/C or TV, $31 (£17) with A/C and TV. AE, DC, MC, V. **Amenities:** Restaurant; bar; pool. *In room:* A/C, TV (in some rooms only).

OUTSIDE IGUAZU

The Yacutinga Lodge and Wildlife Reserve This is the ultimate jungle experience. The fact that you have to make the last leg of the journey there by boat makes you anticipate not so much the heart of darkness, but the heart of another world—a world of giant butterflies, dazzling birds, and hidden jaguar. It is a world where five-star comforts do not exist, so be prepared. But the sacrifices you make (such as hard beds, limited menu, and patchy service) are worth it for a memorable experience. The Yacutinga Lodge is set in 570 hectares (1,410 acres) of *Jungle Book* paradise, run to ensure that its presence has no negative effects on the surrounding environment; you even get to plant a tree before leaving. The decor might look pseudo-Flintstone, but the chunky wood, adobe walls, and tiny colored glass windows are all made from recycled material. Even the coffee table is a discarded tree trunk, redesigned so you can put your fruit juice on it. Set amid this Eden-like Utopia are four-room cabins with decent-size rooms and a wood-fueled fireplace (June–Aug mornings can be chilly). The decor is basic, and don't expect air-conditioning. Hot water runs continuously, but power runs only during certain times of the day. There's a small pool more popular with insects and sunbathing iguanas than people. On hand every day are local guides with extensive wildlife knowledge. They conduct daily tours of the lush reserve, including the spectacular palmetto palm forest. The reserve teems with wildlife, but don't expect to see too much unless you are very still, silent, and lucky. The 3-day package includes just one full-day excursion, because it takes a lot of time to get there. The constant mud, humidity, and water (Wellingtons provided) are not for everyone, but the experience unforgettable. The lodge is 60km (37 miles) from Iguazú Falls.

Iguazú, Missiones. No phone. www.yacutinga.com. 12 units. $350 (£193) for 3 days (2 nights). **Amenities:** Restaurant; bar; pool.

WHERE TO DINE

Dining in Puerto Iguazú is casual and inexpensive, provided you look for a meal outside your hotel. Argentine steaks, seafood, and pasta are common on most menus.

EXPENSIVE

Garganta del Diablo ☆☆ INTERNATIONAL Inside the national park at the Sheraton Internacional Iguazú, this restaurant (the best in the area) serves excellent international and regional dishes. Open for nearly 25 years, it's best known for its magnificent view of Devil's Throat. Enjoy a romantic table for two overlooking the falls, and consider the grilled *surubí* (a mild fish from the river before you) or spider crab on couscous. The wine list includes an excellent Malbec from Altos Los Hormigas.

Parque Nacional Iguazú. © 3757/491-800. Main courses $12–$20 (£6.60–£11); buffet $25 (£14). AE, DC, MC, V. Daily 7am–11pm.

La Rueda *(★ (Finds* ARGENTINE   Nothing more than a small A-frame house with an outdoor patio built from local materials, La Rueda is a delightful place to eat. Despite the casual atmosphere, tables have carefully prepared place settings, waiters are attentive and friendly, and the food—served in large portions—is very good. The diverse menu features pasta, steaks, and fish dishes. Try the *surubí brochette,* a local whitefish prepared with bacon, tomatoes, onions, and peppers, and served with green rice and potatoes.

Av. Córdoba 28. (© 3757/422-531. Main courses $15–$20 (£8.25–£11). AE. Mon–Tues 6:30pm–midnight; Wed–Sun noon–3:30pm.

INEXPENSIVE

El Charo *(Finds* ARGENTINE   Recent renovations have altered this restaurant's previously ramshackle but cozy character. Now large and somewhat soulless, it still produces delicious food, and it's tremendously popular with both tourists and locals. Among the main dishes, you'll find breaded veal, sirloin steaks, pork chops, catfish, and items from the *parrilla* (grill). Also available are salads and pastas such as ravioli and cannelloni.

Av. Córdoba 106. (© 3757/421-529. Main courses $7–$15 (£3.85–£8.25). No credit cards. Daily 11am–1am.

El Quincho del Tío Querido *(★★* PARRILLA   Located in the heart of town, this restaurant serves excellent *parrilla* and fresh river fish such as dorado or *surubí,* along with excellent wines. Open for nearly 20 years, the restaurant also offers live music, including tango and *folklórico.* Shows start every night at 8pm.

Bonpland 110, at Perito Moreno. (© 3757/420-151. Main courses $9–$13 (£4.95–£7.15). AE, DC, MC, V. Daily noon–3pm and 7–11pm.

PUERTO IGUAZÚ AFTER DARK

Puerto Iguazú offers little in the way of nightlife, although the major hotels—including the Sheraton Internacional Iguazú and Hotel Cataratas—often have live music and other entertainment during peak season. Try **Café Central,** Av. Victoria Aguirre 320, a popular bar and restaurant with a small casino, or **La Barranca,** Avenida Tres Fronteras and Costanera (© 3757/423-295), a pub with live music every night. **Cuba Libre,** Paraguay and Brazil, plays tropical beats until late. For better nightlife many people go to Foz do Iguaçu on the Brazilian side (see "Foz do Iguaçu After Dark," below).

2 The Brazilian Side: Foz do Iguaçu *(★ (★*

A visit to the Brazilian side of Iguazú Falls affords a dazzling perspective on the waterfalls. Trails here are not as extensive as on the Argentine side, but the views are no less spectacular. In fact, many people find Brazil's unobstructed panoramic view of Iguazú Falls even more inspiring.

If you decide to stay on the Brazilian side, the Tropical das Cataratas Hotel and Resort (see "Where to Stay," below) is a spectacular hotel at the foot of the national park, overlooking the falls. Alternatively, you could stay in Foz do Iguaçu—the Brazilian counterpart to Puerto Iguazú. Foz is a slightly larger town 25km (16 miles) from Iguaçu National Park, with numerous hotels, restaurants, and shops (along with a slightly larger incidence of poverty and street crime).

Border Crossing

There is currently much confusion among American travelers concerning what their visa requirements are to enter the Brazilian side of the falls. They hear they are required to get a $100 (£55) visa in advance, yet they get there to find American citizens crossing the border without hindrance. Indeed, the law says that citizens from the United States, Canada, and Australia must obtain a visa to enter Brazil, whether for 1 day or 90 days. On the ground, however, some local officials, hotel concierges, tourist agencies, and taxi companies ignore the rule to make an extra buck. Rules are rules, however, and it is illegal to enter a country without the proper papers. If you want to see the Brazilian side of Iguazú Falls, my advice is to get a visa.

You can obtain one on short notice in Puerto Iguazú. Visit the Brazilian Consulate, Av. Córdoba 264 (© **3757/421-348**; Mon–Fri 8am–1pm). The process takes 2 hours and requires a passport photo. You can also apply before traveling, which takes 2 weeks. U.S. citizens should contact the Brazilian Embassy at 3006 Massachusetts Ave. NW, Washington DC 20008 (© **202/238-2700**; www.brasilemb.org). Canadian citizens must contact the Brazilian Embassy at 450 Wilbroad St., Ottawa, ON K1N 6M8 (© **613/237-1090**; www.brasembottawa.org). Australian citizens contact their Brazilian Embassy, at 19 Forster Crescent, Yarralumla, ACT 2600 (© **02/6237-2375**; http://brazil.org.au).

ESSENTIALS
GETTING THERE
BY PLANE   Foz do Iguaçu Airport (© 45/3521-4200) is 11km (6¾ miles) from Foz do Iguaçu, on the Brazilian side. **Airport Varig** (© 45/3521-4292), **Gol** (© 45/3521-4230), and **TAM** (© 45/3521-4242) fly there from Rio de Janeiro and other major Brazilian cities. Public buses make frequent trips to the national park and into town for a small fee.

FROM THE ARGENTINE SIDE   For most nationalities, crossing the border is fairly easy with a passport. Citizens of the United States, Canada, and Australia must obtain a visa to visit Brazil. The visa costs $100 (£55; see "Border Crossing," below). The most convenient way to get from the Argentine to the Brazilian side is by taxi (about $30/£17 round-trip). Buses are considerably less expensive, but less convenient, too. **Tres Fronteras** and **El Práctico** buses make the half-hour trip to Foz do Iguaçu 15 times per day ($1/55p) from the Puerto Iguazú bus terminal; to visit the national park, ask the bus driver to let you off just after the border check, then catch the national park bus.

BY CAR   To avoid border hassles and international driving issues, it's best to take a bus or taxi to the Brazilian side.

VISITOR INFORMATION
Foz do Iguaçu's **municipal tourism office**, at Praça Getúlio Vargas (© 45/3521-1455), is open weekdays from 7am to 11pm. **Teletur** (© 0800/454-516) is a toll-free information service.

SEEING THE BRAZILIAN SIDE OF THE FALLS

The national park entrance to the **Cataratas do Iguaçu** is at Km 17, Rodovía das Cataratas, and the entrance fee is $5 (£2.75). Park your car or get off the bus here and pay your entry fee; private vehicles (except for taxis and guests of the Tropical) are not allowed in the park. From here, you board a shuttle bus bound for the falls. The waterfall path begins just in front of the Tropical das Cataratas Hotel and Resort, which is 11km (6¾ miles) from the national park entrance (if you are taking a taxi, have your driver bring you directly to the Tropical das Cataratas hotel and jump onto the trail from here). You will catch your first sight of the falls from a small viewpoint at the foot of the hotel lawn, from which the path begins. The trail zigzags down the side of the gorge and trundles along the cliff face for about 2km (1.25 miles) past **Salto Santa María, Deodoro,** and **Floriano** falls. There are 275 separate waterfalls with an average drop of 60m (197 ft.). The last catwalk plants you directly in front of the awesome **Garganta do Diablo (Devil's Throat),** where, once again, you will get wet (there's a small store in front where you can buy rain gear and film, if you need it). Back on the main trail, a tower beckons visitors to take an elevator to the top for an even broader panoramic view of the falls. This circuit takes about 2 hours. As you are leaving the park, drop into the **Parque das Aves,** Rodovia das Aves Km 18, a bird park with some fantastic species. Admission is $10 (£5.50).

WHERE TO STAY

Peak season is January and February (summer holiday), July (winter break), Semana Santa (Holy Week, the week before Easter Sunday), and all long weekends. Rates are often substantially discounted in the off season.

EXPENSIVE

Bourbon Foz do Iguaçu *✦✦ Kids*   A full-service resort hotel, the Bourbon is 2.5km (1½ miles) out of town on the road to the falls. All rooms are colorfully appointed; standard rooms in the original wing have light colors and look out over the front of the hotel, while superior rooms have verandas with views over the pool and lawn. The newer wing houses "master" suites with modern furnishings and huge windows. But don't count on spending a lot of time in your room; the real draw of the Bourbon is its leisure space. There's a 1.3km (.8-mile) trail in the woods behind the hotel; keep an eye out for toucans, parakeets, and the colorful butterflies in the aviary. The vast outdoor pool area includes three large pools, one especially for children with lots of play equipment. In high season, activity leaders organize all-day children's activities in the pool or in the Tarzan house, tucked away in the forest.

Rodovía das Cataratas, Km 2.5, Foz do Iguaçu, 85863-000 PR. © **0800/451-010** or 45/3529-0123. www.bourbon.com.br. 311 units. $200–$225 (£110–£124) standard, superior, or master double; $40–$60 (£22–£33) per extra person. Prices include breakfast and dinner. AE, MC, V. Bus: Parque Nacional or Cataratas. **Amenities:** 3 restaurants; huge pool complex (3 outdoor pools, 1 small indoor pool); outdoor tennis courts lit for evening play; sauna; children's programs; game room; concierge; tour desk; car-rental desk; business center; shopping arcade; salon; room service; massage; laundry service; nonsmoking rooms. *In room:* A/C, TV, Internet (master suites only), minibar, fridge, hair dryer, safe.

Tropical das Cataratas Hotel and Resort *✦✦*   The Portuguese colonial hotel (called Hotel das Cataratas for most of its existence), built in 1958 and ideally located in the Brazilian national park, is a UNESCO-declared World Heritage Site. The meticulously kept pink-and-white buildings, on a cliff above the Brazilian falls, have hosted an impressive list of princes and princesses, presidents and ministers, artists and celebrities. The hotel is often fully booked, but if you can get a reservation, its spacious corridors and quiet courtyards promise a relaxing vacation. Deluxe and superior rooms, fitted with two-poster beds, granite- or marble-top tables, and hardwood floors, are far better than standard rooms; make sure you ask for one that has been refurbished so you don't get stuck with a 50-year-old bathroom. Only the presidential suite has direct views of the falls; other rooms stare at trees. The trail to the Brazilian falls is just steps from the hotel entrance; when there's a full moon, magical night hikes can be arranged. The hotel has two commendable restaurants serving Brazilian and international food. Restaurante Itaipú is the more formal choice, while the outdoor Ipe Bar & Grill offers evening entertainment. Although the national park closes to the public after 7pm, people who want to come for dinner at the hotel can get a special after-hours pass at the park entrance.

Parque Nacional do Iguaçu, Foz do Iguaçu, 85863-000 PR. ℂ **0800/150-006** or 45/2102-7000. www.tropical hotel.com.br. 200 units. $363–$436 (£200–£240) double superior; $508 (£279) double deluxe. Children under 10 stay free in parent's room. AE, DC, MC, V. Take the road to Iguaçu Falls, go straight towards the gate; do not turn left into the visitor's area. Identify yourself at the gate. **Amenities:** 2 restaurants; bar; large outdoor pool; tennis court; game room; concierge; tour desk; business center (24-hr. Internet access); shopping arcade; salon; room service; laundry service. *In room:* A/C, TV, minibar, fridge, hair dryer, safe.

MODERATE

Continental Inn ✦ *(Finds)*   Recently renovated, the Continental Inn is a gem. All the rooms are quite comfortable, but the suites are truly outstanding, well worth the extra money. The regular suites have beautiful hardwood floors, modern blond-wood furniture, a separate sitting area, a desk, a table, and a bathroom with a large round tub. The best rooms in the house are the master suites: hardwood floors, king-size bed, fancy linens, a large desk, a separate sitting area, a walk-in closet, and a bathroom with a Jacuzzi tub and a view over the city of Iguaçu. The amenities are top-notch, too: large pool with children's play area, sauna, and game room with video games. Rooms for travelers with disabilities are also available.

Av. Paranà 1089, Foz do Iguaçu, 85852-000 PR. ℂ **45/2102-5000**. www.continentalinn.com.br. 113 units, 102 rooms showers only. $65 (£36) double; $95 (£52) suite; $135 (£74) master suite. In low season 30% discount. Children under 5 stay free in parent's room; children 5 and over $14 (£7.70) extra. AE, DC, MC, V. **Amenities:** Restaurant; large pool; exercise room; sauna; game room w/video arcade; car-rental desk; business center; room service; laundry service. *In room:* A/C, TV, Internet, minibar, fridge, hair dryer, safe.

WHERE TO DINE

You will find a number of pleasant restaurants in Foz do Iguaçu. **Avenida Brasil,** a main artery of the town, is a good place to wander for food stalls, coffee bars, and hearty home-style Brazilian fare.

EXPENSIVE

Restaurante Itaipú—Tropical das Cataratas ✦ BRAZILIAN   The best *feijoada* (a Brazilian black-bean dish) in town is served here, only on Saturday afternoons, in this elegant colonial-style restaurant in the Tropical das Cataratas. A large feast is put out, with white rice, *farofa* (a manioc meal, a very Brazilian ingredient—a bit like tapioca, a bit like cornmeal, it is the most authentic accompaniment to *feijoada*), fried banana, green cabbage, orange slices, and all the *feijoada* you can eat. The big clay dishes of beans and meat are clearly labeled (a vegetarian version is also available). Desserts are sweet and rich; try the various caramelized fruits with coconut.

In the Tropical das Cataratas Hotel and Resort, Km 28, Parque Nacional do Iguaçu. ℂ **45/2102-7000**. Main courses $10–$20 (£5.50–£11). AE, DC, MC, V. Daily 7:30am–11pm. No public transit; easiest to combine eating here with a visit to the falls; the park shuttle will leave you in front of the Tropical.

MODERATE

Clube Maringá ✦ SEAFOOD   One of the most popular seafood restaurants for locals is Clube Maringá. It can be a bit tricky to find, on a dead-end road that leads to the Brazilian border across from Argentina and Paraguay. The food is excellent. The menu is all fish and mostly local. Try the *piapara* fish grilled in a banana leaf or the barbecued dorado. Other dishes include *surubí* sautéed in butter, tilapia skewers, cod pastries, and *surubí a milanesa* (breaded and fried). Even the *sashimi* is made with local tilapia and piapara.

Av. Dourado (just off Av. General Meira s/n, by the Policia Militar). © 45/3527-3472. Main courses $9–$13 (£4.95–£7.15). MC, V. Mon–Sat 11am–11pm. Call ahead for lunch hours; these vary by season. A taxi is recommended.

FOZ DO IGUAÇU AFTER DARK

The best bars and clubs line Avenida Jorge Schimmelpfeng. Try **Tass Bier and Club,** Av. Jorge Schimmelpfeng 450 (© **45/3523-5373**), which acts as a pub during the week and disco on weekends. The **Teatro Plaza Foz,** BR (National Rd.) 277, Km 726 (© **45/3526-3733**), offers evening folkloric music and dance shows celebrating Brazilian, Argentine, and Paraguayan cultures.

3 Resistencia & El Chaco

1,020km (632 miles) NE of Buenos Aires

On of the least visited parts of Argentina, El Gran Chaco is a vast flatland of marsh, savannah, and desert scrubland. It rises gently from the city of Resistencia and runs north and west, taking up huge areas of Paraguay, Brazil, and even Bolivia. Made up of the provinces Chaco and Formosa, the Argentine part is split into two distinct areas. The Wet Chaco is an agriculturally rich prairie land of cotton, soya, and sunflowers. Rivers zigzag across this vast wetland, which is rich in animal life, be it cattle or birds. In protected areas such as Parque Nacional Chaco you will find alligators and, strangely enough, wolves. The population has a strong, vibrant, tribal tradition, mostly comprising the Tuba and Wichi people. Much of the area is inaccessible, with little or no public transport, and prone to frequent flooding. It is definitely 4WD country. To the west, the area becomes known as the Dry Chaco and turns into parched desert scrub with little or no human life. Undoubtedly one of the hottest places on earth, the Dry Chaco has the inviting nickname, "El Impenetrable."

Resistencia, the capital city of Chaco province, is an interesting stopover if you're traveling to Salta from Iguazú or if you are interested in exploring the region further. Originally an Italian colony, this modern town of 400,000 is a thriving commercial center, renowned for its public art, gaining it the name the "City of Statues." Nearby is the beautiful Isla de Cerrito, and farther north the bird-watchers' paradise Parque Nacional Chaco.

ESSENTIALS

GETTING THERE

BY PLANE   Aerolíneas Argentinas (© **0810/222-86527** or 3722/445-550), flies twice a day on weekdays from Buenos Aires to **Resistencia Airport** (© **3722/446-009**); on weekends, there is just one flight a day. The trip takes 1¼ hours. Round-trip fares range from around $245 (£135). The airport is 9km (5½ miles) west of the city. Catch a taxi (for about $5/£2.75); there is no bus service.

BY BUS   The **terminal,** avenidas Malvinas Argentinas and Maclean (© **3722/ 461-098**), is located 2.5km (1½ miles) outside the city. The fastest bus service from Buenos Aires is with **Flecha Bus** (© **11/4000-5200** in Buenos Aires) or **San Cristóbal** (© **3722/465-574** in Resistencia), which takes 12 to 13 hours and costs $35 to $42 (£19–£23) one-way, depending on the seat you choose.

VISITOR INFORMATION

For information on the town and province, contact the **Provincial Tourist Office,** on Santa Fe 178 (© **3722/423-547**; www.chaco.gov.ar/turismo). It is open Monday to Friday from 8am to 8:30pm, Saturday and Sunday 8am to noon.

WHAT TO SEE & DO

Rich with local plant life, the central Plaza 25 de Mayo is huge and worth wandering through. **Museo del Hombre Chaqueño,** Juan B. Justo 280 (© **3722/453-005**), is a small museum telling the story of the native Wichi, Toba, and Mocovi people. **Fogón de los Arrieros,** Brown 350 (© **3722/426-418**), is an art center formed by artists intent on making the city an open-air art gallery. For this reason, you will find works of art by renowned sculptors in the most unlikely of places in the city. **Isla del Cerrito** is a river island and nature reserve 51km (32 miles) north of the city. The eastern end of the island is a popular beach resort with hotel. Northwest of Resistencia by 115 km (71 miles), off route 16, the province's biggest draw is the **Parque Nacional Chaco** (© **3725/496-166** or 3725/499161). This Eden-like paradise of wild orchids and Carayas monkeys covers 15,000 hectares (37,050 acres) of virgin forest. It has over 340 species of birds, and rare pumas and maned wolves prowl amid the foliage. The park is open 24 hours. The visitor center is 300m (984 ft.) from the park entrance.

WHERE TO STAY

The city's best hotel is the three star **Hotel Covadonga,** Guemes 200 (© **3722/ 444-444**; www.hotelcovadonga.com). It has clean rooms and decent facilities such as a pool, sauna, and gym. **Gran Hotel Royal,** Obligado 211 (© **3722/443-666**; www. granhotelroyal.com.ar), is a good alternative.

WHERE TO DINE

La Chimenera, Av. Hernandero 436 (© **3722/437-316**), is a typical *parrilla*. For more variety, try **Marcelino,** J. D. Perón 454 (© **3722/437-316**). **Fusin,** Perú 244 (© **3722/437-316**), is good for pastas and fish.

7

Salta & the Northwest

by Charlie O'Malley

The Northwest of Argentina has too long been regarded as a dusty, indigenous outpost to what is a rich and modern country. Indeed, as you tour the North's red deserts and dusty adobe villages; stand among old, wizened Indian women; or dare to dance *chacareras* at the colorful street carnivals, you might indeed think you were in Bolivia or Peru and not the brash, forward-looking nation of high fashion and *rock nacional* that you have experienced elsewhere. Yet the Northwest is my favorite part of Argentina, a place steeped in history and unafraid to show it. Here you'll find the ruins of ancient civilizations—be it the terraced settlements of the Quéchuan Indians or the mysterious standing stones

of the Tafi tribe. You can gaze upon the wonderful baroque art created by the indigenous people when they were converted to Christianity by Spanish explorers such as Francisco Pizarro and Diego de Almagro. You can follow the narrative of the glorious Gaucho Wars that beat off the Spanish and then gave rise to their own strongmen, such as Martín Guemes and Julio A. Roca. And here begins the Route 40, that epic Andean roadway that forms the backbone of Argentina. In the Northwest alone it passes by vineyards, cactus hills, rain forests, tobacco fields, sugar-cane country, dinosaur parks, and vast empty salt plains. All this and more makes the Northwest of Argentina the very heart of South America.

EXPLORING THE REGION

The Northwest is best explored by car. Although there is bus service between most towns, a car allows you to explore at ease the rainbow-colored mountain ranges of **Humahuaco** or the rugged scenery of **Calchaquies Valley.** Be prepared for long distances and hidden marvels off the beaten track, such as the Indian settlement of **Quilme** and the breathtaking canyons of **Talampaya National Park.** Most cities such as **Salta** and **Jujuy** are best explored by foot, and the wineries of **Cafayate** are easily accessible by bicycle. Three days at a minimum to 5 days should allow you to experience the flavor of the region.

Another way to discover the Northwest is aboard the **Tren a las Nubes (Train to the Clouds)** ✮, a daylong journey that takes you from Salta toward the Chilean border. It runs only from April to November, however, and it's currently suspended indefinitely. For more, see "Train to the Clouds: Delayed until Further Notice," below.

1 Salta ✮

90km (56 miles) S of San Salvador de Jujuy, 1,497km (928 miles) N of Buenos Aires; 1,268km (786 miles) N of Mendoza

With its cloistered nuns and gaucho waiters, gilded churches and mountain mummies, Salta province is a rich mix of all the things that make the Northwest so distinctive.

Here the old meets the new, and the old wins. Time trips by at a more rhythmic pace, like the hoof-clopping music *chacareras,* which pipes from every cafe and car. The city itself (pop. 500,000) is a sunny mix of colonial architecture; friendly, gracious people; colorful history; and indigenous pride. Conservative by nature, Salteños let their hair down during Carnaval (Mardi Gras), when thousands come out for a parade of floats celebrating the region's history; water balloons are also tossed from balconies with great aplomb. Ringed by green hills and blessed with a cooler, more temperate climate, Salta City should be top of your list when you're visiting the area. (That is not to say it does not get hot. High season here is actually the winter months of Apr–Oct).

ESSENTIALS
GETTING THERE
I don't recommend making the long-distance drive to Argentina's Northwest; it's safer and much easier to either fly or take the bus.

BY PLANE Flights land at **Martín Miguel De Guemes International Airport,** RN 51 (© **387/424-2904**), 8km (5¼ miles) from the city center. **Aerolíneas Argentinas** (© **0810/222-86527** or 387/431-0862) and **Andes Líneas Aéreas** (© **0810/122-26337** or 387/416-2600) fly from Buenos Aires (some flights make a stop in Córdoba). Nonstop flights from Buenos Aires take 2 hours and cost between $55 and $100 (£30–£55) each way, depending on the season and availability. A shuttle bus travels between the airport and town for about $3 (£1.65) one-way; a taxi into town will run about $6 (£3.30).

BY BUS The **Terminal de Omnibus,** or central bus station, is at Avenida H. Yrigoyen and Abraham Cornejo (© **387/401-1143**). Buses arrive from Buenos Aires (18 hr.; $60/£33) and travel to San Salvador de Jujuy (2½ hr.; $4/£2.20) and other cities in the region. **Chevalier** (© **387/431-2819**) and **La Veloz del Norte** (© **387/431-7215**) are the main bus companies.

VISITOR INFORMATION
The tourism office, **Secretaría de Turismo de Salta,** Buenos Aires 93 (© **387/431-0950** or 387/431-0640; www.turismosalta.gov.ar), will provide you with maps and information on dining, lodging, and sightseeing in the region. It can also help you arrange individual or group tours. It's open every day from 9am to 9pm. In Buenos Aires, obtain information about Salta from the **Casa de Salta** in Buenos Aires, Sáenz Pena 933 (© **011/4326-1314**). It's open weekdays 10am to 6pm.

FAST FACTS: SALTA
Currency Exchange Exchange money at the airport, at **Dinar Exchange,** Mitre and España (© **387/432-2600;** Mon–Fri 9am–1:30pm and 5–8pm; Sat 10am–3pm), or at **Banco de La Nación,** Mitre and Belgrano (© **387/431-1909;** Mon–Fri 9am–2pm).

Emergency Dial © **911** for police, © **100** for fire, and © **107** for an ambulance.

Hospital Saint Bernard Hospital is at Dr. M. Boedo 69 (© **387/432-030**).

Tour Operators Explore the region with **Saltur Turismo,** Caseros 485 (© **387/421-2012**), or **Incauca Turismo,** Mitre 274 Local 33 (© **387/422-7568;** www.incaucaturismo.com). The tourist office can suggest English-speaking guides.

GETTING AROUND
Salta is small and easy to explore on foot, but be careful; drivers here are pedestrian-blind. The **Peatonal Florida** is Salta's pedestrian walking street—a smaller version of

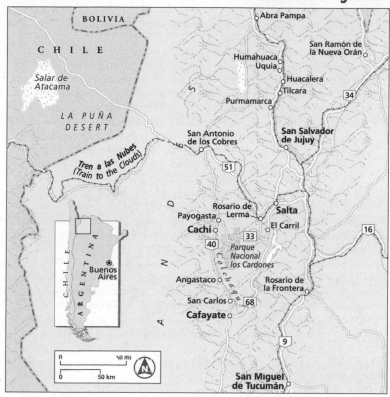

Calle Florida in Buenos Aires—where most of the city's shops are. The main sites are centered on **Plaza 9 de Julio,** with a monument to General Arenales in the center and a beautiful baroque cathedral at its edge. Built in 1858, the **Catedral** is considered Argentina's best-preserved colonial church. All the other attractions here—except the **Salta Tram** and the **Tren a las Nubes**—are within easy walking distance.

RENTING A CAR Noa Rent a Car, Buenos Aires 1 Local 6 (© **387/431-0740**), has subcompacts and four-wheel drives. **Hertz** is at Caseros 374 (© **387/421-7553**) and the airport (© **387/424-0113**). **Avis** is located on Casero 420 (© **387/ 421-2181**) and at the airport (© **387/424-2289**). Following the currency evaluation, cars have become more affordable to rent here, ranging from $45 to $50 (£25–£28) per day.

SEEING THE SIGHTS

Most museums in the Northwest don't have formal admission fees; instead, they request small contributions, usually $1 (55p) or less.

El Cabildo/Museo Histórico del Norte (Historical Museum of the North) First erected in 1582, when the city was founded, the Cabildo has since reinvented itself a number of times. The latest town hall was completed in 1783, typical of Spanish construction—two levels and a tower built around interior patios. The building

Train to the Clouds: Delayed until Further Notice

The **Tren a las Nubes (Train to the Clouds)** ☞ is one of the world's great railroad experiences—a breathtaking ride that climbs to 4,220m (13,842 ft.) without the help of cable tracks. The journey takes you 434km (269 miles) through tunnels, turns, and bridges, culminating in the stunning La Polvorilla viaduct. You will cross magnificent landscapes, making your way from the multicolored Lerma valley through the deep canyons and rugged peaks of the Quebrada del Toro and on to the desolate desert plateau of La Puña. The train stops at the peak, where your tour guide (there's one in each car) will describe the region's topography and check that everyone is breathing fine and not suffering from altitude sickness. In the small town of San Antonio de los Cobres, you'll have a chance to buy handicrafts, ponchos, and other textile goods from the indigenous people. The 14½-hour ride includes a small breakfast, lunch (additional), and a folkloric show with regional music and dance. A restaurant, post office, communications center, and infirmary are among the first-class passenger cars. The ride makes for a fascinating experience, but be prepared for a very long day.

Tren a las Nubes is currently suspended, and a new operator hopes to resume service in June 2007. For more information, contact the tourism office in Salta, **Secretaría de Turismo de Salta,** Buenos Aires 93 (© **387/ 431-0950** or 387/431-0640; www.turismosalta.gov.ar). The train operates from April to November and departs Salta's General Belgrano Station.

A ticket previously cost $68 (£37), not including lunch.

houses the Museo Histórico del Norte (Historical Museum of the North), with 15 exhibition halls related to the Indian, colonial, and liberal periods of Salteño history. Here you will see religious and popular art, as well as works from the Jesuit period and from upper Peru.

Caseros 549. © 387/421-5340. www.museonor.gov.ar Museum: Tues–Fri 9:30am–1:30pm and 3:30–8:30pm; Sat 9:30am–1:30pm and 4:30–8pm; Sun 9:30am–1pm.

Iglesia San Francisco (San Francisco Church) ☞☞   Rebuilt in 1759 after a fire destroyed the original building, the Iglesia San Francisco is Salta's most prominent postcard image. The terra-cotta facade, with its 53m (174-ft.) tower and tiered white pillars, was designed by architect Luis Giorgi. The belfry—the tallest in the Americas—holds the Campana de la Patria, a bronze bell made from the cannons used in the War of Independence's Battle of Salta. A small museum exhibits a variety of 17th- and 18th-century religious images.

Córdoba and Caseros. No phone. Daily 8am–noon and 4–8pm.

Museo de Arqueológia de Alta Montaña (Andean Archaeological Museum) ☞☞   The MAAM, as it has fast become known in Salta, opened its doors on the main plaza in November 2004 to much fanfare. A beautifully restored historic building, the MAAM houses a good collection of Andean textiles woven over the years. This museum is also home to a large research library dedicated to Andean culture and anthropology. The main focus of the museum is its film screen, which shows the

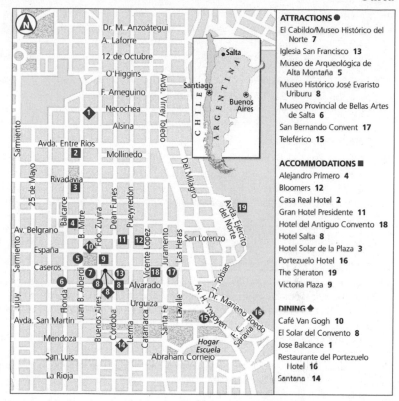

ATTRACTIONS ●

El Cabildo/Museo Histórico del Norte **7**

Iglesia San Francisco **13**

Museo de Arqueológica de Alta Montaña **5**

Museo Histórico José Evaristo Uriburu **8**

Museo Provincial de Bellas Artes de Salta **6**

San Bernardo Convent **17**

Teleférico **15**

ACCOMMODATIONS ■

Alejandro Primero **4**

Bloomers **12**

Casa Real Hotel **2**

Gran Hotel Presidente **11**

Hotel del Antiguo Convento **18**

Hotel Salta **8**

Hotel Solar de la Plaza **3**

Portezuelo Hotel **16**

The Sheraton **19**

Victoria Plaza **9**

DINING ◆

Café Van Gogh **10**

El Solar del Convento **8**

Jose Balcance **1**

Restaurante del Portezuelo Hotel **16**

Santana **14**

recent excavations at Mount Llullaillaco, the highest volcanic peak in Argentina, near the Chilean border. There, three amazingly preserved Andean mummies (over 500 years old) were found in 1999 by a *National Geographic* team of archaeologists, and MAAM was designed for their display. More than 100 other objects were found with the mummies—gold statues and other objects dating back to the Inca era, which will also slowly be featured over the coming years. Already, the locals are affectionately calling this place the *museo de las momias* (mummy museum). Plan to spend an hour here if you want to watch the 30-minute documentary.

Mitre 77. ℂ 387/437-0499. Admission $10 (£5.50). Tues–Sun 9am–1pm and 4–9pm.

Museo Histórico José Evaristo Uriburu ⑆ José Evaristo Uriburu's family, which produced two Argentine presidents, bought this simple adobe house with a roof of reeds and curved tiles in 1810. The street entrance leads directly to a courtyard, characteristic of homes of this era. Exhibits include period furniture and costumes, as well as documents and objects belonging to the Uriburus and General Arenales.

Caseros 479. ℂ 387/428-174. Tues–Sat 9:30am–1:30pm and 3:30–8:30pm.

Museo Provincial de Bellas Artes de Salta (Museum of Fine Arts) ⑆ Colorfully decorated tapestries and other regional works fill this 18th-century Spanish house, which houses a permanent collection of colonial art upstairs, and religious and contemporary art downstairs. Noteworthy pieces include a portrait of Francisco de Uriburu by Spanish painter Joaquín Sorolla y Bastida, and a painting of Salta by Italian Carlo Penutti.

Florida 20. (C) **387/421-4714.** Mon–Sat 9am–1pm and 4–8:30pm.

San Bernardo Convent 𝄞𝄞   Salta's oldest religious building was declared a Historical National Monument in 1941. It's worth a walk by to admire the city's most impressive example of colonial and indigenous art (only Carmelite nuns are allowed to enter). Indigenous craftsmen carved the entrance from a carob tree in 1762.

Caseros near Santa Fe.

Teleférico (Salta Tram) 𝄞   This Swiss-made cable car has been in operation since 1987, ferrying tourists to the top of San Bernardo Hill, 300m (984 ft.) over Salta. At the top, there's not much to do besides take in the panoramic view of the Lerma valley and grab a snack at the casual restaurant. If you miss the last tram, a cheap taxi will return you to the city center.

At the intersection of avs. H. Yrigoyen and San Martín. (C) **387/431-0641.** Admission $3 (£1.65) adults, $2 (£1.10) children. Daily 10am–7:30pm.

OUTDOOR ACTIVITIES & TOUR OPERATORS

The bounty of nature around Salta is staggering. Since most of the landscape is untouched, and there are gorges and canyons and volcanic peaks to negotiate, **trekking** is the most popular outdoor activity in the area. **Adventure Life Journeys,** 1655 S. 3rd St. W., Missoula, MT 59801 (C) **800/344-6118** or 406/541-2677; www.adventure-life.com), offers some of the best-organized treks in the region, usually beginning and ending in Buenos Aires. Their popular 9-day Northwest trek through Salta, Cafayate, and Cachi runs about $1,695 (£932) per person, everything included.

Ecotourism is gaining popularity in the area due to the abundance of wildlife. One-to four-day safaris and bird-watching expeditions are organized by **Clark Expediciones,** Caseros 121, Salta (C) **387/421-5390;** www.clarkexpediciones.com), an excellent local outfitter. Their bird-watching trips run from half a day to 2 days, and the highlight is usually seeing the immense Andean condor soaring over the mountains.

Rafting, windsurfing, and other **watersports** are becoming popular in the Dique Cabra Corral, 70km (43 miles) south of Salta. For more information, contact **Salta Rafting,** Buenos Aires 88 Local 14 (C) **387/401-0301;** info@saltarafting.com), and **Active Argentina,** Zuviria 982 (C) **387/431-1868**).

SHOPPING

Salta province's secretary of tourism does a great job controlling their handmade products—from textiles to bamboo and wood ornaments. After certification, they're sold only at the **Mercado Artesanal,** San Martín 2555 (no phone), open from 9am to 9pm daily. Here, you'll find authentic products—from leather goods to candles—made throughout Salta Province by local artisans. The price is controlled, too, so you don't have to worry about bargaining here. You'll also find beautiful jewelry and silver.

WHERE TO STAY

Salta now has some luxurious accommodations, and prices are still reasonable in comparison with other parts of the country. Options are good both inside and outside the city center. Staying in the city center gives you a chance to walk everywhere. If you're after some peace and quiet, though, consider staying in the nearby village of San Lorenzo or at a ranch just outside the city center.

IN THE CITY CENTER
Very Expensive
Alejandro Primero ✺✺✺ *Value*   Newly opened in April 2006, Salta's second five-star hotel beats the Sheraton for color and charm. Two gauchos greet you as you enter an 11-story glass vaulted building of Andean chic. Carpets are adorned with minia-ture designs of guanacos (llamas), ostriches, and cactus. Corridors are enlivened with leather wall hangings, indigenous art, and the occasional ceramic pot. Rooms are spa-cious with panoramic views, and double glazing ensures the noisy downtown location does not intrude on your *tranquilidad.* The indigenous theme creeps into the room furnishings, with geometric patterns flourishing on armrests, bed heads, and curtains. Named after the local owner's son who died in a car crash, Alejandro Primero offers all the luxury of a top hotel without losing a sense of place and a human touch.

Balcarce 252. ✆ **387/400-0000.** www.alejandro1hotel.com.ar. 167 units. $100–$140 (£55–£77) double; from $150 (£83) suite. Rates include buffet breakfast. AE, DC, MC, V. **Amenities:** Restaurant; bar; lounge; indoor pool; exercise room; sauna; business center w/free Internet; meeting rooms; room service; laundry service; dry cleaning. *In room:* A/C, TV, minibar, hair dryer, safe.

Hotel Solar de la Plaza ✺✺✺ *Finds*   This absolutely charming hotel used to be the residence of one of Salta's well-known families, Patron Costas. The four rooms in the older part of the building were the actual bedrooms of the family members. They have been meticulously transformed into comfortable hotel rooms while retaining their old-world feel—hardwood floors, Jacuzzi tubs, and wrought-iron floor lamps (handmade in Salta). The rooms in the newer wing sport the same decor but with a slightly more modern feel, including marble pedestal sinks in the bathrooms and writing desks made from local wood. Service is gracious and refined, and the public areas are incredibly ele-gant, from the rooftop pool with its adjoining sun deck to the attractive restaurant serv-ing regional specialties with a nouvelle twist. The competent and English-speaking staff can arrange many outdoor activities, including hiking, horseback riding, and bird watching at the nearby Patron Costas ranch.

Juan M. Leguizamon 669. ✆/fax **387/431-5111.** www.solardelaplaza.com.ar. 30 units. $145–$230 (£80–£127) dou-ble; $260 (£143) suite. Rates include continental breakfast. AE, DC, MC, V. **Amenities:** Restaurant; bar; lounge; small outdoor pool; exercise room; sauna; business center; limited room service. *In room:* A/C, TV, minibar, safe.

The Sheraton ✺✺   Salta's first five-star hotel lacks imagination but trumps on loca-tion. The design could be described as very Sheratonesque—bland but luxurious. A plain, cream-colored facade hangs over a dark lobby of stone walls, corduroy seating, and cobbled stones. Bright, terra-cotta hallways lead to an anti-climax, as the spacious rooms are somewhat colorless and sterile. They nevertheless have all the creature com-forts expected of a Sheraton.

What really stands out is the view. The hotel is a U-shaped, seven-story building cut into the side of a hill overlooking the city (a 10-min. walk from the center). Every room offers an invigorating vista of the Andean *pre-cordillera,* and the city's rooftop hodgepodge of terra-cotta tiles, church spires, and bell towers. Guests can admire all this from a large outdoor pool area with wooden decking and a generous-size Jacuzzi.

Av. Ejercito del Norte 330. ✆ **387/432-3000.** www.starwoodhotels.com. 145 units. $138–$185 (£76–£102) double; from $190 (£105) suite. Rates include buffet breakfast. AE, DC, MC, V. **Amenities:** Restaurant; bar; lounge; outdoor pool; exercise room; sauna; business center; meeting rooms; room service; laundry service; dry cleaning. *In room:* A/C, TV, minibar, hair dryer, safe.

Expensive

Casa Real Hotel *(Value* Rooms are very spacious and comfortable, with big picture windows (some overlooking the mountains), large-screen TVs, and firm, comfortable beds. Bathrooms are also large and very clean. The Casa Real boasts a decent-size exercise room and a good-size indoor pool, as well as an attractive restaurant and bar. The staff is friendly and can help arrange transportation and tours.

Mitre 669. © 387/421-5675. www.casarealsalta.com.ar. 83 units. $80–$100 (£44–£55) double; from $107 (£59) suite. Rates include buffet breakfast. AE, DC, MC, V. **Amenities:** Restaurant; bar; lounge; indoor pool; exercise room; sauna; business center w/free Internet; meeting rooms; room service; laundry service; dry cleaning. *In room:* A/C, TV, minibar, hair dryer, safe.

Gran Hotel Presidente *(* This contemporary hotel has attractive guest rooms splashed in rose and apple green, with sparkling white-tile bathrooms. The chic lobby features black-and-white marble with Art Deco furniture and leopard-skin upholstery. The pleasant international restaurant is located on the upstairs mezzanine, and there's a spa with a heated indoor pool, a sauna, a fitness room, and a solarium.

Av. de Belgrano 353. ©/fax 387/431-2022. www.granhotelpresidente.com. 96 units. $110 (£61) double; $170 (£94) suite. Rates include buffet breakfast. AE, DC, MC, V. **Amenities:** Restaurant; small indoor pool; exercise room; sauna; meeting rooms; room service; laundry service; dry cleaning. *In room:* A/C, TV, minibar, hair dryer, safe.

Moderate

Hotel Salta *((Moments* Popular with Europeans, this neoclassical hotel sits in the heart of Salta—facing Plaza 9 de Julio—and makes an excellent base from which to explore the city. Opened in 1890, these are hardly the most modern accommodations you'll find, but the hotel's wood balconies and arabesque carvings, peaceful courtyard, refreshing pool, and beautiful dining room overlooking the plaza considerably heighten its appeal. At $10 more, "A" rooms are larger than standard rooms and have bathtubs, as opposed to just showers. The friendly staff will arrange horseback riding, golf, and other outdoor activities upon request.

Buenos Aires 1. ©/fax 387/431-0740. www.hotelsalta.com. 99 units. From $55 (£30) double; from $200 (£110) suite. Rates include buffet breakfast. AE, DC, MC, V. **Amenities:** Restaurant; bar; pool; sauna; small business center; meeting rooms; room service; massage; laundry service. *In room:* A/C, TV, minibar, safe.

Portezuelo Hotel *(Overrated* The Portezuelo Hotel stands on top of Cerro San Bernardo, a hill just outside the city center. Guest rooms have A-frame ceilings and simple wood decor; unfortunately, they are a bit shabby and drab, and they're not well maintained. The tiny bathrooms desperately need some care. At $10 (£5.50) more, VIP rooms are slightly larger than standard ones and have work desks and safe deposit boxes, but these, too, are devoid of luxury. Stay here only if the other hotels are full.

Av. Turística 1. © 387/431-0104. Fax 387/431-4654. www.portezuelohotel.com. 63 units. From $44 (£24) double; from $62 (£34) suite. Rates include buffet breakfast. AE, DC, MC, V. **Amenities:** Restaurant; bar; outdoor pool; room service; laundry service. *In room:* TV, minibar, hair dryer, safe.

Inexpensive

Bloomers This is not a bed-and-breakfast but a "bed and brunch," indicating the somewhat colorful, bohemian aspect of this boutique hotel. Wacky rugs and arty lamps adorn the five rooms, along with huge ceramic urns and luminous, cube-shaped beanbag-type chairs. One room has a regal flavor with pink walls, an elegantly hung mosquito net, and silk cushions. The bathrooms are a decent size with colorful, mosaic-style tiling. Some rooms are bigger than others (ask for one out front), and only two have air-conditioning. Public spaces include a beautiful garden and barbecue terrace but no pool. The kitchen is for communal use, and the staff is young and friendly, with good English and a little French, courtesy of the French pastry chef. Small and quirky, Bloomers is a unique and charming place to stay in the city center.

Vicente Lopez 129. ⓒ/fax 387/422-7449. www.bloomers-salta.com.ar. 5 units. From $40 (£22) double. Rates include breakfast. AE, DC, MC, V. **Amenities:** Kitchen; laundry service. *In room:* A/C, TV.

Hotel del Antiguo Convento   The humble colonial entrance to this budget hotel might make you think it is a little too budget. But you will be pleasantly surprised as the modern reception area opens out into three courtyards and a garden pool, all decorated with flowers and pots and flagstones. The surrounding rooms are midsize with air-conditioning and TV. The bathrooms are small but sparkling clean and perfectly adequate. The gracious staff and central location make it a good choice for some quality accommodation.

Caseros 113. ⓒ/fax 387/422-7267. www.hoteldelconvento.com.ar. 25 units. From $33 (£18) double. Rates include breakfast. AE, DC, MC, V. **Amenities:** Outdoor pool; laundry service. *In room:* A/C, TV.

Victoria Plaza   If you're in Salta to sightsee, rather than to loll around in sumptuous hotel rooms, then the Victoria Plaza should do just fine. Rooms are stark and simple, but they're clean, comfortable, and cheerfully maintained. Those on the seventh floor and higher enjoy better views for a few dollars more. The hotel has an excellent location next to the main plaza, the Cabildo (town hall), and the cathedral. The cafeteria-like restaurant is open 24 hours, and the hotel offers free airport transfers.

Zuviria 16. ⓒ/fax 387/431-8500. 96 units. From $24 (£13) double. Rates include buffet breakfast. AE, DC, MC, V. **Amenities:** Tiny exercise room; sauna; meeting room; laundry service. *In room:* A/C, TV, fridge.

OUTSIDE THE CITY CENTER
Very Expensive
House of Jasmines 🌺🌺🌺 *Moments*   American actor Robert Duvall and his Argentine wife bought this pristine farmhouse on 120 hectares (296 acres) and converted it into a fantastic inn, worthy of a spread in *House & Garden*. A large photograph of the actor hangs over the beautiful fireplace in the main living room as you enter the house. Each of the seven rooms is different, but all are exquisitely decorated, in keeping with the colonial feel of the house—four-posted beds, antique furniture, and fluffy duvets. Fresh roses (and jasmines in season) will fill your room with a glorious scent. Bathrooms are sparkling and new. Most guests opt to dine in the elegant dining room, and the chef prepares everything from scratch—even the bread is baked on the premises. Miles of trails and open fields surround a magnificent swimming pool and a rose garden. You are a guest here, not a customer, and the staff will do everything to help make you feel at home. Although the owners are American, the staff does not speak English. The farmhouse is close to Salta's airport, about a 15-minute drive from the city center.

Camino al Encon, La Merced Chica. ⓒ/fax 387/497-2002. www.houseofjasmines.com. 7 units. $125–$260 (£69–£143). Rates include continental breakfast. MC, V. **Amenities:** Restaurant; lounge; pristine outdoor pool; room service; laundry service.

Moderate
El Castillo 🌺🌺 *Finds*   A 10-minute drive from downtown Salta, this lovely hideaway feels like it's 100 miles away. Italian immigrant Luigi Bartoletti built it in the late 1800s as a summer home in the style of an Italian *castello*. Some 20 years ago, John Johnston from Alabama purchased the place, lovingly restoring it to its turn-of-the-20th-century glory. The rooms are different but all are comfortable and furnished

with antiques. Room no. 3 has a Jacuzzi tub and large windows with views of the lush grounds. The two-story suite comes with a fireplace and a giant candelabra. The restaurant serves excellent regional specialties. There are countless outdoor activities in the area, and the friendly English-speaking staff will be happy to make arrangements for you.

Camino a la Quebrada, Villa San Lorenzo. ©/fax 387/492-1052. www.hotelelcastillo.com.ar. 8 units. $42–$58 (£23–£32) double; $87 (£48) suite. Rates include continental breakfast. MC, V. **Amenities:** Restaurant; lounge; beautiful outdoor pool; room service. *In room:* TV.

WHERE TO DINE

The Northwest has its own cuisine influenced by indigenous cooking. *Locro* (a corn-and-bean soup), *humitas* (a sort of corn-and-goat cheese soufflé), tamales (meat and potatoes in a ground corn shell), empanadas (a turnover filled with potatoes, meat, and vegetables), *lechón* (suckling pig), and *cabrito* (goat) occupy most menus. Traditional Argentine steaks and pasta dishes are usually available too. In addition to the locations listed below, the Mercado Central, at Florida and San Martín, has a number of inexpensive eateries serving regional food.

MODERATE

Café van Gogh ✿ CAFE   "Our mission is to make everyone feel at home, no matter where they're from," says one staff member, who proudly displays a collection of coffee cups from Argentina, Europe, and North America. This cheeky cafe, surrounded by little white lights on the outside and decorated with van Gogh prints inside, serves pizzas, sandwiches, meats, hot dogs, and empanadas. Come evening, the cafe-turned-bar becomes the center of Salta nightlife, with live bands playing Wednesday through Saturday after midnight. Café van Gogh is also a popular spot for breakfast.

España 502. © 387/431-4659. Main courses $3–$4 (£1.65–£2.20). AE, DC, MC, V. Daily 7am–2am.

El Solar del Convento ✿✿ ARGENTINE   Ask locals to point you to Salta's best "typical" restaurant—the word used to describe places serving traditional Argentine fare—and they won't hesitate with their answer. This former Jesuit convent has long been an outstanding *parrilla* (grill), serving quality steaks (the mixed grill for two is a deal at $4) and regional specialties such as empanadas, tamales, and *humitas*. The 10-page menu also includes beef brochettes, grilled salmon, chicken with mushrooms, and large, fresh salads. Two dining rooms are connected by an A-frame thatched roof, and a medieval-style chandelier hangs from the ceiling. The atmosphere is festive, and, even late on a Sunday night, expect the restaurant to be packed.

Caseros 444. © 387/439-3666. Main courses $3–$6 (£1.65–£3.30). AE, DC, MC, V. Daily 11am–3pm and 8pm–midnight.

José Balcance ✿✿✿ *(Finds* INTERNATIONAL/REGIONAL   Salta's newest and most elegant restaurant opened in 2004, destined to become one of the most talked-about dining establishments in northwestern Argentina. Everything here is done right, to make you feel as though you've come to a very special place—from the exposed stone walls to the exquisite lighting and elegant dark wood tables, to the very efficient service. Andean cuisine with a modern flair is the specialty at José Balcance. Here's where you can try roasted llama meat served with Andean potatoes or quinoa. Or llama medallions with prickly pear sauce. Local goat cheese is drizzled over a "tower" of grilled aubergines and olive tapenade. You can even have llama carpaccio if you're feeling adventurous, although simpler dishes are always available, such as fresh trout roasted with butter and ginger, or chicken curry with vegetables. The menu changes very often, and different world cuisines, in addition to the Andean, are featured occasionally. Order a well-chilled Torrontes white wine to round out your meal.

Mitre and Necochea. ⓒ **387/421-1628.** Reservations recommended. Main courses $6–$9 (£3.30–£4.95). AE, DC, MC, V. Mon–Thurs 9pm–midnight; Fri–Sat 9pm–1am.

Restaurante del Portezuelo Hotel REGIONAL This restaurant in the Portezuelo Hotel offers good views, and the intimate dining room, with large windows overlooking the Lerma Valley, is decorated with regional artwork and tables topped with white linens and silver candles. You won't go wrong with any of the creative entrees, such as trout stuffed with shrimp and cheese, sirloin steak with scalloped potatoes, or grilled chicken with mustard and tarragon. The restaurant also serves regional specialties such as *locro, pastel de choclo* (corn-and-meat pie), empanadas, *humitas,* and tamales. Jazz music occasionally accompanies dinner. Consider a table on the veranda in warm weather.

Av. Turística 1. ⓒ **387/431-0104.** Reservations recommended. Main courses $4–$7 (£2.20–£3.85). AE, DC, MC, V. Daily noon–3pm and 8pm–1am.

Santana ⓐ INTERNATIONAL   This is one of the few international restaurants in Salta with a classic rather than rustic style. The enticing menu features chicken with white-wine cream sauce, lobster with chimichurri sauce, and homemade ravioli with various cheeses. The selection of Argentine wines is rich; ask for a bottle from San Juan or Mendoza.

Mendoza 208. ⓒ **387/432-0941.** Reservations recommended. Main courses $3–$5 (£1.65–£2.75). AE, DC, MC, V. Daily noon–3:30pm and 8pm–midnight.

Viejo Jack II *(Kids (Value* ARGENTINE   An inexpensive local *parrilla* frequented by locals, Viejo Jack II (Viejo Jack I is at Av. Virrey Toledo 145) serves succulent steaks and fresh pastas. Kids have access to a play area as well.

Av. Reyes Católicos 1465. ⓒ **387/439-2802.** Main courses $2–$4 (£1.10–£2.20). DC, MC, V. Daily 12.30–3:30pm and 8pm–1am.

2 A Driving Tour of the Calchaquíes Valley via Cachi & Cafayate

The landscape surrounding Salta resembles the southwestern United States, with polychromatic hills keeping watch over the Lerma Valley. Tobacco, tropical fruits, and sugar cane are the main agricultural products here, and you will see tobacco "ovens" off the side of the road (Marlboro grows Virginia tobacco here through a subsidiary). Heading south from Salta on RN 68 for 38km (24 miles), you'll reach **El Carril,** which is a typical small town of the valley, with a central plaza and botanical garden displaying 70% of the region's flora.

Although you can reach **Cafayate** more quickly by continuing south on RN 68, it is far more interesting to go west on RP 33 for about 2.7km (1¾ miles) after El Carril to **Cabaña de Cabras,** in La Flor del Pago (ⓒ **387/499-1093**), one of the principal goat farms and cheese factories in Argentina. Ducks, geese, and hundreds of goats roam the scenic property, and you can sample the delicious chèvre in the small dining room and cheese shop in the proprietors' home. A bread and jam snack costs only 50¢ (30p); a cheese sandwich is $2 (£1.10); and a glass of local wine is $1.70 (95p). (The kind owners will prepare a multicourse lunch or dinner with advance reservations.) You can also stay over in one of their well appointed rooms for $45 (£25).

Dense vegetation covers the region surrounding El Carril, but the land quickly dries out as you climb RP 33 toward **Piedra del Molino (Mill Rock).** The road narrows from pavement to dirt 10km (6¼ miles) west of El Carril—watch closely for oncoming cars. A small shrine to Saint Raphael (a patron saint of travelers) indicates your arrival at Mill Rock (3,620m/11,874 ft. elevation) and the entrance to **Parque Nacional los Cardones,** a semiarid landscape filled with cacti, sage, and limestone rock formations.

Ten kilometers (6¼ miles) before Cachi lies **Payogasta,** an ancient Indian town on the path of the Inca Road that once connected an empire stretching from Peru to northern Argentina. **Cachi** (see below) is another precolonial village worth a visit for its Indian ruins. From Cachi, take RN 40 south past Brcalito to Molinos, a 17th-century town of adobe homes and dusty streets virtually unchanged from how it must have appeared 350 years ago. Continuing south, consider stopping 9km (5½ miles) before Angastaco at the **Estancia Carmen** (© 368/1569-3005), which boasts spectacular views of the Calchaquíes Valley and its long mountain canyon. Between 9am and 6pm, you can visit the ranch's Inca ruins, rent horses, and peek inside the private church in back, where two 300-year-old mummies rest in peace.

Continue south on RN 40 to **Angastaco,** which may be a good place to spend the night. **Hostería Angastaco,** Avenida Libertad (© 3868/1563-9016), 1km (about ½ mile) west of the village, is popular with European travelers. The simple hotel offers live folkloric music each evening. The staff will help arrange regional excursions and horseback riding. From Angastaco to San Carlos, you will pass the **Quebrada de las Flechas (Arrows Ravine),** with its stunning rock formations, which appeared in *The Empire Strikes Back.* People often stop their cars by the side of the road and climb a bit. Jesuits settled in **San Carlos,** and the church is a national historic monument. **Cafayate** (see below) marks the southern end of this circuit.

Return to Salta along RN 68 heading north, which takes you through the **Río Calchaquíes Valley** and on to the **Quebrada del Río de las Conchas (Canyon of the River of Shells).** The most interesting crimson rock formations are Garganta del Diablo (Devil's Throat), El Anfiteatro (the Ampitheater), and Los Castillos (the Castles), which are all indicated by road signs. Salta is 194km (120 miles) from Cafayate along RN 68, and it shouldn't take more than a few hours to drive.

CACHI 𝆺

Home of the Chicoanas Indians before the Spaniards arrived, Cachi is a tiny pueblo of about 5,000 people, interesting for its Indian ruins, colonial church, and archaeological museum. The Spanish colonial **church,** built in the 17th century and located next to the main plaza, has a floor and ceiling made from cactus wood. The **archaeological museum** is the most impressive museum of its kind in the Northwest, capturing the influence of the Incas and Spaniards on the region's indigenous people. Next to the main plaza, its courtyard is filled with Inca stone engravings and pre-Columbian artifacts. Wall rugs, ponchos, and ceramics are sold at the **Centro Artesanal,** next to the tourist office, on the main plaza (the people of Cachi are well respected for their weaving skills, and the ponchos they sell are beautiful). **La Paya,** 10km (6¼ miles) south of Cachi, and **Potrero de Payogasta,** 10km (6¼ miles) north of Cachi, hold the area's most important archaeological sites.

GETTING THERE   Cachi is 157km (97 miles) west of Salta on RP 33. **Empresa Marcos Rueda** (© 387/421-4447) offers two buses daily from Salta; the trip takes 4 hours and costs $6 (£3.30).

VISITOR INFORMATION   You can pick up maps, excursion information, and tips on restaurants and hotels at the **Oficina de Turismo,** Avenida General Güemes (© **3868/491902**), open Monday through Friday from 8am to 9pm, and Saturdays and Sundays 9am to 3pm and 5 to 9pm.

WHERE TO STAY

Hostal La Paya ⋒   Opened in 2000 on a 19th-century *estancia* (ranch), this rustic inn overlooking the Calchaquíes Valley is a quiet place to walk, read, and relax. Guest rooms have adobe walls and wood-beam ceilings, llama-wool rugs, and mattresses laid on stone frames. You can eat your meals here if you like; all the produce (except the meat) comes from this farm. The owners will also arrange excursions to the nearby mountains, valley, and river.

8km (5 miles) from Cachi, on RN 40 to Molinos. ©/fax **3868/491139**. www.casadecampolapaya.com.ar. 8 units. From $110 (£61) double. Rates include breakfast. No credit cards. **Amenities:** Restaurant; pool; outdoor excursions.

WHERE TO DINE

Confitería y Comedor del Sol REGIONAL   When you walk into this village restaurant, locals are likely to cease their conversations and stare for a minute. Not to worry—they will quickly return to their business once you sit down; many are engaged in the afternoon's current soap opera. The menu is simple, consisting of pastas, *milanesas* (breaded meat cutlets), empanadas, and tamales. This is a great place to have lunch on your way to Molinos.

Ruiz de los Llanos. © **15/6055-149**. Main courses $1–$4 (55p–£2.20). No credit cards. Daily 8am–1am.

CAFAYATE ⋒⋒⋒

The wine town of Cafayate has its own distinct colors—pink dust, red hills, and olive-green mountains. Corn-yellow sand gathers along the curbstones of this sun-kissed village, while donkeys graze on the central plaza, and heaps of unlocked bicycles stand outside schools and the coffee-colored cathedral. Add to this some pretty, palatial-style wineries, luxury lodges, excellent arts and crafts, and stunning vineyard country producing the aromatic white *torrontes* grape, and you can see why this whole area is becoming known as the Tuscany of Argentina.

GETTING THERE   Cafayate lies 194km (120 miles) southwest of Salta on RN 68. **Empresa El Indio** (© **387/432-0846**) offers three buses daily from Salta; the trip takes 3½ hours and costs about $8 (£4.40).

VISITOR INFORMATION   The **tourist office** (© **3868/421470**) is located on the main plaza and provides maps, bus schedules, and lodging recommendations. Open hours are Monday through Saturday from 10am to 6pm.

SEEING THE SIGHTS

Though there are quite a few vineyards to visit in the area, some unexpectedly shut down their guided visits for inexplicable reasons. The most popular time to visit is from February to early April, when the harvest occurs. Most wineries are open daily except Sunday during that time. I've listed below the wineries most likely to be open year-round. Most museums in this area are free or request a small donation (usually no more than $1/55p). Even more interesting are the different workshops producing handicrafts from the area. Mendoza-based wine tour company **Trout and Wine,** Sarmiento 133, Mendoza (© **261/4255613;** www.troutandwine.com), offers excellent personalized tours of the area.

Arte en Telar   This textile workshop offers a fascinating look into the local tradition of hand weaving. Guests can take a tour (usually in Spanish) and watch women work on hand looms in the garden, converting alpaca and wool into scarves and throws. At the front there is a small display of all their products.

Colón 71. No phone. arteentelar@hotmail.com. Mon–Sat 10am–2pm and 4–10pm.

Bodegas Etchart 🍷   Owned by the French giant Pernod-Ricard, this vineyard is one of the region's most important, producing 6,000 bottles of wine per hour—including chardonnay (for which this *bodega,* or wine cellar, is best known), cabernet sauvignon, Tannat, Torrontes (a Muscadet-like white), and Malbec (a dry red). The *bodega* exports its wine to more than 30 countries. One-hour guided tours and wine tastings are offered Monday through Friday from 9am to 5pm, and Saturday from 9am to noon.

Finca La Rosa, 3km (1¾ miles) from Cafayate on RN 40. 🕿 **3868/421310.**

Finca Las Nubes 🍷🍷🍷 *Finds*   One of Argentina's smallest vineyards is strictly family-run and produces some young but excellent wines. This is the last frontier of winemaking, a few kilometers up a dirt road from the center of town. Jose and Mercedes Mounier started their tiny operation 8 years ago, producing 2,000 bottles. In 2004, they produced 30,000 bottles of cabernet-Malbec, Rose de Malbec, and Torrontes. They use no fertilizer on their vines, so the wine is almost organic. If you call ahead, the Mouniers will arrange to serve you lunch or dinner on their lovely terrace overlooking the vineyard. During visiting hours, you'll see the tiny operation up close and personal (including the labeling of bottles and boxes of wine being readied for shipment). The highlight of the 1-hour visit is a wine and cheese tasting. The Mouniers have a comfortable *cabaña* for rent next to the house overlooking the fields for $50 (£28) per night, including breakfast. Wine tours and tastings are free of charge Monday to Saturday 9am to 5pm; call for an appointment outside these hours or to arrange for a meal.

El Divisadero, Alto Valle de Cafayate, 5km (3 miles) from Cafayate (ask for directions from town). 🕿 **3868/422129.** japmounier@yahoo.com.ar. Mon–Sat 9am–5pm.

Michel Torino Bodega La Rosa 🍷🍷   This medium-size *bodega,* open since 1892, produces roughly 10 million liters of wine per year (10,000 bottles per hour); the main products are Malbec, cabernet sauvignon, merlot, chardonnay, and "Michael Torino" Torrontes. The Don David reserve is the vineyard's top selection. They offer guided tours, in Spanish only, Monday through Thursday from 9am to 5pm, and Friday from 9am to 4pm. The *bodega* also has a small guesthouse with charming rustic rooms.

Finca La Rosa, 3km (1¾ miles) from Cafayate on RN 40. No phone. www.micheltorino.com.ar. Mon–Thurs 9am–5pm; Fri 9am–4pm.

Museo de Vitivinicultura (Museum of Grapevines and Wine) 🍷🍷   Part of the Bodega Encantada winery, this museum tells the story of grape growing and winemaking in and around Cafayate. The 19th-century building houses old-fashioned machinery and more modern equipment, as well as agricultural implements and documentary photographs.

RN 40, at Av. General Güemes. 🕿 **3868/421125.** Mon–Fri 10am–1pm and 5–9pm.

Museo Regional y Arqueológico Rodolfo Bravo (Regional and Archaeological Museum) 🍷   This small museum displays ceramics, textiles, and metal objects discovered over a 66-year period by Rodolfo Bravo. Covering a period between the 4th and 15th centuries, these archaeological finds celebrate the heritage of Diaguita-Calchaquíes, and Inca tribes in the region.

Colón 191. © **3868/421054.** Mon–Fri 11am–9pm; weekend hours vary.

Vasija Secreta 🐾   At the entrance of town, this large *bodega* also houses a small but interesting museum with winemaking equipment dating back to 1857. A good collection of black-and-white photos depicts life at the *bodega* in the late 1800s. There are huge oak barrels (ca. 1900) from Nancy, France, and barrels made from local wood that ruined the wine and thus weren't used much. The 1-hour tour ends with a tasting of the various wines, most of them sold to restaurants around Argentina. Vasija Secreta, unlike other *bodegas,* markets heavily for the local market.

RN 40, Valle Calchaquies. © **3868/421850.** Mon–Sat 9am–4pm.

WHERE TO STAY
Cafayate has seen a surge in luxury accommodation, mostly of the wine lodge variety. The town itself still lacks a high-end hotel, but many of the new lodges are within easy walking distance of the village.

Inexpensive
Gran Real   This terribly modest hotel has quiet rooms with very simple furnishings. These rooms, some with pleasant mountain views, are considerably more enticing than the gloomy downstairs lobby and cafe. Popular with Argentine visitors, the Gran Real has an attractive pool and barbecue area, which is its saving grace. Service is friendly. TVs are available, on request, for an additional $3 (£1.65) per night.

Av. General Güemes 128, 4427 Cafayate. © **3868/421231.** Fax 3868/421016. www.granrealcafayate.com.ar. 35 units. $30 (£17) double. Rates include continental breakfast. MC, V. **Amenities:** Restaurant; lounge; nice outdoor pool. *In room:* TV on request.

Hostal Killa 🐾🐾 *(Value*   With a long, rambling courtyard of whitewashed walls, terra-cotta tiles, wind chimes, and chunky wooden staircases, Hotel Killa has a bright Mediterranean feel. Its four buildings contain spacious rooms and small immaculate bathrooms with baths and powerful showers. The eight rooms are decked out with local stone, windowed wardrobes, and indigenous art. Many have a rooftop view of the village. Little touches such as ceramic-face tiles in the walls, the occasional wicker chair in the courtyard, and whiteflower creepers make this one of the most delightful places to stop over while you're touring the area. Owner Martha Chocobar is constantly on hand to help and offer advice on where to go. Everything is sparkling clean, and an upstairs apartment with a small kitchen sleeps four. The hotel is a short walk from the main plaza.

Colón 47, 4427 Cafayate. © **3868/422254.** hostalkillacafayate@hotmail.com. 8 units. $53 (£29) double; $100 (£55) apt for 4. Rates include continental breakfast. No credit cards. **Amenities:** Small lounge.

Villa Vicuña   A crazy mural of some local leprechauns stands in the shaded courtyard, surrounded by 12 simple but well-appointed rooms in a modern building with some colonial touches, such as an arched entrance and street balcony. Opened in January 2006, Villa Vicuña appears brand spanking new, and the rooms are very comfortable, with wooden posted beds, built-in wardrobes, and clean bathrooms of average size (10 have baths). The decor is somewhat mixed, with plastic chairs in one corner of the courtyard and a traditional loom in the other, not to mention the leprechauns.

Nevertheless, if you are looking for a clean, friendly place that's close to the plaza and not too expensive, this one will not disappoint.

Belgrano 76, 4427 Cafayate. © **3868/422145**. www.villavicuna.com.ar. 12 units. $30 (£17) double. Rates include continental breakfast. MC, V. **Amenities:** Restaurant; lounge. *In room:* TV.

WINE LODGES
Expensive
La Casa de la Bodega   The 20km (12-mile) drive to this luxury winery lodge is almost as enjoyable as the destination itself. You drive through a desert of pink sand and cactus sentinels until you reach a twisting road that meanders through purple mountains that resemble melted plasticine. The hotel itself is built of sand-colored brick with lots of tile and wood; the reception desk itself is a huge trunk of the local tree *algarroba*. The eight rooms are large with stone headboards and yet more wood. Indigenous designs hang everywhere. The bathrooms are luxurious, with Jacuzzi and hydro-massage. All the rooms have a mountain view, and four have a balcony. Despite such opulence, there is no mistaking the humble, rural location, with small adobe huts in the distance and the occasional scampering goat and foraging boar to catch your attention. Adjoining the lodge is a small, ultramodern winery producing very decent wine.

RP 68 Km18, Valle de Cafayate. © **3868/421888**. www.lacasadelabodega.com.ar. 8 units. $200 (£110) double. Rates include continental breakfast. MC, V. **Amenities:** Restaurant; lounge; outdoor pool; spa. *In room:* TV.

Patios de Cafayate   Time travel may be impossible, but the very luxurious winery lodge Patios de Cafayate makes a valiant attempt at it. Through a series of leafy, flower-adorned courtyards (the patios in the title) you are transported through several eras. First stop: 18th-century colonial splendour. The main building is a palatial-style villa with fountains and even a tiny chapel for some private worship. Vaulted corridors lead to suitelike rooms with colonial portraits watching you from the corners. Hand-painted flowers creep over walls and tabletops and into very spacious rooms with Egyptian cotton sheets and generous bathrooms with sunken baths. Next stop: the Roaring '20s. You'll feel like Gatsby himself in this high-ceilinged living room with mellow jazz playing from a gramophone and tall windows overlooking the pool. Then jump ahead several centuries down a jasmine walkway, and you're in the futuristic wine spa—a slate-gray cube of modernist indulgence. Among many treatments guests can enjoy while watching colors change in the mountains, the *torrontes* bath of oils, wine, and herbal cures is especially relaxing. Every aspect of Patios de Cafayate is designed to help you "switch frequency"; the only problem is you may never want to switch back.

RN 40 at RP 68 (part of El Esteco winery), 4427 Cafayate. © **3868/421747**. www.luxurycollection.com/cafayate. 30 units. $200 (£110) double. Rates include continental breakfast. MC, V. **Amenities:** International and regional restaurant; lounge, outdoor pool, spa. *In room:* TV.

Moderate
Viñas de Cafayate Wine Resort   Situated 3km (2 miles) outside the town in the mountain foothills, this beautiful, simply designed wine lodge has a commanding view of the valley. The front facade of pillared arches leads to a large courtyard with pond and a splash of purple from some lavender bushes. On either side are 12 rooms, big with minimal decor. They have traditional cane ceilings, king-size beds, terra-cotta tiles, and the occasional tapestry. The bathrooms are spacious and clean, and all have a shower and bath. Bordered by vineyards on every side, you can literally pick a grape and eat it while sunbathing by the pool. The restaurant is somewhat hall-like and bare,

but it serves good traditional food, such as pork ribs with *choclo,* to guests and visitors alike.

25 de Mayo, Camino al Divisadero, Cafayate. (℃ **3868/422272.** www.cafayatewineresort.com. 12 units. $100 (£55) double. Rates include continental breakfast. MC, V. **Amenities:** Restaurant; lounge; outdoor pool.

WHERE TO DINE
El Rancho *ARGENTINE*   This restaurant is the best one on the main plaza, and it's less touristy than La Carreta (below); when locals go out to eat, they come here. The expansive dining room has an authentic bamboo roof, and the fans overhead keep things cool in the summer months. Start with freshly made empanadas, *humitas,* or tamales and a salad, and then move on to oven-baked *cabrito* (young goat) with roasted potatoes. Pastas are made on the premises, served with a variety of meat dishes, including tenderloin, for diners after something simple. They stock decent house wines, served in small jugs, and the short wine list features local vintages.

Vicario Toscano 4. (℃ **3868/421256.** Main courses $3–$6 (£1.65–£3.30). MC, V. Daily noon–3:30pm and 9pm–1am.

La Carreta de Don Olegario REGIONAL   Popular with foreign visitors, this restaurant has a pleasant dining room that lacks elegance, but the kitchen serves an authentic selection of regional dishes, including *cabritos.* Service is unhurried, so plan to enjoy a leisurely lunch or dinner if you come here. Folkloric shows take place in the evenings.

Av. General Güemes 20. (℃ **3868/421004.** Main courses $2–$3 (£1–£1.65). MC, V. Daily noon–3pm and 8–11pm.

Machacha *ARGENTINE*   Opened in September 2006, Cafayate can at last boast a gourmet restaurant that offers more than steak and more than steak. The menu of this wine-themed establishment includes exotic dishes such as llama meat and duck. Platters of smoked cheese and cold meats compete for your attention with rabbit. The wine list is all local, with the very rustic Bodega Nanni for example, or the very alcoholic San Pedro de Yacochuya. All this, along with a pebbled courtyard and regional music, make it a very pleasant eating experience.

Guemes 28. (℃ **3868/422319.** Main courses $15–$20 (£8.25–£11). MC, V. Daily 10am–3pm and 7pm–2am.

3 San Salvador de Jujuy
1,620km (1,004 miles) NW of Buenos Aires; 90km (56 miles) N of Salta

The regional capital of Jujuy, San Salvador—commonly called Jujuy—was established by the Spaniards in 1592 as their northernmost settlement in Argentina. In 1812, during the wars of independence, General Belgrano evacuated residents of the city before Spanish troops arrived—an event known as *éxodo jujeño* (Jujuy Exodus), celebrated each July. Smaller than Salta, the well-preserved colonial town doesn't have a great deal to offer, besides a few interesting museums and a beautiful cathedral surrounding Plaza Belgrano. The Indian market across from the bus terminal offers a good sense of daily life here, with many vendors dressed in traditional costumes selling food, indigenous crafts, and textiles. Jujuy is also the best base from which to explore the Quebrada de Humahuaca (Humahuaca Gorge), which extends to the north (see "Driving the Quebrada de Humahuaca [Humahuaca Gorge]," below). The circuit includes the Cerro de los Siete Colores (Hill of the Seven Colors), the artists' haven Tilcara, and La Garganta del Diablo (Devil's Throat) gorge.

ESSENTIALS

GETTING THERE   Aeropuerto Internacional Horacio Guzmán (© 388/491-1109/05/04) is 32km (21 miles) from town. **Aerolíneas Argentinas** (© 0810/222-8652?) flies from Buenos Aires once a day. Flights from Buenos Aires cost between $150 and $200 (£83–£110), depending on the season and availability.

The **Terminal de Omnibus,** or main bus station, is located at Dorrego and Iguazú (© 388/422-6299). Buses arrive from Buenos Aires and travel to Salta, Tucumán, Catamarca, and other cities in the region. **Flecha Bus** (© 388/424-1056) offers a night service to and from Buenos Aires for $65 (£36) one-way. **Empresa Balut** (© 387/432-0608) makes the 2½-hour trip to Humahuaca (see "Driving the Quebrada de Humahuaca [Humahuaca Gorge]," below), as well as to other cities throughout the region.

If you want to rent a car, I recommend **Renta-Car Noroeste** (© 388/15-685-3697), which operates from the airport, and **Renta-Car Jujuy** (© 388/422-6678), in the city center on Jaime Freire 567.

VISITOR INFORMATION & FAST FACTS   The **regional visitor center** is located at Urquiza 354 (© 388/424-9501), in the old train station. It is open weekdays from 7am to 9pm and weekends from 9am to 9pm.

You can arrange regional tours at **Grafitti Turismo,** Belgrano 601 (© 388/423-4033), open Monday to Saturday 9am to 1pm, and 5 to 9pm. They will exchange money here, too.

Citibank, at the corner of España and Balcare, has a 24-hour ATM and change machine. The bank is open weekdays from 9am to 2pm.

GETTING AROUND   Easy to explore on foot, Jujuy is more compact than Salta, and its major attractions can be visited in a few hours. The bulk of commercial activity takes place around **Plaza Belgrano,** where the Casa de Gobierno, the *cabildo* (town hall), and the cathedral are located. Not to be missed, the **Catedral,** built in 1750, has a baroque pulpit carved in wood by indigenous people. Shopping in Jujuy is concentrated along **Calle Belgrano.**

WHAT TO SEE & DO

Most museums in this area are free or request a small donation (usually no more than $1/55p).

Catedral (Cathedral) ⊛   Successor to an earlier cathedral dating from the 17th century, this beautiful updated version, built in 1763, salvaged the original wood pulpit characteristic of Spanish baroque. The cathedral towers over bustling Plaza Belgrano, where a pottery market takes place during the day.

West side of Plaza Belgrano. No phone. Daily 8am–noon and 5–8:30pm.

Museo Arqueológico Provincial (Provincial Archaeological Museum) ⊛⊛   Archaeological finds here represent over 2,500 years of life in the Jujuy region, including a 2,600-year-old ceramic goddess, a lithic collection of arrowheads, the bones of a child from 1,000 years ago, and two mummified adults. Objects from the Yavi and Humahuaca cultures are also exhibited.

Lavalle 434. © 388/422-1315. Mon–Fri 8am–9pm; Sat–Sun 9am–1pm and 5–9pm.

Museo Histórico Provincial (Provincial Historical Museum) ⊛   This was the house in which Juan Lavalle, an important general during Argentina's formative years, was killed in 1841. The large door through which he was shot is on display, right next to an enormous bust of the Argentine hero. Other exhibits include war materials and documents used during the 25-year struggle for independence in Jujuy.

Lavalle 252. © **388/422-1355**. Mon–Fri 8am–1:30pm and 3–8pm; Sat–Sun 9am–1pm and 4–8pm.

WHERE TO STAY

Accommodations in Jujuy city have not improved much in quality. Yet you're here to see the sights, not to linger in the confines of your hotel. Note that accommodations in San Salvador quickly fill up in July during the *éxodo jujeño* (Jujuy Exodus) celebration. An excellent new option, 15km (9 miles) outside the city, is **Finca Los Lapachos,** Casilla de Correo 18 (© **388/491-1291**), a beautiful estate house with five rooms surrounded by sugar-cane and tobacco fields.

Altos de la Viña *Kids*   This is the best hotel in Jujuy, on a hill 3km (1¾ miles) from the city center. A wealth of outdoor activities on the sprawling property includes volleyball, miniature golf, tennis, and swimming in the outdoor pool. Half of the guest rooms have balconies with terrific views of the city; bathrooms have phones, hair dryers, and good amenities. The best rooms are "VIPs" (only $15/£8.25 more)—they feature classic furniture, impressive woodwork, and linens decorated with country French colors. The hotel has an excellent restaurant and a very friendly staff.

Av. Pasquini López 50, 4600 Jujuy. © **388/426-2626**. www.hotelaltodelavina.com.ar. 62 units. From $80 (£44) double; $120 (£66) suite. Breakfast included. AE, DC, MC, V. **Amenities:** Restaurant; outdoor pool; tennis; volleyball; children's games; room service; massage; babysitting; laundry service. *In room:* A/C, TV, minibar, hair dryer

Jujuy Palace Hotel   If lobbies are any indication of a hotel's quality, then the modern and comfortable furnishings you'll find upon entering the Jujuy Palace prove that the management is committed to maintaining a good face. Recently remodeled, guest rooms are modern and inviting, with locally made lamps, fluffy pillows, and new black-and-white bedspreads. Both the rooms and the bathrooms are rather small. If you'd like space, splurge for the suite, with its separate living area and spacious bathroom. The restaurant is attractive and serves excellent steaks. The hotel is centrally located in front of the cathedral.

Calle Belgrano 1060, 4600 Jujuy. ©/fax **388/423-0433**. www.imagine.com.ar/jujuy.palace. 52 units. $44 (£24) double; $62 (£34) suite. Rates include buffet breakfast. AE, DC, MC, V. **Amenities:** Restaurant; gym; sauna; room service. *In room:* A/C, TV.

WHERE TO DINE

Chung King *REGIONAL*   Despite the misleading name, Chung King is a long-time regional favorite in Jujuy, serving *humitas,* tamales, empanadas, *picante de pollo,* and *pollo al ajillo* (both local chicken and vegetable dishes). On Saturday evenings, local artists perform traditional Northwestern dances here, and the atmosphere is very fun and festive. A pizzeria next door serves delicious oven-baked pizzas.

Alvear 627. © **388/422-8142**. Main courses $3–$6 (£1.65–£3.30). AE, DC, MC, V. Daily 11:30am–4pm and 7pm–3am.

Krysys *Finds REGIONAL*   A giant Coke sign outside marks the entrance to Jujuy's best *parrilla,* serving juicy Argentine steaks. The international menu also has a number of pasta and chicken selections, and the trout is excellent. This is a festive restaurant, where locals come to celebrate good times and special occasions.

Balcarce 272. © **388/423-1126**. Main courses $3–$5 (£1.65–£2.75). AE, DC, MC, V. Mon–Sat noon–3:30pm and 8pm–2am; Sun only for lunch.

Need a Break?
Heladería Pingüino, Belgrano 718 (© 388/422-7247), sells 50 flavors of ice cream and frozen yogurt to cool you down. The small cafe is open daily from 9am to midnight.

La Royal Confitería SNACKS   One of the few places where you can eat any time of day in Jujuy, La Royal serves pizzas, empanadas, sandwiches, and other light snacks. An old grandfather clock ticks along undisturbed by the modern American rock playing over the speakers. Black-and-white photos of American actors decorate the walls of this casual but popular cafeteria, which is packed at breakfast.

Calle Belgrano 766. © 388/422-6202. Main courses $2–$3 (£1.10–£1.65). MC, V. Daily 7:30am–midnight.

Manos Jujeñas 🍴 *Value* REGIONAL   Tables are normally packed at this delightful restaurant specializing in regional dishes such as empanadas, *humitas,* and tamales. The small, two-level dining room is decorated with local crafts and costumes, and soft Andean music plays in the background. You will have an excellent and very inexpensive meal here: Consider the trout from the nearby Yala River or one of the homemade pastas served weekends only. A tall glass of orange juice is only a peso. When it's crowded, be prepared to wait a bit for your food.

Senador Pérez 222. © 388/422-2366. Main courses $2–$4 (£1.10–£2.20). No credit cards. Mon–Sat noon–3pm and 8pm–2:30am; Sun only for lunch.

Restaurante del Hotel Altos de la Viña 🍴 INTERNATIONAL   This is as elegant as Jujuy gets. You'll have to leave the city center to reach this hilltop hotel restaurant, with splendid views of the town below. Folkloric groups occasionally serenade the dining room at dinner, and there are candlelit tables outside in summer. The extensive menu focuses on seafood and homemade pastas: The *trucha rellena*—trout stuffed with shrimp, mushrooms, cognac, and white wine—is among the best choices, as are the pastas, *humitas,* and empanadas. Plan to stay for a long meal, as you'll want to linger over one of the mouthwatering desserts.

Av. Pasquini López 50. © 388/426-2626. Reservations recommended. Main courses $3–$6 (£1.65–£3.30). AE, DC, MC, V. Daily 11am–3pm and 7:30pm–midnight.

4 Driving the Quebrada de Humahuaca (Humahuaca Gorge)

For the first 30 or 40 minutes as you head north on RN 9 from San Salvador de Jujuy, undulating hills reveal fields rich with tobacco and corn and expose the rural economy of Argentina's Northwest. Quechuan women wearing colorful ponchos walk with babies strapped to their backs, while horses, cows, and goats graze on the surrounding vegetation. Look closely and you might spot a gaucho charging after his herd.

As you climb along the Río Grande to Purmamarca, 71km (44 miles) from the region's capital, the land becomes increasingly dry and gives way to striking rock formations. When you arrive at the junction of RP 52 and RN 9, head west for a few kilometers to reach the small colonial hamlet. Framing Purmamarca like a timeless painting, the **Cerro de los Siete Colores (Hill of the Seven Colors)** reflects its beauty onto the pueblo's quiet streets and dusty adobe homes. Try to arrive early—9am is best—when the morning sun shines brightly on the hill's facade and reveals its tapestry of colors.

Heading back to RN 9 and continuing north for 20km (12 miles), you will arrive at the artist's haven of **Tilcara,** with a pre-Hispanic fortress called a *pucará.* Here you will find spectacular panoramic views of the Humahuaca Valley, as well as a trapezoid-shaped monument marking the Tropic of Capricorn. To visit **La Garganta del Diablo (Devil's Throat)**—a steep gorge with a small walkway leading along the rock's edge—leave RN 9 and head east of Tilcara for a short distance. Be careful walking here, as there is only a small rope separating you from the depths below.

Continue north along RN 9, where you will pass the small adobe villages of Huacalera and Uquia. About 42km (26 miles) north of Tilcara lies **Humahuaca,** a sleepy yet enchanting village of only a couple of thousand Indian residents. Its relaxed pace will make Buenos Aires seem light years away. Note that at an elevation of 2,700m (8,856 ft.), you will feel a little out of breath here, and nights are quite cold. Although the nearby Inca ruins of **Coctaca** are best explored with a tour guide, you can visit them on your own or with a taxi ($5/£2.75 round-trip, including driver wait time) by following a dirt road about 10km (6¼ miles) out of Humahuaca. Coctaca is a large Indian settlement that the Spaniards discovered in the 17th century. Although the ruins are hard to distinguish from the rocks and debris, you can make out the outlines of the terraced crop fields for which the Incas were famous. The site is surrounded by cactus and provides excellent photo opportunities.

From San Salvador de Jujuy, you can travel this circuit by bus or by car. If you decide you'd like to stay the night in Humahuaca (126km/78 miles north of San Salvador), a simple but hospitable option is the **Posta del Sol,** Martín Rodríguez at San Martín (© **388/499-7157**), which will arrange horseback and 4WD excursions into the surrounding area. Otherwise, you can easily complete the Humahuaca circuit in a day. Several restaurants within walking distance serve Andean cuisine. I recommend that you ask the manager at Posta del Sol for the best place to dine in town.

5 Tucumán

1,300km (806 miles) NW of Buenos Aires; 320km (198 miles) S of Salta

The Northwest's biggest city, San Miguel de Tucumán is situated in Argentina's smallest province. Tucumán, otherwise known as "the Garden of the Republic" for its steaming variety of colorful vegetation, appears minute when squeezed between its giant neighbors Salta and Catamarca. What it lacks in size, however, it does not lack in variety—be it subtropical jungle or temperate highlands. The city's history and prosperity was built on sugar cane. Though such riches have since diminished, you will find a brash and vibrant, somewhat ramshackle metropolis, famous for folkloric music, nightlife, and—believe it or not—rugby.

ESSENTIALS

GETTING THERE Aeropuerto Internacional Benjamin Matienzo (© **381/426-5072**) is 13km (8 miles) from the city center. **Aerolíneas Argentinas** (© **0810/222-8652**?) flies from Buenos Aires. Flights from Buenos Aires cost between $80 and $200 (£44–£110), depending on the season and availability.

The **Terminal de Omnibus,** or main bus station, is located at Avenida Benjamín Teran and B. Araoz (© **381/422-2221**). Buses arrive from Buenos Aires and travel to Salta, Catamarca, and other cities in the region. If you opt to rent a car, try **Hertz** (© **381/426-4112**) and **Móvil Renta** (© **381/431-0550**) at the airport, and **Avis** (© **381/426-7777**) on 24 de Setiembre 30, near the bus station.

VISITOR INFORMATION & FAST FACTS   The **regional visitor center** is located at Avenida 24 de Setiembre 484 (© **381/430-3644**). It is open weekdays from 8am to 10pm and weekends from 9am to 10pm.

You can arrange regional tours at **Coltravel,** Crisóstomo Alvarez 301 (© **381/ 422-6575;** www.coltravel.com.ar).

Citibank, located at San Martín 859, has a 24-hour ATM and change machine. The bank is open weekdays from 9am to 2pm.

GETTING AROUND   As you may have noticed, every Argentine town has a **Plaza Independencia.** Tucumán's is warranted, however, as it was here that the Declaration of Independence from the Spanish crown was delivered on July 9, 1816. It's a good starting point from which to explore a city where the concept of urban planning does not exist, making it a shambles architecturally. Avoid threading the streets in midday during the summer, as traffic blocks passage, and the heat is unbearable.

WHAT TO SEE & DO

Most museums here are free or request a small donation (usually no more than $1/55p).

Casa de Gobierno   This interesting Art Nouveau building has spacious porticoes. It's visually pleasing to see at night when the building is lit up.

25 de Mayo 90. © 381/484-4000. Mon–Fri 8am–1pm and 3:30–8pm.

Casa Histórica de la Independencia   Here you'll find the original site where independence was declared, though the building is actually a reconstruction; the original was inexplicably destroyed in the late 19th century. A garden light show is included in the tour.

Congreso 151. © 38/431-0826. Mon–Fri 9am–6pm; Sat–Sun 10am–6pm.

Casa Padilla   Four courtyards lie behind a long facade of pillars, cornices, and elaborate railings, in a style known as *casa chorizo* (meaning "sausage house," not because it was a butcher's, but because its length far exceeds its breadth). Inside, you'll find a fairly average museum and crafts fair. The building will be closed for renovations during much of 2007, with no definite re-opening date.

25 de Mayo 36. No phone. Mon–Fri 8am–12:30pm and 4–8pm; Sat–Sun 9am–1pm and 4–8pm.

Catedral (Cathedral) 🎕   This neoclassical-style church is worth seeing for the two bulbous domes on its twin towers. Built in 1756, it was the first church with this particular style in Northwest Argentina.

24 de Setiembre and Congreso. © 381/421-2707. Daily 8am–8:30pm.

Museo Folklórico 🎕🎕   This fascinating little museum displays a wide range of traditional musical instruments (including banjoes made from armadillo shells) and hand-woven outfits.

24 de Setiembre 565. No phone. Mon–Fri 9am–12:30pm and 5–7.30pm; Sat–Sun 9am–1pm and 4–8pm.

WHERE TO STAY

San Miguel has a good selection of accommodations, from luxury hotels to budget lodgings. Whatever you choose, make sure it comes with air-conditioning.

Catalinas Park   This 10-story block of arched eaves, small windows, and a concrete hooded porch has all the appearance of a depressing Saudi hotel. The rooms are decent, however. The design is a mishmash, from padded headboards with carpet, to pine floors and modernist lamps. The standard-size bathrooms have wall-to-wall mirrors and oval washbasins. The corridors are white and bright, as is the restaurant and piano bar. Everything is sparkling clean. A definite extra is the ever-ready helicopter on hand to whisk you in and out as you tour the area.

Av. Soldati 380, T400IHC San Miguel de Tucumán. (©) 381/450-2250. www.catalinaspark.com. 120 units, 13 suites. From $75 (£41) double; $110 (£61) suite. Breakfast included. AE, DC, MC, V. **Amenities:** Restaurant; outdoor pool; gym; sauna, room service; massage; babysitting; laundry service; solarium. *In room:* A/C, TV, minibar, hair dryer.

Hotel Carlos V This three-star hotel has somewhat cramped and old-fashioned rooms, but they're clean and comfortable. Three blocks from the main plaza and with a good restaurant, it is not a bad budget choice.

25 de Mayo 330, 4600 San Miguel de Tucumán. (©)/fax 381/442-1972. www.redcarlosv.com.ar. 60 units. $40 (£22) double; $62 (£34) suite. Rates include buffet breakfast. AE, DC, MC, V. **Amenities:** Restaurant; room service. *In room:* A/C, TV.

WHERE TO DINE

El Fondo REGIONAL This traditional *parrilla* of red-brick walls and large hanging lamps is big and seats over 240 people. What it lacks in intimacy it makes up for in entertainment, with live music and dancing on Fridays, and folklore and comedy on Saturdays.

San Martín 848. (©) 381/422-2161. Main courses $7–$8 (£3.85–£4.40). AE, DC, MC, V. Mon–Sat noon–4pm and 9pm–1am; Sun only for lunch.

Floreal REGIONAL This gourmet restaurant is one of the best in town. The food is traditional Argentine with a Mediterranean twist. The wine list is excellent.

25 de Mayo 560. (©) 381/421-2806. Main courses $5–$10 (£2.75–£5.50). AE, DC, MC, V. Daily 11:30am–4pm and 7pm–3am.

TAFI DEL VALLE

Home of the Tafi tribes before the Spaniards arrived, Tafi del Valle is a high-altitude oasis of rolling green hills, herds of cows, and goat-cheese factories. It is a remarkable place, considering the sweltering proximity of San Miguel de Tucumán. In many ways, the drive here is more interesting than the destination. From the flat plains of sugarcane country, you drive up a twisting road through cloud forests and lemon groves, an area known as **Selva Tucumana.** You pass the fascinating **Reserva Arqueológica los Menhires,** where you'll find a collection of 50 mysterious standing stones from prehistoric times. Tafi del Valle itself is a popular mountain town set by a lake, frequented by Tucumanos, who come to escape the heat and take advantage of the excellent opportunities to fish, hike, and sail. One recommended adventure tourism agency is **La Cumbre,** Avenida Presidente Perón (© **3867/421-768**). If you continue west along the RP307, you pass through the mountain pass of **La Garganta del Diablo** at 3,000m (9,480 ft.) above sea level. Suddenly the landscape changes dramatically, and what was green and temperate is now red and desertlike. If you continue north along the Route 40, you'll reach the ancient Indian settlement of **Quilmes.** Built in the 9th century by the Quilme tribe, these well-preserved ruins once sheltered a population of 5,000 people and resisted invasion by the Spanish for more than a century and a half. On-site is an excellent museum showing mostly the weaponry of this pre-Incan civilization.

GETTING THERE   Tafí del Valle lies 107km (66 miles) west of San Miguel de Tucumán on RP 307. **Empresa Aconquita** (© **3867/422-7620**) offers buses daily; the trip takes 2½ hours and costs $4.50 (£2.50).

VISITOR INFORMATION   There is no tourist office, but it is possible to pick up maps and excursion information at your hotel.

WHERE TO STAY

Estancia Las Carreras   Built in 1718 by the Jesuits, this working *estancia* has one of the oldest farmhouses in the province. Everything is maintained true to its original appearance, down to the whitewashed adobe walls and burgundy-colored tin roof. The rooms are sparkling clean and somewhat utilitarian, yet comfortable and pleasing, with terra-cotta tiles and tassled bed covers. The farm is famous for its cheese-making tradition, which goes back nine generations. They also grow strawberries and raise Jersey cows. Half a mile from the town, it has a stunning mountain backdrop and a countryside feel.

Ruta 325, Km 13. © **3867/421473**. www.estancialascarreras.com.ar. 6 units. From $70 (£39) double. Rates include breakfast. No credit cards.

Posada La Guadalupe   This orange adobe lodge does not lack color: Multicolored sombreros hang on corn-yellow walls, and lamps hang from a ceiling of wooden beams. The rooms are welcoming, with private bathrooms and floral murals. Out front is a large pond, and behind are green rolling hills. A popular restaurant serves regional and international fare, and the delightful tearoom dishes out quality cakes and pastries.

Camino de la Costa 650. © **3867/421329**. www.posadalaguadalupe.com.ar. 9 units. From $60 (£33) double. Rates include breakfast. No credit cards. **Amenities:** Restaurant; pool, solarium.

WHERE TO DINE

El Mangrullo REGIONAL   This traditional *parrilla* has a folkloric theme. The building is made from traditional adobe and stone, with large windows that give a commanding view of the valley.

Ruta 307, Km 62. © **3867/421554**. Main courses $3–$7 (£1.65–£3.85). No credit cards. Daily 8am–1am.

Rancho de Félix REGIONAL   This charming colonial building with cane ceilings serves *locros, humitas*, and empanadas.

Av. Belgrano and Presidente Perón. © **3867/42022**. Main courses $4–$7 (£2.20–£3.85). No credit cards. Daily 8am–1am.

6 La Rioja

1,142km (708 miles) NW of Buenos Aires; 704km (436 miles) S of Salta

As you travel through the province of Rioja, red desert, sand-blasted plains, and giant cactus may give you the feeling you've wandered off the map. This destination has little history of tourism, but plenty to compel the most adventurous travelers, from cheap wine and a rich indigenous tradition to astounding natural scenery. Home to controversial ex-president Carlos Menem, La Rioja City, founded in 1591, is now an untidy mix of colonial town houses, ugly modern offices, and shambolic neighborhoods. Famous for its orange and jacaranda trees, the city is best visited in winter, as midsummer temperatures can reach a wilting 133°F (56°C). Intensely religious people, Riojanos hit the streets every December 31 to celebrate Tinkunaco, the "meeting" of Quechan and Catholic cultures. Though there is certainly enough to do here to fill a day-long visit, I recommend hitting the open road as soon as possible and feasting on sights such as the vineyards of Chilecito or the grand canyons of Talampaya National Park.

ESSENTIALS

GETTING THERE   Aeropuerto Vicente Almandoz Almonacid (© **3822/ 439-211**) is 7km (4 miles) from the city center. **Aerolíneas Argentinas** (© **0810/ 222-86527**) flies from Buenos Aires for $80 (£44) and $200 (£110), depending on the season and availability.

The **Terminal de Omnibus,** or main bus station, is located at España and Artigas (© **3822/425-453**). Buses arrive from Buenos Aires and travel to Salta, Catamarca, and other cities in the region. If you opt to rent a car, try Winer Rent at Santa Fe 642 (© **3822/425-453**).

VISITOR INFORMATION & FAST FACTS   The **regional visitor center** is located at Av. Pelagio B Luna 345 (© **3822/426-384**). It is open weekdays from 7am to 9pm and weekends from 9am to 9pm.

Banco Río faces the main plaza and has a 24-hour ATM. The bank is open weekdays from 9am to 2pm.

GETTING AROUND   The city center is a typical Spanish grid, easy to negotiate by foot, starting at the central plaza. There is not much shade, however, and so it's best to explore the city in the cooler winter months from May to October. The provincial bus system is extensive, but given that most of La Rioja's main attractions (such as Talampaya) are off the beaten track and miles from anywhere, it is best to hire a car— just be sure it has air-conditioning.

SEEING THE SIGHTS

Most museums here are free or request a small donation, usually no more than $1 (55p).

Convento de Santo Domingo   Built in 1623 this church is one of the oldest buildings in Argentina and a fitting memorial to the local indigenous folk who built it. While the Spanish preferred adobe, this church is entirely built of stone with a wooden roof that has withstood the test of time. Especially interesting are the elaborately carved carob doors.

Pelagio B. Luna and Lamadrid. No phone. Mon–Fri 8am–12:30pm and 4–8pm; Sat–Sun 9am–1pm and 4–8pm.

Mercado Artesanal   Here at this crafts market you will find genuine textiles and ceramics made in the area.

Pelagio B. Luna and Catamarca. No phone. Mon–Fri 8am–12:30pm and 4–8pm; Sat–Sun 9am–1pm and 4–8pm.

Museo Folklórico   Located in a rambling house of dark rooms and pretty courtyards built in 1692, this museum offers a ramshackle display of local mythology and customs, be it photographs of giant, holy rocks in the desert, or processions of Indians with mirrored headdresses. Interesting is the medieval-looking wine press made from cowskin or the side room containing silverware from a famous local silversmith.

Pelagio B.Luna 811. No phone. Daily 9am–noon and 3–8pm.

San Huberto Winery   In the town of Anillaco, 90km (56 miles) north of La Rioja city, stands San Huberto Winery. The winery itself is pretty and traditional, and definitely worth a visit as it was once owned by Carlos Menem. Nearby is Menem's house, where you still see the occasional paparazzi with a long-lensed camera lurking by the garden wall.

24 de Septiembre 565. ✆ 011/4303-5404. www.bodegassanhuberto.com.ar. Mon–Fri 8am–12:30pm and 4–8pm.

WHERE TO STAY

As you have probably gathered, La Rioja is not Las Vegas (not yet, at least), and the choice of accommodations does not rise above dubious four-star quality. Nevertheless you will find perfectly acceptable places to stay that may be light on class and luxury but just as light on your wallet.

Naindo Park   This is the best hotel in La Rioja City. Its pink facade with white arches hides a building block of glass that is at once very modern, spotless, and without character. The rooms are smart, the furniture elegant, and the bed covers quilted. The reasonably priced executive suites come with hydro-massage bathtubs. It is located 1 block from the main plaza.

San Nicolás de Bari 475. ✆ 3822/470-700. www.naindoparkhotel.com. 133 units. From $64 (£35) double; $80 (£44) suite. Breakfast included. AE, DC, MC, V. Valet parking. **Amenities:** Restaurant; pool; gym; sauna; room service; massage; laundry service. In room: A/C, TV, minibar.

Plaza Hotel   This six-story modern block faces the main plaza and houses well-appointed rooms of average size. Rooms come with built-in wardrobes and standard bathrooms. Its overall utilitarian feel seems to suit its mostly business clientele. It has a very pleasant rooftop pool overlooking the city.

San Nicolás de Bari 502. ✆ 3822/425-215. www.plazahotel-larioja.com.ar. 65 units. $45 (£25) double. Rates include buffet breakfast. AE, DC, MC, V. **Amenities:** Restaurant; pool; room service. In room: A/C, TV, hair dryer.

WHERE TO DINE

L'Stanza REGIONAL   This small, atmospheric *parrilla* hosts live music. The menu includes seafood, homemade pasta, and red meat. Local paintings hang on the walls, and the overall feel is elegant and well furnished.

Dorrego 164. ✆ 3822/430-809. Main courses $5–$15 (£2.75–£8.25). AE, DC, MC, V. Mon–Sat noon–3:30pm and 8pm–2am; Sun noon–3:30pm.

CHILECITO 🌟🌟

When it comes to Argentine wine production, La Rioja has always been the poorer sister to more famous regions such as Mendoza and Salta. The wine trade here, however, is booming, centered around the laid-back town of Chilecito in the west of the province. One winery worth visiting is the well-known **La Riojana,** La Plata 646 (✆ 3825/423-150; www.lariojana.com.ar). The town itself has little to boast but quaint and dusty colonial streets and a very large statue of Christ overlooking it all. It does surprisingly have the longest cable car in the world, which runs some 34km (21 miles) and once serviced a mine that reached 4,600m (15,088 ft.) high. Now out of order, it is still worth checking out—especially the mechanism and departure station, which houses a museum; it's on Avenida Presidente Perón, Chilecito (no phone). Chilecito's surroundings are what make it so interesting, with its rolling vineyards, giant cactus, stunning valleys, and breathtaking mountain ranges. Excellent adventure tourism options include paragliding and 4WD excursions. Consult the agency **Cuesta Vieja,** Joaquín V. González 467, Chilecito (✆ 3825/423-150). One very scenic route is the **Cuesta de Miranda.** If you continue west through this stunning mountain pass and then follow the RP18 south, you'll eventually reach what is undoubtedly La

Rioja's star attraction, **Parque Nacional Talampaya,** Villa Unión, La Rioja (© **3825/ 470-356;** www.talampaya.gov.ar). Recently declared a UNESCO World Heritage Site, this 215,000-hectare (531,050-acre) park boasts a red moonscape, towering sandstone cliffs, and sculpted rock—some of it painted by prehistoric tribes. Admission is $8.50 (£4.70) with an extra charge of $8.50 (£4.70) or $11.50 (£6.05), depending on which circuit you decide to explore. Not much farther south and over the border into San Juan is the dinosaur park of **Ischigualisto,** also known as Valle de la Luna.

GETTING THERE   On a map, Chillecito might look close to the provincial capital, but the mountains of Sierra de Velasco force all travelers to make a 200km (124-mile) detour south through the town of Patquia.

Empresa La Riojana (© **3822/435-279**) offers four buses daily from La Rioja. The trip takes 3 hours and costs $6 (£3.30).

WHERE TO STAY

Chañarmuyo Estate 冊冊冊   Situated 88km (55 miles) north of Chillecito, this luxury winery lodge, surrounded by high-altitude vineyards and adjoined by a modernist bunker-type winery, is all an adventurous oenophile could wish for. The simple one-story structure contains an entrance lobby of wall-to-wall glass. The rooms are generously sized, with king-size beds sporting earth-red pillows and indigenous patterns bordering the upholstery. The bathrooms are spacious and sparkling, and the view inspiring. Wicker chairs wait on the patio, and inside, the relaxing living room has a purple sofa and multicolored pillows.

Camino al Dique. ©/fax **011/4314-4884.** www.chanarmuyo.com.ar. 6 units. From $150 (£83) double. Rates include breakfast. No credit cards. **Amenities:** Restaurant; pool; outdoor excursions.

Hostería La Antigua   With pink walls and a green roof, tucked away in parkland 2km (1¼ mile) from the town center, Hostería La Antigua is the perfect rustic hideaway. Inside you'll find red bricks and a cozy atmosphere. The rooms are large and airy, with black and white floor tiles and whitewashed walls. Its top attraction, however, is the surrounding garden with fruit orchard and nut trees, complete with delightful pool.

24 de Septiembre. © **3825/422-352.** www.chilecitotour.com/clientes/antigua.htm. 16 units. From $80 (£44) double. Rates include breakfast. No credit cards. **Amenities:** Restaurant; pool; outdoor excursions.

WHERE TO DINE

El Rancho de Ferrito   REGIONAL   The most popular restaurant in town is large and lacking in personality. It makes up for its want of character, however, with great steaks, live music, and the occasional tango show.

Av. Pelagia B Luna 647. © **3825/422-481.** Main courses $5–$8 (£2.75–£4.40). No credit cards. Daily 8am–1am.

8

Córdoba & the Central Sierras

by Charlie O'Malley

The industrious Jesuits made the central province of Córdoba their South American headquarters in colonial times. Their legacy is still reflected in a famous university tradition and a busy, prolific province that produces everything from soya beans and cars to the country's best graduates. For the visitor, there is an abundance of sights to see, be it the very functional and friendly provincial capital or the rolling green hills of the Punilla Valley. Neat, tidy towns with majestic Jesuit ruins contrast with vast agricultural flatlands of rusting cereal silos and wind-battered billboards. Villa Carlos Paz is a well-polished tourist trap with slick resorts offering watersports and golf. In La Cumbre you can stay on a luxury *estancia* and partake in first-class hiking, horse riding, and paragliding. Rally driving is popular, as is the bizarre phenomenon of UFO watching.

Cordobeses are Argentina's best-loved citizens, noted for their lilting accents and sharp sense of humor. They also have a talent for partying, with some notable get-togethers such as Oktoberfest in Villa General Belgrano and a famous traditional music festival in Cosquín every January.

1 Córdoba

713km (442 miles) NW of Buenos Aires; 721km (447 miles) NE of Mendoza

Córdoba, Argentina's second city, is a bustling mix of commerce and colleges. It appears as a bland utilitarian metropolis of red-brick high-rises and boxed balconies with the occasional Jesuit gem. Currently a building frenzy is underway, fuelled by the soya boom. If your first impressions are of a dull Legoland, don't be deceived; beneath it all lies a young, vibrant city with lots of heritage, great bars and restaurants, and a considerable student population intent on having a good time.

This city of 1.3 million inhabitants was created as a stop for Spaniards traveling between Peru and the Atlantic coast. It was founded in 1573 by Jerónimo Luis de Cabrera. The Jesuits arrived at the end of the 16th century, opening Córdoba's university in 1613 and financing their projects by establishing six large *estancias* throughout the region. Today you can follow the "road of the Jesuit *estancias*" by arranging a tour with a local travel agent.

La Cañada, a waterway created to prevent flooding, is one of the city's symbols. Córdoba's most important historical sights line up around Plaza San Martín, including the Cabildo, cathedral, Marqués de Sobre Monte's residence, and the Jesuit Block. The Manzana Jesuítica, as the Jesuit Block is called in Spanish, developed not just as a place of worship, but also as an intellectual and cultural center that produced Argentina's top doctors and lawyers. It includes the Jesuit churches, the university, and a prestigious secondary school. In 2000, it was declared a UNESCO World Heritage

Córdoba

ATTRACTIONS●

Feria Artesanal del Paseo
  de las Artes **8**
Catedral **4**
Manzana Jesuítica **6**
Museo Histórico Provincial
  Marqués de Sobre Monte **12**
Plaza San Martín **11**
The Cabildo **3**

ACCOMMODATIONS■

King David **2**
Windsor Hotel and Tower **10**

DINING◆

La Mamma **1**
La Nieta e la Plancha **7**
L´America **9**
Mandarina **5**

Site and became a historic museum. The city still serves as an intellectual center, increasingly popular to foreign students who wish to study Spanish outside Buenos Aires.

ESSENTIALS
GETTING THERE

BY PLANE   Córdoba is most easily reached by air, and there are numerous daily flights from Buenos Aires. **Aeropuerto Internacional Ing. Ambrosio Taravella** (also called Pajas Blancas; ℰ 351/475-0871/475-0874) sits 11km (6¾ miles) outside town. **Aerolíneas Argentinas** (ℰ 0810/222-86527), **Lade** (ℰ 0810/810-5233), **Sol** (ℰ 0810/444-4765), and **LanChile** (ℰ 0810/999-9526), operate here, with flights to Buenos Aires, Mendoza, Salta, Rosario, and Santiago de Chile. Buenos Aires flights cost approximately $200 (£110). **Gol** (ℰ 0810/266-3131) also flies four times a week from Rio de Janeiro and Sao Paulo, Brazil. **LAB Lloyd Aero Boliviano** (© 351/482-0614) has two weekly flights from Santa Cruz, Bolivia.

Taxis from the airport to downtown cost between $6 and $8 (£3.30–£4.40).

BY BUS   The **Terminal de Omnibus,** or central bus station, is located at Bulevar Perón 380 (© **351/423-3555**). Numerous companies serve destinations throughout Argentina. Travel times are approximately 10 hours to Buenos Aires, 12 hours to Mendoza, 30 minutes to Villa Carlos Paz, and 2 hours to La Falda. A one-way ticket from Buenos Aires should cost no more than $40 (£22); companies constantly offer promotions and change their prices frequently. I recommend you check with the tourism office or the bus station before booking your ticket. A tourism information office is situated in the bus station (© **351/433-1987**).

BY CAR   The drive from Buenos Aires takes approximately 10 hours on RN 9, which is a good road.

CAR RENTAL   To rent a small car costs $60 (£33)per day. Try **Annie Millet-Hertz** (© **351/475-0581/475-0587;** hertzcordoba@arnet.com.ar) or **Avis** (© **351/475-0815/475-0785;** cordoba@avis.com.ar) at the airport, or **Europe Rent a Car,** Entre Ríos 70 (© **351/422-4867**).

VISITOR INFORMATION   Córdoba's **Centro de Información Turística,** in the Cabildo (© **351/434-1227**), offers limited hotel and restaurant information and distributes small city maps. It's open daily from 8am to 8pm in summer, with shorter hours in winter. There are also branches at the airport (© **351/434-8390**) and at the bus station (© **351/433-1987**). They also provide information and maps on the entire region, such as La Falda or La Cumbre.

GETTING AROUND

The old city of Córdoba is easy to explore on foot, with 24 blocks of pedestrian walking streets near the Cabildo. The heart of the old city spreads out around Plaza San Martín, in the southeast quadrant of Córdoba. Most of the historical sights lie in this area. Avenida Colón, which becomes Avenida Olmos, is the city's main street. As a general rule, you should not walk alone in big cities at night. In Córdoba, this is especially true anywhere along the river.

Driving is difficult in the city, and parking is almost impossible downtown. City buses are cheap and abundant, but only *cospeles*—30¢ (15p) tokens available at kiosks around town—are accepted. In Córdoba, taxis are bright yellow, while the safer and similarly priced *remises* (private, unmetered taxis) are light green. As is the case throughout Argentina, it is always safer to hire a *remise* rather than flag a taxi on the streets. This is just an extra measure of security for the visitor—locals have no problems flagging taxis on the street.

FAST FACTS: Córdoba

Area Code The area code for Córdoba is **351.**

ATMs & Currency Exchange Two reliable exchange houses are **Maguitur,** 25 de Mayo 122, and **Barujel,** Rivadavia 97. There is also an exchange booth at the airport called **Global Exchange** (© **351/475-9038**). ATMs are commonplace in the city center, while the main Citibank is located at 25 de Mayo and Rivadavia.

Emergency For a medical emergency, dial © **107**; for police, dial © **101** or 351/428-7000; in case of fire, dial © **100**.

Hospital The Hospital de Urgencias (emergency hospital; © **351/427-6200**) is located at Catamarca and Salta.

Internet Access Telecom, with a branch on almost every corner downtown, provides Internet access for less than $1 (55p) per hour.

Pharmacy **Farmacia Virtual,** 27 de Abril 99 (© **351/411-1101**), is open daily until midnight.

Post Office The main post office, **Correo Argentino,** is on Av. General Paz 201.

Seasons Córdoba can be visited any time of year, although you should expect hot temperatures, stormy weather, and big crowds in January and February, and fairly cold temperatures June through August. In addition to peak summer season, tourist destinations also fill up during Easter week.

WHERE TO STAY

Córdoba offers a wide variety of hotels. No stellar choices are available directly down-town, but better facilities can be found in the satellite towns. Hotels sometimes charge different prices for foreigners than Argentines, so make sure you confirm rates before you book. Prices listed below do not include the 19% tax. Parking is usually free for hotel guests.

Holiday Inn *Value*   One of the city's favorite hotels, this newer Holiday Inn is sim-ilar in quality but substantially less expensive than the Sheraton (p. 236). Okay, there's definitely less marble, but the service is comparable. The hotel lies between the airport and downtown, next to a large shopping complex and near the posh neighborhood of Cerro de las Rosas. Standard rooms are colorful, bright, and airy, with slightly larger rooms on the executive floor. The gorgeous pool is complemented by a fitness center, sauna, and state-of-the-art massage facility. The helpful staff will arrange airport trans-fers, regional excursions, and sports activities upon request. You'll need to take a taxi or *remise* to the city center, about 10 minutes away. The hotel also functions as a con-vention center.

Centro Comercial Libertad: Fray Luis Beltrán and M. Cardeñosa, 5008 Córdoba. © **351/477-9100.** Fax 351/477-9101. www.holidayinncba.com.ar. 144 units. $130 (£72) double; from $215 (£118) suite. Rates include buf-fet breakfast. AE, DC, MC, V. **Amenities:** Restaurant; bar; poolside bar; heated outdoor pool; fitness center; sauna; business center; room service; babysitting; laundry service; dry cleaning. *In room:* A/C, TV, minibar, hair dryer, safe.

King David *Value*   Opened in mid-2004, Córdoba's newest hotel is hands-down the best value in town. In the heart of downtown, just a short walk from all the main attractions, it offers 110 modern and comfortable apartment-suites. Every unit has a separate living area with TV and sofa, a small but fully equipped kitchen with microwave and stove, and a spacious marble bathroom next to the smallish bedroom. The decor is contemporary, with light wood and large windows overlooking the city. The staff can be a little cold and unhelpful but will arrange transportation and tours if requested. When making reservations, be sure to ask for promotional rates, as the hotel often offers weekday discounts.

General Paz 386, 5000 Córdoba. © **351/570-3528.** Fax 351/570-3535. www.kingdavid.com.ar. 110 units. From $60 (£33) apt for 2; $80 (£44) apt for 3; $100 (£55) apt for 4. Rates include buffet breakfast. AE, DC, MC, V. **Amenities:**

Restaurant; bar; tiny outdoor pool; small exercise room; business center w/free Internet; room service; laundry service. *In room:* A/C, TV, minibar, safe.

Sheraton 👁👁   Just outside the city center next to a fashionable shopping mall, this five-star Sheraton is widely considered Córdoba's best hotel. Elevators shoot up the center of the 16-floor atrium lobby, which is decorated with rose-colored marble, California palms, and paintings by national artists. The rooms are spacious, though not huge. They are well appointed with marble tables and desks, large bathtubs, and views of either the city or mountains. Service is first-rate, although the hotel gets crowded when its convention center is booked. The restaurant is fairly standard, offering a la carte or buffet dining. The breakfast buffet is spectacular with local and international fare. The piano bar is good evening fun. The Sheraton offers the most extensive list of amenities of any hotel in Córdoba. Be sure to check their website for Internet-only rates as low as $110 (£61) for a double room.

Av. Duarte Quirós 1300, 5000 Córdoba. ⓒ 351/526-9000. Fax 351/526-9150. www.sheraton.com/cordoba. 188 units. $119–$140 (£66–£77) double; from $280 (£154) suite. Rates include buffet breakfast. AE, DC, MC, V. **Amenities:** Restaurant; piano bar; heated outdoor pool; tennis court; fitness center; sauna; business center; room service; laundry service; dry cleaning. *In room:* A/C, TV, minibar, hair dryer, safe.

Windsor Hotel & Tower 👁   This centrally located hotel is the best choice near Plaza San Martín. Ask for a room in the more modern tower, built in 1999, rather than in the "Classic" section, where the rooms are ridiculously small. Rooms with king-size beds are larger than those with two twins. Also new are the rooftop pool, fitness room, and sauna. The fifth-floor Oxford restaurant enjoys an impressive view of the city, with good international cuisine. Piano music fills the lobby after 9pm, and the hotel staff will organize city tours and mountain excursions.

Buenos Aires 214, 5000 Córdoba. ⓒ/fax 351/422-4012. www.windsortower.com. 82 units. $70–$100 (£39–£55) double; from $120 (£66) suite. Rates include buffet breakfast. AE, DC, MC, V. **Amenities:** 2 restaurants; piano bar; small outdoor pool; fitness center; sauna; business center; room service; laundry service; dry cleaning. *In room:* A/C, TV, minibar, hair dryer, safe.

WHERE TO DINE

In addition to the restaurants listed below, the most elegant *parrilla* in town is **Al Corta,** Figueroa Alcorta 330 (ⓒ 351/424-7452; www.alcortacarnes.com.ar), serving the best cuts of beef in the city, with entrees from $6 to $8 (£3.30–£4.40). The best Italian restaurant is **La Mamma,** at Santa Rosa and La Canada (ⓒ 351/421-2212), with homemade pastas, veal escalopes, and an incredible lasagna (main dishes cost $7–$10/£3.85–£5.50). **La Nieta e' la Pancha,** on Belgrano 783 (ⓒ 351/468-1290), offers typical food such as *locro, humitas,* and empanadas, and here you can also try the ubiquitous *mate* tea so loved by locals.

DOC Vinos y Cocina 👁 *(Moments* ARGENTINE   This small, elegant restaurant is a piece of the Argentine wine world in a brash commercial city. Located in Córdoba city center, DOC Vinos y Cocina is all about fine wines and finer foods. Modern art hangs from pink-washed walls, amid immaculate white tablecloths bearing wine glasses like waiting sentries. Out back there is a small courtyard with pond, and out front is a tiny wine store. The food is surprising, with marvelous pairings such as *matambre* and chutney, chicken breast stuffed with smoked deer and pork ribs with *ñoquis*. Recommended on the wine list is Ruca Malen cabernet sauvignon or Zuccardi Q Tempranillo. If you are in the mood for beer (shame on you), try a bottle of Jerome, one of the best microbrewery beers being made in Argentina.

H. Yrigoyen 562. ℂ **351/460-8012**. Reservations suggested. Main courses $7–$10 (£3.85–£5.50). No credit cards. Tues–Sat noon–3pm and 9pm–1am.

El Rancho Viejo ARGENTINE   A beautiful, traditional *parrilla* situated in the university city. The building is made entirely of stone with a traditional roof and plenty of greenery surrounding it. Their speciality is kid goat.

Av. Rogelio N. Martínez 1900. ℂ **351/468-3685**. Main courses $10–$20 (£5.50–£11). AE, MC, V. Mon–Sun noon–3.30pm and 8.30pm–midnight; Sun 8.30pm–midnight.

Faustino ARGENTINE   This well-appointed *parrilla*-style restaurant is situated in Parque Sarmiento. Its air-conditioned interior is modern and attractive, and the menu offers the traditional-style *asado* with never-ending dishes of delicious beef. The bathrooms are immaculate—down to the ice cubes in the urinals.

Av. del Dante s/n. ℂ **351/460-1853**. Main courses $7–$12 (£3.85–£6.60). No credit cards. Daily noon–3pm and 8pm–1am.

Il Gatto ARGENTINE   This slick, diner-style restaurant has black-and-white photos on red walls, arty square lamps, and giant golden balls to distract your attention from a very pedestrian menu of pizza, pasta, cake, and coffee. Out front is a wooden platform patio to perch upon and watch the busy street traffic go by.

H. Yrigoyen 181. ℂ **351/568-0090**. Main courses $5–$8 (£2.75–£4.40). No credit cards. Mon–Sun 7.30am–1am.

L'America ✸✸ *Finds* INTERNATIONAL   In a beautifully restored 16th-century building, this elegant restaurant has been serving some of the best international dishes in Córdoba since 2000. The young chef at L'America was trained in the United States and loves to combine Argentine ingredients with North American and international flavors, such as the smoked baby back ribs with barbecue sauce, served with jasmine rice. The smoked pork loin wrapped in pancetta is a masterpiece. There's also a good selection of salads and delicious appetizers. The menu changes every 3 months, and the wine list includes hundreds of labels.

Caseros 67. ℂ **351/421-0476**. Main courses $4–$7 (£2.20–£3.85). AE, DC, MC, V. Mon–Sat noon–3:30pm; Tues–Sat 8:30pm–midnight.

Mandarina ✸ ITALIAN   This eclectic restaurant, along the pedestrian walkway Obispo Trejo, is a cornucopia of surreal and occasionally sexual artwork. The city's cultural crowd comes for salads, pizzas, calzones, and pastas, and later for wines, whiskeys, and wacky cocktails. Freshly baked breads and jams prepared with fresh fruits add to Mandarina's appeal. The wine list includes Trapiche, Zucardi, El Portillo, and Chandon.

Obispo Trejo 171. ℂ **351/426-4909**. Main courses $5–$9 (£2.75–£4.95); 3-course set menu lunch $24 (£13). AE, MC, V. Mon–Sat 8am–2pm and 6pm–2am.

San Honorato ARGENTINE   Named after the patron saint of bread bakers, Saint Honorato, this cool Mediterranean-style restaurant used to be a bakery. Needless to say, all the bread is homemade and fresh. The building is an old-fashioned townhouse with lots of atmosphere. The restaurant also has a well-stocked wine cellar with such exclusive wines as Achaval Ferrer and Terrazas de los Andes. It is 10 minutes by taxi from the city center in the upscale district of General Paz.

Corner of Pringues and 25 de Mayo. ℂ **351/453-5252**. Main courses $15 (£8.25). AE, MC, V. Lunch Tues–Fri 12:30–3pm; dinner Mon–Thurs 8:30pm–midnight, Fri–Sat 8:30pm–12:30am.

WHAT TO SEE & DO

Córdoba City Tour (© 351/424-6605) buses explore the main tourist spots in town. The tour lasts 1½ hours, visiting 40 sights, so it is especially good if you're spending only a short time in Córdoba; you'll see a lot in under 2 hours. The double-decker red buses leave from Plaza San Martín every day except Wednesday, at 10am, 4, and 6pm. The tour costs $6 (£3.30). The tourism office also arranges 2-hour **walking tours** of the city, departing at 9:30am and 4:30pm, for $2 (£1.10). Call in advance to arrange a tour in English (© 351/428-5600). In addition to the sights listed below, an excellent antiques and handicrafts fair, **Feria Artesanal del Paseo de las Artes,** opens at Achaval Rodríguez and La Cañada on Saturday and Sunday (3–10pm in winter, 6–11pm in summer).

Catedral   Construction of the cathedral, situated next to the Cabildo, began in 1577 and took nearly 200 years to complete. No wonder, then, that the structure incorporates such an eclectic mix of styles, heavily influenced by baroque. On each of the towers, next to the bells, you will see Indian angels created by—and in the image of—indigenous people of this region. The dome was painted by Emilio Carrafa, one of Córdoba's best-remembered artists. Visitors are free to enter the church but should respect the Masses that take place at various times during the day.

Independencia 72, at Plaza San Martín. © 351/422-3446. Free admission. Daily 8am–noon and 4–7pm.

Manzana Jesuítica   The Jesuit Block, which includes the Society of Jesús' Church, the Domestic Chapel, the National University of Córdoba, and the National School of Monserrat, has been the nation's intellectual center since the early 17th century. Today the entire complex is a historic museum, although the churches still hold Masses, the cloisters still house priests, and the schools still enroll students.

The **Domestic Chapel,** completed in 1668, was used throughout much of its history for private Masses and religious studies of the Jesuits. Having practiced their building skills on the Domestic Chapel, the Jesuits finished the main church, called the **Compañía de Jesús,** in much the same style in 1676. Built in the shape of a Latin cross, the Compañía de Jesús is the oldest church in Argentina. Its nave was designed by a Belgian shipbuilder in the shape of an inverted hull, which was the best way to make use of the short wood beams available for construction at the time. The dome is all wood—no iron is found anywhere—and the beams remain fastened with raw cowhide. The gilded altarpiece was carved in Paraguayan cedar, indicative of baroque design. At each of the church's wings stands a chapel, one of which has often been used for university graduation ceremonies.

In 1613, the Jesuits founded the **National University of Córdoba,** the oldest university in Argentina and one of the continent's longtime academic centers. With most of the university (including the medical and law schools) having moved elsewhere in the city, the majority of rooms here now form part of the historic museum. You can visit the Hall of Graduates, the main university library, and the exquisite Jesuit library holding roughly 1,000 books dating back to the 17th century; the books are primarily in Latin, Greek, and Spanish, with the exception of a complete Bible from 1645 written in seven languages. Many of the original books in the library were secreted to Buenos Aires when the Jesuits were first expelled from the Americas, but some are slowly being returned.

The Jesuit library leads to the **National College of Monserrat,** which opened in 1687 and quickly became one of the country's top public secondary schools. Walking around the cloisters, you can see the classrooms as well as exhibits of early science machines used for mechanics, electronics, magnetics, color, and sound. During the academic year, you will also find students at work here. You can enter the Compañía de Jesús, the university patio, and the Colegio Nacional de Monserrat free of charge. For $1 (55p), you can also visit the Domestic Chapel and the Hall of Graduates.

Obispo Trejo 242. ℂ 351/433-2075. Guided tours in English and Spanish at 10, 11am, 5, and 6pm. Ask in advance for an English guide. Tours $2 (£1.10); otherwise admission is free.

Museo Histórico Provincial Marqués de Sobre Monte 🇫🇫   The largest colonial house to survive intact in Argentina, this historical museum was used as the 18th-century home and office of the first Spanish governor of Córdoba. Completed in 1772, the house showcases the town's early colonial history. The governor's commercial and office rooms were downstairs, with the more intimate family rooms upstairs. An amazing collection of period furniture fills the bedrooms; public spaces display religious paintings, military uniforms, a rifle collection, early saddles and leatherwear, and an 18th-century chamber organ.

Rosario de Santa Fe 218. ℂ 351/433-1661. Tues–Sat 9am–3pm. Admission $1 (55p).

Plaza San Martín and the Cabildo 🇫   The 400-year-old plaza orients the city, with General San Martín facing the direction of Mendoza (from which his army crossed into Chile and later Peru to liberate them from Spanish rule). Exhibitions, fairs, and impromptu markets are frequent events on the plaza. The **Cabildo** stands on the plaza's west side. During the military dictatorship of the late 1970s and early 1980s, the Cabildo functioned as police headquarters and was used, as acknowledged by a small sign along Pasaje Santa Catalina, as a clandestine center for detention, torture, and execution. Today the Cabildo is a friendlier place, used mainly for cultural exhibitions and events.

The Cabildo is located at Deán Funes and Independencia. ℂ 351/428-5856. Tues–Sun 9am–1pm; daily 4–9pm.

OUTDOOR ACTIVITIES

A number of tour and adventure companies offer excursions into the Sierras de Córdoba, where it is possible to mountain climb, hike, mountain bike, horseback ride, hang glide, and fish. Try **Estación Uno** (ℂ 354/349-2924) or **Explorando Sierras de Córdoba** (ℂ 354/343-7901), both of which offer discovery tours into the mountains, bird-watching, horse riding, and overnight camping trips.

Golf is big in Córdoba. Six world-class 18-hole courses are scattered around the city, and an additional two are a half-hour-drive away. The Jockey Club and the Córdoba Golf Club are the most popular. Log on to **www.golfencordoba.com** for detailed information. The site is available in both English and Spanish.

CORDOBA AFTER DARK

The **Cabildo** serves as a cultural center, with occasional evening events including tango on Friday evenings. For $2 (£1.10), you can get a crash lesson in tango at 9:30pm every Friday and then try to dance the rest of the night away. **Teatro Libertador San Martín,** Vélez Sársfield 366 (ℂ 351/433-2319), is the city's biggest theater, hosting mostly musicals and concerts. The smaller **Teatro Real,** San Jerónimo 66 (ℂ 351/433-1669), presents more traditional theater. You can pick up current theater, comedy, and special events information in the "Espectáculos" section of the daily paper, *La Voz del Interior.* **El Arrabal,** Belgrano 899 at Fructuoso Rivera (ℂ 351/460-2990), is a bar that hosts excellent tango, milonga, salsa, and folkloric shows most nights, open daily from 10am.

Touring the Jesuit *Estancias*

The next time you sip a satisfying glass of Argentine wine, thank the Jesuits of Córdoba. These resourceful monks planted South America's first vineyards in Córdoba in the 16th century, as they required wine to celebrate the Eucharist. They also needed priests, and, for this reason, they established a college in the city, one of the earliest on the continent. Córdoba soon became the headquarters of the entire South American arm of the Jesuits. In 1621 the college was renamed the University of San Carlos. By the 18th century, the city was known as Córdoba Docta, or Learned Córdoba, the undisputed cultural capital of the Vice Regency of La Plata.

To fund such expansion, the Jesuits operated six flourishing *estancias* around the province—three near the town of Jesús María. Produce from their orchards, farms, and vineyards not only paid for students' tuition but funded a massive construction project of beautiful churches and residencies. You can still view five of these today, which is a delightful way to get off road and step back in time.

To visit a provincial Jesuit *estancia*, contact the tourist office, hire a car, or sign up with a local travel agent, such as **Stylo Viajes** (Chacabuco 321; © 351/424-6605; www.stylocordoba.com.ar) or **Córdoba Nativo** (27 de Abril 11; © 351/424-5314); www.cordobanativoviajes.com.ar). A 1-day tour to three *estancias* costs $25 (£14). A 2-day tour of all the *estancias* costs $50 (£28). An English-speaking guide costs an extra $7 (£3.85) per day and must be booked in advance.

Estancia de Alta Gracia   Another UNESCO World Heritage Site, Estancia de Alta Gracia is now the town center of a municipality by the same name, 25km (16 miles) southwest of Córdoba city. The *estancia*'s beautiful buildings are situated around the central plaza. On site is an interesting museum known as La Casa del Virrey, named after an ex-resident, Santiago de Liniers, Viceroy of the River Plate.

Av. Padre Viera and Solares. © 3547/421-303. info@museoliniers.org.ar. Admission $2 (£1.10). English guides available. Apr–Nov Tues–Fri 9am–1pm and 3–7pm, Sat–Sun and holidays 9:30am–12:30pm and 3:30–6:30pm; Dec–Mar Tues–Fri 9am–8pm.

Estancia de Caroya   Less grand than Estancia Jesús María nearby, this quaint building with a pretty courtyard and a small Spanish-style chapel is the oldest of all the *estancias*. Built in 1616, it was used as a holiday home for foreign scholars and an arms factory during the independence wars. It still boasts

Culture aside, the next best thing to do in Córdoba at night is do as the locals do and party until sunrise. One of the best bars is **Johnny B. Good,** Av. Hipólito Yrigoyen 320 (© 351/424-3960). Giant cardboard cutouts of Paul McCartney, Bono, and the Edge may unsettle your appetite as you munch through typical American food. Amid all this star power is a very nice cake display. It's pure rock 'n' roll.

the ruins of an abandoned mill and dam. It is a 20-minute walk from Jesús María town center.

Av. 28 de Julio. ✆ 3525/426-701. Admission $2 (£1.10). Mon–Sun 9am–1pm and 2–6pm.

Estancia de Jesús María   Close to the laidback town of Jesús María, 31 miles (19km) north of Córdoba City, this is one of the best conserved and most visited Jesuit *estancias.* The 17th-century church and residence form a U-shape around a well-tended garden. A pond, woods, and small graveyard give the place an idyllic feel. Its history is fascinating; wine made here was the first American wine served to the Spanish Royal family. In the Museo Jesuítico, you'll find colonial objects and paintings, as well as old winemaking equipment. The *estancia* is a 300m (984-ft.) walk from the town. Follow Avenida Juan B. Justo north, turn left onto Cleto Peña, and follow a dirt track until you reach the entrance.

Pedro Oñarte s/n. ✆ 3525/420-126. Guided visits in Spanish at 9, 10, and 11am. Admission $2 (£1.10). Tues–Sun 9am–7pm.

Estancia de Santa Catalina   This was the biggest and most important of all the *estancias.* Now in private hands, it is largely closed to the public but still worth visiting for its beautiful location and the magnificent church on the premises, which is still accessible. The amazing baroque-style interior, funded by cattle raising, is one of the most valued works of colonial architecture in the country. It is approximately 19km (12 miles) west of Jesús María, on an unpaved road.

Road north of Ascochinga. (✆ 3525/421-600. Admission $2 (£1.10). No English guides. Tues–Sun 10am–1pm and 3–7:30pm.

Estancia La Candelaria   To reach this lonely UNESCO World Heritage Site 53km (33 miles) west of La Falda, you must drive across a high-altitude plateau of mountain grass and follow a route through charming rivers and waterfalls. Because of its isolation, it's not as elaborate as its sister establishments. Serving as both sanctuary for Christians and fort against hostile indigenous tribes, it has a more austere feel, yet it's nonetheless charming and majestic. One of its main functions was to provide mules for the long trip to the silver mines of Bolivia. Property of the provincial government, the buildings are undergoing extensive restoration work, but visitors can still explore them.

Cruz del Eje, Valle del Norte y Sierras Grandes. ✆ 351/433-3425. Admission $2 (£1.10). No English guides. Mon–Sun 9am–6pm.

Happy hour takes place weekdays from 7 to 9pm. A number of upscale discos are located in the Chateau Carreras neighborhood; the most popular is Carreras, at Avenida Cárcano and Piamonte. The rest of the city's nightlife is concentrated along Bulevar Guzmán, in the north of the city, and in Nueva Córdoba along Avenida Hipólito Yrigoyen. One of the best disco bars in this area is **Mitre,** Marcelo T. de Alvear 635 (no phone).

The district of Cerro de las Rosas is another haunt for night owls. It is famous for good restaurants such as *parrilla*-style **Rancho Grande,** Av. Rafael Núñez 442 (© **351/481-1529**), and Italian restaurant **Restorante Italiano,** Av. Rafael Núñez 3803 (© **351/482-7730**). Another decent eatery is **Il Gatto,** Av. Rafael Núñez 3856 (© **351/482-7780**). At night, the area is bustling with people frequenting pubs and disco bars all centered around the main drag Avenida Rafael Núñez. **Villa Agur,** Tristán Malbrán 4355 (© **351/481-7520;** www.villaagur.com.ar), is a trendy nightclub in an old and beautiful English-style house, near the Mirador del Cerro, where you can enjoy a great view of the city while you sip on the local brew Fernet with cola. There is also a restaurant and a bar with live music.

Córdoba is famous for its own type of music called *cuarteto.* Panned by the critics and looked down on by rock aficionados, it is nevertheless a catchy, tropical blend of violin, piano, accordion, and bass. It is a foot-tapping alternative to the sometimes bland *rock nacional* you hear everywhere else. You can catch it live at several venues in the city, but beware: It attracts hysterical crowds and it's definitely down-market, for slummers only. For more information, call the **Asociación Deportiva Atenas,** Aguado 775 (© **351/471-5658;** www.atenas.com.ar), the **Estadio del Centro,** Santa Fe 480, or **La Vieja Usina,** Avenida Costanera and Coronel Olmedo (© **351/424-5743**).

2 Villa Carlos Paz ✶

36km (22 miles) W of Córdoba

A quick getaway from Córdoba, Villa Carlos Paz surrounds the picturesque Embalse San Roque. It's actually a reservoir, but vacationing Cordobés and Porteño families treat it like a lake and swim, sail, jet-ski, and windsurf in its gentle waters. Year-round, people come to Villa Carlos Paz to play outdoors by day and party by night, with disco-bound buses transporting the youth of Córdoba back and forth. The city of 44,500 inhabitants really comes alive in January and February, when more than 200,000 tourists a month pay a visit. Live theater, comedy shows, music, and dancing fill the night air, and no one seems to sleep. Yet you don't have to be a nocturnal animal to enjoy Villa Carlos Paz—the area's quiet lakeside resorts are a more serene alternative.

ESSENTIALS

GETTING THERE   The N20 is a fast, new highway (with a 1-peso toll) that goes directly from Córdoba to Villa Carlos Paz. The drive takes no more than 40 minutes, except on Sunday evenings, when Cordobés vacationers return home from the mountains. Bus transportation to Villa Carlos Paz is frequent and reliable. Public bus companies that run to and from Córdoba in about 50 minutes are **El Serra** and **Ciudad de Córdoba,** both costing under $1 (55p). **Fero Bus** and **Caru** travel slightly faster but less often and cost about $1 (55p). Minibuses Services leave from the city bus station and Mercado Sur (Bulevar Illia 175 at Ituzaingo). **Chevallier** buses to Buenos Aires take about 10 hours.

VISITOR INFORMATION   The local **tourism office,** adjacent to the bus station at San Martín 1000 (© **3541/43-6688** or 0810/888-2729), is open in summer from 7am to 9pm and in winter from 7am to 11pm. The staff provides information on hotels, restaurants, and tourist circuits around the city.

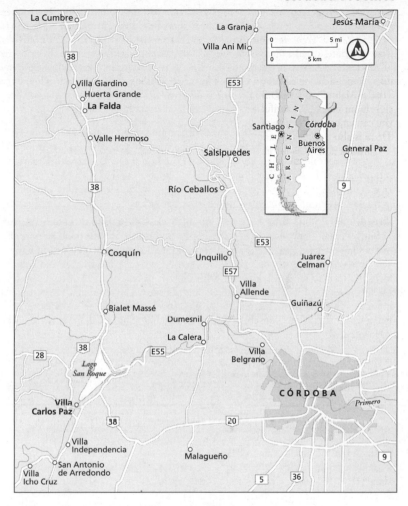

GETTING AROUND Villa Carlos Paz is small and easy to explore on foot. The city is safe to walk in, though you should not walk alone at night. Various car rental agencies are in the bus station.

WHAT TO SEE & DO

There are no special sights in the city, save a 7m-high (23-ft.) cuckoo clock that, for no good reason, has become the city's symbol. Daytime activities focus on the lake and excursions into the surrounding hills. It's not clear why the city allows so many water activities in a reservoir. In any case, swimming, sailing, windsurfing, trout fishing, and—at least, for the time being—jet-skiing are all possible. Villa Carlos Paz is also well positioned for the many driving circuits through the Punilla Valley and into the mountains. These include treks to waterfalls, Jesuit ruins, and mountain *estancias*. Call one of the tourist agencies open at the bus station for more information. In summer, two buses dressed as trains run city tours, including **Bus Panorámico** (© 3541/ 443-4587) and **Trencito Muralito** (© 3541/155-4281). You can call directly for departure times or take them from Avenida San Martin and Belgrano, in front of the bus station and points, or ask at the tourism office. City tours are worthwhile if you don't have time to meander on your own; they're also a good way to get to know the lay of the land before venturing out on your own.

WHERE TO STAY

The area is very well furnished in terms of accommodations. Choices vary from well-run resorts to simple cabins by the side of the road. If you have been overdoing it on Argentine steak and wine, check into **La Posada del Qenti—Health Resort,** on Enrique Zarate 82 (ex Cangallo) 515, Villa Carlos Paz 5152 (© 3541/435-892; www.qenti.com.ar). This plush new villa surrounded by hills is brimming with enthusiastic staff intent on restoring you to your former glory.

Hipocampus Resort & Spa *(Kids*   A bumpy back road leads to this hidden retreat, a white colonial house resembling an old Spanish mission. Its two pools sit on a cliff overlooking the lake, and each of the guest rooms has a balcony with a beautiful water view. Rooms are uniquely decorated, and many have hardwood floors and colorful linens. Bathrooms are small, however, with showers only. The hotel offers a cozy fireside sitting room, as well as a small library and TV area. The restaurant serves regional dishes as well as afternoon tea, and the gracious staff makes this feel more like a B&B than a hotel. Excursions, horseback riding, and hiking trips can all be arranged at the reception desk.

Calle Brown 240, 5152 Villa Carlos Paz. © 3541/421-653. www.hipocampusresort.com.ar. 46 units. $75 (£41) double. Rates include buffet breakfast. AE, DC, MC, V. **Amenities:** Restaurant; 2 outdoor pools (1 heated, 1 for kids); tennis courts; gym; sauna and spa with hydro-massage. *In room:* A/C, TV, fridge, hair dryer, safe.

Lake Buena Vista Resort and SPA *(Kids*   On the shore of San Roque Lake, this modern resort of giant lagoon-type pools and terra-cotta walls is a great place in which to relax and soak up the sun. The apartment-style rooms are light and airy, with large balcony windows, blue-tile floors, and the occasional ceramic urn. The bedrooms are adequate and kitchenettes are well equipped.

Enrique Zárate 82 (ex Cangallo). 5152 Villa Carlos Paz. © 3541/435-892. $96 (£53) double. **Amenities:** Breakfast optional; poolside bar; gym; spa; airport transfers; babysitting; solarium.

Portal del Lago Hotel *(*   The striking wood-frame lobby here leads directly out to the main pool and spacious grounds bordering the lake. The hotel forms a half-moon shape along the banks of the lake, and most of the rooms have water views. Brick walls and dark woods give you the sense of being deep in the mountains, and there are many sitting areas for relaxing. Guest rooms vary in size, although all bathrooms are small; some rooms have two levels and multiple beds to accommodate families. A warm therapeutic pool, sauna, and gym are on the top floor, and a lake-view restaurant extends along the mezzanine of the lobby. The hotel also houses a convention center. The place can be crowded in summer months; try to make reservations in advance. The hotel's many stairs prevent access to those with disabilities.

Gobernador Alvarez, at J. L. Cabrera, 5152 Villa Carlos Paz. © 3541/424-931. Fax 3541/424-932. www.portal-del-lago.com. 110 units. $96 (£61) double. Rates include buffet breakfast. AE, DC, MC, V. **Amenities:** Restaurant; bar; 3 outdoor pools; gym; sauna; room service. *In room:* A/C, TV, safe.

Parque Nacional Quebrada del Condorito

Quebrada del Condorito (www.quebradacondorito.com.ar) is a spectacular 800m (2,624-ft.) ravine and popular haunt for condors and their fledgling offspring learning to fly. It is the most eastern habitat in South America for this giant bird, and the area is littered with waterfalls, sierra grassland, and sloping hills. In 1995, the Quebrada and 40,000 hectares (98,900 acres) of the surrounding Pampa de Achala (a high-altitude plateau) became a national park.

The park's infrastructure is minimal, to say the least. There are three campsites, but they offer little in the way of facilities. Visitors enter the park from La Pampilla, 55km (34 miles) of stunning scenery southeast of Villa Carlos Paz. From two lookout posts, you can sometimes spy the birds bathing beneath waterfalls. The first is called *balcón norte,* and it's a 3-hour walk from the park entrance. The next vantage point is called *balcón sur,* which is another 2 hours into the park. Condors are shy birds, and sightings are not guaranteed, yet the area itself is a very special hiker's paradise. The park is home to 20 animal species unique to the area. **Nativo Viajes** (© 351/4245341) runs an 8-hour trek, in Spanish only, through the park. **Itati Viajes,** 27 de Abril 220, Córdoba (© 351/422-5020; www.itati.com.ar), staffs English-speaking guides who conduct different kinds of tours, all involving trekking and bird-watching. One-day tours start at $40 (£22). This agency also conducts helicopter tours of the province starting at $450 (£248) per hour.

WHERE TO DINE

Let's just say that fine dining is not the reason to come to Villa Carlos Paz. There are a number of good, casual eateries, however, in the city's center. The two best *parrillas* in town are **Carilo,** Yrigoyen 44 (© 3541/431-346), and **La Volanta,** San Martín 1262 (© 3541/422-954). The latter is easy to spot—look for loud green and yellow paint and the carriage sitting on the roof. For excellent Italian dishes, try **Il Gato Trattoria,** at Libertad and Belgrano (© 3541/439-500), and **Parrilla Los Gauchos,** Bv. Sarmiento 1007 (© 3541/432-814), both of which offer fish and meat dishes, too. The latter one has got a beautiful view of the lake. If Mexican is your thing, try **Oaxaca,** Uruguay 93 (© 3541/437-550).

VILLA CARLOS PAZ AFTER DARK

Many young—and even not-so-young—people come to Villa Carlos Paz from Córdoba to drink and dance, and some of the discos arrange private caravans from the city. Expect a late night out—dancing begins after 2am and continues past dawn. By far, the most famous disco is **Keop's,** R.S. Peña and Seneca (© 3541/433-553), with **Zebra Restobar Disco,** Bernardo D'Elia 150 (© 3541/427-130), placing second. **Terrazzo,** Av. Atlántica 400 (no phone), is a trendy disco open only in summer time. For something tamer, visit the **Punta Hidalgo** piano bar, at the corner of Uruguay and Hidalgo (© 3541/421-127). **Casino Carlos Paz** is located at Liniers and Uruguay (© 3541/425-772).

3 La Falda ★

70 km (50 miles) NW of Córdoba

An excellent base from which to explore the Punilla Valley, La Falda (literally, "lap of the mountain") lies between the Valle Hermoso (Beautiful Valley) and the Sierras Chicas. Argentines come here for rest and relaxation, not wild entertainment. Crisp, clean air; wonderful hikes; and quiet hotels are the draw. The city's main tourist site is the once-prestigious (but now decrepit) Hotel Edén, which entertained international celebrities in the early 20th century.

ESSENTIALS

GETTING THERE Frequent buses travel from both Córdoba and Villa Carlos Paz. The most comfortable is **TranSierras** (© **3548/424-666**), costing about $3 (£1.65). If you are driving, you have the option of going first to Villa Carlos Paz and then to La Falda via the N38. Or you can bypass Carlos Paz by taking the new A73, which branches off from the N20 a few miles before Carlos Paz. The trip takes 2 hours from Córdoba.

VISITOR INFORMATION The **tourist office** is inside the old train station at Av. España 50 (© **3548/423-007**). Open daily from 8am to 10pm, it provides city and regional maps as well as hotel, restaurant, and tourist information.

GETTING AROUND You can walk around the small center, but you will probably want to hire a driver, rent a car, or sign up with a tour operator to explore the Sierras Chicas (although you can always hike as well). La Falda's main road is Avenida Edén, which extends from the town center to the old Hotel Edén.

WHAT TO SEE & DO

You come here first and foremost to relax. Once that's accomplished, visit the once prestigious **Hotel Edén** (east end of Av. Edén). During the first half of the 20th century, it hosted the likes of Albert Einstein, the Duke of Savoy, two presidents of Argentina, and other members of Argentine high society. The hotel fell out of favor after World War II, because its owners had been Nazi sympathizers. Boarded up by 1960, the castlelike hotel was left to ruin. The insides have been completely gutted, but, amazingly, the entrance fountain still operates. Guided tours run daily between 10am and 6pm, and there's a bar adjacent to the ghost lobby with pictures of the grand old dame in its day. Outside the city, various adventure agencies offer horseback riding, trekking, mountain biking, hang gliding, and 4WD excursions into the Sierras Chicas. Contact **Polo Tour,** Av. Edén 444 (© **3548/470-795**), for details. You might also consider taking a taxi, which is inexpensive, toward La Cumbre, where numerous handicrafts shops and stands dot the road.

WHERE TO STAY

Hostal L'Hirondelle ★ Never mind the term "hostal"; in this case, it's an architectural distinction, rather than a reference to a budget traveler's dormitory. The house looks like a French chalet, surrounded by gardens and the Sierras Chicas. In a tribute to his poet son, the owner has given each individually decorated room a poet's name. On the second floor, Walt Whitman enjoys a corner view of the pool, courtyard, and nearby mountains. French prints and old bottles and spices decorate the long wood dining room, where guests enjoy half-board (breakfast and dinner) in summer months. Breakfast includes tea, croissants, fruit, cereal, homemade sweets, and fresh juice. For city folks unaccustomed to clear, starry nights, the owner has set up a telescope for celestial viewing. The staff will help you arrange outdoor activities, including hiking and horseback riding, as well as airport transfer upon request.

Av. Edén 861, 5172 La Falda. © 3548/422-825. hostallhirondelle@digitalcoop.com.ar. 21 units. $92 (£51) double in summer, including half-board; half that price in winter with breakfast only. AE, DC, MC, V. **Amenities:** Restaurant; outdoor pool; video and game room; babysitting; laundry. *In room:* TV.

WHERE TO DINE

La Parrilla de Raúl (*★* ARGENTINE   A popular *parrilla* with a distinctive family atmosphere, Raúl's menuless system works like this: First, help yourself to the salad bar, an assortment of mixed vegetable dishes, cabbages, stuffed eggs, candied sweet potatoes, and other delights. As you finish your salad, the first meat course will land on your plate, likely a tender slice of pork with a *cerveza* sauce (yes, beer sauce). Next comes thick *chorizo* and a rich piece of *morcilla* (blood pudding). No stopping here—*costilla* (a beef rib) is next. Ready for more? Following the rib is *matambre*, another delicious morsel of beef. At this point, you can politely request that they stop bringing you meat, or you can wave on more. Request a large soda, and they will bring you a 1.25-liter bottle to help wash it all down. Finish your meal with a trip to the dessert bar, an enticing table of flans, fruits, creams, and the obligatory *dulce de leche*. Then go hit the gym.

Av. Buenos Aires 111. © 351/421-662. Main courses $3–$5 (£1.65–£2.75). No credit cards. Daily noon–3pm and 8:30pm–midnight.

4 La Cumbre (*★*

93km (57 miles) NW of Córdoba

La Cumbre could best be described as Little England, with its cottage-style bungalows, rose gardens, and rolling golf courses. The colony of Anglo-Argentines who settled here were intent on creating their own corner of "that green and pleasant land," and they have done so with considerable success. It must be one of the few towns in South America where the town plaza is quietly forgotten, and the commercial center is situated several blocks away. Famous for its boarding schools and retirement homes, this sleepy town is not for thrill seekers, unless of course you are into first-class paragliding. Other activities include great trekking, horse riding, and golf.

ESSENTIALS

GETTING THERE   The bus station is on General Juan José Valle 50, in the town center. Frequent buses travel from Córdoba. **La Calera** (© 351/452-300) and **TranSierras** (© 351/424-3810) are two companies worth investigating. It costs about $4 (£2.20) and takes around 2 hours. **El Práctico** (© 011/4312-9551) and **General Urquiza** (© 011/4313-2771) are two companies that come from Buenos Aires, a 12-hour trip.

If you are driving, you have the option of going first to Villa Carlos Paz and then on to La Falda via the N38. Other towns you'll pass are Huerta Grande and then Villa Giardino. This is a pleasant trip through the valley, but beware of flash floods in the summer.

VISITOR INFORMATION   The **tourist office** is inside the old train station at Av. Caraffa 300 (© 3548/452-966). Open daily from 7am to midnight, it provides city and regional maps as well as hotel, restaurant, and tourist information. A respected agency specializing in outdoor pursuits in the area is Sendas Travel, Calle Dumas 110, La Cumbre (© 3548/532-177; www.sendastravel.com).

GETTING AROUND   You can easily walk around the small town center but you may soon get bored. Most of La Cumbre's attractions are outside the town, usually up a dirt track, so it is advisable to rent a car or sign up with a tour operator. There is no public transport going east or west.

WHAT TO SEE & DO

La Cumbre is becoming increasingly famous for adventure sports, particularly paragliding. A beauty spot called **Cuchi Corral** is a 300m (984-ft.) cliff that overlooks the Río Pintos valley. Here you'll find a variety of amateurs and professionals hurling themselves into the air and soaring with condors. In 1999, the town hosted the World Paragliding Championship. Other sights worth seeing include **Estancia El Rosario,** 6km (3¾ miles) southeast (© 3548/451-257), home of the ubiquitous *alfajores*—a *dulce de leche* biscuit sandwich popular all over Argentina, and a must-buy souvenir for visiting tourists. In the nearby village of Cruz Chica, you'll find **El Paraíso** (© 3548/491-596), the home of famous Argentine writer Manuel Mujica Lainez and now a museum dedicated to this fascinating character's life. To the north of La Cumbre, near the village of Capilla del Monte, is a mountain known as **Mount Uritorco** popular with trekkers. The mountain is also a mecca for fans of the supernatural, with a reputedly unique energy source and powerful healing properties. The area is famous for UFO sightings as well. You can investigate this phenomenon at a specially built UFO center called OVNI Center, Intendente Cabus 237, Capilla del Monte (© 3548/451-257). Farther east along a dirt track you'll find **Parque Natural Ongamira,** a weird and wonderful moonscape of pink rock amid green rolling hills.

WHERE TO STAY

Dos Lunas 🌸🌸   Sheep graze on the expansive lawn like silent lawnmowers, while a giant circular swimming pool reflects the second moon in the *estancia*'s title. Dos Lunas offers the best of both worlds—a lodge that affords the countryside experience without sacrificing luxury. The century-old building is genuinely pioneer-built, with Prussian blue window shutters, tin roofs, and wrought iron lamps. Yet the interior design is pure urban, boutique chic. Giant, modern rooms have striped bed sheets, subtle lighting, and wicker toilette kits at the end of each king-size bed. Bathrooms are also generously sized, with showers and baths. The dining room is a fabulous salon of red lamps, darkly polished oak furniture, and black roof rafters. The two living rooms are decked out with DirecTV, board games, an honor bar (no barman, just a book to note your liquor consumption), and a library collection that includes the diary of the original owner—an English lady who mostly complained about water problems. The tidy stables exude country glamour, and the horse treks across the 3,000-hectare (7,410-acre) property are both scenic and invigorating. A young Porteño couple named Gonzalo and Lorena run the place with efficient attention to detail and bilingual charm. The *estancia* is situated on a country lane, a 45-minute drive north of La Cumbre.

Alto Ongamira, Todos los Santos, Ischillin. © 011/156-219-5390. www.doslunas.com. 8 units. $300 (£165) double. AE, DC, MC, V. **Amenities:** Restaurant; outdoor pool.

Hotel La Viña   This charming, ivy-covered, red-brick house is a good budget choice. Its leafy location is close to the town center, affording good views of the mountains. The old-style furnishings, cavernous dining room, and bed-cluttered rooms make you feel like you are on a school outing to your grandmother's. The owners, the Zampieri family, make you feel at home, right down to the homemade scones and jam. Some rooms are spacious and pleasant, while others are monastically bare. Everything is perfectly clean and respectable, and the garden pool beckons.

Caraffa 48, La Cumbre. ⓒ 3548/451-388. www.hotellavina.com.ar.19 units. $33 (£18) double. AE, DC, MC, V. **Amenities:** Restaurant; outdoor pool.

Los Cedros (Kids)

A long driveway takes you up to a well-endowed mansion of red tiles and white walls with a glorious pool out front. Family-run Los Cedros consists of three buildings, the oldest of which was built in 1929. Here you will find a well-furnished interior of bright yellow walls, floral curtains, purple sofas, and brick walls. The rooms are of a good size, with built-in wardrobes and large bathrooms (most of which have baths). A sunroom with wicker chairs overlooks the swimming pool, and the dining room in the back has an unhindered view of the Sierra. In the basement, you will find a large activity room with Ping-Pong tables. Staff members are extremely helpful, and the chef is the most famous in La Cumbre.

Av. Argentina 837, La Cumbre. ⓒ 3548/451-028. www.posadaloscedros.com. 25 units. $60 (£33) double. AE, DC, MC, V. **Amenities:** Restaurant; outdoor pool.

Los Potreros (★★)

The Begg family has been farming in this emerald pocket of Argentina for four generations. Their pastoral paradise of 2,000 hectares (4,940 acres), 600 cows, and 140 horses offers the ultimate gaucho experience with a refined, Anglo-Argentine twist. Set high in the Sierras Chicas, the gleaming, white-washed cottage buildings feature old polished stoves, clunky wooden trunks, cozy raftered ceilings, and big welcoming brass beds (water bottles included). What the *estancia* lacks in opulence (it is a genuine *estancia* after all), it makes up for in sparkling cleanliness, well-equipped attention to detail, and superb personal service. At least one member of the family is on hand at all times, and dinner is a heart-warming and gregarious affair in the family dining room. Boasting some of the best horses in Argentina, Los Potreros is a riders' paradise. Guests here are generally the sort who prefer to spend more time in the saddle than in the pool. The six rooms include a cute honeymooners' cottage straight out of a Hans Christian Andersen story. The *estancia*'s address is La Cumbre, but it is actually accessed from a mountain road behind the hotel Eden in La Falda. With that said, it is much easier to get there from the eastern side, via Río Ceballos.

Casilla de Correo 4, La Cumbre. ⓒ 3548/452-121. www.ride-americas.com. 6 units. $260 (£143) per person, all-inclusive including airport pickup. Minimum stay 3 nights. AE, DC, MC, V. **Amenities:** Restaurant; outdoor pool.

WHERE TO DINE

La Cumbre has the usual variety of *parrillas,* and many specialize in kid goat, a local delicacy. **La Casona del Toboso,** Belgrano 349 ([tel **3548/451-439**), is one such place, with a nice cottage house feel and fresh trout on the menu. **La Luna,** Monseñor Pablo Cabrera, Cruz Chica (ⓒ **3548/451-877**), offers something different, with fondue on the menu and an impressive view. **El Pájaro Goloso,** Aerodromo Ruta 38, Km 67 (ⓒ **3548/15-631-885**), has become a hang glider's hangout, with a prime location in the local aerodrome. It's a rickety, informal place that serves fantastic Asian food. Opening hours are erratic, so call ahead.

La Fontana (★) INTERNATIONAL

La Fontana is a bright, cheerful restaurant with excellent food and service. As you wait for your order, the waitress brings a thirst-quenching aperitif of white wine and fruit juice, accompanied by delicious hors d'oeuvres of cheese and sweet corn in tiny cupcakes. The bread is so fresh it is hot, and one variety comes with melted cheese. The menu is a refreshingly eclectic mix, including a zesty Waldorf salad, *parrilla,* homemade pasta, and seafood, including octopus and

Parque Nacional Sierra de las Quijadas

The fossils of winged reptiles and the footprints of ancient dinosaurs are only two of the attractions that may lure you southwest of Córdoba and into the little known province of San Luis. Parque Nacional Sierra de las Quijadas is 155 sq. km (60 sq. miles) of isolated scrubland, gouged by Potrero de la Agua, a 6.4km-wide (4-mile) canyon with red crinkled walls and marvelous rock formations. Here you will find lines of guanacos trodding neatly across the barren land, watched by crowned eagles and falcons and lurking pumas. You will even find tortoises in what is San Luis's only national park.

Facilities are very basic—a free campsite next to a basic canteen. There are two footpaths. One is a 45-minute stroll to a vantage point with spectacular views. The other is a more ambitious 2-hour trek to see a genuine dinosaur footprint. It is advisable to do either trek in the early morning or late evening, as the midday sun can be lethal. The sunsets, however, are amazing. Admission is $4 (£2.20), and opening hours from dawn to dusk. The best agencies that specialize in park tours are situated in San Luis City. **Gimatur,** Avenida Illia y Caseros (© **2652/435-751**), runs tours in Spanish, varying in price from $15 to $25 (£8.25–£14). You can arrange in advance for a translator for an extra $50 (£28). Another company is **Las Quijadas,** San Martín 874, San Luis (© **2652/431-683**). They have specialist guides knowledgeable in archaeology and paleontology, but translations must be pre-arranged.

paella. While this white-walled corner restaurant might have a little too many tables, the atmosphere is very welcoming, the toilets immaculate, and the prices very reasonable. Belgrano and Peperina, Villa Giardino (between La Falda and La Cumbre). © 3548/491-455. Main courses $5–$8 (£2.75–£4.40). No credit cards. Daily noon–3pm and 8:30pm–midnight.

5 Alta Gracia ★

35km (21 miles) SW of Córdoba

Calamuchita Valley, south of Córdoba, is a booming agricultural zone dotted with large reservoirs. Alta Gracia is one of the main towns, situated in the foothills of the Sierra Chica, 35km (21 miles) south of Córdoba. It is famous for its Jesuit-built town center (p. 240), but its commercial center is not so pretty. Once a popular haunt for wealthy Porteños escaping the summer heat, it still boasts some impressive summer villas in the residential zone. The town itself is a good base for hiking, fishing or several lazy rounds of golf.

ESSENTIALS

GETTING THERE   The **bus station** (no phone) is located at C. Paravachasca and Nieto. Every 15 minutes, buses travel from Córdoba. The journey takes 1 hour and cost $1 (55p). **Sarmiento** (© **351/425-5541**) and **Sierras de Calamuchita** (© **351/422-6080**) are two companies worth investigating. The latter runs service farther south to Villa General Belgrano.

VISITOR INFORMATION   The **tourist office** is located at the clock tower, Avenida del Tajamar 1 (© **3547/428-128;** www.altagracia.gov.ar). It's open daily from 8am until noon.

WHAT TO SEE & DO

Alta Gracia's main attraction is the Jesuit *estancia* at its center (p. 240). Although the town has attracted its fair share of the rich and famous over the years, none became quite so well known as a shy school boy with asthma known as Che. **Museo Casa de Ernesto Che Guevara** (Villa Nydia, Avellaneda 501; (© **3547/428-579;** admission $1/55p; Mon–Sun 9am–9pm) is where the legendary revolutionary spent much of his childhood. There you can see some of his personal possessions and correspondence—some addressed to his buddy-in-arms, Fidel Castro. For a good 5km (3-mile) walk, make for the Jesuit ruins of **Los Paredones,** past the poetic Park García Lorca. The walk includes a view of the **Gruta de Lourdes,** a shrine popular with pilgrims in February, and a replica of the famous French grotto. South of town by 37km (23 miles), a large reservoir known as **Los Molinos** is popular for watersports and with fisherman angling for trout and *pejerrey.*

OUTSIDE TOWN

One of the province's biggest festivals is the Oktoberfest in **Villa General Belgrano,** 52km (32 miles) south of Alta Gracia. This German settlement's population was boosted by interned sailors from the Graf Spee in the war years. A quiet leafy resort town most of the time, it comes alive the first half of every October with a beer jamboree spiced up with a generous helping of genuine German sausage. For more information, try the village **tourist office,** Av. Roca 168 (© **3546/461-215;** www. elsitiodelavilla.com).

WHERE TO STAY

During high season—in summer, July, and Easter—rooms fill up and prices jump accordingly. **Hostal Hispania,** Vélez Sarsfield 57, Alta Gracia (© **3547/426-555;** $50/£28 double) is an old residence with large comfortable rooms and a fine verandah overlooking the sierras. The Spanish owners serve delicious tapas. For something more modern, try **Solares del Alto Hotel,** Bv. Pellegrini 797, Alta Gracia (© **3547/429-086;** www.solaresdelalto.com; $50/£28 double, including breakfast, Internet, and gym facilities). **Estancia Potrerillo de la Reta,** Los Paredones, Km 3, Alta Gracia (© **03547/423-804;** www.potrerillodelarreta.com; $140/£77 double) is a plush country club with beautiful wood-panelled bedrooms and a rolling green golf course. Farther south, in Villa General Belgrano, you'll find a charming Swiss-style hotel: **Berna Hotel,** Vélez Sarsfield 86 (© **3546/461-097;** www.bernahotel.com.ar; from $50–$75/£28–£41 double) is an attractive, efficient hotel with a large garden and pool.

WHERE TO DINE

Hispania, Urquiza 90, Alta Gracia (© **3547/426-772**), serves delicious *paella,* washed down with sangria. Highly recommended for dessert is the *crema catalana.* Another restaurant with an international menu, **Morena,** Av. Sarmiento 413, Alta Gracia (© **3547/426-365**), is in a lovely old house. **Brunnen,** Av. Roca 73, Villa General Belgrano (© **3546/461-832**), serves German fare and brews a very decent house beer. Visitors can tour the microbrewery out back.

Mendoza, the Wine Country & the Central Andes

by Christie Pashby

Warm sun, excellent wine and cuisine, and pleasant rural life make Mendoza a delight for the senses and a great place in which to relax and enjoy life. Wild mountains, charming towns, and serene plazas will linger in your memory long after you've returned home. But what you'll probably remember best are the smiles of the Mendocinos. Deeply connected to the land, residents of this delightful city (capital of the province with the same name) and vast province are relaxed, creative, and so very friendly. They feel lucky to live in the "land of *sol y vino*." Indeed, against a stunning backdrop provided by the highest mountains in the Western Hemisphere, Mendoza showers its inhabitants and visitors with sunshine and wine.

Capital of the Province of Mendoza, the city of Mendoza is an oasis amid an almost desertlike high plain—somewhat of a miracle, and a testament to the hard work and determination of local residents. If you consider that only 5% of the entire province is cultivated, and that the area receives around 15 centimeters (6 in.) of rain per year, you'll be grateful for the shade cast by the many giant sycamore trees that line the towns. Thanks to a vast network of aqueducts and dykes, which run through the rural vineyards and even through the heart of Mendoza city, grapes and olives have been harvested to international standards. The most famous grape here is Malbec;

it's of French origin, but it has put Argentine wine on the map.

In the past few years, wine exports have jumped 30%, helped significantly by investors and experts from Europe. Tourism is following suit and booming likewise. Fortunately, it is growing from the ground up. Locals continue to live as always, but now they welcome visitors into their lives—into their homes, their family farms, and their vineyards.

The region affords much to see and do. Start with an orientation day, exploring the town on your own, armed with a good map. Visit the highlights of downtown Mendoza, including the vast San Martín Park. After spending a few days exploring the *bodegas* (vineyards) close to the city, don't miss a day of adventure in the *alta montaña,* or high mountains—rafting, horseback riding or trekking. If you have time, then head out of town and stay in one of the outlying area's enchanting inns. Some of these hotels are close enough to the city center to make them convenient for your entire stay. Blending time in the lovely city of Mendoza with time in the quiet wine towns is ideal.

This picturesque city lies at the heart of the Cuyo, the name of the region that comprises the provinces of Mendoza, San Juan, and San Luis. It was founded in 1561 by Spanish colonialists, and retains an idyllic serenity that has carried over from centuries past.

Mendoza

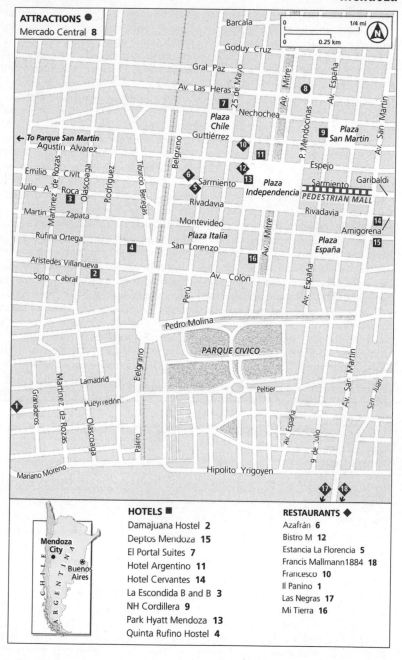

ATTRACTIONS ●
Mercado Central **8**

Barcala
Goduy Cruz
Gral Paz
Av. Las Heras
25 de Mayo
Av. Mitre
Av. España
Av. San Martín
Nechochea
7
8
Plaza Chile
Guttiérrez
P. Mendocinas
9
Plaza San Martín
10
11
12
Espejo
← To Parque San Martín
Agustín Alvarez
Emilio Civit
Julio A. Roca
Martínez de Rozas
Olascoaga
Rodriguez
Tiburcio Beregas
Belgrano
6
Sarmiento
5
13
Plaza Independencia
Sarmiento
Garibaldi
PEDESTRIAN MALL
3
Martín
Zapata
Rivadavia
Rivadavia
Rufina Ortega
Montevideo
Plaza Italia
San Lorenzo
Av. Mitre
14
Amigorena
15
Plaza España
4
16
Aristedes Villanueva
Sgto. Cabral
2
Av. Colon
Perú
Av. España
Pedro Molina
Belgrano
PARQUE CIVICO
Av. San Martín
Sen. Juan
Lamadrid
Peltier
Martínez de Rozas
Granaderos
Pueyrredón
Olascoaga
Pajero
Av. España
9 de Julio
1
Mariano Moreno
Hipolito Yrigoyen
17 **18**

0   1/4 mi
0   0.25 km

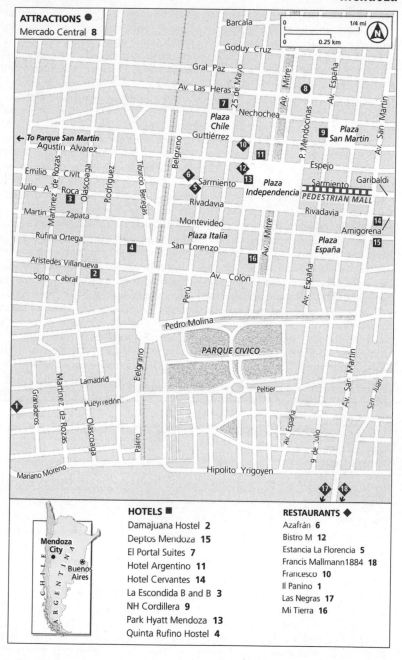

Mendoza City
Buenos Aires
CHILE
ARGENTINA

HOTELS ■
Damajuana Hostel **2**
Deptos Mendoza **15**
El Portal Suites **7**
Hotel Argentino **11**
Hotel Cervantes **14**
La Escondida B and B **3**
NH Cordillera **9**
Park Hyatt Mendoza **13**
Quinta Rufino Hostel **4**

RESTAURANTS ◆
Azafrán **6**
Bistro M **12**
Estancia La Florencia **5**
Francis Mallmann1884 **18**
Francesco **10**
Il Panino **1**
Las Negras **17**
Mi Tierra **16**

Los Caminos del Vino refers to the wine roads that wind their way through the most important wine-producing zones of Mendoza. You should spend at least a day exploring Mendoza's old city—visiting the plazas, and wandering about Parque General San Martín—before heading for the wine route. Choose your own pace when touring the *bodegas* (wineries); two or three visits are possible in half a day. Make a reservation for lunch either at one of the many excellent restaurants in the wine country—or, better yet, a *bodega* itself. Some have truly outstanding restaurants (see later in this chapter). Tours are generally free, although you are encouraged to purchase wine at the end, and some close on Sundays. Reservations are generally required—don't count on being able to just show up at a vineyard. A journey into the magnificent mountains, however, is possible anytime. The best circuit is Alta Montaña, which follows parts of the old Inca trail and Andes railroad through the tall Andes to the border with Chile.

Mendoza also offers a wealth of outdoor activities, ranging from Class III, IV, and V white-water rafting in the Mendoza River to horseback riding, mountain biking, and trekking in the Andes. Tour operators in Mendoza will arrange an itinerary according to your preferences, from part-day outings to multiple-day excursions.

Two-and-a-half hours south of Mendoza is the province's second-largest city, San Rafael. More the size of a large town, it's a laid-back, rural place that has some great outdoor activities nearby, as well as its own share of important *bodegas.*

Las Leñas is a world-class ski resort in the south of the province—playground of Porteños escaping the capital for a snowy retreat. Los Penitentes offers decent runs closer to Mendoza. For the bold and the brave, Mount Aconcagua provides an irresistible challenge, its 6,960m (22,829 ft.) towering above all other peaks in the Western Hemisphere. With a good bit of endurance, money, and time on your hands, the mountain can be conquered.

1 Mendoza ★★★

710km (440 miles) NW of Buenos Aires; 721km (447 miles) SW of Córdoba

Ask a local what she likes best about Mendoza, and she is likely to tell you *la tranquilidad*—the tranquillity of what must be Argentina's loveliest city. It's an artificial oasis, however, receiving no more than 5 days of rain per year. A scarce commodity, water is celebrated in the trickling fountains of the city's many lovely plazas, in the shade of the dyke-supported trees that line the boulevards, and in the tranquil nature of the residents who reap the benefits of the centuries-old roadside canal system. Give yourself time to linger in Mendoza's cafes, plazas, and many fantastic restaurants. This is a city that lives life outdoors, with many public places, cafes, and street-side restaurants that bustle from noon to night.

ESSENTIALS
GETTING THERE
BY PLANE   Mendoza's international airport, **Francisco Gabrielli** (© 261/520-6000), lies 8km (5 miles) north of town on Ruta 40. **Aerolíneas Argentinas** (© 0810/222-86527; www.aerolineas.com.ar) offers seven daily arrivals from Buenos Aires. On Monday mornings, a flight departs from Ezeiza International Airport. **LAN** (© 0810/999-9526; www.lan.com) flies to Mendoza from both Buenos Aires (two times a day) and from Santiago, Chile, once in the morning and once in the evening, making a day trip from Santiago possible.

BY BUS   The **Terminal del Sol** (© 261/431-3001), or central bus station, lies just east of central Mendoza. Buses travel to Buenos Aires (12–14 hr.; $40/£22); Córdoba (12 hr.; $24/£13); Santiago, Chile (7 hr.; $14/£7.70); Las Leñas (7 hr.; $5/£2.75); and other cities throughout the region. **Chevallier** (© 261/431-0235), **Expreso Uspallata** (© 261/421-3309), and **Andesmar** (© 261/431-0585) are the main bus companies.

BY CAR   The route from Buenos Aires is a long (10 hr.) but easy drive on either the RN 7 or the RN 8. Mendoza is more easily reached by car from Santiago, Chile, along the RN 7, although the 250km (155-mile) trek through the Andes can be treacherous in winter, when chains are required. Give yourself 4 to 6 hours to make the journey from Santiago.

VISITOR INFORMATION   Mendoza's **Subsecretaría Provincial de Turismo,** on Av. San Martín 1143 (© 261/420-2800), is open daily from 9am to 9pm. The helpful staff will provide you with tourist information on the entire province, including maps of the wine roads and regional driving circuits. **Municipal tourist offices,** called Centros de Información, are located at Garibaldi near San Martín (© 261/423-8745; daily 8am–1pm), 9 de Julio 500 (© 261/420-1333; Mon–Fri 9am–9pm), and Las Heras 340 (© 261/429-6298; Mon–Fri 9am–1:30pm and 3–7:30pm). They provide city maps, hotel information, and brochures of tourist activities. You will find small visitor information booths at the airport and bus station as well. Information and permits for Aconcagua Provincial Park are available at the **Centro de Informes del Parques,** in Mendoza's Parque San Martín (© 261/420-5052). The office is only open during the climbing season, from December through March. During the rest of the year, you must contact the **Subsecretaría Provincial de Recursos Naturales** (© 261/425-2090). Permits to climb the summit cost $100 (£55), and you must go in person to obtain one. In addition, several websites offer useful tourist information: www.turismo.mendoza.gov.ar, www.aconcagua.mendoza.gov.ar, www.welcomeargentina.com/mendoza, and www.mendoza.com.ar.

GETTING AROUND   You can easily explore central Mendoza on foot, although you will want to hire a driver or rent a car to visit the wine roads and tour the mountains. Taxis and *remises* (private, unmetered taxis) are inexpensive: Drivers cost no more than $10 (£5.50) per hour. Travelers should be wary of walking alone outside the main center of town, especially at night. Traditionally Mendoza is one of Argentina's safest cities, but it has experienced an increase in crime resulting from the economic crisis. Ask your hotel to call a *remise* or radio-taxi, rather than flagging down a taxi on your own. For a *remise,* try **La Veloz Del Este** (© 261/423-9090) or **Mendocar** (© 261/423-6666). For a taxi, call **Radiotaxi** (© 261/430-3300).

If you do rent a car, parking is easy and inexpensive inside the city, with paid parking meters and private lots (called *playas*) clearly marked. Easy to navigate, the city spreads out in a clear grid pattern around Plaza Independencia. Avenida San Martín is the city's main thoroughfare, Paseo Sarmiento is the pedestrian walking street that extends from Plaza Independencia to Avenida San Martín, and Avenida Emilio Civit is the posh residential avenue leading to the entrance of Parque San Martín. Outside the city, road signs are sometimes missing or misleading, and you should pay careful attention to road maps. The main highways are Highway 40, which runs north-south and will take you to Maipú and Luján de Cuyo; and Highway 7, which runs east-west and will take you to the Alta Montaña Route.

Both **Budget** (© 261/425-3114; www.budget.com) and **Hertz Annie Millet** (© 261/448-2327; www.hertz.com) rent cars at Mendoza's airport. Expect to pay about $45 (£25) per day for a compact car with insurance and 200km (124 miles) included. If you reserve the car before arriving in Argentina, you can usually negotiate a similar rate, but with unlimited mileage. **AutoMendoza** (© 261/420-0022; www.automendoza.com), a locally run company, has flexible rates and will drop a car off wherever you need it. Rates start at $30 (£17) per day. You'll get a better deal if you pay in cash.

Mendoza's public bus system is one of the best in the country. Regular buses depart from various stops in town to the outlying wine areas. El Troli, a trolley that follows the main roads in the city, is fun and cheap, at 40¢ (20p) per ride. It's an easy way to get up to Parque San Martín and back.

FAST FACTS: Mendoza

Area Code The area code for the city is **261**. The country code for Argentina is **54**.

ATMs & Currency Exchange ATMs and currency-exchange houses have been plagued by long lines and limited cash since the beginning of the economic crisis. Two reliable exchange houses, both at the corner of San Martín and Catamarca, are **Maguitur** (© 261/425-1575) and **Cambio Santiago** (© 261/420-0277). They are open Monday through Friday from 8:30am to 1pm and from 5 to 8:30pm, and Saturday from 9:30am to 1pm. Major banks, with ATMs that have Cirrus and PLUS access, are located around the Plaza San Martín and along Avenida Sarmiento, including **Citibank** (Av. Sarmiento 20; © 261/449-6519).

Emergency For an **ambulance**, dial © **107** or 261/424-8000; for **police**, dial © **101** or 261/429-4444; in case of **fire**, dial © **100**.

Hospital **Hospital Central** (© 261/420-0600) is near the bus station at Salta and Alem.

Internet Access Internet access in most places costs a meager 1 or 2 pesos (35¢–65¢/20p–35p) per hour. A number of cybercafes run along Avenida Sarmiento; try **Mundo Internet**, Sarmiento 107 (© 261/420-3795), open daily from 8:30am to 1am. **Official Telefónica** and **Telecentro** offices, located all over town, also offer Internet use.

Pharmacy **Farmacia del Puente**, Av. Las Heras 201 (© 261/423-8800), operates 24 hours.

Post Office The main post office, **Correo Argentino** (© 261/429-0848), located at the corner of Avenida San Martín and Colón, is open weekdays from 8am to 8pm.

WHERE TO STAY

Mendoza has some interesting new hotels on the horizon, including three new five-star hotels, which should give the grande dame, the Park Hyatt, a run for its money. Keep an eye out for the new Sheraton, Diplomático, and Caesar chains, scheduled to open in 2008. Also popular are "apart-hotels," or suite-hotels. More than 30 hostels also dot downtown Mendoza. I recommend spending a few nights in town, and then staying at a rural inn amid the vineyards, for a change of pace (see "Touring the Wineries," later in this chapter). More and more *bodegas* are opening up guesthouses, where relaxation and wine are the top draws. Prices quoted are for high season, which in Mendoza is January through March, July, and September through November. Hotel rates are often discounted 15% to 20% in the off season. Prices listed below do not include the 21% tax.

VERY EXPENSIVE

Park Hyatt Mendoza ⟨⟨⟨   Peering majestically over the Plaza de la Independencia, the Park Hyatt opened in 2001, after management restored the original facade of the 19th-century Plaza Hotel and built a seven-floor tower for guest rooms. An award-winning hotel, it is without a doubt the premiere place to stay in town. For the time being, at least, it has no rivals. Sweeping columns of granite and stone showcase the lobby, and an impressive collection of Mendocino art pays tribute to local culture. A concrete courtyard leads to a warm, inviting pool. Guest rooms that face the courtyard are a bit noisy, but the rooms in general are spacious and contemporary. Fluffy duvets and feather pillows blanket the king-size beds. Huge white-marble bathrooms are the size of a standard room in some hotels, with separate bathtubs and showers, and crystal washbasins. The exquisite spa deserves special mention: A professional team of masseurs from Bangkok give wonderful Thai massages, and the spa incorporates Mendocino wines in a variety of treatments, with shampoo based on wine acids and lotion made from grape-seed oil. A well-equipped fitness room, Jacuzzi, sauna, and steam bath are here, too. Serving as a cultural heart of Mendoza, the hotel hosts frequent events, ranging from jazz and music shows to wine fairs and flamenco dances. The breakfast buffet is the best in town. Watch out for overpriced extras such as minibar drinks and Internet connections. Next door, the Regency Casino is Mendoza's nod to Las Vegas. Be sure to check the hotel website for Internet-only rates with a 10% discount.

Chile 1124 (Sarmiento and Espejo), 5500 Mendoza. ℂ 261/441-1234. Fax 261/441-1235. www.mendoza. park.hyatt.com. 186 units. $270 (£149) double; from $350 (£193) suite. Rates include a beautiful buffet breakfast. AE, DC, MC, V. **Amenities:** Restaurant; wine bar; heated outdoor pool; nearby golf; excellent health club and spa; concierge; business center; room service; babysitting; laundry service; dry cleaning. *In room:* A/C, TV, minibar, hair dryer, safe.

EXPENSIVE

El Portal Suites ⟨Kids⟩   These comfortable suites have a clean and modern style. They can sleep from two to five people in a variety of bed setups, and offer a sense of freedom to travelers who want to make themselves at home. They're an especially good option for families. The staff is friendly and helpful, and will deliver local newspapers to your door each morning. Ask for one of the Grand Suites overlooking the Plaza de Chil. These have Jacuzzis, a large patio, and room for up to five people. Bathrooms are large, while kitchenettes range in size. Upstairs, a terrace with an outdoor Jacuzzi offers glorious views, as well as a small gym and a deck for relaxing.

Necochea 661 (Peru and 25 de Mayo), 5500 Mendoza. ℂ/fax 261/438-2038. www.elportalsuites.com.ar. 26 units. AE, DC, MC, V. $93 (£51) double; $125 (£69) triple; $160 (£88) grand suite (sleeps 4–5). Rates include breakfast and parking. **Amenities:** Restaurant; exercise room; outdoor Jacuzzi; business center; room service. *In room:* A/C, TV, Internet, kitchenette, hair dryer, safe.

Hotel NH Cordillera   The NH (New Hotel) Spanish hotel chain caters to business travelers, and this Mendoza property is no different. Opened in late 2002, the NH has four floors of crisp, compact rooms, half of which face Plaza San Martín. The staff describes the hotel's style as minimalist, which fairly well describes their approach to service as well. Yet the NH is efficient and convenient. Stay here because of the hotel's central location and stoic approach, but don't expect many thrills. The restaurant offers a good selection of salads, fresh fish, and meat, but it's closed on Sunday. A computer with free Internet access, next to the bar, is available for guests.

Av. España 1324 (at Gutierrez), 5500 Mendoza. © **261/441-6464.** Fax 261/441-6450. www.nh-hotels.com. 105 units. $145 (£80) double; from $195 (£107) suite. Rates include small buffet breakfast. AE, DC, MC, V. **Amenities:** Restaurant; bar; miniscule outdoor pool; tiny exercise room; sauna; room service; massage room; laundry service; dry cleaning. *In room:* A/C, TV, minibar, hair dryer, safe.

MODERATE

Deptos Mendoza *(Finds)*   Recently built by a transplanted Chilean architect, this sleek new building of steel and brick offers plenty of great value. ("Depto" is short for *departamento,* which is Spanish for "apartment.") Rent a funky studio and slip into a hip and urban way of life; it seems that easy here. On the top floor of this downtown building is the reception desk, which also acts as a lively gallery and a great hang-out spot for those interested in art and design. The apartments are decorated with local art, with a focus on function and lighting. Ceramic tiles, aluminum, concrete, and wood dominate the look. Bathrooms are quite small, with stand-up showers only. Apartment no. 9 is the largest, with a big, sunny terrace, but the street below is quite noisy at night. Two blocks away, another loft sleeps four and has a huge terrace and grill. If you're coming with a group of friends and you love design, this is a great choice. Parking is available nearby for an extra fee of $8 (£4.40)per day.

Leandro N. Alem 41, 5500 Mendoza. © **261/1541-94844.** www.deptosmendoza.com.ar. 12 units. $45–$55 (£25–£30) apt. *In room:* A/C, TV, Internet, kitchenette.

Hotel Argentino *(★★ (Value)*   Cater-cornered from the lavish Park Hyatt (p. 257), and overlooking the Plaza de la Independencia, this hotel is good value in an excellent location. Opened in the spring of 2004, the Argentino offers elegance and comfort at very affordable rates. Forty-four rooms have recently been upgraded; all are furnished with light-wood and black-wood writing desks and chairs, satiny bed covers, and small but sparkling marble bathrooms with showers only. There's also an airy restaurant and an adjacent bar in the bright and expansive lobby. The business center offers free Internet and Wi-Fi access for hotel guests. If you're traveling alone, be sure to ask about their single rates at about 10% off the regular rates. Rates here include all taxes, making it even more of a bargain.

Espejo 455 (at Chile), 5500 Mendoza. © **261/405-6300.** www.argentino-hotel.com. 46 units. $60 (£33) double; $70 (£39) triple. Rates include buffet breakfast. AE, DC, MC, V. **Amenities:** Restaurant; bar; lounge; small outdoor pool; business center; room service; laundry service. *In room:* A/C, TV, minibar, hair dryer, safe.

Hotel Cervantes *(Value)*   A Mendoza classic, this hotel has been run by the Lopez family since 1945, and staff members are old-school hotel professionals. From the outside, the place is baroque and traditional. Inside, rooms are small and a bit stuffy, but they're now tackling floor-by-floor renovations that will include new amenities, new windows, air-conditioners, and a new elevator. There is a lovely new garden out back and ample parking. Ask for a "special" room on the fourth floor for more space and style. The neighborhood is expected to take a turn for the better with the opening of the nearby Sheraton. There's also talk of turning Primitivo de la Reta into a pedestrian street. Parking is available on-site.

Amigorena 65 (San Martín and P. de la Reta), 5500 Mendoza. ℂ 261/520-0400. Fax 261/520-0458. www.hotel cervantesmza.com.ar. 65 units. $56 (£31) double; $105 (£58) suite. Includes breakfast. AE, MC, V. **Amenities:** Restaurant; room service; laundry; Wi-Fi. *In room:* A/C, TV.

La Escondida Bed and Breakfast ⚙

Family-run, friendly, and tranquil, this bed and breakfast is lovely, in a pleasant and convenient neighborhood. La Escondida, as its name suggests, is hidden amid a residential area. It's definitely quiet, even though it's close to the downtown plazas, the nightlife on Calle Arístides, and Parque San Martín, which is only 3 blocks away. All rooms have private bathrooms, a light and airy style, and high ceilings. The building maintains the feel of a colonial home sheltered from the sun. The main floor can be dark, so insist on a room upstairs. The large pool in the back is relaxing, if not always impeccably clean. On-site parking is available at no extra cost.

Julio A. Roca 344 (Martínez de Rosas and Olascoaga), 5500 Mendoza. ℂ 261/425-5202. www.laescondidabb.com. 7 units. $45 (£25) double includes breakfast. No credit cards. **Amenities:** Pool; lounge; spa; Internet. *In room:* A/C, TV.

INEXPENSIVE

Damajuana Hostel *Value* Like a five-star resort at rock-bottom prices, this hostel is located in the heart of the happening Arístides district, in a renovated old family home. It has a huge pool, garden, and barbecue in the backyard, friendly staff and information desk, and a funky bar. It's popular with young travelers and backpackers, and there's always something going on here. Private double rooms are also available for guests who don't feel up to sharing.

Aristides Villanueva 282 (Olascoaga and Rodríguez), 5500 Mendoza. ℂ 261/425-5858. www.damajuanahostel. com.ar. 8 units, all with shared bathrooms. $10 (£5.50) per person in dormitory-style room, $30 (£17) in private double room. Rates include buffet breakfast. No credit cards. **Amenities:** Bar; outdoor pool; laundry; Internet.

Quinta Rufino Hostel ⚙

This may be the classiest hostel in Mendoza. It's tucked in an upscale neighborhood known as La Quinta, yet it's still close to all the action on Arístides. The owners show a lot of love for their work and for their hostel in a renovated old private residence typical of the region. Rooms are sparsely decorated, and the beds are nothing to write home about, but the atmosphere is cheery and relaxed. Considering that all the rooms have a private bathroom, the price is great. Limited onsite parking is available for no extra charge.

Rufino Ortega 142 (Rodríguez and Belgrano), 5500 Mendoza. ℂ 261/420-4696. www.quintarufinohostel.com.ar. 12 units. $28 (£15) double. Rates include breakfast. No credit cards. **Amenities:** Laundry; Internet.

WHERE TO DINE

Mendoza is Argentina's top destination for food lovers. Restaurants here are known around the world, and the food will certainly be a highlight of your trip. As in the rest of Argentina, Mendocinos dine late. Breakfasts of coffee and pastries are served from around 7:30am to 10:30am. Lunch is generally a leisurely meal, running from 11am to 3pm. Restaurants don't usually open for dinner until 8:30pm, and they don't get busy until 10pm. How can you survive? If you must dine before 9pm, stick to hotel-lobby restaurants, which usually open earlier. Or, do as the locals do: Indulge in an afternoon siesta, then satiate your 6pm hunger with a coffee and snack at one of the city's many lovely outdoor cafes. We highly recommend that you soak up the atmosphere at a Mendoza cafe. There are dozens of cafes with outdoor patios along the Sarmiento Peatonal pedestrian street, where the people-watching is world-class. Two of the best are **Bonafide,** Peatonal Sarmiento 102 (ℂ **261/423-7915**), and **Café del Pasaje,** Sarmiento

---

Tips **Take Flight**

The idea of tasting wine by the flight is something relatively new to Mendoza, but the concept has been mastered at **The Vines of Mendoza,** Espejo 567 (© **261/438-1031**). Theirs was the first collective tasting room in the region. Led by charming and bilingual wine experts, tastings include daily samples of some of Argentina's finest—and hardest to find—boutique wines. On Wednesday nights, a local winemaker presents his best *vino tinto,* and on Fridays, it's about bubbly champagne. The indoor terrace is cozy. Likewise, **Wine Club Republic** (© **261/15-541-3892**) meets every Monday at 7pm at the Marcelino Wine Store, at the corner of Benegas and Zapata. It's open to the public, but reservations are required. Both are great places to meet and mingle with expats, other travelers, and local wine lovers.

---

and San Martín (© **261/459-0669**). At Arístides Villanueva 209 try **La Dulcería de la Abuela** (© **261/423-5885**) for delicious sweets. For something funky, **Kato Café** *(★)*, Emilio Civit 556 (© **261/425-7000**), is artsy and hip. And for the classically elegant Mendocino cafe, nothing comes close to **Vía Civit** *(★)*, Emilio Civit 277 (© **261/ 429-8529**). That can be followed by a stroll through the plazas and maybe a stop at a wine bar. Come 9:30 or 10pm, you'll be ready to head out for dinner.

Even if you are staying in the center of town, make at least one trip out to a restaurant in the suburb of Godoy Cruz or in the wine areas (see "Touring the Wineries," later in this chapter), where some of the best cuisine is to be had at restaurants such as La Bourgogne (p. 273) and Terruños (p. 277).

EXPENSIVE

Bistro M *(★★★)* REGIONAL/INTERNATIONAL   A sophisticated international restaurant with French overtones, using regional ingredients, Bistro M created the first open kitchen in South America. Busy chefs attend to the wood-burning oven while crisp waiters attend to you; the most interesting dishes include marinated goat with *chimichurri* (chile and garlic sauce), grilled trout with artichokes and tomato slices, and veal spareribs. The classic Argentine filet mignon served with a drizzle of Malbec reduction is exquisite. Appetizers and salads are elegant and fresh. A spiral staircase climbs past a two-floor wine gallery housing over 450 selected regional wines, some of which are available by the glass. The sommelier will help guide you toward a selection, but don't be surprised if you're steered toward a Malbec. Bistro M has large windows looking out to Plaza Independencia, and an outdoor terrace open in warm weather. After dinner, you can retire to the wine bar upstairs.

Park Hyatt Hotel, Chile 112 (Sarmiento and Espejo). © **261/441-1234.** Reservations recommended. Main courses $12–$18 (£6.60–£9.90). AE, DC, MC, V. Daily 6:30–11am, 12:30–3:30pm, and 8pm–midnight.

1884 *(★★★)* INTERNATIONAL   Some people come to Mendoza just to eat at celebrity chef Francis Mallman's restaurant, inside the Romanesque Bodega Escorihuela—known, among other things, for housing the biggest wine barrel in the province. With fine Argentine meats and fresh local produce, his carefully presented cuisine combines his Patagonian roots with his French culinary training. Local go-tos such as *lechón* (young pork) and *chivito* (baby goat) are classics, and the huge outdoor wooden stove produces an incredible salted chicken. This is simple food prepared in a stripped-down style typical for Mallmann. Dishes are prepared with matching local wine selections, with Malbec and Syrah topping the list. In the summer, request a coveted garden table. For dessert, the *chocolate fanático* will blow your hat off. You can easily combine in the same visit a meal here with a tour of the *bodega*, which also has an art gallery. Tours are offered weekdays every hour from 9:30am to 3:30pm.

Belgrano 1188, Godoy Cruz (at Presidente Alvear). (C) **261/424-2698.** Reservations highly recommended. Main courses $9–$17 (£4.95–£9.35). AE, MC, V. Daily 12:30–3pm, and 8:30pm–midnight.

Francesco Ristorante ITALIAN   Mendoza is populated by Italians, and there are many fine Italian restaurants in town. Francesco, though, is the most elegant and classy. In the kitchen, María Theresa oversees a menu that has impressed for decades. The meat and homemade pasta dishes are equally excellent. The option of combining three stuffed pastas lets you try some of the highlights. Don't miss the tiramisu for dessert. Service is seriously professional here, including a doting sommelier. The outdoor garden is romantic and lovely on both a summer's evening and during a mid-day meal year-round.

Chile 1268 (Espejo and Gutiérrez), Mendoza. (C) **261/429-7182.** www.francescoristorante.com.ar. Reservations recommended. Main courses $9–$15 (£4.95–£8.25). AE, MC, V. Monday through Sunday 7:30pm–1am.

MODERATE

Azafrán (★) *Finds* INTERNATIONAL   This charming restaurant, named after the highly prized and rare saffron spice, is set behind an attractively decorated all wood wine store/cellar. Needless to say, wines are big here, and they have more than 300 different labels for you to choose from. Before you peruse the menu, step into the cellar to discuss your tastes with the friendly on-site sommelier, who'll encourage you to match your food to your wine (not the other way around). Regardless, the food is imaginative, fresh, relaxed, and eclectic. You may start with the house specialty—a platter of smoked meats and cheeses. For entrees, the rabbit ravioli in champagne sauce is delicate and unusual, and the vegetables and tofu baked in a puff pastry will please any vegetarian. Even the steak here is served with a twist—in this case, with sweet potato puréed in a light cream sauce. Given how busy this place almost always is, the service is convivial, and the wood tables and vintage checkered floors give you a sense of dining in an old farmhouse. In warm months, there are a few lovely tables on the sidewalk for alfresco dining.

Sarmiento 765 (Belgrano and Perú). (C) **261/429-4200.** Reservations recommended. Main courses $4–$7 (£2.20–£3.85). AE, MC, V. Mon–Sat 11am–1am.

Las Negras (★) INTERNATIONAL   Stepping through the door into this unobtrusive restaurant in the suburbs of Mendoza, you may be reminded of a chic bistro in Buenos Aires. It's modern, stylish, and hip, with an avant-garde design that includes low tables, couches, and candles. The small menu features items not typical in the region—red tuna with sesame seeds, tandoori duck. The delicate carpaccio is a source of deserved pride. It is all labor-intensive, creative, and unique. Surprise elements include a daily *amuse bouche* and palate cleanser. The wine list is extensive and detailed. It's worth finding this gem, and worth staying for the later-night lounge scene that follows dinner.

Pasteur 177 (at Almirante Brown), Godoy Cruz. (C) **261/424-2008.** Reservations recommended. Main courses $7–$15 (£3.85–£8.25). AE, MC, V. Mon–Sat 8:30pm–1am.

Tips The Real Scoop

Mendocinos love ice cream, and they have some of the best in the country. There are *heladerías* on most every street. The best in town is **Helados Ferruccio Soppelsa** (© **261/422-900**), run by a family of immigrants from the Italian Dolomites. The classics are *dulce de leche*, tiramisu, or strawberry and cream. And check out the *vino*-inspired flavors such as pineapple with Voignier, vanilla with Malbec, and peach with Syrah. They have more than a dozen locations in the Mendoza area, but it's fun to join the local families who gather in the evening at the busy shop on the corner of Belgrano and Sarmiento/Civit. There's also one on the northwest corner of the Plaza Independencia, and another at the Palmares Mall.

Mi Tierra *Moments* ARGENTINE   If, for some unfortunate reason, you don't have time to tour any vineyards in Mendoza, a meal at Mi Tierra will come pretty close to replicating the *bodega* experience. A "thematic restaurant" tucked inside an old downtown house, each room presents the wines of a different local vineyard, including two local heavyweights, Catena Zapata and Chandon, showcasing the vintages, style, and history. You really feel like you've been whisked out to Maipú for dinner. The menu offers local specialties such as goat, young pork, wild boar, and rabbit. The pastas are excellent. For dessert, try the Chardonnay parfait. It's a fun way to spend a leisurely afternoon or evening. Although it's a bit touristy and the food isn't out of the ordinary, the intentions are good, and the building itself is delightful.

Mitre 794 (Pueyrredón and General Lamadrid), Mendoza. © **261/425-0035**. Reservations recommended. Main courses $9–$14 (£4.95–£7.70). AE, MC, V. Daily noon–3:30pm and 8:30pm–12:30am.

INEXPENSIVE

Estancia La Florencia *Value* ARGENTINE   This casual family eatery pays homage to the legendary gaucho, and its two levels mimic a traditional *estancia*. Ask one of the waiters, not one of whom is under 50, for a recommended plate, and he will likely tell you, *"Una comida sin carne no es comida"* (a meal without meat isn't a meal). So choose one of the many varieties of steaks, the *lomo* being the most tender; or order a half-grilled chicken served with a lemon slice. Just remember that a plate of meat is a plate of meat, uncorrupted by green vegetables or anything but potatoes (usually fries). Other accoutrements must be ordered separately. Food is served promptly and without fanfare, and the bill may be one of the lowest you will ever find for what you'll get.

Sarmiento 698 and Perú. © **261/429-3008**. Main courses $5–$8 (£2.75–£4.40). AE, MC, V. Mon–Wed noon–5pm and 8pm–2am; Thurs–Sun noon–2am.

Il Panino *Value* PIZZA   After digging hard to find the best pizza in Mendoza, where you will find great pizza on every block, I landed at this part-restaurant, part-enormous home for what proved to be the perfect meal: The perfectly thin-crusted pizzas are lightly baked, with an emphasis on local fresh ingredients on top—including goat cheese, arugula, fresh herbs, and olives. Look for options such as hearts of palm, asparagus, and sun-dried tomatoes. They've got the right blend of freshness and oozing flavors. They also have wonderful empanadas and Italian sandwiches—and plans to open at lunchtime.

Paso de los Andes 147–153. © 261/428-5922. Main courses $3–$8 (£1.65–£4.40). AE, MC, V. Daily 7pm–1am.

WHAT TO SEE & DO

Mercado Central ★ If you've come to Mendoza to explore food and wine, don't miss the place where locals shop for it. El Mercado Central, the central market, has been in the same location on busy Las Heras street for 120 years and has plenty of atmosphere and lively characters. Stalls offer up fresh produce, and the butchers and fishmongers are the real deal. It's a great place for people-watching. You can also grab quick, cheap snacks such as empanadas, pizzas and sandwiches, and the ingredients for a great picnic.

Corner of Av. Las Heras and Patricias Mendocinas. No phone. Free admission. Mon–Sat 8am–1pm and 4–7pm.

Museo Fundacional ★★ This museum, 3km (1¾ miles) from downtown, displays what remains of the old city, which was ravaged by an 1861 earthquake. Chronicling the early history of Mendoza, the museum begins by looking at the culture of the indigenous Huarpes and continues with an examination of the city's development through Spanish colonization to independence. An underground chamber holds the ruins of the aqueduct and fountain that once provided Mendoza's water supply. Near the museum, the **Ruinas de San Francisco** represent a Jesuit church and school that were used until the Jesuits were expelled from the continent in 1767 and later occupied by the Franciscan Order.

Videla Castillo, between Beltrán and Alberdi. © 261/425-6927. Admission 75¢ (40p). Tues–Sat 8am–8pm; Sun 3–8pm.

Museo Histórico General San Martín ★ Adjacent to the "Alameda," a beautiful promenade under white poplars, the San Martín Library and Museum stands in the spot where General Martí—the legendary liberator who freed Argentina, Chile, and Peru from Spain—had hoped to make his home. The museum's small collection of artifacts pays homage to Argentina's beloved hero, who prepared his liberation campaigns from Mendoza.

Remedios Escalada de San Martín 1843. © 261/425-7947. Admission 75¢ (40p). Mon–Sat 10am–6pm; Sun 10am–2pm.

Parque General San Martín ★★★ Almost as big as the city itself, this wonderful park, designed in 1896 by Carlos Thays (who also designed the Palermo parks in Buenos Aires), extends over 350 hectares (865 acres) with 17km (11 miles) of idyllic pathways and 300 species of plants and trees. A tourist office, near the park's main entrance, provides information on all park activities, which include walking, jogging, bicycling, boating, horseback riding (outside the park's perimeters), and hang gliding. The stunning entrance gates were originally made for the Turkish Sultan Hamid II but ended up as a gift to Mendoza from England. Don't miss the rose garden, the Islas Malvinas soccer stadium (which was built for the 1978 soccer World Cup), or the hustle and bustle at the Club de Regattas. There's even a golf course (see below). A national science museum and zoo (daily 9am–6pm) are located inside the park, and you can also camp here. The best hike leads to the top of Cerro de la Gloria, which, at 960m (3,149 ft.) above sea level, offers a panoramic view of the city and surrounding valley, as well as a bronze monument to the men who liberated Argentina, Chile, and Peru. You can hang glide from the top of the other hill, Cerro Arco.

Main entrance at Av. Emilio Civit and Bologne sur Mer. Free admission. Daily 24 hr.

Plaza Independencia 🗝🗝   The plaza marks the city center, a beautiful square with pergolas, fountains, frequent artisan fairs, and cultural events. Following the 1861 earthquake, the new city was rebuilt around this area. From Tuesday through Sunday, an extensive craft fair gets going about 4pm. On weekend evenings free live concerts and puppet shows take place here. Four additional plazas—San Martín, Chile, Italia, and España—are located 2 blocks off each corner of Independence Square. Each has its own charms, and they're all worth getting to know. Surrounding the square you will find the Julio Quintanilla Theater, the National School, the Independencia Theater, the Provincial Legislature, the Park Hyatt Hotel, and the small Modern Art Museum. During the annual Vendimia Wine Harvest Festival, all major events are staged here.

Av. Mitre (Espejo and Rivadavia). ⓒ 261/425-7279. Admission 75¢ (40p). Mon–Sat 9am–8pm; Sun 4–8pm.

TOUR OPERATORS & OUTDOOR ACTIVITIES

Turismo Uspallata, Las Heras 699 (ⓒ **261/438-1092;** www.turismouspallata.com), runs trips to rural *estancias* and sells bus transfers to all the surrounding areas, including San Rafael and Valle de Uco.

Art lovers can spend the day with local art guide **Cecilia Romera** (ⓒ **261/154-188-800**), who has an insider's access to the top galleries, workshops, studios, and unique exhibits. It's a chance to meet artists face to face, and to explore a blossoming visual arts culture. Customized tours run between $30 and $50 (£17–£28), depending on length.

GOLF   There are three golf courses in the Mendoza area and a few more in the outskirts. The **Club de Campo,** considered the best, has great views of the Andes and opens to the public from Tuesday through Friday. Fees are a bargain at $18 (£9.90) for 18 holes. Club Andino is a course in the middle of the Parque San Martín. The local guides at **TosoBoehler** (ⓒ **261/154-549-005;** www.tosoboehler.com.ar) will help you organize a 1-day or multiday golfing adventure in the Mendoza area. The $75 (£41) admission price covers greens fees, club rentals, a caddy, and a lovely lunch.

HIKING   **Huentata,** Las Heras 680, Mendoza (ⓒ **261/425-3108**), arranges single- or multiple-day hiking trips. Two-hour treks offered by **Argentina Rafting Expediciones,** Primitivo de la Reta 992, office 4 (ⓒ **261/429-6325**), extend from Potrerillos to the waterfall at la Quebrada del Salto, where rappelling is possible. The 2-hour trek costs $25 (£14), including transfer from Mendoza, which adds another 2 to 3 hours to the outing. A full-day hike with transfer and lunch included is $40 (£22).

HORSEBACK RIDING   For those looking to release their inner gaucho, **TosoBoehler** (see above) is a small operator with deep roots in the area's *estancias*. Tours combine a day of horseback riding in the Andes with a gourmet Argentine barbecue. **Argentina Rafting Expediciones** (see above) and **Ríos Andinos,** Ruta 7, Km 64, 5549 Potrerillos (ⓒ **261/431-6074**), offer 2-hour horseback rides for $23 (£13) and full-day rides for $40 (£22) from their bases on Potrerillos.

MOUNTAIN BIKING   In February, cyclists from around the world participate in **La Vuelta Ciclista de Mendoza,** a mini Andean Tour de France, around Mendoza province. **Argentina Rafting Expediciones** (see above) runs 2-hour mountain bike adventures in the rugged Potrerillos area for $25 (£14) and full-day rides for $35 (£19).

SKIING   Perhaps the best place to ski, not just in Argentina but also in South America, is **Las Leñas** (see "Hitting the Slopes in Las Leñas," later in this chapter). Closer to Mendoza, the small resort of **Los Penitentes** (see "The Alta Montaña Driving

Circuit," later in this chapter) offers 23 downhill slopes as well as cross-country skiing. **Portillo** is a much larger and better-equipped ski resort just on the other side of the Chilean border. Eighty kilometers (50 miles) south, **Vallecitos** is the smallest and closest ski resort to Mendoza, but it can be difficult to reach in heavy snow conditions. Obtain information on the province's ski areas from Mendoza's **Subsecretaría Provincial de Turismo** (see "Essentials," earlier in this chapter).

WHITE-WATER RAFTING Mendoza affords the best white-water rafting in Argentina. During the summer months, when the snow melts in the Andes and fills the Mendoza River, rafters enjoy up to Class IV and V rapids. Rafting is possible year-round, but the river is colder and calmer in winter months. Potrerillos, 53km (33 miles) west of Mendoza, has two professional tour operators offering half-day, whole-day, and 2-day trips on the Mendoza River, including direct transfers from Mendoza. These are **Argentina Rafting Expediciones** (see above) and **Ríos Andinos** (see above). Be sure to bring an extra pair of clothes and a towel because you are guaranteed to get soaked. Children under 12 are not allowed to raft. Argentina Rafting has a small restaurant and bar where you can eat and defrost after soaking in the river. Rafting starts at $20 (£11) for 1 hour, and both agencies also offer kayaking ($70/£39 for a full-day kayaking course), horseback riding, trekking, and mountain biking. The 2-day, 60km (37-mile) rafting trip is a Class III and IV excursion offered November through April. It costs $165 (£91), including all meals, camping gear, and transfer from Mendoza. Farther south in San Rafael (see "San Rafael," later in this chapter), there is Class II/III rafting on the Atuel River and perhaps the most extreme rafting in all of Argentina on the wild Río Diamante.

SHOPPING

On Friday, Saturday, and Sunday, an outdoor **handicrafts market** takes place during the day on Plaza Independencia, as do smaller fairs in Plaza España and along Calle Mitre. Thursdays through Saturdays, don't miss the excellent outdoor **antique market** held in Plaza Pellegrini. Regional shops selling handicrafts, leather goods, gaucho paraphernalia, and *mate* tea gourds line Avenida Las Heras. Two of the best are **Las Viñas**, Av. Las Heras 399 (© 261/425-1520), and **Los Andes**, Av. Las Heras 445 (© 261/425-6688). A classier version of the Argentine souvenir shop is **Raíces**, España 1092 (© 261/425-4118). For high-quality leather, visit **Alain de France,** Andrade 101 (© 261/428-5065) or **CuerPiel,** Rioja 601 (© 261/423-7405). More mainstream stores line Avenida San Martín, and Calle Arístides Villanueva is home to upscale fashion boutiques. The city's best shopping mall is **Palmares Open Mall,** on Ruta Panamericana 2650 in Godoy Cruz (© 261/413-9100). Most shops close from 1 to 5pm each day for siesta. You can also buy Mendocine wines at many shops. The least expensive cost a few dollars a bottle, and premiums go for $25 to $80 (£14–£44). Some of the best wine boutiques in town include **Pura Cepa,** Sarmiento 644 (© 261/ 423-8282), and **Sol y Vino,** Sarmiento 664 (© 261/425-6005).

MENDOZA AFTER DARK

Mendoza nightlife is substantially more subdued than Buenos Aires or Córdoba after hours, but a fair selection of bars and nightclubs will capture the attention of night owls. Thursday through Sunday are the biggest nights, when people get started around midnight. It's not La Boca, but there are some great spots to take in tango. On weekend evenings, locals gather at Plaza Pellegrini for a totally authentic, natural tango dancing session, which is not to be missed. Also check out the *milonga* shows at **Teatro**

Las Sillas, San Juan 1436 (© **261/429-7742**). There are a few tango bars in Mendoza, two of which are **C'Gastón,** Lavalle 35 (© **261/423-0986**), and **Abril Café,** Las Heras 346 (© **261/420-4224**).

Start the night at a local wine bar such as **The Vines of Mendoza** (see earlier in this chapter) or at the stunning **Décimo,** Garibaldi 7, Piso 10 (© **261/434-0135**), which is set on the 10th floor of the Gomez building, with the best views in town. The Park Hyatt Mendoza's **Bar Uvas,** Chile 1124 (© **261/441-1234**), begins a bit earlier and offers a complete selection of Mendocine wines, a long list of cocktails, and live jazz and bossa nova groups playing most nights.

The city's best bars line Aristides Villanueva street in the center of town. Try **Lupulo,** A. Villanueva 471 (© **261/15-454-0960**), for microbrewed beers; **Por Acá,** A. Villanueva 557 (no phone), for pizza and microbrewed beers; or **El Abasto,** A. Villanueva 308 (© **261/483-4232**), for good old rock 'n' roll. Most of the serious nightclubs and discos are 10km (6¼ miles) out of town along Ruta Panamericana near Chacras de Coria. **Cacano,** on Aguinaga 1120 (© **261/496-2018),** is a classic. **La Cubana,** on Ruta Panamericano (no phone), is another top disco in this area. Locals flock to **La Reserva,** Rivadavia 32 (© **261/420-3531**), on weekend nights for the drag show at midnight. The **Blah Blah Bar,** Paseo Peatonal Alameda, Escalada 2301 Maipú (© **261/429-7253**), is great for a late-night drink if you're not heading out to the discos. Hip nightclubs do swap places quickly as the hot spot of the moment, and many have unpublished phone numbers.

For you gamblers, the **Regency Casino** at the Park Hyatt, Chile 1124 (© **261/441-1234**), is substantially better than the Casino Provincial, offering blackjack, roulette, poker, and slots. Table bets are $1 to $50 (55p–£28).

2 Touring the Wineries ★★★

Less commercialized than their European and American counterparts, Mendoza's wineries are generally free to visit and easily accessible along wine roads known locally as Los Caminos del Vino. These roads are as enticing as the wine itself, weaving and winding through tunnels of trees to vast dry valleys dominated by breathtaking views of the snowcapped Andes. Some roads climb as high as 1,524m (4,999 ft.) in the High Zone surrounding the Mendoza River, while others lead to lower-level vineyards in the south. Mendoza's wine region is divided into four zones: the High Zone, Mendoza South, Uco Valley, and Mendoza East. We cover the first three: Mendoza East is mostly large industrial vineyards that make Argentine "table wine" (low in both quality and price) and aren't set up for tourists. To the south, San Rafael is a somewhat distant and off-the-beaten track fourth area covered here (see "San Rafael," later in this chapter). Be sure to pick up the essential collection of maps, "Caminos de Las Bodegas." At $5 (£2.75), they're the best investment you'll make in Mendoza. They're available at most hotels and at the wine shops in Mendoza. The mapmakers' new website, www.winemap argentina.com, is an excellent place to get a head start on your planning.

HOW TO SEE THE VINEYARDS

The list of vineyards is enormous, the road maps unfamiliar, and the options endless. How exactly should you plan to make the most of your time in Mendoza? You have choices. First, you can sign up for a fully organized multiday trip led by a local guide

Mendoza Province

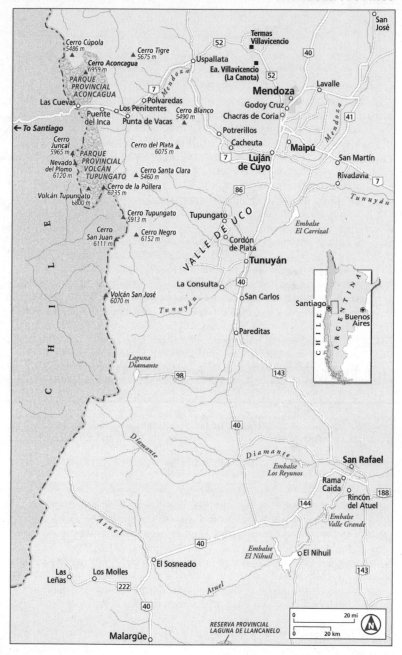

Tips   Taking Wine Home

Argentine wines are becoming more and more popular in North America and Europe, but you won't find many of the best vintages at home yet. Here are some tips for bringing a few bottles home with you.

- Although Customs rules depend on your home country, in general you can take as many bottles back as you can carry, provided they are for personal use. Legally, you are usually allowed to bring three bottles duty-free, but if you bring more (say, up to six), just declare them at Customs. If the charge isn't waived completely, it's usually small, based either on the alcohol-per-liter ratio or on the price of the bottle. More than six bottles and you're likely to be paying a visit to Customs officers, who will tax you.

- Exporting more than a dozen bottles is more complicated. You should discuss the logistics thoroughly with authorities in your country before your trip.

- Due to recent changes in airline security, you need to limit the amount of liquid you take with you as a carry-on. Therefore, I recommend you put the wine bottles in your checked luggage. Pack them well! You can buy wine bags and Styrofoam spacers from wine stores in Mendoza. Try **Pura Cepa,** Sarmiento 644 ((C) **261/423-8282**), or **Marcelino,** at the corner of Zapata y Benegas ((C) **261/429 3648**). They run about $10 (£5.50) each. Many *bodegas* will also help you package special bottles for international travel, and they can help arrange for larger purchases as well. The best option is to buy special boxes with foam hollows for six or twelve bottles. These boxes come with handles for comfortable traveling.

- Another option is to send bottles directly home via a courier service. Ask at the *bodega* or wine store for more information. It runs about $12 (£6.60) a bottle.

- Know that your home state or province determines the regulations you must follow. To be 100% certain you're not treading into dark waters, consult local authorities before your trip.

who takes care of all the logistics and leads you into the heart of the wine land. (See below for details on guides.) You can also just join an organized tour for a day or two. Going on your own is another option. You can hire a *remise* for the day (see earlier in this chapter), call in advance to book your reservations, and head out. Renting a car is another alternative, but beware of drinking and driving! Finally, renting a bike gives the day a leisurely pace.

More and more *bodegas* are opening their doors to tourists; some offer guest rooms—a fabulous trend that is definitely on the rise. If you fall in love with a particular vineyard, ask if they have guest rooms and see if you can stay the night.

The **High Zone** ✸✸✸ that surrounds the Mendoza River includes Luján de Cuyo and parts of Las Heras, Guaymallén, Luján, and Maipú. This first zone is best regarded for its production of Malbec, although cabernet sauvignon, chenin, merlot, chardonnay, and Syrah are all bottled here as well. Many of the *bodegas* in this zone lie within 1 hour's drive of Mendoza, making tours very convenient. I suggest you begin your touring here, where there is great variety and many visitor-friendly *bodegas* to choose from. South of Mendoza, the beautiful **Uco Valley Region** ⚶⚶, including Tunuyán, Tupungato, and San Carlos, produces excellent Malbec, Semillon (a white), and Torrontés (another white, very floral, like a Muscadet, more common in Salta). Allow at least 2 hours to reach this area. It's a long drive but certainly worth the effort. Farthest away, the **Mendoza South Region,** between San Rafael and General Alvear, is fed by the Atuel and Diamante rivers. Its best varieties are Malbec, Bonarda, and cabernet sauvignon. You will need at least a day to visit this region.

The **Mendoza East Region** is the province's largest wine-producing area in terms of quantity (not necessarily quality). The vineyards, irrigated by the Tumuyán and Mendoza rivers, harvest Malbec, merlot, sangiovese, and Syrah, among others. There is little tourism infrastructure here.

With so many wineries (more than 650 at last count), it can be difficult to figure out which to visit. Some are massive, modern industrial complexes funded by foreign investors. Others are traditional "boutique" wineries run by the same family for generations. Most are open from Monday to Friday from 9am to 5pm, and Saturdays 10am to 3pm; some are now open from noon to 3pm on Sundays, although the Sunday visit slots are usually booked up early. Reservations are usually required for visits. Tastings are sometimes free and sometimes cost about $15 (£8.25), which is still a bargain.

TOUR OPERATORS

Local tour operators have the inside scoop on everything from booking rural inns to in-depth presentations on the local wine scene. They can make your time in Mendoza more carefree, helping you navigate the rural roads of Mendoza, and narrowing down the hundreds of *bodegas* to choose from. All you have to do is relax, soak up the gorgeous views, and indulge in some fabulous food and wine.

Tips Make the Most of Your *Bodega* Day!

- Schedule three or four *bodegas* to visit per day at the most. Select a variety of sizes (large, medium, small) and styles (modern, traditional, boutique). Stop for lunch at the middle *bodega* or at a restaurant in the wine areas (see below).
- Rest well the night before you hit the *bodegas.* Tours provide plenty of information and sampling, and you will want to be alert enough to soak it all in.
- The sun is hot in Mendoza, and weather can be dry, given the high altitude. The wineries and cellars can be chilly, however, so bring a sweater, even if it's hot outside.
- Hire a *remise* driver or guide for most days, but treat yourself to 1 day spent roaming the vineyards on bicycle. You will be forced to go at a slower pace and to ride the backroads of the rolling countryside.
- Don't wear perfume or lipstick, which distract from the aroma of the wines.
- Note that many *bodegas* accept only cash for wine purchases, particularly those that do not have on-site restaurants. Be sure to stop by an ATM before heading out.

Sunday Hours

Sunday is a day for Argentines to be with family and have an *asado* barbecue. In Mendoza, as in most of the country, most shops, restaurants, and wineries are not open, with the exception of a handful of *bodegas* and the local mall (Mendoza Shopping Plaza).

Bikes and Wine (© 261/410-6686) rents bikes from the center of wine country in Maipú, provides an easy-to-follow self-guided route map that includes a handful of close-by *bodega* visits, and books you for lunch. They'll also pick you up in downtown Mendoza, give you bikes, reserve your visits at wineries, and include a nice lunch for $30 (£17).

Trout & Wine (© 261/429-8302; www.troutandwine.com) run in-depth and personalized wine tours in Maipú, Uco Valley, and Luján de Cuyo. They know the people behind almost every vineyard in the area, offering a chance to get a more personalized, close-up experience. As their name suggests, they also run fly-fishing tours.

Uncorking Argentina (© 866/529-2861 or 261/429-3830; www.uncorkingargentina. com) is run by a transplanted Californian who has a deep knowledge of wine and friends throughout the local wine country—a "wine educator" whose trips are informative, in-depth, and fun. Each tour package is customized, and wine tours can be combined with cooking classes, spa days, and adventure tours. A 1-day tour costs $110 (£61). All-inclusive 9-day tours start at $2,800 (£1,540). She also teaches short wine-tasting classes if you have a free evening and want to brush up before you head out.

CHACRAS DE CORIA ★★
14km (8½ miles) S of Mendoza

Many travelers use this lovely, leafy suburb of Mendoza as a base for trips to the region. And it's easy to see why: It's convenient to both the city center (20 min. away) and to the *bodegas* area; it has a rich heritage, great restaurants, and a handful of excellent inns; and it's fun and relaxing. This is my first choice for those looking to base their visit away from the hustle of downtown Mendoza.

GETTING THERE
Chacras is accessible via local bus 10, which stops on La Rioja street in downtown Mendoza, or via taxi, which is $5 to $8 (£2.75–£4.40) from downtown. It is feasible to tour the area on a day outing from the city, combining a few *bodegas* and a stroll through the town center—either via the bus, with a driver, in a rented car, or on an organized tour. If you are driving, take the Corredor del Oeste south of Mendoza and follow the signs into the heart of town.

GETTING AROUND
Once you're in Chacras, you can walk to virtually everywhere, including some *bodegas* and some great restaurants.

WHERE TO STAY
Casa Glebinias   Just down the street from Borravino (see below), this quiet inn is a gardener's delight, nestled amid what may be Chacras's greatest botanical display. Rooms are actually separate houses, each with lovely views of the garden outside each

window. Interiors are decorated with an eclectic mix of treasures in a wide range of styles, from Art Deco mirrors and antique window frames, to natural history sketches. All units have a kitchenette, and the staff brings breakfast to your door each morning.

Medrano 2272, Chacras de Coria. (C) 261/496-2116. www.casaglebinias.com. From $110 (£61) suite. MC, V. On-site parking. **Amenities:** Pool; garden; Internet; library. *In room:* A/C, TV, kitchen.

Finca Adalgisa ★★   This is authentic Mendoza: an old family *bodega,* converted into a tranquil and fully authentic inn. Run by the pioneering young *hotelera* Gabriela Furlotti, the inn blends old and new, from the slick modern lounge where you can sample from the *bodega's* limited production of annual Malbecs, to a century-old *casa vieja,* or traditional private residence, where rooms are situated behind an enormous kitchen in the old family home. In the lush backyard, facing the pool, two stone houses have three large suites each. The middle rooms have two stories. Friendly and helpful staff members make you feel at home, and they're willing to help you make reservations at other vineyards or restaurants. Guests can taste wines and dine at the tiny *bodega* adjacent to the old house. The winery still produces a small quantity of wine (6,000 bottles), but they don't market it. If you're not staying here, you may still call ahead and arrange for a visit, including a meal and a wine tasting. Meals run $18 to $23 (£9.90–£13).

Pueyrredon 2222, Chacras de Coria. (C) 261/496-0713. www.fincaadalgisa.com.ar. 11 rooms. $150 (£83) double. MC, V. On-site parking. **Amenities:** Lounge; pool; bicycles; Internet; wine cellar. *In room:* A/C, TV, Wi-Fi, kitchenettes, safe.

Posada Borravino *(Value)*   This stylish and affordable option is modern, yet with a rustic feel. Recently opened by three architects in an old home on a very quiet street, it's only a few blocks from the town square. Interiors are all natural colors, mainly various shades of beige. Quarters are a bit tight; the backyard pool is miniscule. But the staff is very friendly and the common space—which includes a rotating art exhibit— is inviting.

Medrano 2658, Chacras de Coria. (C) 261/496-4445. www.posadaborravino.com. 8 units. $70 (£39) double. MC, V. On-site parking. **Amenities:** Pool; bicycles; grill. *In room:* A/C, TV, Wi-Fi.

Posada Robles de Besares *(Kids)*   This five-room bed-and-breakfast is owned and run by a local family. The owners recently converted this old summer home into a lovely inn. And since they have young kids of their own, they're happy to share the backyard pool, tennis court, and swing set with visiting youngsters, while the parents enjoy the gym or the wine cellar. It's a great value for families.

796 Besares, Chacras de Coria. (C) 261/496-2383. www.roblesdebesares.com.ar. 5 units. $120 (£66) double; $140 (£77) 2-bedroom suite. V. On-site parking. **Amenities:** Pool; tennis court; gym; bicycles; wine cellar. *In room:* A/C, TV.

WHERE TO DINE
Almacén Español SPANISH   This place serves simple Spanish cuisine. Besides classic tapas, which showcase fresh local ingredients, the menu features four types of paella and a wide selection of seafood. On weekends, they host live flamenco and other live music shows.

Darragueira 558, Chacras de Coria. (C) 261/496-1741. Main courses $8–$15 (£4.40–£8.25). AE, D, MC, V. Daily 9pm–1am.

FinisTerre ARGENTINE   In a house dating to 1860, this restaurant aims to replicate a kitchen from that era—with a wood-fueled oven, a traditional circular plough, and *la abuela's* recipes. The kitchen is open to diners who want to meet the cooks and see behind the scenes. Specialties are classic Argentine dishes such as stews and grilled meats. The wine list is good. The lovely outdoor garden is a stage for live music on weekends. They also offer cooking classes.

Italia 5829, Chacras de Coria. © 261/496-1991. www.finisterreargentina.com.ar. Main courses $8–$14 (£4.40–£7.70). AE, MC, V. Thurs–Sat 8pm–1am. Reservations recommended.

Houser CAFE   This German-styled bakery/cafe makes a great stop for an afternoon coffee and a sweet indulgence. Try a sweet lemon loaf, called *budín de limón,* fruit pies, chocolate cakes, or some steaming pastries. The orange juice is freshly squeezed. They change their hours frequently throughout the year, according to season. Generally, however, they are open for breakfast, lunch, and afternoon tea.

Viamonte 5170, Chacras de Coria. © 261/435-2368. No credit cards. Tues–Sun 9am–6pm. Main courses $2–$7 (£1.10–£3.85).

La Piadina 👍 *Finds*   This traditional Italian cantina serves outstanding homemade pastas and pizzas on rustic northern Italian crusts. Low-key and unassuming, it's a place in which to mingle with the locals and to indulge. The pumpkin-stuffed ravioli with mushroom sauce is delicious. Also worth trying are the carrot pappardellis and the tortelloni with ricotta, ham, and walnuts.

Italia 5723, Chacras de Coria. © 261/496-4068. Main courses $7–$15 (£3.85–£8.25). MC, V. Daily 8:30pm–1am.

WHAT TO SEE & DO

An authentic mix of traditional rural life and upscale modern infrastructure character-izes the heart of Chacras, founded in 1600. **Plaza General Espejo,** the delightful town square, hosts an **antiques fair** 👍 on Sunday afternoons. The white-washed neo-colonial parish church, Our Lady of Perpetual Help, faces the plaza. Very good restau-rants are within a few blocks from the center (see above).

The most interesting winery in Chacras is **Bodega y Cava de Weinert,** San Martín 5923 (© **261/496-4676**), a large operation that exports high-quality wines around the world and continues using large oak barrels. It's in a quintessential old Spanish-style villa, and the downstairs tasting room is musky and dark, just as a cellar should be.

To the south of Chacras is the **Museo de Bellas Artes de Mendoza,** San Martín 3651 (© **261/496-0224;** entrance $1/55p), also known as the Museo Fader, after its chief painter, Fernando Fader. Housed in a brick mansion surrounded by a lovely gar-den, rooms are dedicated to national and international artists.

Farther down the same road is **Bodega Lagarde,** San Martín 1745 (© **261/ 498-0011**), one of the oldest and most traditional wineries in Mendoza, with the credo that wines should reflect the vineyards. It is a relaxed, friendly winery that has-n't been slicked up for tourists, so it's a bit untidy. The tour includes a fun lesson in champagne bottling.

CHACRAS DE CORIA AFTER DARK

Some of Mendoza's top nightclubs are in Chacras de Coria, side by side along the Panamericano Highway. Some of the names are ever-changing, but look for La Gua-naca, Pasión, or Cemento.

LUJÁN DE CUYO
17km (11 miles) S of Mendoza

Just south of Chacras de Coria, Luján de Cuyo proudly proclaims itself "La Tierra del Malbec," the land of Malbec. The area's dry, hot weather and high altitudes make it an ideal growing place for full-bodied wines. In the distance, the eternally snow-capped Cordón del Plata mountain range dominates the views. A large area made up of a few towns, this is the place to explore the success and allure of Argentina's most hyped *vino tinto*. The town of Luján de Cuyo, at the center of the region, offers little to visitors except for a few great ice-cream shops.

GETTING THERE
Luján de Cuyo is a vast area. The main *bodegas,* in and around Agrelo and Pedriel, can be accessed by public bus 10 from downtown Mendoza, which takes you into the center of Luján. From there, you need to take a taxi to outlying areas. If you are driving, take Highway 40 south of Mendoza.

GETTING AROUND
If you've arrived by bus, grab a taxi from the center of town to reach the *bodegas.* If you are driving, stick to main roads and follow well-marked signs to each *bodega.* None are too far from a main national or provincial highway, and most are well signed.

VISITOR INFORMATION
The **Visitor Information Center** at 1000 Saenz Pena (© **261/498-1912**) is open daily from 8:30am to 6pm Monday through Friday and on weekends from 10am to 4pm.

WHERE TO STAY & DINE
In addition to the restaurants in this section, many of the *bodegas* listed below in "What to See & Do" also serve lunch.

Cavas Wine Lodge ✦✦ This lodge is an oasis of luxury amid a vast vineyard, with the High Andes serving as a stunning backdrop. Everything here is private, high-end, and the feeling is definitively exclusive. Suites are scattered two by two in spacious adobe bungalows throughout the vineyard, all facing west to the mountains. Inside, rooms are impeccably detailed, with big beds. The ceilings and walls are curved, and bathrooms include soaker tubs. Each unit has a private outdoor hot tub and a stunning upstairs terrace—it's impossible to say which offers a better view of the sun setting behind the Andes. A peaceful spa, a stocked wine cellar, and a first-rate restaurant are on-site as well. The friendly concierge will help you organize any outing, though it is far from town and inconvenient if your goal is to tour a lot. It's ideal, however, for those seeking seclusion and romance. Ask about packages for multiple-night stays.

Costa Flores s/n, Alto Agrelo. © **261/15-454-4118.** www.cavaswinelodge.com. 14 units. $350 (£193) suite. AE, MC, V. On-site parking. **Amenities:** Restaurant; pool; gym; spa; bicycles; wine cellar. *In room:* A/C, TV, Internet, minibar, CD players, fireplace, private deck, private Jacuzzi.

La Bourgogne ✦✦✦ FRENCH This restaurant may be the best one in Mendoza, and it certainly rivals any other in the country. Famed chef Jean-Paul Bondoux has trusted local Federico Zeigler with his signature blend of French techniques and local ingredients. Set inside Carlos Pulenta's modern and serene Vistalba winery, the menu is incredibly creative (cold avocado soup with fennel and onions) and surprising (pumpkin and grapefruit ravioli in prawn broth). Fish of the day is served with watercress, couscous, and wasabi crisps; duck breast is prepared with chestnuts in a Malbec sauce. The wine list is exceptional—don't miss the Vistalba Corte B blends, and don't be shy about asking your waiter or the friendly sommelier for suggestions.

R. Saenz Pena 3531. © **261/498-9421.** www.carlospulentawines.com. Main courses $8–$15 (£4.40–£8.25). AE, MC, V. Daily 12:30–3pm and 8:30–11pm.

Restaurant Cuba 131 ARGENTINE   This restaurant is located deep inside the Bodega Familia Barberis, with recovered barrels serving as tables, floors, and backdrops. It's one of the places, besides an inn, where you can experience a winery at night. All the dishes come off the grill or out of the wood-fired oven. It's only open from November through March, and reservations are required.

Callejón de la Virgen s/n. ✆ **261/154-549275.** Main courses $8–$13 (£4.40–£7.15). No credit cards. Tues–Sun 9pm–1am. Open for lunch with a reservation.

WHAT TO SEE & DO

Luján de Cuyo is home to many, many *bodegas*. We've selected the most visitor-friendly and unique ones, to give you a taste of what is out there. Also worth considering are **Alta Vista** (✆ **261/496-4684;** www.altavistawines.com), **Terrazas de Los Andes** (✆ **261/488-0058;** www.terrazasdelosandes.com), **Norton** (✆ **261/490-9760;** www. norton.com.ar), and **Archaval Ferrer** (✆ **261/425-3812;** www.achaval-ferrer.com).

Bodegas

Catena Zapata 🐾   This strange Mayan temple is the showcase for one of Argentina's most respected and influential winemakers, Nicolás Catena. His journey from California to the top of the crop in Argentina is legendary, and he is usually credited for giving birth to the Malbec boom. The microclimate here is exemplary of the Luján *terroir*. At the end of the tour, visitors receive a complimentary tasting from the well-known Alamos line.

Cobos, Agrelo. ✆ **261/490-0214.** www.catenawines.com. Free tours with standard tasting Mon–Fri 9:30am, 11am, 2pm, and 3:30pm; Sat 9:30am and 11am. Reservation required.

El Lagar Carmelo Patti *Finds*   Patti is the real deal—a winemaker who welcomes each visitor like a family member, while maintaining traditions that date back centuries. A bohemian artist and wine scholar, he'll offer you a tasting straight from the barrel, which is a rarity. Señor Patti's English isn't great, so it's a good idea to bring along a guide if you don't speak Spanish well, to help you appreciate him fully (see "Tour Operators," earlier in this chapter). When it's time for a tasting, see if you can convince Carmelo to uncork a bottle of the 2002 Gran Assemblage blend.

San Martín 2614. ✆ **261/498-1379.** Free tours Mon–Fri 10am–4pm, by reservation only.

Landelia   This new kid on the block makes a refreshing visit and a chance to see a dream become reality. Opened in 2007, it's a new single vineyard estate winery with a natural style that embraces modern ideas. Friendly and open to visitors, they have a special "Barrels Tour" that includes tank and barrel tastings.

Bajo Las Cumbres s/n, Alto Agrelo. ✆ **261/496-1822.** Tour with standard tasting $8 (£4.40) Mon–Sat 9am–5:30pm, Sun and holidays 10am–4:30pm.

Luigi Bosca   One of the most prolific wineries in the country has welcomed tourists for decades—so many tourists, in fact, that buses line up outside to get in. Regardless, it's worth a stop, to see inside a vast operation. Don't miss the champagne either.

San Martín 2044. ✆ **261/498-1974.** www.luigibosca.com. Free tour with standard tasting daily 10:30am, 3pm, and 5pm by reservation only.

Ruca Malen   This is one of many French-owned *bodegas* in the Luján area. The state-of-the-art orange brick building is known for its outstanding four-course *bodega*

Bottle Your Own (& Maybe Buy a *Bodega* While You're at It)

Who wouldn't want to own his or her own piece of the Luján de Cuyo paradise? You can become the proud owner of a vineyard estate, and bottle your own premium wine as part of **Finca Los Amigos** (www.fincalosamigos.com). The Mendoza Vineyard Village is a 150-hectare (370-acre) complex of vines that is to be subdivided into 25 individual vineyards and 50 estate homes. For prices starting at $25,000 (£13,750), potential homeowners can become "vineyard members" with access to an exclusive resort that comes with oenologists to help you impress your friends.

lunches that highlight pairings from the winery's top two lines: Ruca Malen and Kinien. The guides are entertaining, and the atmosphere is posh and generous.

RN 7, Km 1059. ℭ **261/410-6214.** www.bodegarucamalen.com. Reservations required. Free tour with standard tasting Mon–Fri 10am–5pm, Sat 10am–12:30pm.

Tapiz   This winemaker is the creator of the label known as Zolo in North America. Your tour begins with a horse-drawn carriage ride through the property. After a chance to touch and feel the vines, head in for a taste of whatever wine they're featuring that day. All tours are private. The guide, Carolina Fuller, is an unpretentious professional who makes you feel like you were the only visitor. They also have a fabulous lodge and restaurant in Maipú (p. 277).

RP 15, Km 32. ℭ **261/490-0202.** www.tapiz.com.ar. Free tour with standard tasting Mon–Fri at 10am, noon, 2, and 4pm; Sat 10am and noon only. Reservations required.

Vistalba   Carlos Pulenta, the man behind Vistalba, is a star here for his dedication to quality and *terroir.* The winery is a vision of technological wonder, while the downstairs tasting room is stunning, with its natural wall.

R. Saenz Pena 3531. ℭ **261/498-9411.** www.carlospulentawines.com. Free tours start Mon–Sat at 10:30am, noon, 3, and 4.30pm. Tastings run from $5 to $14 (£2.75–£7.70) per person, depending on the label. Reservations required.

Other Attractions

It's not all about wine here in the Land of Malbec. There are also engineering and religious wonders, as well as the chance to explore the mountains around Luján.

The Cipolleti Dike, for instance, is a study of Mendoza's intricate system of aqueducts. Known as *el dique Cipoletti* in Spanish, it's in the Vistalba area of Luján. Built by Cesare Cipolletti in 1895, this dike or diversion dam regulates the flow of the Mendoza River and directs its water into various channels, some heading through the fertile vineyards and other forming the Guaymallén Channel, which moves water through the heart of downtown Mendoza and into all those lovely fountains. The Italian hydraulic engineer who organized the irrigation infrastructure here, as well as aqueducts in Florence and on the Tiber River, is a true Mendozan hero, buried nearby. In the near distance is a major oil refinery run by YPF. You'll likely see this dike if you take a standard 1-day tour of the Mendoza area with one of the operators listed earlier in this chapter. Wine tours also drive nearby and would take a detour if you requested it. You'll also pass nearby if you are on a tour of the Alta Montaña on your way to Potrerillos. If you're in possession of a rental car, this engineering marvel is worth a visit on its own. The dike is situated just south of the Mendoza River and west of the Panamerican Highway 40. Take RP Highway 87.

If you have a spare day and just want to relax, head to the bubbly **Termas de Cacheuta,** RP 82, Km 38, Thermas de Cachueta (ℂ 262/449-0152; www.termas cacheuta.com), for some thermal soaking. There is a natural cave, hydro-massage therapy and a beautiful garden. You can visit for the entire day and have a gourmet lunch for $35 (£19), including transfers from Mendoza. A cheaper option is to bring a picnic and enjoy the nine thermal pools only. With transfers, that runs you $9 (£4.95).

The **Iglesia de la Virgen de Carrodilla** ⓕ, corner of San Martín and Carrodilla, Luján de Cuyo (ℂ 261/435-1667), the home of the patron saint of Mendozan wine, is also worth a visit. This Virgen is displayed in a painting brought from Spain 1811 that shows Mary pushing a cart, with a child in one arm and grapes in the other. The Spaniard believer built a chapel close to his house to house the painting, which is now a popular historic monument. In 1938, she was consecrated the patron saint of vineyards. The adobe-walled church includes wonderful wine-themed murals. The church museum next door has an interesting collection of Catholic artwork. It's open Monday through Saturday from 9am to noon and 4:30 to 7:30pm. The Virgen de Carrodilla is venerated annually during the Vendimia Festival in March. Across the street is an empanada stand where you can grab a snack.

MAIPU
14km (8½ miles) NW of Mendoza

The Maipú region includes vast fields of olives and fruit as well as grape vines. In fact, locals cherish olives every bit as much as grapes here—evinced by the annual National Festival of Olives held in the second half of February each year. If you feel like you are in Tuscany as you roam the shade-lined streets and rural roads, you're not far off the mark: Peek inside any home, and you'll notice that most inhabitants are of Italian descent—which explains their love of good food, good wine, and the good life. Like Luján de Cuyo, Maipú is both a sprawling rural region and a town with the same name.

GETTING THERE
Take a 15- to 25-minute taxi ride from downtown Mendoza, or 30 minutes from the Mendoza airport. Or catch the local bus no. 151 or 160 from the stop on La Rioja street—it'll take you into the center of the town of Maipú. Drivers should head south on Highway 40 and turn east at Juan J. Paso to get to the center. Other turnoffs will take you to outlying vineyards.

GETTING AROUND
Flat and leafy, Maipú is a great place for biking (see "Tour Operators," earlier in this chapter). Alternately, taxis can take you from the bus stop to wherever you need to go.

VISITOR INFORMATION
There is a visitor information center at Ozamis 19 (ℂ 261/492-2448).

WHERE TO STAY & DINE
Almacén del Sur DELICATESSEN   The journey from garden to table is incredibly short at Almacén del Sur. Before seating you, staff members guide you through the herb and vegetable gardens, to demonstrate how fresh the ingredients are. Then you head inside a refurbished farmhouse for your meal. The dishes highlight their gourmet line of deli products sold across the country, including green tomato chutney,

cipolline onions in balsamic vinegar, and rose petal preserve. The five-course lunch is not cheap. If you're on a budget, ask about the simpler alternative.

Zanichelli 709, Coquimbito. © 261/410-6597. www.almacendelsur.com. Lunch menus $15 (£8.25) for 3 courses, $27 (£15) for 5 courses. AE, MC, V. Mon–Sat 12:30–4pm. Reservations highly recommended.

Club Tapiz 🐾   One of the best new lodges in the area is built in an old home, dating to the 1890s, tucked inside a 10-hectare (25-acre) vineyard, which you can explore on bike or on foot, without having to cross a road. The seven guest rooms are simple and tidy, with modern touches, king-size beds, and bright bathrooms. Ask for a room with a window onto the back garden, and be sure to save time for a few hours in the peaceful spa. Rooms start at $125 (£69) a night, including a big buffet breakfast and wine tastings each evening. It's a good deal. The inn is close enough to other *bodegas* to keep you busy for a few days.

Pedro Molina s/n. © 261/496-4815. www.tapiz.com.ar. 7 units. Doubles start at $150 (£83). AE, MC, V. **Amenities:** Restaurant; lounge; pool; spa; games room; business center; Internet; wine cellar. *In room:* A/C, TV.

Terruños Restaurant 🐾🐾 FUSION   Inside the Club Tapiz lodge complex, this restaurant is likewise housed in a restored colonial home. Elegant yet funky, the menu blends French, Italian, and Asian tendencies without distracting too much from the sensational wine list. The pork stuffed with dates in a Malbec sauce is divine, and the young goat cooked in white wine is pure Mendoza. Desserts include a tiramisu truffle and a Malbec parfait. The tea menu is also impressive. On summer nights, ask for an upstairs table on the west side, for killer views. This would be a good midday stop on a tour of Maipú *bodegas*.

Pedro Molina s/n, Russel. © 261/496-0131. Main courses $10–$18 (£5.50–£9.90). AE. Daily noon–3pm and 8:30pm–1am. Reservations required.

EXPLORING *BODEGAS*

In addition to the *bodegas* listed fully here, others worth exploring include **San Telmo** (© 261/499-0050), **Finca Flichman** (© 261/497-2039; www.flichman.com.ar), and the quaint and tiny **Baquero 1886** (© 261/429 3915; www.baquerowineestate.com).

Bodega La Rural 🐾   Founded by Don Felipe Rutini in 1885, this traditional *bodega* maintains an excellent reputation. It's best known for its Trumpeter, San Felipe, and Rutini labels. Next door, the excellent **Museo de Vino** (same contact information), is Latin America's most prestigious wine museum. A great place to start your exploration of Mendoza's wines, it pays tribute to the pioneers of Mendozan wine, and provides information on local geology.

Montecaseros 2625, Coquimbito. © 261/497-2013. www.bodegalarural.com.ar. Free tour with standard tasting. No reservations required. To taste from the Rutini and Felipe Rutini, a reservation is required and fees are charged. Mon–Sat 9am–1pm and 2–5pm.

Carinae Veñedos & Bodega   This *bodega* is receiving a lot of buzz. Owned and run by a very friendly and low-key French couple, Brigitte and Philippe Subra, it's a true boutique *bodega*. Their latest vintages—mostly Malbec, with smaller quantities of Syrah and cabernet sauvignon—have far exceeded any expectations for what was considered a small, unpretentious family project. For an extra $3 (£1.65) a glass, you can sample their award-winning 2004 Carinae Prestige.

Videla Aranda 2899, Cruz de Piedra. © 261/499-0470. www.carinaevinos.com. Tour with tasting $3.50 (£1.95) per person. Daily 10am–6pm.

Familia Zuccardi   Familia Zuccardi is perhaps the most savvy and tourist-friendly *bodega* in the area. They serve lunch, dinner, and even high tea. Their multiday programs give you a deeper understanding of Mendoza's wines and cuisine. This authentic family winery is known for its high production.

RP 33, Km 7.5. *©* 261/441-0000. www.familiazuccardi.com. Free tour and tastings. No reservations required. Mon–Sat 9am–5pm; Sun 10am–4pm.

Tapaus Distillery   This distillery provides a welcome break from grapes. The focus here is on liquor—more precisely, liqueur: brandy, grappa (okay, they use some grapes), and fruit liqueurs. The architecture and design may have your head spinning—if it isn't already.

F. Villanueva 3826. *©* 261/499-0514. www.tapaus.com.ar. Free tour with standard tasting. Mon–Sat noon–6pm. Sun open by appointment only.

Tempus Alba   This is another family establishment dedicated to maintaining a noble, hand-on approach to wine making. Tours are in-depth and detailed. Come in the morning for more personalized attention; afternoons are often swamped with visitors.

Carril P. Moreno 572, Coquimbito. *©* 261/481-3501. www.tempusalba.com. Free tour; tastings $2.50 (£1.40) per glass or 3 glasses for $4.50 (£2.50). Mon–Fri 10am–5pm.

OTHER LOCAL FARMS

In Maipú, numerous farms allow visitors to explore the production of olive oil and indulge in sensual tastings and appreciation courses. **Quinta Generación.** Ozamis Sur 2718 (*©* **261/499-0472**), is a boutique olive oil factory that runs guided tours and tastings. Nearby, **Isabel Agrovivero,** Ceferino 544, Cruz de Piedra (*©* **261/410-6325**), also produces figs, walnuts, and grapes. Their tours are very good, and the shop is stocked with goodies. An old olive oil factory, **Laur** ☆, Videla Aranda 2850, Cruz del Piedra (*©* **261/499-0052**), puts on a show for gourmands—including a presentation on the health benefits of olive oil.

VALLE DE UCO ☆☆
90km (56 miles) S of Mendoza

Everything seems to stand still in the remote, high-altitude Valle de Uco, which may not last for long as word spreads about the incredible wines coming from here (and the incredible characters that have been drawn here to make them). The scenery is divine, and the towns are sleepy and rural, with an old-West feel. The current "it spot" for groundbreaking wines, La Consulta, has attracted luminaries such as Michel Rolland, Paul Hobbs, and the Lurton brothers. Altitude varies from 800m (262 ft.) in Tunuyan to 1200m (3,936 ft.) in Tupungato, some of the highest-altitude wineries in the world. Winters here can be very cold, and summers are warm with cooler nights, which helps produce superior color and tannins. This area makes an excellent day trip from Mendoza.

GETTING THERE
The main towns of Tupungato and Tunuyán can be reached by local bus from the Mendoza bus terminal. If you are driving, take Highway 40 south from Mendoza city. Well-placed signs point you to the major vineyards.

GETTING AROUND
You'll need a car or a hired driver to tour this area. Distances are too great for biking, and local buses are few and far between.

When to Visit

Mendoza is alive four seasons of the year. In winter (June–Aug), you can combine very quiet wine touring with great skiing at Las Leñas (see "Hitting the Slopes in Las Leñas," later in this chapter). In spring (Sept–Nov), the whole area is in bloom. Days are warm, and the air is remarkably aromatic. The hot summer months from December through February require a good sun hat and access to a pool. My personal favorite time to visit is the fall (Mar–May), when the *vendimia* wine harvesting is wrapping up, the alamo and poplar trees glow golden, and the nights are fresh.

WHERE TO STAY & DINE

Numerous hotel plans are in the works for the Valle de Uco, including an inn at the O. Fournier Bodega (see below), and a hotel/spa in Vista Flores, run by the Vines of Mendoza and slated to open in 2008. The best options for now are listed here.

La Posada del Jamón *(Finds* CHARCUTERIE This "ham inn," which started as a sandwich and cold cuts shop, is not what you'd expect to find in this region. Despite its kitschy all-pig theme, it's honest, humble, and a rare find. Come for the sausages, cured meats, head cheese, or pork tenderloin with homemade applesauce (some say it's the best pork in the country). The vegetarian lasagna is also good. The family-run service here is great. In summer, ask for an outdoor table for beautiful views.

RP 92, Km 14, Vista Flores, Tunuyan. ☎ 262/249-2053. www.laposadadeljamon.com.ar. Main courses $4–$12 (£2.20–£6.60). V. Daily noon–4pm, Thurs–Fri 8pm–midnight.

Posada Salentein *☆* Tucked behind the massive Salentein winery complex, this rural posada has an old-time, secluded ranch feel that doesn't overdo the wine theme. Eight comfortable rooms are set in two buildings—a rustic old house and a brighter new one. The upstairs Merlot room has a private balcony. All rooms have kitchenettes. The European owners' art collection is also on display throughout the property. The Argentine-styled menu at the restaurant is very personalized and fresh, for lunch and dinner. This area is particularly gorgeous in the fall when the Alamo trees are golden. This is a fine place in which to get away from it all (including television), with attentive service from the couple who manage the property.

Ruta 89 and Videla, Los Arboles, Tunuyan. ☎ 262/242-9000. www.bodegasalentein.com. 8 units. $108–$180 (£59–£99) double. AE, MC, V. **Amenities:** Restaurant; pool; business center; TV lounge.

Rancho' E Cuero This classic Argentine mountain *estancia* has no frills, no spa, no TVs in rooms, and no five-star restaurant. What it does have is seemingly endless acreage, great hospitality, and plenty of opportunities for adventure—including horseback riding, hikes to glaciers, and fly-fishing. Deep in the mountains and far from the wineries, the lodge is remarkably comfortable. Watch for foxes and guanacos (cousins of the llama) in the hills, and condors in the skies. You need a good vehicle to get here on your own or to arrange a transfer with the lodge directly.

RP 86, Ugarteche, Tupungato. ☎ 261/155-692364. www.ranchoecuero.com.ar. 3 units. $250 (£140) per person per day includes full board and activities. V. **Amenities:** Restaurant; stable; transfers; living room. *In room:* no phone.

Tips   Come to Harvest

If you're going to be in Mendoza between February and April, the Zuccardi family invites you to come pick some grapes at their vineyard, Finca Santa Rosa. This unique program gives wine aficionados a day of hands-on work in the field. After a short tutorial, guests receive scissors and a basket and then set to work for 2 hours. Afterward, the Zuccardis serve a fantastic lunch (with ample wine), followed by a tour and tasting. It's a real bargain at $60 (£33) per person, including lunch, a tour and tasting, and transportation to and from your hotel. Reservations are required (write turismo@familiazuccardi.com or call ✆ 261/441-0000).

Valle de Uco Lodge   This classic Jesuit-style lodge is in the middle of the Valle de Uco, 10 minutes west of Tunuyán. A rustic but upscale country retreat, it encompasses tree-lined paths, expansive gardens, and breathtaking views of the Andes. The eleven double rooms are laid out in two buildings in a U-shape around a pool, garden, and Malbec vines that stretch to the mountains. A charmingly refurbished two-bedroom old adobe farmhouse is at $260 (£143) with breakfast or $360 (£198) with full board. Huge bathrooms, high ceilings, and soft colors characterize the rooms. The restaurant/lounge is a cozy, familiar spot in which to unwind with a sample from the expansive wine cellar.

Calle Tabanera s/n, Colonia de Las Rosas, Tunuyan. ✆ 261/429-6210. www.postalesdelplata.com. 11 units. $200 (£110) double with breakfast, $300 (£165) with full board. AE, MC, V. **Amenities:** Restaurant; wine bar; pool; Internet. *In room:* A/C, TV, safe.

WHAT TO SEE & DO

Wineries flourish in all corners of the Valle de Uco. This "New Napa"—the Mendoza region's "it spot"—is specifically near the village of La Consulta, where vineyards such as Clos de La Siete, San Polo, and O. Fournier are making a big name for themselves. Wineries here are part of a rural countryside that differs from the more urban areas of Maipú and Luján de Cuyo. The colder temperatures make for strong production of Merlot and Pinot Noir wines.

If you are looking for a break from the wine-haze, head to the hills. To the south of the Valle de Uco is the spectacular **Laguna del Diamante** 🐸🐸, well worth a day trip from either San Rafael or Mendoza city itself. At 3,230m (1,059 ft.), this natural reservoir is backed by the gorgeous Maipú Volcano. The scenery is otherworldly. Take a driver and a good truck. It's open for four months in the summer only. **TosoBoehler** (✆ 261/154-549-005) organizes tours in first-rate 4×4s; including a barbecue lunch at the lake, it's $75 (£41) per person.

Bodega Salentein 🐸🐸   This complex is practically a planet of its own. It includes a modern chapel, the Posada inn (see above), the recently-opened and much-heralded Kiika **art gallery** 🐸, a restaurant and gift shop, and, of course, the *bodega* itself. Kiika blends mostly contemporary Argentine art with a bit of the (unnamed) owner's collection of Dutch classics. The exhibition room is ever-changing. Visits to the *bodega* start with a 15-minute film. Guests then walk across to the cross-shaped bodega, which eerily resembles a temple. You wouldn't be the only one who thought of *The Da Vinci*

The Story of Mendoza's Wine

Blessed by rich sunlight and a panorama of snow-filled mountains, Mendoza dominates Argentina's wine-making industry, and it's one of the most successful wine regions on earth. Surrounding the beautiful city of Mendoza, just to the east of the towering Andes, the province accounts for more than 70% of the nation's wine production, and it's the world's sixth-largest producer of grapes.

The Spanish began cultivating Mendoza's wild American vines in the 16th century, and wine production soon dominated the region's economy. They were able to harvest this semiarid land—which receives little natural rainfall—by using a vast irrigation system originally developed by the Incas and extended by the Huarpes, indigenous people from the region. A series of artificial irrigation ditches and canals divert water from the Mendoza, Diamante, Tunuyán, and Atuel rivers, which fill as snow melts in the Andes to nourish the land.

The development of Mendoza's wine industry ebbed and flowed. Wine production stalled in the late 18th century as Spain restricted grape growing to prevent competition with its colonies. The industry was renewed following national independence, as European experts introduced French grapevine stocks and wineries to the region. However, the earthquake of 1861 destroyed most of the existing wineries, and it was not until the opening of a railroad in 1884 that wine production resumed on a significant scale. The railway brought with it many of the founding families of today's wineries, who carried new wine-making techniques and varietals from Italy, France, and Spain. A series of economic crises plagued the industry in the first half of the 19th century, and Mendoza's wines seldom made it farther than the common Argentine table. Some of the wines were so low in quality that soda water was needed to help wash them down, a tradition that continues in some places today, though not because the wine is of poor quality.

In the past decade, wine from Mendoza has finally reached beyond the common table to the international stage. Argentina's National Wine Growing Institute has regulated the country's wine industry and spearheaded quality improvements, with increased focus on the international market. New production techniques, state-of-the-art machinery, advanced irrigation processes, and better grape varieties have combined to bring Mendoza international acclaim. The region's dry, sandy soil; low humidity; and rich sun combine to create wines of high alcohol content and rich fruity character, the most important of which is Malbec, characterized by a powerful fruit bouquet with sweet, dense tannins. Mendocine vineyards grow many other varietals, including cabernet sauvignon, Syrah, Barbera, chardonnay, and sauvignon blanc.

Code or James Bond while touring the underground. Tastings, like everything here, are dramatic. Come to Salentein for the day, and include lunch at the Posada.

Ruta 89 and Videla, Los Arboles, Tunuyan. (C) 262/242-9000. www.bodegasalentein.com. Tour with tasting $3.50 (£1.95) per person, includes entrance to gallery. Reservation required. Mon–Sat 10am–4pm.

Jacques and François Lurton   These two sons of a Bordeaux wine legend have wineries around the world. Here in the Valle de Uco, their *bodega* is a wood, concrete, and stainless steel beauty that fits naturally into the environment. Their Pinot Gris is amongst the best in South America.

RP 94 Km 21, Vista Flores, Tunuyan. (C) 262/249-2067. www.bodegalurton.com. Reservations required. Mon–Fri 10am–5pm.

La Azul   For a very personalized look at a small boutique winery, visit **La Azul.** The grapes have to be very, very good to make it into their exclusive, high-quality selection of wines.

RP 89, Agua Amarga, Tupungato. (C) 262/423-593. www.bodegalaazul.com. Free tours; tastings $10 (£5.50) per person. Reservations recommended. Daily 8:30am–6pm.

Le Clos de los Siete   Led by the infamous and influential Michel Rolland, seven French wine investors, excited by the limitless possibilities to plant without restriction, make up the **Le Clos de los Siete.** Their property in Valle de Uco is divided into seven wine cellars. They'll help you appreciate the freedom that Mendoza affords the world's great winemakers, who elsewhere feel restricted and left to nature's mercy. A visit here will help you put Mendoza in perspective. For tastings, I recommended varietals from the Lindaflor label. For a splurge, ask them to uncork a bottle of the award-winning Clos de los Siete 2003 Malbec/Cabernet/Merlot/Syrah blend.

Clodomiro Silva s/n, Vista Flores. (C) 262/243-2054. www.clos7.com.ar. Free tours; tasting prices depend on the wine and is priced per bottle. Daily 10am–5pm. Reservations required.

O. Fournier   This Spanish-owned company has a remarkable "concept *bodega*" that shows the power of gravity. It's this natural law that makes for outstanding, natural wine. Opened in 2006, the winery has stunned critics with its modern architecture and new twist on technology.

Los Indios, La Consulta, Tunuyan. (C) 262/245-1088. www.ofournier.com. Tour costs $3.50 (£1.95) unless you buy wine or choose a tasting ($2.50–$8/£1.40–£4.40). Reservation required. Daily 9:30am–5:30pm.

3 San Rafael

234km (145 miles) S of Mendoza

Sleepy and rural, San Rafael is a mini-Mendoza minus the hipsters. The main daily activities here include working in a winery, eating ice cream, and riding a bicycle. It's definitely off the beaten track, and you'll need a car and a spirit of adventure to explore the area. It's a long, hot, but rewarding drive from Mendoza.

GETTING THERE

San Rafael is a 1½-hour drive south of Mendoza down Highway 40. The first half of the trip goes through lovely rural towns. The second half crosses a desert wasteland. Many buses leave Mendoza's main terminal heading for San Rafael. **Chevallier** ((C) 2627/446697) and **Andesmar** ((C) 2627/427720) are the main bus companies. **Aerolíneas Argentinas** ((C) 0810/222-86527; www.aerolineas.com.ar) flies five times a week (currently not on Sun or Mon) from Buenos Aires to San Rafael.

GETTING AROUND

The town center is compact and easy to explore on foot. Rural areas will require either a *remise* (call Remises Del Sur at ℭ 2627/430646), rental car, or bicycle. For rental cars, try **Hertz** (ℭ 2627/436959; www.hertz.com) or **Rent A Car San Rafael** (ℭ 2627/437447).

San Rafael is flat, so biking is a great way to explore. To rent a bike, try **Biciletas Rosales** (ℭ 2627/427085) or **Bicipartes** (ℭ 2627/430260). Rates in San Rafael generally run about $7 (£3.85) for a day's rental.

There are many companies that offer transfers out to the fertile Valle Grande and Atuel River, including **Transportes Iselin** (ℭ 2627/446463), which departs from the bus terminal, and **Atuel Travel** (ℭ 2627/429282), which also organizes sightseeing and wine tours.

VISITOR INFORMATION

The municipal Tourism Information Office is at Av. H. Yrigoyen 745 (ℭ 2627/424217). It's open daily 8am to 9pm.

WHERE TO STAY & DINE

In addition to the establishments listed below, don't miss **La Delicia Helados** (Yrigoyen and 3 de Febrero; ℭ 2627/436333), which is great for people-watching and ice cream. A slightly hipper joint is **Sin Fondo,** Yrigoyen 1710 (ℭ 2627/15-545553), with a relatively broad menu for this town; pastas and seafood are the top draws. A classic neighborhood joint, **Tienda Del Sol,** Yrigoyen 1663 (ℭ 2627/425022) serves pizzas, homemade pastas, huge sandwiches, and *minutes*—breaded veal or chicken topped with a choice of jam, cheese, tomato, or all the above.

Finca Los Alamos ℛ   Somewhat of an institution for old-school Argentine literati, this quiet country inn in a fortified old home dates back to 1830. Now, rooms where Borges and others once slept are open to the public for overnight stays. Time seems to stand still at this exclusive rural inn. Adobe-walled rooms are decorated with tapestries and colonial furniture. Beds are a bit creaky, but the bedding is luxurious. The in-house restaurant serves classic homemade fare with a focus on simplicity. Exclusive winery tours and horseback rides through the farm's extensive property are also possible.

Calle Bombal s/n. ℭ 2627/442350. www.fincalosalamos.com. 6 units. $200 (£110) double. MC, V. **Amenities:** Restaurant; pool; games room; wine cellar.

Rocas Amarillas   Thirty beautiful kilometers (19 miles) from San Rafael is a sweet collection of new though rustic two-story cabins on the Atuel River in Valle Grande. Each cabin has a fully equipped kitchen, outdoor grill, and river views. The staff will help you set up adventures, from rafting to climbing.

RP 173, Km 33, Valle Grande. ℭ 2627/15-589285. www.rocas-amarillas.com.ar. 4 units. $30 (£17) cabin. No credit cards. **Amenities:** Grills; picnic area. *In room:* TV, kitchen.

Tower Inn and Suites   In the center of town, the appropriately named Tower Inn is San Rafael's tallest building and only four-star hotel. Rooms are comfortable and fully equipped. The staff is friendly and professional. The kid-friendly Flintstone-style pool has a huge patio. The spa focuses on olive and olive-oil treatments.

Yrigoyen 774. ℭ 2627/427190. www.towersanrafael.com. 89 units. From $110 (£61) double. AE, MC, V. **Amenities:** Restaurant; gym; spa; game room; business center; room service; casino. *In room:* A/C, TV, Internet, safe.

WHAT TO SEE & DO

San Rafael is an oasis irrigated by the Atuel and Diamante rivers. Your explorations will combine both the rivers themselves and the productive oasis they give life to—not to mention the local wineries, which make the most of a shallow mineral soil and a warm climate.

BODEGAS

Bodega Jean Rivier This renovated winery blends old and new with flair and precision. The yield is small and strictly controlled. The owner considers himself a rare classic "grower-winemaker," who straddles what are generally considered separate tasks.
Yrigoyen 2385. © 2627/432676. www.jeanrivier.com. Free tour with tasting. Mon–Fri 8–11am and 3–5pm; Sat 8–11am.

Bodega Valentin Bianchi 𝓡 This traditional family winery is beloved by Argentines throughout the country and very much at the heart of San Rafael. Their modern *bodega* bears the fruits of grapes brought from Italy in 1910 by Mr. Bianchi himself. If you're lucky, you'll get a taste of the exquisite Enzo Bianchi Malbec. They also have a separate cellar that gives champagne-focused tours.
Comandante Torres 500. © 2627/433046. www.vbianchi.com. Free tour; standard tastings $4 (£2.20) or deluxe tasting for $9 (£4.95). Mon–Sat 9am–noon and 2–5pm.

OUTDOOR ADVENTURES

San Rafael's bounty stems from the waters of the Atuel River, which local residents have long used as a playground. The road south from town leads through the scenic walls of the **Atuel Canyon.** The adventure scene is headquartered in the tranquil community of **Valle Grande** 𝓡, which stretches along the river itself. Along the way, you'll find cabins for rent, horseback riding trips, rock climbing, and small restaurants. Many cater to large groups of students. For half-day rafting trips, try **Raffeish** (© 2627/436996) or **Antu Aventuras** 𝓡 (© 2627/439069). Up river from Valle Grande are four imposing hydroelectric dams, and beyond that a massive reservoir called El Nihuil where there are boat rentals, restaurants and beaches.

A new development southwest of San Rafael is **Finca Viña del Golf,** RN 144, Km 674 (© 2627/487027; www.vinasdelgolf.com.ar), which combines a winery, 18-hole golf course, and a planned lodge.

4 The Alta Montaña Driving Circuit

Climbing the mountains on the way to the Chilean border, this excellent driving circuit leads past the magnificent vineyards of Mendoza to breathtaking vistas of the Andes. It is an all-day excursion (at least 5 hr. with no stops) that leads past the Uspallata Valley up to nearly 3,000m (9,840 ft.) at Las Cuevas and the entrance of Aconcagua Park. You can take one of two routes: The easier drive takes you past Potrerillos on the RN 7—a small area along the Mendoza River popular for its whitewater rafting. The more challenging drive (due to winding dirt roads) takes you through the gorgeous natural-springs town of Villavicencio. (We recommend you go Villavicencio on the way and return via Potrerillos on the RN 7, since you don't want to be stuck above Villavicencio at night.) Whichever route you choose, the roads come together in Uspallata, where the circuit continues to Las Cuevas on the RN 7. You can do this tour on your own, but it is easier with a driver who knows the roads. Note that

Roadside Shrines: Folk Saints of Argentina

At first they seem random. But take a closer look, and you'll discover that the roadside shrines dotted along this high mountain road (and along most rural roads in Argentina) are of two kinds: piles of clear water bottles and mazes of red ribbons. In fact, they are intriguing cultural phenomena worshiped by devoted cults, yet still unrecognized by the Catholic Church. The water bottles honor the **Difunta Correa,** considered by many to be worthy of sainthood and capable of performing miracles. During the civil wars of the 1840s, Señora Deolinda Correa followed her husband's battalion through the desert. Carrying water, food, and their baby son in her arms, she died en route of exhaustion, thirst, and hunger; but her baby survived by nursing on his dead mother's breasts. Believers leave bottles full of water to quench her thirst and ask for her protection, which she has been known to offer in abundance to those in need. There is an elaborate shrine in her honor in the town of Vallecito, in San Juan province. Meanwhile, the red ribbons pay tribute to one man: **El Gaucho Gil,** a mythical outlaw cowboy who was said to be a Robin Hood–type character and a conscious objector to civil wars. In 1878, he was hung for his acts of defiance. Just before his last breath, he pledged that he'd become a miracle worker in the afterlife. Hundreds of thousands of Argentines pray to him for miracles, and he keeps them coming back, always leaving offerings in the color of blood. Just exactly why a Gaucho Gil shrine is located where it is remains a bit of a puzzle to non-followers, but many believe they are positioned where miracles have occurred—including narrowly avoided traffic accidents.

a 4WD is preferable, although not a necessity, for the route to Villavicencio. Expect temperatures to drop significantly as you climb the mountain; bring a sweater! It's also a nice idea to bring a picnic. In absence of any lovely restaurant for lunch on a terrace with a view of the peaks, a roadside pullout may be the better option.

HEADING TO USPALLATA VIA VILLAVICENCIO

Although it takes a couple hours longer than heading straight north on RN 7, driving the Ruta 52 takes you to the natural springs of Villavicencio, the source of Argentina's well-known mineral water. If you've ordered bottled water in Argentina, chances are it's Villavicencio. Leaving Mendoza to the north through Las Heras, you'll be driving on the old international road to Chile. After 34km (21 miles), you'll pass the **Monumento Canota,** the spot where generals San Martín and Las Heras split to confront the Spanish at different fronts in 1817. After Canota, you will begin to climb the Villavicencio Valley, and by 40km (25 miles), the road turns to gravel and becomes winding (the road here is known locally as the Caracoles de Villavicencio, or "the snails of Villavicencio"). A small **ranger station** at 50km (31 miles) offers information on the Villavicencio natural reserve, including sources of the mineral water and the region's flora and fauna. Eagles, condors, pumas, mountain cats, foxes, ostriches, guanacos, flowering cacti, and many plants and trees occupy the area.

VILLAVICENCIO
45km (28 miles) N of Mendoza

French-owned Danone purchased the rights to this land and its mineral water, and it is working hard to preserve the integrity of the springs. This explains why the **Hotel Termas Villavicencio,** frequented by Argentina's high society until its closing in 1980, has not reopened. The lush gardens of the Normandy-style hotel, seen on the label of Villavicencio bottles on tables up and down the country, are off limits. Perched against the dusty foothills with oaks and poplars, trickling streams, and wildflowers surrounding it, the hotel's location represents a lush little paradise in the Andes. A small chapel, opened in 1941, lies just behind it. Next to the hotel, you can stop at the Hostería Villavicencio for lunch or a drink.

THE USPALLATA VALLEY

Continuing along the Ruta 52, you will follow the path that San Martín used for his liberation campaign. The dirt road zigzags its way up the canyon, dotted with silver mines exploited by the Spaniards in the 18th century. When you get 74km (46 miles) from Mendoza, you will have climbed to the 3,000m (9,840-ft.) summit. From here, you'll have a magnificent view of Aconcagua and the mountains, and the road begins to improve.

The road from the summit to Uspallata is a breathtaking 28km (17-mile) drive through the **Uspallata Valley.** You will descend into the valley through a small canyon, and when the valley emerges, you'll be treated to one of the most beautiful sights in Argentina. The polychromatic mountains splash light off Aconcagua to your left and the "Tiger Chain" ahead, with occasional clouds painting shadows on some mountains and allowing sun to pour light on others. The curious rock formations surrounding you were filmed for the dramatic setting of *Seven Years in Tibet,* starring Brad Pitt. Just before you arrive in Uspallata, 2km (1¼ miles) north of town, you will see **Las Bovedas**—peculiar egg-shaped mud domes built in the 18th century to process gold and silver for the Spaniards.

HEADING TO USPALLATA VIA POTRERILLOS

This drive is significantly easier than the route through Villavicencio, taking you along the RN 7 through the Precordillera mountains. Follow the signs from downtown Mendoza that point to the REPUBLICA DE CHILE. Potrerillos is a bit of a ghost town along the Río Mendoza, where tour companies arrange white-water rafting, horseback riding, and trekking. There is a gas station here. **Argentina Rafting Expediciones** (see "Tour Operators & Outdoor Activities" on p. 264) has its adventure park off the RN 7. It's a great recharger. There is also a small restaurant. A few kilometers upriver, the new **Pueblo del Río Mountain Resort** (© 261/424-6745; www.pueblodelrio.com.ar) has really nice cabins built with stone and wood that sleep up to eight people each. It has fully equipped kitchens and outdoor grills, and costs $70 (£39) for two people. There's also a good restaurant. This is a great place from which to clear your head after trolling around the wineries, and the **Aires de Montaña Spa,** part of the resort offers all the classic treatments to rejuvenate you. It is the nicest place to stay en route to Aconcagua. The drive continues 41km (25 miles) alongside the Mendoza River to Uspallata.

USPALLATA
58km (36 miles) N of Mendoza

With only 3,500 inhabitants (many of them members of the military), Uspallata is a pretty sleepy place. But this small Andean town surrounded by lovely poplar trees and the biggest mountains in the Americas offers a variety of outdoor activities and makes an excellent base from which to explore the mountains. You can obtain limited visitor information from the **tourist information booth,** open daily from 9:30am to 8:30pm, at the corner of RN 7 and Ruta 52. Gustavo Pizarro is the area's best tour guide, and his **Pizarro Expediciones,** RN 7 (© **2624/20-189**), organizes horseback riding, mountain biking, climbing, and white-water rafting tours. If you need gas or any supplies, get them in Uspallata, which is the last real town before the Chilean border.

WHERE TO STAY & DINE

Hostería Los Condor 👉 Given the town's limited selection of lodgings, Los Condor is probably the best choice. This traditional small-town hotel's location is its best perk. It's steps away from the main intersection and the heart of town. Rooms come in a variety of setups, from simple square singles to large triples. All are bright and spacious, with large bathrooms. There's a rectangular pool outside, and the staff is friendly.

Las Heras s/n, Uspallata. © **262/442-0002.** 23 units. $40 (£22) double. Rates include breakfast. AE, MC, V. **Amenities:** Restaurant; outdoor pool.

Hotel Valle Andino The lodge's greatest merit is its beautiful grounds stretching toward the Andes. A classic mountain retreat, dimly lit and built of wood, it's popular with backpackers and hiking groups. Staff members can organize horseback-riding trips from the hotel. Rooms are stark but modern, some accommodating up to five people. The recreation room has a fireplace and pool table. There's a large new pool in the backyard.

Ruta 7 s/n, Uspallata. © **261/425-8434.** www.hotelguia.com/hoteles/valleandino. 26 units. $6 (£3.30) double. Rates include breakfast. No credit cards. **Amenities:** Restaurant; bar; indoor pool.

Parrillada San Cayetano ARGENTINE This *parrilla* is widely considered the best Argentine grill in town, serving large portions of standard classics such as young goat, chicken, and beef. Behind the YPF gas station, it's a favorite among truckers crossing the border. For $6 (£3.30), servers deliver to your table a small steaming grill loaded with a selection of various cuts. Homemade empanadas and pastas round out the options. The wine list isn't bad, either.

Ruta 7, Km 1105. © **262/442-0149.** Main courses $4–$8 (£2.20–£4.40). No credit cards. Daily noon–2am.

HEADING TO ACONCAGUA FROM USPALLATA

Continuing along the RN 7, you'll drive through the wide U-shape valley carved from ancient glaciers and loaded with minerals such as iron, sulfur, talc, and copper. As you climb the canyon, you will see on your left the first signs of the atrophying **Andes railway**—an old, narrow track from 1902 that lifted an early-20th-century steam train up the mountains. The railroad was abandoned in 1980, due to a political dispute between Chile and Argentina, but it received new vigor in 2006, when presidents Kirchner of Argentina and Bachelet of Chile agreed to start it running again. The $436-million project—necessitated by increased Argentine exportation and increased Chilean demand for imports—should be finished by 2010. The goal is to build a weatherproof line that won't be snowed out, as are hundreds of cargo trucks on this road each winter. No word yet if they will also implement a tourist service, for this is bound to be one of the world's most beautiful train tours.

When you get 20km (12 miles) from Uspallata, you'll come to **Puente Pichueta,** a stone bridge over the Pichueta River commissioned by Fernando VII in 1770 to allow

Hitting the Slopes in Las Leñas

One of South America's top ski destinations, Las Leñas boasts 64km (40 miles) of runs, excellent snow, and typically small crowds. The summit reaches 3,430m (11,250 ft.), with a 1,230m (4,034-ft.) vertical drop. There are 30 runs, with approximately 8% set aside for beginners, 22% for intermediates, and 70% for advanced skiers. The resort's 11 lifts are getting seriously outdated, and there are loud calls for some infrastructure improvements. When the top lift shuts down (as it did for 2 of the season's 4 months in 2006, due to an avalanche), options for experts are limited. When all is running smooth, the lifts here can transport up to 9,200 skiers per hour, which is far more capacity than the town has in accommodations. Consequently, you seldom have to wait in line to get to the top.

Las Leñas is a destination resort—everyone comes on a package that usually includes 1 week of hotel accommodations, lessons, and lift tickets. It has one small grocery store and no nearby town to speak of. Essentially, you must eat all your meals out. It definitely has the feel of a winter wonderland, with no car traffic or high-rises, and hardly any trees. Because the climate is so dry, the powder snow is terrific. In season, it attracts wealthy Porteños and Argentine celebrities, as well as international skiers looking for extreme and challenging off-*piste* terrain, and it has an active nightlife in winter. Local ski instructors are excellent. The majority of people on the slopes are beginner/intermediates, which leaves the advance terrain virtually untouched and ready for exploration. Snow season runs from late June to mid-October. In summer, Las Leñas offers mountain biking, trekking, rafting, and fishing, and hotel prices drop significantly. The resort is most easily reached via a 90-minute flight from Buenos Aires to Malargüe, followed by a 1-hour bus to Las Leñas (68km/42 miles). Alternatively, you can travel by car or bus from Mendoza, which is a 4- to 5-hour drive (399km/247 miles).

The stylish new **Virgo Hotel and Spa** ₢₢ opened in 2005. It is a 105-room minimalist resort that has taken the lead as Las Leñas' best hotel, which definitely gives the resort something to celebrate. Rooms are spacious and bright.

messengers to cross from Argentina to Chile. The road leading to the bridge forms part of the old Inca trail. The lone tree beside the bridge is a nice picnic spot.

LOS PENITENTES
165km (102 miles) W of Mendoza

Los Penitentes is a small resort for downhill and cross-country skiing. Twenty-three slopes accommodate skiers of all levels, and a ski school instructs novices. Skiing is pricier but much better in Portillo, Chile (see below), but if you decide to stay in Los Penitentes, consider lodging at **Ayelan,** Ruta 7, Km 165 (② 261/427-1123), across the street from the ski resort, with basic rooms looking toward the mountains. Doubles cost roughly $75 (£41), including breakfast, and the rustic dining room serves a limited selection of high-quality regional dishes. If you are in Mendoza in winter and like to ski, this makes a good day trip.

Their quadruple rooms are a great value for larger groups. Bathrooms have a Zen-like simplicity with all natural elements and large showers. The spa is so nice you may not even want to hit the slopes, although with a lift just 15m (49 ft.) from the lobby, it's easy to start linking your turns.

The 90-bedroom **Pisces Club Hotel** has well-equipped rooms that accommodate up to three people, though it's not quite the five-star hotel the sign proclaims. A stay here includes breakfast and dinner. Like most of the lodgings here, it is ski-in, ski-out. Following a day of skiing, the hotel provides hot drinks and warming by the fireplace, and the indoor pool, Jacuzzi, and sauna should reinvigorate the remaining cold parts of your body. The restaurant, **Los Cuatros Estaciones,** is the best around. All the hotels offer ski instruction and children's activities, as well as adult activities in the casino and nightclub. After a siesta and then a late dinner, swing by **La Cueva del Esquiador** wine bar and sample from a long and impressive wine list. They have special tastings of Mendozan wine throughout the ski season. As vibrant in the evening as it is on snowy winter days, the place hosts night skiing three times a week and regular concerts, parties, and events.

Las Leñas lies in the southwest of Mendoza province, near the city of Malargüe and close to the Chilean border. To drive from Mendoza, take the RN 40 to the PR 222. Most bookings are done online at www.laslenas.com. **PowderQuest Tours** (www.powderquest.com) offers packages popular with North Americans and Europeans. A 7-night package includes flights from Buenos Aires and excellent guided English-language tours for a few days of wine touring in Mendoza.

Lift tickets run about $46 (£25) per day, with multiple-day passes available. A weekly pass, for example, will run you $245 (£135). Prices for lifts, as well as those for accommodations, depend on the time of the season. September is generally a great time to come—fewer crowds, cheaper prices, and longer days. Great last-minute end-of-season promotions are available as well.

Note: Serious skiers with more time to ski or snowboard should make the trip to **Portillo** (www.skiportillo.com), a much larger and better-equipped resort across the Chilean border. Better yet, head south of Mendoza to Las Leñas (see below).

PUENTE DEL INCA
6km (3¾ miles) W of Los Penitentes

Although it's become somewhat of a tacky tourist trap, the remarkable bridge **Puente del Inca** is nonetheless beautiful. First described in 1646 by the Spanish Conquistadores, it's a natural stone bridge used by the Incas to cross the Río de las Cuevas, about 6km (3¾ miles) past Los Penitentes. With its beautiful display of natural colors, it is believed to have once been a bridge made of ice that was hardened by the thermal springs. Now it's holding a fragile balance between natural cementation and erosion. So it's off limits to visitors—you can look at it, but you can't walk on it. Under the

A Shared Backbone: Crossing into Chile

Trans-Andean neighbors, sometime rivals, colleagues, and "cousins," Chile and Argentina are intricately linked as nations. They share a 5,150km-long (3,193-mile) border from the high deserts of the north to the wilderness of Tierra del Fuego. The busiest border crossing is here at the Paso de Los Libertadores; these border posts are open 24 hours a day for most of the year. In winter, from May 15 to September 1, it's open from 8am to 8pm, or only when the road is open. From here, it's a steep and scenic 3-hour descent to the Chilean capital of Santiago.

bridge, you will see the remains of an old spa that once belonged to a hotel, built in 1917 to capitalize on the thermal springs. That hotel was destroyed in an avalanche in 1965, but, in what many consider a miracle, the adjacent church went unscathed. Natural hot springs still flow underground here, but access is closed to the public. Near the spa, vendors sell handicrafts. **Hostería Puente del Inca** (© 261/429-9953) is the best place to eat here. It's a bit stuffy and seems to be trapped in the 1950s, but the set menu is reliable and well priced at $6 (£3.30).

PARQUE PROVINCIAL ACONCAGUA

Just after Puente del Inca, you will come to the entrance of **Aconcagua Provincial Park.** At 6,960m (22,829 ft.), Cerro Aconcagua is the "Roof of the Americas"—the highest peak not just in South America, but also in the entire Western Hemisphere. From RN 7, you can see the summit on clear days. For a great look at it, get out of the car at the parking lot on the north side of the highway and hike the 15 minutes to Laguna Los Horcones (there is another stellar view from Km 34 on the road between Uspallata and Villavicencio). First climbed in 1897, it is a challenging, although not overly technical climb, where your body battles the stresses of high altitude in an extreme environment. Only highly experienced climbers should even think about this as a goal—it requires fitness, strength, and endurance—as well as a certified local guide. Most people take over 2 weeks to climb, giving themselves at least 1 week to acclimatize to the altitude before pushing for the top. The south face, which gets little sun, is the most treacherous climb. The normal route is along the west side. The main climbing season is in January and February, when dozens of expeditions from around the world converge to tackle one of the prized Seven Summits. The rest of the year, the park is virtually deserted.

The provincial park includes 71,000 hectares (175,441 acres) of stunning high mountain country tucked on the eastern side of the border between Chile and Argentina. To enter the park, however, you must first obtain a permit from the park's "attention center," called Edificio Cuba (© 261/425-2031), inside Mendoza's Parque San Martín. The location where you can buy permits changes periodically, so check with Mendoza's tourism office for additional details. Two-day, 7-day, and 20-day permits are available. With one of the shorter-duration permits, you can hike to the base camps without climbing to the summit. Those hoping to reach the top must buy a 20-day permit, which costs $200 (£110; including emergency medical insurance).

The top guiding company in the park is **Fernando Grajales Expediciones** (© 800/516-6962 or 261/1550-07718; www.grajales.net), which offers 3-day hikes as well as 19-day summit attempts. Another recommended outfitter is **Rudy Parra's Aconcagua Trek** (© 261/431-2000; www.rudyparra.com). Also try **Aymara Adventures** (© 261/420-2064; www.aymara.com.ar), which has horseback-riding trips in the provincial park.

After visiting the park, if you have time to go a bit farther and still make it back to Mendoza before too late, continue on to the official border point. At 4,000m (13,120 ft.) above sea level, it's a wild and wooly place. The famous towering bronze monument Cristo Redentor was erected by the neighboring nations in 1902 after they resolved a territorial dispute. Then return to Mendoza via Potrerillos on the RN 7.

The Argentine Lake District

by Christie Pashby

With its tall peaks and crystalline waters, the Argentine Lake District is one of the world's most spectacular mountain playgrounds, yet it is remarkably unknown and unexplored by foreigners.

The region stretches from the rugged, wild-west town of Junín de los Andes in the north to the emerald waters of Cholila in the south. In between, cottage-lined towns are scattered about, affording plenty of options for overnight stops. A range of travelers will find something of interest here—Alpine adventures, aquatic sports, fabulous wine and cuisine, and cozy chalets and hotels.

Argentines flock here during their twice-annual holidays–to ski in July and August, and to raft in the lakes and hike the mountains in January. The rest of the year, it's *tranquilísimo*. I suggest you schedule your visit when the locals are back at work, during the shoulder-season months of November (spring) and March (autumn)—my favorite time to visit here.

For more information about the region, see **www.interpatagonia.com**.

EXPLORING THE REGION

In this chapter, I have focused both on the Lake District's principal destinations—San Carlos de Bariloche (known here simply as Bariloche), Villa La Angostura, and San Martín de los Andes—as well as stops off the beaten path, such as El Bolsón and Junín de los Andes. This coverage includes numerous national parks, as well as driving tours and boat trips that take in the best of the stunning lakeside scenery. I recommend basing yourself in one of these towns and striking out from there to explore the surrounding wilderness. All the towns described in this chapter offer enough outdoor and sightseeing excursions to fill 1 or even 2 weeks, but 4 to 5 days in one location is ample time for a visit. Based in Bariloche, you can take a day trip south to the crafts fair and lakes at El Bolsón, and then head out for daytime adventures in Nahuel Huapi National Park. Then, take 2 nights to visit San Martín de los Andes and Villa la Angostura. If you're up for it, don't miss the chance to sleep in the backcountry—in either a charming and rustic high-mountain hut, a fly-fishing lodge, or a simple tent, after you've taken in the scenery on horseback. Another interesting route is to make a detour into Chile via the lake crossing from Bariloche, or to organize a boat-bus combination that loops from Bariloche and Villa La Angostura in Argentina, then crosses the border into Chile, then stops in Puyehue, continuing south to Puerto Varas or Puerto Montt, then crosses back into Argentina and Bariloche via the Lake Crossing. Another option is to cross from San Martín de los Andes to Pucón, Chile.

Argentina's Lake District

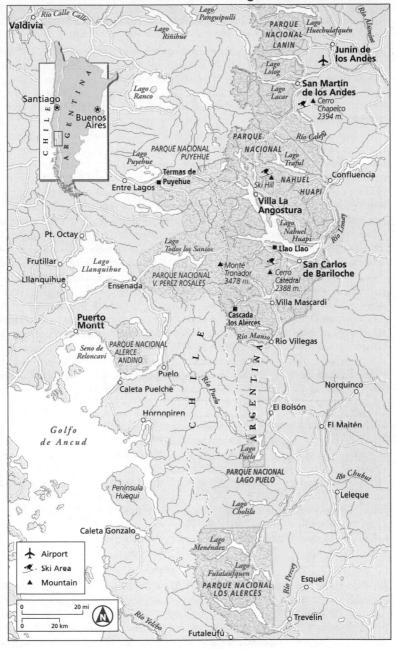

Valdivia

Río Calle Calle

Lago Panguipulli

Lago Riñihue

PARQUE NACIONAL LANIN

Lago Huechulafquén

Río Aluminé

✈ Junín de los Andes

Lago Lolog

Santiago ⊛

CHILE

ARGENTINA

⊛ Buenos Aires

Lago Ranco

Lago Lacar

✈ San Martín de los Andes

▲ Cerro Chapelco 2394 m.

PARQUE NACIONAL PUYEHUE

Lago Puyehue

Termas de ■ Puyehue

Entre Lagos

PARQUE NACIONAL PUYEHUE

PARQUE NACIONAL

Río Calefu

Lago Traful

Confluencia

Ski Hill ✗ ▲

NAHUEL

HUAPI

Villa La Angostura

Pt. Octay

Lago Todos los Santos

Lago Nahuel Huapi

■ Llao Llao

Río Limay

Frutillar

Lago Llanquihue

Llanquihue

Ensenada

PARQUE NACIONAL V. PEREZ ROSALES

▲ Monte Tronador 3478 m.

✗ San Carlos de Bariloche

▲ Cerro Catedral 2388 m.

○ Villa Mascardi

■ Cascada los Alerces

Puerto Montt

Seno de Reloncaví

PARQUE NACIONAL ALERCE ANDINO

Puelo

Caleta Puelche

Río Manso ○ Rio Villegas

CHILE

Río Puelo

ARGENTINA

Norquinco

El Bolsón

Hornopiren

El Maitén

Golfo de Ancud

Lago Puelo

PARQUE NACIONAL LAGO PUELO

Río Chubut

Península Huequi

Lago Cholila

Leleque

Caleta Gonzalo

Lago Menéndez

Lago Futalaufquen

PARQUE NACIONAL LOS ALERCES

Río Percey

Esquel

✈ Airport

✗ Ski Area

▲ Mountain

Río Yelcho

Río Futaleufú

Trevelin

0   20 mi
0   20 km

Ⓝ

Futaleufú

293

1 San Carlos de Bariloche ★★★

1,621km (1,005 miles) SW of Buenos Aires; 180km (112 miles) S of San Martín de los Andes

Just mention Bariloche to an Argentine, and you'll inspire a whimsical sigh. Officially known as San Carlos de Bariloche, this city represents the good life in the national consciousness. With stunning natural scenery and fine cuisine, it's a winter and summer playground for vacationing Argentines, and it's practically a right of passage for Argentine youth to explore nature in the Nahuel Huapi National Park here, with Bariloche in the middle.

Bariloche is blessed with a strategic geographic position. With the rugged plains of the Patagonian Steppe to the east, the towering snowy peaks of the Andes to the west, and the glistening and grande Nahuel Huapi Lake in front, opportunities for adventure are abundant. Even if you're not much of an adventurer, you'll still find plenty of pleasant sightseeing tours, boat trips, boutiques, driving excursions, and fine dining to keep you busy. Or just park yourself wherever the view is good and soak it all in.

The city itself embodies a strange juxtaposition: an urban city plopped down in the middle of beautiful wilderness. Unfortunately, Argentine migrants fleeing Buenos Aires, an evergrowing tourism industry, and 2 decades of unchecked development have left a cluttered mess in what was once an idyllic mountain town. Bits and pieces of the charming architecture influenced by German, Swiss, and English immigration are still in evidence. Visitors to Bariloche are sometimes overwhelmed by its hodgepodge of ugly apartment buildings and clamorous discos, and the crowds that descend on this area from mid-December until the end of February and again during ski season in July. Yet drive 10 minutes outside town, and you'll be surrounded again by thick forests, rippling lakes, and snowcapped peaks that rival the Alps. If you're looking for a quiet vacation, you'd be better off lodging outside the city center, on the road to the Llao Llao Peninsula or in the town of Villa La Angostura (p. 315). On the flip side, Bariloche offers a wealth of services, including the area's largest and best-serviced airport.

ESSENTIALS
GETTING THERE
BY PLANE The **Aeropuerto Bariloche** (© 02944/426162) is 13km (8 miles) from downtown. Buses to the city center line up outside the arrival area; they're roughly scheduled to coordinate with flight arrivals. A taxi to the center costs about $10 (£5.50)—a bargain if you have a group of two or three people. **Aerolíneas Argentinas,** Mitre 185 (© 02944/422548; www.aerolineas.com.ar), runs at least three daily flights from Buenos Aires; in summer, it operates a daily flight from El Calafate as well. **LanArgentina,** Mitre 534 (© 800/999-9526; www.lan.com), runs two or three flights a day from Buenos Aires; LanChile schedules two weekly international flights to Santiago. **LADE,** Quaglia 238, #8 (© 02944/423562; www.lade.com.ar), serves small destinations in the area such as Neuquen and Esquel.

BY BUS The **Terminal de Omnibus** (© 02944/432860) is at Av. 12 de Octubre 2400; a dozen companies serve most major destinations in Argentina and Chile. **Via TAC** (© 02944/434727) schedules three daily arrivals from Buenos Aires and daily service from El Bolsón, Esquel, Mendoza, and Córdoba. **Vía Bariloche** (© 02944/432444) has eight daily arrivals from Buenos Aires (the trip lasts about 20 hr.) and one daily trip from Mar del Plata. **Andesmar** (© 02944/430211) has service from

Mendoza, Río Gallegos, and Neuquén, and service from Osorno, Valdivia, and Puerto Montt in Chile. For long trips, opt for the slightly more expensive (usually $10/£5.50 more) *coche cama* or supercama for chairs that practically become beds. In addition, there's a daily service from San Martín de los Andes via the scenic Siete Lagos (Seven Lakes) route (only during the summer); from Villa La Angostura, try **Ko-Ko** (© **02944/ 431135**).

BY CAR   Motorists can reach Bariloche from San Martín via several picturesque routes. The 200km (124-mile) scenic **Siete Lagos route**, from San Martín de los Andes, follows *rutas* 234, 231, and 237 (avoid this route when it's raining, as the dirt roads turn to mud). The 160km (99-mile) **Paso Córdoba** follows *rutas* 234, 63, and 237. The safest route for night driving or crummy weather, the **Collón Curá** runs 260km (161 miles) along *rutas* 234, 40, and 237; it's the longest route, but it's entirely paved. To get to El Bolsón, follow Ruta 258 south; continue down 40 to get to Esquel. To cross into Chile, take the Puyehue Pass via Ruta 231 (through Villa La Angostura); during periods of heavy snowfall, chains are required. The drive from Buenos Aires will take you upwards of 20 hours, and there are few pit stops en route.

TRAVELING BY BOAT TO CHILE   **Catedral Turismo** offers a spectacular **Cruce de Lagos** journey to the Lake District in Chile. It's a boat-and-bus combination that terminates in Lago Todos los Santos near Ensenada and Puerto Varas. If you're planning to visit Chile, it's a superb option that allows you to take in the beauty of the Andes and the volcanoes, rivers, and waterfalls in the mountain range. I don't recommend making this journey during heavy rain. The trip can take 1 long day or 2 days, with an overnight in the Hotel Peulla or the Hotel Natura in Chile. The trip costs $178 (£98) per person for the boat trip (including lunch), and an average of $135 (£74) double for an overnight at the Hotel Peulla. Book at any travel agency or from Catedral Turismo's offices in Bariloche at Moreno 238 (© **02944/425443;** www.crucedelagos.cl).

GETTING AROUND

BY FOOT   The city is compact enough to explore on foot. Most visitors spend just a few hours touring the city, however, and then use it as a base for exploring the region. The main streets for shopping and tourist agencies are Mitre and San Martín/Moreno. The center of town is the scenic Centro Cívico (Civic Center) plaza. From here, distances are measured in kilometers to the east or west.

BY CAR   Most savvy travelers rent a car to visit this area. You'll need wheels if you're staying outside the city center or planning to explore the sinuous roads that pass through exceptionally scenic landscapes such as the Circuito Chico. All travel agencies offer bus excursions to these areas, which is another way to see them if you don't drive. Rental agencies such as Budget, Dollar, Hertz, and Avis have kiosks at the airport as well as a number of downtown offices: **Budget,** Mitre 106 (© 02944/422482); **AI Rent a Car,** Av. San Martín 127 (© 02944/436041); **Dollar,** Villegas 282 (© 02944/430333); **Hertz,** Quaglia 165 (© 02944/423457); **Bariloche Rent a Car,** Moreno 115 (© 02944/ 427638); and **Localiza,** V.A. O'Connor 602 (© 02944/435374). Rates are reasonable, starting at around $30 (£17) per day. Driving west of town, you have two options: the **directo Pioneros** road that locals use, a few blocks uphill from the lake, or **Bustillo,** the lakeside road. Distances are measured in kilometers away from the Civic Center.

Tips   Bringing a Car into Chile

If you're hoping to do a Lake District circuit combining both the Argentine and Chilean lake districts, be warned that you'll need additional insurance and written permission from the car-rental agency to take the vehicle across the border. If you are planning to drive back to Argentina, you'll have no problems. Few agencies, however, will allow you to leave the car in Chile. I suggest using Budget or Avis for these trips: They're the only companies with offices in numerous towns in both countries, they can offer roadside assistance, and they can quickly provide you with a replacement car if you run into problems. *Note:* The passes into Chile require chains in wintertime.

BY BUS   Bariloche's public bus system is cheap and efficient, whether you're heading to the Cerro Catedral ski resort or exploring the lakeside route of the Circuito Chico. Regular buses depart from calle San Martín, just in front of the National Park headquarters, or from Moreno and Palacios. Bus 20 follows the shores of Lago Nahuel Huapi past the Campanario chair lift to the Llao Llao Hotel and Resort. Bus 10 does the same route but continues past the village at Colonia Suiza. Bus 50 will take you directly to Cerro Catedral. Rides cost less than $1 (55p; just ask the driver).

When navigating the streets of Bariloche, be aware that two streets have similar names, though they are distinct routes: V.A. O'Connor runs parallel to the Costanera, and J. O'Connor bisects it.

VISITOR INFORMATION

The **Secretaría de Turismo,** in the stone-and-wood Civic Center complex between calles Urquiza and Panzoni (© **02944/426784;** securismo@bariloche.com.ar), has general information about Bariloche and is an indispensable resource for accommodations listings, especially during the high season. They also operate an information stand in the bus terminal, open Monday through Friday from 8am to 9pm, and Saturday and Sunday from 9am to 9pm. For information about lodging and attractions surrounding Bariloche, try the **Secretaría de Turismo de Río Negro,** Av. 12 de Octubre 605, at the waterfront (© **02944/423188**); it's open Monday through Friday from 9am to 2pm. Useful tourism information, as well as the best maps and local books, are available at an information kiosk at the corner of Villegas and Moreno, next to the Artisan Market (no phone).

Good websites for all sorts of up-to-date travel information include **www.bariloche.org** and **www.interpatagonia.com.**

The **Club Andino Bariloche,** Av. 20 de Febrero 30 (© **02944/422266;** fax 02944/424579; www.clubandino.com.ar), provides excellent information about hiking, backpacking, and mountaineering in the area. They sell maps and provide treks, mountain ascents, and ice walks led by guides from the Club Andino, as well as rafting, photo safaris, and horseback rides; they are open daily from 9am to 1pm and 6 to 9pm during winter, daily from 8:30am to 3pm and 5 to 9pm during summer. For general information about **Nahuel Huapi National Park,** head to the park's headquarters across the street from the Civic Center (© **02944/423111**), open Monday through Friday from 8:30am to 12:30pm.

FAST FACTS: Bariloche

Banks & Currency Exchange Most banks exchange currency, including **Banco de Galicia,** Moreno and Quaglia (© **02944/427125**), and **Banco Frances,** San Martín 332 (© **02944/430315**). Try also **Cambio Sudamérica,** Mitre 63 (© **02944/434555**).

Hospital **Hospital Privado Regional** is located at 20 de Febrero 594 (© **02944/ 423074**).

Internet Access Internet cafes are on just about every corner—and almost every hotel has Internet access, which is usually free for guests. Try **Cyber-Firenza,** Quaglia 262 Loc. 20 (© **02944/422038**) or **Net & Cappuccino,** Quaglia 220 (© **02944/426128**). The cost is less than $1 (55p) per hour.

Laundry There are two reliable laundromats here: **Mileo,** at Villegas 145 (© **02944/422331**), and **Lavadero Huemul,** on Juramento 36 (© **02944/522067**).

Pharmacy The three main pharmacies in the city center are **Angel Gallardo,** A. Gallardo 701 (© **02944/427023**); **Zona Vital,** Moreno and Rolando (© **02944/ 420752**); or **Nahuel,** Moreno 238 (© **02944/422490**).

Police For emergencies, dial **101.** For other matters, call © **02944/423434.**

Post Office The central post office (no phone) is in the Civic Center, next to the tourist office.

WHAT TO SEE & DO IN BARILOCHE

Bariloche's **Civic Center,** Avenida Juan Manuel de Rosas and Panzoni, is a charming stone and wood complex that houses most municipal offices and tourism services, such as the information center and national park headquarters. The complex, built in 1940, was inspired by the architecture of Bern, Switzerland. Here you'll find the **Museo de la Patagonia Perito Moreno** (© **02944/422309**), open Tuesday through Friday from 10am to 12:30pm and 2 to 7pm, and Saturday from 10am to 5pm. Admission is $1 (55p). The museum has five salons dedicated to the natural science, history, and ethnography of the Bariloche region. The well-tended displays here are intriguing, notably the stuffed and mounted local fauna, such as *pudú* (miniature deer), puma, condor, and more. The second floor has displays of Mapuche artifacts, such as weapons, art, and jewelry, and other artifacts from the colonial period. A small gift shop sells postcards, books, and crafts.

SHOPPING You'll find everything and anything along Bariloche's main street, Mitre, including shops selling souvenirs and Argentine products such as *mate* (tea), gourds, and leather goods. For the region's famous smoked meats and cheese, and other regional specialties such as trout pâté, try the renowned **Familia Weiss,** Mitre 360 (© **02944/424829**), or **Del Turista,** Av. San Martín 252 or Mitre 239 (© **02944/ 422124**). Del Turista also has an enormous array of chocolates and candy, as do other confectioneries up and down Calle Mitre, such as **Abuela Goye,** Mitre 258 (© **02944/ 433861**) and Quaglia 221 (© **02944/422276**); **Bonifacio,** Mitre 171(© **02944/ 425240**); **Mexicana,** Mitre 288 (© **02944/422505**); and **Mamuschka** ⊛, Mitre 298 (© **02944/423294**). Stop by the visitor center for a map of Avenida Bustillo and the Llao Llao Peninsula, which are lined with dozens of shops selling regional specialties.

One of the nicest for lovely home furnishings and accents is **Orígen Arte y Artesanía,** at Bustillo 3.850 (© 02944/442640). Note that generally you are not allowed to take food items such as smoked meats wrapped in plastic outside Argentina.

For local handicrafts predominantly made of wood and wool, stroll the **outdoor artisan market** behind the Centro Civico, held each afternoon except Tuesdays and Wednesdays, from noon to 8 pm (depending on the time of year). It's also worth checking out the indoor **artisan market** on Moreno between Quaglia and Villegas, which is open daily from 11am to 8pm. There is a small shop of all-natural wool products run by a local Mapuche indigenous group. All the vendors are friendly.

TOUR OPERATORS

A plethora of travel agencies offer everything under the sun along the streets of Bariloche. Most tours do not include lunch, and some charge extra for a bilingual guide. The best of the lot includes **Catedral Turismo,** Moreno 238 (© 02944/425443; www.hotelpuertoblest.com.ar), and **Limay Travel,** V.A. O'Connor 710 (© 02944/420268; www.limaytravel.com.ar). Both offer a wide variety of land excursions to El Bolsón, Cerro Tronador, and circuit sightseeing routes. **Huala Adventure Tourism,** San Martín 86 (© 02944/522438; www.huala.com.ar), specializes in adventure sports such as white-water rafting, trekking, and horseback riding, as well as creative and fun multiday outings that combine activities. They can also help with car rentals and hotel accommodations.

PARQUE NACIONAL NAHUEL HUAPI

Nahuel Huapi is Argentina's oldest and most popular national park, with a range of activities for any fitness level. The park surrounds the city of Bariloche, and its headquarters are downtown in the Civic Center (see "Visitor Information," above). The park's main feature is the 3,500m (11,480-ft.) extinct volcano **Tronador (Thunderer),** named for the rumbling produced by ice falling from the mountain's peak. But the park is also known for its glacial-formed Lake Nahuel Huapi (the largest of more than a dozen lakes), as well as its lovely forested peninsulas and its waterways, which are often compared to the channels of southern Patagonia or the fjords of Norway. During

What's with All the Chocolate?

Bariloche is a chocolate-lovers heaven. Within 3 blocks on the main drag, Calle Mitre, dozens of chocolate shops offer tasty little morsels of artisan chocolate. The industry sprang from early Swiss pioneers who settled at the nearby village of Colonia Suiza and saw the potential in all those healthy cows. Classic local flavors include *dulce de leche*, chocolate with lemon, and chocolate with local berries. All the shops are good and produce high-quality chocolate, but the constant lines in **Mamushchka,** Mitre 298 (© 02944/423294), attest to the fact that this shop sells the absolute best chocolate in town. It's worth waiting your turn for the cute red boxes of delicious treats. Mamushka also has a nice smoke-free cafe inside, and a branch at the base of Cerro Catedral ski resort. (Take note of the colorful tile work, by a local artist, on the sidewalk when you walk into Mamuschka).

Nah-Well What?

You're not the only one who has trouble pronouncing the name of Bariloche's stunning lake and national park, **Nahuel Huapi**—that's *nah*-well *wah*-pee. It means Island of the Tiger in the native Mapuche language. With 524 sq. km (204 sq. miles), this stunning lake is more like an inland sea, connecting the lush forests and high peaks of the Andes with the rugged plains of the Patagonian Steppe.

summertime, visitors can take part in day hikes or backpacking trips, with many trails to choose from, or boat out to one of the lake's islands.

The park also has plenty of other outdoor activities, such as rafting, horseback riding, and fishing; during the winter, the park's other dominant peak, **Cerro Catedral,** is a popular ski resort. Easy access to all regions of the park makes Nahuel Huapi popular with visitors seeking mellower activities, such as sightseeing drives and chair lifts to magnificent lookout points. The following information applies to all attractions within Nahuel Huapi and around Bariloche.

THE ROAD TO THE LLAO LLAO PENINSULA 𝒦𝒦𝒦

The **Cerro Campanario** 𝒦 provides possibly the best lookout point in the region, with exceptional views of Nahuel Huapi and Perito Moreno lakes, as well as the ravishing beauty of the Llao Llao Peninsula and the peaks surrounding it. The lookout point is accessed by a 7-minute chair lift ride located 18km (11 miles) outside Bariloche on the road to Llao Llao, meaning you'll have to arrange transportation with a tour, drive a rental car, or take the local bus no. 20, which departs from behind the Centro Cívico on Calle San Martín. A restaurant here offers panoramic views. The office is at Belgrano 41, #B (© **02944/427274**), open daily from 9am to noon and from 2 to 6pm; the cost for the chair lift is $5 (£2.75), and you don't need reservations. Just show up at the chair lift at Avenida Bustillo, Km 17.5, during operating hours.

The Cerro Campanario is along a popular 60km (37-mile) drive around the Llao Llao Peninsula, commonly known as the **Circuito Chico** 𝒦𝒦. This drive affords spectacular views of Nahuel Huapi and Perito Moreno lakes and the snowcapped peaks of Cerro Lopez and Catedral, which tower over the water. Head west out of town on the lakeside Avenida Bustillo. At 18km (11 miles) from Bariloche, the route changes into Ruta 237, loops around the peninsula as Ruta 77, and meets back at Ruta 237 and eventually Bustillo, all the while meandering through dense forest and picturesque bays with outstanding lookout points. There are short hikes en route as well, including a trail through an enchanting *arrayán* (myrtle) forest at the Parque Municipal Llao Llao, and a trail out to the hidden Lago Escondido. Visitors will find *parrilla* (grill) and fondue-style restaurants along the way, as well as the world-renowned **Llao Llao Hotel & Resort** (p. 305). Overlooking the hotel, the lovely **Capilla San Eduardo** 𝒦 displays the unique rustic Andean architecture that so typifies Bariloche. In front of the Llao Llao, **Puerto Pañuelo** is the main dock for boat trips (see below), as well as trips to Puerto Blest and the boat crossing to Chile. Past the Llao Llao, the Ruta 77 continues to a lookout below Cerro Lopez and then descends to Bahía Lopéz, which has a nice beach. Farther along, be sure to stop for a photo-op at the incredibly picturesque Punto Panorámico. Just past the turn-off to Colonia Suiza is **Meli-Hue** (✿ (© **02944/448029;** daily 2:30–8pm), a lovely lavender farm with a small gift shop and fantastic teahouse on the premises. Stop by the tourist information center in town to pick up a detailed Circuito Chico map highlighting restaurants and shops along the way. Again, most tour operators offer this excursion as a bus tour. Another option is to take the local bus along this route, hoping off and on in accordance with the hourly schedule (the tourist information office can also give you a bus schedule).

CERRO OTTO

Walk, bike, drive, or ride a gondola to the top of **Cerro Otto** for sweeping views of Lake Nahuel Huapi, the Llao Llao Peninsula, and the high peaks of Catedral and Tronador. Popular local pastimes include paragliding, trekking, rock climbing, and, during the winter, skiing, tobogganing, and dog sledding. The road up to Cerro Otto takes visitors through a thick forest of pine, beech, and *alerce* (larch) populated with charming chalets. To walk (2–3 hr.) or bike, take Avenida Los Pioneros for about 1km (about ½ mile) and follow the signs to Cerro Otto or Piedras Blancas. Or take the free shuttle bus that leaves from Mitre and Villegas; it runs daily every hour from 10:30am to 4:30pm and drops you off at the gondola base. The **gondola ride** (© **02944/441035**) costs $10 (£5.50) per person and runs January through February and July through August daily from 9:30am to 6pm; the rest of the year, it runs daily from 10am to 6pm. Atop the summit, you'll also find a revolving restaurant (© **02944/441035**). About a 20-minute walk down from the restaurant, the Club Andino runs a cafe at **Refugio Berghof**, a rustic old mountain hut with heaps of character and a small museum about the area's mountaineering history (see "Visitor Information," above, for Club Andino contact information).

COLONIA SUIZA (✿

Don't miss the quaint Swiss pioneer village at Colonia Suiza, out on the Circuito Chico, for their twice-weekly *curanto* cook-ups—a centuries-old style of cooking meat and vegetables deep in the ground. Both a lesson and a delight, *curantos* are held on Wednesdays and Sundays at the main plaza in Colonia Suiza. Founded in 1895 by the Goye and Mermaud families, who crossed into the area from Chile, this is also where Bariloche's chocolate industry was born. It's a tranquil little hamlet with a few restaurants and good campgrounds.

For more local driving tours, see "South of Bariloche," later in this chapter.

BOAT EXCURSIONS

Several boat excursions run from Puerto San Carlos or Puerto Pañelo at Llao Llao. Cost fluctuates between $20 and $30 (£11–£17) per person; to obtain exact prices for any of the following trips and to make a reservation, stop by any travel agency or call © **02944/426784** for more information.

An enjoyable full-day excursion takes you to **Isla Victoria** and the **Bosque Arrayanes** (see also "Villa La Angostura," later in this chapter) by boat from Puerto San Carlos or Puerto Pañuelo. The excursion begins with a 30-minute sail to Isla Victoria, where passengers can disembark for a walk through a conifer forest or ascend to a lookout point atop Cerro Bella Vista via chair lift. The second stop is Península Quetrihué and the Bosque Arrayanes, famous for its concentration of the unusual terra-cotta-colored *arrayán* tree. This handsome "tree" is really a bush, with an odd, slick trunk that is cool to the touch. From Puerto Pañuelo to Isla Victoria, trips leave at 10am and return at 5:30pm; from Puerto San Carlos, trips leave at 9am and return at 6:30pm.

Boat trips also run to **Puerto Blest.** These excursions sail through classic fjords and exuberant vegetation known as the Valdivian Forest, until they reach Puerto Blest. From this point, there is an optional bus ride to Laguna Frías followed by a boat ride to Puerto Frías, then back to Puerto Blest. The return trip to Puerto Pañuelo includes a stop at Los Cántaros Waterfall. Visitors can dine at the restaurant at Puerto Blest or can bring a picnic lunch. These trips are very crowded in the summer. An interesting alternative is to hire a private hiking or naturalist guide (see "Outdoor Activities," below), who will lead you away from the crowds and deep in to the forest while your boat is docked at Puerto Blest. From Puerto Pañuelo, trips to Puerto Blest leave at 10am and return at 5pm; trips from Puerto San Carlos leave at 9am and return at 6pm.

OUTDOOR ACTIVITIES

BIKING   Mountain bike rental and information about bike trails and guided trips in Nahuel Huapi are available from **Bike Way,** V.A. O'Connor 867 (© **02944/424202**); **Bariloche Mountain Bike,** Gallardo 375 (© **02944/462397**); and **Dirty Bikes,** V. A. O'Connor 681 (© **02944/425616**).

FISHING   This region provides anglers with excellent fly-fishing on the Manso, Limay, Traful, and Machico rivers. Fisherman also troll on Lake Nahuel Huapi for introduced species such as brown trout, rainbow trout, and landlocked salmon. Even hardcore anglers will find enough to keep them busy here for weeks on end. The fishing season opens in November and runs through April. You can pick up information and fishing licenses at the **Baruzzi Fly Shop,** Urquiza 250 (© **02944/424922**), or the office of the Parque Nacional Nahuel Huapi in the Civic Center. Bariloche is home to dozens of fly-fishing guides. Be sure to choose one who is fully licensed and provides lunch, transfers, and the appropriate gear. Recommended outfitters are **Martín Freedman** (© **02944/15-550-702;** www.flyfishingpatagonia.com) or the guides at **FlyMaster's** (© **02944/462101;** www.bariloche.com/flymasters). Costs generally run around $300 (£165) per day for up to two people. Trolling and spinning are also available. Tour agencies such as **Huala Adventure Tourism,** San Martín 86 (© **02944/522438;** www.huala.com.ar), offer half-day and full-day fly-casting and trolling excursions.

HIKING   The Nahuel Huapi National Park has a well-developed trail system for day hikes, multiple-day hikes, and loops that connect several backcountry *refugios,* some of which offer rustic lodging. The national park office in the Civic Center provides detailed maps and guides to the difficulty level of each trail. Local hiking guides will share their knowledge and make for a safe and rewarding outing. An excellent multilingual local hiking guide and naturalist is **Max Schoffel** (© **02944/15-669669;** www. patagoniatravelco.com). Another great source for information is the **Club Andino,** Av. 20 de Febrero 30 (© **02944/422266;** www.clubandino.com.ar), which also has trails, guided trekking, ice walks, and climbing trips on Cerro Tronador.

GOLF   There are three golf courses in the Bariloche area. The crème de la crème is the par-70 18-hole course at the **Llao Llao Resort** (© **02944/448530**). Above the shores of Lago Gutierrez, the **Arelauquen Golf Resort** (© **02944/431111**) is the newest 18-hole course in the area. There are 9 holes at the **Pinares Golf Club** (© **02944/ 476122**) on the road to the Llao Llao. Most are open from mid-September through mid-May, and fees run from $25 to $40 (£14–£22).

HORSEBACK RIDING   Horseback rides in various areas of the park are offered by **Tom Wesley Viajes de Aventura,** Mitre 385 (© **02944/435040**), which also has a kid-friendly adventure camp. Rides cost an average of $10 (£5.50) for 2 hours and $15 (£8.25) for 3 hours. **Cumbres Patagonia,** Villegas 222 (© **02944/423283**), has trips to Fortín Chacabuco for $18 (£9.90) per half-day and $30 (£17) per full day, including lunch. For overnight or multiday horseback riding trips, contact **Gatomancha** (© **02944/523009;** www.gatomancha.com).

KAYAK TOURING   Recently, the many fjords of Nahuel Huapi Lake have been tempting visitors to explore in sea kayaks, or touring kayaks. It's a lovely outing that's possible in a variety of weather conditions. Operators such as **Senzi Limiti** (© **02944/520597;** www.slimiti.com) also offer overnight tours, often year-round.

MOUNTAINEERING   Experienced climbers, and those looking for a taste of the high peaks, have plenty of options in Bariloche, including the challenging 3-day climb of Mt. Tronador. Contact **AndesCross** (© **02944/467522;** www.andescross.com) for guiding services.

RAFTING   Various companies offer river rafting on the Río Manso in both Class III and Class IV sections, on either half-day or full-day trips. The average cost for a half-day is $35 to $45 (£19–£25); full-day is $65 to $75 (£36–£41). Easier floats down the Class I Río Limay are also available, for about $25 (£14) for a half-day. Excursions include all equipment, transportation, and a snack or lunch (full-day trips). The two best local rafting companies are **Patagonia Rafting,** San Martín 86 (© **02944/522438**), and **Extremo Sur,** Morales 765 (© **02944/427301**).

SKIING & SNOWBOARDING   Bariloche's main winter draw is the ski resort at Cerro Catedral. When the resort's two former halves joined in 2005, everyone rejoiced. There is more terrain, better lifts, and close to a dozen on-slope restaurants to choose from, making this perhaps South America's greatest ski hill. The scenery is stunning. Lift tickets cost $15 to $40 (£8.25–£22) for adults and $8 to $18 (£4.40–£9.90) for kids, depending on high and low seasons. The season usually runs from June through October, with mid-August by far the busiest time (when all Argentines have their 2-week winter holidays). Heavy snowfalls in September the past few years have helped keep the top sections open well into spring. Regardless, experienced skiers will want to stay high and explore the mountain from Punta Princesa to the south to Piedra del Condor on the north. There is lots of terrain for beginners and intermediates, as well as a snowboard park and tons of events throughout the season. For great slope-side atmosphere and a drop-dead view, have lunch at the traditional Refugio Lynch. Nonskiers can also enjoy the scene thanks to pedestrian lifts, open daily, that ferry passengers to the top. Every July or August, Catedral hosts the **National Snow Party,** with torchlight parades and other events (contact the Catedral ski resort for more information and each year's dates). The bustling Villa Catedral is at the base of the resorts, with a jumble of shops, rental stores, and several lodging options. The nicest ski-in, ski-out hotel is **Pire-Hue Hotel and Resort** (© **029444/460040;** www.pire-hue.com.ar). **Sudbruck Hostería** has a handful of spacious rooms decorated with rustic cypress wood (© **02944/460156;** www.sudbruck.com). Rooms start at about $65 (£36) per night for a double. **Cabañas Antu Pukem** has cabins for six to eight guests; consult them directly for prices (© **02944/460035**).

Catedral is home to a number of good ski instructors. For excellent ski guiding services, ranging from a few days at Catedral to a few weeks touring the many great ski resorts of Patagonia, contact **PowderQuest Tours** (© **888-565-7158** in North America; www.powderquest.com). They have very knowledgeable, experienced, and fun guides.

During the summer, the main gondolas are open to pedestrians for sightseeing Monday to Friday from 9:15am to 4pm.

WHERE TO STAY

If you're looking for luxury, you'll find the most options along Avenida Bustillo, the main road outside town that runs parallel to the lake and leads to the Llao Llao Peninsula. The larger hotels in the city (such as the Panamericano, below) tend to cater to tour groups and aren't especially luxurious or service oriented, but their location is advantageous; staying in town puts you steps from the many excellent restaurants and shops in this tiny metropolis in the mountains. If you're planning to rent a car, then by all means stay outside the city and drive in at your convenience. You can also take the local bus or a quick taxi ride.

A handful of hotels in and around Bariloche are owned by unions and offer discounts to members. These hotels—such as Argentina Libre, Curu Leuvu, Puente Perón, and the larger hotels on Avenida Bustillo toward Llao Llao, including the Amancay and Panamericano (not to be confused with the Panamericano that's downtown)—can take on a clubby workers' atmosphere, which is unpleasing to most visitors. During the high season (Dec 15–Feb 28 and Easter week), prices double. Many hotels consider the winter months of July and August to be a second high season, with prices to match.

The cheapest rates are from March 1 to June 30 and September 1 to December 15. Dates vary; inquire before booking and always ask for promotions or discounts for multiple-day stays. Rates listed here are generally for high season.

WITHIN THE CITY CENTER
Expensive
Hotel Edelweiss 🔆   With its reliable service and huge double bedrooms, this hotel is a solid choice in downtown Bariloche in this price category; just don't come expecting luxury. Double superiors were renovated in 2007 and come with two full-size beds, bay windows, and lake views, as do the suites. Standard doubles are smaller, with a single full-size bed or two twins and a view of a building in the back, but they are just as comfortable and $10 (£5.50) cheaper. The design is pleasant but very run-of-the-mill for a hotel that deems itself a five-star. The suites deserve mention for their gargantuan size, with separate living areas and small bars; suite bathrooms have hydro-massage tubs. An aging penthouse pool with glass walls affords views of Lake Nahuel Huapi. The lounge area has polished floors, leather couches, and fresh flowers; a computer with Internet access is available for a nominal fee. The hotel offers attractive packages and promotional rates, so be sure to inquire when you make your reservations.

Av. San Martín 202, San Carlos de Bariloche. © 02944/445510. Fax 02944/445520. www.edelweiss.com.ar. 100 units. $160 (£88) double superior; from $275 (£151) suite. Rates include buffet breakfast. AE, DC, MC, V. Valet parking. **Amenities:** 2 restaurants; bar; indoor pool; sauna; game room; room service. *In room:* TV, minibar, safe.

Hotel Panamericano *(Overrated*   The massive Hotel Panamericano has long coasted on its reputation as one of Bariloche's premier accommodations, boasting a casino, a lake view, a range of amenities, and an upscale restaurant, QuVé. Its deluxe rating is exaggerated, however, especially when you compare this place to rivals such as the Llao Llao Hotel & Resort (p. 305). Rooms are spacious and comfortable, but the design needs a face-lift, and appointments seem aged, tired, and boring. Lake views are available only above the fifth floor; in fact, the hotel rarely books rooms on the bottom floors unless they're hosting a convention, although they have plenty of tour groups that keep the hotel busy year-round. The back rooms face an ugly building, but they're cheaper. The junior suites are quite nice; they're actually a better deal than the regular suites. They're a tad smaller, but they come with plant-filled balcony patios, outdoor table and chairs, a fireplace, and a living area. A double comes with two full-size beds or one king-size. Inside the lobby, a faux waterfall trickles in the background, and a bar/lounge regularly has live piano music. You can laze around the steamy penthouse pool or exercise in a glass-enclosed exercise room while savoring the lake view; a personal trainer is on hand to offer special ski-oriented workouts in the winter. The hotel has another 100 or so rooms and a casino on the other side of the street, connected by an aerial walkway.

Av. San Martín 536, San Carlos de Bariloche. (©/fax **02944/425846.** www.panamericanobariloche.com. 306 units. $200 (£110) double; $225 (£124) double with lake view; from $430 (£237) suite. Rates include buffet breakfast. AE, DC, MC, V. Valet parking. **Amenities:** 2 restaurants; bar; lounge; indoor pool; exercise room; sauna; room service; massage; laundry service; dry cleaning. *In room:* TV, dataport, minibar, coffeemaker, safe.

Moderate

Hostería Las Marianas 🍴🍴 *(Finds)*   A lovely, cozy inn just a few blocks from the Centro Cívico, Las Marianas is a great choice if you want both the convenience of downtown and the tranquillity of Bariloche. It's a renovated old Swiss-style mansion. The managers are friendly and fun. Beds have luxurious down comforters. The bedrooms aren't large, and bathrooms are particularly tight, but the warmth of the entire place makes up for it. Four new rooms on the top floor have nice views.

24 de Septiembre 218, San Carlos de Bariloche. (©/fax 02944/439874. www.hosterialasmarianas.com.ar. 14 units. $65 (£36) double. Rates include buffet breakfast. No credit cards. **Amenities:** Lounge; laundry service; Internet. *In room:* TV, hair dryer, safe.

Hotel Nahuel Huapi 🍴   This is my favorite of the larger hotels in downtown Bariloche. It's in an older building that underwent a makeover in 2006. More amenities are in the works, including a spa. With 79 rooms, it's a good size. Standard rooms have wood floors and a crisp, clean decor, with off-white and green bedspreads and curtains. The bathrooms are marble and ceramic. The new look is natural, sleek, and simple. The staff is very friendly and helpful, and they have a sense of pride that seems to be lacking among their competitors.

Moreno 252, San Carlos de Bariloche. (©/fax **02944/426146.** www.hotelnahuelhuapi.com.ar. 79 units. From $189 (£104) double. Rates include buffet breakfast. AE, DC, MC, V. **Amenities:** Restaurant; bar; lounge; laundry service; dry cleaning. *In room:* TV, safe.

Hotel Tres Reyes   Directly on the lakefront Costanera, just a few minutes' walk from the Civic Center, this venerable hotel is often overlooked, but it's difficult to understand why. It has a tremendous amount of stark, Scandinavian style, preferred by the Belgian immigrant who built the hotel in 1950, and perhaps that does not appeal to everyone. Nevertheless, the hotel has been superbly maintained, with architectural details such as wood ceilings and beechwood paneling, and the vast lounge area has dozens of chairs and a velvet couch to sink into while you gaze out over the lake. The backyard has a path that meanders through a pleasant garden. All the rooms have been renovated within the past year, with new bedding, paint, curtains, and carpet. All are warm and come with sparkling bathrooms. The look indoors is a bit outdated. Neither slick nor hip, it's still pretty and classic. Lake-view rooms are more expensive, but they might not be as desirable, given that loud traffic speeds by well into the night. During the 1960s, the hotel's red-leather bar was the "in" spot for Bariloche's fashionable set, and it hasn't been altered in the least. The service is very friendly.

Av. 12 de Octubre 135, San Carlos de Bariloche. © 02944/426121. Fax 02944/424230. www.hoteltresreyes.com. 75 units. $70–$130 (£39–£72) double garden view; $74–$150 (£41–£82) double lake view; from $160 (£88) suite. Rates include continental breakfast. AE, DC, MC, V. **Amenities:** Restaurant; bar; room service; laundry service. *In room:* TV, safe.

Inexpensive
Hostería La Pastorella   This cozy little hotel was one of the first in Bariloche, built in the 1930s. Its gingerbread style harks back to the German family who first ran the establishment. The Pastorella is comfortable if a bit stuffy, with a dining area and a sunny lounge and bar that open up onto a lush garden. The rooms are a bit tired, but for the price and location, they're a good value. Some rooms have an extra seating area, although the funny futonlike chairs do nothing to beckon you to take a seat. Try to get a room that looks out over the garden. The hotel is run by a friendly Argentine couple who recently installed a sauna ($3/£1.65 extra). Note that this hotel does not accept children.

Belgrano 127, San Carlos de Bariloche. © 02944/424656. www.lapastorella.com.ar. 12 units. $40–$66 (£22–£36) double. Rates include continental breakfast. No credit cards. **Amenities:** Bar; sauna.

Perikos ⭐ *(Value*   The friendliest hostel in town, this is a great choice not just for youth, but for any traveler on a budget who wants to meet new friends, get off the beaten trail, and explore independently. Perikos has 10 rooms; four doubles, two triples, two that sleep two to four people, and two that sleep six. Their private doubles are a great deal, with their own bathrooms. Breakfast and use of the kitchen is included in the price. Next door, the friendly staff at Overland Patagonia will help you organize excursions. On Friday nights, the hostel organizes a typical *asado* barbecue.

Morales 555, San Carlos de Bariloche. © 02944/522326. www.overlandpatagonia.com. 10 units. $10 (£5.50) for bunk in shared room; $30 (£17) double. Rates include breakfast and use of kitchen. No credit cards. **Amenities:** Kitchen; TV room w/DVD library.

OUTSIDE THE CITY CENTER, ON THE ROAD TO THE LLAO LLAO PENINSULA
As this book goes to press, the newest luxury hotel in Bariloche is opening its doors. **El Casco Art Hotel,** Avenida Bustillo, Km 11.5 (© **11/4815-6952** for reservations in Buenos Aires; www.hotelelcasco.com), will appeal to those who love nature and fine arts. It's a full-service hotel with 33 enormous suites, a spectacular restaurant, and more than 200 masterpieces by prestigious local and international artists.

Very Expensive
Llao Llao Hotel & Resort ⭐⭐⭐ *(Kids*   The internationally renowned Llao Llao Hotel & Resort is one of the finest hotels in Latin America, as much for its magnificent location as its sumptuous, elegant interiors and refined service. Situated on a grassy crest of the Llao Llao Peninsula, and framed by rugged peaks, this five-star hotel was modeled after the style of Canadian mountain lodges, evident in its cypress and pine-log walls, stone fireplaces, antler chandeliers, and barn-size salons. This is *the* place to spend the night if you're willing to splurge for a special evening. The hotel was first built in 1938 but, after burning to the ground, was rebuilt again in 1939. It closed during the 1980s, but recent restorations have renewed its original grandeur

while giving it a fresh and modern feel. A driveway winds up to the hotel, where a discreet security guard monitors traffic: The hotel tries to keep gawkers at a distance, although visitors may come for a drink, afternoon tea, or a meal, but only with a prior reservation. The lounge has glossy wood floors carpeted with incredibly long Oriental rugs, coffee-colored wicker furniture, and soft lights. It's the site of frequent teas and special appetizer hours. The nearby Club House has a daily tea from 4 to 7pm.

From the lobby, every turn leads to another remarkable room, including a "winter garden" cafe whose expansive glass walls look out onto a large patio, the hotel's golf course, and Lake Nahuel Huapi beyond. A monumental hallway adorned with paintings from local artists leads to the rooms. All are decorated in a rustic country design and have gleaming white bathrooms; they're nice, but the style is not as exceptional as one would expect from a hotel of this caliber. Standard rooms are comfortable but quite small; superior suites are split into bedroom and living areas and some come with a wraparound deck and fireplace; a lovely two-bedroom cabin with a splendid view of Lake Moreno is also available. The hotel has a handful of unadvertised standard double rooms without a view. They're reserved for drop-ins who inquire at reception for the cheapest accommodations (no prior reservations are accepted for these rooms). The cheapest, though, can still mean $350 a night in high season. The spa affords views that are nothing less than panoramic. Treatment rooms yield breathtaking lake and mountain vistas. A myriad of daily activities is included in the price of the rooms, from adult watercolor-painting classes to games and events for kids. Transfers to and from the airport and the ski hill are also included. The hotel's fine-dining restaurant, **Los Cesares,** is the best in the Bariloche area (p. 312). Internet access is free for registered guests in the business center.

Av. Bustillo, Km 25. © **02944/448530.** Fax 02944/445789. Reservations (in Buenos Aires): © 11/4311-3434; fax 11/4314-4646. www.llaollao.com. 159 units. $340–$460 (£187–£253) double; $490–$1,150 (£270–£633) suite; $830–$1,320 (£457–£726) cottage. Rates include buffet breakfast. AE, DC, MC, V. **Amenities:** 2 restaurants; bar; lounge; small indoor heated pool; golf course; tennis courts; exercise room; fabulous spa; Jacuzzi; extensive watersports equipment; children's center; video arcade; tour and car-rental desk; business center; shopping arcade; salon; room service; massage; babysitting; laundry service; dry cleaning. In room: TV, safe.

Expensive

Aldebaran ★★ (Finds)   Serenity, silence, and highly personalized service make this remote retreat one of the Lake District's newest treasures. Far off the typical tourist route, each of the 10 rooms here enjoys lovely views across the Campanario Arm of Nahuel Huapi Lake. The design and construction are very natural, from stone and wood walls to cement floors. Thick Mediterranean-style walls have curved ceilings and dark hallways. Rooms are large, with earth-toned blankets, cozy nooks, and a blend of modern and recycled furniture. Rustic bathrooms have large tubs and spotlights. All have either a balcony or a patio. Downstairs, an in/out pool and serene spa are deeply relaxing. Sirius, the inn's boutique bistro, is very good. Ten minutes down a dirt road on the coast of the San Pedro Peninsula, Aldebaran is a compelling hideaway. (Media junkies be warned: Rooms don't have TV.)

Península San Pedro, Av. Bustillo, Km 20.4, San Carlos de Bariloche. © **02944/465143.** www.aldebaranpatagonia.com. 10 units. From $220 (£121) double; $300 (£165) suite. Includes breakfasts, in/out transfer. AE, V. **Amenities:** Restaurant; bar; spa; laundry; dock; TV/DVD room. In room: Hair dryer, safe.

Design Suites ★   Catering to stylish young couples, the newest upscale hotel in Bariloche is unique in many ways. The exterior look is ultramodern, and the location,

2.5km (1½ miles) from town amid a large garden, is excellent. The interior design is contemporary and minimalist, with local materials such as wood, stone, and glass enhanced by a revolving display of local art. Rooms are the largest in town, with light hardwood floors, crisp cream walls, plenty of shelving, and small patios. They may remind you of Ikea showrooms. Ample bathrooms have heated floors. All have either a jetted tub or a full hot tub nestled beneath a bay window. They all have advanced technology appliances, from snazzy little stereo systems to flatscreen televisions. Entrance hallways allow rooms to stay clean and dry. The junior suites have the best views.

The rooms are spread among three buildings, each with an outdoor elevator. Plans for a fourth building with a convention center are in the works. The amenities are certainly handy. The restaurant is open all day, and two daily shuttles run into town or up to the ski hill in winter. Downstairs in the main building is a lovely indoor-outdoor pool. There is an activities desk with helpful attendants who will help you plan your adventures.

Av. Bustillo Km. 2.5, San Carlos de Bariloche. ✆ **02944/457000.** www.designsuites.com. 54 units. Doubles $145–$235 (£80–£129); junior suites $210–$330 (£116–£182). Rates include continental breakfast. AE, MC, V. **Amenities:** Restaurant; bar; in-out pool; gym; spa; sauna; kids club; shop; art gallery. *In room:* TV, hair dryer, safe.

El Sol del Nahuel *Finds* Making full use of a strategic lakeside location, this new inn is bright, cheery, and peaceful. It comfortably lets the lake be the star of the scene. Positioned below the main road, the hotel is protected from traffic noise, unlike many of the other inns along Bustillo. The lobby is reminiscent of an Alpine ski chalet, with a massive fireplace and comfy couches. All rooms have spectacular views overlooking the lake. Rooms are large, with wood floors and neutral colors that let the gorgeous blues of the lake shine. Downstairs, a warm indoor/outdoor pool is open year-round. The grounds also encompass a vast garden with a private beach and barbecue.

Av. Bustillo, Km 5.4, San Carlos de Bariloche. ✆ **02944/520700.** www.soldelnahuel.com.ar. 17 units. **$175** (£96) double. Rates include breakfast. AE, MC, V. **Amenities:** Restaurant; bar; pool; sauna; massage services; garden. *In room:* TV, minibar, safe.

Villa Huinid ★★ The country-style luxurious cabins, suites, and the brand-new main building with three stories of lovely new rooms that make up the newer and very modern Villa Huinid are top-notch choices for travelers looking for independent accommodations outside town. Facing the lake, just 2.5km (1½ miles) from the city center, the complex is backed by a thick forest with a walking trail. There are 12 cabins handcrafted of knotty cypress, and a new hotel complex with 50 high-level rooms. Cabins have stone fireplaces, lovely decks with a full-size barbecue, and a handsome decor of floral wallpaper, plaid bedspreads, craftsy furniture, and other accents such as dried flowers and iron lamps. The units come as four-, six-, and eight-person cabanas with fully stocked kitchens. Some of the hotel's new units have lake views with big bay windows. All accommodations come with daily maid service. The bathrooms are sumptuous, with wooden sinks and hydro-massage baths, and the cabins come with 1½ bathrooms. Also new is an acclaimed restaurant called Batistin, and a large spa with a spectacular pool. The Huinid runs its own transfer van to drive guests into town or to the ski areas in winter. Service here is very good.

Av. Bustillo, Km 2.5. ✆/fax **02944/5235234.** www.villahuinid.com.ar. 62 units. $180–$245 (£99–£135) garden-view double; $220–$295 (£121–£162) lake-view double. Cabins sleeping 2–4 people $230–$360 (£127–£198). AE, DC, MC, V. **Amenities:** Restaurant; lounge; pool; gym; spa; games room; laundry service; Internet. *In room:* TV, fridge, coffeemaker, safe.

CABANAS

The southern shoreline of Nahuel Huapi Lake is dotted with cabin complexes for visitors. Some have only one or two cabanas for rent, while other have up to a dozen. They're a nice way to be self-sufficient, prepare your own meals, and make yourself at home. Some can be very affordable, especially outside the high-season months of January and August. Bungalows and apart-hotels are similar options. Try the fun **El Bosque de los Elfos,** Avenida Bustillo, Km 5 (© **2944/442356;** www.bungalows deloselfos.com.ar), or **Cabañas Abril,** close to Playa Bonita at Aries 160 (© **2944/ 461070;** www.bariloche.com/abril). **Cabañas Arcadia,** at Av. Bustillo 5782 (© **2944/ 441817;** www.arcadiapatagonia.com.ar), has five cabins built in the typical rustic wooden architecture of Bariloche.

WHERE TO DINE

The restaurants in downtown Bariloche, unlike the hotels, are an excellent value. The best are on the road to the Llao Llao Peninsula; even if you're not staying in town, you'll probably find yourself coming here to dine. Service, however, is not a highlight of the dining experience. In the high-season months of July, January, and February, consider eating early (before 9pm) or making a reservation. Otherwise you may spend the evening walking around town looking for a table. We've found the starred restaurants below to offer the best overall service, quality, and variety in the city. But remember to be patient with the waitstaff at the rest of the establishments listed below, and always allow plenty of time for lunch (2 hr.) and dinner (3 hr.).

WITHIN THE CITY CENTER
Expensive

Kandahar ⓐ REGIONAL   Named after the famed European ski race, rather than the Afghani capital, Kandahar is one of the best restaurants in town. In this funky and colorful old house with cozy nooks, the food is creative and fresh. The rosehip soup is a great starter, as is the Kandahar salad with greens from the owner's garden and smoked venison. For main dishes, try homemade pastas such as gnocchi with olives, trout with spinach, rabbit with quince sauce, or peppered tenderloin. The desserts are excellent, including grilled spiced apples with ice cream. This place is always busy so a reservation is essential.

20 de Febrero 628. © 02944/424702. Reservations highly recommended. Main courses $8–$14 (£4.40–£7.70). AE. Daily 8pm–midnight.

Naan ⓐⓐ *(Finds)* FUSION   Hard to find but impossible to forget, Naan is a revelation in Patagonia. The couple (he's the chef, she's the service) that operates this small restaurant inside a house in a leafy neighborhood have traveled the world and brought flavors back to Bariloche. Starters range from Italian and Middle Eastern dishes to Vietnamese and French specialties. Main courses include a lamb curry and a coconut chicken and prawns that will awaken your senses. They also prepare a souvlaki and tofu tempura—practically a revolutionary dish for these parts. And the filet mignon *a la pampa* is divine. Less adventurous diners will delight in the simple, light trout. The view is spectacular, and the vibe is slightly chaotic. They close for holidays in low season, so call before heading out.

Campichuelo 568. © 02944/421785. Reservations required. Main courses $8–$13 (£4.40–£7.15). No credit cards. Jan 1 to pre-Easter and July 10–Sept 30 daily 8–11:30pm; post-Easter to July 10 and Oct 1–Dec 31 Tues–Sun 8–11:30pm.

Moderate

Casita Suiza SWISS   The Casita Suiza lives up to its name with a roster of Swiss dishes, such as smoked pork, sauerkraut, and apple strudel, and a wide variety of international meat and fish dishes. Service is impeccable at this restaurant owned by the children of Swiss immigrants; the owner's mother still bakes fresh cakes and tarts daily using old family recipes. Fondues are an excellent value, at $8 (£4.40) per person. If you like to participate in preparing your meal, choose the *pierrade*, a platter of various meats, sauces, and potatoes that you grill at the table, for $10 (£5.50) per person. Call ahead to see if they're open for lunch, as their daytime hours are erratic.

Quaglia 342. © 02944/426111. Main courses $4–$8 (£2.20–£4.40). AE, DC, MC, V. Daily 8–11:30pm.

Días de Zapata MEXICAN   Bariloche's best Mexican restaurant is surprisingly good and a nice change of pace from *parrillas*. You'll find the usual tacos, fajitas, and nachos on the menu, but you'll also find more uncommon Mexican dishes such as chicken *mole*, Veracruz conger eel, and spicy enchiladas. Every evening, from 7 to 9pm, the restaurant hosts a happy hour, with buy-one-get-one-free drinks. The warm brick walls and Mexican folk art make for a cozy atmosphere; the service is very friendly too. This place packs up quickly, so go early (before 9:30pm) to get a table if you don't want to wait.

Morales 362. © 02944/423128. Reservations recommended. Main courses $3–$6 (£1.54–£3.30). MC, V. Daily noon–3pm and 7pm–midnight.

El Boliche de Alberto *Overrated* STEAKHOUSE   Long considered the best *parrilla* in Bariloche, Alberto seems to have no limits. Some regulars have been coming back for 20 years, and some make the crossing from Chile to have a piece of beef here. The menu is brief, with several cuts of beef, chicken, and sausages; salads; and side dishes such as french fries. The dining area is unpretentious and brightly lit, with wooden tables. A typical *bife de chorizo* steak is so thick you'll need to split it with your dining partner; if you're alone, they can do a half-order for $8 (£4.40). They don't accept reservations, so there is almost always a long line here, which has the waiters rushing diners through their meals in an effort to keep filling tables. Yes, the meat is good. But for the same price, you can go somewhere less touristy and crowded and actually enjoy your meal at a reasonable pace.

Villegas 347. © 02944/431433. Main courses $6–$10 (£3.30–£5.50). AE, MC, V. Daily noon–3pm and 8pm–midnight.

El Boliche Viejo *Moments* REGIONAL   Step back in time to the old Patagonian pioneer days, at this country store dating back more than a century. Little has changed since the days when Butch Cassidy and the Sundance Kid purportedly stopped in for a meal. It's northeast of Bariloche, on the road to Villa La Angostura, past the airport turn-off and the town of Dina Huapi. The menu is pure Patagonian, including lamb slow-grilled on a spit and every cut of beef you could imagine, from T-bone to tongue. This makes a great stop for a midday meal if you are on a sightseeing drive.

Ruta 237 at Limay River bridge. © 02944/468452. Main courses $7–$12 (£3.85–£6.60). MC, V. Daily noon–4pm and 8:30pm–midnight.

Familia Weiss *Moments* *Kids* REGIONAL   The Weiss family is well known all over the region for their outstanding smoked meats and cheeses, which they've been selling from their shop at Mitre 360 for decades. Their restaurant near the waterfront is so architecturally unique you really should at least stop in for one of the locally brewed beers and to view the handsome interiors. The decor includes cypress trunks that form pillars rising from a mosaic floor also made of cypress. Each wall is a patchwork of wood, brick, and ceramic, except the front area, which has large picture windows looking out onto the lake. Details such as papier-mâché lamps and folk art lend the place character.

As for the food, a lot is on offer here, all of it very good. Start off with an appetizer of the smoked meats, seafood, and cheese for which the Familia Weiss is known. There's cheese and beef fondue with five dipping sauces; large, leafy salads; stewed venison with spaetzle; grilled meats with fresh vegetables; homemade pastas; local trout served with ratatouille; and much, much more. A good wine list and a kids' menu make the Familia Weiss hard to beat.

Corner of Palacios and V.A. O'Connor. © 02944/435789. Main courses $5–$12 (£2.75–£6.60). AE, DC, MC, V. Daily noon–1am.

Tarquino ⍟ *(Moments* REGIONAL   Worth visiting for the architecture alone, this friendly family-run grill in front of the leafy Plaza Belgrano feels like a storybook tree-house. After entering through a stunning wooden door that would suit a hobbit, choose a table beside a live towering cypress tree (this is Bariloche's famous rustic building style at its most imaginative). The food is good, especially the beef: standard grill selections such as *bife de chorizo,* a 650-gram (22-oz.) piece of tender flank steak, pork tenderloin, or grilled trout with almond sauce. The servings are large. There is also a salad bar.

24 de Septiembre (corner of Saavedra). © 02944/431601. Reservations recommended. MC, V. Daily noon–3pm and 8pm–midnight.

Inexpensive

El Mundo PIZZERIA   El Mundo serves up crispy pizza in more than 100 varieties, as well as empanadas, pastas, and salads. The sheer number of pies makes the menu a little overwhelming. The pasta is fresh, and they deliver. A large seating area makes El Mundo a good spot for groups.

Mitre 759. © 02944/423461. Main courses $2.50–$5 (£1.40–£2.75). AE, DC, MC, V. Daily noon–midnight.

Friends *(Kids* CAFE   Friends is worth a mention for the fact that it's open 24 hours a day, and it's popular among families with kids. The cafe is embellished with hundreds of antique toys and trinkets, which hang from the ceiling and fill every corner. The menu serves grilled meats and fish, crepes, sandwiches, soups, and salads. There's also pan-fried trout served several different ways and a huge selection of rich, sugary desserts.

Corner of Mitre and Rolando. © 02944/423700. Main courses $2–$4 (£1.10–£2.20). AE, MC, V. Daily 7am–3am.

Las Brasas *(Value* ARGENTINE GRILL   Nothing fancy, Las Brasas is where local Barilochenses come for grilled meat. This simple and family-style restaurant started as a simple take-out joint next door. Order the *parrilla mixta*—the waiter will bring you a grill stacked with a variety of meats and sausages. This goes typically with a mixed salad and French fries. For something lighter, choose the grilled chicken. The quality of the meat and the size of the servings are outstanding.

Elfein 163. © 02944/431628. Main courses $4–$10 (£2.20–£5.50). MC, V. Daily 8pm–midnight.

Rock Chicken FAST FOOD   Bariloche has no McDonalds or any other multina-tional fast-food chain. What they do have is Rock Chicken, a local staple and a great place to grab a quick and cheap bite. The grill is wide open so there is no doubt what is coming your way. Choose from a *choripán* (chorizo sausage on a bun), Milanese (breaded beef), grilled chicken, or a slice of sirloin. Menus usually include a drink (beer or wine) and a choice of salad or French fries.

Rolando 245. ℂ **02944/435669**. Main courses $2–$5 (£1.10–£2.75). No credit cards. Daily 10am–4am.

Vegetariano ℛ VEGETARIAN   If you need a break from the grills, head to this unpretentious, cozy restaurant for a dose of veggies. Recipes are purely homemade. Meals are served as a large and nutritious daily set menu; you can usually choose either fish or a soy patty. The mixed juice is chock-full of vitamins, and the tea served at the end of the meal is delightful. Try to save room for dessert; the sweets here are excellent. The staff is very friendly.

20 de Febrero 730. ℂ **02944/421820**. Main courses $4–$8 (£2.20–£4.40). No credit cards. Lunch Mon–Sat noon–3pm; dinner Mon–Fri 8–11pm.

Vogue ℛ *Finds*   Pronounced "*boh*-geh," this place is a local favorite, known for its hearty helpings of staples such as *milanesas* (breaded veal), more than 50 kinds of pizza and homemade pastas, reliable service, and reasonable prices. Start your meal with a slice of *faena,* a garbanzo patty. Stuffed cannelonis and beef *milanesas* topped with mozzarella and ham are also delicious. They also have some of the best salads in town. It's cramped but packed with locals. They open earlier at dinner.

Palacios 156. ℂ **02944/431343**. Main courses $5–$8 (£2.75–£4.40). MC, V. Daily noon–3pm and 7pm–midnight.

OUTSIDE THE CITY CENTER (EN ROUTE TO THE LLAO LLAO PENINSULA)
Expensive
El Patacón ℛℛ ARGENTINE/REGIONAL   This large restaurant is a 7km (4¼-mile) drive from the city center. El Patacón's unique architecture and mouthwatering cuisine drew Bill Clinton and Argentina's Carlos Ménem to dine here during a presidential meeting several years back—a fact the restaurant is more than happy to advertise. The building is made of chipped stone inlaid with polished, knotty tree trunks and branches left in their natural shape, which form zany crooked beams and pillars. The tables and chairs were handcrafted from cypress driftwood, also kept in its natural form.

Start your meal with a platter of five provolone cheeses, served crispy warm off the grill. Follow it with venison ravioli or goulash, trout in a creamy leek sauce with puffy potatoes, wild boar in wine, or mustard chicken. The *parrilla* serves grilled meats and daily specials, and the *bodega* (wine cellar) offers an excellent selection of wines. The restaurant recently inaugurated an adjacent bar, a fascinating medieval-style lounge with iron chandeliers, and a tremendous fireplace with a tree-trunk mantel, where the staff will welcome you with a cocktail.

Av. Bustillo, Km 7. ℂ **02944/442898**. Reservations recommended on weekends. Main courses $8–$15 (£4.40–£8.25). AE, DC, MC, V. Daily noon–3pm and 8pm–midnight.

Il Gabbiano ℛℛ *Finds* ITALIAN   If Bariloche's dining scene has a sure thing, this outstanding Italian restaurant is it. Located close to the Llao Llao, Il Gabbiano is a labor of love for its owners. It's set inside a bungalow that has a Mediterranean feel, with brick, iron, and stonework reminiscent of a countryside farmhouse. The menu is authentic *italiano.* Antipasti include bruschetti and salmon with grapefruit. Delicate homemade pastas are varied and fresh. Main entrees include *osso bucco,* rabbit with garlic and rosemary, and a simple trout with lemon. The wine cellar has more than 250 labels, including a good selection of European varieties, rare in Patagonia. *Note:* They do not accept any credit cards.

Av. Bustillo, Km 24.3. © 02944/448346. Reservations highly recommended. Main courses $10–$17 (£5.50–£9.35). No credit cards. Wed–Mon 7:30pm–midnight.

Los Cesares 🞷🞷🞷 *Moments* PATAGONIAN FINE DINING   This enchantingly romantic restaurant offers the only fine-dining experience in the Bariloche area. In the luxurious Llao Llao Hotel & Resort (p. 305), the setting is refined and slightly formal, with fireplace, antiques, white tablecloths, and ultracomfortable chairs with armrests. The restaurant prides itself on using the highest-quality ingredients grown locally— from wild game for the main courses to the wild berries for dessert. Specialties include grilled venison with blackberry sauce, almond-crusted local trout (from the nearby lake), and a good selection of Argentine steaks. The excellent wine list features many regional wines for under $18 (£9.90). The white-gloved service is superb, and when you finally get the bill, you'll be pleasantly surprised at how affordable it really is for such an exquisite place.

Av. Bustillo, Km 25. In the Llao Llao Hotel & Resort. © 02944/448530. Reservations required. Main courses $13–$18 (£7.15–£9.90). AE, DC, MC, V. Daily 7:30–11:30pm.

Punta Bustillo 🞷 *Finds* ARGENTINE   In a cozy old cottage on the road out of town, this restaurant is friendly and casual, with a varied menu and an excellent wine list. It's particularly nice on a chilly winter evening. For starters, the squash soup is excellent. They serve the grill standards such as tenderloin and steaks, and grilled venison and lamb as well. Nongrilled dishes include goulash with spaetzle. They also stock a wide selection of microbrewed beers.

Av. Bustillo, Km 5.8. © 02944/442783. Main courses $9–$13 (£4.95–£7.15). AE, MC, V. Daily noon–4pm and 7:45pm–midnight.

BARILOCHE AFTER DARK

Open 24 hours a day, the lakefront wine bar **Trentis Lakebar,** J.M. de Rosas 435 (no phone), is a great place for a cocktail. Bariloche is home to a handful of discos catering to the 16- to 30-year-old crowd. These discos adhere to Buenos Aires nightlife hours, beginning around midnight or 12:30am, with the evening peaking at about 3 or 4am. The cover charge is usually $3 to $4 (£1.65–£2.20) per person, and women often enter for free. Try **Roket,** J.M. de Rosas 424 (© 02944/431940), or **Cerebro,** J.M. de Rosas 405 (© 02944/424965). Earlier in the evening, locals gather at **The Roxy,** San Martín 490 (© 02944/400451), for funky music and big-screen light shows. There are a number of local pubs, including **Wilkenny,** San Martín 435 (© 02944/424444), and **Pilgrim,** Palacios 167 (© 02944/421686). Microbrew pubs are also becoming popular in Bariloche. Downtown, try **Antares,** Elflein 47 (© 02944/431454). **Cervecería Blest,** Avenida Bustillo, Km 11.5 (© 02944/461026), is the oldest microbrewery in Argentina. Next door, **Berlina,** Avenida Bustillo, Km 11.75 (© 02944/523336), is hip and fresh. The **Worest Casino,** Av. San Martín 570 (© 02944/425846), is open from 9am to 5am. The casino hosts live shows every evening. Guests must be over 18 years old; entrance is free. **Cine Arrayán** is a one-screen local cinema at Moreno 39 (© 02944/422860). A more modern cinema is at Shopping Patagonia, Onelli 447 (© 02944/427189). Both often show English-language movies with Spanish subtitles.

2 South of Bariloche ★★

The massive Nahuel Huapi National Park extends to the south of Bariloche in a winding maze of majestic mountains and lakes. Whether you're on a day's drive, as part of an overnight getaway from the hustle and bustle of Bariloche, or en route to a world-class fly-fishing lodge, this area is definitely worth exploring. Driving south out of Bariloche on RN 40, you'll pass tall waterfalls and snowy peaks, edge around emerald lakes, and drop through a deep canyon as you head to El Bolsón. This laid-back town has a microclimate that has drawn nature lovers from around the country since the 1960s.

Heading south from Bariloche, you'll find the lovely **Estancia Peuma Hue** ★ (© 02944/15-501030; www.peuma-hue.com) on the south shore of Lake Gutierrez. With two large houses and two cabins, as well as a slew of outdoor activities such as horseback riding and trekking, this high-end complex is intimate. It's one of the only ways to live a more rural Patagonian experience so close to Bariloche. A 3-day all-inclusive plan starts at $650 (£358) for two people.

Continuing south, you'll pass the **continental divide**—a wide marsh where the water drains north to Lake Gutierrez and then on to the Nahuel Huapi and the Atlantic; and west through Lake Mascardi, over the border to Chile and the Pacific.

A DRIVING TOUR: CERRO TRONADOR, LOS ALERCES WATERFALL & VENTISQUERO NEGRO

This wonderful, full-day excursion takes visitors through lush forest and past hidden lakes (such as the picturesque Lago Mascardi), waterfalls, and beaches to a trail head that leads to the face of **Ventisquero Negro (Black Glacier).** You'll need a vehicle to drive the 215km (133-mile) round-trip road, including a detour to Cascada Los Alerces (Los Alerces Waterfall); it's 170km (105 miles) without the detour. Plan to stop frequently at the various lookout points along the road. Most tour agencies offer this excursion for about $25 to $30 (£14–£17) a person.

At 35km (22 miles) south of Bariloche, you'll reach Villa Mascardi. From here it is possible to take a full-day sailing excursion aboard the *Victoria II*, which takes riders across Lake Mascardi to the Hotel Tronador for lunch, followed by a bus ride up the valley to Pampa Linda and Los Ventisqueros for a trail walk. Visitors return the same way. This excursion can be booked at any travel agency and usually includes transportation from Bariloche, leaving at 9am and returning at 8pm (Nov–Mar only). Or you can leave directly from the dock if you have your own vehicle. The cost, including transportation from Bariloche, is $32 (£18) per person. It shaves off more than an hour of driving along a windy, dusty road.

If you're not taking the sailing excursion, continue past Villa Mascardi and take RP 81, the road that branches off to the right. You must stop at the National Parks gates and pay an entrance fee of $3 (£1.65) for foreigners. Past the turnoff to Pampa Linda and Los Rapidos campsite, continue to the Río Manso bridge, where a road heads left to the Los Alerces Waterfall. A 300m (984-ft.) walk takes you to a vista point overlooking the waterfall. After doubling back, you reach the bridge again, where you head left, continuing along the shore of Lake Mascardi until you reach the **Hotel Tronador** (© 02944/441062; www.hoteltronador.com), where the views of Mt. Tronador are outstanding. The charming log cabin hotel, built in 1929 by a Belgian immigrant family, is backed by high peaks and makes a good spot for lunch or a quiet getaway for overnight visitors. They have 30 rooms; high-season (Jan–Feb) prices for a double start at $95 (£52). The road continues up the valley of the Río Manso Superior, winding through Alpine scenery until reaching the lush and expansive Pampa Linda plains, where there is another inn and teahouse. The final leg ends at a stunning cirque (a steep valley with a lake) draped with vegetation and waterfalls. From here a trail leads to Black Glacier, named for the debris that colors the ice at its terminus. The mountain's power is imposing here. Return to Bariloche the same way you came, and see if you can pick out the heart-shaped Isla Corazón in the middle of Lago Mascardi.

Note that the route to Tronador, RP 81, is a narrow gravel road with restricted hours of transit during the busy summer months. Cars are allowed to travel in towards Tronador in the mornings only (9:30am–2pm), and travel out again in the afternoon only (4:30–7:30pm). Check with the Tourist Information Office before heading out.

EL BOLSON
131km (81 miles) S of Bariloche

A lovely town of 11,000 set amid a lush valley, El Bolsón is equally famous for its artisan's fair and its microclimate, which makes it almost 7° F (4°C) warmer than in Bariloche. On Saturdays throughout the year, and on Tuesdays and Thursdays in summer, El Bolsón hosts a wonderful **Artisan and Produce Market** 🐾🐾 in its central plaza. Stroll the stands for organic fruit, wool sweaters, homemade jams, wooden cutting boards, and microbrewed beer. There are also vegetarian sandwiches, sweet waffles, and delicious Armenian empanadas to grab as snacks. It usually runs from 10am to 4pm. Because El Bolsón is in a basin surrounded by tall peaks, there is great hiking here. One of the most interesting hikes takes you up to the **Bosque Tallado,** a magical forest with sculpted tree trunks. Inquire at the Tourist Information Center, Avenida San Martín and Roca (✆ **02944/492604**), for trail maps and other information.

El Bolsón is also known for its production of hops, its microbreweries, and its annual **Beer Festival,** held each year in late February. South of El Bolsón by 15km (9⅓ miles) is **Lago Puello National Park,** where visitors can swim, boat, hike, camp, and fish.

WHERE TO STAY & EAT
The downtown core has some standard hotels, the best of which is **Hotel Cordillera,** Av. San Martín 3220 (✆ **02944/492235**). Rooms have lovely balconies. Doubles start

Ruta 40: The Road South

The mighty and legendary **Ruta 40** is one of the world's great adventure drives. It takes you along the eastern slope of the Andes from the top of Argentina all the way to the bottom of Patagonia. For travelers with a few extra days, the 3-night Ruta 40 trip organized by **Overland Patagonia** (✆ **02944/438654**; www.overlandpatagonia.com) includes stops at traditional *estancias*, petroglyphs, and untouched national parks, and it costs a budget-friendly $320 (£176) per person. It starts in Bariloche and ends in El Calafate. Don't even think of making this expedition on your own without a 4×4 in excellent condition, stocked with all the necessary supplies. This land is Patagonia off the beaten track.

at $40 (£22). Outside town, you can soak up the authentic El Bolsón lifestyle at **La Casona de Odile,** Barrio Luján, Km 6 (© **02944/492753**), a small inn and restaurant serving French cuisine and local produce. Rooms start at $15 (£8.25), and for $22 (£12) you can include three fabulous meals a day. **Jauja** ✿, Av. San Martín 3261 (© **02944/493505**), is home to an outstanding ice-cream parlor and a good restaurant next door with delicious trout entrees. Vegetarians will love **La Calabaza,** Av. San Martín 2518 (© **02944/492910**), which serves soups, salads, and quiches.

SOUTH OF EL BOLSON

Farther along the road is the village of **Cholila,** where Butch Cassidy and the Sundance Kid hid out and ranched in peace, from 1901 to 1906. They became cherished members of this tiny community. You can still spot the old farmhouse the two fugitives built. South of Cholila, the outstanding **Museo Leleque** (© **02944/451141;** Tues–Thurs 11am–5pm) is 6km (3¾ miles) from town on RP 15. Situated on an enormous ranch once owned by the South-Land Company, and now part of the extensive land-holdings of the Italian clothier family Benetton, this excellent museum focuses on the history of rural Patagonia. Nearby is the **Los Alerces National Park** ✿, one of the world's finest fly-fishing areas. Its majestic giant alerce trees are more than 2,000 years old, and mesmerizing emerald lakes come into view at every turn. **Esquel Outfitters** (© **406/581-1760** in the U.S.; www.esqueloutfitters.com) will hook you up on a dreamy week-long fishing adventure, with accommodations in their luxurious and remote lodge.

3 Villa La Angostura ✿✿

81km (50 miles) N of Bariloche; 44km (27 miles) E of the Chilean border

Villa La Angostura (Narrow Village) takes its name from the slender isthmus that connects the town's center with the Quetrihué Peninsula. The town was founded in 1934 as a collection of simple farmers with small plots of land. These farmers were eventually displaced by out-of-towners who chose this lovely location for their summer homes. Increased boating activity, the paving of the road to Bariloche, increased tourism to Chile (the border of which is just 20 min. from town), and the inauguration of several exclusive hotels and a handful of bungalow complexes have converted Villa La Angostura into a upscale getaway for the rich and famous. Even so, this tiny enclave hosts only a fraction of visitors to the region, unlike Bariloche. This picturesque village is for visitors seeking solitude. Most lodging options are tucked away in the forest on the shore of the Lake Nahuel Huapi, providing beautiful views and quiet surroundings. Like Bariloche, Villa La Angostura is within the borders of Parque Nacional Nahuel Huapi.

GETTING THERE   By Plane   For airport and flight information, see "Getting There," under "San Carlos de Bariloche," earlier in this chapter. To get to Villa La Angostura from the airport, take a taxi or transfer service (about $55–$75/£30–£41). The drive takes about an hour.

By Bus   **Algarrobal Buses** (© **02944/494360**) leave for Villa La Angostura from Bariloche's Terminal de Omnibus about every 3 hours from 8am to 9pm. The trip takes about 1 ½ hours. **Albus** (© **2944/423552**) also goes to Villa La Angostura four times a day.

By Car   Villa La Angostura is a 1-hour drive from Bariloche around the north shore of Lake Nahuel Huapi. Take the coastal road northeast of town past the village at Dina Huapi, and turn left on RP 231.

VISITOR INFORMATION   The Secretaría de Turismo is at Av. Siete Lagos 93 (© 02944/494124), open daily from 8am to 8pm. It offers accommodations listings and prices, and information about excursions around the area. For information about Nahuel Huapi National Park or Parque Nacional Los Arrayanes, try the **Oficína de Turismo** at the pier (© 02944/494152), open Monday through Friday from 11am to 4pm (Wed until 2pm), and Saturday and holidays from 2:30 to 5pm.

WHAT TO SEE & DO
PARQUE NACIONAL LOS ARRAYANES ☆

The Parque Nacional Los Arrayanes is home to the only two *arrayán* forests in the world (although the *arrayán* can be found throughout this region, including in Chile), one of which can be visited at the tip of Península Quetrihué. This fascinating bush grows as high as 20m (66 ft.) and looks to the untrained eye like a tree, with slick cinnamon-colored trunks that are cool to the touch. They are especially beautiful in the spring when in bloom.

The peninsula itself offers a pleasant 24km (15-mile) round-trip moderate hiking and biking trail to the *arrayán* forest. Most visitors either walk (2–3 hr.) or bike (1–2 hr.) half the trail and then boat to or back from the park; you can also take the boat both ways (trip time: 2 ½ hr.). **Catamaran Patagonia Argentina** (© 02944/494229) has a new launch with a cafeteria, and runs daily trips four to five times a day during the summer, depending on demand; cost for adults is $15 (£8.25) round-trip, kids 6 to 12 $8 (£4.40) round-trip; $6 (£3.30) for all ages one-way traveling up the western, more exposed side of the Península Quetrihué. From the interior side, the Bahía Mansa, consider the **Catamaran Futaleufú** (02944/494004 or at the dock 494405; www.bosquelosarrayanes.com.ar). **Bettanso Excursiones** has a 50-person boat with daily departures at 2:30pm, and six to seven trips during the summer for the same price as Paisano (© 02944/495024). Bettanso also offers excursions to Isla Victoria and Puerto Blest, a trip that is described in "Boat Excursions," earlier in this chapter.

Villa La Angostura is a main stop on the popular Ruta de los Siete Lagos. It's also the last stop on the road to the border with Chile.

OTHER OUTDOOR ACTIVITIES

BIKING   Free Bikes, Las Fucsias (© 02944/495047; www.freebikes.com.ar), has a large selection of rental bikes for $1 (55p) per hour, $4 (£2.20) up to 6 hours, and $5 (£2.75) for a full day. They also supply-guide a number of different mountain-bike trips.

HORSEBACK RIDING   Hop on a horse and ride up to the top of the ridge for views of all the area lakes. Organized by a well-known local character, **Cabalgatas Correntoso** (© 02944/624221; www.cabalgatacorrentoso.com.ar) has rides from 2 hours to 9 hours, and overnight pack trips.

FISHING   Anglers typically head to the renowned Río Correntoso for rainbow and brown trout, reached just before crossing the bridge just outside town on Ruta Nacional 231, from the Siete Lagos road. **Banana Fly Shop**, at Arrayanes 282 (© 02944/494634), sells flies and gear, and they provide information and can recommend guides. You may pick up a **fishing license** here or at the Bosques y Parques Provinciales office at the port (© 02944/494157); it's open Monday through Friday from 11am to 4pm, Wednesday until 2pm, Saturday and holidays from 2:30 to 5pm.

SKIING   Villa La Angostura is home to a little gem of a ski resort, **Cerro Bayo,** located about 9km (5½ miles) from downtown. It's a smaller resort than the one at

Cerro Catedral, but the crowds are thinner and the view is wonderful. For those reasons, I almost prefer it. There are 250 skiable acres. About 40% of the terrain is intermediate, and 35% is advanced. To reach it, you'll need to take a long lift from the base up to the summit; during the summer, this same chair lift provides access to an excellent short hike and lookout point. Cerro Bayo has ski and snowboard rental and instruction; the season runs from mid-June to mid-September, although it can get fairly patchy toward the end of the season.

To get to Cerro Bayo, ask your hotel to arrange transportation or hire a taxi for the short ride. Tickets are $18 to $21 (£9.90–£12) for adults, $12 to $18 (£6.60–£9.90) for kids, depending on the season. Kids under 6 and adults over 65 ski free. Half-day tickets, 3-day tickets, and weekly passes are also available. For more information, call © 02944/494189 or visit www.cerrobayoweb.com.

WHERE TO STAY
VERY EXPENSIVE

Las Balsas ⓕ One of the greatest inns in the country, the award-winning Relais & Chateaux–affiliated Las Balsas remains in a class all its own in Villa la Angostura. It has the airs of a country cottage, and an unbeatable lakefront setting (neighbors are among the wealthiest folk in Argentina). From the moment you walk in, you'll feel relaxed and at home. Common areas range from a big-screen TV room upstairs to a living room with a massive fireplace, comfortable couches, and coffeetable books. With only 15 rooms, this place ensures that guests get away from it all. English-speaking staff members are very charming and attentive without being stuffy or condescending, which enhances the air of exclusivity here. There is a strong focus on details, from fresh orange slices by the pool to imported teas. Rooms are not large—this inn was built long before the McMansion-style hotel trends of late—but they make up for their limited size with character. Each room is different, and all have bright windows overlooking the lake; none have televisions. Floors are a bit squeaky on the ground floor. The inn's restaurant is world-class (p. 320). The spa next door doesn't quite match the inn, and the gym should be moved out of the tranquil relaxation area, but the services are specialized and indulgent. Management plans to build more suites in the forest beyond the spa.

Bahía Las Balsas. ©/fax **02944/494308.** www.lasbalsas.com.ar. 15 units. $300 (£165) double; $400 (£220) suite. Rates include continental breakfast. AE, MC, V. **Amenities:** Exquisite restaurant; bar; lounge; indoor/outdoor heated pool; spa; sauna; watersports equipment; room service; massage; babysitting; laundry service. *In room:* Coffeemaker, hair dryer.

EXPENSIVE

Correntoso Lake and River Hotel Completely restored in 2003, the red-roofed Correntoso Hotel has been a landmark on the north shore of Nahuel Huapi Lake for almost a century. Perched above the mouth of the Correntoso River and facing due west across to the Andes, it was founded in 1922 as a fishing destination for Bariloche residents who crossed the lake by boat. Now, it feels like a clean, natural, and fresh fishing lodge. The lobby is stunning, with glass ceilings, large leather couches, and an enormous fireplace. The huge library has big sofas, heritage maps, and another fireplace. The gourmet restaurant is open to the public and worth a visit for the views alone—hotel guests have access to the choicest tables. Down at the dock, there is another less formal restaurant. The property is full of walking trails and berry bushes. All but six of the rooms have fabulous views over the lake. Corner rooms 309 and

409 have the very best views. A new spa is scheduled for 2007. The staff is friendly and casual.

Ruta 234 and Río Correntoso. ⓒ/fax **02944/1561-9728.** www.correntoso.com. 33 units. $221–$239 (£122–£131) double; $318–$392 (£175–£216) suite. Rates include buffet breakfast. AE, MC, V. **Amenities:** Restaurant; bar; lounge; heated outdoor pool; spa; concierge; deck; Wi-Fi. *In room:* TV, fridge (in suites only).

Hostería Puerto Sur ⓐ   The best of a slew of new wood-framed inns that have taken over the formerly exclusive Bahia Manzano area, Puerto Sur is smart. Built into the hill, each room has expansive lake views. The bottom floor has a spa area with an indoor/outdoor pool, gym, and large sauna. All rooms have large bathrooms with big tubs beneath glass ceilings. Rooms on the outside corner have nice private decks, where you can enjoy breakfast if you reserve one ahead of time. Furniture is soft cotton. The bistro-styled restaurant has a cute wine cellar.

Los Pinos 221, Puerto Manzano. ⓒ/fax **02944/475224.** www.hosteriapuertosur.com.ar. 14 units. $163 (£90) double with deck, $150 (£83) without deck. Rates include buffet breakfast. MC, V. **Amenities:** Restaurant; lounge; heated outdoor pool; Jacuzzi; sauna; massage; dock; private beach; TV room. *In room:* TV, safe.

MODERATE

Hostal Las Nieves ⓥ*alue*   The very friendly and energetic Marita Miles owns and runs this lovely lodge, a 5-minute drive from the center of town behind exquisitely manicured gardens (Marita is an avid gardener and has won many awards for her landscaping). The rooms are rustic, simple, and comfortable, with white-washed walls, red-checkered bedspreads, and handmade wooden side tables. The gleaming bathrooms are small but adequate. Apartments are on the upper level and come with kitchenettes, slanted roofs, and wood furniture, including a pair of charming cypress chairs in each unit. There's an outdoor pool in the lovely back garden, and overlooking the front garden is a lounge with a roaring fireplace where you can order drinks from the bar. The ample breakfast buffet is served from 8am onward (until the last guest has been served), and the restaurant serves both lunch and dinner in high season. The tiny "spa" offers shiatsu and other massage options, as well as facials. This is a good option for midrange budgets.

Av. Siete Lagos 980. ⓒ/fax **02944/494573.** www.lasnieves.com. 12 units. $25–$56 (£14–£31) double; $34–$62 (£19–£34) apt. Rates include buffet breakfast. MC, V. **Amenities:** Restaurant; bar; lounge; heated outdoor pool; tiny exercise room; Jacuzzi; sauna; massage. *In room:* TV, fridge (in apts).

Verena's Haus ⓥ*alue*   It can be hard to find something unpretentious in snazzy Villa La Angostura. Verena's is whole-heartedly down to earth. Verena welcomes guests with tea and a tasting from her homemade liqueurs. The European-style inn is loaded with character, including creaky floors. But the rooms are comfortable and all have private bathrooms (no TVs). Breakfasts, with homemade German-style pastries, are excellent. The location, a few blocks from the main street, can't be beat.

Los Taiques 268. ⓒ/fax **02944/494467.** www.interpatagonia.com/verenashaus. 6 units. $25–$36 (£14–£20) double; $34–$62 (£19–£34) apt. Rates include buffet breakfast. MC, V. **Amenities:** Lounge; library.

WHERE TO DINE

Many *parrillas* and cafes line the town's sole main street. The best, however, are either on side streets or are a few minutes' drive outside town.

La Delfina ⓐ CONTEMPORARY ARGENTINE   Tucked inside a cozy old cottage next to the La Escondida Inn at the Bahia Manzano community, La Delfina is a

Tips **Driving to Chile**

Villa la Angostura is the last stop before you head over the Andes and on to Chile via Paso Cardenal Samore, also known as **Paso Puyehue**. The border itself is 64km (39 miles) from town, although driving eastwards you'll hit the Argentine Customs building at 34km (21 miles). It's a spectacular drive through virgin forests in two adjoining national parks (Nahuel Huapi in Argentina and Puyehue in Chile). There are lovely picnic spots and short hiking trails en route. In winter, the drive often requires chains. The border crossing itself involves first exiting Argentina and then entering Chile. Across the border, you're within an hour of lovely spots such as the Thermas de Puyehue hot springs and the delicious seafood restaurants in the city Puerto Montt on the Pacific Coast. Either makes a great day trip from Bariloche or Villa La Angostura. Remember, though, that the border closes at 11pm in summer and at 8pm in winter. If you are renting a car, be sure to tell the rental agency that you plan to drive to Chile—if you reach the border without the proper paperwork, you will have to turn back.

gourmet revelation and full of surprises. The menu changes virtually daily to reflect the chef's whimsical tastes, but staples include a spectacular tenderloin in goat cheese, arugula, and basil, and slow-cooked lamb with red wine and rosehip sauce. The smoked-trout soup with lime cream is also fabulous. During the summer, you can dine outdoors.

Av. Arrayanes 714, Puerto Manzano. © 02944/475313. Reservations highly recommended. Main courses $10–$15 (£5.50–£8.25). AE, MC. Tues–Sun noon–3:30pm and 8:30–11:30pm.

La Encantada *(Finds* PIZZA   This may be the best pizza joint in the Lake District. The trademark here is the thin crusts cooked in the wood-burning oven. Toppings are fresh and creative, including my favorite: arugula, mozzarella, tomato, and olive oil. Another option combines locally smoked salmon with parsley and mozzarella. The menu also includes some unusual empanadas such as one stuffed with rainbow trout, white wine, and hard-boiled eggs. Soups, salads, and pastas are also available. It's a cozy and fun place with great service.

C. Belvedere 69. © 02944/495436. Main courses $4.50–$7 (£2.50–£3.85). No credit cards. Tues–Sun noon–3pm and 8–11:30pm.

La Macarena CONTEMPORARY ARGENTINE   Recently reopened at a new location on the main drag, the menu here is a funky mixture of flavors. Start with the excellent homemade mushroom soup. The fusion-inspired entrees include wild boar cooked in dark beer with sauerkraut and potatoes, venison goulash, or pork with honey and rosemary. There is also a kids' menu, and local classics such as cheese and chocolate fondue.

Av. Arrayanes 44. © 02944/494248. Main courses $9–$13 (£4.95–£7.15). MC, V. Tues–Sun noon–3pm and 8–11:30pm.

Las Balsas *Moments* PATAGONIAN/INTERNATIONAL   A 10-minute drive from town, this enchanting restaurant, on the ground floor of the Las Balsas inn (p. 317), boasts large picture windows overlooking the lake. It is quiet and romantic. With only a few tables and top-notch food and service, it's a fine place from which to sample authentic local flavors. Using only local ingredients, Chef Pablo Campoy seamlessly blends Patagonian and international cuisines to create dishes such as the deer carpaccio with whipped cream cheese, and local greens served with a delicate fresh raspberry dressing. For a main course, trout from the lake is always available, as is a dish made with wild game, such as venison, wild boar, or guanaco (a Patagonian animal similar to the llama), grilled and served with a side such as pureed garbanzo and quinoa. Desserts are exquisite—try the stewed cherries and strawberries with homemade vanilla ice cream and a chocolate brownie. The wine list is extensive and expensive; don't miss the chance to choose your own bottle from the wine cellar. Las Balsas is not easy to find; be sure to ask for detailed directions when you make reservations.

Bahía Las Balsas. ℂ/fax **02944/494308**. Reservations required. Main courses $10–$18 (£5.50–£9.90). AE, MC, V. Daily 8–10:30pm.

Tinto Bistro FUSION   Everything sparkles inside the Tinto Bistro. The lighting is intimate, and the decor is deluxe. Chef Leonardo Andres's food manages to shine as well. An eclectic offering of tapas includes rabbit *escabeche* with endives. The main courses reflect a global palate, with Asian, Middle Eastern, and Mediterranean influences—from garlic-and–lemon grass chicken to Saigon beef and udon noodles with sautéed seafood in vodka-saffron sauce and coconut milk. It's a very exciting and refreshing change, perhaps a bit too spicy for most Argentine palates but interesting to many travelers. A wide selection of *vino tinto*, with more than 150 labels, honors the restaurant's name. For dessert, try Princesa Mia, a honey parfait with flambéed fruits—named, perhaps, after the owner's celebrity sister, Princess Maxima of Holland.

Bv. Nahuel Huapi 34. ℂ **02944/494924**. Main courses $6–$12 (£3.30–£6.60). MC, V. Reservations recommended in high season. Mon–Sat 8pm–midnight.

Waldhaus SWISS/REGIONAL   This little restaurant's gingerbread eaves, notched furniture, and woodsy location will make you feel such as though you're dining in the Black Forest. The location, 6km (3¾ miles) from downtown, makes the Waldhaus less convenient than its main competitor, Rincón Suiza, but the food is slightly better here. In addition to nightly specials, typical menu offerings include wild-mushroom soup, beef fondue, venison marinated in burgundy wine, and typical Tyrolean dishes such as spaetzle with ham.

Ruta Nacional 231, Km 61. ℂ **02944/495123**. Main courses $7–$13 (£3.85–£7.15). MC, V. Summer and winter daily noon–3:30pm and 8pm–midnight; spring and fall daily 8pm–midnight.

4 Driving Bariloche to San Martín

There are four ways to get from Bariloche to San Martín de los Andes. Each has its pros and cons. All head northeast of Bariloche on RN 237, however, with lovely picnic spots and stunning scenery along the way. If you continue along the Limay River, you'll journey past the river's impressive Amphiteatre and the Valle Encantado, with rare volcanic rock formations, including the Dedo de Dios (Finger of God).

The only fully paved route takes you along the gorgeous Limay River to Rinconada and then loops to San Martín via **Junín de los Andes.** This route is the longest, at

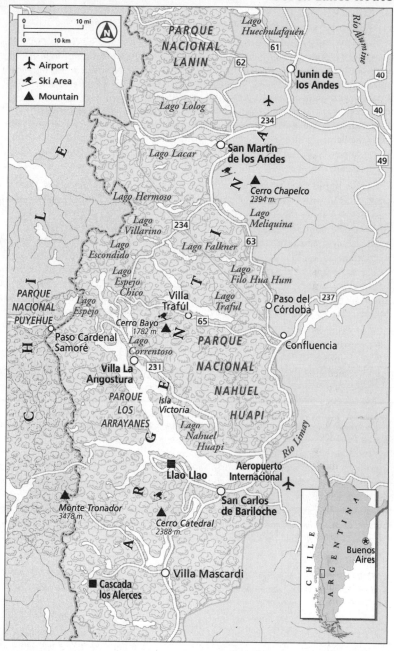

Seven Lakes Route

Airport
Ski Area
Mountain

PARQUE NACIONAL LANIN

Lago Huechulafquén

Río Aluminé

61

62

Junín de los Andes

40

40

234

Lago Lolog

49

San Martín de los Andes

Lago Lacar

Cerro Chapelco
2394 m.

Lago Hermoso

Lago Meliquina

234

Lago Villarino

Lago Falkner

63

Lago Escondido

Lago Filo Hua Hum

Lago Espejo Chico

Lago Traful

Villa Trafúl

Paso del Córdoba

237

PARQUE NACIONAL PUYEHUE

Lago Espejo

Cerro Bayo
1782 m.

65

Confluencia

Paso Cardenal Samoré

Lago Correntoso

PARQUE NACIONAL NAHUEL HUAPI

231

Villa La Angostura

PARQUE LOS ARRAYANES

Isla Victoria

Lago Nahuel Huapi

Río Limay

Llao Llao

Aeropuerto Internacional

Monte Tronador
3478 m.

San Carlos de Bariloche

Cerro Catedral
2388 m.

CHILE

ARGENTINA

Buenos Aires

Villa Mascardi

Cascada los Alerces

(Moments   Villa Traful: A Timeless Mountain Hideout

On what is often referred to as the Circuito Grande (opposed to the Circuito Chico that take you to the Llao Llao), the delightful little village of Villa Traful makes a great day trip from either Bariloche or Villa la Angostura. This lakeside settlement 63km (39 miles) north of Villa La Angostura is home to some 300 people, many descendents of original settlers. The town includes teahouses, campgrounds, and a few cabins for those who want to spend the night.

260km (161 miles), but it's the one I recommend for safety if you are traveling in winter or at night.

The second route takes you also along the Limay River but then heads west on a gravel road just past Confluencia and over the incredibly wild and rugged **Córdoba Pass** before joining the traditional Seven Lakes Route, RP 234. This also takes you past the picturesque Meliquina Lake, where you'll find a teahouse and general store. Soon after Meliquina, turn right on RP 231, the Ruta de los Siete Lagos (see below), to continue to San Martín de los Andes. Turn left to return to Villa la Angostura.

The route that heads through **Villa Traful** at RP 65 can also be done as the "Circuito Grande," a nice day drive from Bariloche, looping through Villa La Angostura. At Confluencia, you head west along the Traful River past the expansive Estancia Primavera, owned by a certain gringo by the name of Ted Turner. It then catches up to RP 231, the Ruta de los Siete Lagos. Again, it's a right turn to San Martín de los Andes and a left turn to Villa la Angostura. The Circuito Grande is 240km (148 miles) total, looping from Bariloche.

Numerous daily buses link along these roads as well. Campers can hop on and off at their own pace.

The classic **Ruta de Los Siete Lagos (Seven Lakes Route),** is a direct trip from Villa La Angostura to San Martín de los Andes. This road is only half-paved, 184km (114 miles) from Bariloche, but it affords many excellent lookouts, short hikes, and picnic spots, and you certainly need a full day to complete the drive to San Martín and back to Villa la Angostura. After leaving the shores of Nahuel Huapi Lake and the town of Villa La Angostura on RP 231, turn north on RP 234. The lakes actually amount to more than seven, starting with Correntoso, Espejo, and Espejo Chico. At the juncture of lakes Villarino and Falkner, the rustic **Hostería Lago Villarino** (© 02972/427483; www.hosteriavillarino.com.ar) is one of the only places to spend the night en route, besides numerous campgrounds. Shortly thereafter, you cross the border into Lanín National Park. You can check Hermoso, Machónico, and Lácar lakes off your list before dropping into the town of San Martín de los Andes.

---

5 San Martín de los Andes ★★

1,640km (1,017 miles) SW of Buenos Aires; 200km (124 miles) N of San Carlos de Bariloche

San Martín de los Andes is a charming mountain town of 35,000 nestled on the tip of Lago Lácar between high peaks. The town is considered the tourism capital of the Neuquen province, a claim that's hard to negate, considering the copious arts-and-crafts shops, gear-rental shops, restaurants, and hotels that constitute much of downtown. San Martín has grown considerably in the past 10 years, yet it hasn't succumbed to the whims of developers as Bariloche has, owing to city laws that limit building height and regulate architectural styles. The town is quieter than Bariloche and decidedly more picturesque, thanks to its timber-heavy architecture and Swiss Alpine influence. Because it's in a valley between two peaks, however, it lacks the majestic lake view. San Martín overflows with activities including biking, hiking, boating, and skiing. The town is also very popular for hunting and fishing—and, believe it or not, some come just to relax. The tourism infrastructure here is excellent, with every lodging option imaginable and plenty of great restaurants.

ESSENTIALS
GETTING THERE
BY PLANE   **Aeropuerto Internacional Chapelco** (© **02972/428388**) sits halfway between San Martín and Junín de los Andes (see later in this chapter) and, therefore, serves both destinations. **Aerolíneas Argentinas/Austral,** Capitán Drury 876 (© **02972/427871**), flies from Buenos Aires. A taxi to San Martín costs about $12 (£6.60); transfer services are also available at the airport for $24 (£13) per person. A taxi to Junín de los Andes costs $20 (£11); transfer services are $2 (£1.10) per person. **By Mich Rent a Car** and **Avis** both have auto rental kiosks at the airport.

BY BUS   The **Terminal de Omnibus** is at Villegas and Juez del Valle (© 02972/427044). **Via Bariloche** (© 02972/422800) runs daily bus service to San Martín de los Andes from Buenos Aires (a 19-hr. trip). **Ko-Ko Chevalier** (© 02972/427422) also offers service to and from Buenos Aires, and serves Villa La Angostura and Bariloche by the paved or by the scenic Siete Lagos route. **Centenario** (© 02972/427294) has service to Chile and also offers daily service to Buenos Aires; Villarrica- and Pucón-bound buses leave Monday through Saturday, and those for Puerto Montt depart Tuesday through Thursday. **Albus** (© 02972/428100; 2944/423552) has trips to Bariloche via the Siete Lagos route (about 3 hr.). Bus service can vary due to season, and it's best to evaluate a coach's condition and services before buying a ticket, especially for trips to and from Buenos Aires.

BY CAR   San Martín de los Andes can be reached from San Carlos de Bariloche following one of three routes. The popular 200km (124-mile) Siete Lagos route takes *rutas* 234, 231, and 237, and sometimes closes during the winter (see above). The 160km (99-mile) Paso Córdoba route takes *rutas* 234, 63, and 237; the longest, yet entirely paved 260km (161-mile) Collón Curá route follows *rutas* 234, 40, and 237. If driving at night, take the paved route. To get to Neuquén (420km/260 miles), take *rutas* 234, 40, and 22. From Chile, take the Tromen Pass (132km/82 miles from Pucón) to Ruta 62, taking you to Ruta 234 and through Junín de los Andes; note that a large portion of this route is on unpaved roads.

GETTING AROUND
San Martín is compact enough to explore by foot. For outlying excursions, tour companies can arrange transportation. **El Sol Rent a Car,** Av. San Martín 461 (© **02944/421870**), will drop a car off in Junín de los Andes (see later in this chapter). **Hertz Rent a Car** is at Av. San Martín 831 (© **02972/430280**) and **Nieves Rent-A-Car** is at Villegas 668 (© **02972/428684**).

Note that two main streets have similar names and can be confusing: Perito Moreno and Mariano Moreno.

VISITOR INFORMATION

San Martín's excellent **Oficina de Turismo** ((C)/fax **02972/427347** and 02972/427695) offers comprehensive accommodations listings with prices and other tourism-related information, and the staff is friendly and eager to make your stay pleasurable. The office is open Monday to Sunday 8am to 8pm, at Rosas and Avenida San Martín, on the main plaza. The **Asociación Hotelero y Gastronomía,** San Martín 1234 ((C) **02972/ 427166**), also offers lodging information, including photographs of each establishment, though service is not as efficient as it is at the Oficina de Turismo. During the off season, it's open daily from 9am to 1pm and 3 to 7pm; during high season, it's open daily from 9am to 10pm.

For information on Parque Nacional Lanín, drop by the park's information center, open daily 9am to noon only, or visit **www.parquenacionallanin.gov.ar**.

A website chock-full of valuable information is **www.smandes.gov.ar**.

FAST FACTS: San Martín de los Andes

Banks & Currency Exchange **Andina International,** Capitán Drury 876, exchanges money; banks such as **Banco de la Nación,** Av. San Martín 687; **Banco de la Provincia Neuquén,** Belgrano and Obeid; and Banco Frances, Av. San Martín and Sarmiento, have automatic tellers and money exchange. All banks are open Monday through Friday from 10am to 3pm.

Emergency Dial (C) **107.**

Hospital **Hospital Regional Ramón Carrillo** is at Avenida San Martín and Coronel Rodhe ((C) **02972/427211**).

Laundry The most convenient laundromats are **Laverap Santa Ana,** Belgrano 618 ((C) **02972/421898**), and **Laverap Drury,** Drury 880 ((C) **02972/428820**).

Police For emergencies, dial (C) **101.** The federal police station is at Av. San Martín 915 ((C) **02972/428249**); the provincial police station is at Belgrano 635 ((C) **02972/427300**).

Post Office **Correo Argentino** is at the corner of General Roca and Coronel Pérez ((C) **02972/427201**).

Taxi **Eco-taxi** ((C) **02972/429421**) has a stand at Plaza San Martín.

Telephone & Internet The fastest computers are at **Cooperativa Telefónica,** Capitán Drury 761, open from 9am to 11pm, where you can also make phone calls. One half-hour of Internet use costs less than $1 (55p).

WHAT TO SEE & DO

San Martín de los Andes's heritage is in agriculture, cattle, and logging, all of which are carefully displayed at the **Museo de los Primeros Pobladores,** J. M. Rosas 750 (no phone), open on Tuesday and Friday afternoons only. Now, San Martín is heavily geared toward tourism; accordingly, its streets are lined with shops selling arts and crafts, wonderful regional specialties such as smoked meats and cheeses, outdoor gear, books, and more. There is a lovely crafts market open most afternoons in the central plaza. Visitors will find most shops on **Avenida San Martín** and **General Villegas.**

For regional specialties and/or chocolates, try **Ahumadero El Ciervo,** General Villegas 724 (© **02972/427361**); **Mamusia,** San Martín 601 (© **02972/427560**); or **Su Chocolate Casero,** Villegas 453 (© **02972/427924**). For arts and crafts, try **Cooperativa De Artesano,** Av. San Martín 1050 (© **02972/429097**).

San Martín is a mountain town geared toward outdoor activities. If you're not up to a lot of physical exertion, take a stroll down to the lake and kick back on the beach. Alternatively, rent a bike and take a slow pedal around town. Pack a picnic lunch and head to Hua Hum.

The vast **Parque Nacional Lanín,** founded in 1937, is the third-largest national park in the country. It has 35 lakes, as well as thick forests, abundant wildlife, and an extinct volcano. The park is still home to more than 50 native Mapuche communities.

Just up the hill above town, the quaint and cozy **Arrayán Tea House** *⭐,* Circuito Arrayán, Km 4 (© **02972/425570**), has the area's best view. Built at a clearing in a cypress forest in 1938 by Renee Dickenson, a spirited young British woman, the house today maintains the same style that first charmed local residents. During the '40s and '50s, this was the hot spot in San Martín, on the old road to Bariloche. Today it's open afternoons for exquisite teas, coffees, and pastries, and for lunch and dinner with a reservation only. Take a taxi up for $3 (£1.65) and walk down.

Cultural events such as plays and concerts are held at the **Sala de Teatro de San José,** Capitán Drury 750 (© **02972/428676**).

The **Red Bus** (© **02972/421185**) runs city tours on a double-decker bus that helps orient visitors and gives a glimpse into the town's history. Tours depart daily at 10:30am and 6:30pm from the Plaza San Martín. The tour costs $5 (£2.75).

TOUR OPERATORS & TRAVEL AGENCIES
Both **Tiempo Patagónico,** Colonel Diaz 751 (©/fax **02972/427113;** www.tiempo patagonico.com), and **Pucará,** Av. San Martín 941 (© **02972/429357;** pucara@ smandes.com.ar), offer similar tours and prices, and also operate as travel agencies for booking plane tickets.

Excursions to the village Quila Quina, via a sinuous road that offers dramatic views of Lago Lácar, cost $7 (£3.85); a longer excursion including Chapelco and Arrayán is $10 (£5.50). Excursions to the hot springs Termas de Lahuenco are $12 (£6.60); scenic drives through the Siete Lagos route are $12 (£ 6.60) to Villa La Angostura and $15 (£8.25) to Bariloche. A gorgeous circuit trip to Volcán Lanín and Lago Huechulafquén goes for $15 (£8.25). Tours do not include lunch, which must be brought along or arranged ahead of time.

OUTDOOR ACTIVITIES
BIKING   San Martín is well suited for biking, and shops offer directions and maps. Bike rentals are available at **Enduro Kawa & Bikes,** Belgrano 845 (© **02972/427093**); **HG Rodados,** Av. San Martín 1061 (© **02972/427345**); and **Mountain Snow Shop,** Av. San Martín 861 (© **02972/427728**).

BOATING   Naviera Lácar & Nonthué (© **02972/428427**), at the Costanera and main pier, offers year-round boat excursions on Lago Lácar. A full-day excursion to Hua Hum includes a short navigation through Lago Nonthué. The cost is $20 (£11) adults, $9 (£4.95) kids 6 to 12 and seniors, plus park entrance fees ($3/£1.65); there's a restaurant in Hua Hum, or you can bring a picnic lunch. Naviera also operates three daily ferry services to the beautiful beaches of Quila Quina (which are packed in the summer) for $9 (£4.95) adults, $6 (£3.30) kids 6 to 12 and seniors. Naviera also rents kayaks for $2 (£1.10) per hour.

To raft the Hua Hum or the Aluminé rivers, get in contact with Tiempo Tours or Pucará (see "Tour Operators & Travel Agencies," above).

DIVING For lake dives, including first-timers, stop by the lakefront **Buceo de los Andes,** Costanera s/n (© **02972/15-550006**).

FISHING INFORMATION & LICENSES **Jorge Cardillo Pesca,** General Roca 636 (© **02972/428372;** cardillo@smandes.com.ar), is a well-stocked fly-fishing shop that organizes day and overnight fishing expeditions to the Meliquina, Chimehuín, and Malleo rivers, among other areas. The other local fishing expert is **Alberto Cordero** (© **02972/421453;** www.ffandes.com), who will arrange fishing expeditions around the area. He speaks fluent English; for more information, visit his website. You can pick up a fishing guide at the **Oficina Guardafauna,** General Roca 849 (© **02972/427091**).

GOLF The new 18-hole golf course at the **Chapelco Golf Resort** (© **2972/427713;** www.chapelcogolf.com), just north of San Martín, was designed by Jack Nicklaus and his son. It's part of an impressive new resort and country club. A full round of 18 starts at $45 (£25).

KAYAKING: The dozens of lakes near San Martín practically call out for kayakers. **Patagonia Traverse** (tel] **02972/15-609102;** www.patagoniatraverse.com) organizes half-day outings in touring or sea kayaks.

MOUNTAINEERING The guides at **Lanín Expedition** (© **02972/429799;** www.laninexpediciones.com) have decades of experience and offer climbing and orientation courses; ascents of Volcán Lanín and Volcán Domuyo; and treks, climbs, and overnight trips in Lanín and Nahuel Huapi national parks. They have creative itineraries for mountaineering.

SKIING The principal winter draw for San Martín de los Andes is **Cerro Chapelco,** one of the premier ski resorts in South America. Just 20km (12 miles) outside town, Cerro Chapelco is known for its plentiful, varying terrain and great amenities. Although popular, the resort isn't as swamped with skiers as Bariloche is. Instead it draws more families. The resort sports one gondola (which takes skiers and visitors to the main lodge), five chair lifts, and five T-bars. The terrain is 40% beginner, 30% intermediate, and 30% advanced/expert. Chapelco offers excellent bilingual ski instruction, ski and snowboard rental, and special activities such as dog sledding. The resort has open-bowl skiing and tree skiing, and numerous restaurants with an Alpine theme. To get here without renting a car, ask your hotel to arrange transportation or hire a *remise* (private taxi).

To drive to the resort from town, follow Route 234 south along Lago Lácar; it's paved except for the last 5km (3 miles). Lift tickets are quite reasonable and vary from low to high season. A 3-day ticket runs $60 to $108 (£33–£59) for adults, and $50 to $88 (£28–£48) for kids. During the summer, the resort is open for hiking and sightseeing, with lift access. For more information, call © **02972/427460** or visit www.sanmartindelosandes.com. The road is usually passable, but you may need chains during heavy snowfall; check before heading up to the resort.

For packages or guided trips with bilingual ski guides, contact **PowderQuest** tours (© **888/565-7158** in North America; www.powderquest.com).

TREKKING   The guides at **Patagonia Infinita** (© **02944/15-510988;** www. patagonia-infinita.com.ar) will take you deep into the Andes along dozens of excellent hiking trails.

WHERE TO STAY

San Martín has many, many *hosterías* and cabanas. And at last, there is a luxury option on the horizon, with the construction of the 80-room Loi Suites at the Chapelco Golf Resort. If you arrive in town without a reservation, your first stop should be the Oficina de Turismo (see above), next to the main plaza, which has an updated list of availabilities and prices. Rates almost double in most places from December 18 to March 1. For more information, go to **www.sanmartindelosandes.gov.ar**.

EXPENSIVE

Ten Rivers and Ten Lakes Lodge ★★ *Finds*   With undoubtedly the best view in all of San Martín, this tiny and cozy log-and-stone lodge is secluded and romantic. Next to the lovely Arrayán teahouse, where fabulous breakfasts are served, this boutique inn originally opened as a lodge for fly-fishers. They still have excellent fishing packages, but anyone is welcome to spend a few nights in the four rooms. Rooms are decorated with an understated luxury that will appeal to nature lovers, as will the absence of TVs. Big tubs, big beds, big windows, and still-unpretentious style characterize the interiors. Each has a lovely patio with Adirondack chairs and views across Lake Lacar. Given the $3 (£1.65) cab ride taking you into town, guests can roam the quaint streets of San Martín yet enjoy the wilderness as well. This is the best splurge in the area. The restaurant next door is open for dinner with reservations only.

Cerro Diaz, Ruta de los Arrayanes. © **011/5917-7710/11.** www.tenriverstenlakes.com. 4 units. $200 (£110) double; $280 (£154) suite. AE, MC, V. **Amenities:** Restaurant; lounge and TV room.

MODERATE

Hostería La Casa de Eugenia ★ *Finds*   Built in 1927, this lovely old building with bright blue trim used to house the local historical society; now it's a bed-and-breakfast. The charming living room with its large fireplace, piano, and colorful sofas leads to five bedrooms, named by color. The *verde* (green) has a skylight that keeps it bright throughout the day; all the rooms have comfortable beds with down comforters and exquisite linens, gleaming white bathrooms, and little else. Five new rooms, as of 2007, blend modern amenities and bright colors with the inn's historic feel. Breakfast is served in the bright dining room overlooking a small park, and the friendly managers can help you plan excursions in and around San Martín.

Colonel Díaz 1186. © **02972/427206.** www.lacasadeeugenia.com.ar. 9 units. $43–$87 (£24–£48) double. Rates include continental breakfast. AE, MC, V. **Amenities:** Lounge; room service. *In room:* No phone.

Hostería Monte Verde   A good value, this simple and clean *hostería* is one of the newer inns in town. The lobby is sparsely furnished with a giant stone fireplace. Skiers will like the large and handy ski storage area right at the door. Rooms are large and comfortable, with new beds. Bathrooms are also spacious. All superior rooms have Jacuzzi tubs and fireplaces. Some of the common spaces still need to be filled in, but the staff is friendly, and no one would feel cramped here.

Rivadavia 1165. © **02972/410129.** www.hosteriamonteverde.com.ar. 16 units. $60–$80 (£33–£44) standards; $80–$95 (£44–£52) superior. No credit cards. **Amenities:** Restaurant; outdoor pool; sauna; grill. *In room:* TV, safe.

La Cheminée ☾ Warm, attentive service and snug accommodations make La Cheminée a top choice, which is why so many foreign travel groups book a few nights here. New owners are toning down the Alpine Swiss design, emphasizing a new more neutral and modern look. Spacious rooms are carpeted and feature wood ceilings and a country design. The room they call a double *hogar* includes a fireplace for $8 (£4.40) more. The best room is the top-floor unit with wood-beamed ceilings. The bathrooms are rather small in all units. The fern-filled lobby's wooden floors are softened by fluffy rugs, and the walls are adorned with oil paintings by local artists; a small gallery has paintings for sale. A new spa and indoor pool are in the works. The hotel is known for its delicious breakfast, adding trout pâté, caviar, and fresh bread to the usual offerings; a restaurant also serves lunch and dinner. It's conveniently located 1 block from the hubbub.

General Roca and Mariano Moreno. ✆ **02972/427617.** Fax 02972/427762. www.hosterialacheminee.com.ar. 19 units. $85–$150 (£44–£83) double. Rates include full breakfast. AE, MC, V. **Amenities:** Restaurant; bar; lounge; outdoor pool; Jacuzzi; sauna; room service; laundry service; Internet. *In room:* TV, minibar.

La Raclette ☾ *Finds* The design of this appealing inn is a cross between something you'd find in Morocco and Switzerland—molded white stucco interiors set off by carved wooden shutters and eaves. It might also be described as a Hobbit House—anyone over 1.8m (6 ft.) tall might have to stoop, the ceilings upstairs are so low. Impressive renovations in 2007 make it appealing to those who like modern design. On a quiet street, La Raclette has a cozy seating area and a bar and restaurant downstairs. The public areas and the rooms have nooks and crannies and lovely modern art on display. Rooms have charisma, and they are remarkably private considering the small room sizes inherent in an old house like this. All baths have jetted tubs. The hotel exudes a lot of warmth.

Coronel Pérez 1170. ✆/fax **02972/427664.** www.laraclette.com.ar. 9 units. $50–$90 (£28–£50) double. AE, MC, V. **Amenities:** Restaurant; bar. *In room:* TV.

Le Chatelet Le Chatelet's spacious bedrooms, charming Swiss design, and full-service amenities are its strength. The classically designed lobby/lounge area is not as cozy as those in other hotels, but the bedrooms are wonderful, with green-and-white bedspreads and queen-size beds. Top-floor rooms have wooden ceilings, triangular windows, lace curtains, and a tremendous amount of walking room; suites are twice the size of doubles and have fireplaces. The hotel offers free use of VCRs and stocks a video and book library in the lobby. Suites come with CD players. The hotel is 2 blocks from downtown on a quiet residential street, and also sports an enclosed backyard with an outdoor pool. There's a new spa. They'll also help you organize excursions. A generous breakfast is served each morning; the restaurant boasts a roaring fire in the evenings and makes a good place to unwind after a day outdoors. Internet access is available for registered guests.

Villegas 650. ✆ **02972/428294.** www.hotellechatelet.com.ar. 31 units. $83–$159 (£46–£88) double; $143–$2,730 (£79–£1,501) suite. Rates include full breakfast. AE, MC, V, D. **Amenities:** Lounge; outdoor pool; exercise room; sauna; game room; room service; laundry service; garage. *In room:* TV.

Le Village This Alpine Swiss–style hotel is similar to La Cheminée and Le Chatelet in design, and it's popular during the off season for its slightly lower prices. The ambience leans toward family style; the staff is extremely friendly, knowledgeable, and eager to help you plan activities. Rooms are average size and carpeted; a few come with a small balcony. Guests can make use of several lounge areas, including a reading area and library, a felt-covered game table, and a TV/VCR. Le Village also has five cabanas with queen-size and twin beds and spacious living areas, although they are not particularly bright. Note that cabanas for six means two will sleep on a sofa bed in the living room. All guests have use of the sauna. An ample breakfast features specialties such as deer and trout and comes served in a pleasant eating area. A *quincho*, or separate barbecue/dining area for groups, allows guests to throw dinners for friends not staying at the hotel. All guests receive 1 hour of free Internet access.

General Roca 816. ©/fax **02972/427698**. www.hotellevillage.com.ar. 28 units (23 doubles, 5 cabanas). $68–$80 (£37–£44) double; $75–$100 (£41–£55) cabana for 4. Rates include full breakfast. AE, MC, V. **Amenities:** Restaurant; bar; sauna; game room; room service; library. *In room:* TV, minibar.

Patagonia Plaza *(Overrated)*   San Martín's only full-service four-star hotel feels bland and generic. Although the public areas are expansive, with lots of windows overlooking the street, the place feels faded overall. Rooms are comfortable and fairly modern, with colorful bedspreads and large windows overlooking the street. Bathrooms are sparkling clean and adequate. There's a small indoor heated pool and sauna, and an ample breakfast buffet is served every morning. This is a good place for a hassle-free overnight stay, steps from all the shops and restaurants, but don't expect luxury or charm. Kids will like the new micro-cinema.

Av. San Martín and Rivadavia. © **02972/422280**. Fax 02972/422284. www.hotelpatagoniaplaza.com.ar. 90 units. $110–$1,850 (£61–£1,018) double. Rates include buffet breakfast. AE, DC, MC, V. **Amenities:** Restaurant; bar; lounge; indoor heated pool; sauna; tour desk; limited room service; massage; laundry service. *In room:* TV.

INEXPENSIVE

Hostería Anay *(Value)*   A convenient location, economical price, and simple yet comfortable accommodations make the Anay a good value in San Martín. The rooms come with a double bed or two twins, and triples and apartments are available for four and five guests. Second-floor rooms have wooden ceilings and ruby-red bedspreads, a lamp here and there, and nothing else, but they're all clean and neat. The bathrooms are older, yet they have huge showers (no bathtubs). Downstairs, the lobby has a large fireplace, a felt-covered game table, and plenty of plants. The sunny, pleasant eating area is a nice spot for breakfast. The hotel is owner operated, with direct and professional service.

Capitán Drury 841. ©/fax **02972/427514**. www.interpatagonia.com/anay. 15 units. $40–$50 (£22–£28) double. Rates include continental breakfast. No credit cards. **Amenities:** Lounge; limited room service; babysitting; laundry service. *In room:* TV.

Residencial Italia   This little hotel, run by a sweet, elderly woman, is simple and kept scrupulously clean; indeed, it is doubtful you'll find even a speck of dust anywhere. It's a good value, given that the price for doubles does not fluctuate during the year. Rooms are modestly decorated in 1950s style. Downstairs rooms are slightly darker; I recommend booking the sunnier upstairs double or one of the two apartments. The apartments are for four and six people, with fully stocked kitchens, and both have large dining tables. There's a tiny eating area for breakfast (for guests only). I don't recommend the sole single room, given its Lilliputian size. In the spring and summer, beautiful roses frame the *residencial*.

Coronel Pérez 799 (at Obeid). © **02972/427590**. 8 units. $32 (£18) double; $45 (£25) triple. Rates include full breakfast. No credit cards. **Amenities:** Laundry. *In room:* TV.

CABANAS

San Martín has more than three dozen cabana complexes, ranging from attached units to detached A-frames. The quality varies somewhat; generally, the real difference between each is size, so always ask if a cabin for four means one bedroom and two fold-out beds in the living room. Cabanas are a great deal for parties of four to six. They're usually less expensive than hotels and come with small kitchens. During the off season, couples will find reasonably priced cabanas; however, many places charge a full six-person price during high season.

On the upscale end (doubles at around $50/£28 in low season, and $110/£61 in high), try the following: **Claro del Bosque** ✦, Belgrano 1083 (© **02972/427451;** fax 02972/428434; www.clarodelbosque.com.ar), is a Swiss Alpine–style building tucked away at the end of a street on a wooded lot. The managers are very friendly and accommodating. If they're fully occupied here (which is common), ask about their brand-new complex of charming apartments nearby. **Appart Niwen** ✦, G. Obeid 640 (© **02972/425888;** www.niwen.com.ar), has similar accommodations and rates, though it's a tad less charming than the cabanas above.

If you'd like to get out of town, try **Paihuen**'s beautiful stone-and-mortar attached cabanas in a forested lot at Ruta Nacional 234, Km 48 (©/fax **02972/428154;** www.paihuen.com.ar). It's is an upscale resort-style complex with one of the best wine bars in the area. **Aldea Misonet,** Los Cipreses 1801 (©/fax **02972/421821;** www.aldea misonet.com), has wood-and-stone attached units that sit at the edge of town; some units overlook a gurgling stream, as does the terrace. Near the lakeshore, **Terrazas del Pinar,** Juez de Valle 1174 (©/fax **02972/429316;** www.interpatagonia.com/terrazasdelpinar), has a children's play area.

Cabanas with doubles ranging from $18 to $65 (£9.90–£36), according to season, include the following: **El Ciervo Rojo,** Almirante Brown 445 (©/fax **02972/427949;** cabanaselciervorojo@smandes.com.ar), has nice wooden cabins; cheaper units have open second-story sleeping areas. **Del Lácar,** Coronel Rohde 1144 (©/fax **02972/427679;** www.interpatagonia.com/dellacar), has several large, detached wooden cabins. **Las Rosas,** Almirante Brown 290 (©/fax **02972/422002;** www.cablasrosas.com.ar), has pretty whitewashed units half a block from the shore. **Le Village** offers cabanas as well as regular hotel rooms (p. 328).

On the edge of town, **Cabañas Arique** ✦ (© **02972/429262;** www.arique.com) are extremely charming, with lots of local wood, fireplaces, and modern kitchens; there's also a small shared barbecue area and a heated outdoor pool. Cabins are $30 to $58 (£17–£32) double, $40 to $68 (£22–£37) for four people.

Note: Prices fluctuate wildly according to who makes the reservation; speak Spanish and you'll likely get a lower rate. Feel free to bargain when making your reservations. Make your final offer if you find the price too high—the owners may very well take whatever you offer, especially during low season.

WHERE TO DINE

San Martín has several excellent restaurants. For sandwiches and quick meals, try **Peuma Café,** Av. San Martín 851 (© **02972/428289**); for afternoon tea and delicious cakes and pastries, try **Unser Traum,** General Roca 868 (© **02972/422319**).

EXPENSIVE

Avataras ✦ *Finds* INTERNATIONAL   Exceptionally warm, friendly service, a kids' menu, and a marvelous variety of international dishes from Hungary to China to Egypt make this restaurant an excellent, if slightly expensive, choice in San Martín. The chefs, youngish transplants from Buenos Aires, whip up exquisite items, such as Indian lamb curry, rabbit with mustard, Malaysian shrimp *sambal,* and filet mignon with four-pepper sauce. The appetizer menu features Scandinavian gravlax and sweetbreads in herb cream. What stands out, however, is Avataras's willingness to please its guests. Although they officially do not serve dinner until 8:30pm, give them 15 minutes' notice, and they'll open earlier for parties as small as two (they'll also open for lunch if you call ahead). The decor includes light beechwood, ferns, Japanese paper lanterns, and an acoustic ceiling made of beige linen. With smoking and nonsmoking sections, the restaurant even sells cigars, which diners may smoke on the premises. Avataras sometimes hosts live jazz music.

Teniente Ramayón 765. ⓒ 02972/427104. Reservations recommended. Main courses $9–$17 (£4.95–£9.35). AE, DC, MC, V. Daily 8:30pm–midnight.

La Tasca ⓕ REGIONAL   La Tasca is a solid choice for its fresh, high-quality cuisine and extensive wine offerings. Regional specialties are the focus, such as venison flambéed in cognac and blueberries, saffron trout, and raviolis stuffed with wild boar. All meats are hand-picked from local ranches by the chef-owner, and the organic cheese is made at a local German family's farm. Mushroom lovers will savor the fresh, gourmet varieties served with appetizers and pasta. Appetizer platters are a specialty here. The cozy restaurant is festooned with hanging hams, bordered with racks of wine bottles, and warmed by a few potbellied iron stoves. It's a bit too bright for a romantic dinner, but great for families, as they have several large tables.

Mariano Moreno 866. ⓒ 02972/428663. Reservations recommended. Main courses $12–$18 (£6.60–£9.90). AE, MC, V. Daily noon–3:30pm and 7pm–1am.

MODERATE

La Fondue de Betty ⓕ FONDUE   A San Martín classic, Betty's friendly service and bubbling fondue pots make it an enchanting place for dinner, especially if you are with friends. Cheese fondue is the classic starter. Follow it with either beef bourguignon (beef in oil), which comes with six sauces, or beef chinoise (beef in broth). Both come with french fries. A local favorite is *bagna cauda,* a Northern Italian fondue of anchovies, garlic, and cream, in which you dip vegetables. The menu also includes some nonfondue dishes, such as tenderloin with mushroom sauce and trout with saffron. The wine list is very good. For dessert, don't miss the chocolate fondue, of course!

Villegas 586. ⓒ 02972/422522. Reservations recommended in winter. Main courses $8–$13 (£4.40–£7.15). No credit cards. Daily 7pm–midnight.

La Reserva ⓕ *(Moments* ARGENTINE   This lovely old stone-and-wood house was transformed into one of the most romantic restaurants in Patagonia, with a stone fireplace, elegant cloth-covered tables, soothing music, and superb service. La Reserva is run by the talented chef Alejandro Marchand, who lets many ethnic cuisines influence him while using mostly Patagonian ingredients. Begin with a cold glass of Argentine champagne to go with an order of tapas—a tasting of cheeses and dried meats. Then move on to grilled trout, tender venison with fresh berry sauce, or chicken breast stuffed with feta cheese and herbs. More than 250 wines are available, including excellent regional wines for under $10 (£5.50) a bottle. Desserts include a divine selection of homemade fruit tarts and ice creams.

Belgrano 940. ⓒ 02972/428734. Reservations recommended. Main courses $6–$10 (£3.30–£5.50). AE, DC, MC, V. Daily noon–3pm and 7:30pm–midnight.

INEXPENSIVE

El Tata Jockey *(Value* PARRILLA/PASTA   This semicasual restaurant is popular for its grilled meats and pastas at reasonable prices. It's possible to order a *parrilla* of assorted barbecued meats and sausages for two; $6 (£3.30) buys you enough food for three diners. The homemade pastas are also a good bet, as is the trout al Jockey, served with seasonal vegetables and a smoked bacon–and–cream sauce. Owned and operated by a friendly, enthusiastic mountaineer, the restaurant is decorated with photos and tidbits taken from his various exploits around the area; the long, family-style tables have checkered tablecloths. El Tata Jockey also offers special menus for groups.

Villegas 657. (*C*) **02972/427585.** Main courses $6–$11 (£3.30–£6.05). AE, MC, V. Daily noon–2:30pm and 8pm–midnight.

La Costa del Pueblo *(Kids* INTERNATIONAL   This restaurant is a good bet, with a lake view and an extensive menu with everything from pastas to *parrilla*. The establishment ran as a cafe for 20 years until new owners expanded it to include a dozen more tables and a cozy fireside nook. La Costa offers good, homemade pasta dishes such as cannellonis stuffed with ricotta and walnuts, grilled meats, pizzas, and sandwiches. A kids' menu and vegetarian sandwiches help please any crowd. The restaurant is a great place to down a cold beer and a platter of smoked cheese and venison while you watch the lake lap the shore. Just don't come here in a rush; service can be really slow.

Av. Costanera and Obeid. (*C*) **02972/429289.** Main courses $2–$6 (£1.10–£3.30). AE, DC, MC, V. Daily 11am–1am.

La Nonna Pizzería PIZZA   La Nonna's pizza, calzones, and empanadas are so good they're sold packaged and ready-to-bake at the supermarket. Toppings generally run the repetitive gamut of ham and onion, ham and pineapple, ham and hearts of palm. But there are a few deviations, such as anchovy, Roquefort, and Parmesan, or mozzarella with chopped egg. La Nonna also offers specialty regional pizzas with trout, wild boar, and deer. Calzone fillings include chicken, mozzarella, and bell pepper. For a quick snack, try one of eight types of empanadas or a piece of *faina*, a traditional and delicious garbanzo bread. La Nonna also delivers.

Capitán Drury 857. (*C*) **02972/422223.** Pizzas $3–$6 (£1.65–£3.30) small, $4–$9 (£2.20–£4.95) large. AE, MC, V. Daily noon–3pm and 8pm–12:30am.

Pura Vida VEGETARIAN   San Martín's only vegetarian restaurant also serves a few chicken and trout dishes (the curried chicken is excellent). This homespun, tiny restaurant has about seven tables, and features meatless dishes such as vegetable chop suey, soufflés, soy and eggplant *milanesas* (breaded filets), and rich flan. The veggie mousaka is a specialty. The vegetarian offerings are not really extensive, but what they do offer is fresh and good. Pastas are not only homemade, but are made from scratch the moment you order, which can mean a long wait.

Villegas 745. (*C*) **02972/429302.** Main courses $4–$6 (£2.20–£3.30). No credit cards. Mon–Sat 12:30–3:30pm; daily 8pm–midnight.

SAN MARTIN AFTER DARK

With its nice outdoor patio and cool wood and stone interior, the **Dublin South Pub,** on the corner of M. Moreno and San Martín (*C*) **02972/424938**), has a huge list of microbrewed beers and cocktails.

4 Junín de los Andes

40km (25 miles) N of San Martín de los Andes

The main draw in the tiny town of Junín de los Andes is fly-fishing. The sport has caught on so well here that now even the street signs are shaped like fish. But it also provides stunning scenery for other outdoor sports such as hiking and boating, and some lovely nearby ranches may appeal to those searching for a rural getaway. Junín is spread out in a grid pattern, a fertile little oasis along the shore of the Río Chimehuín, surrounded by dry pampa. You'll pass through Junín if you're crossing into Argentina from the Pucón area in Chile.

ESSENTIALS

GETTING THERE   By Plane   See "Getting There" under "San Martín de los Andes," earlier in this chapter. It is also common for drivers to arrive in Junín from Pucón, Chile, coming over the gorgeous Paso Tromen.

By Bus   Ko-Ko Chevalier (© 02972/427422) has service from San Martín de los Andes and Buenos Aires. Ko-Ko also has service to Lago Huechulafquén. The **bus terminal** (© 02972/492038) is at Olarama and Felix San Martín.

GETTING AROUND   Most visitors find that the only real way to get around is to rent a car, especially if they've come to fly-fish. Car-rental agencies can be found at the airport and in San Martín (see "Getting Around" under "San Martín de los Andes," earlier in this chapter).

VISITOR INFORMATION   The **Secretaría Municipal de Turismo** is located at Padre Milanesio 596 (© 02972/491160); it's open daily from 8am to 9pm, from 8am to 11pm during the summer.

WHAT TO SEE & DO

Puerto Canoa is the central entrance to the splendid **Parque Nacional Lanín,** 30km (19 miles) from Junín. Here, you'll find a 30-minute interpretive trail and the departure spot for catamaran excursions across Lago Huechulafquén, which looks out onto the snowcapped, conical Volcán Lanín. Río Chimehuín begins at the lake's outlet and offers outstanding fishing opportunities. Several excellent hiking and backpacking trails traverse the area, with a few rustic backcountry huts; you can pick up information at the ranger station at Puerto Canoa. Towering behind Junín is the park's namesake volcano. Volcán Lanín is 3,776m (12,400 ft.) tall. Experienced mountaineers can mount the summit with a licensed guide (see "Mountaineering" under "San Martín de los Andes," earlier in this chapter). If you're in San Martín de los Andes, stop by the park's headquarters, the **Intendencia Parque Nacional Lanín,** Emilio Frey 749 (© 02972/427233).

Visitors can book a tour or rent a car for the 132km (82-mile) return drive to the hot springs **Termas de Lahuen-Co.,** winding through volcanic landscape and past Lake Curruhue. Formerly known as **Termas de Epulafquen,** the hot springs, which include 19 volcanic mud pools, just underwent a major renovation and reopened under the new name in early 2007. For tours, try Huiliches Turismo, Padre Milanesio 570, Local B (© 02972/491670), or ask at the visitor center.

Founded in 1883 but populated by native Mapuches for centuries, Junín is one of the older towns in the area. The **Mapuche Museum,** Ginés Ponte 550 (© 02972/492322), is worth a stop. Nearby, the **Museo Don Mosés,** C. Juarez and San Marín (no phone), is a turn-of-the-20th-century general store that has been totally preserved. Outside town on the road to Volcán Lanín, you can visit the wool and woodworking workshop of the local native Mapuche people at **Reserva Indígena Chiuquilihuin,** open daily from 9:30am to 7:30pm. Take RP 60 towards Tromen, turning right at Km 13. Local guides also run short hikes in the area. Ask at the workshop for more information or book a tour of the Mapuche villages with **Alquimia Viajes** in San Martín (© **02972/491355;** www.alquimiaturismo.com.ar).

FISHING INFORMATION & LICENSES   Visitors can obtain licenses at the **Tourism Office,** the office of the Guardafauna (© **02972/491277**), open Monday to Friday 8am to 3pm; **The Fly Shop,** Pedro Illera 378 (© **02972/491548**); **Bambi's Fly Shop,** Juan Manuel de Rosas 320 (© **02972/491167**); or **Patagonia Fly Fishing,** Laura Vicuña 135 (©/fax **02972/491538**).

WHERE TO STAY & DINE

Junín de los Andes has a few lodges that specialize in fly-fishing, such as the **Hostería de Chimehuín,** Suarez and Avenida 21 de Mayo, on the shore of the Chimehuín River (© **02972/491132;** $12/£6.60 double). Accommodations are basic, including rooms with balconies and apartments, but the atmosphere is friendly and homey, and it has a good breakfast. An excellent fly-fishing lodge is the **San Humberto Lodge,** on a privately owned stretch of the Malleo River (© **02972/491238**), which charges $150 to $240 (£83–£132) for a double, including all meals. The San Humberto consists of six chalets with twin beds, units that are separate from an enormous rustic lodge. The restaurant is excellent, and so are the fishing guides. Run by a British-expat, the similarly rural **Estancia Huechahue** (no phone; www.huechahue.com) is a working cattle ranch open to visitors for day-long and overnight horseback trips. Their eight-room main house doubles as a charming inn. Rates are $270 per guest per night. **Cerro los Pinos,** Brown 420 (© **02972/427207**), is a charming family ranch with close access to the Chimehuín River. Doubles are $12 to $28 (£6.60–£15); they'll arrange a fishing guide for guests. Dining options are limited here; try the **Ruca Hueney,** Milanesio 641 (© **02972/491113**), which serves pasta dishes, venison and, of course, trout.

11

Península Valdés & Southern Patagonia

by Christie Pashby

Drawn to its emptiness, its windswept horizons, and its promise of discovery, many adventurers are driven to Patagonia by the sense that it's the end of the world. A traveler can drive for days without seeing another soul on the vast Patagonian Steppe. The unrelenting wind spins your head in circles, and conspires with the emptiness of the landscape to warp your perception of time and distance and convince you that you're the only human left on the planet. It is a seduction, but also an illusion; people do live here, after all—though just a scant few hardy survivors.

Patagonia's harsh, blustery climate and curious geological circumstances have produced some of the most beautiful natural attractions in the world: the annual congregation of the Southern Right Whale at Península Valdés, the granite towers and expansive glaciers of Los Glaciares National Park, the Southern and Northern Ice Fields with their colossal glaciers, and the flat Steppe, broken by multicolored sedimentary bluffs. Wildlife lovers and divers explore the rugged coastline of the spectacular Península Valdés; mountaineers stage elaborate excursions through rugged territories, only to be beaten back, like their predecessors, by unrelenting storms.

The area has a fascinating human history as well—from the mountaineering accomplishments of early explorers to border disputes among ranching pioneers. The ample presence of gauchos further heightens the air of romanticism that distinguishes the region.

EXPLORING THE REGION

The big challenges in Patagonia are the extreme distances. Destinations can be upwards of 1,000 km (620 miles) apart—and most of those kilometers are on unpaved roads. Yet thanks to modern amenities and air travel, Patagonia is nonetheless easy to travel today. It's entirely feasible to visit Puerto Madryn and Península Valdés on the coast and then head inland to El Calafate and El Chaltén (or reverse), making for a trip that is just over a week long. If you're planning to hike the trails of Los Glaciares National Park, beneath the lofty peaks of Mt. FitzRoy and Cerro Torre, for example, you'll want to spend between 3 and 5 days in El Chaltén. The minimum amount of time for a worthwhile stop at Península Valdés is 3 days. A quick trip to Argentine Patagonia might include 2 days in El Calafate, 2 in El Chaltén, and 3 in Península Valdés. If you want to work in a trip to Chilean Patagonia, add at least another 5 days.

Prices jump and crowds swell during the summer months, from early November to late March, and some businesses open only during this season. In November, the

Península Valdés is busiest with visiting foreigners, who come to see the Southern Right Whales. The southern area around Parque Nacional Los Glaciares is busiest in January and February, but these summer months are not necessarily the best time to visit Patagonia; calmer weather prevails from mid-October to late November, and from mid-March to late April, when the leaves turn golden and rust in the autumn air, and winds generally die down a bit.

EXPLORING PENINSULA VALDES/PUERTO MADRYN

In the middle of Atlantic Patagonia, in the vast province of Chubut, lies the remote and barren Península Valdés, declared a World Heritage Site by UNESCO in 1999.

The bays and shores on this peninsula that juts out into the Atlantic serve as a marine-life preserve for sea elephants. Sea lions are also plentiful, as are the enormous Southern Right Whales, which come in from April to December. Penguins and orca whales also swim past. Visitors come here to see the whales and to walk on the beaches and view the unusual sea elephants up close. Diving trips are also popular.

Other animals that run wild here include guanacos (similar to llamas), *maras* (large wild rabbits), *choique* (similar to an ostrich), and a bevy of birds and smaller animals.

The region is very well controlled—in fact, in some areas, beach access is restricted unless you are with a certified "naturalist guide." When whales are in the bays (which is most of the year), beach activities are not allowed. This is a nature preserve, after all, not a playground. Kayaks are allowed from late December to March only, when the whales are gone. Diving is allowed offshore throughout the year, but only on certified boats with government-sanctioned guides.

On the peninsula itself (the entire area is a national park), the tiny village of **Puerto Pirámides** (100km/62 miles from Puerto Madryn) is the departure point for all the whale-watching and diving trips. Some visitors opt to stay overnight here. But most of the tourist infrastructure is in **Puerto Madryn,** a small, laid-back, beachside city of 70,000 people. The town went from a tiny, sleepy hamlet of 6,000 people to a bustling small city that serves as a center for industrial products in eastern Patagonia. It's the most pleasant base for travelers—a jumping-off point for day trips to the peninsula and to **Punta Tombo** (2 hr. south), where Magellan penguins come to mate every year.

The typical visit to this area includes a travel day; then a jam-packed day tour of the Península Valdés, which could include whale-watching; and a third day to visit Punta Tombo.

Visitors with more than 3 nights available should consider renting a car and spending a few nights at a rural hotel on the peninsula itself, such as Faro Punta Delgada, or in the beach town at Puerto Pirámides. This will allow you to explore the area away from the crowds, and also to relax. You could consider skipping Punta Tombo if you visit the penguin colony at Estancia San Lorenzo instead, on the northern tip of Península Valdés. A car is necessary to explore the peninsula on your own; there is no public bus system, and distances are vast. Most of the roads are not paved, so a 4WD is a good idea.

The capital of Chubut province is the nearby residential town of **Rawson** (only 20,000 inhabitants), where there's not much to see. Nearby, the bigger city of **Trelew** serves as a gateway to the area, with an airport capable of handling bigger jets. Trelew has a good museum and a few hotels, but it's not of much interest to visitors. The Welsh town of **Gaiman** is much more interesting and makes for an excellent afternoon excursion. Settled primarily from 1865 to 1870, this is one of the few places outside of Wales where Welsh is still spoken. Houses here are reminiscent of those in the

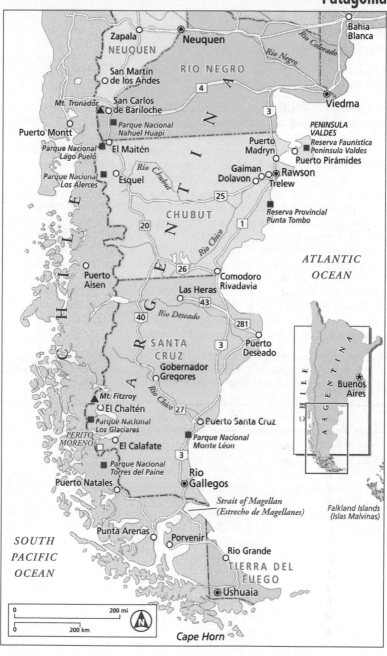

Patagonia

Bahía Blanca

Zapala
Neuquen

NEUQUEN
RIO NEGRO
Río Colorado
Río Negro

San Martín
de los Andes

Mt. Tronador

San Carlos
de Bariloche

Viedma

Parque Nacional
Nahuel Huapi

PENINSULA
VALDES

Puerto Montt

Puerto
Madryn

Reserva Faunística
Peninsula Valdes

Parque Nacional
Lago Pueló

El Maitén

Puerto Pirámides

Parque Nacional
Los Alerces

Esquel

Río Chubut

Gaiman
Dolavon

Rawson

Trelew

A R G E N T I N A

CHUBUT

Reserva Provincial
Punta Tombo

ATLANTIC
OCEAN

Puerto
Aisen

Río Chico

Comodoro
Rivadavia

Las Heras

Río Deseado

Puerto
Deseado

SANTA
CRUZ

Gobernador
Greqores

Río Chico

CHILE

ARGENTINA

Buenos
Aires

Mt. Fitzroy
El Chaltén

Parque Nacional
Los Glaciares

Puerto Santa Cruz

PERITO
MORENO

El Calafate

Parque Nacional
Monte Léon

Parque Nacional
Torres del Paine

Río
Gallegos

Puerto Natales

Strait of Magellan
(Estrecho de Magellanes)

Falkland Islands
(Islas Malvinas)

Punta Arenas
Porvenir

SOUTH
PACIFIC
OCEAN

Rio Grande

TIERRA DEL
FUEGO

Ushuaia

0   200 mi
0   200 km

N

Cape Horn

English countryside. A handful of teahouses offer traditional English tea service (which came in handy when the late Princess Diana visited in 1995).

EXPLORING SOUTHERN ARGENTINE PATAGONIA

The popular image of Patagonia—windswept plains, towering granite spires, hard-working pioneers, endless stretches of dirt road—still exists today in the southern part of Argentina. It's way down there, though. The main tourist center is El Calafate, which is 2,727km (1,691 miles) southwest of Buenos Aires. It's easier than ever to get here, however, which means an increasing number of visitors from North America and Europe are making a pilgrimage to see the glaciers, peaks, and emptiness of Patagonia. The two main destinations in southern Argentine Patagonia are El Calafate—the jump-off point for seeing the beautiful glaciers of Los Glaciares National Park—and El Chaltén, a hiking town at the base of Cerro Torre and Mt. FitzRoy. You could feasibly see this area in a short week, which would give you two full travel days to get there and back from Buenos Aires, from where all international flights depart.

Start in El Calafate, and spend a few days exploring the glaciers—Perito Moreno and the more remote ones such as Upsala. Then head to El Chaltén for some hiking; to make it worthwhile, you need at least 1 full day and 2 half-days there.

Many people visit this area on a trip combined with Torres del Paine National Park, next door in Chile. It's worthwhile, given that they are so close. "Paine," however, as the park is known here, is much busier and more expensive.

You'll also find a growing list of inns and some very good restaurants. If you're anything like me, you'll find yourself deeply moved and inspired by the vast stretches of wilderness unique to this remote part of the world.

1 Puerto Madryn

1,374km (852 miles) S of Buenos Aires; 62km (38 miles) N of Trelew; 1,798km (1,115 miles) N of Ushuaia

A laid-back city of 70,000, Puerto Madryn's population boom came in the mid-1970s. Until then, the city had only 6,000 inhabitants, but the Aloar aluminum factory completely changed the town when it opened its doors here in 1973. Now, there are tile, fish, and ceramic factories on the outskirts of town. Tourism is booming. And Aloar is still expanding. In fact, Puerto Madryn is now one of the fastest-growing cities in Argentina. Mostly used by foreign visitors, the coastal street, Avenida Roca, is lined with restaurants, bars, and hotels. Locals tend to patronize establishments at least 1 block inland. The wide beach is great, with frequently calm waters that make swimming possible from mid-December to mid-March. I also recommend that you take 30 minutes to stroll to the tip of the Old Dock for a great view of the area. The streets a few blocks inland are buzzing with locals. Here you'll find inexpensive clothing stores, and cafes and bars catering more to residents than to tourists. Very few visitors take the time to walk around here, but it's worth meandering in the residential neighborhood for at least an hour. With the bay shimmering in front, there's an easygoing and relaxed feeling about Puerto Madryn, and you may want to spend an extra day relaxing here, before continuing your journey.

ESSENTIALS
GETTING THERE
BY PLANE   LADE (Líneas Aereas del Estado), Roca 119 (© **2965/451256** or 0810/810-5233), has one weekly flight from Buenos Aires aboard a small commuter jet (the flight makes one or two stops along the way) for $170 (£94). Weekly flights

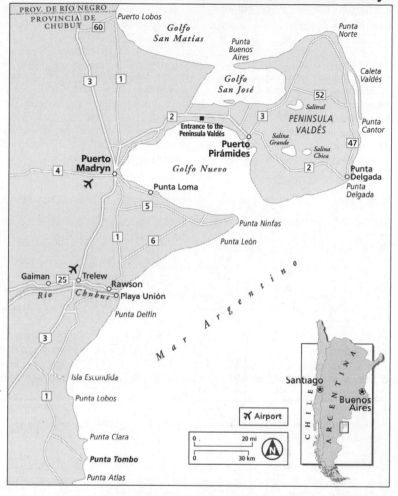

depart from Ushuaia (for $145/£80) and El Calafate (for $115/£63). The fares are much cheaper than those of Aerolíneas Argentinas, but the service is very basic. LADE is the only airline currently operating out of the Puerto Madryn's **Aerodromo El Tehuelche (© 2965/451909)**, saving you an hour-long transfer from the other airport, Trelew (see below).

A taxi from the airport to the center of Puerto Madryn, 10km (6¼ miles) away, should cost no more than $5 (£2.75) for the 10-minute ride.

Most visitors to this region fly into Trelew Airport, **Aeropuerto de Trelew (© 2965/ 433443)**, 62km (38 miles) away. **Aerolíneas Argentinas (© 0810/222-86527)** has three to four daily flights to Trelew from Buenos Aires and several weekly flights from El Calafate and Ushuaia.

A taxi or *remise* from Trelew airport to Puerto Madryn costs $17 to $22 (£9.35–£12), and the trip takes 40 minutes.

BY BUS   The **Terminal de Omnibus** is on García and Independencia. The fastest bus from Buenos Aires takes 19 hours aboard **Andesmar** (© **2965/473764**). The least expensive one-way fare is $60 (£33), but for $5 (£2.75) more you can travel in a reclining *cama* chair. Andesmar also has daily services to Mendoza ($63/£35 one-way, 23 hr.) and Bariloche ($45/£25 one-way, 13 hr.). Other reputable bus companies to try are **QueBus** (© **2965/455805**), **Mar y Valle** (© **2965/472056**), and **Ruta Patagonia** (© **2965/454572**).

VISITOR INFORMATION

You can pick up maps and detailed park information from the **Puerto Madryn Secretaria de Turismo (Tourist Office),** located at Roca 223 (© **2965/453504;** www.madryn.gov.ar/turismo). Their office is open daily from 7am to 9pm.

GETTING AROUND

Puerto Madryn is compact enough that you can pretty much walk everywhere. Taxis are available, however, in case you need them. A trip within the city center should cost no more than $2 or $3 (£1.10–£1.65). Taxis are lined up near the Plaza San Martín, or you can call one at © **2965/472214.** A reputable *remise* company is **Remise Madryn** (España 1560; © **2965/453444**).

Buses run by the company **28 de Julio** (© **2965/472056**) depart every hour for the 45-minute journey to Trelew. The cost is $2.50 (£1.40) one-way. **Mar y Valle** (© **2965/472056**) buses depart the central bus station once a day to Puerto Pirámides on the Península Valdés at 9:30am and return at 6pm, making it handy for independent day-trippers.

You can rent a car at Trelew Airport, at the Puerto Madryn airport, or from the center of Puerto Madryn. **Avis,** Av. Roca 493 (© **2965/475422**), and **Hertz,** Av. Roca 115 (© **2965/474287**), have similar rates of about $50 (£28) per day for a small car. If you think you'll want a car, it's best to book it before leaving home, for the lowest rate. If not, try bargaining at either **Madryn Rent a Car,** Roca 624 (© **2965/452355**), or Fiorassi, Av. Roca 165 (© **2965/456300**), two local companies that offer lower rates if they have cars available. For exploring the Península Valdés, where virtually none of the roads are paved, consider renting a 4WD. Rates start at $110 (£61) per day.

FAST FACTS: Puerto Madryn

ATMs There are quite a few ATMs around town. **Banco Galicia,** Mitre 25 (© **2965/452323**), and **Bansud,** corner of R. Saenz Pena and Marcos A. Zar (© **2965/451489**), are the most conveniently located.

Currency Exchange The Casa de Cambio at Roca 497 (© **2965/455858**) is open until at least 10pm every night.

Emergency Dial © **101** or 451449 for police; © **100** for fire.

Hospital The **Hospital Subzonal** is at R. Gomez 383 (© **2965/451999**).

Internet You'll find many Internet cafes around town. Rates are under $1/55p per hour, and most are open from 8am until midnight. Try **Cyber World,** at Roca 650 (© **2965/475370**), or **El Tucán,** Mosconi 36.

Laundry The laundromat at 2040 Roca (*©* **2965/456-969**) is open Monday to Saturday from 10am to 9pm.

Pharmacy **FarMadryn,** corner of Roca and Belgrano (*©* **2965/474555**), is open 24 hours.

Post Office The main post office for **Correo Argentino** (the official name of the Argentine postal service) is located at Belgrano and Maíz (no phone).

WHERE TO STAY

Puerto Madryn hotels are virtually all situated along the main coastal road, Avenida Roca (which turns into Bulevar Brown farther south), or a few blocks inland. There are a few new establishments in town, including the interesting Hotel Territorio, but most are still family-run, old-fashioned hotels that aren't exactly chic. For the past 4 years, a half-built, giant luxury resort has loomed on the horizon. Rumor has it that Sheraton will take over this white elephant. What's certain is that everyone hopes that someone does something with it soon. Most visitors to Puerto Madryn spend only 2 or 3 nights here. They visit the peninsula one day and Punta Tombo the next, and then fly out. Parking is free at hotels in Puerto Madryn. Prices have soared here over the past few years, especially during the busy months of October and November; some hotels will offer you a cheaper price if you pay in cash. Rates listed here are for high season, September through March.

EXPENSIVE

Hotel Península Valdés *Overrated* For decades, this has been the most expensive hotel in Puerto Madryn, but there is new competition on the block (Territorio, below), and the family that runs the Península Valdés has had to step things up. The lobby has a new look, and the new lounge on the second floor, where breakfast is served, aims for hipness. Many of the rooms have been renovated, including the bathrooms, which are brighter now, though tubs are still tiny. Rooms on the top floor are the most spacious. The charge for "panoramic" rooms with sea views is 20% extra, though it never hurts to ask at check-in for a free upgrade. The panoramic rooms have king-size beds and flatscreen TVs. The most annoying thing about this hotel is the charge for use of the sauna ($14/£7.70) and the unattractive indoor Jacuzzi ($14/£7.70). Internet access from the tiny business center is free, however, and the staff is efficient, if a bit snotty. We recommend the Territorio over this place, if you can afford it. If you are with a tour group or otherwise without a choice but to stay here, however, you will likely find this hotel to be satisfactory, if unimpressive.

Av. Roca 155, 9120 Puerto Madryn. *©* **2965/471292.** Fax 2965/452584. www.hotelpeninsula.com.ar. 70 units. $145 (£80) double; $166 (£91) triple. Rates include buffet breakfast. AE, DC, MC, V. **Amenities:** Bar; lounge; Jacuzzi; sauna; small business center w/free Internet; room service; massage; laundry service. *In room:* A/C, TV, minibar, hair dryer, safe.

Hotel Territorio *©* Finally, classy accommodations have opened in Puerto Madryn. This new hotel is small enough to be classified as an inn (36 rooms), but upscale enough to be a five-star. The hotel itself does not cry for attention, and you may even miss it for how well it blends into the natural setting. It's built in an inconspicuous style with local materials such as stone and tin sheeting. Inside, it's first class.

The lobby, restaurant, and bar look out over the water with towering windows and a sleek, modern look. Rooms are the largest in town, and all face the water. They too feel natural, with washed-cement floors, cream walls, dark-wood furniture, and crisp white linens. Bathrooms are long and narrow, and all have small tubs with ocean views. There is also a spa. Their all-inclusive packages take care of everything: transfers, all meals, park entrance fees, guided excursions, and spa access. Since it just opened in 2006, Territorio remains to be proven dependable. But it is ambitious, comfortable, and very stylish, which is rare in these parts.

Blvd. Brown 3251, 9120 Puerto Madryn. ⓒ 2965/470050. www.atlasdelapatagonia.com.ar. 36 units. $328 (£180) double with breakfast only. 3-day all-inclusive packages start at $1,700 (£935) double. AE, MC, V. **Amenities:** Restaurant; bar; lounge; spa; business center; room service; laundry service. *In room:* A/C, TV, minibar, hair dryer, safe.

MODERATE

Hostería Solar de la Costa *(Finds)*   An oceanfront inn in an upscale neighborhood, the Hostería Solar de la Costa has a breezy feeling. Most of the rooms are doubles with king-size beds, tiny televisions, and clean, compact bathrooms. Rooms that face the ocean cost the same as those facing the garden, so reserve early to get the front ones. Top-floor rooms sleep four and have a fully equipped kitchen and a Jacuzzi. All rooms have air-conditioning. Breakfast includes home-baked breads, pastries, and pies. A big shady garden out back has a barbecue. Overall, this place has a friendly, relaxed feel.

Bvd. Brown 2057, 9120 Puerto Madryn. ⓒ 2965/458822. www.solardelacosta.com. 14 units. $95 (£52) double; $180 (£99) quadruple with kitchen. Rates include breakfast. AE, MC, V. **Amenities:** Laundry; family room; garden; Internet use. *In room:* TV.

Hotel Bahía Nueva (★★)   This is Puerto Madryn's best-kept traditional hotel. The staff is friendly and helpful, and they take great pride in maintaining a spick-and-span hotel. Rooms are pleasant, with wood furnishings and nice tiled baths. Four rooms have sea views; ask at check-in if one is available, and you'll be upgraded at no extra cost. Rooms are simple, with tiny televisions in the corner. Most have small windows. The full breakfast buffet may be the best in town, served in a cheerful dining room on the second floor. The buffet includes fresh fruit and eggs—a rarity in these parts. The ground-level bar area has a pool table and a lovely fireplace in the cozy lounge. The staff is knowledgeable about the area and can help arrange excursions. My main concern is that they have drastically raised their prices without any interior renovations or upgrades to accompany the increase. It is no longer a bargain.

Av. Roca 67, 9120 Puerto Madryn. ⓒ/fax 2965/451677. www.bahianueva.com.ar. 40 units. $129 (£71) double; $170 (£94) triple. Rates include excellent buffet breakfast. AE, MC, V. **Amenities:** Bar; lounge; game room; small business center w/free Internet; laundry service. *In room:* TV.

INEXPENSIVE

Hotel Gran Madryn (★)   Young managers with big plans recently took over this aging family-run hotel, which is still a deal. Get a taste of what is to come in the rooms along the newest wing or in the 11 new superior rooms on the top floor, which all have sea views. These are larger, with new furniture and new safes, and the corner units have Jacuzzi tubs. Bathrooms are bright and clean. The old rooms (there are about 20 left to remodel) have low beds, old fixtures, and simple linens. A half-block from the beach, the location is good. Service is upbeat.

Lugones 40, 9120 Puerto Madryn. ⓒ 2965/472205. www.hotelgranmadryn.com.ar. 43 units. Rates include breakfast. $40 (£22) double; $60 (£33) triple; $75 (£41) superior. AE, MC, V. **Amenities:** Room service; laundry; Internet. *In room:* TV.

> ## *Tips* Call Ahead
>
> Although reservations are not required anywhere in Puerto Madryn, you can usually score a better table and a warmer greeting if you call ahead. Even if you don't arrive exactly on time, the mere fact that your name is on a "list" gives you a bit more leeway with the waitstaff. If you see a table you like (by a window, for example) and you have a reservation, they are more likely to give it to you. If you plan to come around 9:30pm, you'll find most places packed. For earlier diners (7:30–8:30pm), you should have less of a problem.

Hotel Muelle Viejo *(Value* This is one of the best bargains in town. Having remodeled its rooms in late 2004, the Muelle Viejo is ready to take on challengers in the budget category. It has a port-hotel feel, more similar to a pension than an inn, drawing a mixture of sailors, visiting foreigners, and traveling salesmen. Half a block off the main drag, the location is ideal. Most of the rooms now have hardwood floors, small TVs, and brand-new fixtures in the bathrooms. The new bedcovers are blindingly white. A few rooms remain to be overhauled, but the owner insists that the work will be done by mid- to late summer 2007. Just to be sure, ask for a "special" room when you make your reservations, to ensure you land a remodeled one. The two older gentlemen who run the show are entertaining and friendly.

Hipolito Yrigoyen 38–42, 9120 Puerto Madryn. ©/fax 2965/471284. www.muelleviejo.com. 27 units. $38 (£21) double; $50 (£28) triple. MC, V. **Amenities:** Bar; lounge; laundry service. *In room:* TV.

WHERE TO DINE

Fish is big in Puerto Madryn. The fishermen go out into the bay every morning and reel in white salmon, cod, and sole. Meat is double the price here, compared to Buenos Aires, because everything has to be flown or trucked in.

If you are craving meat, the best place is where the locals go—the simple **Estella Parilla,** R. S. Pena 27 (© **2965/451573**). For $9 to $12 (£4.95–£6.60), you can have tenderloin or filet mignon and a salad. A variety of sausages is also available, as well as chicken on the grill. They're open Monday to Saturday from 8pm to midnight and Sunday from noon to 11pm.

MODERATE

Mar y Meseta *★★* SEAFOOD/INTERNATIONAL   This excellent seafood restaurant manages to be both upscale and relaxed, with a kids' menu. Service is top-notch, and the chef uses Patagonian ingredients whenever possible to create his masterpieces. Start with a bottle of cold Argentine sparkling wine and the chef's appetizer platter, consisting of steamed mussels, smoked mackerel, fried cod fingers, and pickled carrots and cauliflower. Move on to what may very well be the most creative dish in Puerto Madryn: fresh local cod baked with Patagonian honey, served on a bed of toasted cinnamon sticks and sweet-potato chips. Other seafood dishes include a mixed grill of seafood and fish for two people for $18 (£10), and a daily selection of fresh grilled fish filets (depending on the catch of the day). The seafood stew is a hearty meal on a cold evening. A good selection of Patagonian and Mendoza wines rounds out a meal here.

Av. Roca 485. © 2965/458740. Main courses $7–$12 (£3.85–£6.60). AE, MC, V. Daily 11am–3pm and 7pm–midnight.

Nativo Sur *&& &ds* REGIONAL/INTERNATIONAL   This is the best beachfront restaurant in town. A small playground for kids faces the pleasant patio area. The main dining room is very rustic, furnished in a purely Patagonian motif with dark local-wood tables and chairs. Even the plates are ceramic and made in Patagonia.

The large windows overlooking the bay give the entire place an airy and relaxed feel. The owners, a husband-and-wife team, work here every day to make sure that every ingredient used is of the highest quality. They buy fish daily from a local fisherman, and vegetables are trucked in fresh from a nearby farm. The focus here is fish—whatever is fresh (usually white salmon, sole, or cod), made to order. The fresh grilled calamari is tender and yummy. The best appetizer is a seafood sampler with calamari, scallops, oysters, prawns, and the like. I highly recommend fish of the day with stir-fried vegetables for $7.50 (£4.15). This place is wonderfully laid back, allowing for a long, leisurely dinner. Service is very friendly and unhurried.

Corner of Brown and Humphreys. © 2965/457403. Main courses $6–$11 (£3.30–£6.05). MC, V. Tues–Fri 8pm–midnight; Sat–Sun noon–3:30pm and 8pm–midnight.

Plácido *&* INTERNATIONAL   Puerto Madryn's fanciest restaurant has a great location in the center of town. An airy, expansive dining room with plenty of windows, large wine glasses, crisp white tablecloths, and heavy silverware set the stage for an elegant evening. Unfortunately, management has overzealously sought out foreign visitors, which has made the cuisine schizophrenic, at best. Paella, cod in hollandaise sauce, Patagonian lamb with rosemary, and shrimp in curry sauce with white rice are just a few of the many main courses available. The wine list is impressive, and service is very refined. If only the food could be simpler and more regional. Stick with simply prepared fresh fish or prawns or the good selection of homemade pastas, and you'll have a memorable meal. The vegetarian tagliattele with wild mushrooms, for example, is delicious. Call ahead and reserve a table by a window overlooking the bay.

Av. Roca 506. © 2965/455991. Reservations recommended. Main courses $7–$11 (£3.85–£6.05). AE, DC, MC, V. Daily noon–3pm and 8pm–midnight.

Taska Beltza *&* BASQUE/SEAFOOD   A local favorite, this spot is hip without being flashy. It's all about good food served in an atmosphere that's not trying to be something it isn't. Chefs garnish local fish and seafood with the classic Basque quartet of seasonings: garlic, lemon, butter, and parsley. Try blackened *merluza* (hake) with red-pepper sauce or *pejerrey* (mackerel). Shrimp with cognac and scallops on the half shell are also excellent. For dessert, don't miss the Beltzan apples. Service can be a bit slow, but it could just be that the staff is that relaxed.

9 de Julio 345. © 2965/474003. Main courses $6–$10 (£3.30–£5.50). AE, MC, V. Tues–Sun 7:30pm–midnight.

INEXPENSIVE

Ambigú *&* *Value* INTERNATIONAL   Elegant but very affordable, Ambigu has a huge menu with a mélange of dishes, ranging from chicken curry to beef chop suey and all kinds of pizzas. The most interesting is the asparagus and provolone pizza with black olives. There's also a limited selection of seafood and fish. It's a fun, boisterous, and informal place that is busy every night. Service can be spotty when they're swamped, but nobody's in a rush here. Order a bottle of Mendoza Malbec to go with your meal, then sit back and watch all the people walk by on the coastal Avenida Roca.

On the corner of Roca and Roque Saenz Pena. © 2965/472541. Main courses and pizzas $7–$12 (£3.85–£6.60). MC, V. Daily noon–2pm and 7:30pm–midnight.

WHAT TO SEE & DO

There's not much to see in Puerto Madryn itself, apart from a couple of museums. Most visitors are here because of the town's proximity to the Península Valdés. If you have time to kill, however, grab a bike or walk up the lovely beach road or stroll the shops along Roca.

Ecocentro 𝕽𝕽   The newest museum in the region is more like an interactive learning center, where you can educate yourself on the marine ecosystems of Atlantic Patagonia. I recommend coming to Ecocentro on your first day in Puerto Madryn, before heading out to the Península Valdés. The view of the ocean is exquisite from this lovely modern building, and the nautical and topographical maps afford deep insight into this region. A tank re-creates a tidal pool, where you can see species that inhabit the coastal areas. A soundtrack plays whale sounds, and a good movie about the Península Valdés explores the habits of Magellan penguins in Punta Tombo, as well as local elephant seals and sea lions. Ask for the English-language handbook to get even more out of your visit. You'll need about 2 hours to visit Ecocentro. A very pleasant on-site cafe serves snacks.

Julio Verne 3784. ℂ **2965/457470.** www.ecocentro.org.ar. Admission $6 (£3.30). Sept to mid-Dec daily 10am–7pm; mid-Dec to mid-Feb daily 5–9pm; call to confirm hours during the rest of the year.

Oceanographic and Natural Sciences Museum   This downtown museum is inside a recently renovated historical home, custom-built to have an excellent view of the comings and goings in the port. Presentations touch on a wide range of subjects— geology, human history, flora and fauna, and oceanography, each in a separate room off a winding stairway. I like that the museum blends marine sciences with the natural history of the Patagonian Steppe, since things in Madryn are so focused on the sea. It is almost exclusively in Spanish but still worth a visit, even if you are touring the area independently without a local tour guide to keep you fully informed.

Domecq García and Menéndez. ℂ **2965/451129.** Admission $2 (£1.10). Mon–Fri 9am–1pm and 3–7pm; Sat–Sun 3–7pm.

PUNTA TOMBO NATIONAL RESERVE

Most visitors spend a day on the Península Valdés and then a day at Punta Tombo National Reserve, the second most visited attraction in Atlantic Patagonia. The largest sanctuary for Magellan penguins, Punta Tombo is 248km (154 miles) south of Puerto Madryn, a 2-hour trip. Every year from September to April (the park is closed May–Aug), up to a million of these penguins return to Punta Tombo to mate. Visitors

---

Tips **Getting to the Ecocentro**

There are four ways to get to the Ecocentro, which is 3km (1¾ miles) south of the center of town. The fastest is by taxi, which will cost around $3 (£1.65). If you have an hour or so, and it's a nice day, walk down the coast to the south, just over the point on the horizon to the museum. Or rent a bike and pedal for about 30 minutes in the same direction. For about 50¢ (30p), you can take the local bus 2 from downtown. It will drop you off just down the hill from the Ecocentro. En route, you'll also pass the Punta Cuevas historical monument to the Welsh settlers as well as the Tehuelche Monument to the area's original inhabitants.

are able to walk just a few feet away from hundreds and thousands of penguins guarding their nests. Baby penguins are visible in December and January. Bird lovers will enjoy views of king and rock cormorants, giant petrels, kelp gulls, and oystercatchers as well.

The drive from Puerto Madryn is on a highway until you pass Trelew; then you head south on RP 1, a monotonous gravel road that seems to go on forever. The entrance to the national reserve is clearly marked, and the entrance fee is $7 (£3.85). Be sure to observe all the posted signs (stopping your car is strictly prohibited except in the designated parking lots). Walkways and handrails point you in the right direction as you explore. Veering off the trail is prohibited, as is going down to the beach. There is a cafeteria at Punta Tombo, but consider bringing a picnic instead. You'll need about 2 hours to visit the reserve and observe the penguins.

TOUR OPERATORS

Puerto Madryn's coastal street, Avenida Roca, is lined with travel agencies. Shop around for a space if you are booking at the last minute. We highly recommend asking for a bilingual guide. Almost all quote the same price for standard tours such as the 1-day Península Valdés or Punta Tomba tours, most of which start at 7:30am (depending on whether you are staying in Trelew or Puerto Madryn) and get you back before dinner. One-day tours of the Península Valdés start at $30 (£17) per person, not including the whale-watching trip (an additional $20/£11) or lunch.

If you have a group of six or more, it is worth while—and surely more relaxing—to take a private tour for the same price, rather than signing up for a standard group tour.

Flamenco Tour, Av. Roca 331 (© **2965/455505;** www.flamencotour.com), is perhaps the largest tour operator in the area. The 1-day guided tour to the Península Valdés lasts from 7:30am to 7pm and includes a stop at the museum, a chance to go on a whale-watching cruise, and guided walks on the Punta Delgada beach and Caleta Valdés, to view the elephant seals.

Huinca Travel, Av. Roca 353 (© **2965/450720;** www.huincatravel.com), has traditional tours in small groups as well as active options, including a nighttime whale-watching tour and mountain biking on the Península Valdés. **NieveMar Tours** *F*, Av. Roca 493 (© **2965/455544;** www.nievemartours.com.ar), has very friendly and knowledgeable guides. They offer the standard Península Valdés tour with a long lunch break, to stretch your legs, at Caleta Valdés; a full day at Punta Tombo; and a 6-hour trip to discover the Welsh heritage of Gaiman. They can also set up multiday tours that include accommodations.

OUTDOOR ACTIVITIES

BIKING   **Huellas y Costas,** Bvd. Brown 860 (© **2965/1568-0515;** www.huellasy costas.com), has guided mountain-biking tours that last from a few hours to 3 days. For short-term bike rentals, try **El Retorno,** Mitre 798 (© **2965/456044**). A 1-day bike rental will cost $10 (£5.50).

DIVING   Most of the diving companies here offer the same tours for the same price. It's a question of whose schedules you like. All have been licensed and have high safety standards. The main draw is swimming with the sea lions and elephant seals, and some also arrange for diving close to the whales. **Aquatours,** Av. Roca 550 (© **2965/ 451954**), offers a variety of diving trips in the bay off Puerto Madryn and also off the Península Valdés.

FISHING   Call **Raúl Díaz** (© **2965/450812**), a seasoned fisherman who will be happy to take visitors out with him on a fishing trip.

GOLF   The **Puerto Madryn Golf Club** (http://golf.madryn.com) is on Ruta 4, on the road to the airport. Call the club manager, Juan González (© **2965/1553-0110**), to arrange your tee times and get detailed information on the rates.

HORSEBACK RIDING   For rides between 2 and 4 hours in the Steppe above Madryn and along the coast, try **GH Cabalgatas** (© **2965/1566-1315**).

KAYAKING   **Huellas y Costas,** Bulevar Brown 860 (© **2965/1568-0515;** www.huellasycostas.com) runs regular sea-kayaking outings from late December through March.

WINDSURFING   You can rent a windsurf board and sail from the **Vernardino Club Mar,** Bulevar Brown 860 (© **2965/455-633**).

PUERTO MADRYN AFTER DARK

This town is very subdued at night. Because most visitors rise at the crack of dawn to head to the Península Valdés, Puerto Madryn shuts down early. The best place for a late-night drink (and light snacks such as pizza and hamburgers for $3–$5/£1.65–£2.75, served until 1am) is **Margarita Pub,** R.S. Peña 15 (© **2965/450454;** daily 5pm–3am; no credit cards), an attractive wood-and-tile lounge with a large bar. All the locals who work as guides during the day come here on weekends—this place is hopping from midnight to 3am on Friday and Saturday. For pool tables and live music, head to **Takos,** P. Escardo 171 (© **2965/1540-1665**).

On summer nights, lots of folk hang out on the beach, at the oceanside **Disco Rancho Cucamonga,** Bulevar Brown and Jenkins (no phone). Downtown, the coolest disco is **Disco La Frontera,** 9 de Julio 254 (no phone).

2 Península Valdés

Most visitors to the peninsula come for the day on guided excursions, aboard small nine-passenger vans. There is enough here, however, to keep you busy for 4 days. If you choose to drive on your own in a rental car, remember that the peninsula is very isolated and barren, and the only gas station is in Puerto Pirámides. Sometimes you can go for hours without seeing another soul. All roads on the peninsula are gravel, and driving is hazardous. Consider renting a 4WD truck for more comfort.

Península Valdés is not a national park but a Natural Protected Area managed by the Province of Chubut. Within its protected borders, families continue to run the ranches that they have managed for more than a century, although some are now turning to tourism. Human activity is restricted, and although tourism is now the major player, the balance game between conservation and recreation is monitored closely.

At the park gates, foreign visitors have to stop and pay an entrance fee of $12 (£6.60) per person (it's good for the length of your stay in the park, be that an afternoon or 3 days). Just past the entrance to the national park (which is about a half-hour's drive northeast of Puerto Madryn), the new **Interpretive Center** makes a good consolation prize if you don't have time for the excellent Ecocentro museum in Puerto Madryn (see above). The Interpretive Center is open from 8am to 8pm daily. Admission is free. The museum shows the history of the Península Valdés, with some good maps and bones and skulls of Tehuelches aboriginals. There's also a huge skeleton of

---

Tips When to Visit

Timing is critical when you're visiting the Península Valdés. If you want to see penguins, forget about coming here between May and August. If you're hoping to watch whales, don't come between mid-December and April. All things considered, the ideal time to visit Atlantic Patagonia is in October or November. The penguins have laid their eggs and are guarding their nests, the whales are happily swimming in the bays with their offspring, and schools in Argentina are still in session, so crowds are thin.

---

a whale and an interesting collection of stuffed animals—a guanaco and a Patagonian fox. The lookout tower is worth a stop.

From the park entrance, after driving east for about an hour on Ruta 2, you'll reach the tiny village of Puerto Pirámides (pop. 202), which is only 2 blocks wide. This is the main launching spot for the whale-watching boats that depart from this area from April to late December. Whale-watching trips cost $20 (£11) per person and last about 1½ hours.

The rest of the year, warmer weather transforms Puerto Pirámides into more of a beach town, with snorkelers, kayakers, and swimmers playing on the wide, sandy beach. It's popular with vacationing Argentines on their summer holidays. The town has a funky, laid-back vibe, with a few small shops and a handful of good restaurants.

The Southern Right Whales that swim past here once verged on extinction (they earned their name because they move slowly and float easily, making them "right" for hunters). Today, these gentle giants gather to mate in these bays just off the peninsula from April to December. They each weigh 35 to 40 tons and measure about 17m (56 ft.) long. About 800 whales show up each year, after feeding in Antarctica for 3 months. Whale-watching trips almost always bring visitors within meters of these very social whales. It's a rare and moving experience.

From Puerto Pirámides, if you continue east on RP 2, you'll reach **Punta Delgada,** a stretch of beach favored by elephant seals from mid-June to late December. You can stop for lunch at the upscale Faro Punta Delgada Hotel (see below) and also take a tour of the light house.

Heading north on RP 47 will bring you to **Caleta Valdés,** which has a cafeteria on the bluff overlooking the ocean. This is where most visitors on excursions eat lunch, so it is very busy from 1 to 3pm. The stairs leading down to the beach take you to another stretch of sand covered by elephant seals, who are usually sleeping. Pleasant interpretive walks with placards explain the natural history of the area, with beautiful views of the Atlantic Coast.

At the northeastern tip of the peninsula is Punta Norte, where hundreds of sea lions congregate from January to June. Orcas can sometimes be seen off this point too, attracted by the sea lions—their favorite snack. Count yourself very lucky if you manage to see the orcas hunting baby sea lions during dramatic high-tide attacks. Just to the west of Punta Norte is **Estancia San Lorenzo** (© **2965/458-444**), which welcomes a colony of up to 200,000 Magellan penguins each year from August to April. Tours are expensive ($35/£19 per person) but worthwhile, because you get to see penguins up close in a very quiet setting. Come early in the morning if possible.

Because the peninsula is barren and dry, you'll be able to spot guanacos; reminiscent of small llamas, they're found only in Patagonia. Because they are so shy, however, they usually run in the opposite direction when they see a car coming. Also keep an eye out for *choiques* (ostrichlike birds); the strange-looking *mara,* which is a rabbit that runs on four-legs like a dog; and lots of sheep. In the middle of the peninsula, three giant salt-flats appear like mirages on the horizon.

In one day, it's possible to quickly sample the area and spot some whales, sea lions, elephant seals, and guanacos. You will spend the bulk of the day in the tour operator's van, however, especially if you are staying in Trelew. Wildlife lovers should plan to spend 2 or 3 days exploring the peninsula. For more information and good interactive online maps, visit **www.peninsulavaldes.org.ar**.

WHERE TO STAY & DINE

The peninsula has a handful of new upscale lodging options—namely ranches or lighthouses that have opened their doors to the public over the past 5 years or so. Most are expensive and offer packages that include all meals and daily activities. They're a relaxing way to really live the wonders of Península Valdés, to see the wildlife in silence, and to get away from it all. I recommend you spend at least 2 nights in any of the following places. Highly recommended, **Estancia La Elvira** (② 2065/474248; www.laelvira.com.ar) is inland, at the working heart of a ranch, which also runs a restaurant overlooking Caleta Valdés. The ranch house has eight large rooms that start at $150 (£83) with breakfast or $270 (£149) for full board. You don't get the coastal views or the ocean breezes here, but you will delight in excellent service and a charming rural facility. At the tiny and elegant **Rincón Chico** (② 2965/471733; www.rinconchico.com.ar; all-inclusive doubles at $275/£151 per night), an eight-room beach house is open to the public. The most visitor-friendly is the **Faro Punta Delgada Country Hotel** ★★ (② 2965/458444; www.puntadelgada.com; all-inclusive doubles at $250/£138 per night), inside a refurbished government lighthouse facility. The setting is beautifully windswept, and the rugged outdoor setting is balanced by the charming staff and nice amenities inside the hotel. Rooms are cozy and country-styled, with blue-gingham bedspreads and simple bathrooms. Guests can explore the lighthouse, which brings a sense of romance to dark evenings, or the many nearby trails that lead to deserted beaches on their own. The bar is a great place to gather and share stories with other travelers in the evening. The restaurant is packed with tourists during the day, but it's much more intimate for breakfast and dinner.

Kayak Expedition: Up Close & Personal with Wildlife

Overnight kayaking is strictly controlled in the Península Valdés area and subject to constant bureaucratic adjustments. Right now, only a handful of operators are licensed to travel the area by sea kayak, and only with very small groups. The best trip is operated by **Whitney and Smith Legendary Expeditions** (② 800/713-6660; www.legendaryex.com), a Canadian company that has been kayaking in the Valdés area for 12 years. Their fully guided 10-day kayaking and camping trip explores the area by sea and land, and includes a night at the Faro Punta Delgada. It's an incredibly special expedition open to people who love camping, who come with a sense of adventure.

3 Puerto Pirámides

100km (62 miles) NE of Puerto Madryn

The only village inside the Península Valdés National Park, Puerto Pirámides is tiny—about 4 blocks. Once a bustling salt-exporting port, today it's a quiet village. It's the sole launching point for the many whale-watching trips that depart from here, from April to late December. During the day, the beach is mobbed with day-trippers, but it's a much more intimate experience in the evening. Some travelers choose to stay here overnight instead of in Puerto Madryn (see above), especially if they have their own transportation. You can venture to other parts of the park much more quickly from here, and you can have the stretch of beach all to yourself in the evening, once the tourists have left. The helpful staff at the **Tourist Information Center** (at the end of the first street; © **2965/495048;** www.puertopiramides.gov.ar) can help you plan your excursions. There is no fresh water here—saltwater is just barely treated before hitting your taps—so you must make an effort to conserve water and drink only bottled water.

ESSENTIALS
GETTING THERE
See "Getting There" under "Puerto Madryn," earlier in this chapter.

BY CAR   You can rent a car in Puerto Madryn or in Trelew. From Puerto Madryn, the trip is 100km (62 miles) and takes about 1½ hours. There's only one road here: Ruta 2.

BY BUS   Daily buses depart Puerto Madryn's terminal at 9:30am and return at 6pm. Contact **Mar y Valle** (© **2965/472065**). The cost is $3.50 (£1.95) each way.

A taxi or *remise* from Puerto Madryn should cost no more than $75 (£41); from Trelew, the cost is $110 (£61).

WHAT TO SEE & DO
See also "Península Valdés," above.

Since Puerto Pirámides is the only town on the peninsula, it's entirely tourist- oriented and, therefore, very expensive. The only gas station on the peninsula is here. Whale-watching tours depart from here, so it is a stopover point for people who are visiting the park. Diving trips also leave from here, and the few hotels are frequently filled with groups of divers from Europe. From late December to late March, when the whales leave the bay, it's possible to kayak and swim, and the area becomes a destination for beach-seeking Argentine vacationers. But the main draw is the whale-watching trips. The cost is about $20 (£11) per person, but if you're staying overnight, I encourage you to bargain with Captain Pinino (see below) to arrange your own excursion. Staying here also gives you best access to the sunset whale-watching trips, which are beautiful. Sometimes you can even hear the whales at night from your room. A few nights here will leave you relaxed and in touch with nature.

Captain Pinino at **Whales Argentina** (★★ (© **2965/495015;** www.whalesargentina.com.ar) has the newest boat around, and he is fun and very experienced. There's usually a group whale-watching trip at around 10:30am daily, but he can arrange private trips later in the day as well.

For kayaking (in the summer), try either **Hydrosport** (© **2965/495065**) or **Moby Dick** (© **2965/495122**). Even if you've never dived before, **Patagonia Scuba**

(© **2965/495030**) will take you out for a first dive, and will take more seasoned divers for night and deep dives. Sand boarding is becoming popular on a hillside overlooking the town, and you can inquire here for sand boards (much like snow boards). Mountain bikes are also available. Ask at the Tourist Information Center (see above).

WHERE TO STAY

Choices are limited in Puerto Pirámides, and prices are very high. There are a handful of private campgrounds in town, but you'll need a tent. Camping is prohibited elsewhere in the peninsula. For other alternatives, see "Where to Stay & Dine" in the Península Valdés section. Rates listed here are for high season, September through March.

Las Restringas   The best and most expensive hotel in the region has 12 rooms, 8 of which are oceanfront with fantastic views. If you're lucky, you might even spot a whale from your private patio. The modern two-story structure, under new management since 2005 and formerly known as Patagonia Franca, is reminiscent of Laguna Beach or La Jolla. The airy lobby and adjacent dining room, with its exposed stone, are pleasant, with an understated elegance. Rooms have tiled floors, wooden beds, wrought-iron lamps, ceiling fans, and sliding French doors that overlook the ocean or the village. Rooms have TVs, but no cable; instead you can borrow movies on DVD. I highly recommend splurging for the sea view; the other rooms are darker and less cheery. Marble bathrooms have bathtubs. The friendly front-desk staff can arrange your excursions and help with transportation. The hotel has one computer with an Internet connection available for guests' use. The on-site restaurant is the best in town, with a daily selection of fresh fish.

1st right as you enter the village, Puerto Pirámides. © **2965/495101**. www.lasrestringas.com. 12 units. $183–$240 (£101–£132) double; $214–$281 (£118–£155) in Nov. Rates include breakfast and either lunch or dinner. AE, MC, V. **Amenities:** Restaurant; bar; tour desk; room service; laundry service. *In room:* TV w/DVD, minibar, hair dryer.

The Paradise Hostería ⟡   A large brick building midway up the hill, the Paradise is friendly and fun. Most of the rooms are basic, with clean and simple white bathrooms, bright bedspreads, ceramic floors, and overhead fans. It is surrounded by a lush green garden. Their two suites are not cheap, but they are probably the best rooms in town, with lovely sea views and large Jacuzzis, which is somewhat gluttonous in a town that has hardly any water access. Staff members are relaxed and helpful and treat guests like family. The restaurant, full of seafaring knickknacks, is popular with locals and has a large menu. Most evenings, it's the liveliest place in town.

2nd right as you enter the village. © **2965/495030**. www.puerto-piramades.com.ar. 12 units. $180 (£99) double; $270 (£149) suite with Jacuzzi and sea view. Rates include breakfast. AE, MC, V. **Amenities:** Restaurant; laundry service; patio.

WHERE TO DINE

Las Restingas (see above) has the best restaurant in the village.

El Refugio ⟡   The owner of this quirky restaurant-bar is a fisherman, so you can be assured that what you're eating is fresh from local waters. Ask what he found that day, and order it. The small dining room, filled with antiques, has a very cozy feel to it. Just behind the restaurant are two snug cabins for rent, at $65 (£36) for a double; they each have tiny kitchenettes, a small but clean bathroom, and a double bed.

Puerto Pirámides. © **2965/495031**. Main courses $5–$9 (£2.75–£4.95). No credit cards. Daily noon–11pm.

La Estación ⊛ This place is a great choice for lunch on a warm day, with a very pleasant patio outside a building with a historic feel. Fresh seafood is the focus, but they also have homemade pastas, salads, and some grilled meats. Note that the restaurant is closed the last week in December.

Puerto Pirámides. © 2965/495047. Main courses $5–$10 (£2.75–£5.50). No credit cards. Daily 10am–11pm.

4 Trelew

67km (42 miles) S of Puerto Madryn

Trelew's airport is the gateway to the region; many travelers pass through here on their way to and from the Península Valdés. The largest city in the region (pop. 100,000), Trelew is industrial and certainly not as charming at its neighbor Puerto Madryn. The town has a pleasant square and an excellent paleontological museum, but little else of interest. The nearby Welsh town, Gaiman, is worth an afternoon visit.

ESSENTIALS
GETTING THERE
Aerolíneas Argentinas (© 0810/222-5627) is the sole operator at **Almirante Zar** airport, 5km (3 miles) from the city center. They fly at least twice daily from Buenos Aires, with extra flights on weekends. Aerolíneas also has several weekly flights from El Calafate and Ushuaia. **28 de Julio** buses (© 2965/472056) arrive every hour from Puerto Madryn at the OmniBus Station, located at 100 Urquiza (© 2965/420121). The cost is $3 (£1.65) one-way. Buses from Buenos Aires take 20 hours and cost $70 (£39) one-way.

VISITOR INFORMATION The tourist office is on the Plaza San Martín, at 387 Mitre (© 2965/420139; www.trelew.gov.ar). The English-speaking agents are very helpful and have lots of maps and information about the Península Valdés and the region. The office is open from 8am to 8pm daily.

GETTING AROUND
A taxi or *remise* from the airport to the city center will cost no more than $3.50 (£1.95). From Puerto Madryn to Trelew, a taxi or *remise* will cost no more than $30 (£17). A taxi from Puerto Pirámides is $105 (£58).

　　Fiorasi Rent-A-Car has offices at the airport and at Urquiza 31 (© 2965/435344) in the city center. **Hertz** has an office only at the airport (© 2965/436-005). The average cost for a compact car is $50 (£28) per day.

WHAT TO SEE & DO
There's not much to see here except for one museum, but if you have a bit of extra time, you may want to take a walk around the pleasant San Martín square.

MEF, Museo Paleontológico Egidio Feruglio (Paleontological Museum Edigio Feruglio)
The MEF, as it is widely known, is one of the best paleontological museums in South America, a must for dinosaur fans. Opened in 2000, it houses an amazing collection of fossils and dinosaur bones. Inside the museum (and visible when you visit) is a working lab where a team of scientists studies and cleans fossils. Try to come here during the week when the scientists are at work (Mon–Fri), and you'll get a sense of how much they do to study just one fossil. An amazing skeleton of a titonausaur, which walked on this land 70 million years ago, fills one room. Other rooms take you

through a chronological order of dinosaur discoveries over the years, from past to present. There's also a good movie with English subtitles showing sea fossils found in Patagonia. You'll need about 1½ hours to visit the museum. The lobby houses a gift shop and a snack bar.

Av. Fontana 140. (℃ 2965/420012. Admission $5 (£2.75). Daily 10am–6pm.

WHERE TO STAY & DINE

The best and most centrally located hotel is **The Rayentray,** San Martín 101 (℃ 2965/434702; www.cadenarayentray.com.ar), just steps from the main plaza. The modern building has 110 rooms that are comfortable but neither luxurious nor elegant, and some complain it is too noisy. There's a small indoor pool, massages available, a restaurant, and a bar. Each of the rooms has a cable TV. The staff is friendly. American Express, MasterCard, and Visa are accepted. The cost is $48 to $60 (£26–£33) for a double.

Up the hill from the main plaza is the older but slightly grander **Hotel Libertador,** Rivadavia 31 (℃ 2965/420220; www.hotellibertadortw.com.ar). The aging rooms with very 1970s mustard-colored drapes and bedcovers have a tiny bit of charm, but not that much; superior rooms are slightly brighter, with off-white curtains and bedcovers. The small bathrooms are clean but in desperate need of a remodel. This is another old-fashioned, family-run establishment that seems to be stuck in time. Doubles are $58 to $65 (£32–£36). MasterCard and Visa are accepted.

The best *parrilla* in town is **El Viejo Molino,** Av. Gales 250 (℃ 2965/428019). In a heritage building, the wood-fired grill offers up classics of sausages, beef, chicken, and lamb. They also serve grilled vegetables and interesting pastas. Main courses cost $6 to $12 (£3.30–£6.60). No credit cards are accepted. They are open from noon to 3pm and from 8 to 11:30pm Tuesday through Sunday.

5 Gaiman

17 km (10 miles) W of Trelew

Just a 10-minute drive west of Trelew, you'll find the lush, green town of Gaiman, settled in 1870 by immigrants from Wales. It's a pleasant place to take a walk and to admire the very English-looking houses. Almost every house in this town of 4,500 residents is open to the public in some way, as a teahouse, a small inn, or some other type of hospitality center. People in Gaiman—many of them descendents of the original families such as the Joneses and Roberts—are both exceedingly friendly and proud. They cling to their unique heritage with the same sense of purpose that brought their ancestors all the way here more than 130 years ago. Gaiman is also known for its singing choirs that blend traditional Welsh tunes with Argentine folk music. Each October, the town hosts the Eisteddfod music and poetry festival, which draws people from Wales and other Welsh communities around the world. Some of the choirs perform at the teahouses (see below).

ESSENTIALS
GETTING THERE

From Trelew, buses such as 28 de Julio (℃ 2965/472056) depart regularly for Gaiman from Plaza Roca. Fewer buses run on the weekends. The trip is about 25 minutes and costs about $3 (£1.65). A *remise* from Trelew to Gaiman should cost around $12 (£6.60). If you are driving, take RN 25 west from Trelew.

High Tea in Gaiman

Most visitors come to Gaiman to have real Welsh tea, a tradition that was built on the difficult life of the early settlers, who came home in the afternoons and found solace in a cup of warm brew sent specially to these outposts from the United Kingdom. The tradition lives on, and it's now shared with the public: The late Princess Diana herself enjoyed tea here in 1995 when she made an official visit. The chair she sat on is displayed inside a lovely house that has become one of the best teahouses in Gaiman: **Ty Te Caerdydd,** Finca 202; (© **2965/491510**), serves Welsh tea complete with sandwiches, scones, homemade jams, cakes, and lemon pie every day from 2 to 8pm. The cost is $8 (£4.40) per person. **Ty Nain,** Yrigoyen 283 (© **2965/491126**) will fill you up with *torta galesa* (Welsh cake) and a bottomless pot of tea, also for $8 (£4.40).The lovely 1890 home is sparkling clean and has a small museum of Welsh-Argentine history out back. Note that the Gaiman tea experience is popular with bus tours; if you are on your own, look for a spot that doesn't have a bus parked out front if you want some personal attention.

WHAT TO SEE & DO

The Welsh museum, **Museo Histórico Regional Gales,** at the corner of Rivadavia and Sarmiento streets (no phone), is an interesting place to get the lowdown on the town and its origins. The Welsh immigrants built the Chubut railway, and the museum is housed in the old railway station. It contains some interesting documents and relics from the late 1800s and early 1900s. Admission is $1 (55p).

If you are keen on continuing to explore the Welsh scene, take a side trip to the nearby village of **Dolavan,** 18km (11 miles) west of Gaiman via RN 25. It's an authentic little farming village, with wooden waterwheels and a historic town center with old brick buildings, including the old mill known here as the **Molino Harinero,** Maipú 61 (© **2965/492290**). Built in 1880, it still operates, has a small cafe serving hearty sandwiches, and opens sporadically for guided tours. The little brick chapel, built in 1917, is typical of the Welsh architecture that blends so naturally with the environment. It's one of a handful of similar constructions that dot the countryside of the Chubut River valley.

WHERE TO STAY

Many of the small teahouses (see above) have a room or two available for rent. They are generally spanking clean. Try the friendly **Hostería Gwesty Tywi,** Jones 342 (© **2965/491292;** from $25/£14 double). The most charming place to stay near Gaiman is the rural **Posada los Mimbres,** Chacra 211, Gaiman (© **2965/491299;** www.posadalosmimbres.com.ar), which is housed on a sprawling farm 6 km (4 miles) from town. There is an old house, built more than 100 years ago, and a new one that is much brighter; both have three doubles that cost $135 (£74) with breakfast included.

6 El Calafate ★★

222km (138 miles) S of El Chaltén; 2,727km (1,691 miles) SW of Buenos Aires

El Calafate is a tourist-oriented town that has seen phenomenal growth in the past 5 years. It's best known for being the base from which to see the spectacular Perito Moreno Glacier. The town hugs the shore of turquoise Lago Argentino, and this location, combined with the town's leafy streets, gives it the feel of an oasis in the desert Steppe. The town's population has grown from 5,000 in 1996 to 20,000 in 2006, and it's heavily dependent on its neighboring natural wonder, Perito Moreno Glacier, as well as the nine daily flights that arrive at the El Calafate International Airport packed with foreign and national tourists. Thousands of visitors come for the chance to stand face to face with this tremendous wall of ice, which is one of the few glaciers in the ice field that isn't retreating (scientists say it is "in balance," meaning it shrinks and grows constantly).

The town was named for the *calafate* bush found throughout Patagonia, which produces a sweet berry commonly used in syrups, ice creams, and jams. As the economy in Buenos Aires deteriorated, following the country's financial collapse in 2001, many Argentines fled to the countryside as well as here, to El Calafate, which had suffered from a tourist-trap mentality for years. Thankfully, this tendency has evolved for the best, as more migrants head south, out of town, to set up efficient and creative businesses meant to serve visitors. The town itself is quite a pleasant little place, but you won't find many attractions here—they are almost all within the confines of Los Glaciares National Park. What you will find, however, are several good restaurants and a charming main street lined with boutiques boasting fine leather goods and shops selling locally manufactured chocolates, jams, and delicious caramel cookies called *alfajores*.

FAST FACTS: El Calafate

ATMs There are only a few ATMs around town. **Banco de la Nación,** Libertador 1133 (*©* **02902/429536**), and **Banco Provincia de Santa Cruz,** Libertador 1285 (*©* **02902/492320**), are the most conveniently located. *Note:* At press time, there was no ATM in El Chaltén. If you're headed there, be sure to withdraw extra dosh in El Calafate.

Currency Exchange The Casa de Cambio Thaler is at 9 de Julio 57 (*©* **02902/ 493245**).

Emergency Dial *©* **101** or 451449 for police; *©* **100** for fire.

Hospital The **Hospital Districtal José Formenti** is at Av. Julio A. Roca 1487 (*©* **02902/491001**).

Internet You'll find many Internet cafes around town. All have fast connections at about $1 (55p) per hour. Try **El Calafate Cyber,** 25 de Mayo 23 (*©* **02902/ 492706**), or the **Cooperativa Telefónica,** Cte. Espora 194 (*©* **02902/491000**), which has the fastest connections, at under $1 (55p) per hour. They are open Monday to Saturday from 8am to midnight, and Sunday from 9am to midnight.

Laundry **El Lavadero** is at 25 de Mayo 43 (© **2965/492182**) and **Lava Andino** is at Cte Espora 88 (© **2965/493980**).

Pharmacy **Farmacia Del Cerro** is at Libertador 1337 (© **02902/491496**).

Post Office The main post office for **Correo Argentino** (the official name of the Argentine postal service) is located at Libertador 1133 (© **02902/491012**).

Taxi There are a number of taxi or *remise* agencies in El Calafate. A good one is **Lago Argentino,** which has an office at the corner of Libertador and 15 de Febrero (© **2962/491479**).

ESSENTIALS
GETTING THERE
BY PLANE   El Calafate's **Aeropuerto Lago Argentino** (© **02902/491220**) is a modern complex that was built in 2000. It's already proving to be too small, though, for the increasing traffic. Service is from Argentine destinations only: **Aerolíneas Argentinas/Austral** (© **11/4340-3777** in Buenos Aires; www.aerolineas.com.ar) has daily flights from Buenos Aires and flights from Bariloche, Trelew, and Ushuaia several times a week. A daily 747 flight also arrives directly from Ezeiza International Airport in Buenos Aires during high season (all flights used to leave from Aeroparque, downtown, and you would have to change airports). Be sure to specify which airport you'd like to fly from. **LAN Argentina** (© **0810/999-9526;** www.lan.com) has recently opened up three flights per week from Buenos Aires, and it's planning to offer more in the future. **LADE** (**Líneas Areas del Estado;** © **0810/810-5233;** www.lade.com.ar) has a weekly flight from Buenos Aires and weekly connection to Puerto Madryn, Ushuaia, and Bariloche.

The airport is 23km (14 miles) from the center of town, which seems like a long way in the wide openness of Patagonia. From the airport, **Aerobús** (© **02902/492492**) operates a bus to all the hotels in town for $4 (£2.20); they can also pick you up for your return trip if you call 24 hours ahead. A taxi into town should cost no more than $9 (£4.95) for up to four people. There's also a Hertz Rental Car desk (© **02902/492525;** www.hertz.com) at the airport. Please note that on the exit from this airport, all travelers are required to pay an airport exit tax of $18 (£10).

BY BUS   El Calafate has a bus terminal on Julio A. Roca, reached via the stairs up from the main street, Avenida del Libertador. To and from Puerto Natales, Chile: **Turismo Zaahj** (© **02902/491631**) has six weekly trips leaving at 1pm. **Cootra** (© **02902/491144**) leaves at 8am. The trip takes 5 to 6 hours, depending on how long it takes to get through border crossing procedures. To get to El Chaltén, three operators have departures at 6am, 1pm, and 6pm. The best is **Chaltén Travel** (© **02902/491833**); also try **Caltur** (© **02902/491842**); or **Interlagos Turismo** (© **02902/491179**). The trip takes approximately 4 hours, but travel time should diminish shortly, once the pavement project on the road between the two towns is complete in 2007. Buy all bus tickets the day before, at least, to ensure you'll get a seat.

BY CAR   Ruta 5, followed by Ruta 11, is paved entirely from Río Gallegos to El Calafate. From Puerto Natales, cross through the border at Cerro Castillo, which will lead you to the famous RN 40 and up to the paved portion of Ruta 11. The drive from Puerto Natales is roughly 5 hours, not including time spent at the border checkpoint.

Southern Patagonia

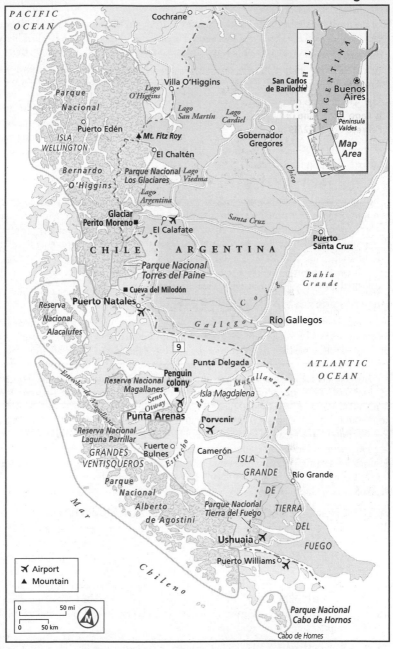

PACIFIC
OCEAN

Cochrane

Parque
Nacional

Puerto Edén

ISLA
WELLINGTON

Bernardo
O'Higgins

Lago
O'Higgins

Villa O'Higgins

Lago
San Martín

Lago
Cardiel

▲ Mt. Fitz Roy

El Chaltén

Parque Nacional Lago
Los Glaciares   Viedma

Lago
Argentina

Glaciar
Perito Moreno ■

El Calafate ✕✈

CHILE

ARGENTINA

Santa Cruz

Gobernador
Gregores

Chico

San Carlos
de Bariloche

Buenos
Aires

CHILE

ARGENTINA

Peninsula
Valdes

Map
Area

Puerto
Santa Cruz

Parque Nacional
Torres del Paine

■ Cueva del Milodón

Reserva
Nacional
Alacalufes

Puerto Natales ○
✈

9

Bahía
Grande

Coig

Gallegos

Río Gallegos

Punta Delgada

ATLANTIC
OCEAN

Reserva Nacional
Magallanes

Penguin
colony ■

Estrecho de Magallanes

Seno
Otway

Punta Arenas ○
✈

Reserva Nacional
Laguna Parrillar

GRANDES
VENTISQUEROS

Parque
Nacional

Alberto
de Agostini

Fuerte ○
Bulnes

Estrecho

de Magallanes

Isla Magdalena

Porvenir ○
✈

Camerón ○

ISLA
GRANDE

DE

Parque Nacional
Tierra del Fuego

TIERRA

Río Grande ○

DEL

Mar

Chileno

Ushuaia ○ ✈

Puerto Williams ○ ✈

FUEGO

Parque Nacional
Cabo de Hornos

Cabo de Hornes

✕ Airport
▲ Mountain

0   50 mi
0   50 km

N

GETTING AROUND

For information about transportation to and from Perito Moreno Glacier, see "Parque Nacional Los Glaciares & Perito Moreno Glacier," later in this chapter. If you'd like to rent a car, you can do so at the **Europcar** office, at Av. del Libertador 1741 (© **02902/ 493606;** www.europcar.com.ar). Rates begin at $50 (£28) per day, including insurance and taxes. There's a brand-new **Hertz** rental car desk (© **02902/492525;** www. hertz.com) at the airport as well. Rental cars may be of interest if you're in a group of four people, and want to cover longer distances of 4 hours or more, including the drive to El Chaltén or Torres del Paine National Park in Chile. Most roads here are unpaved. Most of the town can be explored on foot, although many new hotels are either up a good-size hill or well out of town, so make sure your hotel offers a shuttle. Taxis in El Calafate are reasonably priced.

VISITOR INFORMATION

The city's **visitor information kiosk** is inside the bus terminal. They offer an ample amount of printed material and can assist in planning a trip to Perito Moreno Glacier; they're open October through April from 8am to 11pm daily and May through September from 8am to 8pm daily (© **02902/491090**). All other spots that look like information centers are travel agencies trying to sell tours.

Two good websites for impartial information are **www.elcalafate.com.ar** or the municipal government's site at **www.elcalafate.gov.ar**.

WHAT TO SEE & DO IN EL CALAFATE

El Calafate serves mostly as a service town for visitors on their way to the glaciers (see "Parque Nacional Los Glaciares & Perito Moreno Glacier," later in this chapter), but it does present a pleasant main avenue for a stroll. As expected, there are lots of souvenirs, bookstores, and crafts shops to keep you occupied. Heading out of town on Avenida del Libertador, you'll pass the **Museo Municipal** (Calle G. Bonarelli s/n; © **02902/492799;** free admission), open Monday through Friday from 10am to 9pm, with a collection of farming and ranching implements, Indian artifacts, and historical and ethnographical displays. It's worth a stop if you have the time. The **Los Glaciares National Park Headquarters,** Av. del Libertador 1302 (© **02902/491755**), has a good visitor information center and a lovely garden. And that's about it here in El Calafate, although if you are interested in bird-watching, you could take a short walk to the Bahía Redonda at the shore of Lago Argentino to view upland geese, black-necked swans, and flamingos.

ATTRACTIONS & EXCURSIONS AROUND EL CALAFATE

For information about visiting the glaciers and the national park, see "Parque Nacional Los Glaciares & Perito Moreno Glacier," later in this chapter. Other typical excursions from El Calafate include El Chaltén, for trekking beneath the famous peaks of Cerro Torre and Mt. FitzRoy in 1 day, or a jam-packed day visiting Chile's Torres del Paine National Park. For either of these, try **Patagonia Extrema,** Av. del Libertador 1341 (© **02902/492393**), or **AlwaysGlaciers** (© **011/5031-2869** in Buenos Aires). More and more adventure activities and excursions are popping up in El Calafate, capitalizing on the tourism boom.

HORSEBACK RIDING   Patagonia is horseback-riding heaven, and a number of agencies offer good trips. Whenever possible, try to get away from tours that depart directly from El Calafate. A company called **02902 Cerro Frias,** Av. del Libertador

1857 (© **02902/492808;** www.cerrofrias.com), offers half-day horseback riding trips in the wide-open plains of Patagonia that take you up to a gorgeous view point. Excursions include a spectacular barbecue lunch or dinner.

OFF-ROADING Four-wheel-drives have become a popular way to explore the wilderness around El Calafate. **Mil Outdoor Adventure,** Av. del Libertador 1029 (© **02902/491437**), takes you across rivers, over boulders, along ridges, and up to the El Calafate Balcony for a panoramic view. There are also fossils and rock mazes en route.

MOUNTAIN BIKING Hop on a bike and explore the rolling hills and plains of the Patagonian Steppe. **Patagonia Bikes,** 9 de Julio 29 (© **02902/492767**), rents bikes and offers hour-long biking city tours and half- and full-day bike tours with private guides. It's a good activity if you have an early-afternoon flight out of town.

VISITING AN *ESTANCIA* An excellent day trip takes you to one of the several *estancias,* or ranches, that have opened their doors to the public. They typically run day activities and restaurant services, and some even offer lodging, should you opt to spend the night. They're a lovely way to experience the local history, immerse yourself in the wild landscapes, and live Patagonia as authentically as possible. Most day excursions include a choice of horseback riding, hiking, or bird-watching, as well as a hearty traditional meal, usually of barbecued local *cordero* (lamb). All of the following *estancias* offer meals, excursions such as horseback riding and trekking, and transportation from El Calafate. Most also have museums in the old family ranch homes. Close to town, **El Galpón del Glaciar** (© **02902/491793;** www.elgalpondelglaciar.com.ar) adds traditional *estancia* activities such as sheep-shearing. It's a good spot for an evening visit; dinner shows start at 6pm (reservations recommended). Perhaps the most exclusive ranch in the area is the **Estancia Helsingfors,** open from October to March, located on the shore of Lago Viedma about 150km (93 miles) from El Calafate. Helsingfors offers lodging, horseback riding, overflights, bird-watching, boat trips, and fine dining. It's too isolated and too far from town to visit in 1 day. For more information, contact their offices in Buenos Aires, Av Córdoba 827, 11A (©/fax **011/ 4315-1222;** www.helsingfors.com.ar). My favorite of the bunch is **Estancia Cristina** ✪✪, situated at the end of the remote north arm of Lago Argentino. See "Where to Stay," below, for more information. You take a spectacular 4-hour boat trip to get there, sailing past floating icebergs and the enormous Upsala Glacier. Day trips include a hike with excellent views of Cerro Norte and the Patagonian Ice Cap, a 4WD trip, or a lovely horseback ride. Contact their office in El Calafate at 9 de Julio 57, Local 10 (© **02902/491133;** www.estanciacristina.com).

The meticulously maintained **Estancia Alta Vista** (© **02902/491247;** altavista@cotecal.com.ar), at 33km (20 miles) from El Calafate on the dirt road RP 15 near the beautiful area of Lago Roca, is open October through March and offers ranch activities and fishing. **Estancia Nibepo Aike** (© **02902/492797;** http://nibepoaike.com.ar) is picturesquely nestled on the southeast edge of the national park, about 60km (37 miles) from El Calafate. It's also near Lago Roca, offering fishing and ranch activities October through April. An overnight here is a slightly less than at other local *estancias.*

Closer to town, **Parque De La Bahía,** Padre Agostini and Av. Costaner (© **02902/ 496555**), has a nightly shearing show and in-depth presentation on all things wool-and sheep-related. After a lively demonstration of dogs herding sheep, you get a chance to feed a baby lamb from a bottle, and then head indoors for a hearty lamb dinner with a folklore show.

WHERE TO STAY

New hotels and *hosterías* are opening up every month in El Calafate. The bulk of them are 15-room inns in the outskirts of town. Really good value is hard to find here; most places are capitalizing on the short tourist season. Prices soar from December through February, making October to November and March to April the most economical time to visit.

ESTANCIAS

Eolo Patagonia's Spirit *Finds*   Inspired by the ever-present Patagonian winds, Eolo is a new take on the old-style ranch. Built around a protected courtyard, it is upscale through and through, yet casual and comfortable. Expansive cream-colored rooms have huge windows and a mixture of new and antique furnishings. Bathrooms have refurbished mirrors, vanities, and deep tubs with windows looking out to the vastness. The corner suite has a view of the Torres del Paine on a clear day. No matter which way you look, there are sublime expanses outside with no trace of civilization in sight. Only 25km (15 miles) from El Calafate, and en route to the Perito Moreno Glacier, the location is convenient to town, the airport, and the main tourist attractions, making it much more convenient than Eolo's competitors, and a good place to base a trip lasting from 3 to 5 days. The excellent restaurant is open to the public with reservations. Most people come here as an all-inclusive package that includes the traditional local glacier tours as well as trekking, bird-watching, and horseback riding. Or you can just relax by the indoor heated pool. The unpretentious and flexible staff will call you by name and make you feel at home. For a place with only 17 rooms, Eolo offers a remarkably complete experience, affording a comfortable and luxurious window onto Patagonian life.

RP 11, Km 23, El Calafate. © 02902/492042. Reservations © 11/4700-0075 in Buenos Aires. www.eolo.com.ar. 17 units. 2-night packages start at $338 (£186) per person based on double occupancy; 4-night packages start at $237 (£130) per person based on double occupancy. Rates include all meals, airport transfers, excursions. AE, MC, V. **Amenities:** Restaurant; lounge; indoor pool; sauna; guided excursions; Internet; library; TV room. *In room:* Safe.

Estancia Cristina *Moments*   If seclusion is the new luxury, this *estancia* is the ultimate indulgence. Situated at the end of the north arm of Lago Argentino, it's the well-preserved former ranching outpost of the Masters family, early-20th-century British pioneers. To get here (see "Visiting an *Estancia*," above), you take a spectacular 4-hour boat trip, sailing past floating icebergs and the enormous Upsala Glacier. One- and two-night packages allow you to choose from a selection of day excursions, such as treks, a 4WD trip, or a wonderful horseback ride. Upon return, you'll have the place to yourself, once the day-trippers have headed back to town. At night, the silence and darkness will astound you. Relax in a soaker tub, explore the Masters family museum, roam the English gardens, enjoy bird-watching, or sidle up to the bar for a glass of *vino tinto*. Twelve rooms have been designed to resemble the older ranch buildings, with light green roofs and white walls. Inside, they're clean, spacious, and fresh, with large beds and huge bay windows that open onto the Cerro Norte. The food is excellent, and the service is friendly and charming. The modern facilities (the hotel opened in 2005) don't detract from the history or majestic setting of the place. Both gentle and rugged, new and old, Estancia Cristina is a gem, making it a favorite of so many Patagonian travelers. If you can splurge for just 1 night in Patagonia, do it here.

9 de Julio 57, local 10, El Calafate. ℂ 02902/491133. Reservations ℂ 11/4814-3934 in Buenos Aires. www.estancia cristina.com. From $659 (£362) per person double. Rates include all meals, excursions, and transfers. **Amenities:** Restaurant; bar; hiking trails; Internet; library; museum. *In room:* Safe.

EXPENSIVE

Design Suites *(Overrated)* With a breathtaking setting at the highest point of the Nimes peninsula, overlooking the vast Lago Argentino, this magical hotel bills itself as *the* spot for style and design, popular with fashion-forward Europeans and Porteños. It is certainly creative, with eclectic art and furnishings and nature on display through the massive windows. Common spaces are airy and bright, allowing the natural elements to shine. Still, the look is somewhat unsettled and leaves guests missing the type of hospitality that's typical of Patagonia. Most rooms overlook the lake, with floor-to-ceiling windows covered in draping curtains, huge tubs, king-size beds, and modern bathrooms. This may be the only spot in Patagonia that needs air-conditioning, given that windows don't open enough to counter the constant afternoon sun. Another concern is that rooms aren't soundproof, and the design concepts are inefficient (the bathroom sinks, for example, are beautiful but messy). It has all sorts of amenities, from an indoor/outdoor pool to a small business center. In the evenings, it's a chic spot from which to watch the sunset and drink a martini.

Calle 94 No. 190, El Calafate. ℂ 02902/494525. Reservations ℂ 11/5199-7465 in Buenos Aires. www.designsuites.com. 60 units. $145–$235 (£80–£129) double; $210–$330 (£116–£182) suite. Rates include buffet breakfast. AE, MC, V. **Amenities:** Restaurant; bar; lounge; gym; spa; room service; babysitting; laundry; art gallery. *In room:* TV, DVD, minibar, hair dryer, safe.

Esplendor de Calafate 🎗 Similar to the Design Suites in its effort to be creative and modern, the Esplendor excels with a warm and cozy feeling. This former white elephant was transformed in 2006 into a sleek new multistory hotel with a unique earthy style and stunning windows. It calls itself a boutique inn, but, with 57 rooms, it's quite big. Your eyes are constantly on the move in the vast lobby, with its 20m (66-ft.) ceilings, huge fireplace, long line of computers, and low leather sofas. Rooms are dotted with warm fabrics such as wool and suede, and the crisp microcement floors are surprisingly warm. The curtains, with built-in fabric window slots, give you both privacy and a view. The king beds are covered in crisp white linens and knitted blankets. Bathrooms include stand-up showers, separated sinks, and soaker cement tubs. More towel racks would help. Rooms on the second floor are the largest; third-floor rooms have wooden angled ceilings. The standards are called concept rooms. The suites, for around $15 (£8.25) more, are a real bargain: They have step-in rounded tubs, a living room, and plenty of windows. The hotel restaurant, which specializes in modern European cuisine, is quite excellent, and the gourmet lunch boxes they prepare for guests heading out on day trips are outstanding.

Pte. Perón 1143, El Calafate. ℂ 02902/492454. www.esplendorcalafate.com. Reservations ℂ 11/5217-5700 in Buenos Aires. 57 units. From $194 (£107) double standard; $208 (£114) suite. Rates include buffet breakfast. **Amenities:** Restaurant; bar; business center; laundry service; room service. *In room:* TV, minibar, safe.

Hotel Kosten Aike This downtown hotel offers modern and attractive accommodations. It's as conservative as its main competitor down the street, the Posada Los Alamos (see below). One of the biggest hotels in town, the Kosten Aike makes up for its lack of personal charm with its great location and dependability. Furnishings and artwork imported from Buenos Aires include matching drapes and bedspreads in rust and beige, accented with black geometric squiggles, papier-mâché lamps, iron and rosewood tables and chairs, and petal-soft carpets. All rooms feature large bathrooms. Some rooms are very large, with bay windows; they aren't any more expensive, so ask for one when booking. The airy lobby is inlaid completely with gray stone. With less character than the new inns in town, Kosten Aike is a good option for groups.

Gobernador Moyano 1243, El Calafate. © 02902/492424, or 11/4811-1314 (reservations). Fax 02902/491538. www.kostenaike.com.ar. 80 units. $201–$231 (£111–£127) double. AE, DC, MC, V. **Amenities:** Restaurant; wine bar; fireside lounge; gym; spa; game room; concierge; business center; room service; laundry service. *In room:* TV, dataport, minibar, hair dryer, safe.

Hotel Posada Los Alamos   The Posada Los Alamos is as conservative as a Brooks Brothers suit, perhaps better suited to a golf resort than wild Patagonia. Because of the low-key design of the complex and the slightly aloof service, you can't help the feeling that you're in a private country club or thousands of miles north in Buenos Aires province. The style is classic Argentine: a red-brick exterior fringed with the hotel's namesake alamo trees, plaid carpet, old English furniture, and windows with wooden, triangular eaves. They have just about everything here, including a new spa with a huge pool, wine bar, convention center, and hair salon. There are a number of comfortable lounges in the hotels various buildings, all with large windows looking out onto an expansive (and expensive-to-maintain) lawn. Rooms have ample space, and each has a slightly different color and style. Ask for one that looks out onto the quiet, grassy backyard instead of the dusty dirt road. The hotel's excellent restaurant, La Posta, is reviewed on p. 364. It is a very large complex popular with tour groups.

Gobernador Moyano and Bustillo, El Calafate. © 02902/491144. Fax 02902/491186. www.posadalosalamos.com. 144 units. $253 (£139) double; from $371 (£204) suite. AE, MC, V. **Amenities:** Restaurant; bar; lounge; golf course; tennis court; tour desk; room service; massage; laundry service; dry cleaning. *In room:* TV, minibar, safe.

MODERATE

El Faro del Calafate   A comfortable and friendly midrange option, El Faro is part of the new wave of small *hosterías* that have opened in the past few years on the outskirts of town. With natural colors and furnishings, El Faro tries to fit into the landscape. Rooms are big—especially the triples, which are often available at the same price as doubles. Decor is simple, with plain white walls and bedspreads, small TVs mounted in the corners, and very large bathrooms. A simple breakfast is served in the sunny living area. The staff is particularly friendly, upbeat, and keen to help arrange all excursions. A nice step up from a hostel, it offers plenty of space for you to relax in after a long day exploring Patagonia.

Calle 405 No. 82, El Calafate. © 02902/493899. www.elfarocalafate.com.ar. 10 units. $105 (£58) double; $115 (£63) triple. V. **Amenities:** Lounge; concierge; laundry service. *In room:* TV, hair dryer.

Hostería Lupama   Compact in size but big in heart, this charming new inn above the main part of town takes its name from a local aboriginal chief. You'll be drawn in by the towering windows and lovely wood architecture. The feeling inside is simple but rustic, with touches of wood and stone. Spacious rooms upstairs have nice views, particularly those on the town side, and king-size beds. Separated bathrooms all have jetted tubs. The two junior suites are slightly larger with two-person tubs. You can borrow DVDs from the video library to watch in your own room. The bilingual staff are hardworking and helpful.

Calle 992 No. 19, Villa Parque Los Glaciares, El Calfate. © 02902/491110. www.lupama.com.ar. 14 units. $140 (£77) double; $160 (£88) suite, with continental breakfast included. V. **Amenities:** Restaurant; bar; room service; laundry; Internet; lunch boxes. *In room:* TV w/DVD, minibar, safe.

Kau Kaleshen *Value*   With an excellent location just a block and a half from the main drag, the Kau Kaleshen *hostería* is a simple and charming inn. It's been around long enough to feel warm and authentic. Rooms are all located around the tranquil back garden, some on a two-story yellow-walled building (the top floor rooms have better circulation). They all have rustic brick walls and ceramic floors; it's nothing fancy. Clean white bathrooms are also simple, with stand-up showers only. There is a lovely teahouse out front where breakfast is served, and where nonguests and guests alike can enjoy a $6 (£3.30) *té completo*—afternoon tea with homemade pastries.

Gobernador Gregores 1256, El Calafate. © 02902/491188. www.losglaciares.com/kaukaleshen. $70 (£39) double. Rates include breakfast. **Amenities:** Teahouse; laundry service.

INEXPENSIVE

America del Sur Hostel *&*   This is the best new hostel in El Calafate. Located a 7-minute walk up the hill from downtown, it affords a lovely panoramic view. The service is very friendly, and the vibe laid back. Guests have the choice of a simple bunk bed in a shared room that sleeps up to four people at a time, or one of the newer doubles with private baths. All dorm rooms have private lockers and baths with separate tubs, showers, and toilets that allow for some privacy in an otherwise shared room. There is a big kitchen that all guests are free to cook in; it's an upbeat place in which to mix and mingle with other travelers while saving some cash by dining in. The big common living room has a fabulous panoramic view and a cozy wood-burning fireplace. Extras such as free transfers from the bus terminal and Internet are included.

Puerto Deseado 151, El Calafate. © 02902/493523. www.americahostel.com.ar. 60 beds. $40 (£22) double; $10 (£5.50) bed in shared room. Rates include breakfast. No credit cards. **Amenities:** Restaurant; kitchen; laundry; Internet; luggage storage; transfers. *In room:* Lockers.

Casa de Grillos B and B *Finds*   This small inn, 8 blocks from Avenida del Libertador in the old part of town, is in one of El Calafate's only lush, green areas. Steps from Laguna Nimez and the shores of Lago Argentino, it's somewhat of an oasis and a nice choice for nature lovers who still want the convenience of being within walking distance from town. It's a true bed-and-breakfast, in that a lovely couple rents a handful of rooms in their home. Rooms are cozy, and two of the four have private bathrooms (the other two rooms share). There is a lovely common area for TV watching, Internet surfing, and visiting.

Los Condores 1215, esq. Las Bandurrias, El Calafate. © 02902/491160. www.casadegrillos.com.ar. 4 units. $30–$40 (£17–£22) double, including breakfast. **Amenities:** Internet; library.

WHERE TO DINE

A number of cafes and espresso bars run along the main drag, Libertador, and its side streets. Try **Elba'r,** in the De los Pajaros plaza at 9 de Julio 57 (© 02902/493594). Or the interesting **Borges & Alvarez Libro-Bar,** Av. del Libertador 1015 (© 02902/491464), has a fantastic selection of books to peruse while you sip a *café con leche.* For a light snack, try **Almacenes Patagónicos,** at Av. del Libertador 1044 (© 02902/491042).

MODERATE

Casimiro Biguá *& Moments* REGIONAL   This sleek wine bar and restaurant has quickly become the number-one hot spot in El Calafate. The chic and modern black-and-white decor, thick tablecloths, flickering candles on every table, and young and energetic waitstaff make this place a winner. You can sample one of the many wines while enjoying an appetizer platter of regional Patagonian specialties such as smoked trout, smoked wild boar, and a variety of cheeses. Main courses change frequently but usually range from a simple steak to an elaborate pasta with salmon, cream, and capers in white-wine sauce; there's always a chicken and seafood offering as well. The menu combines Argentine classics such as empanadas and beef with fusion-style dishes such as sesame tuna. It's also an excellent place to try a glass of dry Argentine sparkling wine. A few doors down is the sister restaurant, the town's most upscale steakhouse.

Av. del Libertador 963. ℭ 02902/492590. Reservations recommended. Main courses $6–$15 (£3.30–£8.25). AE, MC, V. Daily 10am–1am.

La Posta ★★ ARGENTINE   Although it's in a building separate from the Posada Los Alamos, the La Posta is considered to be part of that hotel. This has long been considered El Calafate's most upscale restaurant, serving great cuisine and choice wines in a formal, candlelit environment. The menu, printed in four languages, offers well-prepared dishes that effectively blend Argentine and international-flavored fare, such as filet mignon in a puff pastry with rosemary-roasted potatoes, king crab ravioli, almond trout, or curried crayfish. Desserts are superb. A lovely breakfast buffet is served here for guests every morning, and the service both morning and night is exquisite.

Gobernador Moyano and Bustillo. ℭ 02902/491144. Reservations recommended in high season. Main courses $8–$15 (£4.40–£8.25). AE, DC, MC, V. Daily 7pm–midnight.

Sancho Restaurant ARGENTINE   Specializing in local food with Mediterranean influences, this family-run joint is friendly and big. The menu includes good starters. For a break from the red meat, opt for seafood in champagne sauce or an excellent trout stuffed with king crab. Pasta lovers or vegetarians should try the spinach gnocchi with pesto or *pomodoro* sauce. Service is friendly but really slows down when things get busy, as they do most every night from November through March.

25 de Mayo 80. ℭ 02902/492442. Reservations recommended in high season. Main courses $7–$13 (£3.85–£7.15). AE, MC, V. Daily 8pm–midnight.

Toma Wine Bar ★ ARGENTINE/FUSION   This new bistro-style joint gives you a chance to sample the best of Argentina's wine without taking the trip to Mendoza. The front room is chic and intimate, while the back is inside a traditional Patagonian room with whitewashed walls and big windows. Don't choose your food without having a chat with the sommelier, who'll give you some tips and answer any question about his excellent wine list. Start your meal with a creative appetizer such as sweetbreads in honey and soy sauce or goat cheese grilled Provoleta paired with a glass of Syrah. For an entree, try pork with chutney and mashed sweet potatoes paired with a Tempranillo, or king crab with shrimp and saffron sauce that will pair well with a Voignier. More adventurous eaters should try the *ñandú*, a delicious and surprisingly tender cousin of the ostrich. The wine list ranges from big names to boutique vineyards, and you are encouraged to order by the glass, which is a real treat if you've got a few different labels and grapes you're wanting to try. If you love or want to learn more about Argentine wines, this is a great choice. On warm summer days, they open tables on a sidewalk patio.

Av. del Libertador 1359. ℭ 02902/492993. Reservations recommended. $7–$17 (£3.85–£9.35). AE, MC, V. Daily noon–3pm and 6pm–midnight.

INEXPENSIVE

El Puesto PIZZA   El Puesto's brick interior, with its white-lace curtains and old photos, is cozy and inviting, but the restaurant's tiny size means you might have to wait for a table on busy evenings. The former pizzamaker is the new owner, so the 23 varieties of delicious pies are dependably good. There are great pasta options as well. Also on the menu are fresh salads and a couple of steaks. It's a cozy spot with some mildly messy hustle and bustle around the wood-fired oven.

Gobernador Moyano and Av. 9 de Julio. © 02902/491620. Reservations required. Pizzas $2–$6 (£1.10–£3.30). MC. Daily noon–3pm and 8pm–midnight.

La Cocina *Value* BISTRO   This recently expanded restaurant serves bistro-style food, including fresh pastas such as raviolis and fettuccine, fresh trout, and meats prepared simply but well. Try the crepes stuffed with vegetables (known as *cannelloni*) or combinations such as ham and cheese, or meat items such as steak with a pepper-and-mustard sauce. There's a huge list of pasta options as well. Of all the restaurants on the main street with a similar appearance, La Cocina is without a doubt the best. There is something here for everyone, and when it's busy, the friendly staff maintains an upbeat vibe.

Av. del Libertador 1245. © 02902/491758. Main courses $7–$9 (£3.85–£4.95). MC, V. Tues–Sun noon–3:30pm and 7pm–midnight.

La Tablita *Value* STEAKHOUSE   This is 100% typical Argentine food—the stuff that families from Iguazú to Ushuaia enjoy on any given Sunday afternoon. Carnivores need look no farther. La Tablita is all about meat, and it's one of the local favorites in town for its heaping platters and giant *parrilladas* (mixed grills) that come sizzling to your table on their own mini-barbecues. The *parrilladas* for two cost $20 (£11), but they really serve three diners, given the size and assortment of chicken, sausage, beef, lamb, and a few innards you may or may not recognize. The filet mignon is incredibly tender here; at $9 (£4.95), it's one of the least expensive filets that we've ever had. The sunny, airy restaurant can be found on the other side of the bridge that spans the Arroyo Calafate, about a 2-minute walk from downtown.

Coronel Rosales 24. © 02902/491065. Reservations highly recommended. Main courses $3–$7 (£1.65–£3.85). AE, MC, V. Daily 11am–3pm and 7pm–midnight (Wed closed for lunch).

Parrilla Mi Viejo STEAKHOUSE   Mi Viejo is another local barbecue favorite, with enough variety on the menu to satisfy everyone. Mi Viejo (My Old Man) seems to refer to the crusty character manning the lamb barbecue spit at the restaurant's front entrance, serving up weighty, delicious cuts of meat. Three to five diners could eat from a $10 (£5.50) *parrillada* meat assortment, depending on their hunger. The menu also offers trout and salmon dishes and a few interesting plates such as pickled hare. Some decent wine options are less than $10 (£5.50) a bottle. The restaurant is on the main drag, and its dining room is warm and pleasant.

Av. del Libertador 1111. © 02902/491691. Main courses $6–$8 (£3.30–£4.40). MC, V. Daily 11am–3pm and 7pm–midnight.

Pura Vida *Finds* VEGETARIAN/REGIONAL   The friendliest place in town is a short walk from downtown, but it's worth finding. Set in a woodsy location overlooking the lake, it's the best place in El Calafate for home-style cuisine that favors vegetarians. Try the delicious pumpkin soup or the gnocchi in saffron sauce. If you want to try a regional specialty, then go for the *cazuela de cordero* (hearty lamb stew with mushrooms). For dessert, both the rice pudding and the pumpkin ice cream are delicious. Fresh fruit shakes, sandwiches, and afternoon tea with homemade rolls and jams are also offered. Despite the outdated A-frame exterior, the service is laid back, the crowd is young and relaxed, and the view of the lake is divine.

Av. del Libertador 1876. © **02902/493356.** Main courses $5–$12 (£2.75–£6.60). No credit cards. Thurs–Tues 7:30–11:30pm.

EL CALAFATE AFTER DARK

In a rustic old building, **La Zaina,** Gob. Gregores 1057 (© **02902/496789**), is a cafe/bar rich with local atmosphere. The **Shackleton Lounge,** at del Libertador 3287 (© **02902/493516**), gets going a bit later, 3km (1¾ miles) down the road outside town. It has great sunsets, a long list of cocktails, semiregular evening slideshows, and lots of travelers in the crowd swapping tall tales.

---

7 Parque Nacional los Glaciares & Perito Moreno Glacier ⭐⭐⭐

The Los Glaciares National Park covers 600,000 hectares (1.5 million acres) of rugged land that stretches vertically along the crest of the Andes and spills east into rolling steppe. Most of Los Glaciares is inaccessible to visitors except for the park's two dramatic highlights: the granite needles, such as FitzRoy near El Chaltén (covered in "El Chaltén & the FitzRoy Area," below), and this region's magnificent Perito Moreno Glacier. The park is also home to thundering rivers, blue lakes, and thick beech forest. Los Glaciares National Park was formed in 1937 and declared a World Heritage region by UNESCO in 1981. It is a wild, rugged, and yet sublimely beautiful landscape—one that offers up surprise, wonder, adventure, and serenity all at once.

Named after famed Argentine scientist Francisco "Perito" Moreno ("perito" is the title given to someone considered an expert in their field), the famous glacier Perito Moreno is a must-see, as important to Argentine culture and tourism as Iguazú Falls or the Casa Rosada. Few natural wonders in South America are as spectacular or as easily accessed as this glacier. It's just one fingertip in the imposing Patagonian Ice Cap, the fourth largest frozen mass in the world after the two poles and Greenland. Perito Moreno is one of the few glaciers in the world that is not receding. Scientists like to stay that it is "stable," or constantly growing and receding. Around 1900, Perito Moreno was measured at 750m (2,460 ft.) from the Península Magallanes; by 1920, it had advanced so far that it finally made contact with the peninsula where tourists now walk the boardwalk and take in views. Each time the glacier reached the peninsula, which would occur every 3 to 4 years, it created a dam in the channel that drastically altered water levels on either side. Over the period of a few years, the built-up pressure would set off a calving explosion for 48 to 72 hours, breaking the face of the glacier in a crashing fury. The last time this happened was in March of 2006, making news across the country. Perito Moreno is usually reliable for sending a few huge chunks hurling into the channel throughout the day. Sit in silence with your camera ready and you're almost certain to get a fabulous photo opportunity of a calving glacier.

What impresses visitors most is the sheer size of Perito Moreno Glacier—a wall of jagged blue ice measuring 4,500m (14,760 ft.) across and soaring 60m (197 ft.) above the channel. You literally could fit the entire city of Buenos Aires on it. From the parking lot on the Península Magallanes, a series of vista-point walkways descend which take visitors directly to the glacier's face. It's an unforgettable, spellbinding experience,

worth taking in slowly so you can savor the view and capture the ice cracking off in photos or videos. There are opportunities to join an organized group for a walk on the glacier, as well as boat journeys that leave from Puerto Banderas for visits to the neighboring glaciers. In 2007, a major infrastructure expansion project began at the Península Magallanes that will include refurbished boardwalk paths, a new restaurant, and a visitor center.

There are other magnificent glaciers in the national park; all are much harder to access than Perito Moreno but equally stunning. The Upsala Glacier is the largest in South America, and the Spegazzini Glacier has the largest snout of all the glaciers in the park. Onelli, Seco, and Agassiz are also gorgeous. All can be seen as part of the **All Glaciers Tour** organized by René Fernández Campbell, whose main office is at Av. del Libertador 867 (© **02902/492340**).

Glaciology 101

A glacier is a large body of snow and ice that slowly moves down a valley or spreads across a surface due to accumulation and gravity. Glacial ice forms when heavy snowfall crushes first into snow crystals and then into pellets, finally becoming a dense mass that takes on transparency and hardness over time. Heavy precipitation and low temperatures are the most significant factors in glacial growth. Dark lines in the glaciers, called moraines, are produced by rock debris, sand, and clay that accumulate on the ice. They are useful for indicating past positions of the glacier.

GETTING THERE & GETTING AROUND

At Km 49 (30 miles) from El Calafate, you'll pass through the park's entrance, where there's an information booth with erratic hours (no phone; www.calafate.com). The entrance fee is $10 (£5.50) per person. If you're looking for information about the park and the glacier, pick up an interpretive guide or a book from one of the bookstores or tourist shops along Avenida del Libertador in El Calafate.

TO GET TO THE PARK

BY CAR   Following Avenida del Libertador west out of town, the route turns into a well-maintained road that is almost completely paved. From here, it's 80km (50 miles) to the glacier.

BY TAXI OR *REMISE*   If you want to see the glacier at your own pace, hire a taxi or *remise*. The cost averages $70 (£39) for two, $75 (£41) for three, and $100 (£55) for four, although many taxi companies will negotiate a price. Be sure to agree on an estimated amount of time spent at the glacier, and remember that the park entrance fee of $10 (£5.50) per person is not included.

BY BUS   Cal-Tur buses, Av. del Libertador 1080 (© **02902/491368**), leave downtown El Calafate twice a day (8am and 3pm, returning from the glacier at 1 and 8pm), allowing you to explore the glacier lookout area on your own. The bus ride costs a very reasonable $18 (£9.90), plus the $10 (£5.50) park entrance fee. Other buses leave on a similar schedule for similar prices from the bus terminal.

BY ORGANIZED TOUR   Several companies offer transportation to and from the glacier, such as **Interlagos,** Av. del Libertador 1175 (© **02902/491179;** interlagos@ cotecal.com.ar); and **TAQSA,** in the bus terminal (© **02902/491843**). These mini-van and bus services provide bilingual guides and leave around 9am, spending an average of 4 hours at the peninsula; the cost is $35 to $50 (£19–£28) per person, not including lunch. For a more personalized tour (a private car with driver and a bilingual, licensed guide), contact **SurTurismo,** Av. del Libertador 1226 (© **02902/ 491266;** www.surturismo.com.ar); they can arrange for a half-day trip costing $68 to $85 (£37–£47) for two people (prices vary with the seasons).

OUTDOOR ACTIVITIES

You can see the Perito Moreno glacier close up on your own in a half-day's outing by taxi or bus. But several exciting activities in the Perito Moreno region afford a more in-depth and thrilling experience. **"Minitrekking"** (although there is nothing "mini"

How to See the Glacier

Do not miss the chance to see the majestic Perito Moreno Glacier, one of the world's most stunning sites and a great lesson in nature. You've got a number of options for making your visit worthwhile, depending on your time frame and budget.

- Rent a car and drive to the glacier from town. This option is not cheap unless you are a group of four. It's helpful if you have a midday flight.
- Take the local bus that has three departures daily. It's the best budget option, and a good choice if you want to stick to your own schedule.
- Hop on a local tour. This gives you more information and understanding of what you're looking at. But you're stuck with the tour's schedule. Some tours offer a short hike along Icebergs Channel (Canal de los Témpanos) or boat trips along the north wall. Most are bilingual, and some include snacks.
- Sign up for Hielo y Aventura's Minitrekking, to take a walk on the ice and get a good look at its southern wall along the Rico Arm of Lago Argentino. It's a half-day outing; you can include a stroll on the boardwalks.
- For an in-depth and unforgettable exploration of the big white sheet, Hielo y Aventura's Big Ice is the most complete glacier experience. A good level of fitness is required.

about it) takes guests of all ages and abilities for a walk upon the glacier. The trip begins with a 20-minute boat ride across the Brazo Rico, followed by a 30-minute walk to the glacier. From here guests are outfitted with crampons and other safety gear, and then they spend approximately 1½ hours atop the ice, complete with a stop for a whiskey on the thousand-year-old "rocks." This great trip gives visitors the chance to peer into the electric-blue crevasses of the glacier and fully appreciate its size. More experienced, fit, and adventurous visitors can opt for the **Big Ice** 𝒦𝒦 option, which has a more technical approach and gives you much more time (upwards of 4 hr.) to walk on the glacier. Both Big Ice and Minitrekking are organized exclusively by **Hielo y Aventura,** which has its main office at Av. del Libertador 935 (© **02902/492205;** www.hieloyaventura.com). Big Ice costs $115 (£63) including the transfer from El Calafate. Minitrekking will run you $85 (£47) with transfer. Remember, you have to bring your own lunch from town. To save some cash, book directly.

Solo Patagonia, Av. del Libertador 963 (© **02902/491298;** www.solopatagonia.com.ar), offers visitors navigation trips through the Brazo Rico to the face of Perito Moreno, including treks to the base of Cerro Negro with a view of Glacier Negro. Both Solo Patagonia and **Upsala Explorer** 𝒦, Av. 9 de Julio 69 (© **02902/491034**), offer a variety of combinations from Puerto Banderas to Los Glaciares National Park's largest and tallest glaciers—respectively the Upsala and Spegazzini. Upsala Explorer makes a stop at the Estancia Cristina for lunch and offers optional trekking and 4WD trips to the Upsala Lookout. Both companies charge $110 to $165 (£61–£71) for this all-day excursion.

LODGING NEAR THE GLACIER

Los Notros ✶✶✶ *(Moments)*   Few hotels in Argentina boast as spectacular and breath-taking a view as Los Notros—but it doesn't come cheap. This luxury lodge sits high on a slope looking out at Perito Moreno Glacier, and all common areas and rooms have been fitted with picture windows to let guests soak up the marvelous sight. Although the wood-hewn exteriors give the hotel the feel of a mountain lodge, the interior decor is contemporary. Each room is slightly different, with personal touches such as antique lamps and regional photos; crocheted or gingham bedspreads; lilac, peach, or lemon-yellow walls; padded floral headboards or iron bed frames; and tweedy brown or raspberry corduroy chairs. Bathrooms are gleaming white, and premium rooms in the newer wing have whirlpool baths. The older "Cascada bungalow" rooms have very thin walls; if you're a light sleeper, be sure to request a top-floor room or a room in the newer "Premium" (and more expensive) wing.

Inside the main building is a large, chic, and expansive restaurant renowned for serving creative regional cuisine. Upstairs is an airy lounge area with chaise longues positioned in front of panoramic windows; here you'll find a TV room with a selection of nature videos. Guests at the Los Notros must opt for one of the multiple-day packages that include airport transfers, meals, box lunches for expeditions, guided trekking, boat excursions, and ice walks. The guides are great, but hotel service is a bit spotty, and the restaurant is definitely understaffed. Although Los Notros offers 4-night packages, you might find that length of time too long unless you're looking to get away from it all for a while. Note that prices jump substantially during Christmas, New Year's, and Easter week. One-night stays are on request only, and sold only subject to availability; the hotel prefers to sell its rooms to those buying their all-inclusive packages before releasing the rooms to those seeking just an overnight stay. The views are unbeatable, and the rooms comfortable.

Main office in Buenos Aires: Arenales 1457, 7th floor. © **11/4814-3934.** Fax 11/4815-7645. www.losnotros.com. 32 units. $967 (£531) per person for 2-night package Cascada bungalow; $1,145 (£629) per person for 2-night package in double superior; $1,543 (£849) per person for 2-night package in double premium. Rates include all meals and transfers. Room-only rates available by request only, depending on availability. AE, DC, MC, V. **Amenities:** Restaurant; bar; lounge; tour desk; room service; laundry service. *In room:* Minibar.

8 El Chaltén & the FitzRoy Area ✶✶

222km (138 miles) N of El Calafate

El Chaltén is a tiny village of about 500 residents whose lifeblood, like El Calafate's, is the throng of visitors who come each summer. Visitors here, however, are generally more active and adventurous than those who stay only in El Calafate; they include some of the world's greatest mountaineers as well as avid trekkers. This is the second-most-visited region of Argentina's Los Glaciares National Park. It's quite possibly its most exquisite, as well, due to the singular nature of the granite spires that shoot up, torpedo-like, above massive tongues of ice that descend from the Southern Ice Field. In the world of mountaineering, the sheer and ice-encrusted peaks of Mt. FitzRoy, Cerro Torre, and their neighbors are considered some of the most formidable challenges in the world, and they draw hundreds of climbers here every year.

El Chaltén is known as the "trekking capital of Argentina," and it ranks up there with the best trekking destinations in the world. What it offers—excellent trails in spectacularly wild scenery mixed with decent inns and bistros that you can return to at night—is quite rare. Another bonus is that the hiking here doesn't require any serious uphill (or downhill for that matter) climbs, since most trails follow valley floors. Finally, altitude is not a concern, meaning that your lungs should have no problem taking in some of the cleanest air on the planet.

Little more than 10 years ago, El Chaltén counted just a dozen houses and a *hostal* or two, but FitzRoy's rugged beauty and great hiking opportunities have created somewhat of a boomtown. The town sits nestled in a circular rock outcrop at the base of FitzRoy, and it's fronted by the vast, dry Patagonian Steppe. It's a wild and windy setting, and the town has a ramshackle feel. Visitors use El Chaltén either as a base from which to take day hikes or as an overnight stop before setting off for a multiple-day backpacking trip. This area is also remarkably rich in human history, from its hardy early settlers and courageous alpinists, to more recent residents' border disputes with Chile.

El Chaltén is preparing to step into the limelight: Completion of the pavement project on the road that links El Chaltén to El Calafate shortens the trip from 5 hours to just 2½ hours, coinciding with the opening of a new upscale hotel at Los Cerros. Populated by folk with a pioneering spirit, this rough-around-the-edges town has the feeling of a place on the fringe of modernity.

Most visitors come here for 4 days, with 2 travel days on each end. If you take the early morning bus from El Calafate, you'll be here with time for a good half-day hike. Most hotels offer a catering service that prepares box lunches you can take with you on the trail.

The town's layout is somewhat haphazard, but there is a main drag, San Martín, where all the buses stop. Most hotels and restaurants don't have street numbers.

ESSENTIALS
GETTING THERE
BY PLANE   All transportation to El Chaltén originates from El Calafate, which has daily plane service from Ushuaia and Buenos Aires. From El Calafate, you need to take a bus or rent a car; the trip takes from 2 to 2½ hours.

BY CAR   From El Calafate, take RN 11 west for 30km (19 miles) and turn left on RN 40 north. Turn again, heading northwest, on RP 23 to El Chaltén. The only place for a midtrip pit stop is the rustic Estancia La Leona, where you can grab a snack and a coffee.

BY BUS   Buses from El Calafate leave from the terminal, and all cost about $30 (£17) round-trip. **Chaltén Travel,** with offices in El Chaltén in the Albergue Rancho Grande on Avenida San Martín (© **02962/493005;** www.chaltentravel.com), leaves El Calafate daily at 8am and El Chaltén at 6pm. Chaltén Travel can arrange private tours and day trips to outlying destinations, such as Patagonian ranches, as well as summer-only transportation up RN 40 for those crossing into Chile or on to Bariloche. **Caltur,** which leaves from El Chaltén's Hostería Fitz Roy at Av. San Martín 520 (© **02962/491368;** www.caltur.com.ar), leaves El Calafate daily at 7:30am and leaves El Chaltén at 6pm.

VISITOR INFORMATION
There is a $10 (£5.50) fee to enter the park. El Chaltén also has a well-organized visitor center at the town's entrance—the **Comisión de Fomento,** Perito Moreno and Avenida Güemes (© **02962/493011**), open daily from 8am to 8pm. Here you'll find maps, pamphlets, and brief interpretive displays about the region's flora and fauna. In

El Calafate, the **APN Intendencia** (park service) has its offices at Av. del Libertador 1302. Its visitor center is open daily from 9am to 3pm (✆ **02902/491005**).

There is neither a bank nor an ATM in El Chaltén. Many inns, restaurants, and stores don't take credit cards, because phone lines are sketchy. So be sure to stop in for cash at a bank in El Calafate.

OUTDOOR ACTIVITIES
TOUR OPERATORS
Fitz Roy Expediciones ⋆⋆, Lionel Terray 212 (✆/fax **02962/493017**; www.fitzroy expediciones.com.ar), offers a variety of trekking excursions, including a complete 9-day circuit around the backside of the FitzRoy and Cerro Torre peaks on the spectacular Patagonian Ice Cap, for $1,850 (£1,018) per person, all equipment and meals included, as well as 2 nights' lodging in an *albergue*. This is a trip for hardcore adventurers only. They also have an excellent day trip to Lago del Desierto, which includes a short hike or boat cruise and lunch at their adventure camp, which offers rafting trips. The full-day trip costs $75 (£41). **Patagonia Mágica,** Fonrouge s/n (✆ **2962/493066**), rents mountain bikes and can help organize backcountry trips.

BOAT TRIPS
Similar to the Minitreks on the Perito Moreno Glacier, but with less than half the people, you can strap on some crampons and explore the nearby Viedma Glacier from El Chaltén. **Viedma Discovery** ⋆ (✆ **2962/493110**) has four categories of excursions: Viedma Light is a half-day boat trip where you don't step on the ice; Viedma Trek includes a light hike at the base of the glacier; Viedma Ice Trek is a crampons-on trek atop the glacier; and finally, Viedma Pro is an ice trek that includes a short course in ice climbing. All include transfers from El Chaltén, but not lunch—you must bring your own food. Another interesting boat trip is across the remote Lago del Desierto, which despite its name is in one of the most lush valleys in southern Patagonia. See above for booking details.

HORSEBACK RIDING
There's nothing like horseback riding in Patagonia, and two outfitters offer several day excursions: **Rodolfo Guerra,** Las Loicas 773 (✆ **02962/493020**), provides horseback rides and a horsepack service for carrying gear to campsites. Also try the **El Relincho,** Av. del Libertador s/n (✆ **02962/493007**).

HIKING & CAMPING
El Chaltén is Argentina's national trekking capital and home to some very good hiking guides who'll take you out for an afternoon stroll, a full-day trek, or even a multiday hiking expedition. The best can be found at **Mountaineering Patagonia,** whose office is at E. Brenner 88 (✆ **2962/493915**; www.mountaineeringpatagonia.com). Also try Manuel Quiroga at **El Chaltén Mountain Guides** (no phone; www.ecmg.com.ar). They also can arrange more challenging mountaineering objectives, such as climbs of local peaks, multiday treks to Paso Marconi, and week-long traverses of the majestic Southern Ice Field.

Although the trails here are generally very well marked, a local guide will help you to have a much more enjoyable experience. Guides will help you understand the natural history, learn about amazing mountaineering feats that took place in the area, and ensure safety. If you're planning to hike in the park, you'll want to pick up a copy of

Zagier & Urruty's trekking map, *Monte FitzRoy & Cerro Torre,* available at most bookstores and tourist shops in El Calafate and El Chaltén. You'll also need to register at the park service office at the entrance to El Chaltén. The best thing about hiking in El Chaltén is that almost all trails start and end in the town itself, meaning you can return each evening for a hot shower, a nice meal, and a good bed. Two standard half-day hikes leave from town: Laguna Capri, which offers a marvelous view of FitzRoy, and the Laguna Torre Lookout. For full-day hikes, the best are Laguna Torre and Laguna de los Tres. Trails here run from easy to difficult, and they take anywhere from 4 to 10 hours to complete. See below for trail descriptions.

Trails in the El Chaltén Area

The El Chaltén area of Los Glaciares National Park has incredible trails for hikers, not to mention imposing challenges for alpinists and mountaineers. The beauty of this area, besides the stunning scenery, is that the valleys are long and don't require too much uphill or downhill hiking, and you can make it back to town each night to a warm shower and good dinner. While overnight camping trips are available, El Chaltén excels in its proximity to day hike trail heads. Unlike the Torres del Paine hikes, which generally require a few nights of camping, all of the main highlights here can be seen in a few day hikes.

What makes hiking in El Chaltén so good is the varied terrain and the relatively little climbing required to get amazing views. These hikes all leave from town and run from easy to difficult. They'll each allow you to see the famous spires from many angles. The times given are estimates for the average walker from El Chaltén. *Note:* These trips are listed according to difficulty, from easy to strenuous.

Cascada Chorrillo del Salto The easiest and flattest hike in the area, this trail is level and stays along the El Chaltén valley floor. Follow the Rio de las Vueltas riverbank northeast of town to the Chorrillo del Salto waterfall, which emerges from a dense forest. Give yourself an hour each way to walk at an easy pace.

Return is 90 min. 4km (2.5 miles) one-way. Easy.

Cerro Torre Lookout Known as "el Mirador del Cerro Torre" in Spanish, this is a nice half-day hike. The trail head is behind the Los Cerros hotel. After climbing 200m (656 ft.), to get above the El Chaltén valley, you'll stroll along a raging glacial FitzRoy River, through thick beech forests, meeting a spectacular view of the needlelike Cerro Torre, with its namesake lake and glacier in front. This is an excellent way to sample some of the world's finest trekking and a great choice if you arrive midday. Climb off to the left (river side) of the trail for the lookout at Cerro Dos Condores.

Round-trip 3 hr. 3km (2 miles) one-way. Easy/medium.

Laguna Capri 🏕 A bit longer than the other great local half-day hike to the Cerro Torre Lookout, Laguna Capri is the must-see destination for lovers of the FitzRoy massif. The trail leads north from town past Cerro Rosado before heading west towards Mt. FitzRoy. Many trekkers come here as a pilgrimage to one of the world's finest granite mountains, saving some time to scour the walls of FitzRoy with binoculars, to look for climbers. It's a 2-hour hike into the lagoon, following the same trail that leads to the Poincenot camp.

4-hr. return. 7 km (4 miles) one-way. Easy/medium.

Patagonia's Famous Peaks

The Cerro Torre and FitzRoy groups may be two of the alpine world's most recognized skylines, made famous by decades of unbelievable mountaineering feats, and by the U.S.-based Patagonia Inc. clothing company, which chose this horizon as its company's logo. Climbers consider these among the toughest challenges on the planet. They are also a remarkable display of natural beauty with a rich human history of struggle, controversy, and extraordinary achievement. Whether you're a serious climber or a nonclimbing mountain lover, these peaks are sure to inspire. From left to right, here is what's making your jaw drop:

- **Cerro Torre:** At 3,102m (10,174 ft.), this granite needle sticks straight into the sky. Its first ascent has been the subject of debate for 50 years, since photographer and climber Tony Egger disappeared on what climbing partner Cesare Maestri claimed was the first summit. Maestri's account has been long doubted and debated. A recent team of climbers followed the route Maestri described and found it impossible to climb, with no apparent evidence of previous attempts.
- **Cerro Standhart:** The granite needle Standhart at 2,650m (8,692 ft.), is seen as a good warm-up for those attempting the summit of Cerro Torre.
- **Torre Egger:** Named after Tony Egger, who allegedly climbed what was considered the hardest mountain climb in the world with Maestri in 1956. When Egger disappeared on the descent, along with his camera, he shattered the credibility of the summit Maestri claimed.
- **Pico Poincenot:** The big one to the left of FitzRoy group, this spire reaches 3,002m (9,846 ft.).
- **Mt. FitzRoy:** Named for Sir Robert FitzRoy, the Capitan of HMCS *Beagle*, which brought Charles Darwin on his first voyage to South America, this magnetic giant stands 3,405m (11,168 ft.) tall. For generations, the local Tehuelche people have called FitzRoy "El Chaltén," or volcano, because it is almost always covered by clouds, which they confused for smoke. To the left of FitzRoy are the spires Agujas, St. Exupery, and Rafael Juarez. To the right are Mermoz and Guillaumet.

Laguna Torre ✯✯   Continuing past the Cerro Torre lookout (see above), the trail winds its way up the FitzRoy River to the sheltered nook at the D'Agostini campground, which is a good spot for a protected picnic. From here, you climb up over the moraine and face first into the howling wind for a jaw-dropping close-up of Cerro Torre, its glacier, and its milky blue lake. Next to the Torre Glacier, you have a glimpse of the Grande Glacier. This is a 22km (12-mile) round-trip; plan for 3 hours each way. There are also good views of Mt. Solo and the Adela chain en route. If you have time left at the lake, scramble to the north shore of Laguna Torre to Mirador Maestri. For an even fuller day, you can include a hike with crampons on the Torre Glacier as well, though this must be done with a guide from FitzRoy Expediciones (see "Tour Operators," above).

6- to 7-hr. return. 11km (7 miles) one-way. Medium.

Laguna de los Tres ⭐⭐ The best full-day hike in El Chaltén takes you along the Chorrillo del Salto river past the campground at Poincenot, which is probably the best and most centrally located campground in the area, and over the Rio Blanco before the final steep climb (400m/1,312 ft., which will take you an hour) up to the gorgeous Laguna de los Tres, nestled beneath the giant granite walls of Mt. FitzRoy.

10-hr. return. 13km (8 miles) one-way. Medium/difficult.

Pilar-Río Blanco–Poincenot This alternative to the Laguna de los Tres trek starts at Hostería el Pilar and heads back to El Chaltén via Río Blanco. The advantage is that it's a one-way trail (one of the only), so you are not retracing your steps. To make it to Laguna de los Tres, though, you need to get a very early start. You'll need a shuttle one-way to get to the trail head, on the banks of the Río Eléctrico, at Hostería El Pilar, 17km (11 miles) from El Chaltén. Many local companies, including Patagonia Magica (see above), can help you organize this. From here it's a gradual climb to Laguna Capri (see above) before dropping back into El Chaltén.

9 hr. 20km (12 miles) total. Medium/difficult.

WHERE TO STAY

As the distances from El Calafate shrinks, thanks to highway pavement, El Chaltén is taking a swing upscale. Formerly a destination for backpackers and hostel-goers, it now affords interesting new lodging options. And more luxury inns are on the horizon, so stay tuned!

Albergue Patagonia Cozy and friendly, this is the smallest and best hostel in town. Service is caring and helpful, and the place fills up with mountain lovers. A total of 20 beds are spread among different rooms, none of which sleeps more than five. There is a big kitchen for guests to use. The upstairs loft is a nice place to read a book, watch a movie, or chat with fellow travelers. Next door, they are opening a new building with double rooms, each with private bathrooms.

San Martín s/n, El Chaltén. © 2962/493019. 20 dorm beds, 3 private rooms. $30 (£17) double with shared bathroom, $10 (£5.50) dorm room with shared bathroom. No credit cards. **Amenities:** Kitchen; bike rentals; laundry room.

El Puma ⭐ A mainstay that has played host to many mountaineers over the years, El Puma offers comfortable accommodations and friendly service. The owners of this hotel work with the outfitter Fitz Roy Expediciones, which has an office next door. The hotel sits back from the main road and faces out toward snowy peaks, though the view doesn't take in FitzRoy. Inside, warm beige walls and wooden beams interplay with brick, offset with soft cotton curtains and ironwork. Although the common areas have terra-cotta ceramic floors, all rooms are carpeted. The rooms are well designed and spacious; the lounge has a few chairs that face a roaring fire. The staff is very helpful. There's also a good restaurant with wooden tables and a small bar. El Puma is the closest thing to a classic mountain lodge that you'll find in El Chaltén.

Lionel Terray 512, El Chaltén. ©/fax 02962/493095. www.hosteriaelpuma.com.ar. 12 units. $140 (£77) double. Rates include buffet breakfast and transfers from the bus stop. MC, V. Closed Apr–Oct. **Amenities:** Restaurant; bar; lunch catering; excursions; transfers; laundry services.

Hostería El Pilar ⭐ Seventeen kilometers (10 miles) from El Chaltén, Hostería El Pilar has long been popular with trekking groups. It's isolated, but then lovely, peaceful surroundings are what many guests look for when they come to visit the national park. The yellow-walled and red-roofed El Pilar was once an *estancia;* now it's tastefully and artistically decorated with just enough detail to look great without distracting you from the outdoors. The lounge has a few couches and a fireplace, and it's a comfy spot in which to hang out and read a book. Rooms are simple but attractive, with peach walls, comfortable beds, and sunlight that streams through half-curtained windows. Superior rooms are all doubles and have bigger bathrooms. Transfers from El Chaltén are included. Guests normally take their meals at the hotel's restaurant, which serves great cuisine. The hotel offers guided excursions, and it's located next to several trail heads. If you're driving here, keep an eye open for the sign to this hotel, because it's easy to miss. It is open to the public as a teahouse.

Ruta Provincial 23, 17km (10 miles) from El Chaltén. ℂ/fax 02962/493002. 9 units. $108 (£59) double standard; $125 (£69) superior. No credit cards. Open Oct–Apr; rest of the year with a reservation. **Amenities:** Restaurant; bar; lounge.

Los Cerros Del Chaltén ℱ   Owners of the famous Los Notros Hotel have done their best to spiff things up in El Chaltén. The brand-new Los Cerros inn is by far the most luxurious place in town. Throughout, deep oranges and rusts complement the natural surroundings. The common spaces have a new cottage feel, with comfy sofas and tall ceilings The rooms, on either side of green hallways, are large and open to fabulous views stretching above the village and across the valley. Bathrooms come in a variety of set-ups, all with modern fixtures and a jetted soaker tub in which to rest your weary bones. Top-floor premium rooms have sloped ceilings and an alpine chalet feel. There are no TVs or phones in the rooms; but there is a common living room with picture books and a large TV where you can watch movies. I found the service a bit too formal for a laid-back mountain village such as El Chaltén. The restaurant is excellent, particularly the scrumptious baked goods. However, the all-inclusive nature of most packages keep you from discovering the surprisingly fun and funky restaurants of El Chaltén. The downstairs spa is minimal but relaxing enough. Too new to be a sure thing, Los Cerros opens up a whole new option for those who prefer the best.

San Martín s/n, El Chaltén. ℂ 2962/491185. www.loscerrosdelchalten.com. 44 units. 2-night packages $608–$711 (£334–£391) per person in double occupancy. All-inclusive packages include meals, transfers, and select excursions. Room and half-board-only options are also available. AE, MC, V. **Amenities:** Restaurant; lounge; small spa; excursions; gift shop; room service; laundry service; Internet; library; mini-cinema. *In room:* Hair dryer, safe, jetted tubs, no phone.

Nothafagus B and B ℱ *Value*   Owned and operated by a down-to-earth local couple, this B&B is bright, sunny, and well priced. There are seven simple and clean rooms; three are doubles with private bathrooms, and four have shared bathrooms and a mix of beds. The upstairs triple has a huge bathroom. If you like the unpretentiousness of a hostel but want something more mature and quieter (although walls are a bit thin), this is a great choice. There is also a cozy reading room. Hearty breakfast is included.

Hensen s/n, El Chaltén. ℂ 2962/493087. www.elchalten.com/nothofagus. 7 units. $35 (£19) with shared bathroom; $65 (£36) with private bathroom. No credit cards. Open Oct–Apr; rest of the year with reservations only. **Amenities:** Laundry service; library.

WHERE TO DINE

For a casual town where everyone wears a backpack, El Chaltén has surprisingly good dining options. During the winter, only one restaurant valiantly stays open: **La Casita,** Avenida del Libertador at Lionel Terray, in the pink building (ℂ **2966/493042**). La Casita serves average, home-style fare, including sandwiches, meats, pastas, stuffed crepes, and absent-minded service; it accepts American Express, MasterCard, and Visa.

Climbers gather during a stormy day at **Patagonicus,** Güemes at Andreas Madsen (*©* **2966/493025**). Patagonicus serves mostly pizza and enormous salads in a woodsy dining area; no credit cards accepted. It's a good spot for an afternoon coffee. **Fuegia** *⭐*, San Martín s/n (*©* **2966/493019**), has an eclectic, global menu including coconut chicken with cashews and excellent salads. There are also good vegetarian options. In a ramshackle old house loaded with character, **Ruca Mahuida,** at Lionel Terray 501 (*©* **2962/493018**), has the feel of an old alpine hut. The food is pure Patagonian, with stews, trout, and hearty pastas to fill you up after a day on the trail. Diners gather around a handful of tables, making this a great spot to make new friends. Reservations are recommended. For a funky scene with cool music and creative food, head to **Estepa,** at the corner of Cerro Solo and Antonio Rojo (*©* **2962/493069**). The lamb in soft mint sauce, pizzas, and pumpkin sorrentinos are superb.

9 Torres del Paine National Park, Chile *⭐⭐*

113km (70 miles) N of Puerto Natales; 360km (223 miles) NW of Punta Arenas

Across the border from Argentina's Los Glaciares National Park is Chile's prized jewel—a national park so magnificent that few in the world can claim a rank in its class. Torres del Paine is a major tourist destination whose popularity has grown tenfold over the past 5 years. Granite peaks and towers soar from sea level to upward of 2,800m (9,184 ft.). Golden plains and the rolling steppes are home to llamalike guanacos and more than 100 species of colorful birds, such as parakeets, flamingos, and ostrichlike rheas. During the spring, Chilean firebush blooms a riotous red, and during the autumn, the park's beech trees change to crimson, sunflower, and orange. A fierce wind screams through this region during the spring and summer, yet flowers, such as the delicate porcelain orchids and ladyslippers, somehow weather the inhospitable terrain. Electric-blue icebergs cleave from Glacier Grey. Resident gauchos ride atop sheepskin saddles. Condors float effortlessly even on the windiest day. This park is not something you just visit; it is something you experience.

Although it sits next to the Andes, **Parque Nacional Torres del Paine** is a separate geologic formation created roughly 3 million years ago when bubbling magma began growing and pushing its way up, taking a thick sedimentary layer with it. Glaciation and severe climate weathered away the softer rock, leaving the spectacular Paine Massif, whose prominent features are the *Cuernos* (which means "horns") and the one-of-a-kind *Torres*—three salmon-colored, spherical granite towers. The black sedimentary rock is visible on the upper reaches of the elegant Cuernos, named for the two spires that rise from the outer sides of its amphitheater. *Paine* is the Tehuelche Indian word for "blue," and it brings to mind the varying shades found in the lakes that surround this massif— among them the milky, turquoise waters of Lagos Nordenskjold and Pehoé. Backing the Paine Massif are several glaciers that descend from the Southern Ice Field.

Torres del Paine was once a collection of *estancias* and small-time ranches; many were forced out with the creation of the park in 1959. The park has since grown to its present size of 242,242 hectares (598,338 acres), and in 1978 was declared a World Biosphere Reserve by UNESCO for its singular beauty and ecology. This park used to be a backpacker's dream, for adventurous trekkers only. These days, more and more visitors are choosing shorter hikes and fancier lodges, and Torres del Paine is closer to becoming a destination on the beaten path. Hiking along the main trails, you may find yourself in a queue and stumble upon places to spend money at every corner. Still, it's a big place, with big skies and room for many. There are options for everyone, which is why the number of visitors to this park is growing by nearly 20,000 per year.

ESSENTIALS
WHEN TO COME & WHAT TO BRING
This is not the easiest of national parks to visit. The climate in the park can be abominable. Wind speeds can peak at 161kmph (100 mph), and it can rain and snow even in the middle of summer. It is not unusual for visitors to spend 5 days in the park and never see the Towers. On average, the windiest days happen between late November and mid-March, but the only predictable thing about the weather here is its unpredictability. Spring is a beautiful time for budding flowers and birds; during the fall, the beech forests turn colors, which can be especially striking on walks up to the Towers and to the glacier. The winter is surprisingly temperate, with relatively few snowstorms and no wind—but short days. You'll need to stay in a hotel during the winter, but you'll practically have the park to yourself. Summer is, ironically, the worst time to come, especially from late December to mid-February, when the wind blows at full fury and crowds descend upon the park. When the wind blows, it can make even a short walk a rather scary experience or just crazy making. But just try to go with it, rather than fight it, and revel in the excitement of the extreme environment that defines Patagonia.

I can't stress enough the importance of bringing the right gear, especially waterproof hiking boots (if you plan to do any trekking), weatherproof outerwear, and warm layers, even in the summer. The ozone problem is acute here, so you'll need sunscreen, sunglasses, and a hat as well.

VISITOR & PARK ENTRANCE INFORMATION
Your visit to Torres del Paine will require logistical planning, unless you've left it up to an all-inclusive tour or hotel. Begin your research at www.torresdelpaine.cl, an English-language overview of the park and its surroundings, including maps, activities information, events, photos, hotel overviews and links, and more. The park service **CONAF** has a relatively unhelpful Spanish-only website at www.conaf.cl. The park's administration and visitor center are at the southern end of the park (© 61/691931). The park is open year-round from 8:30am to 10pm. The cost to enter is $30 (£17); during the winter, the cost is $10 (£5.50) for adults.

GETTING THERE & AWAY
Many travelers are unaware of the enormous amount of time it takes to get to Torres del Paine. From the Argentine side, semiregular buses run to the park, but most go first to the town of Puerto Natales, where you will need to spend the night before heading to the park. Remember that if you are planning to camp in Torres del Paine, you'll need to buy most of your food in Puerto Natales, since there are very limited grocery options in the park, and you can not take fresh food across the border from Argentina.

BY BUS   To get to Torres del Paine from Argentina by bus, your best bet is to take the regular bus to Puerto Natales, spend the night there, then head into the park the next morning. **Bus Sur Zaahj,** at the Bus Terminal (© 02902/491631), runs this route six days a week, leaving El Calafate at 1pm. **Cootra,** which has an office in

Baquedano 244 (© **02902/491144**), departs El Calafate at 8am. Buy tickets at least the day before to ensure yourself a seat. **Cordillera del Sol,** whose office is at 25 de Mayo 43 in El Calafate (© **02902/492822;** www.cordilleradelsol.com), offers transfers from El Calafate to Torres del Paine directly.

From Puerto Natales, buses to Torres del Paine enter through the Laguna Amarga ranger station, stop at the Pudeto catamaran dock, and terminate at the park administration center. If you're going directly to the Torres trail head at Hostería Las Torres, there are minivan transfers waiting at the Laguna Amarga station that charge about $5 (£2.75) one-way. The return times given below are when the bus leaves from the park administration center; the bus will pass through the Laguna Amarga station about 45 minutes later. Some buses will pick you up from your hotel, but it depends on the relationship your hotel has with the various bus companies, so ask at the hotel reception.

JB, Arturo Prat 258 (© **61/410242**), leaves at 7:30am and 2pm, and returns at 1 and 6:30pm; **Gomez,** Arturo Prat 234 (© **61/411791**), leaves daily also at 7:30am and 2pm, returning at 1pm and 6:15pm; and **Andescape,** Eberhard 599 (© **61/412877**), leaves at 7:30am and 2pm, returning at 1pm and 6pm. The cost is around $15 (£8.25) one-way.

Every day during the summer at 5pm, a bus goes directly from Laguna Amarga to El Calafate, across the border in Argentina. Contact **CalTur** (© **02902/492217** from within Argentina) for more information. It costs $38 (£21), twice as expensive as the bus from Puerto Natales to El Calafate.

BY TOUR VAN   From El Calafate, a handful of similar "Paine in a Day" tours includes one organized by **Chaltén Travel** (© **02902/492212** in El Calafate; www.chaltentravel.com) for $65 (£36). It's a long but unforgettable day. They will also pick you up or drop you off in the park. **Comapa** (© **61/414300;** www.comapa.com) has an 11-hour tour of Paine from Puerto Natales that includes a few short hikes and lunch at the Hostería Lago Grey.

BY CAR   From El Calafate, the direct drive to Torres del Paine is 394km (224 miles). Head south on Ruta 11 to Ruta 40 past the small town at El Cerrito to the border at Cerro Castillo. On the Chilean side of the border, head north on Ruta 9 at Cerro Castillo 84km (52 miles) to the park's administration building, or right/south on Ruta 9 for 63km (39 miles) to Puerto Natales. Be sure to tell the rental car agency that you will be taking your car to Chile, which requires special permits. The drive is 342km (212 miles) long and takes approximately 5 hours.

CROSSING LAGO PEHOE BY CATAMARAN   Day hikers to the Glacier Grey trail and backpackers taking the W or Circuit trails will need to cross Lake Pehoé at some point aboard a catamaran, about a 45-minute ride. The cost is $33 (£18) one-way. Buses from Puerto Natales are timed to drop off and pick up passengers in conjunction with the catamaran (Dec–Mar 15 leaving Pudeto at 9:30am, noon, and 6pm; and from Pehoé at 10am, 12:30, and 6:30pm; in Nov and Mar 16–30 from Pudeto at noon and 6pm, and Pehoé at 12:30 and 6pm; in Oct and Apr, from Pudeto at noon, from Pehoé at 12:30pm; closed May–Sept but service may expand—check with CONAF). Hikers walking the entire round-trip Glacier Grey trail can do so only on the 9:30am boat, returning at 6:30pm from December to March 15. The boat fills up quickly, so try to be there early; it's first-come, first-served.

WHERE TO STAY & DINE IN TORRES DEL PAINE
HOTELS & *HOSTERIAS*

Hostería Lago Grey ⋆   This spruce little white *hostería* is tucked within a beech forest, looking out onto the beach at Lago Grey and the astounding blue icebergs that drift to its shore. It's well on the other side of the park, but the view is better here than at the Hostería las Torres, and they have a transfer van and guides for excursions to all reaches of the park. The 20 rooms are spread out from a main common area, a thoroughly enjoyable place to relax, with a restaurant, outdoor deck, and lounge area. The price suggests more luxurious rooms, but the walls are a tad thin and have little decoration. Also, when the wind whips up, this side of the park is colder. On the plus side, there are plenty of trails that branch out from here, including the stroll along the beach out to the Pingo Valley and the strenuous hike up to Mirador Ferrier. You can also arrange rafting trips down the Rio Grey and kayaking among the icebergs. The transfer van will pick you up from any roadside spot in the park.

Office in Punta Arenas, Lautaro Navarro 1061. ℂ 61/229512. www.turismolagogrey.com. 30 units. Oct–Apr $250 (£138) double; May–Sept $120 (£66) double. Rates include buffet breakfast. AE, DC, MC, V. **Amenities:** Restaurant; lounge; tours.

Hostería Las Torres ⋆⋆ *(Kids)*   This *hostería* sits at the trail head to the Torres on an *estancia* that still operates as a working cattle ranch. Accordingly, the complex includes a low-slung, ranch-style hotel, and there's a large campground and a hostel—meaning a fair amount of traffic comes in and out daily. In the afternoon, horses and the odd cow graze just outside your hotel room door, meaning it's a fun place for kids. The *hostería* is a decent value for its standard rooms, which are far lower in price yet nearly identical to the newer, "superior" rooms. This is an ideal lodge for horseback-riding enthusiasts due to their on-site stables, and its access to the Towers is convenient; however, it is a long drive to the other side of the park. The *hostería* now offers expensive packages that include guided tours, meals, and transportation, much like Explora, and excellent off-season trips to little-explored areas (their 4-night package is just $200/£110 cheaper per person than Explora, so comparison-shop beforehand). Packages run from 3 to 7 nights, or you can pay separately for day trips. Try spending 2 nights here and 2 at Hostería Grey, thereby avoiding the steep price of an excursion there. Las Torres recently inaugurated a small spa, with mud therapy, massage, and sauna. The buffet-style restaurant is above-par, but pricey at $30 (£17) a person for dinner.

Office in Punta Arenas, Magallanes 960. ℂ/fax 61/710050. www.lastorres.com. 56 units. From $149 (£82) double. Rates include buffet breakfast. AE, DC, MC, V. **Amenities:** Restaurant; lounge; spa; tour desk; room service; laundry service; conference rooms; horseback riding.

Hostería Mirador del Payne ⋆   This *hostería* is part of an antique *estancia* just outside the park, and it boasts a commanding view of the Paine Massif rising behind a grassy field and Lake Verde. If you really want to get away from crowds, this is your hotel, although it doesn't put you directly near the park's trail heads. The rooms are in a unit separate from the main lodge, which has a restaurant, bar, and fireside lounge. The *hostería* offers horseback-riding opportunities that include a chance to corral cattle and assist with other ranch duties. Access to the *hostería* is via one of two ways: by a road that branches off before arriving at the park or by a moderate 2-hour trail that leads to the park administration center. Guests arrive by road, but more than a few opt

---

(*Tips*) **Advance Planning**

Due to the soaring popularity of Torres del Paine, it is recommended that travelers book well in advance if they're planning to visit the park between late November and late March. Nearly every business now has a website or, at the very least, an e-mail address, so trip planning is easier than ever. Hotels can be booked directly, and often they offer their own transportation from the airport. At the very least, they can recommend a service to call or e-mail. One-stop local agencies such as **Path@gone Travel,** Eberhard 595 in Puerto Natales (© **61/ 413291;** www.pathagone.com), is a good place for *refugio* reservations, horseback-riding trips, or camping equipment rentals, and they can sometimes offer lower hotel rates at *hosterías* in the park. They can also solve tricky transfer problems. **Turismo Comapa** in Punta Arenas is another all-around company that can book tours, *refugio* stays, and more (Magallanes 990; © **61/200200;** www.comapa.com). They also have an 11-hour "Paine in One Day" excursion for those on a tight schedule.

---

to end their stay here with a horseback ride to the park administration center to continue on to another hotel within the park's boundaries.

Office in Punta Arenas, Fagnano 585. © 61/228712. www.miradordelpayne.com. 20 units. Nov–Mar 15 $195 (£107) double; Mar 16–Oct $160 (£88) double. AE, DC, MC, V. **Amenities:** Restaurant; bar; lounge; tours; laundry service.

Hostería Pehoé ⭐   This is the park's oldest hotel, built before Torres del Paine was declared a national park. It is located near the Explora Hotel, on an island in Lake Pehoé, and it enjoys the same dynamite view of the Cuernos formation. However, none of the rooms here comes with the view because they are located behind the main building in a grove of beech trees. It's an awesome location nonetheless, and it is situated in the middle of the park, cutting down on driving time to either end (the reason for its one star). The guest rooms have been spruced up a bit recently, but they are still too run-of-the-mill for management to charge $160 (£88) for a double during high season. This is the only hotel in the area with satellite TV in rooms. Guests normally take their meals in the hotel's restaurant, which offers so-so fare at above-average prices.

Office in Punta Arenas, Jose Menendezs 918. © 61/244506. www.pehoe.com. 25 units. $260 (£143) double. AE, DC, MC, V. **Amenities:** Restaurant; bar; lounge; tours; laundry service. *In room:* TV.

Hotel Explora Salto Chico ⭐⭐⭐ (*Moments*)   Explora in Patagonia has garnered more fame than any other hotel in Chile, and deservedly so. Few hotels in the world offer as stunning a view as does Explora, perched above the milky, turquoise waters of Lago Pehoé and facing the dramatic granite amphitheater of the Cuernos formation. It is terribly expensive, but worth the splurge if you can afford it. Explora's style is comfortable elegance, and its handsome contemporary interiors belie the rather bland modernist exterior: Softly curving blond-wood walls built entirely from native deciduous beech are a soothing ambience in which to relax after a long hike. A band of picture windows wraps around the full front of the building, and there are large windows in each room— even the bathrooms come with cutouts in the wall so that while you're brushing your teeth, you can still have your eyes on the gorgeous panorama. The furniture was handcrafted using local wood, and the crisp guest rooms are accented with Spanish checkered linens, handsome slate-tiled bathrooms, and warming racks for drying gear. Explora recently expanded to include 20 new guest rooms, meaning it is easier now to get a reservation than before, but the hotel has, in the process, lost a bit of the intimacy it had with just 30 rooms.

Explora is all-inclusive, with prices that cover airport transfers, meals, open bar, and excursions. Every evening, 5 of the 20 full-time guides meet with guests to discuss the following day's excursions, which range from easy half-day walks to strenuous full-day hikes. There are about 15 excursions to choose from, including horseback rides and photo safaris. In the morning, a fleet of vans whisks guests off to their destination and back again for lunch; guides carry picnic lunches for full-day hikes. The set menu is limited to two choices, generally a meat and vegetarian dish, and it must be said that the food quality has at times been uneven—never bad, but not as outstanding as one would expect from a hotel of this caliber. Americans make up a full 50% of the guests, who typically leave thrilled with their visit. Note that the first-day arrival to the hotel is around 6pm, leaving time for a short hike to a lookout point only. And the last day isn't really a day at all, as guests leave after breakfast for the drive back to the airport.

In Santiago, Américo Vespucio Sur 80, 5th floor. (℃ 2/395-2533. Fax 2/228-4655. www.explora.com. 51 units. Packages per person, double occupancy: 4 nights/3 days starting at $3,060 (£1,683); 8 nights/7 days starting at $5,515 (£3,033). Rates include all meals, transportation, gear, and guides. AE, DC, MC, V. **Amenities:** Restaurant; bar; lounge; large indoor heated pool; outdoor Jacuzzi; sauna; massage; laundry service; Internet. *In room:* Minibar.

REFUGIOS & HOSTALES

Four cabinlike lodging units, all with shared accommodation, distributed along the park's Circuit and W trails, are moderately priced sleeping options for backpackers who are not interested in pitching a tent. Although most have bedding or sleeping bags for an expensive rental price, your best bet is to bring your own. The price, at $35 (£19) on average per night (about $63/£35 for room and full board), is not cheap; it's at least three times more than camping. All come with hot showers, a cafe, and a common area for hiding out from bad weather. Meals served here are simply prepared but hearty. Alternatively, guests can bring their own food and cook. Each *refugio* has rooms with two to six bunks, which you'll have to share with strangers when they're full. During the high season, consider booking weeks in advance; although many visitors have reported luck after calling just a few days beforehand (due to cancellations). All agencies in Puerto Natales and Punta Arenas book reservations and issue vouchers, but the best bet is to call or e-mail (shown below).

The first three *refugios* are owned and operated by The Paine Grande Mountain Lodge (www.verticepatagonia.cl/ingles/lodge.htm).

- **Albergue Las Torres:** This lodge is the largest and most full-service *refugio* in the park; it sits near the Hostería Las Torres. You may dine in the hotel or eat simple fare in the *refugio* itself. Horseback rides can be taken from here. Call or book through Fantástico Sur, a division of the Hostería las Torres (℃/fax **61/710050;** albergue@lastorres.com).

- **Refugio Chileno:** This is the least-frequented *refugio* because it is located halfway up to the Towers (most do the trail as a day hike). Hikers will find it more convenient to stow their stuff in the campground at the *hostería,* but, then again, this *refugio* puts you away from the hubbub below. Call or book through Fantástico Sur, a division of the Hostería las Torres (℃/fax **61/710050;** albegue@lastorres.com).

- **Refugio Los Cuernos:** This may be the park's loveliest *refugio*, located at the base of the Cuernos. The wood structure (which miraculously holds up to some of the strongest winds in the park) has two walls of windows that look out onto Lago Nordenskjold. Call or book through Fantástico Sur, a division of the Hostería las Torres (©/fax **61/710050;** albergue@lastorres.com).
- **Paine Grande Mountain Lodge:** This *hostal*-like "lodge" replaces the old *refugio* Pehoé, at the busiest intersection in the park. It is the hub for several of the trail heads to the park administration center, Glacier Grey, and French Valley, as well as the docking site for the catamaran. Utilitarian in style, the hostal has 60 beds, two lounges, and a cafeteria that can serve 120 people. Day walks to Glacier Grey and French Valley can be taken from here. Call or book at © **61/412742;** contact@verticepatagonia.cl.

CAMPING IN TORRES DEL PAINE

Torres del Paine has a well-designed campground system with free and concession-run sites. All *refugios* have a campground, too, and these and other concession sites charge about $15 (£8.25) per person, which includes hot showers, clean bathrooms, and an indoor dining area in which to escape bad weather and eat under a roof. The site at Las Torres provides barbecues and firewood. Free campgrounds are run by CONAF, and they can get a little dingy, with deplorable outhouses. Beginning in March, mice become a problem for campers, so always leave food well stored or hanging from a tree branch. The JLM hiking map (available at every bookstore, airport, kiosk, and travel agency, and at the park entrance) denotes which campgrounds are free and which charge a fee.

TRAILS IN TORRES DEL PAINE

Torres del Paine has something for everyone, from easy, well-trammeled trails to remote walks through relatively people-free wilderness. Which path you choose depends on how much time you have and what kind of walking you're up for. Pick up one of **JLM's Torres del Paine maps** (sold everywhere), or download a map from **www.torresdelpaine.com** to begin planning your itinerary. Walking times shown below are average.

LONG-HAUL OVERNIGHT HIKES

The Circuit The Circuit is a spectacular, long-haul backpacking trip that takes hikers around the entire Paine Massif. It can be done in two ways: with the W included or without. Including the W, you'll need 8 to 11 days; without it, from 4 to 7 days. The Circuit is less traveled than the W because it's longer and requires that you camp out at least twice. I don't recommend doing this trail if you have only 4 or 5 days. This trail is for serious backpackers only, because it involves several difficult hikes up and down steep, rough terrain and over fallen tree trunks. You'll be rewarded for your effort, however, with dazzling views of terrain that varies from grassy meadows and winding rivers to thick virgin beech forest, snowcapped peaks, and, best of all, the awe-inspiring view of Glacier Grey seen from atop the John Garner Pass. If you're a recreational hiker with a 4- to 6-hour hike tolerance level, you'll want to sleep in all the major campgrounds or *refugios*. Always do this trail counterclockwise for easier ascents and with the scenery before you. If you're here during the high season and want to get away from crowds, you might contemplate walking the first portion of this trail, beginning at Laguna Azul. This is the old trail, and it more or less parallels the Circuit, but on the other side of the river, passing the gaucho post La Victorina, the only remaining building of an old *estancia*. At Refugio Dickson, you'll have to cross the river in the *refugio*'s dinghy for $4 (£2.20). To get to Laguna Azul, you'll need to hitchhike or arrange private transportation.

Approximately 60km (37 miles) total. Beginning at Laguna Amarga or Hostería Las Torres. Terrain ranges from easy to difficult.

The W   This segment of the Paine Massif is so called because hikers are taken along a trail that forms a W. This trail leads to the park's major geological features—the Torres, the Cuernos, and Glacier Grey—and it's the preferred multiple-day hike for its relatively short hauls and a time frame that requires 4 to 5 days. In addition, those who prefer not to camp or carry more gear than a sleeping bag, food, and their personal goods can stay in the various *refugios* along the way. Most hikers begin at Hostería Las Torres and start with a day-walk up to the Torres. From here, hikers head to the Los Cuernos *refugio* and spend the night, or continue on to the Italiano campsite near the base of the valley; then they walk up to French Valley. The next stop is Pehoé *refugio*, where most spend the night before hiking up to Glacier Grey. It's best to spend a night at Refugio Grey and return to the Pehoé *refugio* the next day. From here, take the catamaran across Lago Pehoé to an awaiting bus back to Puerto Natales.

Approximately 56km (35 miles) total. Beginning at Hostería Las Torres or Refugio Pehoé. Terrain ranges from easy to difficult.

DAY HIKES

These hikes run from easy to difficult, either within the W or from various trail heads throughout the park. Again, the times given are estimates for the average walker.

Glacier Grey   This walk is certainly worth the effort for an up-close look at the face of Glacier Grey, though warm summers of late have sent the glacier retreating. There aren't as many steep climbs as the trail to Las Torres, but it takes longer to get there (about 3½ hr.). I recommend that hikers in the summer walk this lovely trail to the glacier lookout point, and then take the boat back to Hostería Grey. The walk takes hikers through thick forest and stunning views of the Southern Ice Field and the icebergs slowly making their way down Lago Grey. A turnoff just before the lookout point takes you to Refugio Grey.

3½ hr. one-way. Difficult.

Lago Grey *(Moments)*   Not only is this the easiest walk in the park, but it is one of the most dramatic for the gigantic blue icebergs that rest along the shore of Lago Grey. A flat walk across the sandy shore of the lake takes visitors to a peninsula for a short hike to a lookout point with Glacier Grey in the far distance. This walk begins near the Hostería Lago Grey; they offer a recommended boat ride that weaves past icebergs and then takes passengers to the face of the glacier.

Departing from the parking lot past the entrance to Hostería Lago Grey. 1–2 hr. one-way. Easy.

Lago Pingo *(Finds)*   Lago Pingo consistently sees fewer hikers, and it's an excellent spot for bird-watching for the variety of species that flock to this part of the park. The trail begins as an easy walk through a pleasant valley, past an old gaucho post. From here the trail heads through forest and undulating terrain, and past the Pingo Cascade until it eventually reaches another old gaucho post, the run-down but picturesque Zapata *refugio*. You can make this trail as long or as short as you'd like; the return is back along the same trail. The trail leaves from the same parking lot as the Lago Grey trail.

Departing from the Lago Grey parking lot past the entrance to Hostería Lago Grey. 1–4 hr. one-way. Easy/moderate.

Las Torres (The Towers)　The trail to view the soaring granite Towers is a classic hike in the park but certainly not the easiest. Those who are in decent shape will not want to miss this exhilarating trek. The trail leaves from the Hostería Las Torres and begins with a steep 45-minute ascent, followed by up-and-down terrain for 1½ hours to another 45-minute steep ascent up a slippery granite moraine. Midway is the Refugio Chileno, where you can stop for a coffee or spend the night. Don't give up—the Torres do not come into full view until the very end.

3 hr. one-way. Difficult.

Mirador Nordenskjold　The trail head for this walk begins near the Pudeto cata-maran dock. This trail begins with an up-close visit to the crashing Salto Grande waterfall. Then it winds through Antarctic beech and thorny bush to a lookout point with dramatic views into the French Valley and the Cuernos, looking over Lago Nordenskjold. This trail is a good place to see wildflowers in the spring.

1 hr. one-way. Easy.

Valle Francés (French Valley)　There are several ways to hike this trail. From Refugio Pehoé, you'll pass by the blue waters of Lake Skottsberg and through groves of Chilean firebush and open views of the granite spires behind Los Cuernos. From Refugio Los Cuernos, you won't see French Valley until you're in it. A short walk through the campground leads hikers to direct views of the hanging glacier that descends from Paine Grande, and enthusiastic hikers can continue the steep climb up into the valley itself for a view of French Valley's enormous granite amphitheater.

Departing from Refugio Pehoé or Refugio Los Cuernos. 2½–4½ hr. one-way. Moderate/difficult.

OTHER OUTDOOR ACTIVITIES IN THE PARK
HORSEBACK RIDING

A horseback ride in Torres del Paine can be one of the most enjoyable ways to see the park, especially from the Serrano Pampa for big, bold views of Paine Massif. Both Hostería Las Torres and Explora have their own stables, but only the *hostería* has daily horseback rides, even to the Refugios Chileno and Los Cuernos; its Punta Arenas office is at Magallanes 960 (℃/fax **61/226054**). The full-day trips cost $95 (£52) per person, and they leave from the hotel. For longer, multiday horseback-riding trips, contact **Chile Nativo Expeditions,** Eberhart 230 (℃ **61/411835;** www.chilenativo.com). Chile Nativo can plan custom-made journeys within the park and to little-known areas, some of which include an introduction to the gaucho and *estancia* way of life. Most trips require prior experience.

12

Tierra del Fuego & Antarctica

by Charlie O'Malley

Four hundred years have passed since Ferdinand Magellan cast his eyes on the dark headlands, silver shores, and craggy peaks of Tierra del Fuego. As he sailed past, flames blazed in the darkness along the coastline—bonfires lit by the Yamanas tribe—inspiring him to name the place "Land of Fire." Since then, this windswept island, washed by the Magellan straits to the north and Beagle Channel to the south, has witnessed a rich parade of shipwrecks, penal colonies, gold prospectors, and missionaries. The Yamanas have disappeared, but Chile and Argentina have repopulated the area, while conducting a bad-tempered tug of war over its icy inlets and penguin-populated rocks. This wild, romantic island is now divided in two: Argentina controls the lower eastern coast, and the rest belongs to Chile.

Vast sheep *estancias* (ranch farms) to the north cover a rolling tundra of brown furze and isolated farmhouses. Here the wide, meandering Río Grande holds the biggest sea brown trout in the world, making it a mecca for fly fishers. Farther south, the land rises into forests of beech trees and wind-chopped lakes. The snow-flecked summits of the Andes give way to the bustling pioneer town of Ushuaia. Here you'll find an eclectic mix of resettled Argentines and silver-haired American baby boomers stopping off on cruises bound for Antarctica.

This is the end of the world, which is one reason why thousands of visitors flock here every year, and Tierra del Fuego's tourism industry is booming. They also come for rich coastal wildlife, stunning views, the best seafood in Argentina, and off-season skiing beneath hanging glaciers.

Just when you think you can go no farther, you remember that another continent lies farther south. The coldest place on the planet, Antarctica is the world's hottest destination, and it is from Ushuaia that you get there.

1 Ushuaia

461km (286 miles) SW of Punta Arenas; 594km (368 miles) S of Río Gallegos

Pinned snugly in a U-shaped cove facing the Beagle Channel, Ushuaia is a substantial metropolis of 70,000 people. Colorful clapboard houses with rickety staircases and corrugated roofs at impossible angles are punctuated by the occasional bland block of brick or concrete. All rise steeply into a backdrop of beech trees and spirelike mountain summits. Not only is it the most southerly city in the world (Chilean Puerto Williams is actually farther south but hardly qualifies as a city), it also has the distinction of being the only Argentine city on the other side of the Andes. At its tail end, the mountain range is dragged eastwards by restless tectonic plates that rattle frequently—thus the flexible nature of its architecture, and to reach Ushuaia by car you

Ushuaia

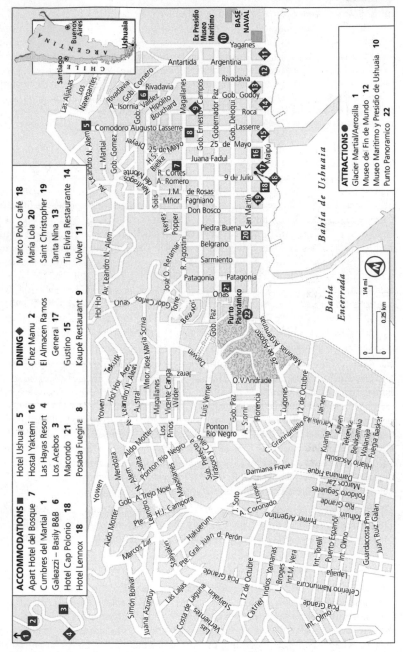

ATTRACTIONS ●
Glacier Martial/Aerosilla **1**
Museo de Fin de Mundo **12**
Museo Maritimo y Presidio de Ushuaia **10**
Punto Panoramico **22**

ACCOMMODATIONS ■
Apart Hotel del Bosque **7**
Cumbres del Martial **1**
Galeazzi – Basily B&B **6**
Hotel Cap Polonio **18**
Hotel Lennox **18**

Hotel Ushuaia **5**
Hostal Yaktemi **16**
Las Hayas Resort **4**
Los Acebos **3**
Macondo **21**
Posada Fueguina **8**

DINING ◆
Chez Manu **2**
El Almacen Ramos
    Generai **17**
Gustino **15**
Kaupé Restaurant **9**

Marco Polo Café **18**
Maria Lola **20**
Saint Christopher **19**
Tanta Nina **13**
Tía Elvira Restaurante **14**
Volver **11**

must cross the Andes. What you find is a frontier town with lots of character and a surprisingly cosmopolitan feel. One hundred years ago, the only people crazy enough to live here were convicts in chains. Indeed, the city owes its existence to the prison: Inmates built the town railway, hospital, and port. Now it attracts Argentines from all over the country, who come for tax breaks and plentiful jobs. Visitors find lots to do—whether it's visiting that same prison, which is now a fascinating museum, or exploring the many attractions of the Beagle Channel. Local residents are welcoming and friendly, with a refreshing hardiness and eccentricity that likely come from living at the end of the world.

ESSENTIALS
GETTING THERE
BY PLANE   The **International Airport Malvinas Argentinas** is 5km (3 miles) from the city (© **02901/431232**). There is no bus service to town, but cab fares are only about $5 (£2.75). Always ask for a quote before accepting a ride. **Aerolíneas Argentinas** (© **0800/222-86527** or 2901/437265; www.aerolineas.com.ar) operates eight or nine daily flights to Buenos Aires, one of which leaves from Ezeiza and stops in El Calafate. Average round-trip fare is $400 (£220). Frequency increases from November to March, when there's also a daily flight from Río Gallegos and twice-weekly flights from Trelew. **LAN Chile** (© **0810/999-9526** or 2901/424244) flies from B.A. once a day on Mondays, Wednesdays, and Saturdays. They also fly from Santiago de Chile on Tuesdays and Thursdays. **Aerovías DAP,** Deloqui 575 (© **2901/431110;** www.aeroviasdap.cl), runs charter flights from Punta Arenas and over Cape Horn. It costs around $3,000 (£1,650) for a group of seven people (round-trip), leaving whenever you want.

BY BUS   There is no bus station in the city. Buses usually stop at the port (Maipú and Fadul). The service from Punta Arenas, Chile, costs $35 (£19) and takes about 12 hours. **Tecni Austral** (© **2901/431408** in Ushuaia, or 61/613423 in Punta Arenas) leaves Mondays, Wednesdays, and Fridays at 5:30am; tickets are sold in Ushuaia from the Tolkar office at Roca 157, and in Punta Arenas at Lautaro Navarro 975. **Tolkeyen,** San Martín 1267 (© **2901/437073;** ventas@tolkeyenpatagonia.com), works with the Chilean company Pacheco for trips to Punta Arenas, leaving on Monday, Wednesday, and Friday at 8am; it costs $50 (£28). To go to Río Grande, try **Lider LTD, Transporte Montiel,** or **Tecni Austral.** They offer eight daily departures, and the $10 (£5.50) trip takes around 4 hours.

BY BOAT   The company **Crucero Australis** operates a cruise to Ushuaia from Punta Arenas and vice versa, aboard its ship the M/V *Mare Australis;* departures are Saturday from Punta Arenas and Wednesday from Ushuaia, from late September to April. See "Cruising from Punta Arenas to Ushuaia," below.

GETTING AROUND
BY CAR   Everything in and around Ushuaia is easily accessible via bus, taxi, or an inexpensive shuttle or tour service. Ushuaia's taxi drivers must be the nation's friendliest, and they're fonts of information concerning the region. The multitude of excursion options obviates the need for a car, though rentals are very reasonable, from $50 to $65 (£28–£36) per day. *Note:* If you decide to drive, pay the small extra fee for enhanced insurance, because basic insurance requires you to pay up to $1,000 (£550) for initial

Cruising from Punta Arenas to Ushuaia

Crucero Australis (www.australis.com) conducts an unforgettable journey between Punta Arenas and Ushuaia aboard its ship, the M/V *Mare Australis*. This cruise takes passengers to remote coves and narrow channels and fjords in Tierra del Fuego, and then heads into the Beagle Channel, stopping in Puerto Williams, on Isla Navarino, and later in Ushuaia, Argentina. The trip can be either a 7-night, 8-day round-trip journey; a 4-night one-way from Punta Arenas; or a 3-night one-way journey from Ushuaia. I recommend that you take just the one-way journey, leaving you to explore a new city and then continue on by air or land from there.

What is unique about this cruise is the intimacy of a smaller ship and its solitary route, which takes passengers to places in Tierra del Fuego that few other travelers have a chance to see. Passengers are shuttled to shore via zodiacs (motorized inflatable boats) for two daily excursions that can include visits to glaciers or a sea elephant rookery, walks to view elaborate beaver dams, or horseback rides. Several excellent bilingual guides give daily talks about the region's flora, fauna, history, and geology. Service aboard the *Mare Australis* is excellent, and the food is quite good. Accommodations are comfortable, ranging from suites to simple cabins. All-inclusive, per-person prices (excluding cocktails) range from $1,200 to $2,200 (£660–£1,210) one-way from Punta Arenas and $3,100 to $5,100 (£1,705–£2,805) round-trip. This cruise runs from early October to late April. For reservations or information, contact their U.S. offices in Miami at 4014 Chase Ave., Suite 202 (© **877/678-3772;** fax 305/534-9276); in Santiago at Av. El Bosque Norte 0440 (© **2/442-3110;** fax 2/203-5173); in Punta Arenas at Av. Independencia 840 (© **61/224256**); or visit www.australis.com.

damage in even a minor accident. **Avis,** Godoy 46, drops its prices for multiple-day rentals (© **2901/436665;** www.avis.com); **Cardos Rent A Car** is at Av. San Martín 845 (© **2901/436388**); **Dollar Rent A Car** is on Belgrano 58 (© **2901/437203;** www.dollar.com); **Localiza Rent A Car** is on Sarmiento 81 (© **2901/437780**); Most of them rent 4×4 Jeeps with unlimited mileage. If you wish to cross into Chile at San Sebastian, you will need a special permission document costing $50 (£28).

VISITOR INFORMATION

The **Subsecretaría de Turismo** have two very helpful and well-stocked offices on San Martín 674 (© **2901/424550** or 0800 333 1476; fax: 2901/432000) and the other one in the tourism Pier, Maipú 505 (© **2901/437666;** fax 2901/430694; www.e-ushuaia.com). They also have a counter at the airport. From November to March, the offices are open daily from 8am to 10pm. The rest of the year they are open Monday through Friday from 8am to 9pm, weekends and holidays from 9am to 8pm. The national park administration office is on Av. San Martín 1395 (© **2901/421315;** Mon–Fri 9am–3pm).

FAST FACTS: Ushuaia

Currency Exchange **Banco Patagonia,** Avenida San Martín and Godoy ((C) **2901/ 432080**), and **Banco Nación,** Av. San Martín 190 ((C) **2901/422086**); both exchange currency and have 24-hour ATMs.

Laundry **Los Tres Angeles,** Rosas 139, is open Monday through Saturday from 9am to 8pm.

Pharmacy **Andina,** Av. San Martín 638 ((C) **2901/423431**).

Post Office **Correo Argentino** is at Avenida San Martín and Godoy ((C) **2901/ 421347**), open Monday through Friday from 9am to 7pm, Saturday from 9am to 1pm; the private postal company **OCA** is at Maipú and Avenida 9 de Julio ((C) **2901/424729**), open Monday through Saturday from 9am to 6pm.

Travel Agency & Credit Cards **American Express** travel and credit card services are provided by **All Patagonia,** Juana Fadul 48 ((C) **2901/433622**).

WHERE TO STAY

It seems that anyone with a large house in Ushuaia is offering rooms, and the plethora of hotels, B&Bs, and cabins can be bewildering. Nevertheless, accommodations are not cheap, and price is often not indicative of quality. It's best to shop around before committing to lodgings. Below are some of the best values in the area.

VERY EXPENSIVE

Las Hayas Resort Hotel 🛇🛇 *(Finds*   Ushuaia's best hotel is on the road to Glacier Martial. If you're looking for elegant accommodations, look no further. This imposing hotel sits nestled in a forest of beech, a location that yields sweeping views of the town and the Beagle Channel. It's at least 3km (1¾ miles) from downtown, however, so you'll need to take a cab, hike, or use one of the hotel's summer-only transfer shuttles. The sumptuous lounge stretches the length of the building; here you'll find a clubby bar, formal restaurant, and fireside sitting area. The rooms are decorated with rich tapestries, upholstered walls, and big and bright bathrooms. The ultracomfortable beds with thick linens invite a good night's sleep. A glass-enclosed walkway leads to one of Ushuaia's few swimming pools and an indoor squash court; the hotel also offers automatic membership at the local golf club. The owner of Las Hayas promotes an air of genteel exclusivity, making the hotel less than entirely suitable for children. Luis Martial, the gourmet restaurant on-site, changes its menu weekly but specializes in black hake and king crab dishes. It is one of the best restaurants in Ushuaia, with excellent service and attention to detail. Downstairs, a more casual restaurant has an indoor garden dining area with a delightful glass atrium. There is a frequent shuttle service to the town center in summer.

Av. Luis Fernando Martial 1650, Ushuaia. (C) **2901/430710.** Fax 2901/430719. www.lashayas.com.ar. 102 units. $262 (£144) double; $235–$321 (£129–£177) suites. Rates include buffet breakfast. AE, DC, MC, V. **Amenities:** 2 restaurants; bar; lounge; indoor swimming pool; exercise room; Jacuzzi; sauna; concierge; room service; massage; laundry service; dry cleaning. *In room:* TV, hair dryer, safe.

EXPENSIVE

Cumbres del Martial 🛇🛇 *(Finds*   With its Hansel and Gretel forest setting, wooden walkways, tin roofs, old-fashioned tea shop (p. 397), and white fences, you might think you have walked into the world of *Anne of Green Gables,* except in this case the gables are a very rich burgundy. Cumbres del Martial must be the most romantic and charming hotel in Ushuaia. At the entrance to the Martial Glaciar, this complex of pristine, immaculate wood cabins forms a leafy view of the bay with the relaxing tinkle of a mountain stream in the background. Long, white Georgian windows illuminate spacious, well-upholstered luxury rooms. Beneath wooden rafters lies a king-size bed fit for an emperor; it's so comfortable you can forget about rising early the next day to make any excursions. On the walls hang charming pictures of cows, sunflowers, and fat old ladies. The bathrooms are generously sized, with separate shower and toilet units and heated towel rails. Above the reception building, a guest's lounge has wing-backed armchairs, grandfather clocks, a small bar, and a computer with free Internet. Below the teahouse is a spa and clubhouse offering saunas and massages. Two larger cabins have chunky log walls, stone floors, and large Jacuzzis. If you want charm, character, and utter indulgence, however, I highly recommend the smaller cabins. This place is perfect for honeymooners, old romantics, and armchair tourists.

Luis Fernando 3560, Ushuaia. ✆ 2901/424779. www.cumbresdelmartial.com.ar. 7 units. $150 (£83) double; $270 (£149) large cabins. AE, MC, V. **Amenities:** Teahouse; bar; spa. *In room:* TV.

Hotel Cap Polonio   This hotel's central location and bustling restaurant, which essentially forms part of the entrance lobby, help to make up for its shortfalls. The bright yellow-and-red exterior sits directly on busy San Martín; for this reason, you'll want to request a room in the rear of the hotel to minimize noise. Rooms are a little old-fashioned, with slightly dowdy shag carpets and frilly bedspreads. And, as with most hotels in town, a single bed is laughably narrower than a twin, and might be uncomfortable for anyone over the age of 10; be sure to ask for a double instead.

Av. San Martín 746, Ushuaia. ✆ 2901/422140. www.hotelcappolonio.com.ar. 30 units. $110–$140 (£61–£77) double. AE, MC, V. **Amenities:** Restaurant; bar; room service. *In room:* TV.

Hotel Ushuaia   This hotel also affords sweeping views, yet it's only an 8-block walk to downtown—convenient for anyone who wants to be closer to restaurants and services. In this price range, the Hotel Ushuaia is one of the city's better values, offering very bright interiors and comfortable, spacious rooms, although it's aging fast. From the vine-draped reception area, long hallways stretch out on both sides; centered in the middle is a second-story restaurant with a lofty, V-shape ceiling from which hang about 100 glass bubble lamps, a style that is somewhat 1970s, but attractive nevertheless. All doubles cost the same but range in three sizes; when making a reservation, ask for the largest double they have; they'll reserve them for single travelers if they have enough vacancies.

Lasserre 933, Ushuaia. ✆ 2901/423051. Fax 2901/424217. 58 units. $110 (£61) double. Rates include buffet breakfast. AE, MC, V. **Amenities:** Restaurant; bar; lounge; room service; laundry service. *In room:* TV.

Los Acebos ⟨★ *(Finds*   If Los Hayas offers a refined and polished atmosphere, Los Acebos is colorful and fun. This upstart sister hotel is across the road from Los Havas, with an equally commanding view of the bay. Opened in March 2006, it has all the style and quality you'd expect from a brand-new hotel—designer sofas in chrome, cube-shaped sofas, and subtle lighting. Splashes of color, such as olive green and scarlet red, give it a bright, welcoming feel. Attention to detail, such as upholstered walls, smooth Portuguese linen, and towel heaters ensure your stay here will be as comfortable as possible. The rooms are large enough for two doubles and a work desk. The sparkling bathrooms have separate shower and toilet units. Los Acebos is a cheerful, family-oriented hotel with lots of space, and it promises to be busy with skiers in the winter.

Av. Luis Fernando Martial 1911, Ushuaia. ℂ 011/4393-0621. Fax 2901/430719. www.losacebos.com.ar. 61 units. $176 (£97) double; $264–$310 (£145–£171) suites. Rates include buffet breakfast. AE, DC, MC, V. **Amenities:** Restaurant; bar; lounge; concierge; frequent shuttle service to town center in summer; room service; laundry service; dry cleaning. *In room:* TV, hair dryer, safe.

Posada Fueguina   Guests at the Fueguina can choose to stay in either hotel rooms or inviting wooden cabanas (without kitchens). In a row on a well-manicured lot, the cabins have freshly painted cream-and-mauve exteriors, which stand out among the clapboard homes surrounding them. Inside, Oriental floor runners, dark glossy wood, and tartan curtains set the tone. Everything on the premises is meticulously maintained. Most rooms are spacious; the second and third floors have good views. The three rooms on the bottom floor are the most recently refurbished. Bathrooms are sparkling clean with modern fixtures. The cabins do not have interesting views, but they're so comfy you won't mind. The hotel is a 3-block walk to downtown.

Lasserre 438, Ushuaia. ℂ 2901/423467. Fax 2901/424758. www.posadafueguina.com.ar. 26 units, 4 cabins. Oct–Apr $130 (£72)double; cabin rates depend on number of guests (see website for details); closed May–Sept. Rates include buffet breakfast. AE, MC, V. **Amenities:** Bar; lounge. *In room:* TV, minibar, hair dryer.

Tierra de Leyendas 🦋🦋   Maia Muriel and Sebastian Garcia Cosoleto met while working at the Marriott in Buenos Aires. They married and traveled the world before opening Tierra de Leyendas in Ushuaia, a hotel that caters to hedonists, foodies, and coastal walkers. Sebastian's experience as a trained chef and Maia's background in the hotel business go to good use here. You can immediately understand how their delightful establishment quickly gained a reputation as one of the best boutique hotels in Argentina, if not South America. This wooden mansion glows with warm, welcoming colors. The entire bottom floor is open plan, comprising a lounge room, restaurant, and reception with huge windows overlooking the bay. A rust-colored sofa contrasts nicely with olive-green walls and corn-yellow staircase. The attention to detail is incredible; they comb the sheepskin seat covers every day, and deliver with breakfast every morning a little note explaining a local anecdote (this is what the legends in the hotel's name refers to). The dining room tables are mini-museum exhibits with indigenous arrowheads and flints beneath the glass dining surface. The five rooms are all named after a local fable. Ask for the Los Yamanas room, with its stunning view and incredibly relaxing, giant hot tub. The small restaurant is open to the public Monday to Saturday, so if you do decide to lodge elsewhere, at least book a table here to experience Sebastian's excellent cooking. The hotel is on the outskirts of town in an upscale residential zone of rolling hills and huge mansions known as Río Pipo. Here you can enjoy a pleasant coastal walk towards the National Park (no path).

Calle Sin Nombre 2387, Ushuaia. ℂ 2901/443565. www.tierradeleyendas.com.ar. 5 units. $120 (£66) double. AE, MC, V. **Amenities:** Restaurant; bar; room service. *In room:* TV, DVD, Jacuzzi.

MODERATE

Apart Hotel del Bosque *Value*   The Apart Hotel del Bosque gives guests a huge amount of space, including a separate living/dining area and a kitchenette. The kitchenette is intended, more than anything, for heating water, not cooking, and so they include breakfast, which is not common for apart-hotels. The 40 guest rooms are spread out much like a condominium complex, each with a separate entrance and maid service. The exteriors and the decor are pretty bland but very clean. Inside the main building, a cozy restaurant serves fixed-price meals on wooden tables. The hotel is in a residential area about a 3-minute walk from downtown.

Magallanes 709, Ushuaia. ©/fax **02901/430777**. www.hostaldelbosque.com.ar. 40 units. Apr–Sept $50 (£28) double; Oct–Mar $80 (£44) double. Rates include continental breakfast. AE, DC, MC, V. **Amenities:** Restaurant; room service; laundry service. *In room:* TV, dataport, kitchen, minibar, hair dryer.

Hotel Lennox *Value*   The hippest lodgings in town, this hotel exudes style and modernity. In the lobby, floor lighting illuminates tall, mirrored walls, punctuated by dark-rock tiles and light-wood panelling. Modish sofas, in moody tones of black and gray, look out onto busy Avenida San Martín. On the third floor, a comfortable and spacious communal room houses more sofas and a widescreen TV. The dining room has elegant, urbane furnishings in red and brown. Here you can enjoy a continental breakfast while taking in fantastic views of the bay. Rooms are small but adequate, and some of the sparkling bathrooms have a Jacuzzi. Be sure to ask for a room at the back facing the bay. The street side can be noisy, and the inward facing rooms (facing a tiny, somewhat overstated "zen garden") can lack privacy. In general, staff members are very friendly, and the hotel's contemporary feel is very refreshing and reassuring.

San Martín 776, Ushuaia. ©/fax **02901/436430**. www.lennoxhotel.com. 30 units. $80 (£44) double. Continental breakfast included. AE, DC, MC, V. **Amenities:** Restaurant; room service; laundry service.

Macondo   This stylish green-roofed boutique hotel has a young, bohemian feel, without sacrificing elegance. Wall-to-wall Georgian windows surround the common room, with a black stone floor and colorful, cubed armchairs. Spacious bedrooms have a loftlike feel, with red roof beams and rafters. Bathrooms are fair-sized with shower enclosures and wooden platforms. Stairs are in the style of a fire escape, leading you down to a second denlike common room with more couches and mattresses. Simple, modern, and attractive, this hotel also boasts a good central location with a great view.

Gobernador Paz 1410, Ushuaia. ©/fax **02901/437576**. www.macondohouse.com. 7 units. $87 (£48) double. Rates include continental breakfast. AE, DC, MC, V. **Amenities:** Room service; laundry service; free Internet and Wi-Fi; TV room.

INEXPENSIVE

Galeazzi—Basily B&B *Value*   Sixteen years ago, Frances Basily's hospitality so overwhelmed an American house guest that he raved she should start a bed-and-breakfast. Twenty minutes after he had left, Frances received a knock on the door, and it was two strangers inquiring about a room, recommended by the insistent American. "They had prices and everything! What could I do?" she asks. Since then, Frances and her husband Alejandro have been receiving a steady stream of guests, some lodging in the family home and others in some well-appointed cabins out back. The house itself is tall, with a picket fence out front guarding a small forest of beech trees. A wooden walkway leads you into a comfortable, if somewhat worn, suburban home of white walls, plants, family photos, and a long dining room table. The house rooms are small and basic and a little gloomy. They offer single beds and a shared bathroom. The cabins are much more spacious with lots more light. Yet you do not come here for simple luxury. What you get instead is a much more elusive sense of welcome and belonging. Everyone in the family speaks perfect English, and they're all very engaging and helpful. The kitchen is accessible, as is the living room sofa and TV, and Internet is free. A fantastic budget option, this bed-and-breakfast is a great introduction to the area, just 4 blocks from the town center.

F. Valdez 323, Ushuaia. © **02901/423213**. www.avesdelsur.com.ar. 5 shared units. $33 (£18) double; $80 (£44) cabin. No credit cards. **Amenities:** Lounge, Internet, kitchen.

Hostal Yaktemi   A decent budget option, Hostal Yaktemi lacks charm and character, but rooms are clean, and the downtown location is convenient. Above some stores on San Martín, accessed by a wooden staircase, rooms are fair-sized with basic furnishings. The velvet-covered headboards are the only nod to luxury, but everything is well maintained, if not exactly sparkling clean. Toilets are adequate, with shower and curtain rail. Each of two apartment units has two bedrooms and a kitchenette with microwave. Centrally heated, the rooms can get a little too warm; bathrooms, which lack ventilation, can be oppressively hot. Cheap and rudimentary, Hostal Yaktemi is fine for an overnight stop en route to somewhere better.

San Martín 626–636, Ushuaia. (© 02901/437437. www.yaktemihostal.com.ar. 13 units. $60 (£33) double. No credit cards.

WHERE TO DINE

Here king crab rules, and you'll find it on all menus, along with other excellent seafood dishes, such as sea bass and mussels. In general, dining out is much pricier here compared to the rest of the country. A dozen cafes are on San Martín, between Godoy and Rosas, all of which offer sandwiches and quick meals. The most popular among them is **Tante Sara,** San Martín 137 (© **2901/435005**), where a two-course meal of salad and ravioli or gnocchi costs $8 (£4.40). A block away, the Tante Sara Café is the place to sip coffee with locals in the afternoon. In addition to the restaurants listed below, you might consider the Hotel Las Hayas's **Luis Martial** (© **2901/430710;** p. 390). It is an excellent choice, with great views and gourmet dining, as well as fixed meals and menus that change weekly. Another notable hotel restaurant is **Tierra de Leyendas,** Calle Sin Nombre 2387, Ushuaia. (© **2901/443565;** p. 392). It is wise to book ahead.

Chez Manu *(Finds)* SEAFOOD/FRENCH   The Chez Manu offers great food and even better views, seen through a generous supply of windows. Two French expats run the place; one of them was once the chef at the five-star resort Las Hayas. True to their roots, they've crafted a French-style menu based on fresh local ingredients. Dishes include black hake cooked with anise and herbs, or Fuegian lamb. Before taking your order, the owner/chef will describe the catch of the day, usually a cold-water fish from the bay, such as abadejo or merluza from Chile. Side dishes include a delicious eggplant ratatouille, made with extra-virgin olive oil and herbes de Provençe. The wine list includes several excellent regional dry whites.

Av. Fernando Luis Martial 2135. (© 02970/432253. Main courses $10–$18 (£5.50–£9.90). AE, MC, V. Daily noon–3pm and 8pm–midnight.

El Almacén de Ramos General COFFEEHOUSE   This recently renovated, 100-year-old general store has a relaxing appeal. The principal room is large and atmospheric, with shelves on either side and a long, low shop counter. Old toys, fabrics, tools, and clothes are on display from floor to ceiling. Family portraits of the original owners hang in a side room, and a piano sits in the corner, along with old-fashioned typewriters. Situated in front of the port, the restaurant's menu offers cheese platters and generous king crab salads. Recommended is a very strong-smelling toasted brie sandwich. It makes for the perfect midmorning coffee stop while you tramp the wet streets of Ushuaia. The wine list is excellent and includes a deservedly pricey Cheval des Andes. In keeping with its old world vibe, the coffeehouse also serves as a bakery, ladies fashion store, and bar with draft beer.

Maipú 749. (© 02901/424317. Main courses $7–$15 (£3.85–£8.25). AE, MC, V. Daily 9:30am–12:30am.

Gustino 𝒸 (Finds) SEAFOOD/ARGENTINE Gustino is the latest gastronomical stopover in Ushuaia. Situated in the Albatros Hotel, this attractive, modern restaurant has glass walls overlooking the bay. Furnishings are clean cut and simple, with soft orange undertones and the occasional wood panel wall or rock pillar. The menu includes homemade lamb pâté and local lamb marinated in Syrah wine. The steaming starter of mussels is so tasty you want to chew on the shells. The highlight of the menu is a lasagna made from pastry layers and smoked salmon. The salmon dish itself comes in a huge slab the size of a sirloin steak. A local wine supplier, the owner Ezequiel puts a lot of attention into his wine list, and his air-conditioned glass and wrought-iron wine cellar has pride of place in the center of the restaurant. (Try the Patagonian Marcus Cabernet Franc.) Service is prompt and attentive. The restaurant is open all day, every day, and makes a good pit stop for a casual coffee or milkshake.

Maipú 505. ✆ 2901/430003. Main courses $10–$18 (£5.50–£9.90). AE, MC, V. Daily 8am–midnight.

Kaupé Restaurant 𝒸𝒸𝒸 ARGENTINE FINE DINING This is one of the best restaurants in Ushuaia, for its superb cuisine, lovely view, and warm, attentive service. The menu is brief, but the offerings are delicious. Don't start your meal without ordering a sumptuous appetizer of king crab wrapped in a crepe and bathed in saffron sauce. Main courses include seafood, beef, and chicken; sample items include tenderloin beef in a plum sauce or a subtly flavored sea bass steamed in parchment paper. Kaupé offers a special "sampler" with appetizers, a main dish, wine, dessert, and coffee for $57 (£31) per person. The extensive gourmet wine list ranges in price from $8 to $38 (£4.40–£21); there's also wine by the glass. Finish it all off with a sorbet in a frothy champagne sauce. Kaupé's dining area is cozy, and candlelit tables exude romance.

Roca 470. ✆ 02901/422704. Reservations recommended on weekends. www.kaupe.com.ar. Main courses $10–$17 (£5.50–£9.35). AE, MC, V. Nov–Apr daily noon–2pm and 6–11pm; June–Oct dinner only daily 7–11pm.

Marcopolo Café Restaurant INTERNATIONAL This casual restaurant is a good place for lunch, for both its varied menu and busy atmosphere. The softly lit dining area has warm yellow walls and beige linen tablecloths, offset by artsy ironwork knickknacks, colorful candles, and watercolor paintings. The menu will satisfy most tastes, with creative concoctions as well as simple, familiar items such as chef salads and shrimp cocktails. Try a local specialty, such as trout stuffed with king crab or Fuegian lamb in a flaky potato pastry. There's also fresh, homemade pasta with a choice of six sauces. Open early for breakfast, the Marcopolo also has a cafe menu of sandwiches, soups, and pastries, which can be ordered all day.

Av. San Martín 746. ✆ 02901/430001. Main courses $10–$17 (£5.50–£9.35). AE, MC, V. Daily 7:30–10:30am, noon–3pm, and 8pm–midnight.

Maria Lola 𝒸 (Moments) ARGENTINE This laid-back, relaxing restaurant is situated on a hill, 4 blocks from main street San Martín. In a modern house with large windows, it overlooks the bay, with the town's clapboard church in the foreground. The dining area is large and spacious, and the decor is modern if a little bare. The clientele are a healthy mix of locals and visitors. They come for a seafood menu, which includes the ubiquitous king crab, homemade pasta, and enormous desserts of cream and fresh fruit. The bar has a very decent wine list. Maria Lola may not leave you speechless gastronomically, but it makes for very pleasant evening dining. Its charm is in its understatement.

Deloqui 1048. ✆ 2901/421185. Main courses $7–$16 (£3.85–£8.80). AE, MC, V. Mon–Sat noon–3pm and 7pm–midnight.

Tante Nina ★ *Finds* SEAFOOD/ARGENTINE   For the best atmosphere and water views in the center of town, Tante Nina is your best bet. The elegant dining room has huge picture windows overlooking the bay, handsome wooden chairs, and white table-cloths. This place is becoming very popular since it opened a year ago, and many members of the local elite choose to dine here. Specialties are the seafood casseroles (known as *cazuelas*), most of which come with fresh king crab (all for $12/£6.60). There's a delicious Hungarian-style *cazuela* with king crab, tomatoes, cream, and mushrooms; a long list of fish prepared many different ways; and, of course, grilled chicken, tenderloin, and the very interesting pickled Patagonian rabbit, for the adventurous. For dessert, try the homemade almond ice cream or luscious lemon sorbet. Service is refined, if slightly aloof, and the diners tend to be on the older side.

Gobernador Godoy 15. (*C*) **2901/432444.** Reservations recommended for dinner in high season. Main courses $8–$18 (£4.40–£9.90). AE, MC, V. Daily 11am–3pm and 7pm–midnight.

Tía Elvira Restaurante ARGENTINE BISTRO   Tía Elvira is part restaurant, part mini-museum, with walls adorned by antique photos of the region and various artifacts collected by the owners during their 30 years in business. The menu features fairly straightforward Argentine dishes such as grilled meats, but the restaurant serves mostly simple seafood preparations, including king crab, trout, sea bass, and cod in a variety of sauces, such as Roquefort or Parmesan. Homemade pastas include lasagna and stuffed cannelloni. The restaurant is on the waterfront, with up-close views of the canal and the pier. It caters mostly to foreign tourists.

Maipú 349. (*C*) **2901/424725.** Main courses $8–$18 (£4.40–£9.90). MC, V. Daily noon–3pm and 7–11:30pm.

Volver ARGENTINE   It is worth stopping by here just to see this crazy, kitschy restaurant on the waterfront. Volver is inside a century-old yellow tin-pan house. Old newspapers and signs wallpaper the interiors, which are also packed with oddball memorabilia, photos, football shirts, gadgets, trinkets, and antiques. The food is pretty good. The menu includes regional dishes such as trout, crab, lamb, plus homemade pastas. King crab comes a dozen different ways, in soups, casseroles, or with a side sauce. Desserts are primarily crepes with local fruits such as calafate. Two complaints: For a relatively pricey restaurant, the service can be awful, and the toilets aren't very clean or well maintained.

Maipú 37. (*C*) **2901/423977.** Main courses $12–$20 (£6.60–£11). MC, V. Daily noon–3pm and 7:30pm–midnight. Closed for lunch Mon.

WHAT TO SEE & DO IN & AROUND TOWN

Because Ushuaia rests on a steep hill, most businesses, traffic, and people seem to converge on the main street that lies at the bottom, Avenida San Martín. You will soon tire of walking up and down this busy thoroughfare, however, so it's worth making the effort to climb up and explore the city's other streets. The best way to get a feel for the landscape is to walk to the city park and up to the **Punto Panorámico,** a great lookout point, from where you get sweeping views of the city and the channel. The trail, which begins at the southwestern end of Avenida San Martín, is free. For a port town with lots of tourism, the city's coastal stretch is disappointingly undeveloped; some parts are very ugly, in fact, and the pier is closed to casual strollers.

Glacier Martial/Aerosilla *Finds*   Glacier Martial is a pleasant excursion that sits in Ushuaia's backyard. Avenida Luis Fernando Martial winds 7km (4¼ miles) up from town to the base of a beautiful mountain amphitheater. From here, a chair lift takes you on a thrilling ride to the small Glacier Martial ($8/£4.40). It's a long walk up the road, and there are no buses to take you there. Visitors usually hire a taxi for $4 (£2.20) and walk all the way back down, or arrange for the driver to pick them up later. At the base of the chair lift, don't miss a stop at **La Cabaña** ⭐ (© **2901/ 424257**), an excellent teahouse with a wraparound outdoor deck and mouthwatering cakes and pastries (see Cumbres del Martial on p. 390).

Av. Luis Fernando Martial, 7km (4¼ miles) from town. No phone. Admission $8 (£4.40) adults, $1 (55p) children under 9. Daily 9:45am–7pm.

Museo del Fin de Mundo ⭐ The main room of this museum displays an assortment of Indian hunting tools and colonial maritime instruments. There's also a natural history display of stuffed birds and a "grandfather's room" set up to resemble an old general store, packed with antique products. But the strength of this museum is its 60 history and nature videos available for viewing, and its reference library with more than 3,650 volumes, including a fascinating birth record. Its store has an excellent range of books about Patagonia for sale.

Maipú 175. © 02901/421863. Admission $3 (£1.65) adults, 60¢ (35p) students, free for children under 14. Daily 9am–8pm.

Museo Marítimo y Presidio de Ushuaia ⭐ (Moments) Ushuaia was populated primarily by the penal colony set up here in the late 1800s for hundreds of Argentina's most dangerous criminals. The rehabilitation system consisted of forced labor to build piers and buildings, and creative workshops for teaching carpentry, music, tailoring, and other trades—all of which, coincidentally, fueled the local economy. The museum offers a fascinating look into prisoners' and prison workers' lives through interpretive displays and artifacts. Here you can dwell in the cells of mass murderers and teenage anarchists and read about their unenviable existence in what must have been a grim place. The on-site restaurant serves "prison" meals and other theme items. The maritime museum displays famous ships and shipwrecks from the area.

Yaganes and Gobernador Paz. © 2901/437481. Admission $30 (£17) adults, free for children under 5. Daily 9am–8pm.

OUTDOOR ACTIVITIES

BOATING The best way to explore the Beagle Channel is by boat. Numerous companies offer a variety of trips, usually in modern catamarans with excellent guides. Many of them run kiosks near the pier; you'll see a cluster of them by the water. The most popular excursion is a half-day cruise of the Beagle Channel to view sea lions, penguins, and more. **All Patagonia Viajes y Turismo,** Juana Fadul 48 (© **2901/ 433622;** allpat@tierradelfuego.org.ar), is an excellent tour company that can arrange the exact itinerary you want. **Motonave Barracuda** (© **2901/437066**) leaves twice daily for its 3-hour trip around the channel for $30 (£17) per person, stopping at Isla de Lobos, Isla de Pájaros, and a lighthouse. **Motovelero Tres Marías** (© **2901/ 436416**) also leaves twice daily and sails to the same location; they accommodate a maximum of nine guests at a time, and they add an hour-long walk, crab fishing, cognac, and an underwater camera to the package, for $36 (£20) per person. Most companies visit the teeming penguin colony and pull the boats up to the shore where travelers can close in tight to watch these marvelous animals. It's $65 (£36). **Pira Tur,** B. Yaganes Casa 127 (© **2901/15604646**), offers walking tours onto the colony with controlled groups. **Motovelero Patagonia Adventure** (© **2901/15465842**) has an 18-passenger maximum and leaves daily; it visits the sea lion colony and includes a walk on the Isla Bridges for $20 (£11). This company also works with the Aventuras Isla Verde in the park for a full-day sail; inquire at their kiosk. **Ushuaia Boating,** Gob. Godoy 190 (© **2901/436193;** www.ushuaiaboating.com.ar), operates a small, speedy ferry to Chilean Puerto Williams. It costs $300 (£165) round-trip.

FISHING   For a fishing license and information, go to the **Club de Pesca y Caza,** Av. San Martín 818 (no phone). It costs about $10 (£5.50) for foreigners per day.

SKIING   Ushuaia's ski resort, **Cerro Castor** (© **2901/499302;** www.cerrocastor. com), is surprisingly good, with more than 400 skiable hectares (988 acres), 15 runs, three quad chairs and one double, a lodge/restaurant, and a slope-side bar. Day tickets cost $18 to $30 (£9.90–£17), depending on low or high season. The resort is open from June 15 to October 15. To get there, take the shuttle buses **Pasarela** (© **2901/ 433712)** or **Bella Vista** (© **2901/443161**); the fare is $7 (£3.85).

TOUR OPERATORS

One of the better agencies in town, **All Patagonia Viajes y Turismo,** Juana Fadul 48 (© **2901/433622;** allpatagonia@allpatagonia.com), is the local American Express travel representative. It acts as a clearinghouse; if they don't offer a trip themselves, they'll arrange an excursion with other outfitters. They can also reserve excursions in other destinations in Argentina and Chile. All Patagonia offers three glacier walks for those in good physical condition, impressive scenic flights over Tierra del Fuego ($60/£33 per person for 30 min.), and treks and drives in its Land Rover with nature guides. They also arrange a bus and boat trip to Harberton and the penguin colony ($65/£36 per person), and they are one of the few agencies to operate afternoon tours of the national park. It is a very good company to approach if you're not sure what you want. **Canal Fun & Nature,** Rivadavía 82 (© **2901/437395;** www.canalfun.com), specializes in "unconventional tourism." It's a great company to choose if you're hankering after some hair-raising adventure. They staff excellent guides who provide 4WD trips and walks culminating with a barbecue. You'll marvel at the capabilities of a Landrover and the guides' driving skills as they push these vehicles to the limit through muddy roads and even into lakes. *Warning:* It's not for the faint-hearted. The company also leads kayaking and nighttime beaver-watching trips, and they'll custom-build a trip for you. They run private tours only on request. **Rumbo Sur,** Av. San Martín 350 (© **2901/430699;** www.rumbosur.com.ar), and **Tolkeyen,** San Martín 1267 (© **2901/437073;** ventas@tolkeyenpatagonia.com.), are two more-conventional operators that deal with larger groups and arrange more classic excursions, such as a city tour and guided visits to the national park and Lagos Escondido and Fagnano.

USHUAIA AFTER DARK

Nocturnal activities are somewhat sedate in this city. That is not to say it is completely dead, however, and there are some good bars to help you wash down that king crab dinner with some locally brewed beer. Two to try are **Dreamland,** 9 de Julio and Deloqui (© **2901/421246**), and **Dublin Irish Pub,** 9 de Julio 168 (© **2901/430744**).

Kua   With its cushioned mini-amphitheater facing a giant, shoreline view of the bay, Kua is certainly the most avant-garde of Ushuaia's nightspots. The metal bar counter goes well with the ironclad menus, and the decor is a hip arrangement of chunky wooden furniture, colored-glass beading, and wrought-iron bar stools, in which design definitely trumps comfort. The bar brews its own beer, and patrons can view the fermenting tanks through a glass panel beneath the dining room. The restaurant offers standard fare (main courses $12–$20/£6.60–£11), but its main attraction is the bar with regular live music and theater performances. And here is the ultimate compliment—the toilets are reassuringly clean and immaculate. The bar is located 2km (1¼ miles) east of the city center. It's open Tuesday to Sunday from 5pm until 2am. Av. Perito Moreno 2232. © **2901/437396. MC, V.**

Saint Christopher   The location couldn't be better—right on the waterfront with fabulous views of the bay and mountains, from the large windows that wrap around the entire building. Yet, like its namesake—the rusting hulk in the bay (a foundered ship)—the Saint Christopher has a certain worn-down, roadhouse feel. The decor has certainly seen better days. Yet this is *the* place, in these parts, for a late-night drink, dance, or meal (main courses $5–$9/£2.75–£4.95). A live band usually plays on weekends, and the place fills up with young Argentines looking to live it up and sing along to some popular *rock nacional.* It's open daily from 11am until 4am (5am Fri–Sat). Maipú 822. © **02901/422423. AE, MC, V.**

EXCURSIONS AROUND USHUAIA

One of the most intriguing destinations around Ushuaia is the **Estancia Harberton,** the first ranch founded in Tierra del Fuego. Now run as a museum, it affords a fascinating glimpse into the area's pioneering past. The tour begins with a walk through a small nature reserve, where the guides discuss, in good English, the different plants from the area. The *estancia*'s missionary founders are buried in the graveyard, and nearby are some reconstructed houses used by the original natives. Just as interesting is the mothballed shearing shed, a marvelous step back in time to when the *estancia* was a thriving sheep farm. There is also a curious natural history museum of marine life bones and fossils. (*Note:* To visit the museum, you must make reservations in advance; it's not included in the ordinary tour.) The ranch is located on the shore of the Beagle Channel, accessible by road or boat. The entrance fee is $5 (£2.75) April through October and $6 (£3.30) November through March. Most travel agencies in town provide transportation to the *estancia,* 90km (56 miles) from Ushuaia, for an average cost of $65 (£36) per person plus the entrance fee, provided you are among a group of four or more. Roughly from October to April, several tour companies offer a catamaran ride to the *estancia,* a 6-hour excursion for $75 (£41) per person; try **All Patagonia,** Juana Fadul 48 (© **2901/433622**). Tour groups will also arrange a boat excursion to a **penguin colony** from the *estancia,* an add-on excursion that costs about $62 (£34) per person.

After the turnoff for Estancia Harberton, RN 3 begins to descend down to **Lago Escondido,** a beautiful lake about 60km (37 miles) north of Ushuaia. It provides a quiet spot for relaxation or for fishing the mammoth trout that live in the lake.

A Ride in the Park

If you don't feel like walking but still want to take in the sights at Parque Nacional Tierra Del Fuego, you can ride **El Tren del Fin del Mundo,** a vapor locomotive replica of the train used to shuttle prisoners to the forest to chop wood (© **2901/431600;** www.trendelfindelmundo.com.ar). It can be very touristy, however, drawing big crowds. The train departs from its station (with souvenir shop and cafe) near the park entrance three times daily. The 1-hour, 50-minute round-trip journey costs $20 (£11) for adults, $33 (£18) for first class, $3 (£1.65) for passengers 4 to 14, and free for children under 4.

Monster Trout on the Río Grande

The north of Tierra del Fuego is a brown plain of gentle, undulating hills, and meandering rivers, punctuated by the occasional lonely *estancia*. It is a serene and desolate place without so much as a tree or a hedge for miles. Indeed, for many years, the only things you could find here were hardy ranchers, thousands of sheep, and wild herds of graceful guanacos.

One of those hardy ranchers decided to introduce trout to the local rivers, with the aim of creating a diversion for himself and his fly-fishing friends. Little did John Goodall know, when he first slipped some fingerlings into the gentle waters of the Río Grande back in the 1930s, that the area would become world famous for its trout. It's now a place of annual pilgrimage for thousands of fly-fishing fanatics. The trout thrived on the river, but they did even better when they discovered the rich Antarctic fishing grounds out to sea. The **sea run brown trout** had found its ideal habitat and grown accordingly; anglers are astounded to find fish as heavy as 30 pounds. Many say the Río Grande is the world's top location for fishing this type of trout.

Overfishing depleted stocks in the mid-1980s. In response, several *estancias* that controlled the upper Río Grande introduced strict conservation methods and catch-and-release restrictions. Their methods worked, and now those same *estancias* enjoy a steady stream of visitors seeking luxury accommodations on their fishing trips. The most famous is **La Villa de Estancia María Behety,** owned by the affable Alejandro Menéndez, who must be one of the few people in the world who can boast a river named after his family. The elegant family home, with a sparkling blue roof and commanding glass porch, has six opulent rooms. When guests are not fishing, they can partake of Alejandro's 10,000-bottle wine cellar and magnificent full-size snooker table—a relic of the Anglo-Argentines who used to work here. The property has another more modern but just as welcoming **Estancia María Behety Lodge** closer to the river that accommodates 12.

Estancia La Despedida is another popular fishing lodge. This ample log cabin offers very comfortable rooms and an inviting lounge with bar. The charismatic owner Danny Lajous speaks perfect English and regales guests with stories about the area. Nearby **Posada del Guanaco,** a sparkling farmhouse of pine floors and terra-cotta rugs, attracts visitors who are not necessarily here to fish but want to indulge in other pursuits such as horseback riding and bird-watching, or who simply enjoy the magnificent silence and peace here.

All four lodges work exclusively through a Californian outfitter called **The Flyshop Inc,** 4140 Churn Creek Rd., Redding, CA 96002 (© **530/ 222-3555;** fax 530/222-3572; www.theflyshop.com). All-inclusive 1-week packages start at $4,795 (£2,637) per person; it's $2,650 (£1,548) for those who choose not to fish. All the *estancias* are close to the town of Río Grande, 180km (112 miles) north of Ushuaia.

PARQUE NACIONAL TIERRA DEL FUEGO

Parque Nacional Tierra del Fuego was created in 1960 to protect a 63,000-hectare (155,610-acre) chunk of Patagonian wilderness that includes mighty peaks, crystalline rivers, black-water swamps, and forests of *lenga,* or deciduous beech. Only 2,000 hectares (4,940 acres) are designated recreation areas, some of which offer a chance to view dams built by the beavers that were introduced to Tierra del Fuego in the 1950s. Another eyebrow-raiser is the multitude of rabbits that roam the park.

It's the only Argentine national park with a maritime coast, but chances are you won't be blown away by it if you've been traveling around southern Argentina or Chile. Much of the landscape is identical to Patagonia's thousands of kilometers of mountainous terrain, but it does afford easy and medium day hikes to let you stretch your legs, breathe some fresh air, take a boat ride, or bird-watch. In some areas, the road runs through thick beech forest and then abruptly opens into wide views of mountains whose dramatic height can be viewed from sea level to more than 2,000m (6,560 ft.). Anglers can fish for trout here in the park but must first pick up a license at the **National Park Administration office,** Av. San Martín 1395 (© **2901/421315;** Mon–Fri 9am–3pm), in Ushuaia. The park service issues maps at the park entrance showing the walking trails here, ranging from 300m (984 ft.) to 8km (5 miles); admission into the park is $7 (£3.85). Parque Nacional Tierra del Fuego is 11km (6¾ miles) west of Ushuaia on RN 3. Camping in the park is free; there are no services, but potable water is available. At the end of the road to Lago Roca, there is a snack bar/restaurant. At Bahía Ensenada, you'll find boats that take visitors to Isla Redonda, where there are several walking trails. The cost is about $8 (£4.40), or $15 (£8.25) with a guide. All tour companies offer guided trips to the park, but if you just need transportation there, call these shuttle bus companies: **Pasarela** (© **2901/433712**) or **Bella Vista** (© **2901/443161**). The round-trip cost $10 (£5.50).

2 Puerto Williams, Chile

Puerto Williams is the southernmost town in the world, though it functions primarily as a naval base with a population of less than 2,500 residents. The town occupies the northern shore of Isla Navarino in the Beagle Channel, an altogether enchanting location framed by towering granite needles called the "Teeth of Navarino." Its Argentine neighbor Ushuaia has a much more burgeoning tourism infrastructure. Apart from a few hiking trails and a museum, Puerto Williams doesn't offer much to do, but adventurers bound or returning from kayak trips around Cape Horn use the town as a base. And really, there is a certain cachet to setting foot in this isolated village and knowing you're at the end of the world.

The best way to visit Puerto Williams is via the *Mare Australis* cruise ship, or any other ship that gives you an afternoon or a day to explore this far-flung locale. The Yamana culture, which so perplexed the first Europeans in their ability to withstand their harsh environment with little clothing, is long gone; but visitors may still view the last vestiges of their settlements and a well-designed anthropological museum in town.

GETTING THERE

BY AIR Aerovías DAP, O'Higgins 891 (© **61/223340** in Punta Arenas, or 61/621051 in Puerto Williams; www.aeroviasdap.cl), operates charter flights from Punta Arenas or Ushuaia to Puerto Williams and on to Cape Horn.

BY BOAT   **Ushuaia Boating,** Gob. Godoy 190, Ushuaia (© **2901/436193;** www. ushuaiaboating.com.ar), runs a small, speedy ferry service to and from Puerto Williams. The cruise ship *Mare Australis* makes a stop here; for information, see "Cruising from Punta Arenas to Ushuaia," earlier in this chapter. The passenger and cargo ferry **Transbordadora Austral Broom** offers cheaper passage to Puerto Williams, with a 34-hour journey from Punta Arenas (Av. Bulnes 05075; © **61/ 218100;** www.tabsa.cl). During the summer, the ferry leaves Punta Arenas four times a month on Wednesday and returns on Saturday; sleeping arrangements consist of reclining seats ($140/£77 adult one-way) and bunks ($170/£94 adult one-way). Kids receive a 50% discount. **Victory Adventure Travel,** based out of Puerto Williams at Teniente Munoz 118, #70 (© **61/621092;** www.victory-cruises.com), specializes in sailing journeys around the Beagle Channel and Cape Horn, and as far away as Antarctica. The schooner-style ships are not luxurious, but they are warm and comfortable, and their small size allows for a more intimate, hands-on journey than the *Mare Australis.* A 7-day trip starts at $198 (£109) per person, per day. **Sea & Ice & Mountains,** in Puerto Williams (office located in the Coiron Guesthouse; © **61/ 621227;** www.simltd.com), is a German-run agency with a six-passenger yacht that takes visitors on 5- to 7-day journeys around Cape Horn and past the Darwin mountain range; contact the agency for prices. For general travel agency needs, including city tours, airline tickets, and hotel reservations, contact **Turismo Akainij,** Uspashum 156 (© **61/21173;** turismoakainij@hotmail.com).

WHAT TO SEE & DO

The **Museo Maurice van de Maele,** Aragay 01 (© **61/621043**), is open Monday to Thursday and Saturday from 10am to 1pm and 3 to 6pm, featuring a good collection of Yaghan and Yamana Indian artifacts, ethnographic exhibits, and stuffed birds and animals. The museum's docent is an anthropologist, naturalist, and all-around expert in the region; he is usually on hand to provide tours in the area. About 3km (1¾ miles) southeast of Puerto Williams on the main road, at the La Virgen cascade, is a medium-level **hiking trail** with an exhilarating, sweeping panorama of the Beagle Channel, the Dientes de Navarino mountain range, and Puerto Williams. The hike takes 3 hours round-trip. One of Chile's best backpacking trails, the **Dientes de Navarino Circuit,** is here, thanks to an Australian who blazed the trail in 1991. The circuit is 53km (33 miles) in length and takes at least 4 days to walk; the difficulty level is medium to high. The trail is open only from late November to April; otherwise, snow makes this walk dangerous and disorienting. The best map is JLM's *Tierra del Fuego* map, sold in most shops and bookstores.

WHERE TO STAY & DINE

The pickings are slim but reasonably priced; however, note that travelers will not find luxury in Puerto Williams. Basic, clean accommodation can be found at the **Hostería Camblor,** Calle Patricio Cap Deville 41 (© **61/621033;** hosteriacamblor@terra.cl), which has modern rooms for $30 (£17) or $50 (£28) per person (including meals and transfer). Some rooms come with a kitchenette. The Camblor also has a restaurant that occasionally serves as the local disco on Friday and Saturday nights, so noise could be a problem. Another simple but comfortable place is the **Hostal Yagan,** Piloto Pardo 260 (© **61/621334;** hostalyagan@hotmail.com), with doubles for $25 (£14). For dining, try the convivial **Club de Yates Micalvi** (© **61/621041**), housed in an old supply ship that is docked at the pier. It serves as the meeting spot for an international crowd of adventurers sailing around Cape Horn. Or try the Hostería Camblor's restaurant or **Los Dientes de Navarino** (© **61/621074**), on the plaza. Also try the **Restaurant Cabo de Hornos,** Ricardo Maragano 146 (on the second floor; © **61/ 621232**), for Chilean specialties.

3 Antarctica

The coldest spot on the planet is one of the hottest destinations for travelers seeking the next great adventure. Antarctica is its own continent, but the hook of the Antarctic Peninsula is closest to the tip of South America, and so the majority of visitors depart for Antarctica from Ushuaia.

Antarctica is home to exotic wildlife and landscapes that are equally savage and beautiful. Be prepared for ice like you've never seen it: monumental peacock-blue icebergs shaped in surreal formations, craggy glaciers that crash into the sea, sheer ice-encrusted walls that form magnificent canals and jagged peaks that jut out of icy fields. A major highlight here are the penguins—colonies of several hundred thousand can be found nesting and chattering away throughout the area. Humpback, orca, and minke whales are often visible, nosing out of the frigid water, as are elephant, Weddell, leopard, and crabeater seals. Bird-watchers can spend hours studying the variety of unique seabirds that reside here, including petrels and albatrosses.

Most importantly, Antarctica sits at the "end of the world," which is reason alone to compel many people to venture here. Like the early explorers who first visited this faraway continent in the 1800s, travelers today revel in the chance to explore a pristine region where relatively few humans have stepped foot before. But Antarctica's remoteness comes with a toll: No matter how you get here, it's not cheap. The tediously long travel time, amid sometimes uncomfortable conditions, heightens the price that this region exacts from travelers. Nevertheless, many of Antarctica's 30,000 yearly visitors would agree that it's worth the effort.

A BRIEF HISTORY

The history of exploration and the discovery of the Antarctic continent are littered with claims, counterclaims, tall tales, intrigue, and suffering. Captain James Cook discovered the South Sandwich and South Georgia Islands in 1773 (a part of Antarctica, these islands are a British possession), but he never spotted the Antarctic continent. He did, however, set off a seal-hunting frenzy, after reporting the large colonies he found there; it's estimated that sealers eventually discovered around a third of the islands in the region. Two sealers were the first to actually step foot on the continent: the American John Davis at Hughes Bay in 1821, and the British James Weddell at Saddle Island in 1823. During a scientific expedition in 1840, the American navy lieutenant Charles Wilkes finally concluded that Antarctica was not a series of islands and ice packs, but rather a contiguous landmass.

The South Pole eluded explorers for another 90 years, until Norwegian Roald Admudsen and his well-prepared five-man team reached it on December 4, 1911. Amundsen's arrival at the pole accounted for one of history's most remarkable expeditions ever. His feat, however, was eclipsed by tragedy: His rival, the British captain Robert Scott, reached the pole 33 days later, only to find Amundsen's tent and a note. Scott and his party, already suffering from scurvy and exposure, froze to death on their return trip, just 18km (11 miles) from their ship.

No other destination has held such cachet for adventurous explorers. In 1915, the Irish explorer Ernest Shackleton, deemed Antarctica "the last great journey left to man." Shackleton attempted to cross the Antarctic continent but never achieved his goal: Pack ice trapped and sank his boat. The entire party miraculously survived for 1 year on a diet of penguin and seal, before Shackleton sailed to South Georgia Island in a lifeboat to get help.

Today, 27 nations send personnel to Antarctica to perform seasonal and year-round research. The population varies from 4,000 people in the summer to roughly 1,000 in the winter. A total of 42 stations operate year-round, and an additional 32 run in summer only. The stations study world climactic changes and can be instrumental in improving the environment. In 1985, for instance, researchers at the British Halley station discovered a growing hole in the ozone layer. This prompted the Montreal Protocol in 1987 to cut back on CFC emissions.

PLANNING YOUR TRIP TO ANTARCTICA
VISITOR INFORMATION
Numerous websites offer helpful information about Antarctica. A few of the best are:

- **www.iaato.org**: This is the official website of the International Association Antarctic Tour Operators. It is important that your tour group be a member of the IAATO. Most cruise operators are members. Membership in the organization ensures a safe and environmentally responsible visit to Antarctica. Statistics, general information, and news can be found on this website.
- **www.70south.com**: This site includes links to other Antarctica-oriented websites, as well as weather and event information and message boards.
- **www.antarcticconnection.com**: This site offers travel information, tour operator links, and Antarctica-related items for sale, including maps and videos.

ENTRY REQUIREMENTS
No single country claims Antarctica as its territory, so visas are unnecessary. You will need a passport, however, for unscheduled stops and for your first stop in either Argentina or Chile (see chapter 2 for information about entry requirements).

WHEN TO GO
Tours to Antarctica are conducted between November and March—after March, temperatures dip to lows of –100°F (–38°C), and the sun disappears until September. The opposite is true of the summer months (Dec–Mar), and visitors can expect sunlight up to 18 to 24 hours a day, depending on where you are in Antarctica. Summer temperatures near the Antarctic Peninsula vary between lows of 5°F to 10°F (–15°C to –12°C), and highs of 35°F to 60°F (2°C–16°C).

What you see during your journey to Antarctica may depend on when you go. November is mating season for penguins and other birds, and visitors can view their offspring in December and January. The best months for whale-watching are February and March.

SAFETY
EXTREME WEATHER   Cold temperatures, the wind-chill factor, and perspiration conspire to prohibit the human body from keeping itself warm in Antarctica. Travelers need to outfit themselves in the highest-quality outdoor clothing available. Tour operators are constantly amazed at how under-prepared people can be when they visit

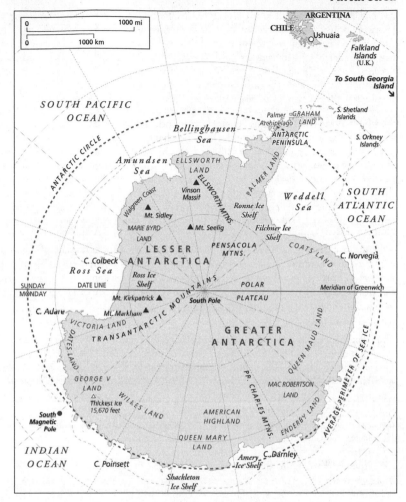

Antarctica, and so they will provide clients with a packing checklist. Ask your tour company if it provides its guests with waterproof outerwear or if you are expected to bring your own. The thin ozone layer and the glare from snow, water, and ice make a high-factor sunscreen, a hat, and sunglasses imperative as well.

SPECIAL HEALTH CONCERNS *Everyone* should bring anti–motion sickness medication on their trip to Antarctica. If you are suffering from a special health problem or taking prescription medication, bring a signed and dated letter from your physician for medical authorities in case of an emergency. Delays of up to 4 weeks aren't uncommon on guided trips to the interior, so visitors should seriously consider the extremity of such a journey, submit themselves to a full medical exam before their departure, and bring the quantity of medication necessary for a long delay.

MEDICAL SAFETY & EVACUATION INSURANCE   All passenger ships have a physician onboard in the event of a medical problem or emergency; however, passengers should discuss an evacuation policy with each operator. Emergency evacuation can be hindered by bad weather, and anyone with an unstable medical condition needs to keep this in mind. Also, check your health insurance to verify that it includes evacuation, because it can be unbelievably expensive. From the Shetland Islands alone, it costs $40,000 (£22,000) to evacuate one person.

GETTING THERE
BY SHIP

Few would have guessed that the collapse of the Soviet Union in the early 1990s would spawn tourism in Antarctica. But when Russian scientific ship crews found themselves without a budget, they spruced up the ships' interiors and began renting the vessels out to tour operators on a rotating basis. These ships (as well as others that have since come on the market) are specially built for polar seas, complete with antiroll stabilizers and ice-strengthened hulls. A few of these ships have icebreakers that can chip through just about anything.

Before you go, it helps to know that a tour's itinerary is a rough guide of what to expect on your journey. Turbulent weather and ice conditions can cause delays or detours. Wildlife sightings may prompt your group to linger longer in one area than the next. The ship's crew and the expedition leader of your tour will keep you informed of any changes to the program.

Typical Itineraries

Tour companies offer roughly similar trajectories for cruises to Antarctica, with the exception of a few over-the-top cruises. (Got 2 months and $60,000/£33,000?) Then Quark Expeditions conducts a full circumnavigation of Antarctica.) Apart from the destinations listed below, cruises attempt to land at research stations when it's convenient. Most Antarctic cruises leave from Ushuaia, in Argentina, but a tiny fraction leave from New Zealand. Chile used to be a departure site for Antarctica, but few if any travelers now leave from Chile; those who do make the journey aboard a military ship. Plan to leave from Ushuaia; it's the fastest departure point.

Remember to factor in 2 days to cross the Drake Passage (4 days total for the return trip, if you're traveling to the Antarctic Peninsula). During this time, you won't do much more than hang out, relax, take part in educational lectures, and suffer through occasional bouts of seasickness. Cruises typically last 8 to 13 days for the Antarctic Peninsula, and 18 to 21 days for journeys that include the Subantarctic Islands. Seasoned travelers have frequently said that 8-day trips are not much of a value; consider tacking on 2 extra days for a 10-day trip.

THE ANTARCTIC PENINSULA   This is the easiest site to visit in Antarctica. Due to its rich variety of wildlife and dramatic scenery, it makes for a magnificent introduction to the "White Continent." If you have a short amount of time and/or a limited budget, these trips are for you.

All tours stop at the **South Shetland Islands.** Historically, sealers and whalers used these islands as a base; today they're home to research stations, colonies of elephant seals, and a variety of nesting penguins and sea birds. Popular sites here are **King Island, Livingston Island,** and **Deception Cove**—a collapsed, active volcanic crater with bubbling pools of thermal water.

Tours continue on to the eastern side of the Antarctic Peninsula, making stops to view wildlife such as Weddell and leopard seals and vast colonies of Adélie, chinstrap, and Gentoo penguins. At the peninsula, sites such as the **Lemaire** and **Neumayar** channels afford camera-worthy views of narrow, sheer-walled canals made of ice and rock. At **Paradise Harbor,** calving icebergs theatrically crash from the harbor's main glacier, and throughout the area, outlandishly shaped gigantic icebergs float by. Other popular stops include **Port Lockroy,** a former British base that is now run as a museum; **Cuverville** and **Rongé** islands, with their penguin colonies; and **Elephant Island,** named for the huge, sluglike elephant seals that inhabit it.

THE POLAR CIRCLE   Ships with ice-breaking capabilities can transport guests past the Antarctic Circle and into the zone of 24-hour sunlight. The highlight here is **Marguerite Bay,** with its abundant orca, minke, and humpback whales, and multitudinous Adélie penguins. These cruises typically stop for a fascinating tour of research stations, both ultramodern and abandoned ones.

THE WEST SIDE & THE WEDDELL SEA   Longer tours to the peninsula might include visits to its west side, known as "iceberg alley" for the mammoth, tabular chunks of ice floating by slowly. Stops include the rarely visited **Paulet Island,** an intriguing crater island, and **James Ross** and **Vega** islands, known for their nesting colonies of Adélie penguins.

An even longer trip (or simply a different itinerary) takes travelers to the distant **Weddell Sea,** which is blanketed with a vast expanse of pack ice, looking much like a frozen sea. But that's just one of the highlights here; the real reason visitors pay extra time and money to reach this white wonderland is because of the colonies of emperor penguins that reside here. Rugged mountains and glaciers are also part of the view.

SUBANTARCTIC ISLANDS   Tours to the Subantarctic Islands begin or end with a trip to the Antarctic Peninsula and the Shetland Islands, which is the reason why these tours run 18 to 21 days. A few of these faraway islands are little visited by tourists, and they instill a sense of adventure in the traveler for their remoteness and fascinating geography, not to mention their important historical aspects.

The first stop is usually the **Falkland (Malvinas) Islands,** to view bird life, especially king penguins, and to tour the Victorian port town of Stanley. Some tours fly directly from Santiago, Chile, to the Falklands, and then begin the sailing journey there.

One of the most magnificent places on earth, **South Georgia Island** is surely a highlight of this trip. Its dramatic landscapes, made of rugged peaks, fiords, and beaches, are home to a staggering array of wildlife. South Georgia Island is also subject to unpredictable weather. Trip landings here risk cancellation far more frequently than other sites. Some tours tack on visits to the **South Orkney Islands** (with their dense area of Antarctic hairgrass—an indigenous flowering plant) and the actively volcanic **South Sandwich Islands.**

Tour Operators

Prices vary depending on the length of the trip, the company you choose, and the sleeping arrangements you require. A 9-day journey in a room with three bunks and a shared bathroom runs about $4,500 (£2,475) per person. A 21-day journey with lodging in a corner-window suite runs between $12,000 (£6,600) and $15,000 (£8,250) per person. Shop around to find something to suit your needs and budget.

Prices include passage, meals, guides, and all excursions. Some tours offer scuba diving, kayaking, overflights, or Alpine trekking, usually at an additional cost. When researching trips, also consider the size of the ship: Tour companies offer space for anywhere from 50 to 600 passengers. Most travelers like to share their space with fewer people; even for those who enjoy the camaraderie of a crowd, more than 100 to 150 guests is overkill. The International Association Antarctic Treaty Organization limits landings to 100 people, meaning large ships must conduct landings in turns.

A few well-known tour operators include:

- **Abercrombie & Kent,** 1520 Kensington Rd., Suite 212, Oak Brook, IL 60523-2141 (© **800/544-7016** or 630/954-2944; fax 630/954-3324; www.abercrombiekent.com). Like Quark, A&K offers deluxe journeys, with trips that last 14 to 18 days.

- **Antarctica Cruises,** Guido 1852, Office B, 4th Floor, Buenos Aires C1119AAB (© **54-11/4806-6326;** fax 54-11/4804-9474; www.antarcticacruises.com.ar). Based in Buenos Aires, Zelfa Silva and her husband Gunnar are seasoned Antarctica travelers and expert trip-planning consultants.

- **Aurora Expeditions,** 182A Cumberland St., The Rocks, NSW 2000, Australia (© **02/9252-1033;** fax 02/9252-1373; www.auroraexpeditions.com.au). This Australian company organizes a variety of educational, photographic, and climbing tours for small groups.

- **Geographic Expeditions,** 2627 Lombard St., San Francisco, CA 94123 (© **800/777-8183** or 415/922-0448; fax 415/346-5535; www.geoex.com). Tours vary between 11 and 28 days, with small boat cruising, trekking, and climbing options.

- **Lindblad Expeditions,** 720 Fifth Ave., New York, NY 10019 (© **800/397-3348** or 212/765-7740; www.expeditions.com). This venerable Swedish-run company was the first to bring tourists to Antarctica. It offers 11- to 28-day tours, with trekking.

- **Mountain Travel Sobek,** 1266 66th St., Emeryville, CA 94608 (© **888/687-6235** or 510/594-6000; fax 510/525-7710; www.mtsobek.com). This well-respected company has been operating Antarctic tours for 15 years. They offer 11- to 21-day tours, with zodiac rides.

- **Oceanwide Expeditions,** 15710 JFK Blvd., Suite 850, Houston, TX 77032 (© **800/453-7245;** fax 281/987-1140; www.oceanwide-expeditions.com). This Dutch company operates a variety of journeys aboard its own ship.

- **Peregrine Adventures,** 258 Lonsdale St., Melbourne, VIC 3000, Australia (© **1300/854444** in Australia, or 03/9662-2700 outside Australia; fax 03/9662-2442; www.peregrine.net.au). This Australian company is the only operator that doesn't charge solo travelers a single supplement.

- **Quark Expeditions,** 980 Post Rd., Darien, CT (© **800/356-5699** or 203/656-0499; www.quarkexpeditions.com). This highly esteemed company offers the industry's most outrageous trips, including complete circumnavigations.

BY PLANE

Apart from working for a research station, one of the few ways to get out and really explore the Antarctic continent is by plane. A handful of companies offer a small selection of astonishing, out-of-this-world journeys to the Antarctic interior and beyond.

Flights to the Antarctic can be divided into two distinct categories: flights that access man-made airstrips on certain islands close to the peninsula, and flights that

> ## ⸜Tips⸝ Last-Minute Reduced Fares to Antarctica
>
> Some travel agencies in Ushuaia offer reduced fares for last-minute bookings, but it is by no means guaranteed. Be prepared to hang around Ushuaia for up to 2 weeks without any certainty that you will score a berth. If you do, however, prices can be 10% to 50% lower than the advertised rate. Two agencies to try are **All Patagonia,** Juana Fadul 26, Ushuaia, Argentina (© **2901/433622;** fax 2901/430707; www.allpatagonia.com) and **Rumbo Sur,** Av. San Martín, Ushuaia, Argentina (© **2901/421139;** fax 2901/434788; www.rumbosur.com.ar). Note that the best time to snag discounted rates is late November to early December, before the onset of the high travel season in southern Argentina.

penetrate the frigid interior, relying on natural ice and snow runways for landing areas. The logistics involved in flying to the Antarctic are complicated, to say the least, and fuel becomes an issue. Make no mistake: Air travel to the Antarctic is a serious undertaking. The rewards, however, can be unforgettable.

From Punta Arenas, Chile, King George Island on the peninsula is the preferred destination. The island houses a number of research stations, some of which can be visited. It boasts extraordinary wildlife and sightseeing opportunities. The average stay is 1 or 2 days, but weather delays can alter itineraries.

The severity of the landscape and the remoteness of the Antarctic interior call for special considerations when you're planning and preparing for an unexpectedly prolonged stay. All travelers attempting a trip to the interior should be aware of the extreme climatic conditions. Travel delays caused by severe weather are the norm. These trips, however, represent adventure travel in its purest form.

Tour Operators

Prices vary depending on the company and the destination. In general, flights to the peninsula are much cheaper than those to the interior. As expected, these all-inclusive trips can cost anywhere from $15,000 to $38,000 (£8,250–£20,900) per person, depending on the destination. Logistical support for extended expeditions can easily run to over $40,000 (£22,000). Prices typically include transportation, meals, and guides.

- **Adventure Network International,** 4800 N. Federal Hwy., Suite 307D, Boca Raton, FL 33431 (© **801/266-4876** or 561/347-7523; fax 801/266-1592; www.adventure-network.com). This company began as a private plane service for climbers headed for Vinson Massif, the highest peak in Antarctica. They now include several 7- to 22-day tours, such as flights to the South Pole and the Transantarctic and Ellsworth mountain ranges, an emperor penguin safari, and a 60-day ski trip to the South Pole. Activities planned during these trips can include hiking, skiing, and skidoo trips; overnight camping; and ice hockey, igloo building, and just about anything else related to ice.
- **Aerovías DAP,** O'Higgins, Punta Arenas (© **61/223340;** fax 61/221693; www.aeroviasdap.cl). This small Chilean airline specializes in charter flights to the peninsula, in particular King George Island.

Appendix A: Argentina in Depth

by Michael Luongo

Argentina is a nation that once was among the wealthiest in the world. It long reigned as the preeminent power on the South American continent, both economically and militarily. Every building in Buenos Aires, every legend emerging from the Pampas, every abandoned church in the missions, overgrown with vines, tells of this vast country's glorious past. Even the faces on the streets of Argentina's cities are a reflection of a history full of accidents, desires, and the sheer force of a nation's will to shape itself and its perception within the outside world.

1 Settlement & Colonization

Well before the arrival of Europeans, several distinct indigenous groups populated the area now called Argentina. The Incas had made inroads into the highlands of the Northwest. Most other groups were nomadic hunters and fishers, such as those in the Chaco, the Tehuelche of Patagonia, and the Querandí and Puelche (Guennakin) of the Pampas. Others (the Diaguitas of the Northwest) developed stationary agriculture. The Mapuche Indians, a warrior tribe based at the very bottom of Patagonia in both Argentina and Chile, were the only Indian tribe never conquered by the Spanish.

The Argentina we know today took shape only after repeat attempts at colonization by the Spanish. Much of Spain's effort was initially aimed at staving off Portuguese expansion in what today is Brazil. The first European known to have laid eyes on the area that would become Buenos Aires was Juan Díaz de Solís, who sailed up what is now the Río de la Plata and named it the Mar Dulce, or Sweet Sea. Ferdinand Magellan retraced the route in 1520, thinking he had stumbled upon a passageway that would take him to the Pacific Ocean. Sebastian Cabot returned on a treasure hunting expedition in 1526. An exchange with local Indians yielded trinkets of gold and silver, and so Cabot renamed the Mar Dulce the Río de la Plata, or River of Silver, in expectation of riches he hoped to find. And then he returned to Spain to convince the crown that more wealth was to be had in the region.

In 1535, Spain—victorious after having conquered Peru, yet aware of Portugal's presence in Brazil—sent an expedition, headed by Pedro de Mendoza, to settle the region. Mendoza was initially successful in founding Santa María del Buen Aire, or Buenos Aires (1536), but the lack of food proved fatal. Mendoza, mortally ill and discouraged by Indian attacks, sailed for Spain with a hundred of his men in 1537. He died on the way, and his body was cast out to sea.

The Spanish had greater success in other parts of the country. In 1573,

Jerónimo Luís de Cabrera founded Córdoba in central Argentina. The city was a Jesuit stronghold, and the religious order established the Universidad Nacional de Córdoba in 1613, one of the oldest universities in South America. Córdoba remained an important city through much of colonial Argentina. To this day, it's Argentina's most important education center, where one out of five residents is a student.

Mendoza, in the shadows of the Andes, was settled in 1561 by Pedro del Castillo. He had pushed into the region from an expedition based out of Santiago, in modern Chile. In 1535, the Spaniards began exploring the Northwest, as they expanded down through the recently conquered Inca empire, and founded the city of Salta in 1582.

In 1580, Juan de Garay resettled Buenos Aires. His expedition sailed from Asunción in Paraguay down the Paraná River. At the time, Asunción was a significant city within the Spanish Empire, and Jesuit missions on the border of what is today Argentina, Brazil, and Paraguay thrived, providing economic output and the ability to control the frontiers. Garay had with him about 45 men and, uniquely, one woman, Ana Díaz. Díaz's role has been obscured by time, and it is unknown whether she was a prostitute from Asunción who accompanied the troops or whether she should be exulted as a female conquistador. In any case, a woman's touch on the expedition proved to be the charm. Upon the second attempt to colonize, the city continued to grow into a permanent, though small, colonial establishment. Ana Díaz's colonial landholdings were on what is today Calle Florida.

While today Buenos Aires is the cultural and political capital of Argentina, it was a backwater region for a long time during the colonial period. More important were Córdoba, Salta, the Jesuit missions, and other parts of the country closer to Lima and Asunción, the centers of power in the Spanish Empire. Buenos Aires was logistically important in defending the lower half of the Spanish Empire from the Portuguese. Constant skirmishes continued between the two empires, with neighboring Uruguay as a disputed territory. Tiny Colonia, across the Río de la Plata from Buenos Aires, passed back and forth, and its buildings reflect the styles of the two ruling powers. With access to the Río de la Plata and the open Atlantic, however, it was inevitable that Buenos Aires—at first a lonely outpost on the edge of the vast Pampas—would grow to be one of the continent's most important cities.

2 Independence & Warfare

All revolutions are political as well as economic, and Argentina's was no exception. By the late 1700s, Buenos Aires was the preeminent port within the region, and cattle hides became a major component of the economy. The trade, however, was heavily taxed and strictly regulated by the Spanish crown, and so smuggling and circumventing became the norm, along with illicit trade with the British. Downtown Buenos Aires is still riddled with underground tunnels. Many of them opened directly to what had been the port area along the Río de la Plata, and cargo passed untaxed through them during this time period. To this day, it is not clear whether the Jesuits may have built them, even farther back, as secret passageways. In any case, the merchants' desire to end taxation began to foment, feeding a greater drive for overall political independence.

Indirect trade was not enough for the British. Sensing that the Spanish Empire was weakening, they attacked Buenos Aires in 1806 and 1807. The battles were known as the Reconquista and the Defensa. These battles are memorialized in the names of the streets of Buenos Aires that feed into the Plaza de Mayo, which were the routes the Argentine armies used to oust the British. Able to defend themselves without the aid of Spain, many Argentine-born Europeans began to debate the idea of self-government in Buenos Aires.

The Revolution of Buenos Aires was declared on May 25, 1810, marking the beginnings of the independence movement. On July 9, 1816 (Nueve de Julio), Buenos Aires officially declared its independence from Spain, under the name United Provinces of the Río de la Plata. Several years of hard fighting followed before the Argentines defeated the Spanish in northern Argentina, and the Europeans remained a threat until Perú was liberated by General José de San Martín, considered the national hero of Argentina, and later by Simón Bolívar, from 1820 to 1824. With Lord George Canning as their main representative, Britain officially recognized Argentina's independence. Argentina's relationship with this European world power would, however, remain tenuous.

Spain's defeat, however, did not mean that Argentina had peace. Boundaries and the power structure were still unclear. Strongmen with private armies, called caudillos, controlled remote regions, as was the case in other areas of South America after independence. Even with a national constitution, the territory that now constitutes modern Argentina was frequently disunited until 1860. The national debate included the question of whether Buenos Aires would be the new capital.

The internal and external struggles were brutal, changing both the physical and ethnic structure of the country. In 1864, the War of the Triple Alliance (also known as the Paraguayan War), broke out between Paraguay and an alliance of Argentina, Brazil, and Uruguay. Paraguayan president Francisco Solano López saw himself as an emperor and hoped to give the country an Atlantic port. The war, which devastated Paraguay, lasted 6 years, and was among the bloodiest fighting ever on South American soil.

Of the three countries fighting Paraguay, Argentina recovered from the war most quickly, and it served as an impetus for unification. From this point on, Argentina was the most powerful and wealthy country on the continent—and remained so for nearly 80 years.

Modern Argentine historians dispute this subplot, but the Argentine army fought its battles by placing black soldiers at the front lines, where they faced immediate slaughter, ahead of white soldiers. For this reason, Argentina, unlike much of South America, is home to few descendants of slaves brought from Africa.

Argentina's ethnic makeup was further altered in the late 1870s by General Julio Argentino Roca's Campaign of the Desert. Essentially, he drew a line out from Buenos Aires and slaughtered virtually every Indian within it. He claimed to do so in the name of national defense and the economy, in light of the fact that some Indian populations stole cattle and attacked the various estancias and forts within the Pampas and upper Patagonia. The destruction of the native population further consolidated Buenos Aires's control of the hinterlands, and led to a wave of new ranches and estancias and the unimpeded development of the railroads. Now only within the north and the very south of Argentina (areas untouched by Roca) do Indians exist in any substantial numbers.

It was these two specific genocidal policies—toward descendants of African and indigenous South American folk—

that laid the ground for the largely white and European culture that Argentina was to become. Needless to say, however, Argentines have a sensitive relationship with this period and often gloss over it in historical accounts. Many historians account for the lack of an African population by arguing that blacks died out naturally, or simply intermarried with the millions of white immigrants until pure Africans no longer existed.

The fact that Africans existed in Argentina is most evident, however, in the nation's most important cultural contribution to the world—the tango. Like all musical and dance forms native to the Americas, it owes its roots to slave culture. Photographs of gauchos from the late 1800s also show that many were clearly of African descent. The overwhelmingly white society of greater Buenos Aires that tourists see today was not simply the proud result of millions of Italians and Spaniards descending from boats after a long Atlantic voyage, but was instead a deliberate government policy of genocide.

3 Buenos Aires, the Capital

Genuine unification of Argentina did not occur until 1880, 300 years after the permanent founding of Buenos Aires. On this anniversary, the city was officially made the capital. The return of San Martín's body that year, to a permanent tomb within the Catedral Metroplitano on Plaza de Mayo, solidified and symbolized the city's absolute authority.

From then on, Buenos Aires experienced a period of explosive growth and wealth, laying the foundations for the glory days that Argentines remember about their country. Trade with Europe expanded, with cattle and grain from the newly conquered hinterlands serving as the main exports. Millions of immigrants came from Italy, Spain, and other countries, filling the city's slums, primarily in the southern sections of La Boca and San Telmo. To this day, there are almost as many Italian last names as Spanish in Argentina. Even the language spoken in Argentina seems almost like Italian-accented Spanish, with its rhythm and pitch. *Lunfardo,* the street dialect associated with tango, owes many of its words to immigrant Italian.

The exponential growth of this time means that Buenos Aires—unlike in Salta, Córdoba, and other old Argentine cities—retains few colonial buildings besides its churches. In fact, by the late 1800s, the capital made a conscious effort to completely rebuild much of its cityscape, following a pattern loosely based on Haussman's plans for rebuilding Paris under Second Empire France. Much of this was to be done in time for the 1910 Independence Centennial celebrations.

Developers laid new boulevards over the original Spanish colonial grid. The most important was Avenida de Mayo, which opened in 1893 and would serve as the government procession route, linking the Casa Rosada or Presidential Palace on its eastern end with the new Congreso on its western terminus. Lined with Beaux Arts and Art Nouveaux buildings, according to the styles of the time, it became the cultural and nightlife center of the city. Diagonal Norte and Diagonal Sud were also laid out (though not completed for many years later). The widest boulevard in the world, 9 de Julio, was planned in 1888 as well, but its construction didn't begin until 1937. Technically, it remains incomplete.

The majority of Buenos Aires's most iconic structures were built at this time—the Teatro Colón, the Water Palace, the Subway System, Congreso, Retiro Station, and the innumerable palaces and mansions that still line the streets in the northern sector. For nearly 30 years, the city was an ongoing construction site, as it forcefully rebuilt itself with a European image. While Argentina had the wealth and resources to pay for the massive rebuilding, however, it lacked the know-how and had to import its talent, labor, and even materials from Europe. The capital's planners, architects, and engineers came from the Old World, bringing with them the beautiful structural materials that now grace the city. A sticking point for many years was the fact that the British built and controlled the railroads.

Today, as a visitor mindful of Argentina's past several decades of political and economic chaos, it is difficult to make sense of the ostentatiously built infrastructure that remains from this earlier time. In essence, between 1880 and 1910, Argentina assumed the height of its wealth and power. Built at great expense of labor, money, and determination, Buenos Aires was the imperial capital of a country hungry to assert its importance on the world stage. Indeed, at the turn of the last century Argentina was one of the 10 wealthiest countries in the world.

4 The Cultural Growth of the 1920s & 1930s

The economic expansion, wealth, and sense of power Argentina had during this time laid the groundwork for strong cultural growth by the 1920s and 1930s. During this period, traditions that had always existed among the lower classes within Buenos Aires bubbled to the surface and came into international recognition. Tango has its roots in slave culture, and immigrants (mostly Italian) adopted the dance as they moved to Argentina. While the dance had always been associated with the slums of the lower classes, one man changed all of that. In 1917, Carlos Gardel, who began his career singing as a child in Buenos Aires's Abasto Market, recorded what is considered the first important tango song—"Mi Noche Triste," which launched him to stardom. Throughout the 1920s, Gardel toured in France. Seeing that Parisians accepted tango, the upper classes within Argentina began to embrace it as well. By the middle of the 1920s, tango became the country's most important musical form; its history and eventual acceptance internationally is akin to the rise of jazz in the United States. Gardel recorded numerous songs and toured Europe, South America, and the United States, making musical movies along the way. He died young, at the age of 44, on June 24, 1935, in a plane crash in Colombia, which solidified his status as one of Argentina's most important cultural icons.

The same period saw a flowering of literature and live theater. Jorge Luis Borges published short stories that often spoke of the struggles of the gangsters and lower classes in Buenos Aires and other parts of Argentina. Along with other colleagues, Borges launched the short-lived literary magazine Proa in 1924. By the 1930s, amid political chaos, eminent civil war, and repression in Spain, Buenos Aires became the preeminent center of Spanish language culture. Among the most important Spanish artists who came during this period was the playwright Federico García Lorca, who lived in Buenos Aires briefly between 1933 and 1934, staying at the Castelar Hotel on Avenida de Mayo.

The 1930s were also a golden age for Argentine radio and cinema. Many stars came of age at this time, including Tita Morello and Libertad Lamarque. The Argentine film industry's only South American rival was in Rio de Janeiro. Even there, however, stars such as Carmen Miranda, long before Hollywood discovered her, emulated the style of Buenos Aires movie stars who set the trends on the continent. By the 1930s, Avenida Corrientes was also widened, many theaters moved to this new location, and many new ones opened.

Viewed from the edges, the city of Buenos Aires glittered as the cultural capital of Argentina, pulling many a young man and woman in from the provinces to seek fame. In 1934, one teenage girl from the city of Junín in the Province of Buenos Aires would come to do just that, changing Argentine history forever with her determination beyond the obvious glamour of the stage and screen. Though accounts differ as to exactly how Maria Eva Duarte came to Buenos Aires—whether she was escorted by members of her family or by her purported lover, Augustin Magaldi, one of the country's top tango singers—she was in Buenos Aires for her very first time at the tender age of 15. With little but her looks, charm, and persistence, Ms. Duarte moved through a succession of jobs and men in theater, radio, and film. Many claimed she lacked talent, but with her connections, she became a force to be reckoned with. Various bosses hired her knowing only who her current powerful boyfriends were. Eventually, with success as an actress, she would meet her most powerful boyfriend of all.

5 The Perón Years

Few eras of Argentina's history play into its modern-day politics like the Perón era. In 1943, the military overthrew Argentina's constitutional government in a coup. Perón was put in charge of the National Labor Office, making him popular among the working class. Unique among members of the military, he had a flare for public relations, courting members of the media as well as young stars. Even during this period, he was revealing what would eventually be part of his persona: He is often the only member of the military smiling in photographs.

Perón's popularity was anchored by an earthquake that occurred on January 15, 1944, in San Juan, a city near Mendoza in the shadows of the Andes. Ten thousand people died and nearly half the city was left homeless. The tragic event became the ultimate public relations opportunity for Perón, as he rallied support for the region. Perón arranged a fundraiser for the victims of the earthquake with a star-studded concert in Luna Park, a stadium in Buenos Aires. Legend has it that at this event, he met 24-year-old actress Eva Duarte, changing Argentina's history forever. (In fact, photographic evidence makes clear that the two had met before, in Buenos Aires.)

Fearing his rise to power, the military government arrested Perón and imprisoned him on Juan García Island in the Tigre Delta. A near revolt occurred in Buenos Aires, and the government quickly released him. On October 17, 1945 (the most important date in the Peronist calendar), Perón spoke to a crowd gathered from a balcony at the Casa Rosada and announced that elections would be forthcoming. Feeling the need to legitimize their relationship with elections pending, Eva and Perón married secretly in Los Toldos, the town of her birth, using the civil registry. They later married in a Catholic ceremony in La Plata, the provincial capital of Buenos Aires Province. Ordinarily, the Catholic church would not have sanctioned the marriage, given Duarte's reputation as a "tainted" woman, but the priest was a relative of Perón's.

Perón became president in 1946 in an election marked by fraud and brutality on both sides. Though Juan was technically the power, he could not have retained his popularity without Eva (nicknamed Evita by the people) at his side. Knowing that their power was based in worker's unions, the couple launched numerous economic and work initiatives, many along the lines of communist-style 5-year plans, and employment and wages spiked under the new regime.

The modern middle class of Argentina, now weakened by more recent economic policies, owes its existence to this period. Eva used her position to create the Eva Perón Foundation, which was as much a public relations tool as a charity service for the first lady. Under the official economic plans and the foundation, contributions were forced from workers and the wealthy alike; land, buildings, and factories were seized from the oligarchs; and the railroads, formerly in the hands of the British, were nationalized in lieu of payment for unpaid war debts owed by Great Britain to Argentina. Throughout the country, the couple built hospitals, schools, and playgrounds for lower-class citizens and their children. One children's park, the Ciudad de los Niños in La Plata, served as the model for Walt Disney when he designed Disney Land in California. The popularity of the power couple soared among the poor, but the two were despised by the upper classes and the military alike.

After Evita's long insistence, women received the right to vote in 1947, and the presidential elections of 1951 were the first in which women participated. Wanting to legitimize her power within the government, Evita sought to be vice president on the 1951 election ballots, but Perón forced her to decline. Stricken with cervical cancer, Evita was dying, and forfeiting this final fight worsened her health. She voted in the elections from her hospital bed. She was so weak for the inaugural parade through Buenos Aires that they doped her up with pain killers and strapped her body to a wood frame, hidden by an oversized fur coat, so she could wave to crowds.

On July 26, 1952, Evita finally died. A 2-week mourning period ensued, and millions poured into Buenos Aires to pay their final respects. More than a dozen people died and hundreds were injured in the commotion as mourners lined up for days to view Evita's body in its glass coffin. Knowing that without Evita his days might soon be over, Perón commissioned a monument to her, which was never completed, and had her body embalmed to be preserved forever.

A period of economic instability ensued, exacerbated by Perón's own policies. He had, in essence, robbed the country of its wealth by spending on social causes (and siphoning much for his own use). In 1955, the military deposed Perón and stole Evita's body, sending it on a journey that lasted nearly 17 years before it resurfaced. Images of the Peróns were banned in Argentina; even uttering their names was an offense.

Perón bounced through several countries—Paraguay, Panama, Venezuela, the Dominican Republic—before finally settling in Spain, ruled by his longtime ally Francisco Franco. During his time in Panama, he met his future third wife and vice president, Isabel Martínez, a nightclub dancer.

While Perón was exiled in Spain, Evita's body was returned to him, and his power base in Argentina strengthened, allowing his return to the presidency in 1973. Still, his arrival was wrought with chaos. Gun battles broke out at Ezeiza Airport when his plane landed, leaving several of his followers and rivals dead. When he died in 1974, Isabel replaced him. Neither as strong as her husband nor his previous wife, Isabel could not hold onto the country for very long. She took on the nickname Isabelita, to bring back the memory of her predecessor, and, as an occultist, she supposedly held séances over the coffin of Evita in order to absorb her power. Despite her efforts, terrorism and economic instability persisted during her short reign, and on March 24, 1976, she was deposed in a military coup.

6 The Dirty War & Its Aftermath

The regime of Jorge Rafael Videla, established in the Junta, carried out a campaign to weed out anybody suspected of having Communist or Peronist sympathies. (Ironically, it was in this period that Evita was finally laid to rest in her current tomb in Recoleta Cemetery.) Congress was closed, censorship imposed, and unions banned. Over the next 7 years, during this "Process of National Reorganization"—a period now known as the Guerra Sucia (Dirty War) or El Proceso—between at least 10,000 and 30,000 intellectuals, artists, activists, and others were tortured or executed by the Argentine government. The mothers of these *desaparecidos* (the disappeared ones) began holding Thursday afternoon vigils in front of the presidential palace in Buenos Aires's Plaza de Mayo as a way to call international attention to the plight of the missing. Although the junta was overturned in 1983, the weekly protests continue to this day in Buenos Aires and in other large cities in the country.

With the Argentine population growing increasingly vocal about human rights abuses and the increasingly worsening economy, the military dictatorship sought a patriotic distraction.

Argentines have long laid claim to the Falkland Islands, known locally as the Islas Malvinas. The basis for the claim is that the territory, which was used for a penal colony beginning in 1828, was part of the Spanish Empire that Argentina conquered when it won independence. Argentina's early military rivals for power over the islands included both Britain and the United States. Argentina proved to be too young a nation with too little power to control such a remote region: The British seized the islands in 1833 by simply sending warships and a gentlemanly note to the Argentine commander in charge, José María Pinedo.

The taking of the Falklands had always been a sticking point among Argentines. In the early 1980s, Argentine President Leopoldo Galtieri assumed that invading the Falklands would be easy and bring much needed support to his government. Galtieri believed the invasion would go almost unnoticed by the United Kingdom (unbelievable in retrospect) because the U.K. didn't really want the islands and would not tolerate a loss of life to protect its far-flung turf. At the United Nations, Argentina had made several attempts to bring up their claim to the Falklands before the invasion, without any response from Great Britain.

The Argentines tested the waters by first invading the South Georgia Islands on March 19, 1982. On April 2, Galtieri launched the full-fledged invasion of the Falklands. The invasion was ill-fated, ill-planned, and tragic; nearly 900 people died in the short war. Most of Argentina's military forces remained on the Chilean border out of concern that British ally Augusto Pinochet of Chile would use the war as a reason to invade his eastern neighbor. Losses were heaviest on the Argentine side, including the sinking of the battleship *General Belgrano* with nearly 300 sailors aboard. Officially, neither side declared war on the other during the entire dispute. While no other powers contributed to the military effort, much of Latin America sided with Argentina, while Europe and the United States sided with Great Britain.

The war was a diplomatic nightmare for the United States, whose Monroe Doctrine, penned nearly 180 years before, technically required it to declare war on Great Britain. The war meant the end of the military regime, however, and the solidification of power for Great Britain's Prime Minister Margaret Thatcher. Virtually forgotten in the greater world, it's almost a joke among English-speaking nations that Argentina would challenge one of the world's greatest naval powers. But the war is a serious issue for Argentines, who still lay claim to the Falklands.

Galtieri's defeat brought about his greatest fear: the collapse of his government. An election in 1983 restored constitutional rule and brought Raúl Alfonsín, of the Radical Civic Union, to power. In 1989, political power shifted from the Radical Party to the Peronist Party (established by Juan Perón), the first democratic transition in 60 years. Carlos Saúl Ménem, a former governor from the province of La Rioja, won the presidency by a surprising margin.

A strong leader, Ménem pursued an ambitious but controversial agenda with the privatization of state-run institutions as its centerpiece. With the peso pegged to the dollar, Argentina enjoyed unprecedented price stability, allowing Ménem to deregulate and liberalize the economy. For many Argentines, it meant a kind of prosperity they had not seen in years. The policies had a dark side, however. The new money controls devastated local manufacturing, and the country's entire export market virtually dried out. World financial crises in the late 1990s, including those in Mexico, East Asia, Russia, and Brazil, increased the cost of external borrowing and further made Argentine exports and industries uncompetitive. The chasm between rich and poor widened, squeezing out much of the middle class and eroding the social support systems put in place over the decades. This destroyed investor confidence, and the national deficit began to soar. Ménem was seen as a corrupt purveyor of cheap glamour. His wife, Cecilia, the former Miss Chile and Miss Universe, was hated by many and regarded as a trophy wife. Rumor has it that members of his government had a hand in the bombings of the Israeli Embassy and the AIMI Jewish Community Center bombings. Some of the accusations bear a racial tinge, given that he was Argentina's first president of Arabic descent.

After 10 years as president—and a constitutional amendment that allowed him to seek a second term—Ménem left office. By that time, an alternative to the traditional Peronist and Radical parties, the center-left FREPASO political alliance, had emerged on the scene. The Radicals and FREPASO formed an alliance for the October 1999 election, and the alliance's candidate, running on an anti-corruption campaign, defeated his Peronist competitor.

Less charismatic than his predecessor, President Fernando de la Rúa was forced to reckon with the recession the economy had suffered since 1998. In an effort to eliminate Argentina's ballooning deficit, de la Rúa followed a strict regimen of government spending cuts and tax increases recommended by the International Monetary Fund. However, the tax increase crippled economic growth, and political infighting prevented de la Rúa from implementing other needed reforms designed to stimulate the economy. With a heavy drop in production and steep rise in unemployment, an economic crisis was looming.

The economic meltdown arrived with a run on the peso in December 2001, when investors moved en masse to withdraw their money from Argentine banks. Government efforts to restrict the run by limiting depositor withdrawals fueled anger through society, and Argentines took to the streets in sometimes violent demonstrations. De la Rúa resigned on December 20, as Argentina faced the worst economic crisis of its history. A series of interim governments did little to improve the situation, as Buenos Aires began to default on its international debts. Peronist President Eduardo Duhalde unlocked the

Argentine peso from the dollar on January 1, 2002, and the currency's value quickly tumbled. Within a few months, several presidents came and went in the ensuing crisis, and several citizens died in street protests throughout the country. The country's default to the IMF was the largest in history.

Argentina's economic crisis severely eroded the population's trust in the government. Increased poverty, unemployment surpassing 20%, and inflation hitting 30% resulted in massive emigration to Italy, Spain, and other destinations in Europe and North America. Anyone who had the passport to do so fled to Miami, Milan, and Madrid in particular. *Piqueteros* and *cartoneros,* the protestors and the homeless, became a visible presence throughout Buenos Aires and other large cities, as the unemployed in rural areas picked garbage for a living. Many of the protestors, it is claimed, have been paid off or fomented by various factions in government seeking to further destabilize the country and bring visible chaos to the streets.

Ironically, those who could not flee the country in the midst of the economic chaos stayed behind and built a stronger nation. While under Ménem, Argentina idolized Europe and the United States; now citizens had to look to their own historical and cultural models, the things that were authentically Argentine. The tango—long expected to die out as a dance for the older generation—found new enthusiasts among the young. It had always been seen as a dance that alleviated pain, and there was more than enough of that to go around.

Expensive ingredients for cuisine could no longer be imported, and so young chefs had to create using material grown in the country—even ingredients dating back to the time of the Incas. Meat, of course, remained the center of the Argentine palate. The explosion of new cooking ideas was most exemplified by the emerging restaurant scene in Buenos Aires's Palermo Viejo neighborhood, where new chefs became national celebrities. Full cafes and restaurants seemed to deny that there was any economic crisis at all. Young designers, unable to show on the runways in Europe, and young women, unable to afford imported fashions, created a new market for strictly Argentine fashion innovations. Argentina's abundant leather and its own locally produced textiles became the material of choice. Artists, unable to find real jobs anyway, had time to explore their creative impulses.

The country further stabilized by 2003, with the elections of Nestor Kirschner, the governor of the Province of Santa Cruz in Patagonia, a province made wealthy by oil exploration. Kirschner had proven his economic savvy by sending the province's investments overseas just before the collapse of the peso. A left-wing Peronist, he saw many of his friends disappear under the military regime. Viewed by some as a proponent of open government, he has reopened investigations into this dark period in Argentina's history and also begun to go after the most corrupt of Ménem's regime. A consolidator of power, he and his wife—Cristina Fernandez de Kirschner, a senator in her own right representing the Province of Buenos Aires—are together the country's most important political couple. Under Kirschner, economic stability has returned, with exports of soy, oil, and meat pumping the economy, now that the fall of the peso has proven to have a silver lining. Learning from past mistakes, Kirschner has not allowed the country's destiny to be shaped solely by Europe and the United States. Much of the raw material Argentina produces is bound up in new trade agreements with China and other Asian economies. Tourism has become the third most important economic sector under his administration. While she has made no official declaration, rumors abound that Ms. Kirschner will run for president herself in 2007—a nod to the aspirations of a first lady who came to power more than half a century before her.

Beholding the images of Argentina's chaos, with police shooting protestors in 2002, no one would have imagined the relatively stable and happy Argentina we experience today. But now you hold this book in your hand, and you are one example of the millions who have come to Argentina as a guest, heralding an era of growth unseen here for more than 130 years. On the dawn of Argentina's bicentennial celebrations, a new era in the nation's history has begun.

Appendix B:
Survival Spanish

Argentine Spanish has a rich, almost Italian sound, with the double "ll" and "y" pronounced with a "j"-like sound. So *llave* (key) sounds like "*zha*-ve" and *desayuno* (breakfast) sounds like "de-sa-*zhu*-no." *Usted* (the formal "you") is used extensively, and *vos* is a form of "you" that's even more familiar than *tú* (informal "you"). Peculiar terms you may come across only in Argentine include: *bárbaro* (very cool); Porteño (a resident of Buenos Aires); *pasos* (steps in a tango); *bandoneón* (a cousin of the accordion, used in tango music); and *subte* (the Buenos Aires subway). **Uruguayan Spanish** closely resembles the Spanish spoken in Buenos Aires.

BASIC WORDS & PHRASES

English	Spanish	Pronunciation
Good day	**Buenos días**	*bweh*-nohss *dee*-ahss
How are you?	**¿Cómo está?**	*koh*-moh ehss-*tah*
Very well	**Muy bien**	mwee byehn
Thank you	**Gracias**	*grah*-syahss
You're welcome	**De nada**	deh *nah*-dah
Goodbye	**Adiós**	ah-*dyohss*
Please	**Por favor**	pohr fah-*bohr*
Yes	**Sí**	see
No	**No**	noh
Excuse me (to get by someone)	**Perdóneme**	peh-*doh*-neh-meh
Excuse me (to begin a question)	**Disculpe**	dees-*kool*-peh
Give me	**Déme**	*deh*-meh
Where is . . . ?	**¿Dónde está . . . ?**	*dohn*-deh ehss-*tah*
the station	**la estación**	lah ehss-tah-*syohn*
a hotel	**un hotel**	oon oh-*tel*
a gas station	**una estación de servicio**	*oo*-nah ehss-tah-*syohn* deh sehr-*bee*-syoh
a restaurant	**un restaurante**	oon res-tow-*rahn*-teh
the toilet	**el baño**	el *bah*-nyoh
a good doctor	**un buen médico**	oon bwehn *meh*-dee-coh
the road to . . .	**el camino a/hacia . . .**	el cah-*mee*-noh ah/*ah*-syah

English	Spanish	Pronunciation
To the right	**A la derecha**	ah lah deh-*reh*-chah
To the left	**A la izquierda**	ah lah ees-*kyehr*-dah
Straight ahead	**Derecho**	deh-*reh*-choh
I would like . . .	**Quisiera . . .**	kee-*syeh*-rah
I want . . .	**Quiero . . .**	*kyeh*-roh
to eat	**comer**	koh-*mehr*
a room	**una habitación**	*oon*-nah ah-bee-tah-*syohn*
Do you have . . . ?	**¿Tiene usted . . . ?**	*tyeh*-neh oo-*sted*
a book	**un libro**	oon *lee*-broh
a dictionary	**un diccionario**	oon deek-syoh-*nah*-ryoh
How much is it?	**¿Cuánto cuesta?**	*kwahn*-toh *kweh*-stah?
When?	**¿Cuándo?**	*kwahn*-doh?
What?	**¿Qué?**	kay?
There is (Is there . . . ?)	**(¿)Hay (. . . ?)**	eye
What is there?	**¿Qué hay?**	keh eye
Yesterday	**Ayer**	ah-*yer*
Today	**Hoy**	oy
Tomorrow	**Mañana**	mah-*nyah*-nah
Good	**Bueno**	*bweh*-noh
Bad	**Malo**	*mah*-loh
Better (best)	**(Lo) Mejor**	(loh) meh-*hor*
More	**Más**	mahs
Less	**Menos**	*meh*-nohss
No smoking	**Se prohibe fumar**	seh pro-*hee*-beh foo-*mahr*
Postcard	**Tarjeta postal**	tar-*heh*-tah poh-*stahl*
Insect repellent	**Repelente contra insectos**	reh-peh-*lehn*-teh *cohn*-trah een-*sehk*-tohss

MORE USEFUL PHRASES

English	Spanish	Pronunciation
Do you speak English?	**¿Habla usted inglés?**	*ah*-blah oo-*sted* een-*glehss*
Is there anyone here who speaks English?	**¿Hay alguien aquí que hable inglés?**	eye *ahl*-gyehn ah-*kee* keh *ah*-bleh een-*glehss*
I speak a little Spanish.	**Hablo un poco de español.**	*ah*-bloh oon *poh*-koh deh eh-spah-*nyol*
I don't understand Spanish very well.	**No (lo) entiendo muy bien el español.**	noh (loh) ehn-*tyehn*-doh mwee byehn el eh-spah-*nyol*

English	Spanish	Pronunciation
The meal is good.	**Me gusta la comida.**	meh *goo*-stah lah koh-*mee*-dah
What time is it?	**¿Qué hora es?**	keh *oh*-rah ehss
May I see your menu?	**¿Puedo ver el menú (la carta)?**	*pweh*-doh vehr el meh-*noo* (lah *car*-tah)
The check, please.	**La cuenta, por favor.**	lah *kwehn*-tah, pohr fah-*bohr*
What do I owe you?	**¿Cuánto le debo?**	*kwahn*-toh leh *deh*-boh
What did you say?	**¿Cómo? (colloquial expression for American "Eh?")**	*koh*-moh?
I want (to see) . . .	**Quiero (ver) . . .**	*kyehr*-oh (vehr)
a room	**un cuarto** or **una habitación**	oon *kwar*-toh, *oon*-nah ah-bee-tah-*syohn*
for two persons	**para dos personas**	*pah*-rah dohss pehr-*soh*-nahs
with (without) bathroom	**con (sin) baño**	kohn (seen) *bah*-nyoh
We are staying here only . . .	**Nos quedamos aquí solamente . . .**	nohs keh-*dah*-mohss ah-*kee* soh-lah-*mehn*-teh
one night	**una noche**	*oo*-nah *noh*-cheh
one week	**una semana**	*oo*-nah seh-*mah*-nah
We are leaving . . .	**Partimos (Salimos) . . .**	pahr-*tee*-mohss (sah-*lee*-mohss)
tomorrow	**mañana**	mah-*nya*-nah
Do you accept . . . ?	**¿Acepta usted . . . ?**	ah *sehp* tah oo *sted*
traveler's checks?	**cheques de viajero?**	*cheh*-kehss deh byah-*heh*-roh
Is there a laundromat?	**¿Hay una lavandería?**	eye *oo*-nah lah-*bahn*-deh-*ree*-ah
near here?	**cerca de aquí?**	*sehr*-ka deh ah-*kee*
Please send these clothes to the laundry.	**Hágame el favor de mandar esta ropa a la lavandería.**	*ah*-gah-meh el fah-*bohr* deh mahn-*dahr ehss*-tah *roh*-pah a lahlah-*bahn*-deh-*ree*-ah

TRANSPORTATION TERMS

English	Spanish	Pronunciation
Airport	**Aeropuerto**	ah-eh-ro-*pwer*-toh
Flight	**Vuelo**	*bweh*-loh
Rental car	**Arrendadora de Autos**	ah-rehn-dah-*doh*-rah deh *ow*-tohss
Bus	**Autobús**	ow-toh-*boos*

English	Spanish	Pronunciation
Bus or truck	**Camión**	kah-*myohn*
Local bus	**Micro**	*mee*-kroh
Lane	**Carril**	kah-*reel*
Baggage (claim area)	**Equipajes**	eh-kee-*pah*-hehss
Luggage storage area	**Custodia**	koo-*stoh*-dyah
Arrivals gates	**Llegadas**	yeh-*gah*-dahss
Originates at this station	**Local**	loh-*kahl*
Originates elsewhere	**De Paso**	deh *pah*-soh
Stops if seats available	**Para si hay lugares**	*pah*-rah see eye loo-*gah*-rehss
First class	**Primera**	pree-*meh*-rah
Second class	**Segunda**	seh-*goon*-dah
Nonstop	**Sin Escala**	seen eh-*skah*-lah
Baggage claim area	**Recibo de Equipajes**	reh-*see*-boh deh eh-kee-*pah*-hehss
Waiting room	**Sala de Espera**	*sah*-lah deh eh-*speh*-rah
Toilets	**Baños**	*bah*-nyoss
Ticket window	**Boletería**	boh-leh-teh-*ree*-ah

NUMBERS

1 **uno** (*ooh*-noh)
2 **dos** (dohs)
3 **tres** (trehss)
4 **cuatro** (*kwah*-troh)
5 **cinco** (*seen*-koh)
6 **seis** (says)
7 **siete** (*syeh*-teh)
8 **ocho** (*oh*-choh)
9 **nueve** (*nweh*-beh)
10 **diez** (dyess)
11 **once** (*ohn*-seh)
12 **doce** (*doh*-seh)
13 **trece** (*treh*-seh)
14 **catorce** (kah-*tor*-seh)

15 **quince** (*keen*-seh)
16 **dieciseis** (dyeh-see-*sayss*)
17 **diecisiete** (dyeh-see-*syeh*-teh)
18 **dieciocho** (dyeh-*syoh*-choh)
19 **diecinueve** (dyeh-see-*nweh*-beh)
20 **veinte** (*bayn*-teh)
30 **treinta** (*trayn*-tah)
40 **cuarenta** (kwah-*ren*-tah)
50 **cincuenta** (seen-*kwen*-tah)

60 **sesenta** (seh-*sehn*-tah)
70 **setenta** (seh-*ten*-tah)
80 **ochenta** (oh-*chen*-tah)
90 **noventa** (noh-*behn*-tah)
100 **cien** (*syehn*)
200 **doscientos** (doh-*syehn*-tohss)
500 **quinientos** (kee-*nyehn*-tohss)
1,000 **mil** (meel)

Index

AARP, 22
Abasto (Buenos Aires)
  accommodations, 89
  restaurants, 121–122
Abercrombie & Kent, 34, 40, 408
Abril Café (Mendoza), 266
Accommodations, 5–6, 26–27
Aconcagua Provincial Park, 290–291
Active vacations, 37–39
Adventure Life Journeys, 210
Adventure Network International, 409
Adventure trips, organized, 34–35, 39–41
Aerovías DAP, 409
AGUITBA (Asociación de Guías de Turismo de Buenos Aires), 35
Aires de Montaña Spa, 286
Air travel, 25–26, 30–31
Alain de France (Mendoza), 265
All Patagonia Viajes y Turismo (Ushuaia), 398
Alta Gracia, 250–251
Alta Montaña driving circuit, 284–291
Alto Palermo Shopping Center (Buenos Aires), 135
American Express, 35
  Buenos Aires, 60
Amerika (Buenos Aires), 150
Amsterdam (Mar del Plata), 159
Andean Archaeological Museum (Salta), 208–209
Andes railway, 287
Angastaco, 216
Antarctica, 12, 403–409
Antarctica Cruises, 408
Antares (Bariloche), 312
Antu Aventuras (San Rafael), 284
Archaeological museum (Cachi), 216

Arelauquen Golf Resort, 301
Argentina Rafting Expediciones, 264, 286
Argentine Open Polo Championships, 18
Arte en Telar (Cafayate), 218
Artesano Platero (San Antonio de Areco), 185
Ashanti Leather Factory (Buenos Aires), 139
Asociación Argentina de Cultura Inglesa (Buenos Aires), 144
Asociación Argentina de Polo (Buenos Aires), 134
ATMs (automated teller machines), 16
Atuel Canyon, 284
Aurora Expeditions, 408
Avenida Corrientes (Buenos Aires), 131
Avenida Santa Fe (Buenos Aires), 135
Aymara Adventures, 291

Backpacking, 38
Backroads Active Vacations, 34–35, 40
Bahía López, 299–300
Baquero 1886 (Maipú), 277
Bariloche, 294–312
  accommodations, 303–308
  banks and currency exchange, 297
  getting around, 295–296
  Internet access, 297
  nightlife, 312
  outdoor activities, 301–303
  restaurants, 308–312
  shopping, 297–298
  sights and attractions, 297–301
  south of, 313–315
  tour operators, 298
  traveling to, 294–295
  visitor information, 296

Barrio Histórico (Colonia del Sacramento, Uruguay), 173, 174
Barrio Norte (Buenos Aires)
  accommodations, 63
  restaurants, 99
Bar Uvas (Mendoza), 266
Basílica y Convento de San Francisco (Buenos Aires), 133
Beer Festival (El Bolsón), 314
Beith Cuer (Buenos Aires), 142
Belgrano (Buenos Aires), restaurants, 110–111
Berlina (Bariloche), 312
Bettanso Excursiones, 316
Biblioteca Nacional (Buenos Aires), 133
Bikes and Wine (Mendoza), 270
Biking and mountain biking, 38
  Bariloche, 301
  El Calafate, 359
  Mendoza, 264, 270
  Puerto Madryn, 346
  San Martín, 325
  Villa La Angostura, 316
Bird-watching
  Iguazú Falls area, 195
  Parque das Aves (Foz do Iguaçu, Brazil), 201
  Parque Nacional Chaco, 204
  Quebrada del Condorito, 245
Black Glacier, 313
Blah Blah Bar (Mendoza), 266
Boat trips and cruises
  Antarctica, 406
  to Chile, from Bariloche, 295
  El Chaltén area, 372
  Lake Mascardi, 313
  Lake Pehoé, 379
  Llao Llao, 300–301
  Montevideo, Uruguay, 175–176
  Puerto Williams, Chile, 402
  from Punta Arenas to Ushuaia, 389
  San Martín, 325–326
  Tigre delta, 166

Boat trips and cruises *(cont.)*
  Ushuaia, 397–398
  Villa La Angostura area, 316
Boca Juniors stadium (Buenos Aires), 123, 126, 134
Bodega Jean Rivier (San Rafael), 284
Bodega Lagarde (Chacras de Coria), 272
Bodega La Rural (Maipú), 277
Bodega Salentein (Tunuyan), 280, 282
Bodegas Etchart (near Cafayate), 218
Bodega Valentin Bianchi (San Rafael), 284
Bodega y Cava de Weinert (Chacras de Coria), 272
Borello Travel & Tours, 33
Bosque Arrayanes, 300
Bosque Tallado, 314
Bosque Vivero Dunícola Florentino Ameghino (Miramar), 159
Botanical Gardens (Buenos Aires), 127
British Arts Centre (Buenos Aires), 144
British Clock Tower (Buenos Aires), 131
Buemes Travel Services (Montevideo, Uruguay), 176
Buenos Aires, 9–10, 55–151
  accommodations, 63–89
  American Express, 60
  area code, 61
  business hours, 61
  currency exchange, 61
  emergencies, 61
  getting around, 58–60
  language, 61
  layout of, 57–58
  nightlife, 144–151
  post offices, 61
  restaurants, 89–122
  safety, 61
  shopping, 134–144
  sights and attractions, 123–134
  spectator sports and outdoor activities, 134
  suggested itinerary, 42–43
  taxes, 62
  taxis, 59–60
  telephone, 62
  tipping, 62
  traveling to, 56–57
  visitor information, 60
  websites, 58

Buenos Aires News, 150
Business hours, 35
Bus travel, 31–32
Butterfield and Robinson, 34, 40

Cabaña de Cabras (La Flor del Pago), 215
Cabildo
  Buenos Aires, 129
  Córdoba, 239
  Montevideo, Uruguay, 178
  Salta, 207–208
Cacano (Mendoza), 266
Cachi, 216–217
Cafayate, 3, 215, 217–221
Café Central (Puerto Iguazú), 199
Café Misterio (Montevideo, Uruguay), 183
Café Tortoni (Buenos Aires), 146
Calchaquíes Valley, 215–221
Calle Florida (Buenos Aires), 131, 135
Calle Lavalle (Buenos Aires), 131
Calle Perú (Buenos Aires), 131
Caminito (Buenos Aires), 123
Camping
  El Chaltén area, 372–375
  Torres del Paine National Park (Chile), 383
Campo Argentino de Polo (Buenos Aires), 134
Canal Fun & Nature (Ushuaia), 398
Cándido Silva (Buenos Aires), 138
Capilla San Eduardo (Llao Llao), 299
Carinae Veñedos & Bodega (Cruz de Piedra), 277
Carnaval, 18
Car rentals, 32–33
  surfing for, 27
Car travel, 32
  driving rules, 35–36
  driving tours
    Alta Montaña, 284–291
    Bariloche to San Martín, 320–322
    Calchaquíes Valley, 215–221
    Circuito Chico, 299
    Llao Llao Peninsula, 299–300
    Quebrada de Humahuaca (Humahuaca Gorge), 224–225
    south of Bariloche, 313–315

Casa de Brown (Colonia del Sacramento, Uruguay), 174
Casa de Gobierno (Tucumán), 226
Casa Histórica de la Independencia (Tucumán), 226
Casa López (Buenos Aires), 142
Casa Mario Leather Factory (Montevideo, Uruguay), 179–180
Casa Padilla (Tucumán), 226
Casa Rosada (Buenos Aires), 128–129
Cascada Chorrillo del Salto, 373
Casino Carlos Paz (Villa Carlos Paz), 245
Casino Miramar, 160
Catamaran Futaleufú, 316
Catamaran Patagonia Argentina, 316
Cataratas do Iguaçu (Brazil), 201
Cataratas Turismo (Iguazú Falls), 194
Catedral (Cathedral)
  Córdoba, 238
  Jujuy, 222
  Montevideo, Uruguay, 178
  Tucumán, 226
Catedral de la Inmaculada Concepción (La Plata), 163
Catedral Turismo (Bariloche), 295, 298
Catena Zapata (Luján de Cuyo), 274
Cellphones, 29–30
Centro Artesanal (Cachi), 216
Centro Cultural de Borges (Buenos Aires), 145
Centro Cultural Recoleta (Buenos Aires), 128, 145
Cerebro (Bariloche), 312
Cerro Aconcagua, 290
Cerro Bayo, 316–317
Cerro Campanario, 299
Cerro Castor, 398
Cerro Catedral, 299
Cerro de los Siete Colores, 224
Cerro Otto, 300
Cerro Standhart, 374
Cerro Torre, 370, 372–374
Cerro Torre Lookout, 373
Cerro Tronador, 298–299, 313, 314
Cervecería Blest (Bariloche), 312
C'Gastón (Mendoza), 266
Chabeli (Buenos Aires), 142
Chaco province, 203–204
Chacras de Coria, 3, 270–272

Chandon Bar (Buenos Aires), 150
Chapelco Golf Resort (near San Martín), 326
Chicharron Disco Bar (Buenos Aires), 150
Children, families with, 24
Chile
    bringing a car into, 296
    crossing into, 290
    driving to, via Paso Puyehue, 319
    traveling by boat from Bariloche to, 295
Chilecito, 230–231
Chocolate (Mar del Plata), 158
Cholila, 315
Cine Arrayán (Bariloche), 312
Cipolleti Dike (Luján de Cuyo), 275–276
The Circuit (Torres del Paine), 383–384
Circuito Chico, 299
Circuito Superior/Circuito Inferior (Iguazú Falls), 193
City Zoo (La Plata), 163
Civic Center (Bariloche), 297
Clark Expediciones (Salta), 41, 210
Climate, 17
Club Andino Bariloche, 296, 300, 301
Club de Campo (Mendoza), 264
Coctaca, 225
Colegio Nacional de Buenos Aires (Buenos Aires), 129–130
Colonia del Sacramento (Uruguay), 3, 173–175
Colonia Suiza, 300
Colón Theater (Buenos Aires), 133–134, 146
Compañía de Jesús (Córdoba), 238
Congreso (Buenos Aires), 133
    accommodations, 83–85
    restaurants, 99–101
Contemporary Art Museum (La Plata), 163
Convento de Santo Domingo (La Rioja), 229
Córdoba, 232–242
    accommodations, 235–236
    ATMs and currency exchange, 234
    getting around, 234
    Jesuit estancias, 240–241
    nightlife, 239–242
    outdoor activities, 239

restaurants, 236–237
seasons, 235
sights and attractions, 238–239
traveling to, 233–234
visitor information, 234
Córdoba Nativo, 240
Córdoba Pass, 322
Cousiño Jewels (Buenos Aires), 139
Coyote (Mar del Plata), 159
Credit cards, 17
Crucero Australis, 389
Cruises. See Boat trips and cruises
Cuareim (Montevideo, Uruguay), 183
Cuba Libre (Puerto Iguazú), 199
Cuchi Corral, 248
CuerPiel (Mendoza), 265
Cuesta de Miranda, 230–231
Cuesta Vieja (Chilecito), 230
Currency and currency exchange, 15–16
    Montevideo, Uruguay, 178
Customs regulations, 14–15

Dance clubs and discos
    Bariloche, 312
    Buenos Aires, 150
    Mar del Plata, 158–159
    Mendoza, 266
    Montevideo, Uruguay, 183
    Puerto Madryn, 347
    Villa Carlos Paz, 245
Dardo Rocha Cultural Center (La Plata), 163
Décimo (Mendoza), 266
De la Abundancia/Artesanos (Montevideo, Uruguay), 179
De Los Padres Lake and Hills (Mar del Plata), 155
Del Turista (Bariloche), 297
Día de la Tradición (San Antonio de Areco), 18, 184
Dientes de Navarino Circuit (Chile), 402
Difunta Correa, 285
Dique Cabra Corral (Salta), 210
Disabilities, travelers with, 21–22
Divino Beach (Mar del Plata), 159
Dolavan, 354
Domestic Chapel (Córdoba), 238

Draghi Museum and Shop (San Antonio de Areco), 184–185
Dreamland (Ushuaia), 398
Drugstores, 36
Dublin Irish Pub (Ushuaia), 398
Dublin South Pub (San Martín), 332
Duo (Punta del Este, Uruguay), 173

Ecocentro (Puerto Madryn), 345
Ecological Preserve (Buenos Aires), 130
Ecotourism, Salta, 210
El Abasto (Mendoza), 266
El Arrabal (Córdoba), 239
El Arranque (Buenos Aires), 147–148
El Beso Nightclub (Buenos Aires), 148
El Bolsón, 314–315
El Cabildo. See Cabildo
El Calafate, 355–366
    accommodations, 360–363
    getting around, 358
    nightlife, 366
    outdoor activities, 358–360
    restaurants, 363–366
    sights and attractions, 358
    traveling to, 356
    visitor information, 358
El Carril, 215
El Cencerro (Capilla del Señor), 187–188
El Chaco, 203–204
El Chaltén and FitzRoy area, 3–4, 370–377
Electricity, 36
El Galpón del Glaciar (near El Calafate), 359
El Gaucho Gil, 285
El Lagar Carmelo Patti (Luján de Cuyo), 274
El Museo Histórico Nacional (Buenos Aires), 131
El Niño Bien (Buenos Aires), 148
El Nochero (Buenos Aires), 142
El Ombú de Areco (San Antonio de Areco), 188
El Paraíso (Cruz Chica), 248
El Paraíso, Zoo (Mar del Plata), 155
El Querandí (Buenos Aires), 146
El Rosario de Areco (San Antonio de Areco), 188–189

El Tren del Fin del Mundo
(Ushuaia), 399
El Viejo Almacén (Buenos
Aires), 126, 147
Embassies, 36
Emergencies, 36
Entry requirements, 13–14
Escorted tours, 33–35
Escuela Argentina de Tango
(Buenos Aires), 145
Esquel Outfitters, 315
Esquina Carlos Gardel (Buenos
Aires), 147
Estadio Boca Juniors (Buenos
Aires), 123, 126, 134
Estancia Alta Vista (near
El Calafate), 359
Estancia Carmen, 216
Estancia Cristina (near
El Calafate), 359
Estancia de Alta Gracia, 240
Estancia de Caroya
(Córdoba), 240
Estancia de Jesús María
(Córdoba), 241
Estancia de Santa Catalina
(Córdoba), 241
Estancia El Rosario
(La Cumbre), 248
Estancia Harberton, 399
Estancia Helsingfors (near
El Calafate), 359
Estancia La Candelaria
(Córdoba), 241
Estancia La Despedida, 400
Estancia Nibepo Aike (near
El Calafate), 359
Estancia Peuma Hue, 313
Estancias (ranches)
near Buenos Aires, 187–189
near El Calafate, 359–361
Jesuit, in Córdoba, 240–241
Estancia San Lorenzo (Penín-
sula Valdés), 348
Euro Tur, 34
Experience Patagonia, 41
Explorador Expediciones
(Iguazú Falls), 194
Ezeiza International Airport
(Buenos Aires), 56

Falkland (Malvinas)
Islands, 407
Familia Weiss (Bariloche), 297
Familia Zuccardi (Maipú), 278
Families with children, 24
Faro de Punta del Este
(Uruguay), 170

Feria Artesanal del Paseo de
las Artes (Córdoba), 238
Fernando Grajales Expedi-
ciones, 291
Fiesta de las Murgas (Buenos
Aires), 18
Finca Flichman (Maipú), 277
Finca Las Nubes (near
Cafayate), 218
Finca Los Amigos (Luján de
Cuyo), 275
Finca Viña del Golf (near San
Rafael), 284
Fishing, 38
Alta Gracia, 251
Bariloche, 301
Junín, 334
Junín de los Andes, 333
Puerto Madryn, 347
Río Correntoso, 316
San Martín, 326
Tierra del Fuego, 400
Ushuaia, 398
FitzRoy, Mt., 374
FitzRoy area, 370–377
Fitz Roy Expediciones, 372
Fogón de los Arrieros
(Resistencia), 204
For Export (La Plata), 163
Foz do Iguaçu (Brazil), 199–203
French Valley (Torres del
Paine), 385
Frommers.com, 26

Gaiman, 336, 338, 353–354
Galería Alvear (Buenos
Aires), 138
Galería El Solar de French
(Buenos Aires), 138
Galería Ruth Benzacar (Buenos
Aires), 139
Galerías Pacifico (Buenos
Aires), 135
Garganta del Diablo (Devil's
Throat)
Iguazú Falls, 193, 194
Jujuy, 225
Tafi del Valle, 227
Garganta do Diablo (Brazil), 201
Gaucho Gil, 285
Gaucho Parade (Salta), 18
Gay and lesbian travelers,
23–24, 150, 159
General Rudecindo Alvarado
(Miramar), 160
Geographic Expeditions, 408
Gimatur (San Luis City), 250
Glacier Grey (Torres del
Paine), 384

Glacier Martial/Aerosilla,
396–397
Gloria Lopes Sauqué (Buenos
Aires), 142
Go! (Mar del Plata), 159
Golf
Bariloche, 301
Buenos Aires, 134
Córdoba, 239
Mendoza, 264
Miramar, 160
Puerto Madryn, 347
San Martín, 326
near San Rafael, 284
Gran Bar Danzon (Buenos
Aires), 150
Grupo de Teatro Catalinas Sur
(Buenos Aires), 145
Gruta de Lourdes (Alta
Gracia), 251
Guevara, Ernesto Che, Museo
Casa de, 251

Hard Leather (Buenos
Aires), 142
Health concerns, 19–21
Antarctica, 404–406
Health insurance, 19, 21
Helados Ferruccio Soppelsa
(Mendoza), 262
Henry J. Beans (Buenos
Aires), 150
High Zone (Mendoza), 268–269
Hiking and trekking, 37–38
Bariloche, 301
El Chaltén area, 372–375
Mendoza, 264
Parque Nacional Los
Arrayanes, 316
Puerto Williams, Chile, 402
San Martín, 327
Torres del Paine National Park
(Chile), 383–385
Hipódromo Argentino de
Palermo (Buenos Aires), 134
Hipódromo de San Isidro
(Buenos Aires), 134
History of Argentina, 410–420
Holidays, 17–18
Horseback riding, 39
Bariloche area, 302
El Calafate, 358–359
El Chaltén area, 372
Mendoza, 264
Puerto Madryn, 347
Torres del Paine National Park
(Chile), 385
Villa La Angostura, 316

Horse racing, Buenos Aires, 134
Hotel Edén (La Falda), 246
H.Stern (Buenos Aires), 139
Huala Adventure Tourism
  (Bariloche), 41, 298, 301
Huentata (Mendoza), 264
Humahuaca, 225
Humahuaca Gorge (Quebrada
  de Humahuaca), 224–225

Iglesia de la Virgen de Carro-
  dilla (Luján de Cuyo), 276
Iglesia Matriz (Colonia del
  Sacramento, Uruguay), 174
Iglesia San Antonio
  (Miramar), 160
Iglesia San Francisco (Salta), 208
Iguazú Falls/Puerto Iguazú,
  190–200
    accommodations, 194–198
    Brazilian side of the falls (Foz
      do Iguaçu), 199–203
    getting around, 192–193
    outdoor activities, 194
    traveling to, 192
    visiting the national park,
      193–194
    visitor information, 192
    wildlife viewing, 195
Iguazú Jungle Explorer, 194
Insurance, 18–19
Internet access, 27–28, 36
    Montevideo, Uruguay, 178
Inti Raymi, 18
Isabel Agrovivero (Cruz de
  Piedra), 278
Ischigualisto, 231
Isla del Cerrito, 204
Islas Malvinas War Memorial
  (Buenos Aires), 131
Isla Victoria, 300
Itati Viajes (Córdoba), 245
Itineraries, suggested, 42–54

Jacques and François Lurton
  (Tunuyan), 282
James Ross Island, 407
Japanese Garden (Buenos
  Aires), 127
Jesuit estancias, Córdoba,
  240–241
Jewelry, Buenos Aires, 139
Johnny B. Good (Córdoba),
  240–241
Jorge Newbery Airport (Buenos
  Aires), 56

Jujuy, 221–224
Julio Bocca and Ballet Argentino
  (Buenos Aires), 145
Junín de los Andes, 320, 322,
  333–334

Kayaking, 39
    Bariloche area, 302
    Península Valdés, 349
    Puerto Madryn, 347
    Puerto Pirámides, 350
    San Martín, 326
    Ushuaia, 398
Keop's (Villa Carlos Paz), 245
The Kilkenny (Buenos Aires), 150
Kua (Ushuaia), 398–399

La Azul (Tupungato), 282
La Bamba (San Antonio de
  Areco), 189
La Barranca (Puerto
  Iguazú), 199
La Boca (Buenos Aires)
    restaurants, 120–121
    shopping, 135
    sights and attractions,
      123, 126
La Boca Fair (Buenos Aires), 138
La Cañada (Córdoba), 232
La Casa de Becho (Montevideo,
  Uruguay), 183
La Cubana (Mendoza), 266
La Cumbre (Tafi del Valle), 227,
  247–250
La Falda, 3, 246–247
Lago Escondido, 399
Lago Grey (Torres del
  Paine), 384
Lago Pingo (Torres del Paine),
  384–385
Lago Puello National Park, 314
Laguna Capri, 373
Laguna del Diamante, 280
Laguna de los Tres, 375
Laguna Torre, 374
The Lake District, 10, 292–334
La Mano (Punta del Este,
  Uruguay), 170
Landelia (Luján de Cuyo), 274
La Paya, 216
La Plata, 162–164
La Reserva (Mendoza), 266
La Rioja, 228–231
La Riojana (Chilecito), 230
Las Bovedas, 286
Las Cañitas (Buenos Aires), 127

Las Leñas, 288–289
Las Quijadas (San Luis City), 250
Las Torres (Torres del Paine), 385
Las Viñas (Mendoza), 265
Laur (Cruz de Piedra), 278
La Villa de Estancia María
  Behety, 400
La Viruta (Buenos Aires), 148
La Vuelta Ciclista de
  Mendoza, 264
La Zaina (El Calafate), 366
Leather Corner (Punta del Este,
  Uruguay), 173
Le Clos de los Siete (Vista
  Flores), 282
Legislatura de la Ciudad
  (Buenos Aires), 129
Les Amis, 34
Limay Travel (Bariloche), 298
Lindblad Expeditions, 408
Links Miramar, 160
Llao Llao Peninsula, 299–300
Llao Llao Resort golf
  course, 301
Los Alerces National Park, 315
Los Andes (Mendoza), 265
Los Glaciares National Park,
  258, 366–370
Los Molinos (Alta Gracia), 251
Los Paredones (Alta Gracia), 251
Los Penitentes, 288–289
Lost-luggage insurance, 19
Louis Vuitton (Buenos
  Aires), 143
Lower Circuit (Iguazú Falls), 193
Luigi Bosca (Luján de Cuyo), 274
Luján de Cuyo, 272–276
Luna Park (Buenos Aires), 145
Lupulo (Mendoza), 266

Maipú, 276–278
MALBA-Colección Constantini
  (Buenos Aires), 131–132
Malvinas (Falkland) Islands, 407
Mambo (Buenos Aires), 150
Mamushchka (Bariloche),
  297, 298
Manzana Jesuítica (Córdoba),
  232–233, 238
Manzanas de las Luces (Buenos
  Aires), 129
Mapuche Indians, 325, 333,
  334, 410
Mapuche Museum (Junín), 333
Mar del Plata, 152–159
Mar del Plata Casino, 154
Mar del Sud, 160

Margarita Pub (Puerto
  Madryn), 347
Marguerite Bay, 407
Mariachi (Montevideo,
  Uruguay), 183
Markets. *See also* entries
  starting with Mercado
  El Bolsón, 314
Martín García Island
  (La Plata), 166
Medical insurance, 19, 21
MEF (Museo Paleontológico
  Egidio Feruglio; Trelew),
  352–353
Meli-Hue, 300
Mendoza, 10, 252–291
  accommodations, 256–259
  currency exchange, 256
  emergencies, 256
  getting around, 255–256
  Internet access, 256
  nightlife, 265–266
  restaurants, 259–263
  shopping, 265
  suggested itinerary, 49–52
  tour operators and outdoor
    activities, 264–265
  traveling to, 254–255
  visitor information, 255
  wineries. *See* Wineries and
    vineyards, Mendoza
Mendoza East Region, 269
Mendoza South Region, 269
Mercado Artesanal
  La Rioja, 229
  Salta, 210
Mercado Central (Mendoza),
  263
Mercado del Puerto (Montevideo, Uruguay), 179
Meteorological Station (Punta
  del Este, Uruguay), 170
Metropolitan Cathedral
  (Buenos Aires), 129
Michel Torino Bodega La Rosa
  (near Cafayate), 218
Microcentro (Buenos Aires)
  accommodations, 66–73
  restaurants, 112–117
  shopping, 135
  sights and attractions,
    130–131
Milongas (tango dance clubs),
  Buenos Aires, 147–149
Mirador Nordenskjold (Torres
  del Paine), 385
Miramar, 159–161
Miramar Synagogue, 160
Mitre (Córdoba), 241

Molino Harinero (Dolavan), 354
Money matters, 15–17
Monserrat (Buenos Aires)
  accommodations, 73–76
  restaurant, 111
Montevideo (Uruguay), 175–183
  accommodations, 180–182
  area code, 178
  getting around, 176
  nightlife, 183
  orientation, 176
  restaurants, 182–183
  shopping, 179–180
  sights and attractions,
    178–179
  tour companies, 176, 178
  traveling to, 175–176
  visitor information, 176
Monumento Canota, 285
Mountaineering and rock
  climbing, 38
  Aconcagua Provincial
    Park, 290
  Bariloche area, 302
  El Chaltén area, 372–374
  San Martín, 326
Mountaineering Patagonia, 372
Mountain-Travel Sobek, 34, 40,
  408
Municipal Art Museum
  (La Plata), 163
Municipal Hall (San Antonio de
  Areco), 184
Murillo 666 (Buenos Aires), 143
Murillo Street Leather District
  (Buenos Aires), 142
Museo Arqueológico Provincial
  (Jujuy), 222
Museo Casa de Ernesto Che
  Guevara, 251
Museo de Arqueológia de Alta
  Montaña (Salta), 208–209
Museo de Arte Contemporáneo
  (Montevideo, Uruguay), 178
Museo de Arte Oriental
  (Buenos Aires), 132
Museo de Bellas Artes de Men-
  doza (Chacras de Coria), 272
Museo de Ciencias Naturales
  (La Plata), 163
Museo de la Patagonia Perito
  Moreno (Bariloche), 297
Museo del Azulejo (Colonia del
  Sacramento, Uruguay), 174
Museo del Fin de Mundo
  (Ushuaia), 397
Museo del Hombre Chaqueño
  (Resistencia), 204

Museo del Mar
  Mar del Plata, 155
  Punta del Este, Uruguay, 170
Museo de los Primeros Pobla-
  dores (San Martín), 324
Museo de Vino (Coquimbito),
  277
Museo de Vitivinicultura
  (Museum of Grapevines and
  Wine; Cafayate), 218
Museo Don Mosés (Junín),
  333–334
Museo Evita (Buenos Aires), 132
Museo Folklórico (La Rioja), 229
Museo Folklórico
  (Tucumán), 226
Museo Fundacional
  (Mendoza), 263
Museo Histórico del Norte
  (Salta), 207–208
Museo Histórico General San
  Martín (Mendoza), 263
Museo Histórico José Evaristo
  Uriburu (Salta), 209
Museo Histórico Nacional
  (Buenos Aires), 131
Museo Histórico Provincial
  (Jujuy), 222–223
Museo Histórico Provincial
  Marqués de Sobre Monte
  (Córdoba), 239
Museo Histórico Regional
  Gales (Gaiman), 354
Museo Leleque (near
  Cholila), 315
Museo Marítimo y Presidio de
  Ushuaia, 397
Museo Maurice van de Maele
  (Puerto Williams, Chile), 402
Museo Municipal (Colonia del
  Sacramento, Uruguay), 174
Museo Municipal (El
  Calafate), 358
Museo Municipal de Bellas
  Artes "Juan Manuel Blanes"
  (Montevideo, Uruguay), 179
Museo Nacional de Arte Deco-
  rativo (Buenos Aires), 132
Museo Nacional de Bellas Artes
  (Buenos Aires), 132–133
Museo Nacional de Historia
  Natural (Montevideo,
  Uruguay), 179
Museo Paleontológico Egidio
  Feruglio (MEF; Trelew),
  352–353
Museo Portugués (Colonia del
  Sacramento, Uruguay), 174

Museo Provincial de Bellas Artes de Salta, 209–210
Museo Regional y Arqueológico Rodolfo Bravo (Cafayate), 218–219
Museo Ricardo Güiraldes (San Antonio de Areco), 185
Museum of Fine Arts (Salta), 209–210
Museum of the Gaucho (San Antonio de Areco), 185

Nahuel Huapi National Park, 296, 298–299, 313
National College of Monserrat (Córdoba), 238–239
National Gay Pride (Buenos Aires), 18
National History Museum (Buenos Aires), 131
National parks. See entries starting with Parque Nacional
National University of Córdoba, 238
Nativo Viajes, 245
Naval Museum (La Plata), 166
New York (Montevideo, Uruguay), 183
Nightlife, 1
Northeast, 10
The Northwest, 10, 205–231
Nuestra Señora de la Candelaria (Punta del Este, Uruguay), 170

O. Fournier (Tunuyan), 282
Obelisco (Buenos Aires), 131
Oceanographic and Natural Sciences Museum (Puerto Madryn), 345
Oceanwide Expeditions, 408
Off-roading, El Calafate, 359
Oktoberfest, Villa General Belgrano, 251
Olitas Tours (Mar del Plata), 155
Once (Buenos Aires), restaurants, 121–122
100% Uruguayo (Punta del Este, Uruguay), 173
Opera Bay (Buenos Aires), 150
Orígen Arte y Artesanía (Bariloche), 298
Outdoor activities, best outdoor adventures, 4–5
Outlet (Buenos Aires), 143

Outlet de Cuero (Buenos Aires), 143
Overland Patagonia, 305, 314

Package tours, 33–35
Palacio (Buenos Aires), 150
Palacio Municipal (La Plata), 163
Palacio Salvo (Montevideo, Uruguay), 179
Palacio Taranco (Montevideo, Uruguay), 179
Paleontological Museum Edigio Feruglio (Trelew), 352–353
Palermo (Buenos Aires)
   restaurants, 101–110
   sights and attractions, 126–127
Palermo Viejo (Buenos Aires), 127
   accommodations, 88
Pallarols (Buenos Aires), 138
Palmares Open Mall (Mendoza), 265
The Pampas, 10
Paradise Harbor, 407
Paragliding, 230, 248, 300
Parque das Aves (Foz do Iguaçu, Brazil), 201
Parque De La Bahía (near El Calafate), 359–360
Parque de la Costa (La Plata), 166
Parque General San Martín (Mendoza), 263
Parque Nacional Chaco, 204
Parque Nacional Lanín, 325, 333
Parque Nacional Los Arrayanes, 316
Parque Nacional los Cardones, 216
Parque Nacional los Glaciares, 258, 366–370
Parque Nacional Nahuel Huapi, 296, 298–299, 313
Parque Nacional Quebrada del Condorito, 245
Parque Nacional Sierra de las Quijadas, 250
Parque Nacional Talampaya (La Rioja), 231
Parque Nacional Tierra del Fuego, 401
Parque Nacional Torres del Paine (Chile), 377–385
Parque Natural Ongamira, 248
Parque Provincial Aconcagua, 290–291

Parque San Martín (San Antonio de Areco), 185
Parque Tres de Febrero (Buenos Aires), 127
Paseo del Bosque (La Plata), 163
Paseo Del Cuero (Buenos Aires), 143
Paseo Victórica (Tigre), 165
Pasión Argentina-Diseños Etnicos (Buenos Aires), 143
Paso Cardenal Samore, 319
Paso Puyehue, 319
Patagonia, 10, 12
   southern, 338
   suggested itineraries, 43–48, 52–53
Patagonia Travel Company, 41
Patio Bullrich (Buenos Aires), 135
Paulet Island, 407
Payogasta, 216
Pehoé, Lake, 379
Penguins, 348, 397, 399, 403, 404, 406, 407
Península Valdés, 335–338, 340, 345–349
Peregrine Adventures, 408
Perito Moreno Glacier, 366
Pico Poincenot, 374
Piedra del Molino, 216
Pilar-Río Blanco-Poincenot Trail, 375
Pilgrim (Bariloche), 312
Pinares Golf Club, 301
Pizarro Expediciones, 287
Plaza Arellano (San Antonio de Areco), 184
Plaza Artigas (Punta del Este, Uruguay), 170, 173
Plaza Bar (Buenos Aires), 151
Plaza Central (Miramar), 160
Plaza Colón (Mar del Plata), 154
Plaza Congreso (Buenos Aires), 133
Plaza de Mayo (Buenos Aires)
   restaurants near, 94
   sights and attractions, 128–130
Plaza Dorrego (Buenos Aires), 126
Plaza Dorrego Bar (Buenos Aires), 151
Plaza General Espejo (Chacras de Coria), 272
Plaza Independencia (Mendoza), 264

Plaza Independencia (Montevideo, Uruguay), 179
Plaza Mayor (Colonia del Sacramento, Uruguay), 174
Plaza Moreno (La Plata), 163
Plaza San Martín (Buenos Aires), 130–131
Plaza San Martín (Córdoba), 239
Plaza Serrano Fair (Buenos Aires), 135, 138
Plaza Victoria Casino (Montevideo, Uruguay), 183
Polar circle, 407
Polo, 134
　Argentine Open Polo Championships, 18
Polo Tour (La Falda), 246
Por Acá (Mendoza), 266
Portillo (Chile), 265
Port Lockroy, 407
Portuguese Museum (Colonia del Sacramento, Uruguay), 174
Posta del Sol (Humahuaca), 225
Potrerillos, 286
Potrero de Payogasta, 216
PowderQuest Tours, 41, 289
Presidential Museum (Buenos Aires), 129
Puente del Inca, 289–290
Puente Pichueta, 287–288
Puente Viejo (San Antonio de Areco), 185
Puerto Blest, 301
Puerto de Frutos (La Plata), 166
Puerto Iguazú. See Iguazú Falls/Puerto Iguazú
Puerto Madero (Buenos Aires)
　accommodations, 76–77
　restaurants, 94–96
　sights and attractions, 130
Puerto Madryn, 336, 338–347
Puerto Pañuelo, 299–301
Puerto Pirámides, 336, 350–352
Puerto Punta del Este (Uruguay), 170
Puerto Williams (Chile), 401–403
Punta del Este (Uruguay), 167–173
Punta Delgada, 348
Punta Hidalgo (Villa Carlos Paz), 245
Punta Shopping (Punta del Este, Uruguay), 173
Punta Tombo National Reserve, 336, 345–346

Punto Panorámico (Ushuaia), 396
Pura Cepa (Mendoza), 265

Quark Expeditions, 408
Quebrada de Humahuaca (Humahuaca Gorge), 224–225
Quebrada de las Flechas, 216
Quebrada del Condorito, 245
Quebrada del Río de las Conchas, 216
Quebrada del Salto, 264
Quilmes (Tafí del Valle), 227
Quinta Generación (Maipú), 278

Raffeish (San Rafael), 284
Raíces (Mendoza), 265
Rawson, 336
Recoleta (Buenos Aires)
　accommodations, 77–81
　restaurants, 96–99
　shopping, 135
　sights and attractions, 127–128
Recoleta Cemetery (Buenos Aires), 128
Recoleta Cultural Center (Buenos Aires), 145
Recoleta Fair (Buenos Aires), 138
Regency Casino (Mendoza), 266
Regions of Argentina, 9–12
República de los Niños (La Plata), 163
Reserva Arqueológica los Menhires (Tafí del Valle), 227
Reserva Indígena Chiuquilihuin, 334
Resistencia, 203–204
Restaurants, best, 7–8
Río Grande, 400
Ríos Andinos (Mendoza), 264
Roket (Bariloche), 312
Romera, Cecilia, 264
Rossi & Caruso (Buenos Aires), 143
The Roxy (Bariloche), 312
Ruca Malen (Luján de Cuyo), 274–275
Rudy Parra's Aconcagua Trek, 291
Ruinas Casa del Gobernador (Colonia del Sacramento, Uruguay), 174

Ruinas Convento San Francisco (Colonia del Sacramento, Uruguay), 174
Ruinas de San Francisco (Mendoza), 263
Rumbo Sur (Ushuaia), 398
Ruta de Los Siete Lagos, 322
Ruta 40, 314

Safety, 36
　Montevideo, Uruguay, 178
Saint Christopher (Ushuaia), 399
Sala de Teatro de San José (San Martín), 325
Salón Canning (Buenos Aires), 148–149
Salsón (Buenos Aires), 150
Salta, 3, 205–215
　accommodations, 210–214
　currency exchange, 206
　getting around, 206–207
　outdoor activities and tour operators, 210
　restaurants, 214–215
　shopping, 210
　sights and attractions, 207–210
　traveling to, 206
Salta Tram (Teleférico), 210
Salto San Martín (Iguazú Falls), 193
San Antonio church (Miramar), 160
San Antonio de Areco, 183–187
San Antonio de los Cobres, 208
San Antonio de Padua (San Antonio de Areco), 184
San Bernardo Convent (Salta), 210
San Carlos, 216
San Carlos de Bariloche. See Bariloche
San Francisco, Ruinas de (Mendoza), 263
San Francisco Church (Salta), 208
San Huberto Winery (La Rioja), 229–230
San Ignacio (Buenos Aires), 129
San Luis, 250
San Martín
　accommodations, 327–330
　banks and currency exchange, 324
　getting around, 323

nightlife, 332
outdoor activities, 325–327
restaurants, 330–332
shopping, 324–325
sights and attractions, 324–325
tour operators and travel agencies, 325
traveling to, 323
visitor information, 324
San Martín de los Andes, 3, 322–332
San Rafael, 282–284
San Salvador de Jujuy, 221–224
San Telmo (Buenos Aires)
accommodations, 82–83
restaurants, 117–120
shopping, 135
sights and attractions, 126
San Telmo (Maipú), 277
Say Hueque Tourism, 33–34, 166, 185
Scuba diving, 38
Puerto Madryn, 346
Puerto Pirámides, 350–351
San Martín, 326
Sea & Ice & Mountains (Puerto Williams, Chile), 402
Seasons, 17
626 Cueros (Buenos Aires), 144
Selva Tucumana (Tafi del Valle), 227
Senior travelers, 22–23
Señor Tango (Buenos Aires), 147
Seven Lakes Route, 322
Shackleton Lounge (El Calafate), 366
The Shamrock (Buenos Aires), 151
Silvia Freire, Espacio de Arte y Cultura (Buenos Aires), 145
Skiing, 39
Bariloche area, 302–303
Las Leñas, 288–289
Mendoza, 264–265
San Martín, 326
Ushuaia, 398
Skiing villa, Villa La Angostura, 316–317
Smoking, 36
Snowboarding, 39
Bariloche area, 302
Sobremonte (Mar del Plata), 159
Soccer, Buenos Aires, 134
Sol y Vino (Mendoza), 265
South Georgia Island, 407
South Orkney Islands, 407
South Sandwich Islands, 407

South Shetland Islands, 406
Student travelers, 24–25
Stylo Viajes (Córdoba), 240
Sun exposure, 20
Surfing, 38

Tafi del Valle, 227–228
Tango, 1, 149
Tango dance clubs (milongas), Buenos Aires, 147–149
Tango lessons, Buenos Aires, 149
Tango shows, Buenos Aires, 146
Tapaus Distillery (Maipú), 278
Tapiz (Luján de Cuyo), 275
Tass Bier and Club (Foz do Iguaçu, Brazil), 203
Taxes, 36–37
Teatro Coliseo (Buenos Aires), 146
Teatro Colón (Buenos Aires), 133–134, 146
Teatro Gran Rex (Buenos Aires), 146
Teatro Las Sillas (Mendoza), 265
Teatro Libertador San Martín (Córdoba), 239
Teatro Municipal General San Martín (Buenos Aires), 146
Teatro Nacional Cervantes (Buenos Aires), 146
Teatro Nuevo Argentino (La Plata), 163
Teatro Opera (Buenos Aires), 146
Teatro Plaza Foz (Foz do Iguaçu, Brazil), 203
Teatro Presidente Alvear (Buenos Aires), 146
Teatro Real (Córdoba), 239
Teatro Solís (Montevideo, Uruguay), 179, 183
Teleférico (Salta Tram), 210
Telephone, 37
Tempus Alba (Coquimbito), 278
Tequila (Buenos Aires), 150
Termas de Cacheuta, 276
Termas de Lahuen-Co., 333
Terrazzo (Villa Carlos Paz), 245
Tierra del Fuego, 12, 386–403
The Tigre Delta, 164–167
Tilcara, 225
Tipping, 37
Tolkeyen (Ushuaia), 398
Torre de Jesús (La Plata), 163
Torre Egger, 374
Torre Monumental (Buenos Aires), 131

Torres del Paine National Park (Chile), 377–385
accommodations and restaurants, 380–383
getting there and away, 378–379
hiking and trekking, 383–385
horseback riding, 385
visitor and park entrance information, 378
when to come and what to bring, 378
TosoBoehler (Mendoza), 264, 280
The Towers (Torres del Paine), 385
Train to the Clouds (Tren a las Nubes), 208
Transbordadora Austral Broom (Puerto Williams, Chile), 402
Travel Dynamics International, 33
Traveler's checks, 16–17
Traveling to Argentina, 30–33
Travel insurance, 18–19
Travel Line, 166
Trekking, 37–38. See Hiking and trekking
Salta, 210
Trelew, 336, 352–353
Tren a las Nubes (Train to the Clouds), 208
Trench Gallery (Punta del Este, Uruguay), 173
Trentis Lakebar (Bariloche), 312
Tribunales (Buenos Aires), accommodations, 85–88
Trip-cancellation insurance, 18–19
Tristán Narvaja (Montevideo, Uruguay), 179
Tronador, 298–299, 313, 314
Trout & Wine (Mendoza), 217, 270
Tucumán, 225–228
Turismo Uspallata (Mendoza), 264
Ty Nain (Gaiman), 354
Ty Te Caerdydd (Gaiman), 354

Uco Valley Region, 269
Uncorking Argentina (Mendoza), 270
UNESCO-Colonia headquarters (Uruguay), 174
Upper Circuit (Iguazú Falls), 193
Uritorco, Mount, 248

Ushuaia, 386–401
  accommodations, 390–394
  excursions around, 399–401
  getting around, 388–389
  nightlife, 398–399
  outdoor activities, 397–398
  restaurants, 394–396
  sights and attractions,
    396–397
  tour operators, 398
  traveling to, 388
  visitor information, 389
Uspallata, 286–287
Uspallata Valley, 286

Valdivian Forest, 301
Vallecitos, 265
Valle de la Luna, 231
Valle de Uco, 278–282
Valle Francés (Torres del Paine),
  385
Valle Grande, 284
Vasija Secreta (Cafayate), 219
VAT (value-added tax), 36–37
Vega Island, 407
Ventisquero Negro, 313
Victory Adventure Travel
  (Puerto Williams, Chile), 402
Viedma Discovery (El Chaltén),
  372
Villa Biarritz fair (Montevideo,
  Uruguay), 179
Villa Carlos Paz, 3, 242–245
Villa General Belgrano, 251
Villa La Angostura, 3, 315–320
Villa Ortiz Basualdo (Mar del
  Plata), 155
Villa Trafúl, 322
Villavicencio, 285–286
Villa Victoria (Mar del Plata),
  154–155

The Vines of Mendoza, 260,
  266
Virgen de Carrodilla, Iglesia de
  la (Luján de Cuyo), 276
Visitor information, 12–13
Vistalba (Luján de Cuyo), 275
Vivero Dunícola Florentino
  Ameghino (Miramar), 160

W, The (Torres del Paine),
  384
Waikiki (Mar del Plata), 154
Water, 37
Watersports, Salta, 210
Websites, 12–13
  traveler's toolbox, 29
Weddell Sea, 407
Whales Argentina (Puerto
  Pirámides), 350
Whale-watching
  Península Valdés, 336, 346,
    348
  Puerto Pirámides, 350
Whitewater rafting, 39
  Bariloche area, 302
  Mendoza, 265
  Salta, 210
  San Martín, 326
  San Rafael, 284
Whitney and Smith Legendary
  Expeditions, 41, 349
Wi-Fi access, 28
Wilderness Travel, 35, 40
Wildland Adventures, 35, 40–41
Wildlife viewing. See also Bird-
  watching; Whale-watching
  Iguazú Falls area, 195
  Parque Nacional Chaco, 204
  Península Valdés, 348, 349
  Quebrada del Condorito, 245
  suggested itinerary, 52–54
Wilkenny (Bariloche), 312

Windsurfing, 39
  Puerto Madryn, 347
  Salta, 210
Windsurfing/kite-surfing, 39
Wine Club Republic (Mendoza),
  260
Wineries and vineyards (bode-
  gas)
  Cafayate, 217–219
    wine lodges, 220–221
  Chilecito (La Rioja), 230
  Mendoza, 266–282
    Chacras de Coria,
      270–272
    Luján de Cuyo, 272–276
    Maipú region, 276–278
    San Rafael, 284
    taking wine home, 268
    tips on visiting wineries,
      269
    tour operators, 269–270
    Valle de Uco, 280, 282
    when to visit, 279
Wine shops, Buenos Aires, 144
Wine tasting, 2, 94, 260
Women travelers, 24
Worest Casino (Bariloche), 312
World Tango Festival (Buenos
  Aires), 18

Yacutinga Lodge and Wildlife
  Reserve (Iguazú), 198

Zebra Restobar Disco (Villa
  Carlos Paz), 245
Zoological Gardens (Buenos
  Aires), 127
Zoos
  Buenos Aires, 127
  La Plata, 163
  Mar del Plata, 155

FROMMER'S® COMPLETE TRAVEL GUIDES

Alaska
Amalfi Coast
American Southwest
Amsterdam
Argentina & Chile
Arizona
Atlanta
Australia
Austria
Bahamas
Barcelona
Beijing
Belgium, Holland & Luxembourg
Belize
Bermuda
Boston
Brazil
British Columbia & the Canadian
  Rockies
Brussels & Bruges
Budapest & the Best of Hungary
Buenos Aires
Calgary
California
Canada
Cancún, Cozumel & the Yucatán
Cape Cod, Nantucket & Martha's
  Vineyard
Caribbean
Caribbean Ports of Call
Carolinas & Georgia
Chicago
China
Colorado
Costa Rica
Croatia
Cuba
Denmark
Denver, Boulder & Colorado Springs
Edinburgh & Glasgow
England
Europe
Europe by Rail
Florence, Tuscany & Umbria

Florida
France
Germany
Greece
Greek Islands
Hawaii
Hong Kong
Honolulu, Waikiki & Oahu
India
Ireland
Israel
Italy
Jamaica
Japan
Kauai
Las Vegas
London
Los Angeles
Los Cabos & Baja
Madrid
Maine Coast
Maryland & Delaware
Maui
Mexico
Montana & Wyoming
Montréal & Québec City
Moscow & St. Petersburg
Munich & the Bavarian Alps
Nashville & Memphis
New England
Newfoundland & Labrador
New Mexico
New Orleans
New York City
New York State
New Zealand
Northern Italy
Norway
Nova Scotia, New Brunswick &
  Prince Edward Island
Oregon
Paris
Peru
Philadelphia & the Amish Country

Portugal
Prague & the Best of the Czech
  Republic
Provence & the Riviera
Puerto Rico
Rome
San Antonio & Austin
San Diego
San Francisco
Santa Fe, Taos & Albuquerque
Scandinavia
Scotland
Seattle
Seville, Granada & the Best of
  Andalusia
Shanghai
Sicily
Singapore & Malaysia
South Africa
South America
South Florida
South Pacific
Southeast Asia
Spain
Sweden
Switzerland
Tahiti & French Polynesia
Texas
Thailand
Tokyo
Toronto
Turkey
USA
Utah
Vancouver & Victoria
Vermont, New Hampshire & Maine
Vienna & the Danube Valley
Vietnam
Virgin Islands
Virginia
Walt Disney World® & Orlando
Washington, D.C.
Washington State

FROMMER'S® DAY BY DAY GUIDES

Amsterdam
Chicago
Florence & Tuscany

London
New York City
Paris

Rome
San Francisco
Venice

PAULINE FROMMER'S GUIDES! SEE MORE. SPEND LESS.

Hawaii

Italy

New York City

FROMMER'S® PORTABLE GUIDES

Acapulco, Ixtapa & Zihuatanejo
Amsterdam
Aruba
Australia's Great Barrier Reef
Bahamas
Big Island of Hawaii
Boston
California Wine Country
Cancún
Cayman Islands
Charleston
Chicago
Dominican Republic

Dublin
Florence
Las Vegas
Las Vegas for Non-Gamblers
London
Maui
Nantucket & Martha's Vineyard
New Orleans
New York City
Paris
Portland
Puerto Rico
Puerto Vallarta, Manzanillo &
  Guadalajara

Rio de Janeiro
San Diego
San Francisco
Savannah
St. Martin, Sint Maarten, Anguila &
  St. Bart's
Turks & Caicos
Vancouver
Venice
Virgin Islands
Washington, D.C.
Whistler

FROMMER'S® CRUISE GUIDES

| Alaska Cruises & Ports of Call | Cruises & Ports of Call | European Cruises & Ports of Call |

FROMMER'S® NATIONAL PARK GUIDES

Algonquin Provincial Park	National Parks of the American West	Yosemite and Sequoia & Kings
Banff & Jasper	Rocky Mountain	Canyon
Grand Canyon	Yellowstone & Grand Teton	Zion & Bryce Canyon

FROMMER'S® MEMORABLE WALKS

| London | Paris | San Francisco |
| New York | Rome | |

FROMMER'S® WITH KIDS GUIDES

Chicago	National Parks	Toronto
Hawaii	New York City	Walt Disney World® & Orlando
Las Vegas	San Francisco	Washington, D.C.
London		

SUZY GERSHMAN'S BORN TO SHOP GUIDES

France	London	Paris
Hong Kong, Shanghai & Beijing	New York	San Francisco
Italy		

FROMMER'S® IRREVERENT GUIDES

Amsterdam	London	Rome
Boston	Los Angeles	San Francisco
Chicago	Manhattan	Walt Disney World®
Las Vegas	Paris	Washington, D.C.

FROMMER'S® BEST-LOVED DRIVING TOURS

Austria	Germany	Northern Italy
Britain	Ireland	Scotland
California	Italy	Spain
France	New England	Tuscany & Umbria

THE UNOFFICIAL GUIDES®

Adventure Travel in Alaska	Hawaii	Paris
Beyond Disney	Ireland	San Francisco
California with Kids	Las Vegas	South Florida including Miami &
Central Italy	London	the Keys
Chicago	Maui	Walt Disney World®
Cruises	Mexico's Best Beach Resorts	Walt Disney World® for
Disneyland®	Mini Mickey	Grown-ups
England	New Orleans	Walt Disney World® with Kids
Florida	New York City	Washington, D.C.
Florida with Kids		

SPECIAL-INTEREST TITLES

Athens Past & Present	Frommer's Exploring America by RV
Best Places to Raise Your Family	Frommer's NYC Free & Dirt Cheap
Cities Ranked & Rated	Frommer's Road Atlas Europe
500 Places to Take Your Kids Before They Grow Up	Frommer's Road Atlas Ireland
Frommer's Best Day Trips from London	Great Escapes From NYC Without Wheels
Frommer's Best RV & Tent Campgrounds in the U.S.A.	Retirement Places Rated

FROMMER'S® PHRASEFINDER DICTIONARY GUIDES

| French | Italian | Spanish |

THE NEW TRAVELOCITY GUARANTEE

EVERYTHING YOU BOOK WILL BE RIGHT, OR WE'LL WORK WITH OUR TRAVEL PARTNERS TO MAKE IT RIGHT, RIGHT AWAY.

To drive home the point, we're going to use the word "right" in every single sentence.

Let's get right to it. Right to the meat! Only Travelocity guarantees everything about your booking will be right, or we'll work with our travel partners to make it right, right away. Right on!

Here's a picture taken smack dab right in the middle of Antigua, where the guarantee also covers you.

The guarantee covers all but one of the items pictured to the right.

For example, what if the ocean view you booked actually looks out at a downright ugly parking lot? You'd be right to call – we're there for you. And no one in their right mind would be pleased to learn the rental car place has closed and left them stranded. Call Travelocity and we'll help get you back on the right track.

Now, you may be thinking, "Yeah, right, I'm so sure." That's OK; you have the right to remain skeptical. That is until we mention help is always right around the corner. Call us right off the bat, knowing that our customer service reps are there for you 24/7. Righting wrongs. Left and right.

Now if you're guessing there are some things we can't control, like the weather, well you're right. But we can help you with most things – to get all the details in righting,* visit **travelocity.com/guarantee**.

*Sorry, spelling things right is one of the few things not covered under the guarantee.

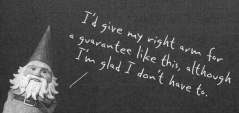

I'd give my right arm for a guarantee like this, although I'm glad I don't have to.

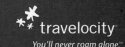

travelocity

You'll never roam alone.™

IF YOU BOOK IT, IT SHOULD BE THERE.

Only Travelocity guarantees it will be, or we'll work with our travel partners to make it right, right away. So if you're missing a balcony or anything else you booked, just call us 24/7. 1-888-TRAVELOCITY.

travelocity

You'll never roam alone